CONSUMING SPLENDOR

Consuming Splendor is a fascinating study of the ways in which the consumption of luxury goods transformed social practices, gender roles, royal policies, and the economy in seventeenth-century England. Linda Levy Peck charts the development of new ways to shop; new aspirations and identities shaped by print, continental travel, and trade to Asia, Africa, and the East and West Indies; new building, furnishing, and collecting; and the new relationship of luxury, technology, and science. As contemporaries eagerly appropriated and copied foreign material culture, the expansion of luxury consumption continued across the usual divide of the Civil War and the Interregnum and helped to propel England from the margins to the center of European growth and innovation. Her findings show for the first time the seventeenth-century origins of consumer society and she offers the reader a new framework for the history of seventeenth-century England.

LINDA LEVY PECK is Columbian Professor of History at the George Washington University. She has published extensively on politics, society, and culture in seventeenth-century England. She is the author of *Northampton: Patronage and Policy at the Court of James I* (1982), *Court Patronage and Corruption in Early Stuart England* (1990) and the editor of *The Mental World of the Jacobean Court* (1991).

CONSUMING SPLENDOR

Society and Culture in Seventeenth-Century England

LINDA LEVY PECK

CAMBRIDGE
UNIVERSITY PRESS

CAMBRIDGE UNIVERSITY PRESS

Cambridge, New York, Melbourne, Madrid, Cape Town, Singapore, São Paulo

CAMBRIDGE UNIVERSITY PRESS

The Edinburgh Building, Cambridge CB2 2RU, UK

Published in the United States of America by Cambridge University Press, New York

www.cambridge.org
Information on this title: www.cambridge.org/9780521842327

First published 2005

Printed in the United States of America

A catalogue record for this book is available from the British Library

ISBN-13 978-0-521-84232-7 hardback
ISBN-10 0-521-84232-8 hardback

To my friends and family

Contents

Illustrations

Acknowledgments

The completion of *Consuming Splendor* coincides with that special season of celebration and consumption that begins with Thanksgiving and lasts through the turning of the year. While this book provides much evidence of luxury and shopping, it begins, as it ought, by giving thanks.

First of all, I wish to thank the John Simon Guggenheim Foundation, the Huntington Library, the National Humanities Center, where I was Delta Delta Delta Fellow, and the George Washington University, which provided me with fellowships to pursue this project. I am especially grateful to Roy Ritchie, W. M. Keck Foundation Director of Research at the Huntington Library, who invited me to be the Fletcher Jones Distinguished Fellow in 1996–97 and to Dean William Frawley who, by naming me one of the first Columbian Research Scholars at George Washington University in 2003–2004, enabled me to complete this book.

Many friends and colleagues have provided insight and thoughtful comment throughout this project. I must begin by thanking two scholars in particular who provided invaluable support from its inception. Stanley Engerman not only read successive drafts of this manuscript and offered important suggestions but discussed these issues with his inimitable knowledge, endless patience, and unfailing good humor. Barbara J. Harris supported this project from its beginning, discussed it at length, and read the final manuscript with a fine eye for argument and language.

Several scholars read most or all of the complete manuscript. John Morrill, always a fine reader, read the entire manuscript and provided invaluable advice. Malcolm Smuts provided significant comments that pointed to important conceptual issues. A. R. Braunmuller provided the literary scholar's insight and enriched the scope of the book. Barbara Taft read an early draft of the chapter on luxury and war and provided her always sharp and insightful comments. Ian Archer, David Armitage, Pauline Croft, Barbara Donagan, Margot Finn, John Guy, Cynthia Herrup, Caroline Hibbard, Barbara Ballis Lal, Margerie Lightman, Fritz Levy, Lena Cowen

Orlin, J. G. A. Pocock, James Robertson, Paul Seaver, Barbara Shapiro and Bob Tittler will all find traces of our conversations in these pages. I am grateful too to the anonymous readers for Cambridge University Press whose analyses were most helpful. I especially wish to thank my editors, Bill Davies and Michael Watson, for their enthusiastic support of this project, my copyeditor, Jacqueline French, who turned typescript into book with scrupulous care, and Elizabeth Davey, who oversaw its production.

I benefited from the helpful comments of participants at seminars and conferences at which I presented work in progress. I thank Gary Taylor for the invitation to be the Strode lecturer at the University of Alabama; Wm. Roger Louis for his invitation to the University of Texas British History seminar, David Cressy for his invitation to Ohio State University, and Pauline Croft for the invitation to speak to the England seminar at the Institute of Historical Research on the occasion of the retirement of Conrad Russell.

I was fortunate to be able to work in archives on both sides of the Atlantic and I wish to thank the curators and librarians at Arundel Castle, the British Library, the Bodleian Library at Oxford, Castle Howard, Chatsworth, the Centre for Kentish Studies, the Folger Shakespeare Library, the Guildhall Library, Hatfield House, the Huntington Library, Nottingham University Library, the Public Record Office, the University of Texas at Austin Library, the Royal Society, and the Westminster Archives.

I thank the Marquess of Salisbury, the Duke of Norfolk, the Duke of Devonshire, and the Duke of Sutherland for permission to quote from their manuscripts. I am particularly grateful to Robin Harcourt Williams, Archivist and Librarian to His Grace, the Marquess of Salisbury, for his advice and help on the Hatfield House Manuscripts; John Martin Robinson, Archivist and Librarian to His Grace, the Duke of Norfolk, and Mrs. Sara Rodger, Archivist at Arundel Castle, for advice on the Arundel Manuscripts; and Peter Day, Librarian to his Grace, the Duke of Devonshire, for advice on the manuscripts at Chatsworth.

To Mary Robertson, Curator of Manuscripts at the Huntington Library, and to Georgianna Ziegler, Reference Librarian at the Folger Shakespeare Library, go my particular thanks.

I especially want to thank Gail Kern Paster, Director of the Folger Shakespeare Library, who suggested an exhibition on luxury based on this book and Rachel Doggett, Curator of Books and Exhibitions at the Folger Shakespeare Library, co-curator of the Folger exhibition. Rachel

Doggett helped me to identify many of the Folger prints and manuscripts reproduced here for which I am most grateful.

Claire Vincent and Jessie McNab, Curators in European Sculpture and Decorative Arts at the Metropolitan Museum of Art, advised me on the museum's seventeenth-century English holdings. I am grateful to Joaneth Spicer, Curator of Renaissance and Baroque Art at the Walters Gallery, and to Geoffrey Fisher of the Conway Library of the Courtauld for their advice on objects reproduced in this volume. Antony Griffiths, Curator of Prints, the British Museum, provided helpful advice on prints and woodcuts.

I thank the University of Pennsylvania Press for permission to reproduce some material I published in "Building, Buying, and Collecting in London, 1600–1625," in Lena Cowen Orlin (ed.) *Material London, ca. 1600* (Philadelphia: University of Pennsylvania Press, 2000), pp. 268–89, and *Albion* for material from "Luxury and War: Reconsidering Luxury Consumption in Seventeenth-Century England," *Albion*, 34 (Spring 2002), 1–23, my presidential address to the North American Conference on British Studies, in 2000.

My friends and family have provided constant support. To them, and especially to my dear mother, go my greatest thanks. Finally, I wish to thank two physicians, Dr. Judith Allen and Dr. Wende Logan-Young, whose specialties lie far from British history. In 1994 I was treated for early breast cancer because of their wise and proactive practice of medicine. I cannot thank them enough.

I, of course, remain responsible for the errors that remain in this volume.

List of abbreviations

Add. Mss.	Additional Manuscripts
BL	British Library
CSPD	Calendar of State Papers Domestic
CSPV	Calendar of State Papers Venetian
Folger	Folger Shakespeare Library
HEH	Henry E. Huntington Library
HMC	Historical Manuscripts Commission
PCC	Prerogative Court of Canterbury
PRO	Public Record Office
TRHS	*Transactions of the Royal Historical Society*

Consuming Splendor

Beginning in 1607, three years after the repeal of England's last sumptuary law, James I enthusiastically endorsed a domestic silk industry. In 1608, borrowing French policy, the King ordered all those of ability

to purchase and plant 10,000 mulberry trees at the rate of six shillings the hundred containing five score plants. There shalbe published in print a plaine instruction and direction for the increasing of the said mulberry trees, the breeding of the silkworms, and all other things needful for the perfecting of a work every way so commendable and profitable.[1]

Although James claimed that he would lose revenues because of reduced customs duties on imported silk, the King dismissed such concerns in the name of industry, science, honor, and plenty.[2]

The Perfect Use of Silk-Wormes and their Benefit, translated by Nicholas Geffe, appeared in 1607. A projector with ties to the Attorney General, Francis Bacon, Geffe argued that an English silk industry "will clothe our backs sumptuously and fill our purses royally ... our private profits and public benefit are deeply interested therein ... we may as well be silke-masters as sheepe-masters."[3] Both Geffe's work and William Stallenge's *Instructions for the Increasing of Mulberie Trees* of 1609, which included the King's order, contained woodcuts showing readers how to cultivate mulberries, raise silkworms, and spin silk. The project to create a domestic silk industry became, by the 1620s, a colonial enterprise, fervently pursued into the 1660s and beyond. Within this discourse, silk was described as rich and solid, not vain and luxurious. Yet the Jacobean goal of swathing

---

[1] PRO SP 14/26/6.

[2] William Stallenge, *Instructions for the Increasing of Mulberie Trees* (London, 1609, a translation of Jean-Baptiste Letellier's *Memoires et instructions pour l'establissement des meuriers* [Paris, 1603]). Olivier de Serres, *The Perfect Use of Silk-Wormes and their Benefit ... Done out of the French original of D'Olivier de Serres Lord of Pradel into English by Nicholas Geffe Esquire* (London, 1607).

[3] De Serres, *The Perfect Use of Silk-Wormes and their Benefit*, pp. 10–11.

English bodies in silk while promoting trade and industry contrasted vividly with the classical and biblical discourses that condemned luxury. Instead, these tracts anticipate Nicholas Barbon's *A Discourse of Trade* (London, 1690) and Bernard Mandeville's *The Grumbling Hive, or, Knaves Turn'd Honest* (London, 1705) which argued that private vices produced public benefit.

The story of seventeenth-century England is often told as a tale of the unique triumph of Protestantism, parliamentary sovereignty, and law over absolute monarchy and Counter-Reformation Catholicism through civil war and glorious revolution. *Consuming Splendor* tells a different story: of new ways to shop; of royal sponsorship of luxury trades and manufactures; of new aspirations, shaped by print and travel, which found expression in buying, building, furnishing, and collecting; of the reinvention of identities through new artifacts; of the transformation of meaning as objects moved across cultures and into new contexts; and of the way in which early science underpinned luxury consumption. Analyzing luxury consumption from the perspective of the early seventeenth century, *Consuming Splendor* stresses continuities across the usual divide of the Civil War and Interregnum. It offers an additional narrative for seventeenth-century studies,[4] one that focuses on the cultural mentalities and political strategies that supported luxury consumption and sponsored cultural borrowing throughout court, city, and countryside.[5] The result helped propel England from the margins to the center of European growth, improvement, and innovation.

Luxury commodities circulated throughout society from the merchant who imported them, to the retailer who sold them, the purchaser who bought them, the client who presented them to his patron, and the poor who wore them as second-hand goods. English demand for luxuries imported from Europe and Asia grew strongly from the 1540s. Sir Thomas Smith complained about imports in 1549 in ways that resembled complaints seventy-five years later.[6] William Harrison's *The Description of England* (London, 1587), documented in striking detail the growth in the

---

[4] Timothy Hampton quotes Jean Rousset "one might see drawn several parallel seventeenth centuries," in "Introduction: Baroques," in "Baroque Topographies: Literature/History/Philosophy," *Yale French Studies*, 80 (1991), 6.

[5] See R. Malcolm Smuts, "Material Culture, Metropolitan Influences and Moral Authority in Early Modern England," in C. Curtis Perry (ed.), *Material Culture and Cultural Materialisms in the Middle Ages and the Renaissance* (Turnhout, Belgium: Brepols, 2001), pp. 203–24.

[6] Sir Thomas Smith, *A Discourse of the Commonweal of this Realm of England*, attributed to Sir Thomas Smith, ed. Mary Dewar (Charlottesville: Published for the Folger Shakespeare Library by the University Press of Virginia, 1969).

consumption of goods for the body as well as for the home. Travelers such as Thomas Platter in 1599 wrote in awe of jewelry and gold and silver plate on display at the goldsmiths in Cheapside.[7] Demand for new goods and openness to other cultures challenged the negative identifications of luxury goods with the foreign, the popish, and the decadent, staples of Elizabethan prescriptive literature.[8] Under James I, the contest between moralizing prescription and legislation on the one hand and demand on the other tilted in favor of luxury consumption.

This book addresses why the English became enamored of foreign wares and how they appropriated artifacts and skills from abroad in ways that transformed their economy and culture. It studies the acts and meanings of consuming, the knowledge and agents that made it possible, and its effect on the expression of the self, gender, social relationships, ideology, and the economy. Examining the period from *c.* 1600 to *c.* 1670, before "the long eighteenth century," it offers a new time frame and a different set of agents to explain this transformation.[9] Within this larger agenda, *Consuming Splendor* focuses on London, the hub of national and international networks of exchange, the center of political power, the locus of luxury shopping, and promoter of technical and scientific improvement. It draws attention to but does not address in detail the very important issues of local consumption of luxuries, already studied by Joan Thirsk, Craig Muldrew, Margaret Spufford, Ronald Berger, and Nancy Cox.[10] Furthermore, the significant relationship of luxury and the church warrants closer study than has been possible here. As we shall see, the church's teachings were generally hostile to luxury consumption. Yet in the early

[7] Clare Williams (ed.), *Thomas Platter's Travels in England, 1599* (London: Jonathan Cape, 1937), p. 157.
[8] Sara Warneke, *Images of the Educational Traveler in Early Modern England* (Leiden: E. G. Brill, 1995), analyzes the negative image of the sixteenth- and seventeenth-century traveler. See, for example, Joseph Hall, *Quo Vadis? A Just Censure of Travel as It Is Commonly Undertaken by the Gentlemen of Our Nation* (London, 1617).
[9] Woodruff D. Smith, *Consumption and the Making of Respectability, 1600–1800* (London: Routledge, 2002); Arjun Appadurai (ed.), *The Social Life of Things: Commodities in Social Perspective* (Cambridge: Cambridge University Press, 1986); Mary Douglas and Baron C. Isherwood, *The World of Goods: Towards an Anthropology of Consumption* (New York: Basic Books, 1979). John Brewer and Roy Porter (eds.), *Consumption and the World of Goods* (London: Routledge, 1993).
[10] Ronald M. Berger, *The Most Necessary Luxuries: The Mercers' Company of Coventry, 1550–1680* (University Park: Penn State University Press, 1993). Nancy C. Cox, *The Complete Tradesman: A Study of Retailing, 1550–1820* (Aldershot, Hampshire: Ashgate Publishing, 2000). Joan Thirsk, *Economic Policy and Projects: The Development of a Consumer Society in Early Modern England* (Oxford: Clarendon Press, 1978). Craig Muldrew, *The Economy of Obligation: The Culture of Credit and Social Relations in Early Modern England* (Houndsmill, Basingstoke: Palgrave, 1998). Margaret Spufford, *The Great Reclothing of Rural England: Petty Chapmen and their Wares in the Seventeenth Century* (London: Hambleden Press, 1986).

1. Cheapside, filled with goldsmiths' shops, was the most important shopping street in the City of London. Hugh Alley, who painted the food markets of London at the end of Elizabeth's reign, shows vendors selling food in the middle of the avenue.
The Folger Shakespeare Library Ms. V. a. 318, f.15, Hugh Alley, *A Caveatt for the citty of London.* "Cheapside," Manuscript, 1598.

2. Silver vessels exhibited on the buffet displayed the status and wealth of their owners. These flagons, once thought to have belonged to Sir Edward Coke, were represented in the famous painting by Gerritsz, "Still Life of the Paston (Yarmouth) Collection."
The Metropolitan Museum of Art, Metalwork, Silver-English, London, 16th century, pair of flagons, silver gilt, H. 12 1/4 in. (1597), that belonged to the Coke and Paston families. Gift of Irwin Untermyer, 1968 (68, 141, 142, 143). Photograph, all rights reserved, The Metropolitan Museum of Art, Neg. #193576.

seventeenth century, clerical emphasis on the "beauty of holiness" and church building, and the laity's practice of donating silver plate and lavish textiles for worship and building elaborate pews and tombs for display, made the church an important site for the consumption of luxury goods. Finally, throughout this work, luxury denotes "the habitual use of, or indulgence in what is choice or costly, whether food, dress, furniture, or appliances . . . or surroundings," definitions that were current in the seventeenth century.[11]

---

[11] See the definition of "luxury" in the *Oxford English Dictionary*, 2nd edn, prepared by J. A. Simpson and E. S. C. Weiner (Oxford: Clarendon Press, 1989), Vol. IX, p. 128. Daniel Roche, "Between a

THE LANGUAGE OF LUXURY

The ancients and early Christians subjected luxury and luxury goods to withering attack as the scourge of virtue: decadent, effeminate, sinful, and subversive. In *The Idea of Luxury*, Christopher Berry points out that the traditional moralistic view, from Aristotle to the early seventeenth century, differentiated between needs and wants, privileging the first and casting a dubious eye on the second.[12] The Stoics located luxury in a discourse of war and peace, arguing that luxury took root at a time of peace and prosperity marked by the influx of goods from Asia to fill houses and banqueting tables. Pliny the Elder worried that luxury goods brought by conquest might lead to corruption and the decline of the Roman Empire.[13] Classical and biblical sources associated luxury with the subversive influence of the "other": women, favorites, foreigners, and upstarts.

At the same time, Roman moralists believed that luxury undermined office and hierarchy. Because luxury raised fears of both social mobility and the corruption of the state, sumptuary legislation from the Romans to the Elizabethans sought to maintain sharp distinctions between status groups. Thus, in 1337 no man was allowed "to wear any facings of silk or furs but such as could expend an hundred pounds a year." Two centuries later in 1566 "No man under the degree of a knight or of a lord's room . . . shall wear any hat or upper cap of velvet . . . on pain to forfeit ten shillings."[14]

The condemnation of luxury because it undermined virtue, military strength, and hierarchy continued into the seventeenth century and beyond. For instance, English writers expressed unease about collecting arts and antiquities, even those, such as the diplomats Sir Henry Wotton and Sir Thomas Roe, who were its keenest promoters. Wotton feared that interest in continental art and architecture would be thought popish, morally corrupt, and identified with Counter-Reformation Italy. Roe expressed concern that collecting might be perceived as effeminate.

'moral economy' and a 'consumer economy': clothes and their function in the 17th and 18th centuries," in Robert Fox and Anthony Turner (eds.), *Luxury Trades and Consumerism in Ancien Régime Paris: Studies in the History of the Skilled Workforce* (Aldershot, Hampshire: Ashgate Publishing, 1998), p. 227, "Need varies according to different economic, social, and cultural status – mimetic values were not reserved to the rich."

[12] Christopher J. Berry, *The Idea of Luxury: A Conceptual and Historical Investigation* (Cambridge: Cambridge University Press, 1994).

[13] Sorcha Carey, "The Problem of Totality, Collecting Greek Art, Wonders and Luxury in Pliny the Elder's *Natural History*," *Journal of the History of Collections*, 12 (2000), 1–13.

[14] Frank Warner, *The Silk Industry of the United Kingdom: Its Origin and Development* (London: Drane's, 1921), p. 626.

Sending antiquities to the Earl of Arundel, he wrote defensively that the Ottomans "deliver them to us for our corruption to divert us from the thought or use of arms. But they are absurdly mistaken; for civility and knowledge do confirm, and not effeminate good and true spirits."[15]

To many contemporaries, the peace and prosperity of the Jacobean regime that began in 1603 proclaimed weakness rather than strength. Thomas Mun, the most famous contributor to the economic debate in the 1620s, wrote that "silks, sugars, and spices" were "unnecessary wants … piping, potting, feasting, fashions, and mis-spending of our time in idleness and pleasure contrary to the law of God, and the use of other nations hath made us effeminate in our bodies, weak in our knowledge, poor in our treasure, decline in our valour, unfortunate in our enterprises, and condemned by our enemies."[16]

Yet even among the Stoics, the notion of decorum called for appropriate consumption according to status. By the sixteenth century, Roman decorum, or what the English called "state," created a space for magnificence and splendor. Magnificence became a term of praise associated with office, title, and state in which elaborate buildings, clothing, plate, and retainers defined high-ranking nobles and officials, almost always male.[17]

Magnificence, praised by fifteenth-century Northern humanists, continued to be celebrated in the seventeenth century.[18] Indeed, magnificence and splendor were matched virtues: "magnificence is manifest in public architecture, splendor expresses itself in the elegance and refinement with which one lives his life within buildings."[19] Giovanni Botero's *The Magnificence of Cities* was translated into English in 1606.[20] In 1634 Giles Fleming exhorted contributions for the repair of St. Paul's in a sermon

---

[15] Quoted in David Howarth, *Lord Arundel and his Circle* (New Haven: Yale University Press, 1985), p. 88.

[16] Quoted in Berry, *The Idea of Luxury*, pp. 103–104. Charles Davenant, writing in the second half of the century as a defender of the East India Company, agreed that silks "serve 'luxury' and, as such, they are not only superfluous but also pernicious in that they stimulate vanity and an illimitable desire for their possession." John Sekora, *Luxury: The Concept in Western Thought, Eden to Smollett* (Baltimore: Johns Hopkins University Press, 1977); Werner Sombart, *Luxury and Capitalism*, trans. W. R. Dittmar (Ann Arbor: University of Michigan Press, 1967).

[17] Mary E. Hazard, "A Magnificent Lord: Leicester, Kenilworth, and Transformation in the Idea of Magnificence," *Cahiers Elizabethains*, 31 (1987), 11–35; John Newman, "Inigo Jones and the Politics of Architecture," in Kevin Sharpe and Peter Lake (eds.) *Culture and Politics in Early Stuart England* (Stanford: Stanford University Press, 1993), p. 270.

[18] Simon Thurley, *The Royal Palaces of Tudor England: Architecture and Court Life, 1460–1547* (New Haven and London: Yale University Press, 1993), p. 11.

[19] Richard Goldthwaite, *Wealth and the Demand for Art in Italy, 1300–1600* (Baltimore and London: Johns Hopkins University Press, 1993), p. 249.

[20] Giovanni Botero, *The Magnificence of Cities* (London, 1606), Title page, p. 13, and dedication. F. J. Fisher cites Botero in "The Development of London as a Centre of Conspicuous Consumption in the Sixteenth and Seventeenth Centuries," *TRHS*, 4th series 30 (1948), 37–50.

entitled *Magnificence Exemplified*.[21] In 1654 John Ogilby appropriated "magnificence and splendor" to advertise his new edition of Vergil.[22] Balthazar Gerbier, Caroline tastemaker, merely repeated this language forty years later in his *On Magnificence in Buildings* (London, 1662).

If magnificence, signifier of high estate and office, called for the public display of lavish clothes, retainers, houses, and plate, luxury goods, often available to anyone who could pay, remained suspect to critics. Did luxury, as a product of an expanding economy, undermine magnificence and splendor, the marker of hierarchy? Such a simple developmental model appears problematic when we listen closely to contemporaries, as we shall see throughout this book. Instead, as the range of luxury goods expanded alongside the section of the population who felt entitled to use them, luxuries found acceptance when they were re-labeled as rich, new, innovative, curious, rare, fine, refined, polite, comfortable, and imported.

Christopher Berry argues that a demoralization of luxury took place in the second half of the seventeenth century as it was increasingly placed in a discourse of trade and commerce. As luxury loses its immoral overtones, Berry suggests, "luxury and fashion are acceptable because they stimulate consumption, which in turn generates trade and employment."[23] Thus, in 1690 Nicholas Barbon criticized Thomas Mun for upholding sumptuary legislation. Barbon stressed the economic importance of consumption, especially the clothing and the building trades. Clothing, Barbon wrote, provided work for "the glover, hosier, hatter, seamstress, tailor, and many more, with those that make the materials to deck it; as clothier, silk-weaver, lace-maker, ribbon-weaver, with their assistance of drapers, mercers, and milliners, and a thousand more." Building offered work for even larger numbers: "the chiefest promoter of trade; it employs a greater number of trades and people, than feeding and clothing."[24]

This study demonstrates that the demoralization of luxury had already begun in Jacobean England. Luxury and necessity, wants and needs, which stirred theoretical debates in the eighteenth century, were, after all, always matters of interpretation. Elizabeth, Lady Compton, heiress to Sir John Spencer the City merchant and Lord Mayor, saw luxury goods as

[21] Giles Fleming, *Magnificence Exemplified: and the repair of St Paul's exhorted unto* (London, 1634).
[22] Katherine S. van Eerde, *John Ogilby and the Taste of his Times* (Folkestone, Kent: Dawson, 1976). Sarah L. C. Clapp, "The Subscription Enterprise of John Ogilby and Richard Blome," *Modern Philology*, 30 (1932–33), 365–79.
[23] Berry, *The Idea of Luxury*, pp. 104, 112. Berry cites Sombart, *Luxus und Kapitalismus* (Munich, and Leipzig, 1913), pp. 138–41.
[24] Quoted in Berry, *The Idea of Luxury*, p. 117.

a carefully calibrated expression of wealth, status, and personal autonomy, available to women as well as to men. She specifically identified her own honor with clothing, servants, coaches, jewelry, charity, and splendid interiors, many of which usually formed the trappings of magnificence.

When her father died in March 1609/1610, Lady Compton wrote a long letter to her husband describing the change in spending that their new wealth required. She wanted a larger allowance of L1,600 a quarter, twenty gowns, "six of them excellent good ones, eight of them for the country, and six other of them very excellent good ones," and L600 quarterly for charity. She wanted horses of her own and additional servants, two gentlewomen, eight gentlemen, and two footmen. She required two coaches drawn by four horses: her own coach had to be lined with velvet and laced with gold, her gentlewomen's coach laced with scarlet. Her gentlemen usher required his own horse so as not to crowd her in her coach. Lady Compton requested L2,200 in cash, payment of her debts, and new jewelry. "I would have L6,000 to buy me jewels, and L4,000 to buy me a pearl chain." Then she turned to house and home to describe rich and elaborate furnishings far from the gloomy interiors often labeled "Jacobean."

Also I will have all my houses furnished, and all my lodging chambers to be suited with all such furniture as is fit; as beds, stools, chairs, suitable cushions, carpets, silver warming pans, cupboards of plate, fair hangings, and such like. So for my drawing chamber in all houses, I will have them delicately furnished, both with hangings, couch, canopy, glass, carpet, chair, cushions, and all things there unto belonging.

She concluded "I pray, when you be an earl, to allow me L1000 more than now desired, and double attendance."[25] It is said that, shortly after he inherited his father-in-law's wealth, Compton had a nervous breakdown. He recovered to become Earl of Northampton in 1618. One observer noted that Compton had transformed his father-in-law's house in Bishopsgate "into a gay court, the old usurer himself being forgotten."[26]

In addition to labeling luxuries as excellent, suitable, and delicate, contemporaries re-labeled some luxury imports as staples of the English economy instead of foreign commodities. Indeed, in 1641, in a debate on trade in the House of Commons, Sir Thomas Roe, longtime ambassador to

---

[25] Godfrey Goodman, Bishop of Gloucester, *The Court of King James the First*, ed. John S. Brewer, 2 vols. (London: Richard Bentley, 1839), II, pp. 127–32. When traveling, her laundresses, chambermaids and grooms would be sent ahead "that the chambers may be ready, sweet, and clean." Lady Compton advised her husband to pay his debts, build Ashby House, buy land, and never to loan money to Thomas Howard, Earl of Suffolk.

[26] *CSPD 1603–10*, p. 602, 19 April 1610, Francis Smith to John Nicholas.

the East Indies and to Turkey, praised the East India direct and re-export trade as the key to England's economic health. "Nothing exported of our own growth hath balanced our riotous consumption at home but those foreign commodities which I call naturalized, that is the surplus of our East India trade, which being brought home in greater quantity than are spent within the kingdom, are exported again and become in value and use as natural commodities."[27]

In contrast, some contemporary moralists continued to rail against luxury, effeminacy, and the commodification of honor from the pulpit to city comedies despite the increasing importance of worldwide trade to the economy. Sumptuary bills continued to be introduced in parliament up to 1640. One member of parliament in 1621 argued on behalf of sumptuary legislation by saying that "God did not attire our first parents with excrements of worms."[28] But none passed. Instead of statute, the Crown turned to prescription. In 1610 James I noted "the necessity of taking some politic order gainst excess of apparel."[29] While Francis Bacon advised the reintroduction of sumptuary legislation, the Privy Council in 1622 settled for hopes of "less vanity in the expence of silks and foreign stuffs."[30] The King's subjects eagerly embraced the new, the rare, the curious, and the modern in the early seventeenth-century England with the partial blessing of the Crown.

LUXURY AND THE HISTORIANS

The history of consumption has been connected to issues of power, gender, colonialism, construction of the self, the transformation of the domestic and public spheres, and the relationship of art and the economy.[31] Werner Sombart famously argued that luxury consumption led to the rise of capitalism in early modern Europe.[32] European historians, such as Richard Goldthwaite and Lisa Jardine, have placed luxury consumption

---

[27] *Sir Thomas Roe, His Speech in Parliament. Wherein he Sheweth the cause of the decay of coine and trade in this land, especially of merchants trade. And also propoundeth a way to the House, how they may be increased* (London, 1641).

[28] Quoted in Negley Boyd Harte, "State Control of Dress and Social Change in Pre-Industrial England," in D. C. Coleman and A. M. John (eds.), *Trade, Government and Economy in Pre-Industrial England: Essays Presented to F. J. Fisher* (London: Weidenfeld and Nicholson, 1976), p. 149.

[29] *Ibid.*, p. 150.   [30] *Ibid.*, pp. 150–51.

[31] See note 9 above and Michael North and David Ormrod (eds.), *Art Markets in Europe, 1400-1800* (Aldershot, Hompshire: Ashgate Publishing, 1998); Richard L. Bushman, *The Refinement of America: Persons, Houses, Cities* (New York: Knopf, 1992).

[32] Sombart, *Luxury and Capitalism*, pp. 58–171.

at the heart of economic and cultural change in the Renaissance, as has Simon Schama for the Dutch Golden Age.[33]

British consumption studies, led by Neil McKendrick, John Brewer, and J. H. Plumb's paradigmatic work, *The Birth of a Consumer Society*, and the series of volumes of essays edited by John Brewer, locate the arrival of new goods, new modes of shopping, and the reshaping of identities through consumables in the "long" eighteenth century, underlining the connection of the consumer revolution to the industrial revolution. According to this view, eighteenth-century luxury consumption, fueled by new wants and new wares purchased by middle-class consumers, marked a sharp departure from the court-centered consumption of previous centuries.[34] Maxine Berg's Luxury Project at the University of Warwick has explored important aspects of eighteenth-century luxury consumption in several conferences and two edited volumes.[35] Woodruff Smith has recently analyzed the connection of consumption and respectability by linking international trade to middle-class consumption in the late seventeenth and eighteenth centuries.[36] Recent review essays have, however, perceptively challenged these prevailing paradigms and questioned their focus on the eighteenth century.[37] Still, little of the new work analyzes the significant role of luxury consumption in the early seventeenth century.

While historians of sixteenth-century England, such as F. J. Fisher, Joan Thirsk, and, more recently, Craig Muldrew, have emphasized the importance of conspicuous consumption, consumer industries, and credit, seventeenth-century English historians have not in the main attended to the issue of luxury consumption. Most of the rich archival studies of

---

[33] Richard Goldthwaite, *Wealth and the Demand for Art in Italy, 1300–1600*; Lisa Jardine, *Worldly Goods: A New History of the Renaissance* (New York: W. W. Norton, 1996); Simon Schama, *The Embarrassment of Riches: An Interpretation of Dutch Culture in the Golden Age* (New York: Knopf, 1987).

[34] Brewer and Porter, eds., *Consumption and the World of Goods*; John Brewer and Susan Staves (eds.), *Early Modern Conceptions of Property* (London and New York: Routledge, 1995); Ann Bermingham and John Brewer (eds.), *The Consumption of Culture, 1600–1800: Image, Object, Text* (London: Routledge, 1995).

[35] Maxine Berg and Helen Clifford (eds.), *Consumers and Luxury: Consumer Culture in Europe, 1650–1850* (Manchester: Manchester University Press, 1999). Maxine Berg and Elizabeth Eger (eds.), *Luxury in the Eighteenth Century: Debates, Desires, and Delectable Goods* (Basingstoke: Palgrave, MacMillan, 2003).

[36] Smith, *Consumption and the Making of Respectability, 1600–1800*.

[37] Sara Pennell, "Consumption and Consumerism in Early Modern England," *Historical Journal*, 42 (1999), 549–64. Mary Louise Roberts, "Gender, Consumption and Commodity Culture," *American Historical Review*, 103 (1998), 817–44; Craig Clunas, "Modernity Global and Local: Consumption and the Rise of the West," *American Historical Review*, 104 (1999), 1497–1511; Cissie Fairchilds, "Consumption in Early Modern Europe: A Review Article," *Comparative Studies in Society and History*, 35 (1993), 850–58.

the last twenty years have looked elsewhere. Thus the debate over revision-ism and post-revisionism has galvanized political historians for the last two decades.[38] Important political and religious debates of the seventeenth century continue to be fruitfully explored.[39] The New British History has turned attention to the archipelago and the making of the British state.[40] Popular politics, reading practices, print and culture have been closely examined.[41] Social and economic historians, working within a larger chrono-logical framework of the early modern, defined as 1500–1650 or 1500–1700, have mainly focused on demography, community studies, gender, and poverty.[42] The traditional bifurcation of seventeenth-century studies at the Civil War continues: political historians of the sixteenth and seventeenth centuries often end their work in 1640 or 1642, while Civil War historians focus on the period 1640–1660, obscuring continuities across the century. As a result, the "long" eighteenth century reaches back to 1660 or even 1650.

In contrast, historians of towns, especially of London, have much to say about seventeenth-century consumption, from the seminal work of F. J. Fisher to the work of Ian Archer, Jeremy Boulton, Peter Clark, Vanessa Harding, Derek Keene, David Harris Sacks and Paul Seaver.[43] Recent work by Jules Lubbock, David Kuhta, and Toby Barnard on material culture, Pauline

---

[38] Conrad Russell, *Parliaments and English Politics, 1621-29* (Oxford: Clarendon Press, 1979) is at the center of a literature that includes important work by Tom Cogswell, Richard Cust, Ann Hughes, Mark Kishlansky and Kevin Sharpe.

[39] Peter Lake and Michael Questier, *The Anti-Christ's Lewd Hat: Protestants, Papists and Players in Post-Reformation England* (New Haven: Yale University Press, 2002).

[40] John Stephen Morrill, "The British Problem *c.* 1534–1707," in Brendan Bradshaw and John Stephen Morrill (eds.), *The British Problem, c. 1534–1707: State Formation in the Atlantic Archipelago* (Basingstoke: Macmillan, 1996), pp. 1–38; Michael J. Braddick, *State Formation in Early Modern England, c. 1550–1700* (Cambridge: Cambridge University Press, 2000); Steven C. A. Pincus, "Reconceiving Seventeenth-Century Political Culture," *Journal of British Studies*, 38:1 (1999), 98–111.

[41] Tim Harris (ed.), *The Politics of the Excluded, c. 1500–1850* (Basingstoke and New York: Palgrave, 2001); Kevin M. Sharpe, *Reading Revolutions: The Politics of Reading in Early Modern England* (New Haven: Yale University Press, 2000); Lois G. Schwoerer, *The Ingenious Mr. Henry Care, Restoration Publicist* (Baltimore: Johns Hopkins University Press, 2001); Melinda S. Zook, *Radical Whigs and Conspiratorial Politics in Late Stuart England* (University Park: Pennsylvania State University Press, 1999).

[42] Keith Wrightson, *Earthly Necessities: Economic Lives in Early Modern Britain* (New Haven: Yale University Press, 2000); Peter Clark (ed.), *The Cambridge Urban History of Britain*, Vol. II: *1540–1840* (Cambridge: Cambridge University Press, 2000); Sara Heller Mendelson and Patricia Crawford, *Women in Early Modern England, 1550–1720* (Oxford: Clarendon Press, 1998).

[43] Fisher, "The Development of London as a Centre of Conspicuous Consumption," 37–50; David Harris Sacks, *The Widening Gate: Bristol and the Atlantic Economy, 1450–1700* (Berkeley: University of California Press, 1991); Lena Cowen Orlin (ed.), *Material London, ca. 1600* (Philadelphia: University of Pennsylvania Press, 2000), especially David Harris Sacks, "London's Dominion: The Metropolis, the Market Economy, and the State" pp. 20–54; Derek Keene, "Material London in Time and Space," pp. 55–74; Ian Archer "Material Londoners," pp. 174–92; Paul Seaver, *Wallington's World: a Puritan Artisan in Seventeenth-Century London* (Stanford, CA: Stanford University Press, 1985).

Croft, Kevin Sharpe, and Malcolm Smuts on court culture, and David Ormrod, and John Styles on art, design, and economics contribute to a new direction in seventeenth-century studies.[44]

Recently, Jan de Vries, drawing on the Enlightenment debate over luxury, contrasted "Old" and "New Luxury" in the seventeenth-century Dutch Republic.[45] "New Luxury" consumption differed from earlier forms of consuming, he suggests, because its middle-class exponents aimed at sociability and comfort rather than aristocratic distinction and display. "New Luxury" consumption was urban not courtly. "New Luxury" was based on innumerable choices presented by a growing economy and choices made by many more people.

I argue here, however, that the highly differentiated categories of "Old Luxury" and "New Luxury" are difficult to overlay on seventeenth-century English practice. The contrast between "Old Luxury" and "New Luxury" fails to connect consumption patterns and Crown policies of the late sixteenth and early seventeenth centuries with those of the late seventeenth century. The English elite borrowed manners, mentalities, artifacts, products, skills, and trade from abroad throughout the seventeenth century and, as a result, increased domestic demand for luxury goods and reconfigured earlier patterns of trade. Indeed, overlapping relationships of old luxuries and old consumers, old luxuries and new consumers, new luxuries and old consumers, new luxuries and new consumers all suggest that the binary division of "Old Luxury" and New is too simple.

Twenty-five years ago, Joan Thirsk showed that popular and diversified consumer industries expanded in the English countryside in the sixteenth and early seventeenth centuries.[46] More recently, Craig Muldrew explored how extensive credit networks underlay that consumption.[47] Lorna

---

[44] Jules Lubbock, *The Tyranny of Taste: The Politics of Architecture and Design in Britain, 1550–1960* (New Haven: Published for the Paul Mellon Centre for British Art by Yale University Press, 1995); David Kuhta, *The Three-Piece Suit and Modern Masculinity, England, 1550–1850* (Berkeley: University of California Press, 2002); Kevin Sharpe, *Remapping Early Modern England: The Culture of Seventeenth-Century Politics* (Cambridge: Cambridge University Press, 2000); R. Malcolm Smuts, *Culture and Power in England, 1585–1685* (New York: St. Martin's Press, 1999); Toby C. Barnard, *Making the Grand Figure: Lives and Possessions in Ireland, 1641–1770* (New Haven: Yale University Press, 2004); Pauline Croft, *Patronage, Culture and Power: The Early Cecils* (New Haven: Yale University Press, 2002); North and Ormrod (eds.), *Art Markets in Europe, 1400–1800*; Michael Snodin and John Styles, *Design and the Decorative Arts: Britain, 1500–1900* (London: Victoria & Albert Museum, 2001).

[45] Jan de Vries, "Luxury in the Dutch Golden Age in Theory and Practice," in Berg and Eger (eds.), *Luxury in the Eighteenth Century*, pp. 41–56.

[46] Thirsk, *Economic Policy and Projects.*   [47] Muldrew, *The Economy of Obligation.*

Weatherill and Carole Shammas documented the diffusion of modest consumer goods in early modern England and America.[48] The Centre for Metropolitan History has looked in detail at the acquisition of skills from 1500 to 1750.[49] Nevertheless, important studies of the proliferation of luxury goods as "new" continue to focus on the eighteenth-century market. If new, where, we might ask, did those consumers of the sixteenth and seventeenth centuries go? I suggest they went shopping.

INCREASING DEMAND

England's population increased by over a million between 1601 and 1651 sustained by new crops and methods that allowed farmers to extend land under cultivation.[50] The early seventeenth century saw a significant increase in the importation of luxury goods, including textiles, wine, and food. While the value of imports to London was the same in 1600 as it had been in 1560, by 1620 it was 40 percent higher. The value of imported silk fabrics more than doubled between 1560 and 1622 to L79,530.[51] This growth in demand for imported luxury goods stemmed from several sources: faster population growth amongst the aristocracy (nobility, baronets, knights, and well-to-do gentry) than the rest of the population; increasing agricultural rents that provided more disposable income, and the increase in honors and titles granted by King James so that more people not only desired but also practiced the life of the aristocracy.[52]

Peace with Spain in 1604 fostered the expansion of English trade. In addition, currency manipulation on the continent caused merchants to bring back luxury goods rather than bullion in exchange for exports of English cloth. "All these monies our merchants now bestow in silks with the Italians and return none in specie because the silks yield them more

---

[48] Lorna Weatherill, *Consumer Behaviour and Material Culture in Britain, 1660–1720* (London: Routledge, 1988); Carole Shammas, *The Pre-Industrial Consumer in England and America* (Oxford: Clarendon Press, 1990).

[49] David Mitchell (ed.), *Goldsmiths, Silversmiths and Bankers: Innovation and the Transfer of Skill, 1550–1750* (London: Centre for Metropolitan History, 1995).

[50] Christopher G. A. Clay, *Economic Expansion and Social Change: England, 1500–1700*, 2 vols. (Cambridge: Cambridge University Press, 1984).

[51] *Ibid.*, II, pp. 123–24. Clay draws his statistics from the Millard thesis of 1956 which is the only study of the import trade.

[52] Lawrence Stone, *The Crisis of the Aristocracy, 1558–1641* (Oxford: Clarendon Press, 1965); Felicity Heal and Clive Holmes, *The Gentry in England and Wales, 1500–1700* (Stanford: Stanford University Press, 1994). On population growth in London see Vanessa Harding, "The Population of London 1550–1700: A Review of the Published Evidence," *London Journal,* 15 (1990), 111–28.

profit in their returns."[53] English merchants, responding both to currency changes and diversification of the economy, not only enhanced the import market for luxury goods but also expanded the re-export market underpinned by their increasing control of Italian trading networks and trade to the East and West Indies.[54] The Crown created the farthing token project in 1613 to provide small change for commercial transactions.[55] In the midst of the cloth crisis, as imports increased and exports decreased between 1617 and 1622, King James, the Privy Council, and Parliament took part in an important economic debate over international trade, especially the role of the East India Company.[56] The Venetians complained in the 1630s that "The Londons [sic] do the greatest harm to Venetian cloth as they not only imitate its colours, but can sell at a lower price, thus tempting the middle and lower classes to buy them."[57]

Revitalized Italian luxury manufacturing, especially of silks and the finest velvets, found a ready market in England. Christopher Clay points out that the symbols of aristocratic status changed; while the gentry kept fewer servants, they increased the number and variety of their material goods including, "chimney pieces and plaster work, furniture, hangings, carpets, pictures, plate, pewter, brass and glassware … dress and elaborate coaches. The very rich always retained a fondness for imported goods."[58]

Yet demand came from all regions and sectors of society. Jan de Vries points to an "industrious revolution" at the end of the sixteenth century. Even though their wages fell, working families, including men, women, and children, appear to have increased their production in order to continue and expand consumption.[59] In small towns and rural areas, mercers and haberdashers offered their customers new textiles and a bit of silk and velvet. The accounts of the Longs of Whaddon in Wiltshire include lace, silk, and taffeta for a doublet and hose.[60] Retailers with larger businesses could expect London mercers to bring wares into the countryside.[61]

---

[53] Quoted in B. E. Supple, *Commercial Crisis and Change in England, 1600–1642: A Study in the Instability of a Mercantile Economy* (Cambridge: Cambridge University Press, 1959), p. 91.

[54] *Ibid.*, pp. 90–93.

[55] *CSPD 1611–18*, pp. 140, 141, 175, 180, 184, 215, 237, 258, 322, 387, 456.

[56] Supple, *Commercial Crisis and Change in England, 1600–42*, pp. 197–201; Joyce Appleby, *Economic Thought and Ideology in Seventeenth-Century England* (Princeton: Princeton University Press, 1978).

[57] Quoted in Supple, *Commercial Crisis and Change in England, 1600–42*, p. 160.

[58] Clay, *Economic Expansion and Social Change*, II, p. 25.

[59] Jan de Vries, "Between Purchasing Power and the World of Goods: Understanding the Household Economy in Early Modern Europe," in Brewer and Porter (eds.), *Consumption and the World of Goods*, pp. 85–132.

[60] BL Add. Mss. 15,567, Accounts 1604-, f. 95.

[61] Berger, *The Most Necessary Luxuries*; Cox, *The Complete Tradesman*; Spufford, *Petty Chapmen*.

Litigation for debt shows consumption at all levels of society.[62] Local mercers sold luxury goods, petty chapmen carried them on their backs, and news of fashions spread through letters, print, and visits, linking the farthest parts of the kingdom with London.[63] Even more important were orders to London merchants and travel to London. The gentry spent increasing amounts of time in the capital where the profusion of goods were on display.

Imported goods increasingly appeared in London shops, which served a widening range of the well-to-do. The fashion for elaborate clothing ensured that men as well as women made up the audience for London's increasing abundance and diversity of luxury wares. The numbers of new goods increased rapidly from the sixteenth century on. In 1507 the Book of Rates listed 300 commodities which had to pay customs. By 1558 the number had grown to 1100.[64] The Book of Rates of 1613 included duties on window glass, looking glasses, and hourglasses, from France, Flanders, and Venice. Gloves of all sorts arrived from Spain and Italy. The most expensive, wrought with gold and silver, came from Milan and Venice and paid a duty of 30 shillings the dozen pair. Tapestry, velvets, virginals, and sugar appeared in greater numbers in Jacobean England. Silks of all kinds, from Paris, Granada, Naples, and Spain were available. Naples silk, the most luxurious, paid duties of twenty-six shillings eight pence a pound.[65] In 1647, between the first and second civil wars, an ordinance required that new imports including "a certain silk stuff called Sarsenets of Genoa, and other silk stuff called pranella and all other silk stuffs of the like fabrics or goodness be henceforth rated."[66]

Over the course of the century new manufactured goods, such as watches, clocks, pictures, prints, scientific instruments, were imported and sold not only to the ruling family but to the well-to-do more generally. At the same time, exotic products, such as tobacco, coffee, chocolate, and tea, penetrated the English market. In 1634, for instance, Lord Coventry

---

[62] Muldrew, *The Economy of Obligation.*
[63] Richard Cust, "News and Politics in Early Seventeenth-Century England," *Past & Present,* 112 (1986), 60–90; F. J. Levy, "How Information Spread Among the Gentry, 1550–1640," *Journal of British Studies,* 21 (1982), 11–34; Susan E. Whyman, *Sociability and Power in Late-Stuart England: The Cultural Worlds of the Verneys, 1660–1720* (Oxford: Oxford University Press, 1999).
[64] Cox, *The Complete Tradesman,* pp. 8–9; there were more than 1,800 ratable goods by 1784. Nancy C. Cox, "Objects of Worth, Objects of Desire: Towards a Dictionary of Traded Goods and Commodities 1550–1800," *Material History Review,* 39 (1994), 24–41.
[65] Folger Shakespeare Library, *Book of Rates* (London, 1613).
[66] Thomason tracts, E. 419 (29), p. 20, 16 December 1647.

issued thousands of licenses to retail tobacco.[67] Nevertheless, clothing, textiles, and building dominated luxury consumption.[68]

London was the engine that drove consumption between 1500 and 1700 as F. J. Fisher so tellingly argued decades ago.[69] Since 1980, important studies of sixteenth- and seventeenth-century London have explored the demography, sociology, economy, politics, and culture of the capital.[70] Between 1550 and 1650, as the city grew to the third largest in Europe, perhaps one in eight of the English spent some time in London.[71] From the middle of the sixteenth century on, London had become the center for luxury production "with an exceptionally high density of skilled workers in an unprecedented range of trades."[72] While seventeenth-century England is often associated with the country house in poetry, politics, and architecture, more and more members of the nobility and gentry spent more and more time in London. As we shall see, despite King James's policy to encourage them to return to their counties, the greatest built palaces on the Strand; others boarded with barber-surgeons and innkeepers. The Duke of Bedford built Covent Garden to house them; the Royal Exchange and the New Exchange catered to their love of finery; by the end of the century, Charles Cheyne and Sir Hans Sloane developed Chelsea as an aristocratic enclave. In fact, early Stuart efforts to send nobility and gentry back to the country to take up their duties as local governors clashed with other royal initiatives to build luxury housing and shopping districts in the capital.

[67] I am grateful to Conrad Russell for this reference to the Conway Papers.

[68] On seventeenth-century industries, see Thirsk, *Economic Policy and Projects*; Sybil Jack, *Trade and Industry in Tudor and Stuart England* (London: Allen and Unwin, 1977); and A. L. Beier, "Engine of Manufactures: The Trades of London," in A. L. Beier and Roger Finlay, *London 1500–1700: The Making of a Metropolis* (London and New York: Longman, 1986), pp. 141–67. On interior decoration see Peter M. Thornton, *Seventeenth-Century Interior Decoration in England, France and Holland* (New Haven: Yale University Press, 1978); John Styles, "The Goldsmiths and the London Luxury Trades, 1550 to 1750," in Mitchell (ed.), *Goldsmiths, Silversmiths and Bankers*, p. 119.

[69] F. J. Fisher, *London and the English Economy, 1500–1700*, (ed.) P. J. Corfield and N. B. Harte (London: Hambledon Press, 1990).

[70] See Ian Archer, *The Pursuit of Stability: Social Relations in Elizabethan London* (Cambridge: Cambridge University Press, 1991); Beier and Finlay, *London 1500–1700: The Making of a Metropolis*; Roger Finlay, *Population and the Metropolis: The Demography of London, 1580–1650* (Cambridge: Cambridge University Press, 1981); Jeremy Boulton, *Neighbourhood and Society: A London Suburb in the Seventeenth Century* (Cambridge: Cambridge University Press, 1987); Harding, "The Population of London 1550–1700," 111–28. Orlin, *Material London, ca. 1600*; Whyman, *Sociability and Power in Late Stuart England*; Julia F. Merritt (ed.), *Imagining Early Modern London: Perceptions and Portrayals of the City from Stow to Strype 1598–1720* (Cambridge: Cambridge University Press, 2001); Mark Jenner and Paul Griffiths (eds.), *Londinopolis: Essays in the Cultural and Social History of Early Modern London* (Manchester: Manchester University Press, 2000).

[71] Boulton, *Neighbourhood and Society*; Roger Finlay, *Population and the Metropolis*.

[72] Styles, "The Goldsmiths and the London Luxury Trades, 1550–1750," pp. 114–15.

While the import of luxury goods was not new – oriental luxuries, for instance, had been imported in the fifteenth century[73] – these increasingly diverse luxury imports of the seventeenth century appeared as both fruit and stimulus of expanding travel and trade networks by the English within Europe, the Atlantic world, and the known continents. The result, driven by demographic growth and increasing profits from land and trade, brought new wares into new kinds of shops.

The well-off increasingly identified themselves as cosmopolitan through the appropriation of continental luxuries. Shaking off aspects of cultural isolation at the end of the sixteenth century, they sought to share in a Western European culture which was expressed in what they read, how they lived, what they wore, where they went, what they built, and who they imagined themselves to be. New artifacts helped to craft reinvented identities. English society as a whole used new as well as traditional luxury goods as gifts to mark relationships between patron and client, master and servant, and good neighbors.

The literature on luxury consumption asserts an independent taste for the middle class rather than a trickle down of aristocratic taste. *City Merchants and the Arts, 1670–1720* puts this question explicitly by asking whether merchant taste followed aristocratic taste or aristocratic taste followed merchant taste?[74] I suggest an integrated approach. In the late sixteenth century and early decades of the seventeenth century, new goods from Asia appeared in England first in the houses and inventories of those at court with closest connections to the King. The privileges of these great importers from the Indies and the Levant depended on royal favor. The desire for and use of imported goods by the titled and wealthy rested on merchant networks and ambassadorial gift-giving. Privy councillors such as Henry Howard, Earl of Northampton, and the favorite Robert Carr, Earl of Somerset, had lacquered chests by 1615. William Cecil, Lord Burghley, and Queen Elizabeth had received a collection of porcelain ewers and bowls in the 1580s. Somerset had a collection of porcelain and the Duke of Buckingham did too by the 1620s. The Countess of Arundel, Rubens's first English patron, furnished Tart Hall, her suburban villa, with Indian furnishings. She displayed an extensive collection of porcelain on shelves around her new "Pranketing House" designed for entertaining.[75] The

---

[73] Ronald Findlay, "Globalization and the European Economy: Medieval Origins to the Industrial Revolution," in Ronald Findlay and Kevin O'Rourke (eds.), *Commodity Market Integration, 1500–2000* (Cambridge, MA: National Bureau of Economic Research, 2001), pp. 1–46.

[74] Mireille Galinou (ed.), *City Merchants and the Arts, 1670–1720* (Oblong: Corporation of London, 2004), p. xi.

[75] See chapter 5 below.

houses of leading merchants and their families, such as Lady Noell, displayed collections of porcelain and Asian lacquer in the 1660s. Wealth, influence, power, knowledge, and cosmopolitan identity made these new goods desirable; merchants, ambassadors, retailers, and artisans made them available to consumers beyond the court.

In reaction to increasing imports, the Crown met widespread domestic demand for luxury goods by deliberately developing domestic luxury industries. It aimed not only to bring the great nobility under its sway through conspicuous consumption at court, as Norbert Elias argued,[76] but, just as importantly, to diversify the economy through patents of monopoly that promised to substitute domestic production for a wide range of imports. After all, in exchange for luxury goods, English merchants traditionally exported textiles, alabaster and ashes, hats and herring, Irish mantles and animal skins, and new and old shoes![77] Early Stuart policy aimed not only to enhance trade but to create luxury manfactures at home.

Patents for new manufacturing processes proposed to provide work for a growing population and to increase their skills through encouraging immigration or by copying continental practice. Dating back to the 1570s, patents began to be systematically recorded from 1617. Many in the period from 1617 to 1640 were for luxury goods.[78] While patents are not necessarily an index of successful invention, they do show the desire to claim innovation. There were more patents issued in the 1620s and 1630s than there were between 1660 and 1680.[79] In the 1640s and 1650s writers like Walter Blith, William Petty, and Samuel Hartlib urged improvement, emphasizing the importance of the transfer of skills.[80] The Crown's efforts to create luxury industries at home aimed to stem imports not to monopolize luxury. Unlike *ancien régime* France there was no attempt to create exclusive workshops or goods available to the Crown alone or to control design solely for the sake of the court in seventeenth-century England.[81]

The import of skilled labor proved instrumental in transforming the English economy from the late sixteenth century to the late seventeenth

---

[76] Norbert Elias, *The Court Society* (Oxford: Blackwell, 1983).

[77] *The Rates of Merchandizes as They Are Set Down in the Book of Rates* (London, 1613), Folger, STC 7690.8.

[78] *Chronological Index of Patents of Invention Applied for and Patents Granted* (London, 1854). Oxford, Bodleian Library, Bankes Mss. See chapter 2 below.

[79] B. R. Mitchell, *British Historical Statistics* (Cambridge: Cambridge University Press, 1988), p. 438.

[80] Walter Blith, *The English Improver Improved*, 2nd edn (London, 1652), p. 235; on Petty and Hartlib, see chapter 8 below.

[81] See Leora Auslander, *Taste and Power: Furnishing Modern France* (Berkeley: University of California Press, 1996).

century. French Protestants, fleeing persecution during the French Wars of Religion, and Flemings from the Dutch war with the Spanish, migrated to England or were expressly imported to bring new skills to the clothing industries. In 1565 Thomas Howard, the fourth Duke of Norfolk, received a royal license for "30 Dutchmen of the Low Countries of Flanders" along with their families, to make "bays, arras, says, tapestry, mockadoes ... and such other outlandish commodities as hath not been used to be made within our realm of England." The mayor of Norwich had sought these new workers because "the commodities of worsted making is greatly decayed ... great number of poor of the city were set on work by spinning, weaving, dying."[82] Although they brought skills in goldsmithing and bookmaking, many of the Huguenots who settled in England had not necessarily worked in the clothing trades before they arrived. But the development of Huguenot enclaves in London and regional centres such as Norwich helped newcomers to learn textile skills. The second wave of Huguenot settlers after the Revocation of the Edict of Nantes in 1685 settled especially in Spitalfields, the center for silk textile trades.[83] In addition, in the early seventeenth century, glass workers from Murano worked both in England and Scotland, and the Virginia Company sent skilled labor from Italy, France, and Albania to the colony of Virginia.[84]

Luxury producers, including goldsmiths, jewelers, coach makers, silk weavers, and lacquerers among others, according to John Styles, relied not only on craftsmen from abroad but also on imported designs from France, Germany, and the Netherlands.[85] In *Art and Decoration in Elizabethan and Jacobean England,*[86] Anthony Wells-Cole has shown the crucial impact of Low Countries design on English decorative goods. Continental architecture books and their engraved details by Serlio, Vredeman de Vries, and other continental writers, published in the late sixteenth century, provided patterns that influenced English builders from the middle of the sixteenth century to the late seventeenth century.[87]

---

[82] Quoted by B. A. Holderness, "The Reception and Distribution of the New Draperies in England," in Negley Boyd. Harte (ed.), *The New Draperies in the Low Countries and England* (Oxford: Oxford University Press, 1997), pp. 217–18, 220.

[83] Clay, *Economic Expansion and Social Change*, II, pp. 39, 81–82, and Lien Bich Luu, "French-Speaking Refugees and the Foundations of the London Silk Industry," *Proceedings of the Huguenot Society,* 26 (1997), 564–76.

[84] See chapter 2 below.

[85] Styles, "The Goldsmiths and the London Luxury Trades, 1550–1750," pp. 116–18.

[86] Anthony Wells-Cole, *Art and Decoration in Elizabethan and Jacobean England: The Influence of Continental Prints, 1558–1625* (New Haven: Yale University Press, 1997).

[87] See chapter 5 below.

The rage for luxury goods, which had taken shape in the first half of the seventeenth century, continued during the English Civil War and Interregnum, now turned in new directions by the exigencies of war and exile. Although lacking for the 1640s and 1650s, trade statistics show that between 1640 and 1663, exports doubled.[88] The disruption of the two civil wars must have been temporary and, indeed, masked remarkable continuation of growth in imports and exports, with a dip perhaps, in the mid-1640s. Other evidence suggests that the English Civil War and religious ideology made little dent in luxury consumption and, indeed, fostered it.

GENDER AND LUXURY

Contemporary moralists, playwrights such as Ben Jonson, and analysts from Werner Sombart to Daniel Roche have identified women as agents of novelty, fashion, and economic change.[89] Elizabeth Kowaleski-Wallace and Karen Newman have examined the prominent theme of women as shoppers in eighteenth-century literature.[90] *Consuming Splendor* argues that the representations of sexual encounters and sexual gaze of customer and wench, lady and merchant, gallants and their amours were already in place in the early seventeenth century. Criticism of women shopping in public, analyzed by Judith Walkowitz and Erika Rappaport for the nineteenth and twentieth centuries, had its counterpart in seventeenth-century complaint literature.[91] In her extensive study of defamation cases, Laura Gowing has shown that women were at risk from accusation of looseness when they strayed from home or into the gardens on the edge of town.[92]

In practice, of course, women at all social levels made consumption decisions for the household and some engaged in the retail trades. Despite the limitations of coverture, which, interpreted strictly, meant that women could not make contracts, over the course of the seventeenth century married women, who had no standing in common law, were allowed to buy increasing amounts of luxury goods to support their husband's and

---

[88] Clay, *Economic Expansion and Social Change*, II, p. 143, Table 12.

[89] Sombart, *Luxury and Capitalism*. Daniel Roche, "Between a 'moral economy' and a 'consumer economy,'" p. 223.

[90] Elizabeth Kowaleski-Wallace, *Consuming Subjects: Women, Shopping and Business in the Eighteenth Century* (New York: Columbia University Press, 1997).

[91] Judith R. Walkowitz, "Going Public: Shopping, Street Harassment, and Streetwalking in Late Victorian London," *Representations*, 62 (1998), 1–30; Erika Rappaport, *Shopping for Pleasure: Women in the Making of London's West End* (Princeton: Princeton University Press, 2000).

[92] Laura Gowing, "'The Freedom of the Streets': Women and Social Space 1560–1640," in Jenner and Griffiths (eds.), *Londinopolis*, pp. 130–51.

family's status.[93] Women's luxury consumption took place in public as well as in private. Jacobean and Caroline women attended the theatre often without their husbands or male relatives, walked in public gardens, and went to the Royal and New Exchanges. As we have seen, in cases where they were wealthy enough, wives made explicit demands on their husbands for specific sorts of luxury goods. At the same time, men took a prominent role alongside women in shopping for and consuming luxury goods. Indeed, some contemporaries worried that luxury consumption challenged the boundaries of gender roles, fostered effeminacy, and thereby undermined martial spirit and the political and social order.

Luxury goods offered all individuals the means to project political and economic power, to veil, to shape, and draw attention to the body, to redefine their identity, and to construct their sense of self. Those places and spaces where luxury was on display, from the royal court to the home, from the market to the church, provided the social ties around which connections were formed between king and subjects, household and family, friends and neighbors, petitioners and God. In particular, new public places in which to walk, to talk, to linger, to flirt, and to shop, such as the Exchanges, the Mulberry Gardens, the Spring Gardens, and Hyde Park, suggest a new public sphere well before the emergence of the mid-seventeenth-century coffeehouse and the eighteenth-century salon.

PRESENTING THE ARGUMENT

Consuming Splendor, tracing themes of luxury consumption and cultural borrowing from the early seventeenth century through to the Restoration, presents an additional approach to seventeenth-century studies and contributes to three important debates: the first on the development of luxury consumption and its agents, the second on luxury and gender, and the third on the importance of foreign imports to the domestic economy.

Luxury consumption grew unevenly from the sixteenth century, supported by a matrix of monarchy, aristocracy, and merchants. The policies of James I at the beginning of the seventeenth century provided significant support for London-centered luxury. Examining those mentalities that made the English eager borrowers of technological improvement and

---

[93] Margot C. Finn, "Women, Consumption, and Coverture in England, *c.* 1760–1860," *Historical Journal,* 39 (1996), 703–22. For case law on necessaries see *Baron and Feme: A Treatise of Law and Equity Concerning Husbands and Wives,* 3rd edn (London, 1738); *Stroud's Judicial Dictionary of Words and Phrases,* ed. John S. James, 4th edn. 5 vols. (London: Sweet and Maxwell, 1973), III, pp. 1734–35.

foreign products, *Consuming Splendor* demonstrates that building, buying, and collecting went on during and despite the English civil wars and the Interregnum.

Chapter 1 examines the creation of a new infrastructure for the sale of luxury goods. The chapter documents how the well-to-do bought luxury goods through networks and agents between London and the countryside. It goes on to demonstrate the emergence of retail shopping as entertainment in the early seventeenth century and examines the issue of gender and shopping as well as the role of women as patrons, consumers, and shopkeepers. Chapter 2 analyzes persistent efforts in the early seventeenth century to transfer continental styles and continental technology in a wide variety of luxury manufactures. The chapter suggests that the state's policy of import substitution went hand in hand with its promotion of luxury in the name of plenty, employment, and honor.[94] The Crown explicitly brought colonial economies into efforts to expand domestic production of luxuries. It also argues that the silk project generated a trade literature that promoted luxury manufactures and consumption as a public good decades before Nicholas Barbon and Bernard Mandeville. Chapter 3 examines how new wants were created and explores the roles of information, emulation, and agency in consumption. It looks specifically at the relationship of print, travel, and education to luxury consumption. Chapter 4 analyzes seventeenth-century collecting as a specific case of luxury consumption. It considers the role of ambassadors, merchants, and other agents in importing goods and shaping taste, the problem in overcoming labels of effeminacy and Catholicism, and the recasting of natural and artificial artifacts as luxury goods. Chapter 5 looks at building and rebuilding in London and the countryside between 1603 and 1640, the circulation of continental architectural manuals, and the importation of continental styles and their diffusion to the countryside through the work of Inigo Jones and the Smythsons.

Chapter 6 considers how luxury consumption developed during the English Civil War. It demonstrates that trade grew while armies clashed. Exile offered royalists the opportunity to appropriate continental material culture. An active secondhand art market emerged in the midst of the Protectorate and building recommenced after 1650 in earnest. Its variety and extravagance suggest a multiplicity of styles, increasing consumption,

---

[94] See Jacob Viner, "Power Versus Plenty as Objectives of Foreign Policy in the Seventeenth and Eighteenth Centuries," in David Armitage (ed.), *Theories of Empire, 1450–1800* (Aldershot: Ashgate Variorum, 1998), pp. 277–305.

and significant continental borrowing. Chapter 7 uses the commission for a funeral monument as a case study to locate luxury consumption in church, to look at the appropriation of continental design in an urban setting by a country gentleman who spent part of the Interregnum in Italy. This chapter details the negotiations between patron, agent, architect, sculptor, and marble cutters to make a Baroque funeral monument for an Anglican parish church situated in a fashionable London suburb. The monument, designed by Bernini's son, Paolo, with a life-size sculpture by Antonio Raggi, is the only Bernini workshop tomb in Britain.[95] Chapter 8 analyzes the Royal Society's promotion of luxury manufactures through its program for a history of trades and city planning. It also examines the influence of science on notions of aristocratic identity and the transformation of scientific instruments into luxury goods. The conclusion returns to the question of the emergence of new wants and new wares in the seventeenth century and their influence on social and cultural change and economic transformation.

---

[95] Aidan Weston-Lewis (ed.), *Effigies and Ecstasies: Roman Baroque Sculpture and Design in the Age of Bernini* (Edinburgh: Scottish National Gallery, 1998), which examines British sculpture, omits all reference to it.

"I must have a damasked pair of spurs": shopping in seventeenth-century London

When James VI appointed Robert Lord Spencer to install the Duke of Wurtemberg with the Order of the Garter in Stuttgart in 1603, consuming splendor was the first thing on Spencer's mind. Descended from a family that had made an immense fortune in wool, he had recently been granted a barony by the new king. Spencer used luxury goods to reinforce and enhance his own status in what Daniel Roche has called "the culture of appearances." Splendid clothing, houses, and interiors projected wealth and power and articulated a sense of self constructed through luxury goods as well as lineage. Such cultural concerns had important economic consequences. Roche argues that the urban nobilities of ancien régime France were "a stimulus to building, trade, and circulation as they engaged in the prestige expenditure dictated by their need to retain and display their rank."[1]

Grand court portraits of the sixteenth and seventeenth centuries, from the iconic portraiture of Queen Elizabeth to Van Dyck's over life-sized portraits of the aristocracies of Antwerp, Genoa, and England represented power and status through intricately embroidered and bejeweled clothes and accessories. Painters often painted the clothes not the person.[2] Portraits of Queen Elizabeth, based on a few sittings over the course of her long reign, added patterns of her face to elaborate gowns and artifacts that commented on her virginity and imperial strength.[3] Jacobean portraits,

---

[1] Daniel Roche, "Between a 'moral economy' and a 'consumer economy': Clothes and their function in the 17th and 18th centuries," in Robert Fox and Anthony Turner (eds.), *Luxury Trades and Consumerism in Ancien Régime Paris: Studies in the History of the Skilled Workforce* (Aldershot, Hampshire: Ashgate Publishing, 1998), p. 224; Daniel Roche, *The Culture of Clothing: Dress and Fashion in the "Ancien Régime,"* trans. Jean Birrell (Cambridge: Cambridge University Press, 1994), p. 7, quote on p. 184. Ann Rosalind Jones and Peter Stallybrass, *Renaissance Clothing and the Materials of Memory* (Cambridge: Cambridge University Press, 2000).

[2] See, for example, Van Dyck's preparatory drawing in *Country Life*, (4 October 1990), 130. Oliver Millar, "Viewing a Stuart Legacy," *Country Life*, 184 (4 October 1990), 126–31.

[3] Sir Roy Strong, *The Cult of Elizabeth: Elizabethan Portraiture and Pageantry* (London: Thames and Hudson, 1977).

such as the series of Philip Larkin's carpet paintings, celebrated a variety of extravagant styles of court dress for both male and female courtiers. Even as painting styles changed in the 1620s and 1630s, portraiture continued to pay significant attention to dress and ornament. Thus, Van Dyck painted Anna Wake and Marie Louisa de Tassis holding extravagant ostrich feathers while he portrayed Lady Anne Carr moving toward the viewer while putting on her gloves.[4]

Portraits incorporated the wonders of new worlds and the beginnings of colonial trade. Paul Van Somer painted Anne of Denmark in a gown embroidered with silkworms. Pocahontas's portrait in Jacobean court dress circulated in print. Van Dyck portrayed William Feilding, Earl of Denbigh, in Indian costume with an Indian guide and Queen Henrietta Maria with an orange tree and a monkey. Daniel Mytens painted King Charles and Queen Henrietta Maria accompanied by an African servant as well as Jeffrey Hudson, the court dwarf.[5] Peter Lely continued the motif in the 1650s, painting Elizabeth, Duchess of Lauderdale, with an African. But behind these formal presentations of self through luxury and exotic goods lay the more ordinary and shifting practices by which these effects were achieved, that is, by shopping.

Shopping gathered almost all levels of society, the Crown, the great nobility, gentry, merchants, townspeople, and country people, in patterns of exchange that included gift-giving and the purchase of the fruits of international trade and domestic production. Goods were given and then given away, sold and resold. Gifts circulated and re-circulated throughout society, marking political and social relationships and access to political favor, celebrating special events such as New Year's Day, and concluding ambassadorial appointments and trade negotiations.

The presentation of increasingly valuable and diverse new luxury goods, such as pictures, porcelain, and coaches, as well as the traditional silver plate and deer, characterized seventeenth-century court patronage.[6] Richard Delamain, a mathematician who sought the position of tutor to Prince Charles in 1634, sent him silver arithmetic tables as a New Year's present.[7] While gifts were ostensibly freely given, recipients immediately calculated

---

[4] See Sir Roy Strong, *The English Icon: Elizabethan and Jacobean Portraiture* (London: Paul Mellon Foundation for British Art, in association with Routledge and Kegan Paul, 1969).

[5] Kim F. Hall, *Things of Darkness: Economies of Race and Gender in Early Modern England* (Ithaca: Cornell University Press, 1995), pp. 231, 236, 239.

[6] Linda Levy Peck, *Court Patronage and Corruption in Early Stuart England* (London: Unwin Hyman, 1990).

[7] HEH Ellesmere Mss. EL 6521, January 1634/35. My thanks to Barbara Donagan for this reference.

their value, and, in the case of ambassadorial chains, weighed them and
sometimes found them wanting.[8] Sir John Coke, Secretary of State, kept
close tabs on his plate, which increased in value and variety every year. Cups,
sugar boxes, livery pots, trenchers, escalloped fruit dishes, basins and ewers,
of Italian, Spanish, and Nuremberg work proliferated as his importance in
the government increased. In 1632 he received New Year's gifts from the
Merchant Adventurers, the Turkey Company, the Muscovy Company, the
French Company, the East India Company, and the fishermen of Yarmouth.
King Charles's gift to Coke was a gilt cup with cover weighing fifteen and
one half ounces which Coke exchanged for two porringers.[9] The Earl of
Salisbury received a coach and four from the Earl of Northumberland.[10]
Gifts marked life passages, especially birth, marriage, and death. The
Countess of Shrewsbury sent ermine to her son-in-law, the Earl of
Arundel, for the christening of his son;[11] the Earl of Salisbury sent a suite
of imported hangings worth L1500 to the royal favorite, Robert Carr, Earl of
Somerset, on the occasion of his marriage;[12] and Dorothy Shirley detailed
bequests of coach, jewels, and hangings to her nieces in her 1620 will.[13]

Purchase had its own rules and performance. Customers negotiated
directly with shopkeepers and agents acted on instructions and orders
given to them orally or through letters. To bargain or, as they called it,
"to cheapen," was a skill important enough to be taught. The commodity
that emerged from these negotiations depended on availability, fashion,
and information provided by agents and merchants, who claimed superior
knowledge, whether the purchase was for canvas doublets suitable for
summer or a funeral monument imported from Rome. Shopping offered
agency and sociability to men and women of all incomes. T. S. Willan
described in detail England's inland trade and the work of the merchants
who linked capital and countryside.[14] Craig Muldrew has analyzed the web

---

[8] On gift-giving see Marcel Mauss, *The Gift: Form and Functions of Exchange in Archaic Societies*, trans.
Ian Cunnison (Glencoe, IL: Free Press, 1954); Peck, *Court Patronage and Corruption*, pp. 38–39;
Natalie Zemon Davis, *The Gift in Sixteenth Century France* (Madison: University of Wisconsin
Press, 2000); Sharon Kettering, *Patrons, Brokers, and Clients in Seventeenth-Century France* (New
York: Oxford University Press, 1986).

[9] BL Add. Mss. 69,877, Coke Papers, series II, ff. 21–22v, 35–37, 38–38v, 42–42v, 47v, 52–55v.

[10] Penry Williams, *The Tudor Regime* (Oxford: Clarendon Press, 1979), p. 106.

[11] Folger, Talbot Corr, X. d. 428 (1), (2), Thomas Howard, Earl of Arundel, to Elizabeth, Countess of
Shrewsbury.

[12] BL Add. Mss. 75,352, John Tailor to Francis Clifford, Earl of Cumberland, 18 January 1613–14.

[13] John Gough Nichols, *The Unton Inventories* (London: Printed for the Berkshire Ashmolean
Society, 1841).

[14] T. S. Willan, *The Inland Trade: Studies in English Internal Trade in the Sixteenth and Seventeenth
Centuries* (Manchester: Manchester University Press, 1976).

of relationships of sales, credit, and debit that linked sixteenth-century communities.[15] Imbedded in these credit relationships, an expanding number of shops sold increasing numbers of goods, many of them imported.[16] New and fashionable goods attracted shoppers from the country girl who wanted "London silk" from the local draper and haberdasher to the well-to-do gentleman who adopted metropolitan taste alongside or instead of traditional magnificence based on liveried servants and hospitality.[17] Merchants used their knowledge to tailor goods such as Venetian glass and Chinese porcelain to the home market.[18] At the same time, contemporary representations of shopping in sermons, plays, courtesy literature, and court cases dwelt on the dangers of shopping and commodification through the bargaining away of virtue and estate.

For Spencer, as for so many contemporaries, clothing made the man and identity began with the coat of arms. To purchase the rich apparel and accessories for this important embassy, Spencer drew up an extensive memo for his steward, Stephen French: "Things to be bought for me by French at London."[19] For his packhorses he required "a sumpter [baggage] saddle, a sumpter, and a blue sumpter cloth with my arms and supporters embroidered upon it. The griffin's head, helmet, and crest upon it." For his page, he wanted "one suit of taffeta, one suit of satin of light colours and a hat and a feather." The footmen required two jackets of a "sad [dark] blue velvet lined with white taffeta with flowers embroidered front and back." To provide the embroiderer with the pattern of the family arms, Spencer instructed French to "take the view of these in the parlour window."

Some of Spencer's purchases would not have been misplaced in a Jacobean satire on men's love of finery. Sumptuous fabric in abundance was more important to Spencer than novel cut; the richer the better both inside and out. For himself he asked for "a white satin doublet of the same fashion that my old one is," paired with cloth of gold hose, silk stockings, and garters. Further, "I would have a satin jerkin of any colour laid on as

---

[15] Craig Muldrew, *The Economy of Obligation: The Culture of Credit and Social Relations in Early Modern England* (Houndmills, Basingstoke: Palgrave, 1998).

[16] Muldrew, *The Economy of Obligation*, pp. 52–53.

[17] Rev. J. J. Fowler, "The Account Book of William Wray," *The Antiquary*, 32 (1896), 54–57, 76–81, 117–19, 212–14, 242–44, 278–81, 316–17, 346–47, 369–75, 374.

[18] BL Sloane Mss. 857, Michael Mersey, John Greene to Alessio Morelli in Venice, 1667–71; Claire Le Corbellier and Alice Cooney Frelinghuysen, *Chinese Export Porcelain* (New York: Metropolitan Museum of Art, 2003).

[19] BL Add. Mss. 75,303, unfoliated. When the Earl of Dorset was planning an embassy to France he showed Elizabeth Raleigh "his brave and rich apparel and his page's clothes." She urged her brother to send one of his sons to serve as page, "it will do the boy much good to see France." BL Add. Mss. 72,709, Elizabeth Lady Raleigh to her brother Sir Nicholas Carew, f. 6.

thick with silver lace, of a strong round lace, as may be of a fashion as I shall appoint." He also wanted "as much black lace as Tuckey (his tailor) shall appoint for the lacing of my black velvet cloak." Accessories were key: "I must have a damasked pair of spurs," he wrote, as well as "a fine small pair of French hangers" for his sword, and two beaver hats. He requested a jewel, perhaps for a gift, in the form of a rose, with each point a ruby or, if rubies were not available, then all of diamonds, at a cost of no more than L100. Status anxiety and concern for the proper performance of the rituals of his embassy marked Spencer's consumption. He ordered French to find out "what allowance the Earl of Rutland had from the King" and, in particular, the size of the company that Rutland took with him and their manner of table and plate on a similar mission.[20]

Spencer, who kept a diary and account book of his four-month journey to Wurtemberg for the investiture, brought gifts to the Duke.[21] In return, the Duke marked the honor that King James bestowed upon him by lavishing on Spencer an elaborate and highly wrought set of gilded plate. The set included a great basin and ewer, a high cup with cover and a double cup, all three gilt and "wrought with curious works"; two flagon pots; two dozen gilt spoons; two dozen plates all of parcel gilt; three dozen silver dishes parcel gilt, "one pie plate parcel gilt full of square holes"; six gilt fruit bowls; and "twelve silver forks to eat withal of parcel gilt."[22]

The Duke of Wurtemberg's glittering plate continued to be recorded in the Spencer family's inventories for many decades.[23] Such inventories detailed lists of silver and linen, whether newly bought, inherited, second-hand, in good condition or worn, in the pawn shop, or at the goldsmith's for remodeling to a more fashionable design. Displayed on the buffet and used for important dinners, silver plate was given pride of place because it was not only a luxury good but easily convertible into ready money.[24] Luxury goods circulated in the train of families as they moved back and forth from city to country. Silver, linens, and pictures were sent from one house to another to provide the appropriate "splendor" for aristocratic life.

[20] BL Add. Mss. 75,303, Althorp Papers.
[21] BL Add. Mss. 75,304, includes the journal of the trip; BL Add. Mss. 75,303 is the account book for the journey.
[22] BL Add. Mss. 75,303.
[23] BL Add. Mss. 75,326, Spencer inventories: see 20 September 1610; 10 June 1624; 12 February 1635/36.
[24] On silver, see Philippa Glanville, *Silver in Tudor and Early Stuart England: A Social History and Catalogue of the National Collection, 1480–1660* (London: Victoria and Albert Museum, 1990) and her introduction to David Mitchell (ed.), *Goldsmiths, Silversmiths and Bankers: Innovation and the Transfer of Skill, 1550–1750*, Centre for Metropolitan History, Working Papers Series, no. 2 (London: Centre for Metropolitan History, 1995), p. 2.

From Sheffield, the Earl of Shrewsbury ordered his Countess, the famous Bess of Hardwick, to "take order for the plate, damask, diaper, napkins and sheets for here is neither damask nor diaper napkins in the house."[25] One Spencer inventory for Althorp of "plate brought from London the 10th of June 1611" included six triangle silver trencher salts "at every corner the Spencer arms and crest."[26] The Spencers displayed their arms and badges everywhere in their plate, movables, clothes, and windows. But they were not alone. Luxury goods offered ways to display arms in the sixteenth and seventeenth centuries. Sir Thomas Ramsay, Mayor of London in 1577 and a member of the Grocer's Company, left an extensive amount of gilt, parcel gilt, and silver plate in his Lombard Street mansion including four basins and ewers with his own arms or that of the grocers and a gold ring with his arms.[27] A 1590s tract criticized an actor for sporting a coat of arms tricked up not by the heralds but by a painter-stainer.[28]

Spencer's expedition celebrated the "world of goods" and the important role of objects in structuring social exchange that intertwined public ritual and personal identity.[29] Spencer's exchange of elaborate artifacts with the Duke of Wurtemberg aimed formally to cement international Protestant political networks. At the same time, luxury consumption, by offering outward display and inward reassurance, reinforced individual status and aspiration. Spencer, said to be one of the richest men in England, sought to match or outdo a member of the old nobility, the Earl of Rutland, and he used luxury goods to underwrite his family's move from the ranks of the gentry to the nobility. Luxury consumption was, of course, not new; it persisted in good times and bad, including the aftermath of the Black Death.[30] But Spencer's purchases took place not in a depressed economy

---

[25] Folger, X. d. 428 (99), c. 1575, George Talbot, Earl of Shrewsbury, to Elizabeth Countess of Shrewsbury.

[26] BL Add. Mss. 75,326, addition to inventory for Althorp, 20 September 1610.

[27] F. W. Fairholt, "On an Inventory of the Household Goods of Sir Thomas Ramsay, Lord Mayor of London, 1577," *Archaeologia*, 40 (1866), 311–42.

[28] Linda Levy Peck, *Northampton: Patronage and Policy at the Court of James I* (London: Allen and Unwin, 1982), p. 158.

[29] Mary Douglas and Baron C. Isherwood, *The World of Goods: Towards an Anthropology of Consumption* (New York: Basic Books, 1979); Richard Goldthwaite, "The Empire of Things: Consumer Demand in Renaissance Italy," in F. W. Kent, Patricia Simons (eds.), *Patronage, Art and Society in Renaissance Italy* (New York: Oxford University Press, 1987), pp. 153–76. Simon Schama, *The Embarrassment of Riches: An Interpretation of Dutch Culture in the Golden Age* (New York: Knopf, 1987). See Louis Montrose, "Gifts and Reasons: The Contexts of Peele's *Araygnement of Paris*," *English Literary History*, 47 (1980), 433–61.

[30] Ronald Findlay, "Globalization and the European Economy: Medieval Origins to the Industrial Revolution," in Roger Findlay and Kevin O'Rourke (eds.), *Commodity Market Integration, 1500–2000* (Cambridge, MA: National Bureau of Economic Research, 2001), pp. 1–46.

but in the midst of an active market for luxury goods in both city and country.

Sumptuary legislation enacted over the centuries to reinforce order, hierarchy, and status distinction had long lain unenforced and ended in 1604.[31] Imports of luxury goods grew rapidly in the early seventeenth century. Up until 1660 raw silk was second only to wine in the value of imports. After 1660 it was surpassed only by wine and sugar.[32] This expanding market, with the introduction of new goods and the recycling of old, brought new forms of display and new modes of shopping.

This chapter examines the practice and culture of shopping for luxury goods in seventeenth-century London. First, it shows how the well-off in the countryside ordered luxury goods from London and thereby helped to strengthen the national demand for luxury goods well before the consumer revolution of the "long" eighteenth century.[33] These long-distance shoppers often knew exactly what they desired, in quality, color, and price. They organized gift-giving through London merchants and depended on credit in London and the countryside to underpin their consumption. Second, the chapter analyzes new modes of shopping that appeared in London in the late sixteenth and early seventeenth centuries. The emergence of the English boutique situated in the early seventeenth-century shopping mall had a significant impact on luxury consumption by making shopping an important leisure activity. In particular, leases provide important evidence about the New Exchange merchants, their shops, and specialties. The Civil War disturbed but did not disrupt this new luxury shopping. Third, the chapter examines the nuances of gender and shopping. Well-to-do men and women congregated in the Old and New Exchanges. While creating an important new public space for women as shoppers, shopkeepers, and servants, alongside similar sites such as theaters and public gardens,[34] the

[31] Negley Boyd Harte, "State Control of Dress and Social Change in Pre-Industrial England," in D. C. Coleman and A. H. John (eds.), *Trade, Government and Economy in Pre-Industrial England: Essays Presented to F. J. Fisher* (London: Weidenfeld and Nicholson, 1976), pp. 148–49.

[32] Christopher G. A. Clay, *Economic Expansion and Social Change: England 1500–1700*, 2 vols. (Cambridge: Cambridge University Press, 1984), II, pp. 156–57, Tables XVII and XVIII.

[33] Nancy C. Cox, *The Complete Tradesman: A Study of Retailing, 1550–1820* (Aldershot, Hampshire: Ashgate Publishing, 2000), p. 3, notes that "To date few have attempted seriously to push back the seeds of change to the period before the Restoration in 1660. Dorothy Davis and Joan Thirsk are notable exceptions."

[34] See Linda Levy Peck, "Women in the Caroline Audience: The Evidence from Hatfield," *Shakespeare Quarterly*, 51 (2000), 474–77; Michael Neill, "'Wits Most Accomplished Senate': The Audience of the Caroline Private Theaters," *Studies in English, Literature* 18 (1978), 341–60; Richard Levin, "Women in the Renaissance Theatre Audience," *Shakespeare Quarterly*, 40 (1989), 165–74; *The Autobiography of Anne Lady Halkett*, (ed.) J. G. Nicholls, Camden Society, new series (London,

New Exchange reinforced a complaint literature that linked gender and shopping. These innovations in retailing undermine the contrast often drawn between court and middle-class consumption, complicate the notion of the "feminization" of consumption, and demonstrate how luxury shopping became entertainment.

SHOPS AND SHOPPING

In the Middle Ages, most English people had bought consumer goods at fairs, from peddlers, or from pushcarts. By the eighteenth century, the "nation of shopkeepers" had an internal market which helped fuel the Industrial Revolution.[35] In the sixteenth and seventeenth centuries, shops were often in craftsmen's houses: the front room, which opened to the street, was used for sales, the back served as a warehouse, and the shop owner lived above the business. Shops frequently ringed the open market in market towns and tradesmen sold "through the window," following the medieval practice, according to Nancy Cox, that markets should be open and goods on view in order to prevent fraud.[36] The greatest number of shops sold clothing and its accessories whether first- or secondhand. London shops overflowed with cloth. Thomas Bulmer, citizen of London and draper, who died in 1594, had a shop and three warehouses filled with silks and cottons.[37]

The growth of towns supported the expansion of luxury goods. While some cities like Coventry suffered because its mercers failed to adjust to the new market for luxuries, other regional towns flourished.[38] Between 1602 and 1604, William Bourchier, third Earl of Bath, exchanged fruit and horses with his neighbors, had his viol mended and a scabbard made for

---

1875), p. 3. Thomas Dekker wrote, "The theater is your poet's Royal Exchange." Thomas Dekker, *The Gull's Horn Book* (London, 1609), quoted in James Knowles (ed.), *The Roaring Girl and Other City Comedies* (Oxford: Oxford University Press, 2001), p. xiii.

[35] On shopping see Hoh-Cheung Mui and Lorna H. Mui, *Shops and Shopkeeping in Eighteenth-Century England* (London: Routledge, 1989); Dorothy Davis, *Fairs, Shops and Supermarkets: A History of English Shopping* (Toronto: Toronto University Press, 1966); Alison Adburgham, *Shopping in Style: London from the Restoration to Edwardian Elegance* (London: Thames and Hudson, 1979); Margaret Spufford, *The Great Reclothing of Rural England: Petty Chapmen and Their Wares in the Seventeenth Century* (London: Hambledon Press, 1986); Ian Archer, *The History of the Haberdashers' Company* (Shopwyke Hall, Chichester, Sussex: Phillimore & Co., 1991), pp. 21–31.

[36] Cox, *The Complete Tradesman*, pp. 77–83. See also Kathryn Morrison, *English Shops and Shopping: An Architectural History* (New Haven, CT: Published for the Paul Mellon Centre of Studies in British Art by Yale University Press, 2003), chapters 1 and 2.

[37] BL Add. Mss. 28,714.

[38] Cox, *The Complete Tradesman*, pp. 44–58 and Ronald Berger, *The Most Necessary Luxuries: The Mercers' Company of Coventry, 1550–1680* (University Park: Penn State University Press, 1993).

his silver dagger locally in Barnstaple, while he ordered books from London and attended plays in the metropolis.[39] The Countess of Huntingdon ordered taffeta, Dutch serge, and watered satin from London and her husband, the fifth Earl, paid L23–3–6 for his new velvet suit and other clothing. In August and September, 1627, the Earl traveled to Bath for his health. He bought tobacco along the way and paid for music in Coventry and Cirencester. Once in Bath, he rented a house for L9 a week, purchased glasses and hourglasses, paid the doctor and the apothecary, bought cloth for his gown, lace for his ruffs, and shoes, gave a shilling to three singing men, and bought four dozen tobacco pipes, spending L500 in all on the trip.[40] Within England goods were dispersed through petty chapmen and retail shops that spanned the countryside and catered to the desire of all who had disposable income for luxury goods such as expensive textiles and housewares.[41] Between 1649 and 1672, over 6,500 businesses used shop tokens as small change in transactions.[42]

London, however, continued as the center for the most important purchases of the well off and the stylish.[43] In 1622 James I's daughter, Elizabeth of Bohemia, now in exile at the Hague, received luxury goods from London worth L543–8–4 including embroidery, Spanish gloves, scarves, curling irons, and pictures painted by Peter Oliver.[44] The Countess of Bedford and Sir Albertus Morton shopped for Elizabeth, paying, for instance, L50 "to the embroiderer for a scarf which my Lady Bedford sent the Queen."

The Earl and Countess of Cumberland placed orders in London for clothing, furnishings, and luxury goods for their house and stables in the North. They included their neighbors' requests for new wares and the mending of old along with their own shopping list.[45] These far-flung customers were eager for fashionable new wares such as coaches, watches, and imported textiles. London craftsmen moved quickly to meet these

---

[39] BL Harl. 4258, Steward's Account for the Earl of Bath, 1602–04. The Earl received gifts of stags, rabbits, and rare fruit, including pears, plums, and damascenes while he borrowed horses from his neighbors and gave money to poor Irish and poor French and had a trumpeter go to Exeter "about my Lord's business," f. 10.

[40] HEH, Hastings Mss., HAF, Box 8, nos. 20, 34, 37, 38. No. 32 lists the expenses of the journey to Bath, 2 August–28 September, 1627.

[41] Spufford, *Petty Chapmen*; Fowler, "The Account Book of William Wray," 54–57, 76–81, 117–19, 212–14, 242–44, 278–81, 316–17, 346–47, 369–75.

[42] Willan, *The Inland Trade*, p. 85.

[43] F. J. Fisher, "The Development of London as a Centre of Conspicuous Consumption in the Sixteenth and Seventeenth Centuries," *TRHS*, 4th series 30 (1948), 37–50. Roche, "Between a 'moral economy' and a 'consumer economy,'" p. 227.

[44] Folger, Ms. Add. 727, Ms. list of Elizabeth of Bohemia's expenses for Christmas quarter 1622.

[45] BL Add. Mss. 75,352, John Ecton to Thomas Little, 16 May 1613.

3. Tradesmen in London in the middle of the seventeenth century created their own tokens as a mode of advertising and of small change.
The Folger Shakespeare Library, ART H-P Alb nos. 6, 8, 32, tradesmen's tokens: Mary Long in Russell Street, Covent Garden, her half penny (recto and verso); The Seven Stars (recto and verso); The White Hart (recto and verso).

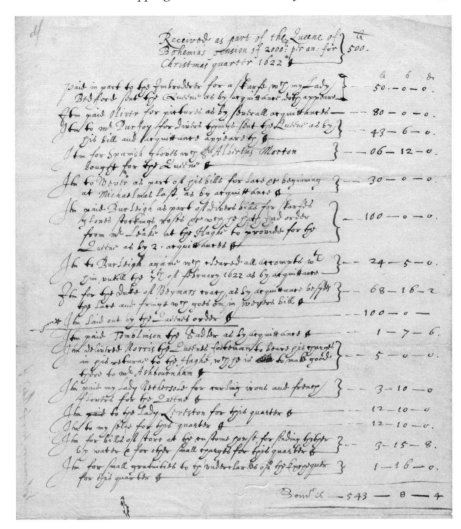

4. Elizabeth of Bohemia, King James's daughter, lived in exile at the Hague during the Thirty Years' War. This manuscript lists the purchases made for her in London by Lucy, Countess of Bedford, and Sir Albertus Morton, of embroideries, miniatures, scarves, and gloves.
The Folger Shakespeare Library, Ms. Add. 727, Elizabeth of Bohemia, List of the Queen's disbursements for the Christmas quarter, 1622. Manuscript, 1622.

desires. One early Stuart goldsmith, Simon Hackett, imported French enamel cases into which he put English watch movements.[46]

[46] Metropolitan Museum of Art. I am grateful to Claire Vincent, curator of the department of European decorative arts, for this reference.

5. Simon Hackett, a watchmaker of London, imported fine French enamel cases into which he placed English watch movements for the English market.

The Metropolitan Museum of Art, Horology, English (London), 17th century (*c.* 1632–40), Simon Hackett (act. 1630–60), watch, glass, enamel, gold, gilded brass, steel, partly blued, diam. 1–1 1/2 in. (3.8 cm). Gift of J. Pierpont Morgan, 1917 (17. 190. 1477). Photograph, all rights reserved, The Metropolitan Museum of Art, Neg. #40111.

In 1613 John Ecton, acting for the Earl and Countess of Cumberland, sent close to L140 of goods from London to York. He assured the Countess that he had followed her instructions to drive a hard bargain.[47]

I observed the direction in that letter very punctually ... beating down the prices ... I hope everything is so done as will answer their honors' expectations, as well for the stuffs and colors as for the prices for after we had sought and searched almost all the shops in Cheapside ... the first shop we were at, and whither he [the tailor] carried me ... was Mr. Barnes ... where we had as good or better choice than elsewhere. We could not mend our markets nor save a penny in the pound of that we were demanded there in any of the places wheresoever we went.

Mr. Barnes, the mercer, whom Ecton favored, had a high-ranking clientele. On one occasion he supplied Robert Cecil, Earl of Salisbury, ten and one-half yards of black uncut figured satin to line a velvet gown at a total cost of L74–16–3.[48]

Lack of cash on hand did not preclude shopping. Well-to-do dealers in luxuries, especially goldsmiths, not only carried a variety of the latest goods but also extended credit, which was particularly important for high-ranking but hard-up aristocrats such as the Cumberlands. Ecton worried about paying the bills "so exceeding scant and short it is with us here." But he turned to the next purchase, the Earl's request to decorate the coach with curtains. He needed only to know the size and material the Earl desired.[49]

Ecton also acted as London purchasing agent for the Cumberlands' untitled neighbors. Robert Sodaby [Sotheby] ordered three yards of white china taffeta which "we cannot get in all this town." He sent instead "a scarf which with good husbandry got for 14s." He asked Little to show it to Sodaby to see "if it will serve him for his white china scarf." If the price was too dear "or the colour not pleasing," Ecton asked him to send it back again, presumably for return or resale. But Ecton could not send Robert Hughes his watch

because it is not yet so well mended but that it will often stand still ... the watchmaker cannot by any means mend it without new making of some of the wheels for which he asketh as much as the watch is worth. He hath had it ever since

[47] BL Add. Mss. 75,352, John Ecton to Thomas Little, 16 May 1613.

[48] Hatfield, Cecil Mss., Accounts 160/1, 1610: "Mr. Barnes the mercer his bill for stuffs for your honors own wearing, 7 December 1609."

[49] BL Add. Mss. 75,352, Ecton to Little, 16 May 1613. Coach makers subcontracted the work to other businesses in London. John Styles, "The Goldsmiths and the London Luxury Trades, 1550–1750," in Mitchell (ed.), *Goldsmiths, Silversmiths and Bankers*, p. 114.

I received it, till yesterday, and it hath stood [stopped] three or four times since I had it, pray him therefore to advise me what he would have me do therein.[50]

Gift exchange, which permeated seventeenth-century society, often depended on London shopping. While Ecton was solicitous of the Countess of Cumberland's purse, John Tailor, the Cumberlands' man of business, understood that a luxurious gift might be a political necessity. Tailor's letters in 1613 and 1614 are filled with discussions of the impending Cockayne project for a home finishing industry for cloth and the connection of the Howards with the favorite, Robert Carr, Earl of Somerset. At the time of the Earl of Somerset's wedding to Frances Howard in 1613, everyone of note was expected to give the royal favorite a gift. Tailor informed Cumberland that

It is said the king declared himself plainly that he thought no man did love him that did not show his love at this time to my Lord of Somerset and so Mr. Dackombe and Mr. Ashton took up L100 worth of plate in silver dishes and presented them unto him in your Lordship's name in a very good fashion for which Mr. Ashton gave his bond to be paid next term, they did it out of their loves ... nor do I yet see how to pay it. He [Somerset] took it very thankfully from your lordship. Never were there so many and so great gifts presented to a subject before.[51]

A traditional gift, silver plate was often re-circulated or sent to be melted into ready money or to be made into something new.[52] King James recycled the plate presented to him as New Year's gifts as gifts to others. He also sold extraordinary Tudor pieces to Muscovy and then had them copied, adding the Scottish thistle to the Tudor rose.[53] Spencer's "curiously wrought gilt plate" from the Duke of Wurtemberg was more costly than Cumberland's silver dishes purchased in London. Nevertheless, the latter served their purpose. Along with the gift of plate, Tailor drafted a letter to Somerset in Cumberland's name in order, as he said, to leave nothing undone in procuring the favorite's support for Cumberland's claims to the manor of Bewcastle.[54] Tailor wrote on another occasion: "I wish your Lordship had a good horse for my Lord of Somerset, Mr. Dackombe will deserve one as well. I strive to gain rather than lose friends."[55]

---

[50] BL Add. Mss. 75,352, Ecton to Little, 16 May 1613.
[51] BL Add. Mss. 75,352, John Tailor to Francis, 4th Earl of Cumberland, 18 January 1613/14.
[52] See Glanville, *Silver in Tudor and Early Stuart England*, pp. 19–68.
[53] Elspeth Moncrieff, "Politics and Plate: English Silver from the Kremlin," *Apollo*, 133 (1991), 50–52.
[54] BL Add. Mss 75,352, John Tailor to Francis, 4th Earl of Cumberland, 27 January 1613–1614.
[55] *Ibid.*, 31 January 1613–14.

Debt and honor, credit and reputation intertwined with consumption.[56] Tailor, like Ecton, blanched at the cost of the Cumberlands' conspicuous consumption and the lack of funds on hand.

I receive not one penny of money, nor shall this month. God knows how it will fall out then between the merchants and me. These things your Lordship writes for comes to a great deal of money. They are and shalbe sent, all, I hope your Lordship will see my credit preserved else can I not be able to do you that service I desire.[57]

Tailor's ability to purchase luxuries for Cumberland depended on his own credit and honor.[58]

Tailor tried to cut costs by supplying ready-made instead of custom-made goods and exchanging the Earl's old clothes for new, contributing thereby to the lively secondhand clothing market.[59] Tailor tried to convince the Earl that a gown of wrought velvet might have drawbacks. "How will your Lordship have your new gown lined and trimmed? If the outside be of wrought velvet, carriage will (I fear) hurt such a gown. Your Lordship said you would send up your other gown to be exchanged toward it. I shall not forget a saddle."[60] Tailor sent the Earl a ready-made saddle with its furniture already gilded (unlike Spencer's custom-made saddle), "which if your Lordship like not I suppose George Hodgson can colour it." He obtained the best plush in London for Cumberland's gown. Costing twenty-two shillings a yard, the tailors claimed that it was lighter and neater than unshorn velvet. "I borrow money because I would buy all at the best hand. Your Lordship shall have the bills for the parcels and prices of all things bought now and last term which comes to a good deal of money."[61]

In another level of society and a different part of the country, dwelt Sir Hugh Smith of Long Ashton, near Bristol, a well-to-do country gentleman, justice of the peace, and deputy lord lieutenant, whose merchant family had become landed gentry in the course of the sixteenth century. One of many country gentlemen knighted as King James traveled to London in 1603, Sir Hugh's marriage to Elizabeth Gorges allied him with a family

---

[56] Muldrew, *The Economy of Obligation*, pp. 148–57.

[57] BL Add. Mss. 75,352, John Tailor to Francis, 4th Earl of Cumberland, 27 January 1613–14.

[58] Muldrew, *The Economy of Obligation*, pp. 148–57.

[59] On the secondhand market and the theatre see Jones and Stallybrass, *Renaissance Clothing and the Materials of Memory*. On the eighteenth century see Beverly Lemire, "Consumerism in Pre-industrial and Early Industrial England: The Trade in Secondhand Clothes," *Journal of British Studies*, 27 (1988), 1–24; Roche, "Between a 'moral economy' and a 'consumer economy,'" p. 226.

[60] BL Add. Mss. 75,352, John Tailor to Francis Clifford, 4th Earl of Cumberland, 18 January 1613–14.

[61] BL Add. Mss. 75,352, John Tailor to Francis Earl of Cumberland, 27 January 1613–14.

with court connections. In 1605 he accompanied the Earl of Hertford on a diplomatic mission to the Archduke of the Spanish Netherlands.[62] Although described as difficult, ill, and misanthropic, Sir Hugh maintained his interest in London fashion. His godson, Stephen Smith, who had rooms at Lincoln's Inn, acted as his personal shopper in London in 1620. Working from Sir Hugh's list, Stephen selected clothes and accessories to complement Sir Hugh's "good leg" and described how his new purchases would work with clothing he already had. Steven described current fashions in detail and exchanged old boots for new.

I have sent you your cassock and canvas doublet. Your tailor and I considered that canvas was only fit for summer and therefore have buttoned it according to the fashion now in request. It is not only suitable to your scarlet hose but will agree as well with any other cloth hose you have. Canvas doublets are now much in request and they are all made plain or trimmed with white lace as this is, for it is accounted somewhat piebald to trim a white doublet with trimming of different colour. If I could have contrived it so as to have made the canvas doublet fit to have been worn under a cassock I had done it: but it is not a winter wear and therefore I shall put you to the charges of a new satin doublet against winter. I have sent you a pair of Spanish leather boots in exchange of your russet boots, and have exchanged also your two pair of shoes for one. You shall receive likewise two pair of welted boothose which I think without comparison are the finest and longest for tops in London. I caused them to be made with long tops because I know that you have a good leg.[63]

Three days later, Stephen Smith reported that he had sent "a ruff with cuffs, a girdle, and a pair of hangers of the newest fashion and such as are now in use by men of the best fashion."[64] The shopping was complete with the purchase of a red outfit and a beaver hat. Beaver, a recent import, had quickly become popular and remained expensive.

On 5 July 1620 Smith wrote:

Hedges the carrier hath a scarlet suit for you in a box trimmed up as plainly as the fashion would admit, and as neatly as your tailor's invention or my furtherance could enable him to it … Since you were pleased to approve of my judgement in the choice of a beaver and to command my pains therein I have sent you one as good and fashionable as my credit could procure … Your old servant Mr. Samuel tells me you are too good a customer to lose, and therefore to continue his credit

---

[62] J. H. Bettey, *The Rise of A Gentry Family: The Smyths of Ashton Court, c. 1500–1642* (Bristol Branch of the Historical Association, Bristol University, 1978), pp. 14–15. J. H. Bettey (ed.), *Calendar of the Correspondence of the Smyth Family of Ashton Court, 1548–1642* (Gloucester: Printed for the Bristol Record Society by Alan Sutton, 1982).

[63] Folger, X. c. 49 (2), Smith Correspondence, Stephen Smith to Sir Hugh Smith, 14 June 1620.

[64] *Ibid.*, (3), Smith Correspondence, 17 June 1620.

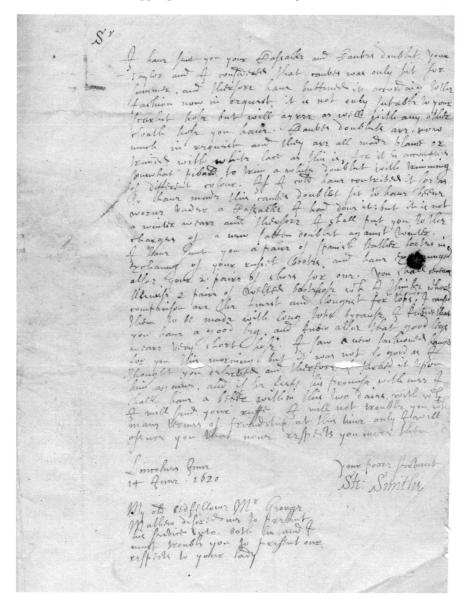

6. Stephen Smith of Lincoln's Inn shopped for clothing for his godfather, Sir Hugh Smith. In this letter, Smith describes the current fashion in doublets and discusses the scarlet hose to complement his godfather's "good leg."

The Folger Shakespeare Library, Ms. X. c. 49 (2), Stephen Smith. Autographed letter, signed to Sir Hugh Smith, 14 June 1620.

with you hath willingly exchanged your black boots for a russet pair which you shall find in the box.[65]

Smith commented on the King's efforts to change the fashion because of the high cost of beaver. "The king (as the report saith) will take order by proclamation that no beavers shall be worn but by men of certain quality and that himself, the prince and my Lord of Buckingham will give the first example of wearing felts."[66]

The Spencers, Cumberlands, and Smiths and their neighbors are examples of consumers all over England who bought luxury goods in London and participated in the growing national market that linked international trade with city and country. Their energetic shopping for luxurious textiles, curtains, coaches, and plate brought fashion to the north and west, upheld status, and forged their political connections at court. While the Cumberlands' fortunes suffered, the Spencers' rose, and Sir Hugh Smith lapsed into melancholy, they all continued to shop enthusiastically in London.

THE NEW EXCHANGE

In the course of eight weeks, between 13 October and 6 December 1608, Lady Frances Cecil bought seven pairs of shoes including three of orange tawny and two of marigold.[67] With such exotic colors, these shoes must have matched particular outfits or even masque costumes. Indeed, the colors, from costly dyes, helped to make them objects of cost and rarity. Lady Frances appears to have shopped at home or through agents. In the same period, her brother, William Cecil, Lord Cranborne, bought twelve pairs of long perfumed gloves at three shillings a pair, two pairs of long cordovan perfumed gloves, and two pairs of perfumed leather gloves fringed with crimson and silver fringe.[68] Since gloves were a favorite gift, Cranborne may have been buying some of them as presents. He also paid an embroiderer for his work on a new doublet, hose, and cloaks and bought new swords.[69]

It is little wonder that their father, Robert Cecil, Earl of Salisbury, who was currently spending large sums on building and furnishing Hatfield House, would recognize the growing market for a diverse range of luxury goods bought by his own children. Cecil also held the farms of the customs on silk and the new draperies. The creation of the New Exchange in 1609

---

[65] *Ibid.* (4), 5 July 1620.   [66] *Ibid.*   [67] Hatfield, Cecil Mss. Bills 34 A and B.
[68] *Ibid.*   [69] *Ibid.*, November, 1608; 1609.

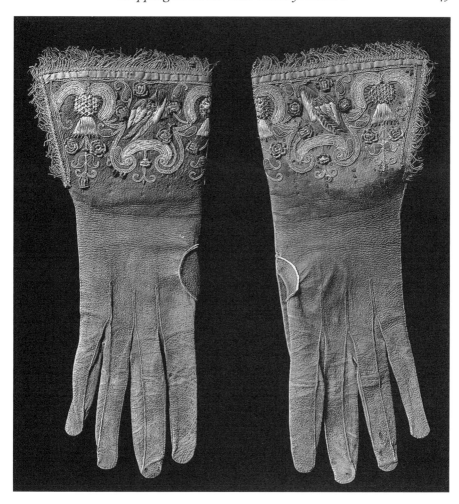

7. Gloves were a favorite gift in the seventeenth century. These display the Scottish thistle, emblem of King James VI of Scotland and I of England.
The Metropolitan Museum of Art, Textiles-Embroidered, English, 17th century, gloves (pair, leather, silk and metal thread, *c.* 1620, supposed to have belonged to King James I, with thistle,) Rogers Fund, 1929 (29.23.13–14). Photograph, all rights reserved, The Metropolitan Museum of Art.

was Cecil's own form of import substitution as well as diversification of the fortune his family had accumulated from office.[70] Well-to-do drapers, milliners, haberdashers, painter-stainers, tiremakers, seamstresses, and

[70] On Cecil's investments see Lawrence Stone, *Family and Fortune: Studies in Aristocratic Finance in the Sixteenth and Seventeenth Centuries* (Oxford: Clarendon Press, 1973), pp. 3–115. Hatfield Cecil Mss. Legal 38/11. "Draft of a letter patent granting to the Earl in consideration of his having built Britain's

8. Wenceslaus Hollar, the most prominent engraver of the early and middle seventeenth century created prints for the commercial market while on the continent in the 1640s. The Folger Shakespeare Library, ART Vol. D86, no. 1, Wenceslaus Hollar, *Byrsa Londoniensis* . . . *The Royall Exchange of London* (1644).

perfumers took up leases.[71] The Earl of Salisbury's children bought clothes from the merchants in the New Exchange including Humphrey Bradbourne, a milliner, who had a large corner shop, and George Blennerhasset, citizen and haberdasher, who had two shops, the George, and the Black Beak.[72]

Historians have ascribed the emergence of luxury retail shopping, separated from manufactures, to the eighteenth century or the late seventeenth century when, in fact, it can be found much earlier.[73] Houses on London Bridge contained small shops dating back at least to the fourteenth century.[74] Cheapside, the great shopping street in the City of London, contained shops for goldsmiths, mercers, and sellers of leather goods. On ceremonial occasions, such as the entree of Marie de Medici in 1639, Cheapside became the stage for her welcome to the City.[75] Mercers, drapers, and furniture makers also had shops nearby in Paternoster Row. In addition to the many food markets throughout the City, Cornhill provided a market for secondhand clothes.[76]

Thomas Gresham's Royal Exchange, which opened in the City in 1570, proved a new departure in luxury consumption. Modeled after the Antwerp Burse, the Royal Exchange brought together merchants in international trade.[77] Thomas Platter, the continental traveler, reported in 1599, "all kinds of fine goods are on show; and since the city is very large and extensive, merchants having to deal with one another agree to meet together in this palace where several hundred may be found assembled twice daily ... buying, selling, bearing news, and doing business generally."[78]

Burse a license to sell merchandise there, especially new draperies, to open a hall and levy hallage." It does not appear that the patent passed. Cox, *The Complete Tradesman*, pp. 29 and 23n. The *OED* cites Edward Misselden's 1622 list of Old and New draperies.

[71] Hatfield, Cecil Mss. Estate Papers, Box R5.

[72] Hatfield, Cecil Mss. Box H4, 163, Ladies Elizabeth and Diana Cecil bought ribbon from Henry Bradbourne and stockings from George Blennerhasset. See also Estate Papers, Box F3, "Things bought for Lady Diana in the Bourse."

[73] See Mui and Mui, *Shops and Shopkeeping in Eighteenth-Century England*, p. 7.

[74] Vanessa Harding and Laura Wright (eds.), *London Bridge: Selected Accounts and Rentals, 1381–1538* (London: London Record Society, 1995).

[75] Jean Puget de la Serre, *Histoire de l'Entree de la Reine Mere du Roy ... dans la Grande Bretaigne* (London, 1639).

[76] *Hugh Alley's Caveat: The Markets of London in 1598, Folger. Ms. V. a. 318*, (eds.) Ian Archer, Caroline Barron, and Vanessa Harding, London Topographical Society, 137 (1988), pp. 9, 90. On medieval shopping, see Derek Keene, *Cheapside Before the Great Fire* (London: Economic and Social Research Council, 1985). Derek Keene, "A new study of London before the Great Fire," *Urban History Yearbook*, 11 (1984), 11–21.

[77] Ann Saunders (ed.), *The Royal Exchange* (London: London Topographical Society, 1997).

[78] *Thomas Platter's Travels in England*, 1599, ed. Clare Williams (London: Jonathan Cape, 1937), p. 157.

The Royal Exchange included two floors of shops which Queen Elizabeth admired when she opened the Exchange. The shops were small, five feet by seven and one-half feet and, at first, Gresham had trouble filling them. But, by the end of the century there was a waiting list.[79] Only one inventory for a shop in the Royal Exchange survives. Thomas Deane, a haberdasher, moved his goods from his very comfortable house to a kiosk in the Royal Exchange at its opening in 1570. Deane sold the small goods necessary for clothes, such as ribbons and points that joined one part of an outfit to another, silk thread for embroidery, and linen for seams. Although his shop was small, Deane was well-to-do and he left a substantial estate.[80]

While the Royal Exchange attracted merchants and city wives, it also tried to lure those of higher rank. In Thomas Heywood's *If You Know Not Me, You Know No Body, the Second Part*, written in the 1620s, the author lauds the Royal Exchange. Gresham, now one of the play's characters, is asked "And what of this part that is overhead?" He responds:

> There is more ware than in all the rest,
> Here like a parish for good citizens
> And their fair wives to dwell in, I"ll have shops
> Where every day they shall become themselves
> In neat attire, that when our courtiers
> Shall come in trains to trace old Gresham's Burse
> They shall have such a girdle of chaste eyes
> And such a globe of beauty round about,
> Ladies shall blush to turn their vizards off,
> And courtiers swear they lied when they did scoff.[81]

To showcase luxury goods and global commodities Salisbury commissioned the New Exchange for the Strand in the heart of the new aristocratic West End.[82] The New Exchange marked a significant departure in consuming because of its location: it was suburban (i.e. outside the City) and private, a shopping mall located close to the court and to new aristocratic housing that Salisbury and the Earl of Bedford developed in St. Martin's Lane, Covent Garden, and elsewhere in the parish of St. Martin

[79] Saunders (ed.), *The Royal Exchange*, pp. 44–45.
[80] Kay Staniland, "Thomas Deane's shop in the Royal Exchange," in Saunders (ed.), *The Royal Exchange*, pp. 59–67.
[81] Thomas Heywood, *If You Know Not Me, You Know No Body, the Second Part with the Building of the Royal Exchange* (London, 1633), E2v.
[82] Stone, *Family and Fortune*, pp. 95–109, provides the fullest description of the building of the New Exchange. See also Hatfield, Cecil Mss. Estate Papers, Box R5, Leases of 1633; Westminster Archives, 10/356, Parish Rate books 1632.

in-the-Fields.[83] As the London elite moved west in the seventeenth century, shops and shopkeepers moved west as well.[84] Not surprisingly, the New Exchange was viewed with apprehension by City merchants. On 30 June 1608 the Lord Mayor and Aldermen of London sent Salisbury a petition complaining that "if a pawne" be erected as proposed, it will "in time draw mercers, goldsmiths and all other chief traders ... out of the city ... to the great decay of the trade within the city."[85] Undeterred, Salisbury proceeded.

To compete with Thomas Gresham's Royal Exchange, the New Exchange emphasized its connection with the court through the display of the arms of the King, the Queen, the Prince of Wales, and Salisbury himself.[86] Maximilian Colt, who carved the tomb of Queen Elizabeth, carved statues of the apostles for the facade. King James opened the new market in 1609 dubbing it "Britain's Burse." Some called it "England's Rialto," a reference to the famous bridge of shops in Venice. The terms Burse and Rialto signified the far-flung cultural borrowing on display at the New Exchange. At the opening, the royal family, the King, Queen, Prince Henry, the Duke of York, and Princess Elizabeth, received goods from Asia. John Taylor of London, a merchant, provided "Indian toys" for the entertainment at Britain's Burse.[87]

Porcelain from China was an exciting new import.[88] The Portuguese had established the trade in the sixteenth century. A rarity in late sixteenth-century England, porcelain arrived in England through gift, trade, and plunder. Queen Elizabeth and William Lord Burghley had been presented with porcelain-covered cups and a ewer with English mounts in the 1580s. The Dutch East India Company took over the trade route at the beginning of the early seventeenth century. A major shipment of perhaps as many as 100,000 pieces of porcelain in its distinctive blue and white colors arrived in Amsterdam in 1604. The Dutch East India Company ordered European shapes such as "mustard pots, saltcellars, and wine pots."

---

[83] Hatfield, Cecil Mss., Accounts 35/2 1638, St. Martin's Lane, List of tenants, rents paid, and fines agreed. Salisbury's tenants included Sir John Bankes, the Attorney General, and Sir Theodore Turquet de Mayerne, the court physician.

[84] Lawrence Stone, "The Residential Development of the West End of London in the Seventeenth Century," in Barbara C. Malament (ed.), *After the Reformation: Essays in Honor of J. H. Hexter* (Philadelphia: University of Pennsylvania Press, 1980), pp. 167–212.

[85] Quoted in Stone, *Family and Fortune*, p. 97.   [86] Hatfield, Cecil Mss., Bills 40–44, 1609.

[87] HMC *Salisbury*, XXIV, 168.

[88] Le Corbellier and Frelinghuysen, *Chinese Export Porcelain*, p. 11; John Ayers and Oliver Impey, and J. V. G. Mallett, *Porcelain for Palaces: The Fashion for Japan in Europe, 1650–1750* (London: Oriental Ceramic Society, 1990), pp. 56–59.

9. Inigo Jones drew a design for the Earl of Salisbury's New Exchange showing the two floors of retail space. The finished building differed somewhat from this original. Worcester College, Oxford, Inigo Jones, The New Exchange, drawing of 1608. Reproduced by permission of the Provost and Fellows of Worcester College, Oxford.

10. The Portuguese controlled the porcelain trade from China to Europe in the 16th century. This ewer, based on a Turkish shape, was one of several presented to William Cecil, Lord Burghley, in the 1580s. By 1600 the Dutch East India Company had taken over the trade.

The Metropolitan Museum of Art, Metalwork-Silver in Combination, English (London), Chinese, 16th century (*c.* 1585), ewer, porcelain, silver gilt, one of set owned by William Cecil, Lord Burghley, H. 13 5/8 in. (34.6 cm), Rogers Fund, 1944 (44.14.2). Photograph, all rights reserved, The Metropolitan Museum of Art.

Nevertheless they urged that designs be made "in the Chinese manner" because "Dutch paintings on porcelain are not considered strange nor rare."[89]

Porcelain, like silk and glass, was beautiful and refined, its manufacture secret, and its desirability great. In the late Elizabethan period and the early seventeenth century, owners added silver and gilt mounts to frame their porcelain vessels – or cover their cracks – and displayed them on the buffet or in the cupboard. Nevertheless, the massive imports of wares from China in the early seventeenth century turned it from a rarity into a luxury good not only coveted but also owned by many. Indeed, English potters copied porcelain designs in earthenware. Jacobean inventories list increasing amounts of porcelain. According to Philippa Glanville, "in Exeter a quarter of the inventories between 1610 and 1643 mentioned carrack or china wares and by 1643 an Exeter man paid 23 shillings for eleven dishes, a ewer and basin and a . . . vinegar spout."[90]

In "The Entertainment at Britain's Burse," Ben Jonson praised the abundance on display and proclaimed the New Exchange the greatest magazine in Europe. Jonson focused on the profusion of manufactured luxury goods, especially china and glass products from the East brought by English trading companies. James Knowles suggests that China and its luxury goods "suffused the Jacobean imagination."[91] Jonson's shop boy cries out, as he might at a country fair or a city market: "What do you lack? What is't you buy? Very fine China stuffs, of all kinds and qualities? China chains, China bracelets, China scarves, China fans, China girdles, China knives, China boxes, China cabinets . . . looking glasses . . . concave glasses, crystal globes, waxen pictures . . . purslane [porcelain] dishes." His master corrects his cry to suit the sensibilities of its desired audience. "Peace Sirrah. Do it more gently. What lack you nobilities?"[92] The success of the New Exchange depended on a broad customer base drawn by the luxurious and the exotic, the new and exclusive. At the same time, china shops suggested places of assignation, a theme taken up repeatedly by seventeenth-century playwrights from Jonson himself in *Epicoene*, written

---

[89] *Ibid.*   [90] Glanville, *Silver in Tudor and Early Stuart England*, pp. 348, 351.
[91] James Knowles, "Jonson in China: Maritime Trade with China," paper presented to the National Maritime Museum and Institute of Historical Research seminar series, 25 January 2000.
[92] James Knowles, "Jonson's Entertainment at Britain's Burse," in Martin Butler (ed.), *Re-presenting Ben Jonson: Text, History, Performance* (Houndmills, Basingstoke: Macmillan, 1999), pp. 114–51. Jonson made fun of speculation about the purpose of the new building – a public bank, a pawnshop, a storehouse for corn, an arsenal, a private library, or "studies for young returned travelers and the walk below for them to discourse in."

within months of "The Keykeeper," to William Wycherley in *The Country Wife* of 1675.[93]

After the economic downturn in 1614, Salisbury had difficulty filling all the shops and engaged his merchant associates such as Sir William Garway to lease them. Garway soon returned them to the Earl.[94] In the 1620s, his son, the second Earl, turned the upper floors into flats.[95] But, by the 1630s, the New Exchange proved a successful venture. Salisbury renewed leases and claimed fines from haberdashers, seamstress shops, and tiremakers. Some retailers had several shops in both the lower and the upper parts of the Exchange. Some complained that they had a poor location, that their neighbors were selling the same sorts of goods, and that the fines asked by Salisbury's agents were too steep. Nevertheless, almost all renewed their leases in 1633.[96] While some shopkeepers were described as citizens of London, many, including Martha Jelley, Thomas Southerne, and Humphrey Bradbourne, were neighbors of their clients, living in the growing parish of St. Martin's, paying assessments alongside their aristocratic neighbors.[97]

The architecture of shopping at the New Exchange provides important surprises. Shopping took place both on the piano nobile and at street level. Seats and benches were built into the outer wall next to the street and an Office of Assurance at the Burse was furnished with wainscoting.[98] At ground level, the street was newly paved. We might, therefore, expect shops at ground level to be the most coveted and to pay the highest rents. Later in the seventeenth century expanses of plate glass invited window shopping. But the rents for shops on the lower level, facing the street, were the lowest. "The shops next the street are not so good by a third part as those on the other side of the outer space and all the shops on the inside are double the value of any in the outer space."[99] According to the New Exchange leases of 1633, the most prized shops were those on the upper level and in the interior, especially the larger shops at the corners. Most shops were 10 or

---

[93] *Ben Jonson* (eds.) Charles Harold Herford and Percy Simpson, 11 vols. (Oxford: Clarendon Press, 1925–52), X, p. 11. I am grateful to A. R. Braunmuller for this point. See A. R. Braunmuller, "Shakespeare's Fellow Dramatists," in Stanley Wells and Lena Cowen Orlin (eds.), *Shakespeare: An Oxford Guide* (Oxford: Oxford University Press, 2003), pp. 55–67.

[94] HMC *Salisbury*, XXIV, 232, Christopher Keighley to -, before March, 1616–17. Hatfield, Cecil Mss., Deeds, 149/28.

[95] HMC *Salisbury*, XXIV, 264, eight plans of parts of Britain's Burse, *c.* 1627. On 15 August 1627 Thomas Styles agreed "to build eleven tenements in the second and upper story of the Burse."

[96] Hatfield, Cecil Mss., Estate Papers, Box R5 (1633–34).

[97] Westminster Archives, 10/356, bridge assessments, 1632.

[98] Hatfield, Cecil Mss., Accounts 160/1, 1610: charges of building at Britain's Burse, L617–10–6.

[99] Hatfield, Cecil Mss., Estate Papers, Box R5 (1633–34).

11 feet in length, but the corner shops were 15 feet. The Earl of Salisbury's agents kept tight control of the leasing of this inner sanctum.[100]

All the shops in the New Exchange were larger than those on London Bridge, Cheapside, and the Royal Exchange. Rents were also slightly lower than at the Royal Exchange, L6 rather than L7–10, and leases were much shorter, eleven years, rather than twenty-one. The Royal Exchange had 120 shops, the New Exchange had 100. The hours of trade at the New Exchange lasted from 6.00 a.m. to 8.00 p.m. in summer, and 7.00 a.m. to 7.00 p.m. in the winter. The Royal Exchange in the City closed at 6.00 p.m.[101]

The establishment of the Royal and New Exchanges created a new architecture in London for consuming imported goods, encouraged new shopping practices, and created a new public sphere.[102] While the opening of Britain's Burse has been well documented, the changing modes of shopping that the Exchange introduced have not been examined. Seventeenth-century luxury shopping was redesigned: in public but away from the dirt, noise, and weather. Passersby dropped in, attracted by the luxury book and print trades as well as clothing and accessories. Instead of markets and shops in the open, the Exchanges deliberately enclosed its customers in a separate social space that brought together different status groups. Shopping was at once private and seductive, and public and on display. Both Exchanges made shopping an entertainment. In particular, the New Exchange recreated the country house Long Gallery in a setting of urban shops. It provided well-to-do men and women the opportunity to shop in private and, at the same time, to parade publicly, to see and be seen. As a result, the process of buying luxury goods fostered community and conversation as much if not more than it reinforced status distinction and difference.

Moreover, shopping in the New Exchange, like going to the theater and walking in the Mulberry and Spring Gardens, offered well-to-do women the opportunity to appear in public, to socialize with male and female friends, and to make their own purchases, outside the usual constraints of patriarchal control and despite the legal constraints on their right to make contracts. The Exchanges created a public sphere, before the emergence of

---

[100] Stone, *Family and Fortune*, pp. 95–109; Hatfield, Cecil Mss., Estate Papers, Box R5, Leases of 1633; Westminster Archives, 10/356.

[101] Saunders (ed.), *The Royal Exchange*; Stone; *Family and Fortune*, pp. 95–109. John Stow, *A Survey of the Cities of London and Westminster, and the Borough of Southwork*, 2 vols. (London, 1598), I, pp. 96, 192–93.

[102] Jürgen Habermas, *The Structural Transformation of the Public Sphere*, trans. Thomas Burger (Cambridge, MA: MIT Press, 1991), pp. 27–56.

the coffeehouse in the 1650s in which women could participate in public life and commerce alongside men.[103] Coaches clogged London streets as men and women went shopping.[104] As a result, an explosion of complaint literature claimed that such public spaces were dens of vice.

Salisbury planned the New Exchange to celebrate the wide variety of luxury goods now available in London. According to his regulations, the New Exchange was to contain haberdashers, stocking sellers, linen drapers, goldsmiths, milliners, perfumers, silk mercers, hookmakers, stationers, booksellers, confectioners, girdlers, sellers of china, pictures, maps, and prints. Whether retailers of all of these goods took up leases is unclear. Certainly by the 1630s most shops were in the hands of the clothing trades. Salisbury's regulations required retailers to focus on a single trade. Despite complaints from other retailers, enterprising shopkeepers brought in other goods regardless of custom and regulation.[105] Shops such as the Acorn, the Anchor, the Gilded Bell, the Half Moon, and the Seven Stars provided signs that would be recognizable to all.

What could the New Exchange shops have looked like? Thomas Middleton's London play, *The Roaring Girl* of 1611, describes retail shops side by side: "The three shops open in a rank: the first an apothecary's shop, the next a feather shop, the third a sempster's shop. Mistress Galliport in the first, Mistress Tiltyard in the next, Master Openwork and his wife in the third."[106] Salisbury's accounts include payments for benches, tables, and cupboards.[107] But, there is virtually no visual evidence of the interior of shops in early seventeenth-century England.[108] A print of Christopher Wren's Mercer's Hall, rebuilt after the Great Fire, has generous ground-floor shops with glass fronts, built-in shelving, and counters but it dates from the 1680s.[109] A portrait of a London linen draper, by a Flemish artist, presents a well-to-do mercer in a large shop. A male servant displays long bolts of cloth on shelves to well-dressed male customers while outside a

---

[103] *Ibid.*, pp. 27–56.

[104] [Henry Peacham], *Coach and Sedan, Pleasantly Disputing for Place and Precedence* (London, 1636).

[105] Hatfield, Cecil Mss., Estate Papers, Box R5.

[106] Thomas Middleton and Thomas Dekker, "The Roaring Girl or Moll Cutpurse," in Knowles (ed.), *The Roaring Girl*, Act I, scene iii.

[107] Hatfield, Cecil Mss., Accounts 160/1, 1610.

[108] On shop architecture, see Morrison, *English Shops and Shopping*.

[109] Eric de Mare, *Wren's London* (London: The Folio Society 1975), pp. 81, 128. British Museum, Mercer's Chapel with adjoining shops and houses as rebuilt after the Fire. Engraving from William Morgan, *London Survey'd*, 1681/2. On eighteenth-century shop design, see Claire Walsh, "The Design of London Goldsmiths' Shops in the Early Eighteenth Century," in Mitchell (ed.), *Goldsmiths, Silversmiths and Bankers*, pp. 96–111.

11. Abraham Bosse made a series of satirical engravings on contemporary French culture. This engraving, after Corneille's *La Galerie du Palais*, shows fashionable women and gallants shopping at boutiques similar, perhaps, to those in the New Exchange.
The Metropolitan Museum of Art, Abraham Bosse (1604–76), "Gallery of the Palais Royale," etching, Rogers Fund, 1922 (22.67.16). Photograph, all rights reserved, The Metropolitan Museum of Art.

vinter and his clients contemplate a glass of wine. It is dated *c.* 1690.[110] Neither of these is a template for the New Exchange.

Contemporary prints of the arcaded shops of the Palais de Justice in Paris may provide the closest model for the shops in the Exchanges. Abraham Bosse's 1630s etching based on Corneille's comedy, *La Galerie du Palais*, shows three shops, side by side, selling books, fans and gloves, and laces. Its satirical verses identify the shops as "boutiques." Smiling retailers look on while gallants and elegantly dressed young women saunter or shop. Moreover, Bosse's satire provides suggestive evidence not only about the look of the New Exchange but also about the type of shopping it encouraged.[111] The accessories displayed on the back wall of the boutique, including clothing, lace, fans, and gloves, were celebrated not only in Jacobean comedy but also, as we have seen, in the grand portraits of the period.

Francis Carter, the Surveyor of the New Exchange,[112] provides direct evidence of consuming practice. A Clerk of the King's Work and an associate of Inigo Jones, Carter had become an architect, working first for Prince Henry and then for the King.[113] At Salisbury's request, he provided estimates about the cost of enclosing the Exchange and adding more shops in 1628. Carter's insightful comments on early seventeenth-century shopping provide us with one of our few descriptions of the New Exchange in operation before Samuel Pepys's *Diary*.

Carter describes the way the New Exchange "worked" in his memorandum to Salisbury. His keynote was sociability and impulse shopping. The covered Burse with its sheltered walk surrounded by luxury goods on display was a place to meet and to spend both time and money. Its downstairs arcade attracted passersby. Carter wrote to Salisbury sometime before 1636:

---

[110] Museum of London, Egbert van Heemskerk the Younger, "Portrait of a Mercer" (*c.* 1690). *The Compleat Tradesman* (London, 1684), Wing H96A, describes how to lay out a shop. My thanks to Rachel Doggett for this citation.

[111] In contrast to this interpretation, James Knowles suggests that the shop in the entertainment at the opening of the New Exchange "has a strongly shrine-like quality comparable to the design for an unidentified entertainment which depicts a female figure or statue surrounded by votive lights," Knowles, "Jonson's Entertainment at Britain's Burse," pp. 114–51. On the display of goods in eighteenth-century shops in Paris, see Carolyn Sargentson, "The Manufacture and Marketing of Luxury Goods: The *Marchands-Merciers*, of Late Seventeenth and Eighteenth Century Paris," in Fox and Turner (eds.), *Luxury Trades and Consumerism in Ancien Régime Paris*, p. 134, in which small goods were hung on chains hanging outside the shop. See also Nicole Villa, *Le XVII Siècle vu par Abraham Bosse, Graveur du Roy* (Paris: Les Editions Roger Dacosta, 1967), p. 23. See plate 85, "La Galerie du Palais."

[112] Stone, *Family and Fortune*, p. 106.

[113] Howard Colvin, *The History of the King's Works*, 6 vols. (London: HMSO, 1975–82), I, pp. 133–34.

I understand by M. Knightley that your Honor is minded to enclose the foreside of Britain's Burse with doors, windows in the arches and with ten shops more on the inside, which work I made an estimate of the charge: which as I remember was L145. I crave leave of your Honor that I may set down some doubts I have in the proceeding of this work. I know that the enclosure of the arches for the night will be very good and it cannot be well without them: but for the shops, I fear [it] will do more harm to the other shops that are up already than themselves will profit: for they will make the walk so narrow (which is now the grace of the Burse) that but few or none will walk or come in it whereas now it begins to be an appointed place of meeting, for men to walk and stay on for another and, in that staying, a man sees one thing or other that he will buy, as I know by my own experience and proof. If it were so enclosed as is determined ere one man then went through it, two would pass by in the street and never come in, which would be a great hinderance both to the fore walk and back walk too, and I dare warrant would hinder a third part of the buyers, for then there would be no chapmen but they that came of set purpose which are not half the buyers.[114]

Carter argues that adding shops would narrow the broad walkway, key to its attraction and profit. Carter also suggests that men were an important part of the audience at the New Exchange in the 1620s as they proved to be in Pepys's day forty years later. Indeed, shopping at the Exchange was an activity undertaken with enthusiasm by both men and women. The Exchanges provided a public space in which to meet business associates, discuss politics, make appointments, buy, gossip, and flirt.

The New Exchange added new specialities in the 1630s. "French wares," Parisian styles and accessories, some sold by Huguenot shopkeepers, reflected the influence on fashion of the new queen, the French princess Henrietta Maria. In 1638 the Queen's perfumer, Jean-Baptiste Ferreine, opened a 15-foot shop in the "upper part of the Burse adjacent to the westside [of] the great window" and agreed to build the shop "according to my Lord's model."[115] In competition, milliners at the Royal Exchange claimed that the Queen herself frequented their shops.[116] At the New Exchange, Martha Jelley, a widow, sold French wares in her seamstress shop, the Acorn, on the side of the Exchange next to Durham House. French wares were also carried by Thomas Southerne, a draper, and David Pope, a haberdasher. William Dyer, who had a shop named The Globe,

---

[114] Hatfield, Cecil Mss., General 101/17. My thanks to Robin Harcourt Williams for help with this letter.
[115] Hatfield, Cecil Mss., Estate Papers, Box R5. HMC *Salisbury*, XXIV, 274.
[116] Some Royal Exchange merchants suggested placing their shops close together so that the Queen might not have to go too far to do her shopping. Saunders (ed.), *The Royal Exchange*, p. 89.

complained that Southerne sold French wares and gloves, two trades in one shop, despite the regulations.[117]

Women played an important role in this new retail market as shop owners as well as servants and consumers. In the 1630s women who leased shops in their own name comprised more than ten percent of the shop-owners in the New Exchange. Susan Clifford had a seamstress shop; Mrs. Hasset was a perfumer.[118] Mary Blithman rented the Moon and Seven Stars. Anne Porter had a shop called the Chair next to the middle door. Sarah Hearde, wife of shopkeeper John Hearde, had a shop as a tiremaker or dressmaker. Mrs. Elizabeth Deloubell had a shop on the north side of the Inner. Mrs. Calcott had the warehouse; Mary Knight had the tire shop called the Cork (Cock); Elinor Southworth and Katherine Bryers also had shops.[119]

In 1638, as part of its effort to control the numbers of gentry living in London and Westminster, the Privy Council insisted that Salisbury return the upper space of the New Exchange from tenements into shops. He promptly complied.[120] New leases required owners to convert them into retail spaces "according to his Lordship's model." Although no model, whether a drawing or in three dimensions, appears to have survived, Salisbury aimed at uniformity, regularity, and decorum. He ordered that "there shalbe no range above head to hang out commodities nor any for show . . . allowed that shall exceed or extend two foot from the front of any of the shops of and within the upper part of the Burse . . . And that there shall be nothing set upon any stalls to raise wares withal above one foot . . . in height."[121] He insisted on Sunday closing and prohibited shut-tlecock, cards, and dice. Beggars and boys were to be kept out. Tenants had access to the Burse either by water or land and had the use with other tenants "of the privy or house of easement."[122] Only the feather makers could use fire and they had to tile the floors of their shops for safety.

Tenants bore the cost of converting the tenements into shops which amounted to L20 or more.[123] The Earl also issued regulations that forbade signs to dangle and sought to control relations among the shopkeepers.[124]

---

[117] Hatfield, Cecil Mss., Estate papers, Box R5.   [118] *Ibid.*   [119] *Ibid.*

[120] See Lawrence Stone, "Inigo Jones and the New Exchange," *Archaeological Journal*, 114 (1957), p. 119. Hatfield, Cecil Mss., Estate Papers, Box R5.

[121] Hatfield, Cecil Mss., Deeds, 41/2, Articles concerning the Upper Part of the Burse, 24 December 14 Charles I. Similar regulations were issued in 1657. Deeds, 146/2.

[122] Hatfield, Cecil Mss., Deed 106/21, Indenture 20 April 22 James I between Hugh Pope and William Earl of Salisbury.

[123] Hatfield, Cecil Mss. Box R5.   [124] Hatfield, Cecil Mss., Box R5, 14 November 1639.

After Salisbury issued these regulations, several tenants banded together to request that he consult them as a group before making any further changes in the conditions of their tenancies.[125]

While it was easy enough to lease the shops at the end of the 1630s, during the Civil War some trade fell off. In the 1640s the Earl leased some of the shops for a half year, rather than the three or five years that he had earlier demanded and received.[126] Some shopkeepers petitioned Salisbury to be released from their leases because of the unsettled conditions. Despite the dislocation of the Civil War, Salisbury tried to collect fines from his tenants. In 1647 tenants on the lower level refused as a group, offering instead fines of one and a half to two and one quarter years depending on where they were located. Once again, inside shops, even on the lower level, commanded a higher rent than those outside. Significantly, the tenants required Salisbury to eliminate the shop in front of the large window so that all the shops could have better light.[127] In the end Salisbury agreed to their demands.

Tenants of the New Exchange claimed that trade had become bad in "these unhappy times." Anne Segar pointed out in 1646–47 that she had been a tenant for eighteen years. She had a lease for twenty-one years but the time had been cut in half in the 1630s when Salisbury required them to turn their space into shops. She dutifully did so, at her own cost, but now was unable to trade. Thomas Hammond took over the shop on 10 May 1647.

If petitions like Anne Segar's provide evidence of a downturn in retailing during the Civil War, other leases tell a different story. Lessees from the 1630s such as the Popes, the Chaplins, the Sears, the Bales, the Cliffs, the Cantons, the Draytons, and the Blennerhassets continued to rent their shops in 1647. Newcomers joined them while London was under the control of the New Model Army. In October 1647, for example, Katherine Dallison of St. Martin in-the-Fields, seamstress, took over a shop in the inner space of the upper part of the New Exchange.[128] The wills

---

[125] *Ibid.*

[126] *Ibid.* On 19 December 1639 Thomas Johnson of the Strand took a lease for five years of the shops in the lower part of Britain's Burse late in the tenancy of William Gophered at the yearly rent of £12. Mary Turpin, spinster, took a shop in the lower part of Britain's Burse in the occupation of John Wattinson for half a year for £3 on 2 October 1644.

[127] Hatfield, Cecil Mss., General 66/13; 72/14.

[128] HMC *Salisbury*, XXIV, 281 and note. Anne Segar to William, Earl of Salisbury, before 10 May 1647; 289, Benjamin Copley to William, Earl of Salisbury, before 4 December 1668. Other petitions include those from John Rowe and George Franklin who wished to give up their shops sometime before 1668, pp. 288–89. Hatfield, Cecil Mss., Estate Papers, Box R5.

of some of the shopkeepers in the 1650s point to prosperity. Hugh Pope, painter-stainer of Covent Garden, had had a shop at the New Exchange since at least 1625. He left L1,000 to his eldest son as well as an interest in his shop. He also owned property in Covent Garden and St. Martin in-the-Fields.[129] Josias Fendall, a joiner, left his daughter L1,000 provided she make a suitable marriage.[130]

The New Exchange prospered in the early 1650s as the end of war promoted continuing consumption. Articles of 1657 required tenants not to "make any of the shops less than nine feet in length." Regulations prohibited fast food: tenants faced fines if they called in any "butcher, apple woman, herb woman, fruit or fish seller or any such like people." But perfumers could call in rose sellers.[131]

At the Restoration, the New Exchange continued to be a fashionable place to shop for imports and finery and to have luxurious textiles made into clothes. As Samuel Pepys's *Diary* makes clear, the New Exchange was a destination, a place of entertainment and alternative to the theatre. Pepys himself was addicted to theatre, attending more than 400 plays in the space of ten years.[132] But, if no play was on, Pepys went to the New Exchange or the Royal Exchange. Pepys shopped with and without his wife, drank coffee, and arranged assignations with shop girls.[133]

The New Exchange continued to be a place for men to meet their friends, bump into acquaintances, talk business and politics, and shop, much as Francis Carter had described it in the 1620s. On 23 June 1662, for example, Pepys went "at noon to the exchange to meet Dr. Williams who sent me [. . .] notice of his going into the country tomorrow, but could not find him. But meeting with Francis Moore, my Lord Lambert's man formerly, he and two or three friends of his did go to a tavern, and there they drank, but I nothing but small beer."[134] On 7 October 1662 Pepys went to the New

[129] Hatfield, Cecil Mss., Deed 100/21 22 James I. *Index of Wills Proved in the Prerogative Court of Canterbury*, vol. VII, 1653–56, ed. Thomas M. Bragg and Josephine Skeate Moir (London: The British Record Society, 1925), Hugh Pope gentleman, Covent Garden, St. Martin in-the-Fields, Middlesex, 1656, f. 93; PROB11/253.

[130] *Index of Wills Proved in the Prerogative Court of Canterbury*, vol. VII, Josias Fendall, joiner, 1653, f. 221. PCC PROB 11/229. He required that her mother, her eldest brother, and a family friend certify the choice in writing, although he allowed it to be decided by two out of three.

[131] Hatfield, Cecil Mss., Deeds 146/2.

[132] C. Thomas Long, "Samuel Pepys, Devoted Theatergoer: Faithful Client, Luxury Consumer or Ambitious Businessman?" Paper Presented at Western Conference on British Studies, Denver, Colorado, 11 September 2000.

[133] Samuel Pepys, *Diary of Samuel Pepys, A New and Complete Transcription*, ed. Robert Latham and William Matthews, 11 vols. (Los Angeles and Berkeley: University of California Press, 1970–83), *passim*.

[134] *Ibid.*, III, p. 118.

Exchange. "While my wife was buying things, I walked up and down with Dr. Williams, talking about my law businesses."[135] On 10 April 1663, "home to dinner, and then by water abroad to Whitehall ... Met my wife and walked to the New Exchange; there laid out 10s upon pendants and painted leather gloves very pretty and all the mode."[136] On 5 October 1663, "and so to the New Exchange, and there met Creed, and he and I walked two or three hours, talking of many businesses, especially about Tangier."[137]

Pepys shopped both for himself and his wife. After dinner on 12 October 1663 Pepys made the rounds of the Exchanges and Cheapside looking for lace. "Thence by coach to the Old Exchange and there cheapened some laces for my wife; and to ... the great lace-man in Cheapside, and bought one, cost me 4l the more by 20s than I intended, but when I came to see them I was resolved to buy one and wearing with credit. And so to the New Exchange and there put it to making."[138] On 4 November 1663 Pepys left his wife at home making marmalade while he went to the New Exchange and other shops to bring home "a case I bought of the trunk makers for my periwig."[139]

The New Exchange made luxury shopping an important, indeed a central, social event for well-to-do Londoners and visitors. In 1666 Samuel Sorbière described it this way: "It is on a great avenue named the Strand; and it contains two galleries doubled one above the other, with eight ranges of mercers boutiques. I leave you to think if one finds there merchandise as beautiful as the beautiful merchants."[140]

Whatever diversity Salisbury had planned in 1609, by 1693 the New Exchange was made up almost entirely of milliners and seamstresses, along with four canemen and two perfumers. A survey of 117 shops in the Burse in 1693 lists the lessee, the tenant, the inhabitant, the old sign, the new sign, the trade specified in the lease, and the trade actually practiced in the shop.[141] The shops now ranged in size from six feet to fifteen feet. Some obviously had been divided and the size of the shops and the counter, whether eight or nine feet, became the subject of a lawsuit.[142] Most continued to rent for L6 as they had in the 1630s. The largest shops belonged to four milliners, one cane man, and one gown seller, while

---

[135] *Ibid.*, III, p. 215.   [136] *Ibid.*, IV, p. 100.   [137] *Ibid.*, IV, p. 324.   [138] *Ibid.*, IV, p. 332.
[139] *Ibid.*, IV, p. 363.
[140] Quoted in E. Beresford Chancellor, *Annals of the Strand, Topographical and Historical* (London: Chapman & Hall, 1912), p. 108.
[141] Hatfield, Cecil Mss., General 50/4.   [142] Hatfield, Cecil Mss., Legal 231/23.

one was empty. Claytons, Popes, and Constables, who had shops in the 1630s, continued to sell in the New Exchange.[143]

The shop signs also sent a specific political message signaling the triumph of the Glorious Revolution. The Pomegranate became the Prince of Orange, the Flying Horse became the King's Head, the Golden Hind became the Prince's Arms, the Acorn became the Prince George and the Globe became the Princess Anne.[144] But patriotism could not overcome location. As aristocratic neighborhoods moved west, the New Exchange found itself left behind. Since it had never become a meeting place for merchants like the Royal Exchange, when it lost its clientele, it lost its raison d'être. Once in the vanguard of the urban development of the West End, the New Exchange was torn down in 1737.

GENDER AND SHOPPING: REPRESENTATIONS

Shopping had long been thought to be subversive of the social order by inverting gender roles and encouraging illicit sex. Contemporaries and later analysts identify women as agents of novelty, fashion, and economic change.[145] Sexual desire and desire for luxury goods intertwined in prints, imaginative literature, contemporary psychology, and retail practice. Women who frequented shops as buyers, owners, or servants were accused by contemporaries of illicit behavior. For example, Laura Gowing describes the accusations against shopkeeper Sara Powell: she met married men, had "fiddlers all night in her shop," and her "night walking and day walking got her no good names."[146] Elizabeth Kowaleski-Wallace examines the prominent theme of women as shoppers in eighteenth-century literature and the trope of women succumbing to the blandishments or seduction of the merchant.[147] But representations of the sexual encounter and sexual gaze of customer and wench, lady and merchant, gallants and their amours were already in place in the early seventeenth century. Shopping in public brought criticism in the seventeenth century as it did in the

---

[143] Hatfield, Cecil Mss., General 50/4.   [144] *Ibid.*

[145] Werner Sombart, *Luxury and Capitalism*, intro. Philip Siegelman, trans. W. R. Dittmar (Ann Arbor: University of Michigan Press, 1967); Roche, "Between a 'moral economy' and a 'consumer economy'," p. 223. Karen Newman, *Fashioning Femininity and English Renaissance Drama* (Chicago and London: University of Chicago Press, 1991).

[146] Laura Gowing, *Domestic Dangers: Women, Words and Sex in Early Modern London* (Oxford: Clarendon Press, 1996), p. 85.

[147] Elizabeth Kowaleski-Wallace, *Consuming Subjects: Women, Shopping, and Business in the Eighteenth Century* (New York: Columbia University Press, 1997).

nineteenth and twentieth centuries.[148] The attack on female agency needs
to be located beside women's and men's own subjective understandings of
new practices of consumption.

The persistent rediscovery of women's role in shopping from the early
modern period to the present depends in part on the recycling of a political
discourse that dates back to the ancients. Although, as we have seen, men
swarmed to the Exchanges, representations of women and luxury based on
classical and Christian authors shaped seventeenth-century literature.
Moralists invoked the ancients: luxury was the abandonment of nature
according to Seneca, the fount and origin of evil according to Sallust, the
equivalent of slavery according to Ambrose, and the source of female
insurrections according to Livy.[149] In Genesis, Eve ate the apple because
she desired unnecessary knowledge and thereby committed "the sin of
luxury."[150]

In 1605 Pierre Erondelle, a French Huguenot, wrote *The French Garden*,
purportedly to teach ladies French, through suggestive French and English
dialogues that included bargaining with the mercer, the silk man, the
draper, the hosier, and the goldsmith.[151] Thus, a lady whose husband is
away decides to go shopping at the Royal Exchange with male and female
friends: "We may take a turn in the Exchange. It is not far hence, for I must
buy a silk waist-coat, which I have lost in play to M. de sur-amour, against a
velvet muff . . . . Give me my mask, and go fetch my fan." The dialogue,
"For to Cheapen," sets the stage for discussion of both cost and easy virtue.
The lady's male companion fancies the linen seller's servant. "This maid
doth invite us to it by her tongue which she hath as free, as any that I ever I
heard." The lady responds "seeing that you affect her we will see what she
will furnish us for your sake."

Visiting the mercer, the lady commands "show me the best velvet you
have." Enumerating all the types and colors he has on hand, "plain velvet,
raised velvet, pinked, wrought velvet," and "the best satin that is in this

[148] Judith R. Walkowitz, "Going Public: Shopping, Street Harassment, and Streetwalking in Late
    Victorian London, *Representations*, 62 (1998), 1–30; Erika Rappaport, *Shopping for Pleasure: Women
    in the Making of London's West End* (Princeton, NJ: Princeton University Press, 2000). See also
    Laura Gowing, "The Freedom of the Streets: Women and Social Space, 1560–1640", in Paul
    Griffiths and Mark S. R. Jenner (eds.), *Londinopolis: Essays in the Cultural and Social History of
    Early Modern London* (Manchester and New York: Manchester University Press, 2000), 130–51.
[149] John Sekora, *Luxury: The Concept in Western Thought, Eden to Smollett* (Baltimore: Johns Hopkins
    University Press, 1977), p. 21.
[150] *Ibid.*, pp. 24, 28.
[151] Pierre Erondelle, *The French Garden: For English Ladies and Gentlewomen to Walk in . . . thirteen
    dialogues in French and English* (London, 1605). Juliet Fleming, "The French Garden: An Introduction
    to Women's French," *ELH* 56 (1989), 19–51.

town, it is full of silk, the colour is fair and fresh," he concludes "Have you no need of my cloth of gold or silver?" The lady decides "yes, I must have some." They bargain over ten yards of cloth of gold. The mercer requests L4, the lady offers 50 shillings, and they settle on L3. The lady sends her page "to the shop on the other side of the street to buy silk, gold and silver lace, the largest silk ribbons to make roses and knots, narrow ones, gold and silk fringe, some laces and some points."

Later, searching for a particular goldsmith's shop, the lady asks directions: "I pray you look to the sign if it be the green dragon." Once there, after looking at a diamond costing 500 crowns, the lady requests pearls. "Show me the biggest pearls, the most oriental and the roundest that you have. How sell you this?" The goldsmith says that the pearl will cost L3. Once again they bargain and the lady agrees to buy enough pearls to make a "cackenet," a necklace.

Those gems for sale in the seventeenth century, emeralds, rubies, diamonds, topaz, and oriental pearls, came from the Americas and Asia as well as all parts of Europe.[152] Both men and women bought jewelry because, like plate, it represented a family's investment. In 1631, for example, William, Earl of Down's inventory included "a little cabinet with certain things and jewels" worth L3,020. In contrast, his plate was worth only L560, his pictures worth L67, while his 2,200 sheep were worth L1,300.[153] Hannibal Gamon, in "The Goldsmith's Storehouse," stressed that in the Old and New Testament precious stones represented "purity and chastity of undefiled life."[154]

Yet Erondelle reduces the importance of jewelry in contemporary society to avarice. In *The French Garden*, as the lady and the goldsmith discuss the virtues of precious stones, he concludes "the precious stones Madame have many great properties, but that which is most profitable unto us, it is the force they have to transport the money from your purse into ours."[155] The suggestive situations of *The French Garden* which satirize women's shopping and seduction and merchant's greed reflect imagery with a long history. Indeed, it was a representation purveyed with vigor by Stuart playwrights from Jonson to Wycherley.

---

[152] Sir Robert Eric Mortimer Wheeler, *The Cheapside Hoard of Elizabethan and Jacobean Jewellery* (London: Museum of London, 1925), pp. 37–38, 62.
[153] Bodleian Library, Ms. North c 47, "Inventory of William Earl of Down late of Wroughton in the county of Oxon, 8 June 1631."
[154] Folger, Hannibal Gammon, "The Goldsmith's Storehouse," f. 60v.
[155] Erondelle, *The French Garden*, 8th, 9th, and 10th dialogues.

The issue of gender and shopping is more complex. While women played an important role in retailing as consumers, shopkeepers, and servants, men made up an important part of the market for luxury goods. Indeed, some contemporaries worried that luxury consumption challenged the boundaries of gender, fostered effeminacy in men, and undermined the social and economic order. Landlords who were supposed to be overseeing their lands, tenants, and local government were caught up in the heady pursuit of London luxuries.

Ben Jonson wrote *Epicoene, or the Silent Woman* in 1609–10 shortly after he wrote the laudatory entertainment for the opening of the New Exchange.[156] Like the *French Garden*, *Epicoene* satirizes women who consume luxuries and the men who match them in love of finery. Morose's search for the perfect wife, one who is completely silent and obedient, provides a major theme of the play. To test Epicoene's claim of silence, he pretends to love fashion and luxury and to want a wife eager to compete in the fashion stakes.

I do also love to see her whom I shall choose for my heifer to be the first and principal in all fashions, precede all the dames at court by a fortnight, have her council of tailors, lineners, lace-women, embroiderers, and sit with 'em, sometimes twice a day upon French intelligences, and then come forth varied like Nature, or oft'ner than she, and better by the help of Art ... how will you be able, lady, with this frugality of speech, to give the manifold (but necessary) instructions for that bodice, these sleeves, those skirts, this cut, that stitch, this embroidery, that lace, this wire, those knots, that ruff, those roses, this girdle, that fan, the tother scarf, these gloves? Ha, What say you, lady?

Epicoene replies, "I'll leave it to you, sir".[157]

Jonson connects blurred gender boundaries and shopping. As women became increasingly visible in public, in shops, at the theater, public gardens, plays, shows and the court, they were attacked for losing their virtue, claiming masculine agency, and expressing their opinions. Jonson assails "The Collegiates," "an order between courtiers and country madams, that live from their husbands and give entertainment to all the Wits ... Cry down or up what they like or dislike in a brain or a fashion with most masculine or rather hermaphroditical authority, and every day

---

[156] Ben Jonson, *Epicoene, or the Silent Woman*, in *Ben Jonson*, V, pp. 139–271. My thanks to Alan Farmer for this reference. On *Epicoene* see Karen Newman, "City talk: Femininity and commodification in Jonson's *Epicoene*," in *Fashioning Femininity and English Renaissance Drama*, pp. 129–43. Ian Archer, "Material Londoners?" in Lena Cowen Orlin (ed.), *Material London ca. 1600* (Philadelphia: University of Pennsylvania Press, 2000), pp. 174–92.

[157] Jonson, *Epicoene*, Act II, scene v, lines 67–80, pp. 194–95.

gain to their college some new probationer."[158] The Collegiates urge Epicoene to insist on "a coach and four horses ... And go with us to Bedlam, to the china-houses and to the Exchange."[159] Jonson drew on Juvenal's Satires to denounce the untrustworthiness of women, but he goes beyond the classical author to add his own satirical comment on contemporary luxury and its consequences. His diatribe reflects the increasing trade in luxury textiles and variety of silver for both the buffet and dinner service.

She must have that rich gown for such a great day, a new one for the next, a richer for the third; be served in silver; have the chamber filled with a succession of grooms, footmen, ushers, and other messengers besides embroiderers, jewelers, tire-women, sempsters, feather men, perfumers; while she feels not how the land drops away, nor the acres melt, nor foresees the change when the mercer has your woods for her velvets."[160]

Such expenditures were not, of course, merely the product of Jonson's misogynist imagination. In 1638 Lady Elizabeth Cecil spent L174 "being in the Queen's masque at Christmas" at the tiremaker, the feather maker, the embroiderer, and shoemaker, where she bought, among other things, a vizor, masking ruff, and embroidered gloves.[161]

Epicoene attacks both aristocratic men and women for wasting the family fortune in conspicuous consumption. Sir Amorous La Foole "has a lodging in the Strand for the purpose, or to watch when ladies are gone to the china-houses or the Exchange, that he may meet ''em by chance and give 'em presents, some two or three hundred pounds' worth of toys."[162] Sir Amorous, too, is a great consumer of fashion which undermines his masculinity if not his virility. He proudly declaims his role in the army sent to Ireland, but, even more, his clothes:

Knighted in Ireland ... I had as fair a gold jerkin on that day as any was worn in the Island Voyage or at Caliz [Cadiz] ... and I came over in it hither, showed myself to my friends in court and after went down to my tenants in the country and surveyed my lands, let new leases, took their money, spent it in the eye of the land here, upon ladies – and now I can take up at my pleasure.[163]

---

[158] *Ibid.*, Act I, scene i, lines 72–78, pp. 166–67, in Hereford and Simpson (eds.) *Jonson*.
[159] *Ibid.*, Act IV, scene iii, lines 19–23, p. 228.
[160] *Ibid.*, Act II, scene ii, lines 101–108, pp. 181–82.
[161] Hatfield, Cecil Mss., Accounts 127/8, Account of the Privy Purse for one year ending at Michaelmas 1638.
[162] Jonson, *Epicoene*, Act I, scene iii, lines 36–40, p. 174.   [163] *Ibid.*, Act I, scene iv, lines 57–64, p. 176.

In the seventeenth century, male costume was often as elaborate as women's attire. King James created a starch monopoly that supported the fashion for ruffs for both men and women.[164] Decades later John Evelyn chastised exuberant male clothing that he claimed was effeminate.

It was a fine silken thing which I spied walking th'other day through Westminster Hall, that had as much ribbon on him as would have plundered six shops, and set up twenty country peddlers. All his body was dress't like a may pole . . . whether he were clad with this garment, or (as a porter) only carried it was not to be resolv'd . . . . Behold we one of our silken chameleons and aery gallants, making his addresses to his mistress, and you would sometimes think yourself in the country of the Amazons, for it is not possible to say which is the more woman of the two.[165]

Elaborately rich clothing masked status and gender difference and demonstrates the widespread use of aristocratic clothing whether at first or secondhand throughout the social order. The theatre purchased and recycled clothes and Philip Henslowe had a secondhand clothes business.[166] Evelyn complained, "How many times have I saluted the fine man for the master, and stood with my hat off to the gay feather, when I found the bird to be all this while but a daw."[167] Yet Evelyn claimed to love variety and appears to recall Jonson's *Epicoene* and its classical references when he wrote that he liked the wearing of a "stately and easy vest within doors and the cloak without. Nor am I of so Morose and particular a humor, that, with Seleucus, I would allow of no ornaments, or significant changes."[168]

Shopping became a potential sexual encounter not only in Jacobean plays but in Jacobean shops. When Robert Gray, a London mercer, traveled to fairs in Bristol and Exeter to buy and sell cloth, his wife and sometimes her mother looked after the business. In letters between 1606 and 1618, Gray gave orders for his shop, his money, and his servants. In particular, Gray sought to control the sexuality of his customers and of "Wench," his female employee. Gray urged his wife

to be as much in the shop as you well may and put the folks in mind of their business other ways it will not be well performed by them . . . see that when any of the folks doth go forth of doors you know whether they go and that they make no

---

[164] Peck, *Northampton*, pp. 67–69.

[165] John Evelyn, *Tyrannus or the Mode with a Discourse of Sumptuary Laws* (London, 1661); reprinted in *The Writings of John Evelyn*, (ed.) Guy de la Bedoyere (Woodbridge, Suffolk: Boydell Press, 1995), pp. 166, 170.

[166] Jones and Stallybrass, *Renaissance Clothing and the Materials of Memory*, p. 176ff.

[167] Evelyn, *Tyrannus or the Mode*, pp. 163–72.   [168] *Ibid.*

longer stay then needs they must, and when they receive any money pray your mother to take it, that it doe not lie about the shop.

Gray wrote that he "would not have Wench forth of doors if any chapmen should come the while . . . I pray see that when any of our customers come to London that Wench be very careful to serve them that are good men; and for the other let them go."[169] Coming to the end of one trip in 1613 he wrote his wife to "tell the folks that I write you I shalbe at home on Saturday because they will be the more mindful of their business, but it will be the Thursday after this doth come to your hands."[170] In Gray's shop, men made the purchases and threatened the virtue of the shop girl.

Yet, many representations of shopping focused on women as consumers. An English engraving of a woman buying shoes at home, perhaps by Richard Gaywood, is an unrecorded copy of one of "Les cordonniers," Abraham Bosse's series of engravings on contemporary French manners done in the 1630s. Bosse presents a well-to-do woman in a languorous pose in her large chamber hung with portraits and lined with tapestries, her dressing table embellished with a looking glass and toilet set, a new French fashion. She reaches for a luxurious shoe proffered by the shoemaker who kneels at her feet. Nearby a man and a woman converse. Underneath the scene are a set of satirical verses that connect women, luxury, sensuality, and shopping. The English version, which is less accomplished, shows the woman in English costume similar to those engraved by Wenceslaus Hollar *c.* 1640.[171] It presents the same satire of luxury, consumption, and women.[172]

Indeed, seventeenth-century representations, whether Jacobean city comedy, Caroline satire, or civil war tracts, attacked women who shopped whether at home and in public. In *The Lady of Pleasure* (1637), set on the Strand, James Shirley attacked women's appetites for luxury and, like Jonson, linked gender and shopping. Aretina has abandoned the country for the city. Criticized for "your change of gaudy furniture and pictures, of this Italian master, and that Dutchman's," her "vanities of tires," "prodigal embroideries," banquets, and perfumes, Aretina responds by identifying luxury consumption with her honor and "the liberty I was born with . . . The practice and tract of every honorable Lady authorize me." Her new neighbor, Celestial, demands a coach lined with crimson plush

---

[169] Quoted in Willan, *The Inland Trade*, pp. 123–25. [170] Quoted in *ibid.*
[171] See Antony Griffiths, *The Print in Stuart Britain, 1603–89* (London: British Museum Press, 1998), pp. 110–15.
[172] I am grateful to Antony Griffiths for advice on this print.

with double gilded nails, the "harness covered with needlework" and new hangings, "fresher and more rich . . . of a finer loom, some silk and silver." To her steward, who seeks to limit her expenses, she declaims, "must I be limited to please your honor? Or for the vulgar breath confine my pleasures . . . my entertainments shall be oftener, and more rich, who shall control me? I live in the Strand."[173] Equations of liberty and libertine, accusations of luxury and sin in contemporary prescriptive literature aimed to bring women back under control. Diatribes such as "News from the New Exchange" (1650) attacked new shopping practices by accusing both serving wenches and aristocratic women who frequented the New Exchange of prostitution.[174] In his Restoration comedies, William Wycherley continued to use the Exchange and the public gardens to satirize sex and shopping. In *Love in a Wood* (1672), published by Henry Herringham, whose shop, The Blue Anchor, was in the New Exchange, the protagonist claimed that he had followed his love to "the Park, Playhouse, Exchange."[175] In *The Country Wife* (1675), Mrs. Pinchwife, newly come to London, inquires about the best fields and woods to walk in. "Why sister, Mulberry Garden and St. James Park; and for close walks the New Exchange."[176] A cynic, Harcourt comments "all women are like these of the Exchange, who, to enhance the price of their commodities, report to their fond customers offers which were never made 'em."[177]

WOMEN AND LUXURY CONSUMPTION

Women at all social levels made consumption decisions for the household and some engaged in the retail trades. Lorna Weatherill's study of 420 women's inventories analyzes the new goods that proliferated in the seventeenth century including mirrors, books, clocks, and new utensils. Weatherill shows that women in the Restoration period owned books in equal proportions to men and had more looking glasses and clocks, although gentry women tended to have fewer than women in the retail

---

[173] James Shirley, *The Lady of Pleasure* (London, 1637), B2, B3, B3v, C2, C2v, C4, C4v, Act I, Scene I, and Act I, Scene II. See A. R. Braunmuller, "Shakespeare's Fellow Dramatists," p. 65.

[174] Henry Neville, *News from the New Exchange Or the Commonwealth of Ladies* (London, 1650); see also *New News from the Old Exchange* (London, 1650). James Grantham Turner examines the literary attack on women frequenting the New Exchange from the 1650s on in "'News from the New Exchange,': Commodity, Erotic Fantasy, and the Female Entrepreneur," in Ann Bermingham and John Brewer (eds.), *The Consumption of Culture, 1600–1800: Image, Object, Text* (New York: Routledge, 1995), pp. 419–39.

[175] Willam Wycherley, *Love in a Wood* (London, 1672), Act II, scene ii.

[176] William Wycherley, *The Country Wife* (London, 1675), Act II, scene i.   [177] *Ibid.*, Act III, scene ii.

trades. Women had more pictures than men, in the main portraits and landscapes, and many had prints. Prints provided embroidery patterns and decoration as well as aiding religious devotion. "The new and decorative goods appear more often in women's inventories than in the men's of the same occupation, with the exception of china and utensils for hot drinks . . . A far higher proportion of women than men among the trades-people and large farmers had pictures, looking glasses and table linen as well as books."[178] Plate continued to be prized too. In 1662, Grace Benet commanded her husband, "I want a thing; such a one as your mother had to put sugar in; they are to be bought at the goldsmiths; they are made of silver and they used to call them sugar chests. If you buy one let it be of the biggest size as is usually made."[179]

Despite contemporary strictures against women shopping, in the 1610s and 1620s great noble families had no qualms about their wives and daughters shopping in public. In the 1620s the Countess of Salisbury sent Mrs. Franklin, the nurse or governess, to accompany her daughter Lady Elizabeth Cecil to the Burse[180] while Mrs. Terwhit laid out seven shillings for Lady Diana Cecil for things bought there. Bills show footmen accompanying Lady Salisbury from the Old Exchange and waiting on Lady Elizabeth to Cheapside in the 1630s.[181]

Between 1610 and 1613 Margaret Spencer, Robert Spencer's next to youngest daughter, then about twenty, made periodic trips to London where she bought taffeta, silk, silk thread, and ribbon, accessories such as gloves and hats, and jewelry, including earrings and bracelets. She gave presents for New Year's, christenings, and weddings, spent a little on gambling and charity, and bought ink and paper. Many of her purchases reflect Jacobean metropolitan fashion based on imports, including her white beaver hat with a white band costing L3, a pair of velvet galoshes, and furred gloves. She also bought a black velvet mask, an Italian falling band and cuffs, Italian work cuffs, a "French lace round ruff and ruff cuffs," a black glass chain, a yellow fan and a silver handle, and a little looking glass. She purchased London luxuries as New Year's gifts including the velvet galoshes that she bought for Lady Despencer for fifteen shillings, velvet slippers for her brother Anderson, and a chain for her niece. Despite her wealth, she had things mended and updated, an old fan tinted, her

[178] Lorna Weatherill, "A Possession of One's Own: Women and Consumer Behavior in England, 1660–1740," *Journal of British Studies*, 25:2 (1986), 131–56.
[179] Hatfield House, Cecil Papers, General 72/35, Grace Bennet to Simon Bennet, 5 May 1662.
[180] Hatfield, Cecil Mss., Accounts 123/7.   [181] Hatfield, Cecil Mss., Bills 189, 1637–38.

earrings changed, her nightgown altered, and ten pairs of silk stockings dyed. She spent repeatedly on starch for her many ruffs and bands. While the court was in mourning for the death of Prince Henry in 1612, she bought black bugle roses, a black handle and fan, two dozen black points, black cobweb lace, and a black glass chain. She also bought two pairs of pistols for twenty-two shillings.

At both Althorp and London, she cultivated her own refinement. In London she paid Thomas Adson for dancing lessons at 12d a piece for six weeks for a total of L3 and she took virginal lessons. Even as she gave gifts she received them including exotic and desirable fruit such as oranges from Lady Holland, plums from Mr Knightly's man, and pears from the "old chandler," as well as books. She went sightseeing and paid a woman "for showing of me Sir Thomas Wharton's house."

When she came to London the next year in 1613, she bought more feathers, ribbons, and lace. She paid for the "making my French petticoat" and mending another, bought a little enameled purse, paid for shoes, ruffs, and "Italian work pearls to make a band," six pair of white gloves, and needles. Upon her departure from London she "left behind to pay for 21 pair of sheets that were left fowl, 5s-3d."[182]

Anne Lady Halkett recalled in her diary in the 1650s that she had only frequented the theater and public gardens in the company of women friends, family members, or chaperones. Nevertheless, she remembered such public expeditions with pleasure.

And so scrupulous I was of giving any occasion to speak of me, as I know they did of others, that though I loved well to see plays and to walk in the Spring Gardens sometimes (before it grew something scandalous by the abuse of some), yet I cannot remember three times that ever I went with any man besides my brothers; and if I did, my sisters or others better than my self was with me. And I was the first that proposed and practised it, for three or four of us going together without any man and everyone paying for themselves by giving the money to the footman who waited on us, and he gave it into the playhouse. And this I did first upon hearing some gentlemen talking what ladies they had waited on to plays, and how much it had cost them; upon which I resolved none should say the same of me.[183]

Lady Halkett had found the way to autonomy by organizing women to go to the play together, paying their own way, and using their own footman, not their fathers, brothers, husbands, or suitors, to pay for the tickets. Her

---

[182] BL Add. Mss. 62,092, Margaret Spencer Account Book, 1610–13. She died in 1613.
[183] *The Autobiography of Anne Lady Halkett*, (ed.) John Gough Nichols (Westminster: Printed for the Camden Society, 1875), p. 3.

self examination in her diary captures both female agency and self-doubt encouraged by prescriptive literature and a regime that had closed the public theaters.

Women participated in the public life of metropolitan London in many ways. They owned and worked in retail shops and bookstores, purchased goods for the household and themselves, created groups to attend public entertainments, attended plays as teenagers, bought books and prints, presented gifts, walked in public gardens, and participated in the circulation of news. They served and petitioned at court, pursued family lawsuits, and visited in town. During the English Civil War, women took up public political roles as royalists, parliamentarians, and leaders of religious sects. Prescriptive literature fought back through intense criticism of women in public, at the Exchanges, and as shopkeepers. But by the end of the seventeenth century, woman writers such as Mary Astell claimed the rights of citizenship for women.[184] The circulation of luxury goods provided not only the objects for private display but one route to public participation in the life of the state.

CONCLUSION

Early seventeenth-century shops displayed the diverse goods now available though increasing imports from Europe and the East and West Indies. Cultural borrowing of European dress, accessories, and manners reinforced the economic boom in imported goods. Shopping was, moreover, transformed by a new built environment in the early seventeenth century. This new architecture of desire, which fostered sociability and emulation, not only offered new wares but encouraged new wants.

While the New Exchange aimed at an elite audience, its location in town made conspicuous consumption available even to the passerby. The emergence of new modes of luxury shopping that engaged the interest of Queen, civil servant, courtiers and city wives alike, linked court and town with well-to-do consumers in a new social formation. This dynamic expansion of luxury goods quickly reached the countryside where consumers were as up to date on new fashions and new textiles as on the political news. Courtiers and officeholders bought the tapestries, jewels, and furnishings that had belonged to their newly deceased friends. The secondhand market in goods re-circulated aristocratic clothing to those of lower status.

---

[184] Mary Astell, *Astell Political Writings*, (ed.) Patricia Springborg (Cambridge: Cambridge University Press, 1996).

Sir Hugh Smith's russet boots found their place in the fashion food chain. As his subjects joined in an exuberant buying spree for imported goods, King James turned his attention to import substitution to foster domestic luxury industries, first silk, glass, and tapestries and, later, lacquer, porcelain, paper, and scientific instruments, as we shall see in the next chapter.

CHAPTER 2

"We may as well be silke-masters as sheepe-masters": transferring technology in seventeenth-century England

When James I's favorite, Robert Carr, Earl of Somerset, fell from power in 1615, an inventory revealed his glittering array of clothing: fifty doublets and hose of silk, satin, and velvet embroidered with silver and gold thread, as well as twenty-five cloaks. These included "one crimson cloak and suit of uncut velvet all embroidered with crimson silk" and "a doublet of black silk mockadoe."[1] The French courtier had a similar wardrobe: at the court of Henry IV "a man is not much esteemed if he has not twenty-five or thirty garments of different patterns which he changes every day."[2] Courtiers spent more on clothing than on pictures.[3] As we saw in the previous chapter, the increasing desire for luxurious textiles among the English expanded far beyond the court in the late sixteenth and early seventeenth centuries and was supplied by the expansion of shops and shopping both in London and the countryside.[4]

In the early seventeenth century, both Henry IV and James I sought to benefit from such luxurious display by systematically promoting domestic luxury manufactures, including silk. Both the English and French states strove to transfer technology from Italy and the Low Countries by importing skilled weavers and using the cheap labor of women and children. In both countries, kings, courtiers, and merchants urged their populations to create the raw materials for the silk industry. King James repeatedly invoked the

---

[1] Folger, L. b. 638, Somerset Inventory, f. 3v; Alfred John Kempe, *The Loseley Manuscripts* (London: J. Murray, 1836), 408–09.

[2] Quoted in Salvatore Ciriacono, "Silk Manufacturing in France and Italy in the XVIIth Century: Two Models Compared," *Journal of European Economic History*, 10 (1981), 178.

[3] R. Malcolm Smuts, "The Court and its Neighborhood: Royal Policy and Urban Growth in the Early Stuart West End," *Journal of British Studies*, 30 (1991), 117–49.

[4] Craig Muldrew, *The Economy of Obligation: The Culture of Credit and Social Relations in Early Modern England* (Houndmills, Basingstoke: Palgrave, 1998), pp. 15–59; Nancy C. Cox, *The Complete Tradesman: A Study of Retailing, 1550–1820* (Aldershot, Hampshire: Ashgate Publishing, 2000), *passim*; Ronald M. Berger, *The Most Necessary Luxuries: The Mercers' Company of Coventry, 1550–1680* (University Park: Penn State University Press, 1993); Eric Kerridge, *Textile Manufactures in Early Modern England* (Manchester: Manchester University Press, 1985), pp. 214–25.

success of Henry IV in promoting sericulture to support his own efforts. In its infancy in the 1580s, the English silk-weaving industry, aided by the skills of Huguenot silk weavers based in Spitalfields, had become an export industry with an important place in French and Italian markets by the end of the seventeenth century.[5]

Advocates of an English silk industry left traditional concerns about luxury behind. Their efforts to create the raw materials for the silk industry led to sustained and strenuous sponsorship of the crop in the New World as a replacement for tobacco. Critics had labeled luxury as debilitating, wasteful, effeminate, and immoral. By 1652 Samuel Hartlib claimed that cultivating silk would civilize native Americans by giving them the means to buy English goods.

The Indians seeing and finding that there is neither art, skill or pains in the thing: they will readily set upon it, being by the benefit thereof enabled to buy of the English (in way of truck for their silk bottoms) all those things they most desire, so that not only their civilizing will follow thereupon, but by the infinite mercy of God, their conversion to the Christian faith, the glory of our nation.[6]

English commodities and English trade, by their ability to create and satisfy desires and to incorporate indigenous peoples in networks of exchange, would become the foundation of the nation's civilizing mission. Indeed, colonial demand for silk products augmented the home market in the 1660s. By the eighteenth century the English silk industry proved successful and by the nineteenth, the silk industry became "the world's first modern factory industry."[7]

This chapter looks at the English Crown's promotion of domestic luxury industries from the beginning of the seventeenth century. The glass, tapestry, and silk projects reflected the policy of improvement and technology transfer that characterized the Jacobean regime. The glass project produced an English industry, based on coal, not wood, that copied continental fashion, cut prices on beer, wine, and window glasses, and produced crystal. The tapestry works produced the most prestigious art works of the early

---

[5] Gigliola Pagano De Divitiis, *English Merchants in Seventeenth-Century Italy* (Cambridge: Cambridge University Press, 1997); Chistopher G. A. Clay, *Economic Expansion and Social Change: England 1500–1700*, 2 vols. (Cambridge: Cambridge University Press, 1984), II, 22; Henry Heller, *Labour, Science and Technology in France, 1500–1620* (Cambridge: Cambridge University Press, 1996).

[6] Samuel Hartlib, *The Reformed Virginian Silk-Worm, or a rare and new discovery of a speedy way and easy means found out by a young lady in England . . . for the feeding of silk-worms in the woods, on the mulberry tree leaves in Virginia* (London, 1652), title page.

[7] S. R. H. Jones, "Technology, Transaction Costs, and the Transition to Factory Production in the British Silk Industry, 1700–1870," *Journal of Economic History*, 47 (1987), 75.

seventeenth century. The silk project produced a little-known literature in support of luxury consumption sixty years before Nicholas Barbon and eighty years before Bernard Mandeville wrote their well-known works on the benefits of conspicuous consumption. Stuart policy was driven not by ideology but by practical efforts to address immediate economic problems.[8]

JACOBEAN POLICY ON MANUFACTURES

James I stated his concern with manufacture and trade from the beginning of his reign in proclamations, pamphlets, and projects. Instead of merely decrying vanity and excessive apparel, the Crown fostered the domestic manufacture of silk, glass, tapestries, and other luxury goods in order to create employment, develop a skilled labor force, diminish import costs, create crops for new colonies, and claim honor for itself by rivaling Italy and France in industries associated with the glories of China and Persia.[9]

Improvement and diversification of the economy had become hallmarks of English economic policy from the 1540s and especially from the middle of the Elizabethan period to the Civil War and beyond.[10] The Crown used several instruments, the best known of which were patents of monopoly.[11] In the 1630s Attorney-General John Bankes received proposals to produce a wide variety of luxury goods such as glass, gold and silver thread, Latin wire, sword blades, cases for looking glasses, paper, and beaver hats. Bankes's papers also included many requests for charters of incorporation or other favors from London tradesmen and artificers of luxury goods including tobacco pipe makers, glovers, leather sellers, and pewterers.[12] In what Joan Thirsk has called the "scandalous phase," James I and Charles I allowed courtiers to serve as brokers for patents and licenses that often promoted rent-seeking, that is, profit from licensing, rather than new kinds

---

[8] See Joan Thirsk, *Economic Policy and Projects: The Development of a Consumer Society in Early Modern England* (Oxford: Clarendon Press, 1978); John Cramsie, "Commercial Projects and the Fiscal Policy of James VI and I," *Historical Journal*, 43 (2000), 345–64; Lars Magnusson, *Mercantilism: The Shaping of an Economic Language* (London: Routledge, 1994); Linda Levy Peck, *Northampton: Patronage and Policy at the Court of James I* (London: Allen and Unwin, 1982), pp. 122–45.

[9] See Jacob Viner, "Power Versus Plenty as Objectives of Foreign Policy in the Seventeenth and Eighteenth Centuries", in David Armitage (ed.), *Theories of Empire: 1450–1800* (Aldershot: Ashgate Variorum, 1998), pp. 277–305.

[10] Thirsk, *Economic Policy and Projects, passim.*

[11] Great Britain, Commissioners of Patents for Inventions, *Titles of Patents of Invention, Chronologically Arranged from March 2, 1617 (14 James I) to October 1, 1852 (16 Victoriae),* ed. Bennet Woodcroft (London: Eyre and Spottiswoode, Queen's Printing Office, 1854). Hereafter cited as *Chronological Index of Patents.*

[12] Oxford, Bodleian Library, Bankes Mss., cited in Linda Levy Peck, *Court Patronage and Corruption in Early Stuart England* (London: Unwin Hyman, 1990), pp. 140, 266–67.

of production.[13] But scandal has obscured the long-term importance of these projects for trade, industry, profit-seeking, and changing views of the economy.

King James's most successful initiatives shared common strategies: to copy continental practice and appropriate continental design; to import skilled workers and designers from Italy, France, and the Low Countries; to train English workers; to create a domestic industry that would meet the luxury needs of the well-to-do; and, ultimately, to create an export industry. The glass patent and Mortlake tapestry works proved among the most successful.

Sir Robert Mansell, Vice Admiral of the Navy, became one of the glass patentees in 1615. The Earl of Suffolk commented on "this good commonwealth's work which His Majesty hath so prudently seen into."[14] In the period from 1615 to 1617 the glass monopoly took up a sizeable amount of the time the Privy Council addressed to the matter of patents.[15] King James's proclamation granting Mansell the monopoly and prohibiting the import of foreign glass stressed the importance of saving timber for the navy and ensuring "that matters of superfluity do not devour matters of necessity and defence." The King suggested that "it were the less evil to reduce the times unto the ancient manner of drinking in stone, and of lattice-windows, than to suffer the loss of such a treasure." But he went on to celebrate modern civility marked by new commodities.

Yet God hath so provided by the comfort and encouragement which We are accustomed to give to new and profitable inventions, as the civility of the times may be maintained; and nevertheless, this great mischief restrained and avoided . . . there hath been discovered and perfected a way and means to make glass with seacoal, pit cole and other fuel without any manner of wood, and that in as good perfection for beauty and use as formerly was made by wood.[16]

The success of the English industry depended on the transfer of skills from Italy and the change to coal in the production of glass. Technology

---

[13] See Thirsk, *Economic Policy and Projects, passim*; Peck, *Court Patronage and Corruption*. On rent-seeking see, for example, Robert Ekelund and Robert Tollison, *Mercantilism as a Rent-Seeking Society: Economic Regulation in Historical Perspective* (College Station, Texas: Texas A & M University Press, 1981).

[14] *CSPD 1611–18*, p. 207, 17 November 1613, W. H. Price, *The English Patents of Monopoly* (Cambridge, MA: Harvard University Press, 1913), p. 73.

[15] *Acts of the Privy Council 1615–16*, pp. 469–73; *Acts of the Privy Council, 1616–17*, pp. 233, 290–91, 420.

[16] *Stuart Royal Proclamations*, (ed.) James F. Larkin and Paul L. Hughes, 2 vols. (Oxford: Clarendon Press, 1973), I, 342, "A Proclamation touching Glasses," 23 May 1615. A further proclamation of 1620 reinforced the glass monopoly and the prohibition on the import of foreign glass, "A Proclamation restraining the importation of any sort of glass from beyond seas," 25 February 1620, I, 464.

transfer occurred through the migration of skilled labor, the circulation of manuscript and printed designs, and the exchange of models and artifacts.[17] Venetian artisans came to England in the sixteenth century. Jacob Verzilini, a glass worker from Murano, who had worked in Antwerp, proved most successful in creating a domestic glass industry after receiving a patent from Queen Elizabeth in 1574.[18] When Mansell received the patent to import Venetian techniques of glassmaking, he brought back Muranese glassmakers to create the home industry and to teach their skills to domestic workers.[19] Mansell's patent was one of many monopolies that Parliament attacked in 1621 for raising prices and limiting free trade.[20]

The Venetians tried to prevent their workers from imparting the secrets of the trade. In 1621 the Venetian ambassador wrote encouragingly to the Doge and the Senate that Parliament's concern for free trade would undercut the glassmakers' monopoly.

In the Lower House, after long negotiation, which I did not fail to assist, they have decided that glassware from Murano may come freely to this kingdom. I hope that the Upper House will agree to this for the reasons which I have already reported. If that happens, it will benefit your Serenity's subjects not a little while it will strike a mortal blow at the furnaces here.[21]

The Doge and Council wanted a more direct approach and urged the ambassador to threaten the Muranese artisans "who are teaching the art of glassmaking in that kingdom ... that they will render themselves much more worthy of obtaining some favour from us if they will decide to leave England."[22] Some Muranese who had come to England to work for Mansell later moved to Scotland and to Virginia. The Venetian ambassador wrote in 1622, "those of Murano who have introduced into these realms and taught the art of glass and crystals ... have already set up new furnaces in Scotland ... It is most necessary to keep an eye upon this ... as I understand that it is spreading to France, Flanders, Amsterdam, and even to Virginia."[23] Mansell kept his patent despite the Statute of

---

[17] W. Patrick McCray, "Creating Networks of Skill: Technology Transfer and the Glass Industry in Venice," *Journal of European Economic History*, 28 (1999), 301–33.

[18] Eleanor S. Godfrey, *The Development of English Glassmaking 1560–1640* (Chapel Hill, NC: University of North Carolina Press, 1975), pp. 28–33.

[19] *Ibid.*, p. 82.   [20] PRO SP 14/162/231B lays out the case against the Mansell patent.

[21] *CSPV 1621–23*, p. 55, 28 May 1621 Girolamo Lando, ambassador in England to the Doge and the Senate.

[22] *Ibid.*, p. 269, 21 March 1622.

[23] *Ibid.*, pp. 308–9, 29 April 1622. Lando wrote of Virginia, "they hope for even better results from improved cultivation of the soil and from the arts recently introduced, and they even sent some Muranese from London for glass work," p. 424, 21 September 1622, "Relation of England of Girolamo Lando."

Monopolies of 1624 because the law exempted innovative projects that supported new industries.[24] By 1640 the English industry successfully produced a variety of glass for the home market.[25] As a result, imports of glassware by both English merchants and aliens declined.[26]

In 1641 Mansell defended his patent to the Long Parliament by stressing the fashion, variety, and new low price of the glass he produced, the increase of employment, the transfer of skills and new specialties, and the saving of timber. Despite the increasing cost of materials, he claimed that he had reduced the cost of beer and wine glasses, looking glasses, spectacles, and window glasses. Crystal beer glasses "made by me (which never were before in this kingdom) and of all fashions that are desired and bespoken, were heretofore sold for eighteen shillings the dozen and are now sold for nine shillings the dearest." Crystal wine glasses, "made by me, were formerly sold for sixteen shillings per dozen, and are now sold for five shillings six pence per dozen and the dearest being of extraordinary fashion for seven shillings per dozen." Ordinary beer glasses now cost four shillings a dozen down from six shillings; the cost of wine glasses declined from four shillings to two shillings and six pence. Mansell had also standardized the size and price of window glass and claimed to have created a new domestic industry to grind and polish looking glasses and spectacles.[27] Nevertheless, like other monopolies, Mansell's patent was canceled by the Long Parliament.

The English glass project, already successful before the Civil War, continued to grow during the Restoration. In 1662 Christopher Merrett, a member of the Royal Society, translated and published Antonio Neri's *The Art of Glass*, a practical treatise on how to make glass, in which he discussed the improvements in glass production in the previous decades.[28] Venetian glass continued to have a niche in the English market for luxury goods. English importers Michael Mesey and John Greene, who imported Venetian glass in the 1660s and 1670s, sent detailed instructions to Alessio Morelli in Venice, of the shapes and patterns of Venetian glass to produce

[24] See the Statute of Monopolies, 21 James I, c. 3 (1624), in *The Statutes of the Realm*, 11 vols. (London: G. Eyre and A. Atrahan, 1810–22) IV, see part 2, 1586–1624.

[25] See Godfrey, *The Development of English Glassmaking*, pp. 29, 82, 250, 252, 255–56.

[26] A. M. Millard, "The Import Trade of London, 1600–1640" (Ph.D. thesis, University of London, 1956), p. 227.

[27] Robert Mansell, *The True State of the Businesse of Glasse of All Kindes, as it now standeth both in the price of glasse and materialls, how sold these fifteen yeers last past*, (London, 1641), f. 4.

[28] Antonio Neri, *The Art of Glass … translated into English, with some observations on the author; whereunto is added an account of the glass drops made by the Royal Society, meeting at Gresham College* (London, 1662); McCray, "Creating Networks of Skill," 301–33, 316–26.

THE
Art of Glaſs,

WHEREIN

Are ſhown the wayes to
make and colour Glaſs, Paſtes, Ena-
mels, Lakes, and other Curioſities.

Written in *Italian* by *Antonio Neri*, and
Tranſlated into *Engliſh*, with ſome
Obſervations on the Author.

Whereunto is added an account of the
Glaſs Drops, made by the Royal Society,
meeting at *Greſham College*.

L O N D O N,
Printed by *A. W.* for *Octavian Pulleyn*, at
the Sign of the *Roſe* in S^t. *Pauls*
Church-yard. *M DC LXII.*

12. Efforts to make glass in England drew on the skills of Italian glassmakers, especially Venetians. Christopher Merrett, a member of the Royal Society, translated Neri's *Art of Glass* in 1662 and described the experiments on glass conducted by the Society.

The Folger Shakespeare Library, 141–042q, Antonio Neri, *The Art of Glass...with some observations on the author*; trans. Christopher Merrett (London, 1662).

for English consumers.[29] In the 1670s George Ravenscroft successfully produced leaded crystal for the home market.[30]

By 1709 Joseph Shaw found most English manufactures outstripped French. Where they did not, he eagerly sought to acquire French technology.

I had been searching into all their manufactures and impartially compared 'em with ours, and found the advantage much on our side; till I came hither and found out the looking-glass manufacture which surpasses anything in England, or perhaps in the universe ... I wish some of 'em were enticed over hither.[31]

Shaw's desire to bring back artisans continued the process of appropriating skilled labor from abroad that prevailed throughout the sixteenth and seventeenth centuries.

Tapestry had long been admired in England and Ireland and long collected. Henry VIII and Cardinal Wolsey amassed collections of important Renaissance tapestries which rivaled those of the great houses of Europe.[32] Wolsey's tapestries became much sought after in later generations. Tapestries identified as Wolsey's appear in the 1614 inventory of the goods of the Jacobean privy councillor, Henry Howard, Earl of Northampton.[33]

Efforts to create a British tapestry industry depended almost entirely on the immigration of Flemish tapestry workers and the appropriation of continental designs and designers.[34] In the 1530s an Irish tapestry factory was established by Piers, Earl of Ormond, who brought Flemish artificers to Kilkenny.[35] In the middle of the sixteenth century Ralph Sheldon founded a tapestry works using Flemish workers. The Sheldon works produced maps of counties and London, the crest and arms of great nobles such as the Earl of Pembroke, cushions for chairs and window seats, and

[29] BL Sloane Mss. 857, copies of letters from Michael Mesey and John Greene to Alessio Morelli at Venice, London, 1667–71.
[30] Godfrey, *The Development of English Glassmaking*, p. 134.
[31] Quoted in John Lough, *France Observed in the Seventeenth Century by British Travellers* (Stocksfield, Northumberland, and Boston: Oriel Press, 1984), p. 58.
[32] Thomas P. Campbell, *Tapestry in the Renaissance: Art and Magnificence*, Metropolitan Museum of Art (New Haven: Yale University Press, 2002).
[33] E. P. Shirley, "An Inventory of the Effects of Henry Howard, K. G., Earl of Northampton, Taken on his Death in 1614, Together with a Transcript of his Will," *Archaeologia*, 42 (1869), 347–78.
[34] Wendy Hefford, "Flemish Tapestry Weavers in England, 1550–1775," in Guy Delmarcel (ed.), *Flemish Tapestry Weavers Abroad: Emigration and the Founding of Manufactures in Europe* (Louvain, Belgium: Louvain University Press, 2002), pp. 43–61. D. C. Coleman, *Industry in Tudor and Stuart England* (London: Macmillan, 1975), p. 29.
[35] William George Thomson, *A History of Tapestry from the Earliest Times until the Present Day* (London: Hodder and Stoughton, 1906, 1930), p. 276.

larger pieces for the Earl of Leicester. These tapestries supplemented rather than replaced imports.[36] Religious persecution in the 1570s and 1580s brought repeated waves of Flemish, Dutch, and Huguenot émigrés to England, including arras workers or weavers. Some of them worked for the Crown while others set up their own workshops.[37]

King James established the Mortlake tapestry works to rival the best in Europe. To do so, he explicitly imitated Henry IV who established French tapestry manufactures with two Flemish weavers in 1607. In 1619 James presented "an abstract of the contract between Henry IV and Marc de Comans and Francois de la Planche" to a royal commission.[38] The commissioners then recommended that Sir Francis Crane become the director of Mortlake, import Low Country tapissiers, particularly those who directed the French works, and use English orphan boys as apprentices.[39] Mortlake not only took over the techniques of Low Countries tapestry works, it imported leading Flemish tapestry makers and copied Italian and Flemish designs. In 1620 Van Male, secretary to the ambassador of the Spanish Netherlands, wrote to Archduke Albert that "the principal masters of this art . . . are coming over daily from Brussels or elsewhere."[40] Francis Cleyn, the Low Countries artist, arrived in the 1620s to oversee Mortlake's designs and remained as designer at Mortlake until 1658.[41] Rubens and Van Dyck may have provided designs.[42] Mortlake produced tapestries for the Crown, the great nobility, and an international audience. It was financed in part by the sale of offices, specifically sergeants at law, that characterized the Jacobean patronage system.[43]

"The Acts of the Apostles" by Raphael was the most important tapestry commission in the sixteenth century. In 1515 Pope Leo X had commissioned Raphael to create a set of cartoons for tapestries which were made in Brussels. The tapestries cost 2,000 ducats. Raphael received 1,000 ducats

---

[36] Thomson, *A History of Tapestry*, pp. 264–70, and Anthony Wells-Cole, "The Elizabethan Sheldon Tapestry Maps," *Burlington Magazine*, 132 (June 1990), 392–401; "Some Design Sources for the Earl of Leicester's Tapestries and Other Contemporary Pieces," *Burlington Magazine*, 125 (May 1983), 284–85.

[37] Hefford, "Flemish Tapestry Weavers in England," pp. 43–61.

[38] On the Mortlake tapestry works see Thomson, *A History of Tapestry*, p. 47. Wendy Hefford, "Prince Behind the Scenes," *Country Life*, 184 (4 October 1990), 132–35; Hefford, "Cardinal Mazarin and the Earl of Pembroke's Tapestries," *Connoisseur*, 195 (1977), 286–90; Hefford, "The Duke of Buckingham's Mortlake Tapestries of 1623," *Bulletin du CIETA*, 76 (1999), 90–103; Laurence Martin, "Sir Francis Crane," *Apollo*, 113 (1981), 90–96. Cardinal Mazarin and Louis XIV both had Mortlake tapestries.

[39] Thomson, *A History of Tapestry*, pp. 278–80.

[40] Hefford, "Flemish Tapestry Weavers in England," pp. 43–61.

[41] *Ibid.*; Thomson, *A History of Tapestry*, p. 282.　　[42] Thomson, *A History of Tapestry*, pp. 285, 309.

[43] Peck, *Court Patronage and Corruption*, pp. 116–23.

for the design. Engravings made in 1516 brought the designs to a wider European audience.[44] Francis I and Henry VIII had copies in the 1530s and 1540s.[45] By the middle of the century, the designs were being used for majolica and Limoges plates, while copies of the tapestries continued to be made in the Low Countries later in the sixteenth century.[46] During his trip to Spain in 1623, Prince Charles urged that the cartoons, then in Genoa, be purchased for Mortlake.[47] Indeed, Raphael's cartoons became the basis for Mortlake's most important work. But Mortlake also produced other series based on sixteenth-century Flemish designs, such as "Vulcan and Venus" and "Hero and Leander." It also copied Henry VIII's tapestry series called "The Months," used copies of Charles I's pictures, and works by Gulio Romano.[48]

King Charles bought many sets of Mortlake tapestries as did great nobles and officials such as the Earl of Pembroke and John Williams, Bishop of London. Buckingham supported the new works and in return received three sets of tapestries including "The Months" and "Vulcan and Venus."[49] Buckingham appears to have received his sets of tapestries as a gift to maintain Mortlake in the King's favor.[50] But domestic consumption was not the only aim. Mortlake created sets of tapestries for export. For example, Francis Crane wrote to Buckingham: "I am gone to Mortlake to meet the Persian Ambassador to see whether we may not establish some trade of our commodity into those parts."[51]

During the English Civil War and Protectorate, Mortlake continued to function and sold tapestries at home and abroad. The Prince of Orange wanted a set in the early 1640s.[52] Oliver Cromwell held onto the King's tapestries while selling his pictures. He hung the Acts of the Apostles in the State Rooms at Hampton Court.[53] In the 1650s Mortlake sold tapestries to the Earl of Rutland and in the 1660s to the Earl of Bedford.[54] Henry Mordaunt, Earl of Peterborough, bought a series called the Daughters of Niobe or The Royal Horses. A royalist, Mordaunt inherited his title in 1643

---

[44] Sharon Fermor, *The Raphael Tapestry Cartoons: Narrative, Decoration, Design* (London: Scala Books in Association with the Victoria and Albert Museum, 1996), pp. 9–12, 24; John K. G. Shearman, *Raphael's Cartoons in the Collection of Her Majesty the Queen, and the Tapestries from the Sistine Chapel* (London: Phaidon, 1972), see especially pp. 138–39, 145–48.

[45] Shearman, *Raphael's Cartoons*, pp. 143–144. [46] *Ibid.* [47] *Ibid.*, pp. 145–46.

[48] Thomson, *A History of Tapestry*, pp. 282–87.

[49] Hefford, "The Duke of Buckingham's Mortlake Tapestries of 1623," pp. 90–103.

[50] *Ibid.* [51] Laurence Martin, "Sir Francis Crane," *Apollo*, 113 (1981), 90–96.

[52] Hefford, "Flemish Tapestry Weavers in England," pp. 54–55.

[53] Thomson, *A History of Tapestry*, pp. 350–54.

[54] Hefford, "Flemish Tapestry Weavers in England," pp. 54–55.

and sought to rally support for the King in 1648. His set may have been produced in the 1650s or even after the Restoration.[55]

In 1663 Parliament opened tapestry making to all. Although Mortlake had faded by the 1670s, the Raphael cartoons continued to be regarded as central to the history of art. Displayed in a new gallery designed by Christopher Wren by 1699, Jonathan Richardson praised them as a sign of English greatness in 1725. "The cartoons of Raphael at Hampton Court ... are generally allowed by foreigners and those of our own nation who are the most bigoted to Italy or France, to be the best of that master as he is uncontestably the best of all those whose works remain in the world."[56]

Beyond glass and tapestry, Stuart industrial policy fostered new fashions in interior decoration through domestic production. Thus, gilded leather panels on walls, alternatives to hangings and tapestries, had already appeared in Holland and France in the late sixteenth century. In 1596, Sir Henry Unton, ambassador to France in the 1590s, had leather wall hangings in his study.[57] By 1614 the Earl of Northampton lined his rooms with gilded leather.[58] Aletheia Talbot, Countess of Arundel, had red and yellow leather floor covers which matched coordinated hangings.[59] In 1638 the Crown granted Christopher Hunt a patent for the sole way of embroidering or "huffling of gilded leather fit for hangings or other furniture for houses."[60] William Billingsly received the sole right for his process of pointing or stamping cabinets, bedsteads, playing tables, and other furniture with liquid gold and silver.[61] The more elaborate soft furnishings of the 1630s also required specialized cleaning. Peter Ladore received a patent for the art of glossing plain and figured satins made within this realm, and ... glossing and refreshing such plain and figured satins made beyond the seas and imported as shall take wet in any way.[62] These initiatives all sought to create domestic industries to satisfy the demand for luxury goods. Several became successful by 1640 and beyond.

[55] Wendy Hefford, "Cleyn's Noble Horses," *National Art-Collections Fund Review*, 87 (1990), 97–102.

[56] Quoted in Fermor, *The Raphael Tapestry Cartoons*, pp. 22–24.

[57] John Gough Nichols, *The Unton Inventories* (London: Printed for the Berkshire Ashmolean Society by John Bowyer Nichols and Son, 1841), p. 3.

[58] Shirley, "An Inventory of the Effects of Henry Howard," pp. 347–78.

[59] Lionel Cust, " Notes on the Collections Formed by Thomas Howard, Earl of Arundel and Surrey, K. G.," *Burlington Magazine*, 20 (1911), 97–100, 233–36, 341–43; Arundel Castle Mss. Inventory 1, "An Inventory of all the parcells of Purselin, Glasses & other goods now remayning in the Pranketing Roome at Tart Hall, 8 Sept. 1641"; David Howarth, "The Patronage and Collecting of Aletheia, Countess of Arundel, 1606–54," *Journal of the History of Collections*, 10 (1998), 125–37.

[60] *Chronological Index of Patents*, #118, 17 July 1638 (Christopher Hunt).

[61] *Ibid.*, #121 (William Billingsley).   [62] *Ibid.*, #123 (Peter Ladore).

13. The Mortlake tapestry works, created by James I, produced large tapestry series based on the cartoons of Raphael and its own designer, Francis Cleyn. Henry Mordaunt, a royalist exile, purchased these Mortlake tapestries in the 1650s or 1660s, after his return to England.

The Metropolitan Museum of Art, Textiles-Tapestries, English, *c.* 1650–70, Francis Cleyn (1582–1658), Mortlake Tapestry, *The Seizure of Cassandra by Ajax*, 1653–60, with arms of Henry Mordaunt, 2nd Earl of Peterborough. Gift of Christian A. Zabriskie, 1937 (37.85). Photograph, all rights reserved, The Metropolitan Museum of Art.

84

King James was recognized by contemporaries as a patron of new industries. Sir Francis Bacon, the Attorney General, who oversaw the granting of patents, hoped that "in your time many noble inventions may be discovered for man's use."[63] One program for the Banqueting House ceiling devised in the mid-1620s suggested that, in addition to honoring the King's learning and the Union of the Crowns of England and Scotland, one large square present "Peace with a Caduceus in one hand, & a little Statua in the other, attended on by those particular Arts which began to take root in this King's time, expressing his providence therein."[64]

"A PROFITABLE PLEASURE": CREATING RAW MATERIALS FOR THE SILK INDUSTRY

New glass and tapestry works illustrate the Jacobean encouragement of new manufactures. Silk displays the drive to control raw materials as well as to support a new industry. In the late sixteenth and early seventeenth centuries, English merchants increasingly brought back luxury goods rather than bullion in exchange for their sale of English cloth.[65] The Levant Company purchased silk from the eastern Mediterranean, which it later augmented with imports from Italy. In 1559 silk fabrics had comprised 3.3 percent of the imports to London; they doubled in the 1590s.[66] By 1622 silk fabric had grown to 5.1 percent of all imports. The increase in the import of raw silk was even more dramatic. In 1559, 1.1 percent of imports was silk; by 1622 it had risen to 7.5 percent. In 1622 London-imported silk was worth L118,000. By 1640 this had reached L175,000, in the 1660s L263,000 and, by the end of the century, L344,000, amounting throughout the century to 23–29 percent of the total value of imports.[67] Silk, either raw or "thrown into thread for the weavers at Spitalfields and elsewhere to work on" became the most valuable of all the raw material imports throughout the middle and later seventeenth century.[68]

---

[63] Quoted in Lisa Jardine and Michael Silverthorne (eds.), *The New Organon* (Cambridge: Cambridge University Press, 2000), introduction, p. xxvii; Francis Bacon, *The Letters and Life of Francis Bacon*, 7 vols., (ed.) James Spedding (London: Longman, Green, Longman and Roberts, 1861–74), VII, p. 130; Bacon to James I.

[64] Quoted in Gregory Martin, "The Banqueting House Ceiling: Two Newly-Discovered Projects," *Apollo*, 139 (1994), 34.

[65] Millard, "The Import Trade of London, 1600–1640," chapters 5 and 6. Barry Supple, *Commercial Crisis and Change in England 1600–1642: A Study in the Instability of a Mercantile Economy* (Cambridge: Cambridge University Press, 1959); Ralph Davis, *The Rise of the English Shipping Industry in the Seventeenth and Eighteenth Centuries* (London: Macmillan, 1962).

[66] Clay, *Economic Expansion and Social Change*, II, 39, 125.   [67] *Ibid.*, 125, 157.

[68] *Ibid.*, 161.

14. The silk trade was a major component of the Italian economy. Jan van der Streit, known as Stradanus, a Flemish artist working in Italy, produced a series of engravings showing how the secret of silk making was brought by monks from the east to the Roman emperor, how mulberry trees were used to raise silkworms, and how aristocratic women embroidered with silk.
The Folger Shakespeare Library, ART Box S895, no. 3, Jan van der Streit, from his *Vermis Sericus*, Antwerp, 1600?, engravings of silk works and, silk making.

At the beginning of the century, Lionel Cranfield did a thriving business importing textiles from the continent. On 15 June 1600, his agent, Richard Rawstorm, wrote about the uncertainty of prices.

I have shipped only the velvet and taffeta for, having no order from you, durst buy nothing in regard they yield such base prices there and here are kept up at the old prices. By all likelihood they will not fall this year by reason of this cold summer, which so much hinders the springing forth of the leaf that they write out of Italy there are no mulberry leaves for the silk worms to feed on, so that silk will be very scant and is thought will this next Frankfort mart be as dear if not dearer than the last. But the alteration of the weather may yet yield some remedy.[69]

Expensive and much coveted, silk production was uncertain, because of the volatility in the cost of imports. As a result, the Medici, the Valois, and the Stuarts all tried to create domestic silk industries in order to control the raw materials on which it was based.

Silk, silkworms, and mulberry trees formed the basis of an industry whose materials from China and Persia had long been admired in Europe. Jan van der Streit, known as Stradanus, a Bruges artist working in Florence, represented the contemporary interest in raising silkworms and creating home-grown silk industries in a series of late sixteenth-century engravings. Dedicated to the Medici Duke of Florence and published in Amsterdam *c.* 1600, the engravings show the presentation of silk to Emperor Justinian in the sixth century by Persian monks who had brought back the secret "that silk was produced by a species of worms, the eggs of which might be transported with safety and propagated in his dominions."[70] Stradanus illustrated how silk was produced.[71] Adult men brought in the mulberry branches, women and children tended the worms and pulled the thread from the cocoons, and aristocratic women embroidered silk textiles.

The French silk industry had developed in the early sixteenth century through the skills of Milanese artisans.[72] In the 1590s Henry IV built silk works and imported foreign workers to produce silk at the same time that he planted mulberry trees in the Tuilleries.[73] His minister, Sully, opposed the initiative, forecasting that "time and practice will teach you that France

[69] HMC, *Sackville*, II, p. 26, 15 June 1600, Emden, p. 17.

[70] César Moreau, *Rise and Progress of the Silk Trade in England from the Earliest Periods to the Present Time* (London, 1826).

[71] Folger, Jan van der Streit, *Vermis Sericus*, Antwerp, 1600? BL Sloane Pr XXXV. Hans Sloane, collected these tracts on silk as well as the original prints at the end of the seventeenth century.

[72] Samuel Sholl, *A Short Historical Account of the Silk Manufacture in England* (London, 1811), p. 1.

[73] Moreau, *Rise and Progress of the Silk Trade in England*, pp. 4–5, citing Francois Eudes de Mézeray, *A General Chronological History of France* (London, 1683); see Sholl, *A Short Historical Account of the Silk Manufacture in England*.

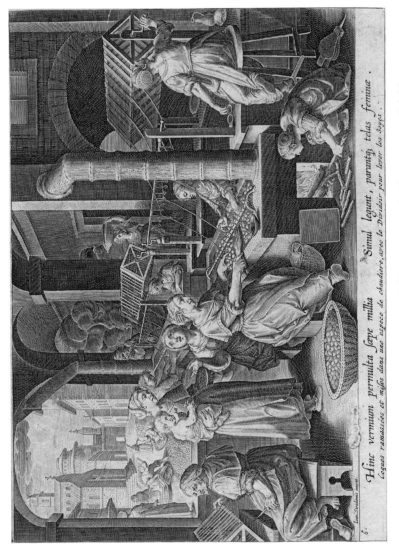

15. Stradanus shows urban silk production in which labor was provided by women and children. The Folger Shakespeare Library, ART Box S895, no. 6, Jan van der Straet, from his *Vermis sericus*. Antwerp, 1600?, engravings of silk works and silk making.

is not ready for such baubles." Echoing the classical critique of luxury, Sully asserted that luxury manufactures encouraged weakness and excess and would, therefore, ruin the state.[74]

In contrast, Barthelemy de Laffemas, a member of the royal household, was an enthusiastic promoter of sericulture and the silk industry.[75] He urged the prohibition of imports, especially from Italy, and the growing of mulberry trees in France. For labor, the silk industry could rely on women and children. To ensure home-grown silk, Laffemas advocated requiring all property owners to grow two to four mulberry trees an acre. Providing directions on the cultivation of silkworms, he hoped that each parish would plant 3,000–4,000 mulberry trees with profits of millions of livres.[76] The implementation of Laffemas's project proved difficult. Merchants soon complained of the difficulty of securing 400,000 mulberry trees and the silkworm eggs.[77] This problem in infrastructure would prove an obstacle in the English industry too.

French writers in the 1590s also pressed for a domestic silk industry. In 1598 Olivier de Serres, in his expansive work on agriculture, *Le Theatre d'Agriculture et Mesnage de Champs* (Paris), described methods of raising mulberry trees in order to cultivate silkworms. Louis Turquet de Mayerne, a French Huguenot historian, known for his work on constitutional monarchy, wrote a treatise in 1599 celebrating merchants and calling for the promotion of the silk industry. Like Laffemas, he urged the King and the nobility to plant mulberry trees.[78] His son, Sir Theodore Turquet de Mayerne, who studied medicine at Montpellier where medicine and botanical studies were strongly linked, became physician to James I in 1611. In 1603 Henry IV sponsored the work of the Parisian silk merchant, John Baptiste Letellier, *Memoires et instructions pour l'establissement des meuriers, et art de faire la soye en France* (Paris, 1603). Along with specific instructions, the book included four woodcuts showing how to dry the leaves and spin the silk.[79] One drew on the Stradanus engravings.

[74] Heller, *Labour, Science and Technology in France, 1500–1620*, pp. 161–62.

[75] Charles Woolsey Cole, *French Mercantilist Doctrines Before Colbert* (New York: Richard R. Smith, 1931), pp. 85–90.

[76] *Ibid.*, pp. 85–90.   [77] *Ibid.*, p. 96.

[78] Heller, *Labour, Science and Technology in France, 1500–1620*, pp. 165–66.

[79] Charles E. Hatch, Jr., "Mulberry Trees and Silkworms: Sericulture in Early Virginia," *The Virginia Magazine of History and Biography*, 65 (1957), 3–61, is the only historian to discuss these images. He assumes that they appeared for the first time in John Bonoeil's 1622 tract. The woodcuts of silkworms and spinning in later English pamphlets are copied from the four in Letellier's work of 1603. See *Catalogue Bibliothèque National*. I am grateful to Rachel Doggett of the Folger for advice on these woodcuts.

Henry IV's important initiatives in developing the silk industry have been described variously as mercantilist, as a response to contemporary labor problems, and as the product of the Calvinism of his chief ministers.[80] In contrast, King James's direct borrowing of Henry IV's assumptions, methods, and implementation have generally gone unnoticed.

In 1599 Thomas Moffett wrote an elaborate poem, *The Silkewormes and their Flies*.[81] Describing the silkworms he had seen when he was in Tuscany in 1579, Moffett exhorted his countrymen to display their greatness by wearing silk.

> Rise hearts of English race.
> Why should your clothes be coarser than the rest?
> Whose features, tall, and high aspiring face
> Aim at great things, and challenge even the best,
> Beg countrymen no more in sackcloth base,
> Being by me of such a trade possest
> That shall enrich yourselves and children more
> Than ere it did Naples or Spain before.[82]

However tongue in cheek, such sentiments signaled an important change in attitudes toward luxury goods at the end of the Elizabethan period.

That same year, William Lee had developed a loom on which to knit or weave silks. Lee had the support of Lord Hunsdon, one of Elizabeth's courtiers, in his effort to get a patent.[83] Worried that the invention would put weavers out of work, the queen limited Lee's patent to silk stockings which "appealed only to a small number of my subjects."[84] Her advisors cautiously calculated which type of imported silk, tufted taffeta or woven silk, would cost her a greater loss in customs duties.[85]

Contemporary interest in producing the raw materials for the silk industry burgeoned in the first decade of the seventeenth century even as

---

[80] On Henry IV's policy see Heller, *Labour, Science and Technology in France, 1500–1620*, pp. 160–64, 168, 170–74.

[81] Thomas Moffett, *The Silkewormes and their Flies* (London, 1599), facsimile edn, (ed.) Victor Houliston (Binghamton, New York: Medieval and Renaissance Texts and Studies Society, 1989), pp. xii–xiii. Moffett relies on Marcus Hieronymus Vida, *De Bombyce* (Rome, 1527) dedicated to Isabella d'Este. An even earlier poem, *Bombyx*, was published in Rome in the 1490s.

[82] Moffett, *The Silkewormes and their Flies*, pp. xviii, 70. Moffett's poem drew praise from Nathaniel Baxter in 1606 in his *Sir Philip Sydneys Ouránia* (1606).

[83] Frank Warner, *The Silk Industry of the United Kingdom: Its Origin and Development* (London: Drane's, 1921).

[84] *Ibid.*, p. 536.   [85] *Ibid.*, p. 627.

the Crown abandoned support for sumptuary legislation.[86] King James took a direct hand in the effort to create a domestic silk industry. The initial failure of that effort has led English historians to consider it one more unlikely project. Thus T. G. Pugh notes it "failed after its short-lived success."[87] Peter Thornton suggests that "nothing permanent seems to have come from this last project."[88] In fact, serious efforts to raise mulberry trees and raise silkworms stretched from James I's letter to the justices of the peace in 1607, to the Virginia Company's initiatives from 1607 to the 1620s, to Samuel Hartlib in the 1650s and to the Royal Society in the 1660s. Merchants, virtuosi, and scientists alike enthusiastically supported this Stuart agenda despite changes in government. Samuel Hartlib, the Calvinist promoter of universal improvement, and Henry Oldenburg, Secretary of the Royal Society, lauded King James I as the author of sericulture in England.

The Jacobean court displayed its commitment to a domestic silk industry at court and in London. King James expanded the Mulberry Gardens located on four acres on the current site of Buckingham Palace. Munton Jennings, "Keeper of the Garden at Theobalds," was granted L50 "for making a place for the silkworms and for providing mulberry leaves."[89] Richard Lecavill, Groom of the Chamber, got three months' expenses "whilst travelling about with the king's silkworms ... withersoever his Majesty went."[90]

The courtly aspects of silk growing continued throughout the reign. In 1609 Queen Anne had her portrait painted in a gown embroidered with silkworms.[91] In 1616 she commissioned Inigo Jones to design an elegant silkworm house at Oatlands. Two stories high, the building had four small rooms downstairs, and a 400 square foot room above with shelves for the silkworms. The room was decorated with wainscoting of "oval and arched panels, a wrought frieze, and a portal." A large west window had Anne's coat of arms "painted in glass." Two rooms had carved mantles and chimneys; the roof had tiles and gables; three rooms had paved floors.

---

[86] Negley Boyd Harte, "State Control of Dress and Social Change in Pre-Industrial England," in D. C. Coleman and Arthur H. John (eds.), *Trade, Government and Economy in Pre-Industrial England: Essays Presented to F. J. Fisher* (London: Weidenfeld and Nicolson, 1976), pp. 148–49.

[87] T. B. Pugh, "A Portrait of Queen Anne of Denmark at Parham Park, Sussex," *The Seventeenth Century*, 8 (1993), 171.

[88] Peter M. Thornton, *Baroque and Rococo Silks* (London: Faber and Faber, 1965).

[89] *CSPD 1611–18*; p. 592, 8 November 1618.

[90] *CSPD 1611–18*, p. 555, [18?] July 1618; Warner, *The Silk Industry*, pp. 537–38.

[91] Pugh, "A Portrait of Queen Anne of Denmark," 170–71. I am grateful to Helen Payne for this reference.

William Pottington received L28 for providing shelves.[92] Jones's silkworm house stood near his new gate which is visible in the background of the portrait of the Queen at Oatlands.[93]

The post of royal gardener was quite desirable. John Bonoeil, author of an important 1622 tract on sericulture for Virginia, became keeper of the royal gardens, vines, and silkworms at Oatlands. After his death, John Tradescant took over the Oatlands gardens. Tradescant also tended the Mulberry Gardens in London with an annuity of £100 a year. By 1640 the new Keeper of the Mulberry Gardens, Lord Goring, paid L1,000 to Sir Walter Aston to hold the Mulberry Gardens and house in fee farm.[94]

Such courtly display of silkworms and mulberry trees was closely linked to the promotion of a domestic industry. Within the court, however, there were conflicting interests. Robert Cecil, Earl of Salisbury, had the grant of duties on imported silk. Lionel Cranfield served as his agent. When it became apparent that a home industry was being promoted through James's leading Scottish courtier, the Duke of Lennox, Salisbury hedged his investment by importing mulberry trees. Indeed, he planted 500 mulberry trees at Hatfield House.[95]

"PRIVATE PROFITS AND PUBLIC BENEFITS": THE LITERATURE OF LUXURY PRODUCTION

The promotion of the silk industry celebrated luxury commodities and the wearing of silk by the English nation as a whole. The print campaign on silk in England from 1603 to the 1670s drew on mercantile language familiar to contemporaries and later scholars from writings in support of the East India Company in the 1620s.[96] It stressed the importance of international trade, import substitution, and employment, especially for poor women and children. Supplying the demand for luxury goods, it argued, would provide both private profits and public benefit. Colonies

---

[92] This paragraph is drawn from Prudence Leith-Ross, *The John Tradescants, Gardeners to the Rose and Lily Queen* (London: P. Owen, 1984), p. 94.

[93] *Ibid.*   [94] *Ibid.*, pp. 93–94. Oxford, Bodleian Library, Bankes Mss. 65/63, 1 July 1640.

[95] Leith-Ross, *The John Tradescants*, p. 42.

[96] On mercantilism see Magnusson, *Mercantilism: The Shaping of an Economic Language*; Lynn Muchmore, "Gerald de Malynes and Mercantile Economics," *History of Political Economy*, 14 (1969), 336–58; Lynn Muchmore, "A Note on Thomas Mun's 'England's Treasure by Forraign Trade,'" *Economic History Review*, new series, 23 (1970), 498–503; J. D. Gould, "The Trade Crisis of the Early 1620s and English Economic Thought," *Journal of Economic History* 15 (1955), 121–33; Supple, *Commercial Crisis and Change in England, 1600–1642*; Joyce Oldham Appleby, *Economic Thought and Ideology in Seventeenth-Century England* (Princeton: Princeton University Press, 1978).

promised both raw materials and markets for finished goods. Yet the silk literature emerged earlier than the East India literature in the context of peace and plenty rather than the contraction of the cloth industry in the late 1610s and early 1620s.

The Duke of Lennox and his appointees, a group of French gardeners and goldsmiths, controlled the mulberry project. M. Forest, whose real name was François de Verton, played a key role in the project. Verton presented King James with a manuscript on silk production sometime after November 1605 which drew on Serres and reproduced the Letellier woodcuts of 1603. Now in color, these prints had been redrawn to show a couple in Jacobean clothes spinning silk.[97] In the aftermath of the Gunpowder Plot, Verton suggested that James had been saved from danger by God for "some great and splendid good." As a result, his subjects would enjoy not only happiness and peace but also abundance in all sorts of goods.[98]

Adopting the project with great enthusiasm and vigor, King James ordered all "those of ability" to plant mulberry trees and used the printing press to promote the project beginning in 1607. In his "Instructions for the Increasing of Mulberry Trees and the Breeding of Silk Worm for the Making of Silk," James stressed the success of the King of France and ordered the lords lieutenant, deputy lieutenants, and justices of the peace to sell mulberry plants to all landowners.[99] "Require the landowners to purchase and plant 10,000 mulberry trees, which will be delivered to purchasers in March or April next, at the rate of six shillings the hundred. A book of instructions on mulberry trees and silkworms is to be published meanwhile, for encouraging the silk trade in England." Although he would actually lose revenues because of the reduction in custom duties on imported silk, the King eschewed such concerns in the name of honor and plenty.

all things of this nature tending to plantations, increase of science, and works of industry, are things so naturally pleasing to our own disposition, as we shall take it for an argument of extraordinary affection towards our person . . . our brother the French king hath, since his coming to that Crown, both begun and brought to perfection the making of silks in his country, whereby he hath won to himself honour, and to his subjects a marvellous increase of wealth. [We] would account it no little happiness to us if the same work which we began among our people with no less zeal to their good (than any Prince can have to the good of theirs) might in our time produce the fruits which there it hath done.[100]

---

[97] BL Royal Ms. 16 E xxvi, François de Verton, "Traicté des proprietez des meuiers, & Instruction par le gouvernement des vers a soye."
[98] *Ibid.*, ff. 2–2v.   [99] PRO SP 14/26/6.
[100] William Stallenge, *Instructions for the Increasing of Mulberie Trees* (London, 1609).

By this figure is shewed the fashion of the Engine, how to wind off the silke from the cods, with the furnaces and cawtherns for that purpose.

16. Olivier de Serres, the French agriculturalist, described how to raise silkworms. His work was translated into English by Nicholas Geffe. Geffe used woodcuts published by Jean-François Letellier in 1603 showing how to raise silkworms and spin silk. These woodcuts were repeatedly used in the English literature on silk up through the 1650s.

The Folger Shakespeare Library, STC 22249, Olivier de Serres, *The Perfect Use of Silk-Wormes and their Benefit*, trans. Nicholas Geffe (London, 1607).

King James promoted the publication of Nicholas Geffe's translation of Olivier de Serres's book, *The Perfect Use of Silk-Wormes and their Benefit*.[101] The work incorporated Letellier's woodcuts (1603) showing how to care for silkworms, harvest raw silk from the cocoons, and spin the silk. Indeed, every major English tract on silk between 1607 and 1655 reproduced the prints from the 1603 French edition of Letellier.

Nicholas Geffe, who came from a Berkshire gentry family, had contacts at court both with Robert Cecil, Earl of Salisbury, Secretary of State, and Sir Francis Bacon, the Attorney General.[102] An inveterate projector,[103] Geffe dated *The Perfect Use of Silk-Wormes* "20 May 1607 from Bacon House." The title page displayed the royal coat of arms on the title page and began with dedicatory poems to Geffe by Michael Drayton, George Carr, and Robert Godwin. They celebrated the trade and manufacture of silk. Drayton emphasized the peace brought by King James and imagined the foreign envy of a domestic silk industry.[104]

Geffe added his own *Discourse . . . of the Meanes and Sufficiencie of England, for to Have Abundance of Fine Silke, by Feeding of Silke-wormes within the Same* to his translation of Serres. He argued, in language not unlike that of Nicholas Barbon and Bernard Mandeville, that private desires for luxury promoted the public good. The silk project "will clothe

---

[101] Olivier de Serres, *The Perfect Use of Silk-Wormes and their Benefit . . . Done out of the French original of D'Olivier de Serres Lord of Pradel into English by Nicholas Geffe Esquire* (London, 1607), STC 22249.

[102] In 1604, while at the Court of Augmentations for Cecil, Geffe was arrested for debt and appealed for help to both Cecil and Bacon. On his behalf, Cecil wrote to the Masters of Requests in whose court the case was heard. HMC *Salisbury*, V, p. 84, Nicholas Geffe to Sir Robert Cecil, 14 January 1594–95; *Salisbury*, XIV, p. 273, Geffe to the Queen undated [1596–1603]; *Salisbury*, XVI, p. 187, Geffe to Cecil, 29 July 1604; p. 217, Geffe to Cecil, August 1604; p. 324, Geffe to Cecil, 4 October 1604. See Lena Cowen Orlin, "Boundary Disputes in Early Modern London," in Lena Cowen Orlin (ed.), *Material London, ca. 1600* (Philadelphia: University of Pennsylvania Press, 2000), pp. 370–72 for Geffe's boundary dispute with his London neighbors.

[103] Geffe proposed a grant for the uncovering of concealed lands both to Queen Elizabeth and King James. HMC *Salisbury*, XX, p. 296 (1608 or later). On 1 July 1616, Geffe and Henry Wingham of Felbrigg, Norfolk, received a special license to make "oil and pitch and soap with sea coals for one and twenty years." In the same month he wrote a strongly worded rejoinder to Sir Edward Coke's attack on the King's power to grant monopolies. *CSPD 1611–18*, p. 380, 11 July 1616. Sherburn to Carleton, enclosing "Accusations and articles of capital injustice, praemunire and high treason against Sir Edward Coke, for the judgement given by him in the King's Bench, 13 Jac I, to the diminution of the King's prerogative, classing His Majesty with his own subjects, supporting his conclusions by forged seditious reports, and by his judgement, disabling the King from giving or receiving grants. If his offenses be examined they will be found greater than Cardinal Wolsey's." PRO SP 14/87/9, I and II.

[104] Geffe, *Discourse . . . of the Meanes and Sufficiencie of England, for to Have Abundance of Fine Silke, by Feeding of Silke-Wormes within the Same . . . For the general use and universal benefit of all those his Country-men which embrace it* (London, 1607).

By this figure is fhewed the portraits of the cods, and the Butterflies com
forth of them, to engender and lay their egs vpon black Serge, Chaml
let, Tammey or fuch like ftuffes as hath been faid.

17. The woodcuts published by Geffe also incorporated parts of Stradanus's *Vermis sericus*. The Folger Shakespeare Library, STC 22249, 02r, Olivier de Serres, *The Perfect Use of Silk-Wormes and their Benefit*, trans. Nicholas Geffe (London, 1607).

our backs sumptuously, and fill our purses royally … our private profits and public benefit are deeply interested therein."[105] Geffe wrote,

we are not ignorant of the store of silk continually used in this realm, amounting yearly to a mass of money which strangers fleece from us, that within a small time we may keep in our purses, by having silk sufficient here at home … we may as well be silke-masters as sheepe-masters … Let us therefore turn our idle wastes and lost grounds into woods of mulberries, let us plentifully plant them with trees, as we are now abundantly filled with people.[106]

The great design would benefit both landowners and the poor. The nobility and gentry would make "thousands of crowns" and "keep their hands from the … tradesman's book," that is from buying on credit. Silk production would also relieve the poor

wherewith our country will in time be too much pestered, unless some new invented necessary employment supply their wants; than which the making of silk in England … cannot give better occasion … weaving satins, velvets, taffetas, and divers sorts of other silken stuffs, by which disposing them the industrious will be ready and willing to work, or being idle, loiterers may be compelled.[107]

Enticing and, if necessary, forcing, the poor into the silk-weaving industry would reduce theft and begging. As a result, "the gallows might cease from his weighted burthens of lamentable spectacles, which there suffer torments of death for petty matters, by which strangers judge us a wicked or cruel nation, regard we hang more in a year than others do in seven."[108] Geffe's argument for a domestic silk industry linked consumption to production and emphasized the creation of a disciplined labor force.

Unfortunately, England had no mulberry trees, whether black, white, or red, although early explorers had found the red mulberry growing in the wild in Virginia.[109] Geffe urged massive and continuing import of mulberry trees. He himself offered "within five years to furnish England with ten millions of white Mulberry plants or upwards which may be generally dispersed, for the good and benefit of the whole kingdom."[110] Later commentators suggested that the English silk project failed because it imported black rather than white mulberry trees but, in fact, either can support silkworms under the proper conditions.[111]

In August 1609 François de Verton undertook to import silkworms and mulberry trees "whereby an exceeding great benefit will redound as well to

---

[105] Geffe, *Discourse*, pp. 10–11.   [106] *Ibid.*   [107] *Ibid.*, p. 13.   [108] *Ibid.*
[109] Hatch, "Mulberry Trees and Silkworms," 44–47.   [110] Geffe, *Discourse*, p. 3.
[111] John Feltwell, *The Story of Silk* (New York: St. Martin's Press, 1990).

all sorts of laboring people as to others."[112] He traveled through the Midlands and East Anglia to see whether the plants had actually been distributed.[113] To induce the English to buy the trees, de Verton showed them "spinners at work."[114] The Frenchman reported to Salisbury that most of the lord lieutenants of the counties and their deputies had indeed put the project into practice. He visited Herefordshire, Suffolk, Norfolk, Cambridge, Huntington, Bedford, Buckinghamshire, Northampton, Warwick, Leicester, Nottingham, Derby, Stafford, Chester, and Lancaster. In each county he met with the Lord Lieutenant or some of the deputy lieutenants. Thus, at Norwich, Sir Arthur Hevingham persuaded him to stay eight days.[115] In Cambridge, the Lord of Bath was an enthusiastic purchaser but in Buckinghamshire the deputy lieutenants proved less cooperative. De Verton met the Earls of Southampton, Essex, Pembroke and Montgomery on his tour. The Earls of Rutland, Burghley, Shrewsbury, and Derby and Lord Cavendish all purchased trees but Lords Darcy and Paget did not.[116] Salisbury later challenged de Verton's claims to have extensive nurseries in France.[117] De Verton continued to claim that he had 500,000 mulberry trees in France.[118]

William Stallenge, a customs official and early keeper of the King's Mulberry Gardens, became a major promoter of the planting of mulberry trees.[119] Stallenge had been the licensee of the Geffe translation of Serres.[120] In 1609 he published a translation of Letellier's "Instructions," again reproducing the illustrations from the 1603 French edition. He also published the King's letter to the lord lieutenants and their deputies and promised that his instructions would prove concise and successful.[121] Henry Peacham, author of the *Compleat Gentleman*, called Stallenge "the first author of making silk in our land."[122] King James gave Stallenge, who was

[112] HMC *Salisbury, 1609–12*, p. 124. De Verton was granted the sole right to bring in as many mulberry trees as he wished free of custom.

[113] *CSPD 1603–10*, p. 540, François de Verton to Salisbury; PRO, SP 14/47/109 and 110. Warner, *The Silk Industry*, p. 538. John Stow, *Annales or a General Chronicle of England*, 2nd edn. (London, 1632), p. 894.

[114] *CSPD 1603–10*, p. 540.

[115] PRO SP 14/47/109 and 110. "of toutefois I ne fiez pas distribution de plus de la moitie."

[116] *Ibid.*, 109.   [117] *CSPD 1603–10*, p. 540.

[118] PRO SP 14/47/110. De Verton appears to say that he distributed "cent mil" (100,000) plants.

[119] *CSPD 1603–10*, p. 562, 25 November 1609, King James issued a warrant to pay Stallenge L935 for enclosing ground near Westminster Palace for planting mulberry trees; by 20 December 1609 the King owed Stallenge L435 for mulberry plants.

[120] *Ibid.*, p. 344, 5 January 1607; *CSPD 1611–18*, pp. 126, 194.

[121] Stallenge, *Instructions for the Increasing of Mulberie Trees*, "To the Reader."

[122] Quoted in introduction to Moffett, *The Silkewormes and their Flies*.

also Searcher in the Port of London, a seven-year grant to import mulberry seeds and set them in any part of the realm.[123]

John Stow recorded that Stallenge and De Verton worked together to promote the silk project.[124] "This year he [William Stallenge] and Monsieur Verton, by order from the king, planted mulberry trees in most shires of England." Stallenge claimed that the distribution of the mulberry trees ordered by King James had indeed been carried out.

> Those young plants of a year old mentioned in His Majesty's letters have been delivered in every shire according to his highness's pleasure. But if any man would have any mulberry trees of 3, 4, 5, or 6 year old, or mulberry seeds to be sown in their gardens … let him repair unto M. Forest, His Majesty's servant at the Duke of Lennox his lodging at the Court, or else in Milford Lane near Temple Bar, at one M. Braband his house, or else at M. Been, goldsmith, dwelling in St. Martin's Lane near Cheapside: or at M. Nicholas the Queen's gardener at Somerset House, deputies of the said M. Forest.

In 1611 Stallenge received L258 for expenditures for mulberry leaves and sweetwood for His Majesty's silkworms. That year he produced nine pounds of silk.[125]

While these early efforts to raise mulberry trees did not succeed in England, the quest for a domestic silk industry remained strong throughout the century. The project then turned in two different directions: the first, to replace the tobacco crop in Virginia with silk, a view promoted from James I to John Locke; second, to sponsor the manufacture of raw silk into silk textiles in England.

"TENDING TO PLANTATIONS": SILK PRODUCTION IN VIRGINIA

Historians have often assumed that efforts to grow silkworms in England ended in failure shortly after the King enthusiastically presented his proposals between 1607 and 1609. In fact, James himself again took up his pen on behalf of the industry in 1622 but this time in Virginia rather than England. Interest in cultivating silk in Virginia dated back to Hakluyt's plan for Raleigh and Roanoke, drawing upon the success of the Spanish,[126] and the Virginia Company pressed sericulture on its planters as early as 1607.[127] Shipments of

---

[123] *CSPD 1603–10*, p. 398, 23 January 1608.

[124] Stow, *Annales or a General Chronicle of England*, p. 894.

[125] *CSPD 1611–18*, p. 29, May? 1611; 7 May 1611.

[126] Wesley Frank Craven, *The Southern Colonies in the Seventeenth Century, 1607–1689* (Baton Rouge: Louisiana State University Press, 1949), pp. 20, 45, 55.

[127] For an extensive discussion of these efforts see Hatch, "Mulberry Trees and Silkworms," 3–61.

silkworms arrived in Virginia in 1613.[128] In 1619, the Virginia Company supplied French "vine dressers" and cuttings from French vineyards and ordered each household to plant ten. In the same year, John Ferrar told the court of the Virginia Company that the silkworm seed would soon be sent.[129] The silk project was just one aspect of the efforts to produce raw materials in the colonies and to to underwrite trade with native Americans.[130]

John Bonoeil, another Frenchman, held the office of Keeper of Silkworms at Whitehall and Greenwich after Stallenge.[131] He published a treatise on sericulture at the request of Sir Edwin Sandys in 1620 and republished it in 1622 with the Letellier woodcuts. King James again wrote the preface while the Earl of Southampton added his endorsement. In *His Majesty's Gracious Letter to the Earl of Southampton, Treasurer, and to the council and company of Virginia here, commanding the present setting up of silk works, and planting of vines in Virginia*, the King and Southampton stressed the importance of silk as a substitute for tobacco. The Virginia Company sent large numbers of Bonoeil's tract to Virginia for distribution to every family. Noting that the Virginia soil naturally produced mulberry trees, James declared it

a design of so much honour and advantage to the public, we have thought good, as at sundry times, so now more particularly to recommend it to your special care, hereby charging you . . . to take speedy order that our people there, use all possible diligence in breeding silkworms and erecting silk works, and that they rather bestow their travail in compassing this rich and solid commodity than in that of tobacco, which, besides much unnecessary expense, brings with it many disorders and inconveniences.

James required Southampton, "Treasurer for our Plantation in Virginia," to have Bonoeil's directions "put into practice throughout our plantations there." Silk and wine were described as valuable not vain, which "brought to their perfection will infinitely redound to the honour, benefit, and comfort of the colony and this whole kingdom."[132]

Bonoeil wrote his tract in the midst of the economic debate stimulated by the crisis in the cloth trade. The debate stretched from the Privy Council and Parliament into print. The Crown considered whether treasure was

---

[128] Craven, *The Southern Colonies in the Seventeenth Century*, pp. 45, 115, 140–43.
[129] A. L. Maycock, *Nicholas Ferrar of Little Gidding* (London: SPCK, 1963), pp. 83–84.
[130] Craven, *The Southern Colonies in the Seventeenth Century*. p 141.
[131] *CSPD 1611–18*, p. 246, 21 July 1614.
[132] John Bonoeil, *His Majesty's Gracious Letter to the Earl of Southampton, Treasurer, and to the council and company of Virginia here, commanding the present setting up of silk works, and planting of vines in Virginia* (London, 1622).

wasted through the export of bullion and "superfluity in expenditure." The Council discussed edicts against "excess in apparel," to increase the value of coins, and to encourage trade.[133] Thomas Mun, Gerard Malynes, and Edward Misselden debated whether or not international trade, even a triangular trade of goods between the East and West Indies and England, might be more profitable than the heaping up of bullion.

Citing Mun and Misselden in the course of his tract on silk, Bonoeil placed sericulture in this economic and global context. He contended that merchants could import silk from Persia and Virginia to make England the great entrepôt for silk. "These silks are the sinews of the Persian State, by which treasure, the Sophy is enabled still as he doth to wage war with the Turk ... I need not tell you, by the way, how hopeful a trade this is to the East India Company." In the margin Bonoeil wrote "see Master Mun's and Master Misselden's books on this." He went on "For by this means great store of clothes may be vented there, multitudes of poor set on work, and England enriched and made in time the magazine for silks. And by this fetching silk still from the fountain head in Persia, the Turk shall be deprived of this great tribute ... and the Persian, by this trade, be the more enriched and strengthened against the Turk to the common good of Christendom."[134] Poor women and children, whose labor was cheap and docile, offered the best labor force for silk production. In Italy, the poor raised silkworms, dividing the silk according to shares.

Bonoeil's tract drew on the French tracts by Serres and Letellier as well as his own experience. He too referred to the innovation of Henry IV: "It is not above twenty years, since these silkworms were generally set up in France, Henry the great with great wisdom appointing commissioners for that purpose." Bonoeil's friends from Languedoc, the French "vignons" sent to Virginia in 1619 "to make silk and dress vines," told him that Virginia was filled with mulberry trees, "the tallest and broadest that ever they saw in any country." Virginia might prove to be more productive than France or Italy. "Such quantity of silk may easily be made in Virginia (if there were store of hands) as in a very short time it would serve all Christendom. What an honour and wealth it would be to this Kingdom of England, all men may judge." In addition to silk, Bonoeil also recommended rice and sugar as crops for Virginia.[135]

Bonoeil encouraged the British to enforce a trade zone with its colonies, to diversify colonial and domestic products, and prevent competition.

---

[133] *CSPD 1619–23*, pp. 210–11; PRO SP14/130. (1620?).
[134] Bonoeil, *His Majesty's Gracious Letter*, pp. 63–64, 73.   [135] *Ibid.*, pp. 68, 69, B2.

He urged all the colonists to participate in producing silk: "every one in Virginia, men and women too, from the highest to the lowest in some proportion, must know it and practice it." Virginia should produce the raw material for home manufacturing in England and not produce cloth of its own or import it from elsewhere. Here the Spanish policy, provided a model:

To balance the commodities well of all his dominions, for the good of all, the planting for wines and oils in the West Indies, upon good reasons, were inhibited. The like he doth in Brasilia, who though they have store of ginger there, yet may it not be carried from thence into Spain, for fear of impoverishing them of S. Domingo, whose chiefest trade it is to get their livings by. And the like doth Great Britain for you here, which suffers no sheep to be carried thither, that cloth might be made there, but so orders it for the good of both, that you here shall have from thence, her native commodities, and her manufactures only, and use no foreign merchandise, but such as is for health or like necessity, for which you return the proper commodities of Virginia hither.[136]

Like Mun, Bonoeil argued that economic strength increased from expanding international trade networks, not from amassing bullion. Although Mun's famous work, *England's Treasure by Forraign Trade*, was not published until 1664, he laid out much of his argument in a petition he printed on behalf of the East India Company as early as 1628.[137] Bonoeil's tract, which cited Mun and Misselden, was published even earlier, in 1622, on behalf of the Virginia Company. While the silk project did not produce great quantities of silk, it did create a literature on silk production almost as active as that supporting the East India Company.

In response to the Virginia Company's vigorous pressure on the settlers to cultivate silkworms, the colonial assembly ordered householders to plant mulberry trees for seven years. In 1625 Samuel Purchas, in *Purchase his Pilgrimes* reprinted the King's and Southampton's letters.[138] Despite these strenuous efforts, silk growing in Virginia proved difficult. Charles turned his attention to domestic production and issued proclamations

---

[136] *Ibid.*, pp. 80–81.
[137] Muchmore, "Gerald de Malynes and Mercantile Economics," 336–58; Muchmore, "A Note of Thomas Mun's 'England's Treasure by Foreign Trade,'" 498–503; Gould, "The Trade Crisis of the Early 1620s and English Economic Thought," 121–33; Magnusson, *Mercantilism*.
[138] Louis B. Wright, "The Lure of Fish, Fur, Wine and Silk" in *The Dream of Prosperity in Colonial America* (New York: New York University Press, 1965), pp. 21–40. Wright notes that "silk making never became a profitable enterprise in the English colonies, although the delusion persisted for two centuries," p. 36.

incorporating the silk throwsters,[139] permitting the use of hard silk in some manufactures,[140] and requiring royal seals to guarantee quality.[141]

Of course, many remained suspicious of swathing all the English in silk. The Massachusetts Bay colony articulated its worries about the rich clothing worn by those of lower status and moved to prohibit it in 1633. Denouncing the "great superfluous and unnecessary expenses occasioned by reason of some new and immodest fashions," the General Court banned some settlers from wearing "silver, gold, and silk laces, girdles, hatbands." Again in 1651, they announced their "utter detestation and dislike that men or women of mean condition, educations, and callings should take upon the garb of gentlemen, by the wearing of gold or silver lace, or buttons or points at their knees, to walk in great boots, or women of the same rank to wear silk or tiffany hoods or scarfs."[142]

PROMOTING SILK PRODUCTION IN THE REPUBLIC AND PROTECTORATE

Despite the assertions of Frank Warner and Maurice Ashley that English puritans thought silk was a worldly vanity,[143] and opposed "luxurious living,"[144] the attitudes and practices of the Commonwealth and Protectorate proved complex. The Council of State could be understanding. In 1651 it instructed the Committee of Examiners to deliver to the Countess of Devonshire the imported silks that they had seized if she paid the duties.[145] More importantly, the author of *Observations on the Decay of Trade* saw the public benefit of luxury consumption. He found himself torn between those "well affected" and those "mechanics and retailers" who depended on the gentry's purchase of "superfluous garments and ornaments." While parsimony might advance individual families, it

stops the revenue and destroys the peace of the state. The former party hath a private thrift ... the second an open expensiveness which, since it maintains the people, contributes much to tax and excise ... That party ... resolve to live no more in

---

[139] *Stuart Royal Proclamations* II, pp. 630–35.   [140] *Ibid.*, pp. 611–13.   [141] *Ibid.*, pp. 630–35.

[142] Quoted in Stephen Innes, "Puritanism and Capitalism in Early Massachusetts," in J. A. James and Mark Thomas (eds.), *Capitalism in Context: Essays on Economic Development and Cultural Change in Honor of R. M. Hartwell* (Chicago: Chicago University Press, 1994), pp. 110–11.

[143] Warner, *The Silk Industry*, p. 539.

[144] Maurice Ashley, *Financial and Commercial Policy under the Cromwellian Protectorate* (London: Frank Cass, 1962), pp. 36–7.

[145] Warner, *The Silk Industry*, p. 639.

the City ... and will likewise further repair their estates by reducing garments and ornaments. If this ... exodus from the city ... proceed, the livelihood of retailers and mechanics will be lost and native excise and customs on imports be reduced.[146]

Moreover, the creation of a Republic did not end the promotion of the cultivation of raw silk as a crop in Virginia. As Cromwell's Western Design, the effort to conquer the West Indies, took hold, there was renewed interest in silk cultivation in Virginia and other southern colonies.[147] But the revival of interest in sericulture was not just Cromwellian. John Ferrar and his daughter Virginia, royalists and longtime supporters of the Virginia Company, also participated in a flurry of pamphlets on the subject in the 1650s.[148]

In 1650, for example, Edward Williams wrote *Virgo Triumphans or Virginia richly and truly valued* in which he argued that the production of silk, that beneficial, comfortable, and profitable crop, promised honor, industry, glory, and happiness.[149] In another tract that same year, *Virginia's Discovery of Silk-Worms with their Benefit and the implanting of Mulberry Trees*, Williams addressed Virginia merchants, adventurers, and planters, arguing that cultivating the silkworm, along with the vine, olive, and almond, would make them rich. Williams reprinted the Letellier/Geffe woodcuts and referred to Bonoeil's work of 1622.[150]

Samuel Hartlib, the unflagging advocate for universal reformation who was keenly interested in husbandry throughout the 1640s and 1650s,[151] repeatedly celebrated sericulture. "The silk-trade (unless we will be deaf to reason and experience) cannot be denied the precedency of all trades that are at this day a foot, in either world: and that in regard of its great and certain gain in so small a time." He warmly recalled King James's effort to

[146] Ashley, *Financial and Commercial Policy under the Cromwellian Protectorate*, citing Thurloes Papers, Bodleian, Rawlinson M. a 45, f. 293. The excise tax was first imposed in 1643 on a variety of goods including luxuries like silk. Clay, *Economic Expansion and Social Change*, II, p. 264.

[147] Craven, *The Southern Colonies in the Seventeenth Century*, pp. 250–51.

[148] *Ibid.*, pp. 251–53. Additional pamphlets include William Bullock, *Virginia Impartially Examined and Left to Publick View* ... (London, 1649); *A Perfect Description of Virginia* (London, 1649); Edward Williams, *Virginia: More Especially the South Part Therof* (London, 1650).

[149] BL B 626(1). He urged the Rump to support his plan in language that would not have come amiss in a dedication to the recently executed Charles. Calling the Rump "your Grandeurs" and lauding "your most vigorous luster," he urged them to adopt his agenda because of the "interest of that Nation you have so happily restored to its just and native liberty."

[150] Edward Williams, *Virginia's Discovery of Silk-Worms with their Benefit and the Implanting of Mulberry Trees* (London, 1650), A4–A4v, p. 71.

[151] Charles Webster, *The Great Instauration: Science, Medicine, and Reform, 1626–1660* (London: Duckworth, 1975).

establish a silk industry in England.[152] "It is not only my opinion that silkworms will thrive here; but the solid judgement of King James and his Council confirmeth the same; as you may see by his letter to the deputy lieutenants of every county wherein also many weighty reasons are contained to convince men of the same; which letter followeth anon."[153]

Hartlib published "A Rare and New Discovery" in 1652 presenting the work of Virginia Ferrar. "The Experiment of a virtuous Lady ... for the breeding of silk worms ... addressed unto the planters of Virginia is set forth to encourage both them and others to set upon this work, to benefit themselves and the Nation thereby."[154] Virginia Ferrar (1626–87) was the daughter of John Ferrar and niece of Nicholas Ferrar, Secretary to the Virginia Company and a close friend of Sir Edwin Sandys.[155] Brought up at Little Gidding, Nicholas Ferrar's famous Anglican community, Virginia was named after the colony. Both her father and uncle supported new industries in the colony. John sent over German carpenters to oversee sawmills in 1620. In 1621 John and Nicholas considered organization of iron works and, later in the year, organized the manufacture of glass and beads.[156] Indeed, Nicholas sent out the French vignons to whom Bonoeil referred in his treatise of 1622.[157] Furthermore, Virginia Ferrar took a close interest in Virginia colonial affairs.[158]

Virginia Ferrar's work reflects the interest of Stuart women in botanical studies.[159] Hartlib argued that Ferrar's experiments demonstrated that silkworms could be raised in the wild in Virginia, required little capital or labor, and promoted trade with the Indians. Fed in the forests, silkworms would within forty days "present their most rich golden-coloured silken fleece, to the instant wonderful enriching of all the planters there, requiring from them neither cost, labor, or hindrance in any of their other employments whatsoever." Virginia illustrated a map of the colony with the trees and plants that grew there.[160]

---

[152] Samuel Hartlib, *His Legacie or an Enlargement of the Discourse of Husbandry in Brabant and Flanders wherein are bequeathed to the Commonwealth of England more outlandish and domestic experiments and secrets in reference to universal husbandry* (London 1651).

[153] BL E628 (11) Hartlib 1651, p. 69. In another tract of 1655, *The Reformed Common-wealth of Bees. Presented in severall letters and observations to Samuel Hartlib, esq. with the Reformed Virginian Silk-worm ...* (London, 1655), Hartlib once again referred to James I's letter and noted that it was out of print.

[154] Hartlib, *A Rare and New Discovery of a Speedy Way ... for the Feeding of SILK-WORMS IN VIRGINIA* (London, 1652), "To the Reader."

[155] Maycock, *Nicholas Ferrar of Little Gidding*, pp. 167–68.   [156] *Ibid.*, pp. 83–84.

[157] *Ibid.*, pp. 167–68.   [158] *Ibid.*   [159] Geffe, *Discourse*, p. 6.

[160] I am grateful to Kathleen Lynch for drawing the map to my attention. George Neely, *A Short History of the Clare College Mission, Rotherhithe* (Ramsgate: Church Publishers, 1964).

In the same decade, the Virginia legislature adopted policies to encourage the crop, revived the Virginia Company law that required "the planting of a specified number of mulberries . . . and offered bounties for the production of silk and other crops beside tobacco."[161] Edward Digges, son of Sir Dudley Digges, the parliamentarian and member of the Virginia Company, imported Armenians to oversee silk production.[162] Francis Yeardley wrote to John Ferrar in 1654 of his plans to experiment with silk, as well as olives and wine, in the Carolinas.[163] At the Restoration, the Crown, building on Cromwell's Navigation Acts, moved once again to diversify the colony's economy and to encourage the production of silk.[164]

Strong continuity thus links James I's efforts in the first decade of the seventeenth century to the policy to raise mulberry trees in the 1650s. This continuing interest, rather than demonstrating an unexpected link between Calvinism and proto-industrialism or the appropriation of court culture by puritans, suggests an impressive and pervasive concern to promote domestic luxury industries in order to put people to work, diversify the economy, expand trade, and integrate the colonies into the economic system of the mother country. The language of the silk industry promoters celebrated riches, glory, honor, desire, comfort, emulation, and cheap labor. They provided a significant and influential challenge to the moralistic view of luxury and luxury goods of their contemporaries. These were themes reiterated in English policy and economic literature into the Restoration.[165]

In the 1660s the newly established Royal Society took an interest in raising silkworms and promoted it in print. The first issue of its *Philosophical Transactions* published "An Extract of a Letter, containing some observations, made in the ordering of silk-worms, communicated by that known virtuoso, Mr. Dudley Palmer, from the ingenuous Mr. Edward Digges." Digges offered a small amount of his Virginian silk. "I did hope with this to have given you assurance, that by retarding the hatching of seed, two crops of silk or more might be made in a Summer: but my servants have been remiss in what was ordered, I must crave your patience till next year."[166]

Later in the same volume, Henry Oldenburg, the Secretary, reported on a recent French treatise by Monsieur Isnard, *Instructions for the Planting of*

---

[161] Craven, *The Southern Colonies in the Seventeenth Century*, p. 253.   [162] *Ibid.*, pp. 252–53.
[163] *Ibid.*, p. 317.   [164] *Ibid.*, p. 314–17.
[165] See Appleby, *Economic Thought and Ideology in Seventeenth-Century England*; Steven C. A. Pincus, "Neither Machiavellian Moment Nor Possessive Individualism: Commercial Society and the Defenders of the English Commonwealth," *AHR* 103 (1998), 705–36.
[166] Royal Society, *Philosophical Transactions*, I, pp. 26–27.

White Mulberries, the Breeding of Silkworms, and the Ordering of Silk, in Paris, and the circumjacent places. Oldenburg admiringly recalled the mercantilist program of Henry IV and described how Louis XVI had revived the silk project in Paris and ordered new publications of instructions on silk production and trade. Like Samuel Hartlib, Oldenburg warmly applauded James I's efforts to establish a silk industry in England, urging that

the design, which the English Nation once did entertain of the increasing of mulberry-trees, and the breeding of silk-worms, for the making of silk within themselves, may be renewed, and that encouragement, given by King James of glorious memory for that purpose (witness that letter which he directed to the Lords Lieutenants of the several shires of England) and seconded by His Most Excellent Majesty, that now is, be made use of, for the honour of England and Virginia, and the increase of wealth to the people thereof: especially since there is cause of hope, that a double silk-harvest may be made in one summer in Virginia, without hindring in the least the tobacco-trade of that Country.[167]

By the 1660s, however, the aim was not to replace tobacco with silk but to develop silk alongside it. Enthusiasm did not flag in Virginia. Reverend Alexander Moray wrote to Sir Robert Moray, his relation and president of the Royal Society, in 1665 that he planned to plant 10,000 mulberry trees in Virginia.[168] In 1668 Charles II received a gift from Barbados with "four hundred weight of silk raised there as a gift to the king."[169]

"WORKS OF INDUSTRY"

Tudor and Stuart policy aimed to provide work for a growing population. Work was a centerpiece of contemporary project literature. The earliest statute regulating silk manufactures dates from 1455 and mentioned "a company of silk women in England," working on small pieces of embroidery and thread.[170] In the fifteenth and sixteenth centuries silk weaving was prestigious, and practitioners included aristocratic women. The Crown made little effort to create a large-scale industry. In contrast, James I sought to support a skilled labor force in the early seventeenth century. He issued a proclamation against faulty dyeing in 1612[171] and supported Sir Philip

---

[167] *Ibid.*, pp. 87–91.   [168] Craven, *The Southern Colonies in the Seventeenth Century*, pp. 314–15.
[169] Warner, *The Silk Industry*, p. 539, gift from Barbados.
[170] Sholl, *A Short Historical Account of the Silk Manufacture in England*, p. 2. See 33 Henry VI, c. 5.
[171] By the King, "Whereas we have been informed of the great fraudes and deceits used in dying all kinds of silk (London, 1612), STC 8479.

Burlamachi in his efforts to bring over foreign "silk-throwsters, silk-dyers and broad-weavers."[172] Thomas Mun reported in the 1620s that hundreds were employed in "winding, twisting, and weaving silk in London." The silk throwers were incorporated in 1629. Charles I issued two proclamations, in 1630 and in 1638, regulating silk manufactures. He noted in the first "that the trade of silk within this realm, by the importation thereof raw from foreign parts, and throwing, dying and working the same into manufactures here at home is much increased within a few years past."[173] The import of raw silk increased between 1603 to 1640 but fewer silk fabrics were imported in the same period as English manufactures picked up.[174] By the middle of the seventeenth century the women in the industry were of lower status and poorly paid. Indeed, most project literature called for women and children because they were docile and cheap labor.

The silk industry benefited enormously from the arrival of Huguenot silk workers who migrated to London during the French Wars of Religion in the 1580s. Another wave of skilled craftsmen arrived after the Revocation of the Edict of Nantes in 1685.[175] The Crown fostered this skilled labor force. During the Restoration, it banned imports in order to improve the market position of the domestic industry.[176]

Silk manufacturing grew during the 1660s and Parliament removed regulations of labor, wages, and numbers of looms. For example, in 1662 it passed "An Act for Regulating the Trade of Silk Throwing." Referring to the incorporation of the silk throwers in 1629, the statute enlarged their charter because "the said trade is of singular use and very advantageous to this common wealth by employing the poor, there being employed by the said Company (as is expressed in their Petition) above forty thousand men, women, and children who otherwise would unavoidably be burthensome to the places of their abode." The statute opened membership in the Company to "every person" who were "masters of the said art, trade or mystery" within London. Moreover, it broke down wage and price regulation and insisted on employers' freedom to negotiate rates and wages with employees: "their respective members shall be left at liberty to contract with their respective employers and also with the person that they employ at such rates as they . . . shall agree upon."[177] In 1667 and 1668, in addition to freeing producers from wage regulation, Parliament repealed the

---

[172] Moreau, *Rise and Progress of the Silk Trade in England*, p. 4.   [173] *Ibid.*
[174] Millard, "The Import Trade of London, 1600–1640," p. 226.
[175] Clay, *Economic Expansion and Social Change*, II, p. 39.   [176] *Ibid.*
[177] Warner, *The Silk Industry*, pp. 632–33.

Caroline statute limiting the size of looms "which is an hindrance to the growth and improvement of the said art and a restraint to the working of silks in this kingdom ... and puts the traders in that commodity upon a necessity of using foreign thrown silk."[178] In 1674 a pamphlet, *The True English Interest: or an Account of the Chief National Improvements*, proclaimed that "in Spitalfields and London suburbs the production of silk, satin, and velvets arrived at great perfection."[179]

Condemnation of luxury continued as production increased. John Locke denounced "the luxury of Courts ... inferior Grandees found out idle and useless employments for themselves and others subservient to their pride and vanity and so brought honest labor in useful and mechanical arts wholly into disgrace." He recommended that governments "suppress the arts and instruments of luxury and vanity."[180] Nevertheless, in 1674 Locke put up L500 to join the Earl of Shaftesbury and Maurice Hunt "for trade in the buying and selling of raw silk."[181]

In the next decade, in 1681, a pamphlet written on behalf of the East India Company recapitulated the growth of the English silk industry, the development of London as an entrepôt for the silk trade, the creation of a skilled labor force, and the promotion of consumption through changing fashion.

I am credibly informed the number of families already employed therein in England doth amount to above 40,000. Now what should hinder but that in a few years more, this nation may treble that number in such manufactures; since the East India Company have of late years found out a way of bringing raw silk of all sorts into this kingdom cheaper than it can be afforded in Turkey, France, Spain, Italy or any other place where it is made. In so much as, with East Indian silks, we serve Holland, Flanders and some other markets from England.

The author justified the bringing in of Indian silks, which were plain or striped, and cheaper "than they can make them at home. Whereas in England our silk manufacture consists not in these plain silks but in flowered silks and fancies, changed still as often as the fashion alters."[182]

---

[178] Warner, *The Silk Industry*, p. 629. Charles II granted a patent for the use of waste silk.

[179] *The True English Interest: or an Account of the Chief National Improvements* (London, 1674); W. English, "A Survey of the Principal References to Fashion Fabrics in the Diary of Samuel Pepys," *Journal of the Textile Institute*, 40 (1949), 23–37.

[180] Ian Harris, *The Mind of John Locke: A Study of Political Theory in its Intellectual Setting* (Cambridge: Cambridge University Press, 1994), p. 129.

[181] Cited in K. H. D. Haley, *The First Earl of Shaftesbury* (Oxford: Clarendon Press, 1968). p. 228.

[182] *A Treatise Wherein is Demonstrated that the East India Trade is the most National of all Foreign Trade* (London, 1681), quoted in Warner, *The Silk Industry*, pp. 630–31.

New ways to spin silk spurred new patents. John Barkstead, a London mercer, received one in 1678 "for an engine for throwing silk whereby the same may be wrought as cheap and as well as in any part beyond the seas."[183] In 1692 a group of merchants and silk throwers claimed that "with great expense and industry," they had found a "useful and cheap way, by engines, of winding the finest raw silk which was formerly brought ready wound, spun, and twisted from Italy." They proposed to bring raw silk from Italy, Turkey, and other countries, and by that means to employ vast numbers of poor people and save considerable sums of money paid for imports "already twisted from foreign parts."[184] The Crown continued its interest in the silk project. Queen Mary investigated the condition of the industry in 1693 as well as the amount of silk available.[185] By the end of the century, English imitation of the French and Italians had borne fruit, if not in producing raw silk, in processing and re-exporting it. Concentrated in Spitalfields, silk weaving became so successful that English exports challenged both the French and Italians by 1700.[186]

Most significantly, in 1716 Thomas Lombe and his brother John brought back plans from Italy for a silk factory. In 1718 they took out a patent for three engines copied from Italian plans "one to wind the finest raw silk, another to spin, and another to twist the finest Italian silk into organzine."[187] In 1721 the Lombe mill was finished. Lombe's silk mill in Derby was the first silk factory based on water power. It was five stories high. Daniel Defoe described it as having "26,586 wheels and 97,746 movements, which work 73,726 yards of silk-thread every time the water wheel goes round."[188]

When Lombe asked Parliament to extend his patent, it declined. Instead the government offered him L14,000 to provide a model of his silk-throwing machine to the public. With the expiration of Lombe's patent, others erected similar mills. "The Factory Age in Britain may therefore be said to have commenced in the silk industry with the erection of factories."[189]

In conclusion, from 1603 on, the English Crown actively promoted luxury trades through the establishment of new industries such as glass,

---

[183] *Chronological Index of Patents of Invention*, #265, 18 April 1678. Jones, "Technology, Transactions Costs, and the Transition to Factory Production," 71–96.

[184] Quoted in Warner, *The Silk Industry*, p. 633.   [185] *Ibid.*, pp. 540–41.   [186] *Ibid.*

[187] *Chronological Index of Patents of Invention*, #422, 9 September 1718.

[188] Quoted in Jones, "Technology, Transaction Costs, and the Transition to Factory Production," 75–96. See W. H. Chaloner, *People and Industries* (London: Frank Cass, 1963), pp. 8–20 on Thomas Lombe.

[189] Jones, "Technology, Transactions Costs, and the Transition to Factory Production," 76–77.

tapestry, and silk, through the import of skilled labor, especially from Italy, France, and the Low Countries, and through the dissemination of knowledge and information via print. The silk industry drew on the transfer of French technology, on skilled Huguenot labor, and on new royal policies. James I was determined to emulate and outstrip the French through plantations, science, and industry. Although mulberry trees failed to take profitable root in England, new commercial policies and industries did. The language of silk cultivation, from Nicholas Geffe in 1607 to Samuel Hartlib and Virginia Ferrar in the 1650s and Henry Oldenburg in the 1660s, celebrated riches, trade, honor, glory, cheap labor, private interest, and public benefit. They praised silk as a rich, profitable, and endlessly desirable luxury good. Whatever debate there might be about the consumption of silk, there was little or none about its production. Silk epitomized the luxury goods of all sorts that were in great demand and the Crown moved to meet that demand and, indeed, to foster it.

CHAPTER 3

"What do you lack? What is't you buy?" Creating new wants

In 1612 Benvenuto Italiano, who had taught Italian in London for nine years, published *The Passenger*, which he dedicated to Henry, Prince of Wales. Containing dialogues in Italian and English about travel, lodging, and eating, *The Passenger* commented on contemporary fashion, manners, and spending, not unlike Erondell's *The French Garden* of 1605. In one dialogue, as Entrepelus and Alatheus walk through the city, Entrepelus suggests "Why let us to the court, for there we shall meet with our friends, gentlemen, and acquaintance, who will tell us some news." Alatheus agrees but offers another reason, "I would we might there rather to see new fashions than hear news." Entrepelus assents and develops their desires more fully. "I would fain go to a place where we might no less hear, than see and contemplate some rare thing." Alatheus amplifies the sentiment, "This is both mine and, as I think, every man's desire else, for to behold ordinary things gives but little satisfaction to the eye and yields much less to the understanding."[1]

Intense curiosity, appetite for news at home and abroad, interest in the new and the extraordinary, whether marvelous or monstrous, permeated early seventeenth-century culture and helped to underpin the creation of new wants that were at the heart of the expansion of luxury in the seventeenth century.[2] Benvenuto suggests that the court was an important site of both the rare and the fashionable, the one enviable, the other

---

The quotation in the chapter title is cited by James Knowles, "Jonson's *Entertainment at Britain's Burse*," in Martin Butler (ed.), *Re-presenting Ben Jonson: Text, History, Performance* (Houndmills, Basingstoke: Macmillan, 1999), p. 134.

[1] Benvenuto Italiano, *The Passenger of Benvenuto Italian Professor of his Native Tongue, for These Nine Years in London* (London, 1612). The Cambridge University Library copy was part of the Arundel library given to the Royal Society in 1667 and later sold. See Linda Levy Peck, "Uncovering the Arundel Library at the Royal Society: Changing Meanings of Science and the Fate of the Norfolk Donation," *Notes and Records of the Royal Society, London*, 52 (1998), 3–24.

[2] On the marvelous see Stephen Greenblatt, *Marvelous Possessions: The Wonder of the New World* (Oxford: Clarendon Press, 1991); Peter G. Platt (ed.), *Wonders, Marvels and Monsters in Early Modern Culture* (London and Newark, Delaware: University of Delaware Press, 1999).

available even more to men than to women. Court culture, rather than being closed and inward-looking, was open to the gaze of the onlooker and directly connected to the wider world of London consumption. Prince Henry and those who served him were known for their interest in continental travel, languages, manners, fortifications, and fashions.[3]

Contemporaries aspired not merely to material goods but also to the cultural messages embedded within them. "French wares" in the New Exchange, Venetian glass, Flemish tapestry, China scarves, Italian building design, textiles, and scientific instruments, Parisian interior furnishings, and rarities, wonders, and inventions, drawn from trade to the East and West Indies, Asia, and Africa, marked their purchasers as fashionable, cosmopolitan and, in some cases, modern. The "endless desires," met by these luxury objects helped to support status, shape identities, promote creature comforts, enlarge sociability as well as to advance the economy. "The wants of the mind are infinite," wrote Nicholas Barbon in 1690. "Man naturally aspires and as his mind is elevated, his senses grow more refined, and more capable of delight; his desires are enlarged, and his wants increase with his wishes, which is for every thing that is rare, can gratify his senses, adorn his body and promote the ease, pleasure and pomp of life."[4] Benvenuto wrote eighty years before but surely agreed with him.

The import of luxury goods had grown strikingly since the middle of the sixteenth century. The practical multiplication of wants met by diversity of goods was, as we have seen, well underway in the early seventeenth century. This chapter turns from the expansion of imports, the retail sale of luxury goods, and the Crown's policy of promoting luxury industries to look at a few specific channels of information that helped to cultivate new wants, specifically through personal contact, print, reading, and travel. Many Englishmen and women proved eager for the sights and sounds of faraway places. The reach of these desires was global.

INFORMATION

How were new wants created? First, purchasers, agents, wholesalers, and retailers exchanged information about new goods orally and visually, in person and letter. These informal exchanges about fashion and new goods

---

[3] See Sir Roy Strong, *Henry, Prince of Wales, and England's Lost Renaissance* (London and New York: Thames and Hudson, 1986); Michael G. Brennan (ed.), *The Travel Diary (1611–1612) of an English Catholic ... Sir Charles Somerset* (Leeds: Leeds Philosophical and Literary Society, 1993), introduction.

[4] Quoted in Christopher J. Berry, *The Idea of Luxury: A Conceptual And Historical Investigation* (Cambridge: Cambridge University Press, 1994), p. 112.

can occasionally be glimpsed. We have already seen that the Countess of Cumberland knew what she wanted from Cheapside. Retailers, such as Mr. Barnes, the mercer in Cheapside who sold expensive textiles to Salisbury and the Cumberlands, counseled customers and their agents on what to buy, and Sir Hugh Smith's tailor advised that his canvas doublet should be edged with lace. Agents, friends, and servants served as the transmitters of information and intermediaries in these important exchanges.

Moreover, shopping and sociability created wants that the purchasers did not know they had. We have already seen the importance of the Exchanges as sites for impulse shopping. Retail shopping had become part of leisure entertainment for well-to-do men and women. Humphrey Mildmay, brother of Sir Henry Mildmay, Master of the King's Jewel House, lived on St. John's Street in the City. He sought out John Tradescant's collections of rarities, attended plays, visited Chelsea and Putney, and frequented Westminster Hall, "saw how full it was, and came home." Mildmay stored his two "furred coats with Mr. Thomas Longhorne, his Majesty's furrier to be kept there until winter." On 5 July 1633 he recorded in his diary, "My Lady Bennet dined here, and after dinner I went with her to my cost to the Hen and Chickens where I took up of Mr. Taylor nine yards of new stuff that must cost me fifty four shillings from thence to Newgate market where in a shop I spent in woodwork as trenchers etc. the sum of nineteen shillings."[5] But how did country purchasers know what to buy? Richard Cust and Fritz Levy have traced how political news spread amongst the gentry in the late sixteenth and early seventeenth centuries linking the farthest parts of the kingdom with London. News of fashions spread the same way, through letters, through circulation of print and manuscripts, and through visits.[6]

Second, importers, such as the Levant Company, the Merchant Adventurers, and the East India Company, introduced new goods in the late sixteenth and early seventeenth centuries that were tailored to the European and English markets. The tonnage of English merchant shipping almost doubled between 1582 and 1629.[7] Alongside the increasing spice trade and luxury textiles from Europe, English merchants developed

---

BL Harl., 434, Folger 600, Humphrey Mildmay's Diary, transcription, pp. 1, 15, 16.

[6] Richard Cust, "News and Politics in Early Seventeenth-Century England, *Past & Present*, 112 (1986), 60–90; Fred J. Levy, "How Information Spread Among the Gentry, 1550–1640," *Journal of British Studies*, 21 (1982), 11–34; Susan E. Whyman, *Sociability and Power in Late-Stuart England: The Cultural Worlds of the Verneys, 1660–1720* (Oxford: Oxford University Press, 1999).

[7] Ralph Davis, *The Rise of the English Shipping Industry in the Seventeenth and Eighteenth Centuries* (London: Macmillan, 1962), p. 10.

trading links with Asia, Africa, and the New World. As demand for English exports of the old draperies declined, merchants brought back not bullion but new goods from their more extensive trading networks in the East and West Indies: pepper and spices from Southeast Asia, indigo, textiles, and silk from India and Persia, and increasing amounts of sugar and tobacco from the West Indies.[8] The Dutch East India Company imported porcelain from China and, later, Japan, which reached the English market in the early seventeenth century. Because of the cost of transport over such long distances, merchant interest was often in the most valuable luxuries available.[9]

English merchants used Indian imports to trade for other goods in Southeast Asia and Africa and re-exported Indian goods from London to the continent.[10] English merchants had begun to participate in the African slave trade by 1619. Although the slave trade only became an important part of the economy after 1660, Africans appeared as household servants in English portraits by the 1620s and 1630s.[11] The cotton trade expanded strongly between 1613 and 1630.[12] By the 1650s the English East India Company began to alter the patterns of Indian calicos much more often to increase demand for new patterns more quickly and regularly.[13] Luxury goods became the trophies of global trade beyond the gift-giving of great kings, tsars, and mughals. At home, they enhanced the social status of those of position and those who sought to climb. Imports from the East and

[8] Davis, *The Rise of the English Shipping Industry*; see also Ralph Davis, *English Overseas Trade, 1500–1700*, prepared for the Economic History Society (London: Macmillan, 1973); Ralph Davis, *The Rise of the Atlantic Economies* (Ithaca, NY: Cornell University Press, 1973); Christopher G. A. Clay, *Economic Expansion and Social Change: England, 1500–1700*, 2 vols. (Cambridge: Cambridge University Press, 1984).

[9] James Knowles, "Jonson in China: Maritime Trade with China," paper presented to the National Maritime Museum and Institute of Historical Research seminar series, 25 January 2000; John Ayers, Oliver Impey, and J. V. G. Mallet, *Porcelain for Palaces: The Fashion for Japan in Europe 1650–1750* (London: Oriental Ceramics Society, 1990), pp. 56–59, 74–75, 84, 105, 138, 229; Meera Nanda, *European Travel Accounts During the Reigns of Shahjahan and Aurangzeb* (Kurukshetra: Nirmal Book Agency, 1994), p. 60.

[10] Alfred P. Wadsworth and Julia de Lacey Mann, *The Cotton Trade and Industrial Lancashire, 1600–1780* (Manchester: Manchester University Press, 1931).

[11] See Kim F. Hall, *Things of Darkness: Economies of Race and Gender in Early Modern England* (Ithaca, NY: Cornell University Press, 1995); Peter Erickson and Clark Hulse (eds.), *Early Modern Visual Culture: Representation, Race, and Empire in Renaissance England* (Philadelphia: University of Pennsylvania Press, 2000).

[12] Wadsworth and de Lacy Mann, *The Cotton Trade and Industrial Lancashire, 1600–1780*.

[13] K. N. Chaudhuri, *The East India Company: The Study of an Early Joint-Stock Company, 1600–1640* (London: Frank Cass, 1965), p. 194. K. N. Chaudhuri, *The Trading World of Asia and the English East India Company, 1660–1760* (Cambridge: Cambridge University Press, 1978). Peter M. Thornton "Bizarre Silks," *Burlington Magazine*, 100 (1958), 265–70.

West Indies were on display alongside French clothes and Italian textiles in retail shops in London and the provinces.

By the 1650s and 1660s, chocolate, coffee, and tea from Latin America, Africa, and Asia became available in London.[14] They were at first enthusiastically promoted in print for their medicinal purposes. Captain James Wadsworth, who had served at the Spanish court and in the Spanish army in Flanders, translated *Chocolate, or, An Indian Drink by the wise and moderate use whereof health is preserved, sickness diverted and cured especially the plague of the guts, vulgarly called the new disease* (London, 1652). Henry Stubbe, physician to the King and to Lord Windsor in Jamaica, wrote *The Indian Nectar or a Discourse Concerning Chocolate* (London, 1662). Stubbe described how chocolate had spread from America to Spain, Portugal, Italy, France, Germany, England, Persia, and Turkey. Physicians recommended it to the "general usage of the nobility and populace of both sexes." Stubbes also wrote an extensive report to the Royal Society from Jamaica in which he discussed the dangers of turning chocolate into a luxury dessert, presumably made with sugar.[15]

That liquor, if it were well made and taken in a right way, is the best diet for hypochondriacs and chronic distempers and the scurvy, gout, and stone, and women lying in and children new-born ... And many other distempers, that ever come into Europe; but that 'tis now rather used for luxury than physic ... and so cook'd now, as if it were to be transformed into a caudle or custard.[16]

These important new groceries provided the impetus for new public spaces, such as the coffee house, new types of silver and ceramics, including chocolate, coffee, and tea pots, porcelain dishes, and silver spoons, and new gendered social rituals. The Aztec religious ceremony, which included drinking chocolate and smoking tobacco, appeared in new forms in the coffeehouses of Madrid, Amsterdam, and London and the Japanese tea

---

[14] Woodruff D. Smith, *Consumption and the Making of Respectability, 1600–1800* (London and New York: Routledge, 2002).

[15] Smith, *Consumption and the Making of Respectability, 1600–1800*, p. 122, suggests that the addition of sugar to tea, coffee, and chocolate occurs late in the seventeenth century. Stubbe's reports suggest that chocolate was already transformed into sweets in the 1660s. See Sidney Mintz, *Sweetness and Power: The Place of Sugar in Modern History* (New York: Viking, 1985) and Steven Topik and W. G. Clarence-Smith, *The Global Coffee Economy in Africa, Asia and Latin America, 1500–1989* (Cambridge: Cambridge University Press, 2003).

[16] Henry Stubbe, "The Remainder of the Observations Made in the Formerly Mention'd Voyage to Jamaica," *Philosophical Transactions*, 3 (1668), 721–22. In the 1680s books appeared promoting coffee, tea, chocolate, and tobacco including John Chamberlayne, *The Natural History of Coffee, Thee, Chocolate, Tobacco ... collected from the writings of the best physicians and modern travellers* (London, 1682).

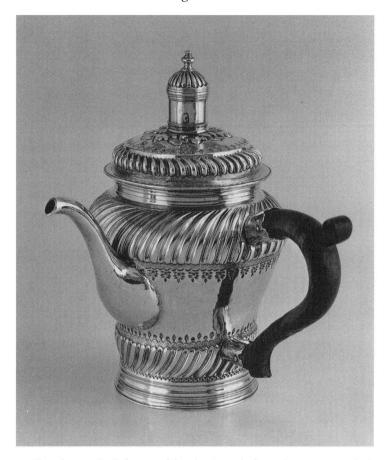

18. Chocolate, a drink borrowed by the Spanish from the Aztecs, reached England in the 1650s where it was encouraged for its medicinal properties. In the later seventeenth century, the chocolate pot's special form, with a stirrer in the top of the pot, appeared amongst the silverplate on display in English homes. The Metropolitan Museum of Art, Silver, English (London), 17th century (1697–98), Isaac Dighton, goldsmith (act. 1673–1707), chocolate pot, silver H. 7 3/4 in. Gift of George O. May, 1943 (43.108 a,b,c,). Photograph, all rights reserved, The Metropolitan Museum of Art.

ceremony materialized in the refined English woman's presiding over the family tea table.[17] Foreign imports thus transformed consumer culture long before the consumer revolution of the eighteenth century.[18]

---

[17] On coffee and tea see Smith, *Consumption and the Making of Respectability, 1600–1800*, pp. 121–29. Thomas Povey wrote a report on "Chai" for the Royal Society in the 1660s, transcribed in BL. Sloane 1039 (Hooke Papers), f. 139. (1686).

[18] See Kathleen Wilson, "The Good, the Bad and the Impotent: Imperialism and the Politics of Identity in Georgian England," in Ann Bermingham and John Brewer (eds.), *The Consumption of*

19. Sugar had long been imported into England but the sugar trade expanded in the seventeenth century with English colonies in the Caribbean devoted to raising sugar cane. Sugar boxes became part of the luxury display on the buffet.

The Metropolitan Museum of Art, Metalwork-Silver, English (London), 17th century, sugar box, silver, L. 8 in. (20.3 cm) (1673–74). Gift of Irwin Untermyer, 1968 (68.141.161). Photograph, all rights reserved, The Metropolitan Museum of Art.

Third, foreign artisans and masters in a whole range of decorative arts including gold, silver, textiles, glass, tapestry, masonry, and marble brought imported patterns to their trades. As we have seen, Francis Cleyn brought new tapestry designs to Mortlake. Continental architecture books with their engraved details by Serlio, Vredeman de Vries, and others provided patterns that influenced English builders from the middle of the sixteenth century to the late seventeenth century.[19] Low Countries prints dominated the English market.[20] Anthony Wells-Cole points out that Robert Smythson used designs published by Vredeman de Vries for the building of Longleat in the 1580s.[21] The Longleat masons provided similar details for other houses and funeral monuments.[22] From plaster work to embroidery, continental

---

Culture: 1600–1800: Image, Object, Text (London: Routledge, 1995); Toshio Kusamitsu, "'Novelty, Give us Novelty': London Agents and Northern Manufacturers," in Maxine Berg (ed.), *Markets and Manufacture in Early Industrial Europe* (London and New York: Routledge, 1991), pp. 114–38.

[19] See chapter 5 below.

[20] Anthony Wells-Cole, *Art and Decoration in Elizabethan and Jacobean England: The Influence of Continental Prints, 1558–1625* (New Haven: Yale University Press, 1997).

[21] *Ibid.*, p. 133.   [22] *Ibid.*, p. 139.

prints were adapted to fill English homes. Thomas Trevilian's Common-place book, 1608, includes many patterns for needlework and marquetry.[23]

Indeed, print translated designs into a mode usable not only by artisans but also by English consumers. In 1615 Crispijn Van de Passe, the Low Countries artist who later worked in London, engraved and published a book of flowers, entitled *Jardin de Fleurs*.[24] The Folger's copy includes a plate of a carnation pricked out for application to cloth for decoration.[25] By the 1620s London print sellers offered prints specifically to apply to trenchers and tobacco boxes, and to put up as wallpaper.[26] In the 1630s printers began to advertise their wares.[27] Thus, in 1637, Mr. Dainty advertised "the four seasons of the year. All sorts of birds, beasts, flowers, fruits. As also all sorts of things that are cut in copper, either coloured or not, fit for gentlewomen's works and schools. Where you may be sure of the best at the lowest rates."[28] In the 1650s Peter Stent advertised his prints: "Books of drafts of men, birds, beasts, flowers, fruits, flies, fishes, etc . . . 1 book of birds sitting on sprigs: 12 plates; 1 book of beasts; 1 book of branches, 11 plates; 1 book of flowers, 12 plates for cheese trenchers . . . 6 plates of Mr. Marshal's for trenchers."[29] William Marshall, whose work Stent advertised, produced over 200 prints between 1617–48.[30] Design based on foreign imports brought together the influence of merchants and consumers in the creating and fulfilling of new wants.

Hannah Wooley described how to use prints bought in a shop to make wallpaper and decorate tableware in 1674. Combining individual invention and social emulation, Wooley's directions emphasized the values of fancy, imagination, delight, and refinement "To adorn a room with prints," for example, she suggested buying black and white prints, cutting out the figures, and applying them to the prepared wainscoting.

Be sure to put the things flying above, and the walking and creeping things below, let the houses and trees be set sensibly, as also water with ships sailing as you put them on observe that they have a relation one to another. If you employ your fancy well, you may make fine stories, which will be very delightful, and commendable;

---

[23] Folger, V. b. 232, Thomas Trevilian, Commonplace book, 1608.

[24] Crispijn van de Passe, *Jardin de Fleurs* translated into English as *A Garden of Flowers* (Utrecht, 1615).

[25] I am grateful to Rachel Doggett for showing me this print.

[26] Antony Griffiths, *The Print in Stuart Britain, 1603–1689* (London: British Museum Press, 1998), pp. 21–22, 107–108, 31, 32, n. 31.

[27] *Ibid.*, pp. 14, 17, 105, 107.

[28] The ad is contained in Martin Billingsley, *A Copie Book Containing a Variety of Examples of All the Most Curious Hands Written, 2nd edn* (London, 1637).

[29] Peter Stent, *A Catalogue of Plates and Pictures that Are Printed and Sould by Peter Stent, dwelling at the sign of the White Horse in Guilt-spur Street* (London, 1654). I am grateful to Rachel Doggett for this citation. See Griffiths, *The Print in Stuart Britain*, p. 107.

[30] Griffiths, *The Print in Stuart Britain*, p. 163.

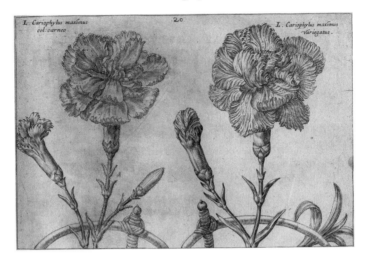

20. Continental prints were used in England for decoration such as wallpaper, embroidery, and appliqué. This engraving of a carnation shows that the flower has already been pricked out for application to paper for embroidery.
The Folger Shakespeare Library, SB450 P2 F7 1615 Cage, Crispijn van de Passe, *Jardin de fleurs* (Utrecht, 1615?) (flower picked out for engraving).

21. The reverse clearly shows the prick marks for applying the design to paper for transfer to needlework patterns.
The Folger Shakespeare Library, SB450 P2 F7 1615 Cage, Crispijn van de Passe, *Jardin de fleurs* Utrecht, 1615? (flower picked out for engraving).

also gardens, forests, landskips, or indeed anything you can imagine for there is not anything to be named, but you may find it in prints, if you go to a shop that is well stored . . . it makes a room very lightsome as well as fine.[31]

In seventeenth-century interiors, the rich had elaborate beds adorned at each corner with urns filled with feathers. Wooley taught her wide audience how to imitate them, specifically how "to make feathers of worsted which do look very like natural feathers, for the corners of beds."[32] Print democratized fashion while it canonized elite taste. At the same time, prints created new wants, centered around the body, the home, and sociability.

"THINGS PRINCIPALLY TO BE OBSERVED IN EVERY COUNTRY"

We turn now to the role of travel, both virtual and real, in creating new wants. Travel and its literature brought other cultures and other continents to English consumers. The results helped to sharpen curiosity, deepen desire for new goods, proffer new standards of comfort, and provide new ways to express individual identity. In the following sections, we look at the increasing interest in travel expressed in travel diaries, books, and libraries from the late Elizabethan period to the Restoration. After examining the practice of seventeenth-century travel, we look at the intense curiosity focused on Africa by the Royal Society and the Royal Africa Company. In the chapters that follow, we will look more specifically at the translation of cultural exchange into consumer goods.

Who went and why? Where did they go? These were questions asked by John Stoye in his classic *English Travelers Abroad, 1604–1667*[33] in which he addressed the Grand Tour, the role of tutors and ambassadors, and the education of some of the elite in European universities. In addition, we will ask, in this chapter and those that follow, what they brought back from their travels. For, despite disapproval of things foreign found in prescriptive literature, many English men and women enthusiastically borrowed manners, values, and goods from abroad throughout the seventeenth century. While many traveled, most did not. Nevertheless, books, prints, and continental and East and West Indies goods in the home market helped to create domestic demand for imported luxury goods. Increasingly, English merchants and policymakers sought to gain control over trade routes, the work of indigenous peoples, and

---

[31] Hannah Woolley, *A Supplement to the Queen-Like Closet; or a Little of Everything Presented to All Ingenious Ladies and Gentlewomen* (London, 1674), pp. 70–71. Smaller tasks included decorating glass-plates for sweetmeats or biscuits with color prints.

[32] Woolley, *A Supplement to the Queen-Like Closet*, p. 73.

[33] John Stoye, *English Travelers Abroad, 1604–1667: Their Influence in English Society and Politics* (New Haven: Yale University Press, 1989).

raw materials. Curiosity, travel, and consumption brought together the over-lapping interests of aristocrats, merchants, and scientific academies.

Travel, its history, literature, and mentality, has generated much work on the Grand Tour, colonial encounters, post-colonial, and feminist readings of travel writings.[34] The discovery of the "new," and of the "other" had long been in process as Europeans encountered Asia and America.[35] Less atten-tion, perhaps, has been paid to the encounter with new sorts of luxury goods which were brought back by travelers in the seventeenth century and the luxury industries they helped promote at home.[36] Real continental journeys and virtual travel, through continental books, prints, clothes, buildings, and drawings, underwrote luxury consumption. The individual's encounter with the novel, whether new or antique, created desire for "curiosities" and goods. For some, continental travel was interwoven with those merchant networks importing luxury goods. As the well-to-do enjoyed the Grand Tour, the sights and sounds of the Rialto, and the Palais Royale, British merchants took over trading networks in Europe and employed skilled labor from abroad. Furthermore, the Crown moved to exploit its holdings in India and Africa to satisfy the home market and to create luxury goods at home.

English travelers of the sixteenth and seventeenth centuries had an extensive and enthusiastic didactic literature to point out what to see and how to interpret what they saw when they traveled on the continent. That literature showed a strong interest in other cultures. Commentators advised travelers to keep their own diaries and an early seventeenth-century manuscript amongst the Spencer papers provides an outline.[37] The author divides "Things Principally to be Observed in Every Country," into four sections: situation, quality, inhabitants, and "the king or prince and his disposition." Situation addressed geography, cities, and military forts.

---

[34] On manuscript travel diaries see John Marciari, *Grand Tour Diaries and Other Travel Manuscripts in the James Marshall and Marie-Louise Osborn Collection*, Yale University Library Gazette, occasional supplement 2 (New Haven, CT: Beinecke Rare Book and Manuscript Library, 1999); on secondary literature, see Stoye, *English Travelers Abroad, 1604–1667*; Edward Chaney, *The Grand Tour and the Great Rebellion: Richard Lassels and "The Voyage of Italy" in the Seventeenth Century* (Geneva: Slatkine, 1985); Edward Chaney, *The Evolution of the Grand Tour: Anglo-Italian Cultural Relations since the Renaissance* (London: Frank Cass, 1998). See the special issue on women and travel, *Women's Studies*, 26 (1997); Elizabeth Bohls, *Women Travel Writers and the Language of Aesthetics, 1716–1818* (Cambridge: Cambridge University Press, 1995); Chloe Chard and Helen Langdon (eds.), *Transports: Travel, Pleasure and Imaginative Geography, 1600–1830* (New Haven: Yale University Press, 1996); Antoni Maczak, *Travel in Early Modern Europe* (Cambridge: Polity Press, 1995).

[35] See Lisa Jardine, *Worldly Goods: A New History of the Renaissance* (New York: W. W. Norton, 1996).

[36] But see *ibid.* and Marcy Norton, "New World of Goods: A History of Tobacco and Chocolate in the Spanish Empire, 1492–1700" (Ph.D. thesis, University of California, 2000).

[37] BL Add. Mss. 75,350. (Althorp Papers), unfoliated, "Account of France; historical and geographical" (early seventeenth century?).

Quality considered climate, resources, mines, land, cattle, and "what strange things of nature are therin to be found." Observations on the "inhabitants" should include their stature, "colour," apparel, religion, and military capability. The author advised the diarist to inquire into the King, his court, religion, customs, revenues, alliances, whether he was given to war or peace, and whether he was "beloved of his subjects or no." The diarist should note the principal men, their wealth, and royal favor and the condition and quality of the common people. In addition, the traveler should ask "what merchandise they trade out of the country and what they chiefly bring in."[38] When Robert Lord Spencer went on his embassy to Wurtemberg in 1603, he kept a travel diary. One of the few to survive from the early seventeenth century, Spencer listed the military forts and places he passed, lauded the French nobility, and disparaged the peasantry.[39]

Demographics, politics, culture, and economy persisted as the primary aims of travel writing throughout the century. Books such as *A Direction for Travailers taken out of Justus Lipsius and enlarged for the behoofe of . . . the Yong Earle of Bedford, being now ready to travell* (1592), and Robert Dallington's *A Method for Travel Shewed by Taking the View of France as it Stood in the Year . . . 1598* (London, 1605) underpinned an expansive notion of travel as education especially for royal service. One owner bound Dallington's 1605 volume with Henry Blount, *A Voyage into the Levant* (London, 1636) and Sir Anthony Sherley, *His Relation of His Travels into Persia* (London, 1613).[40]

Francis Bacon in his *Essays* (1597, 1612) and James Howell in his *Instructions for Forreine Travell* (1642) were among the many who advised the sixteenth- and seventeenth-century English on travel. Like the author of the Spencer manuscript, Bacon urged gentlemen to keep travel diaries and encouraged attention to country, customs, politics, and people. In addition, Bacon and others focused on the importance of learning other languages as the mark of the cultivated traveler, both for royal service and personal enrichment.[41] Howell, writing in 1642 as many royalists went into exile, focused not only on language and politics, but also on the "preeminence of the eye."[42] Through their gaze, travelers saw, evaluated, and appropriated the foreign.

---

[38] BL Add. Mss. 75,350, Althorp Papers.

[39] Spencer's travel diary, BL Add. Mss. 75,350, Althorp Papers: see Brennan (ed.), *The Travel Diary of Sir Charles Somerset*, who points out the rarities of such diaries, pp. 1–2.

[40] Folger STC 6203, copy 4.

[41] Sir Francis Bacon, *The Essayes or Counsels, Civill and Morall* (ed.), Michael Kiernan (Oxford: Clarendon Press, 2000), pp. 56–58, 208–210.

[42] James Howell, *Instructions for forreine travell* (London, 1642). A second edition was published in 1650.

But travel included mental transport as well as physical.[43] Before people traveled, they bought, read, exchanged, and collected news and books from abroad.[44] Across the length and breadth of England, people corresponded about national and international news and wanted more.[45] Thomas Hobbes's friend, Robert Mason, a Cambridge don, commented in 1623 on Gondomar, the Spanish ambassador, the Spanish match, war in Bohemia, and the apostasy of Marcantonio De Dominis, Archbishop of Spalato, who had turned Protestant in exchange for favor at James I's court and turned Roman Catholic when that favor was not enough. Mason asked Hobbes to continue to send him news in language not unlike *The Passenger.*

I would be loth to be thought of so great a stranger to the Commonwealth I live in as not to know what the greater sort of men do, that wish a prosperous success to the designs of their prince and country ... 'tis no matter though it be at the sixth, seventh, or fiftieth hand ... My ambition reaches no further than the Exchange, W. Barret's shop, or the middle aisle in Paul's.[46]

The Exchanges, as we have seen, provided a public space, in which shopping for clothes accompanied shopping for information. Newsletter writers clustered in St. Paul's while booksellers set up shop in St. Paul's churchyard. Mason wanted court and continental news from William Barret, a printer active from 1607–24, who was known for his production of translations and works on travel, which he sold at his shop in St. Paul's churchyard, the Green Dragon.[47]

Barret published Bacon's works; Thomas Coryat's *Coryat's Crudities* (1610); John Florio's translation of Montaigne's *Essays* (1613); *A True Relation and Journall of the Manner of the Arrivall and Magnificent Entertainment given to ... Prince Charles ... at Madrid* (1623); and notable books on the East Indies and Virginia as well as George Sandys's works

---

[43] See, for example, Chard and Langdon (eds.), *Transport: Travel, Pleasure and Imaginative Geography, 1600–1830.*

[44] Kevin Sharpe, *Reading Revolutions: The Politics of Reading in Early Modern England* (New Haven: Yale University Press, 2000); Cust, "News and Politics in Early Seventeenth-Century England," 60–90.

[45] Cust, "News and Politics in Early Seventeenth-Century England," 60–90; Fred J. Levy, "How Information Spread Among the Gentry," 11–34.

[46] Thomas Hobbes, *The Correspondence*, (ed.) Noel Malcolm, 2 vols. (Oxford: Clarendon Press, 1994), I, p. 14.

[47] Peter W. M. Blayney, *The Bookshops in Paul's Cross Churchyard*, Occasional Papers of the Bibliographical Society, 5 (London: Bibliographical Society, 1990); Hobbes, *The Correspondence*; Ronald Brunlees McKerrow, *A Dictionary of Printers and Booksellers in England, Scotland, and Ireland ... 1557–1640* (London: Printed for the Bibliographical Society, 1910).

on the Middle East and Turkey, *A Relation of a Journey Begun Anno Domini 1610 ... containing a description of the Turkish Empire, of Egypt, of the Holy Land, of the remote parts of Italy and islands adjoining* (London, 1615).[48]

Even as they embraced travel and the revelation of the new, these works often reflect the seduction of the foreign and the fear of succumbing to the luxurious desires they created. Coryat described Mantua as "ravishing his senses" but added that the inhabitants were idolaters.[49] Compared to England, Sandys wrote, "all other countries are in someways defective ... foreign additions only tending to vanity and luxury."[50] William Lithgow of Lanark, who traveled through France, Italy, Greece, and Turkey between 1609 and 1612, contrasted Paris, populated with thieves, with London, "the best governed city on the whole face of the earth." Although he lauded the antiquities of Rome, and the laws of Venice, he condemned the sodomy he found everywhere, especially in Turkey. He described Istanbul as "a painted whore." It looked beautiful from afar, "the covertures [roofs] being erected like the back of a coach after the Italian fashion with guttered tile" but within was "stinking deformity." Nevertheless, its situation, including its wines, fruit, and climate made it "the paradise of the earth."[51] Despite such mixed feelings, seventeenth-century libraries reflect strong interest in language and travel literature. Most English libraries of some size had a substantial portion of foreign books.[52] As the seventeenth century progressed, the percentages of English books increased. But imported books provided information about foreign countries while their prints provided continental models for building, decorating, engineering, and manufactures.

Two libraries created by famous travelers demonstrate these interests. Thomas Hobbes put together a library in the 1610s and 1620s for Lord William Cavendish with whom he traveled on the continent in 1614–15.[53]

---

[48] Barret also published *An Historical and True Discourse of a Voyage Made by the Admiral Cornelis Matelife, the Younger into the East Indies* (London, 1608) and *A True Declaration of the Estate of the Colony in Virginia* (London, 1610).

[49] *Coryat's Crudities*, 2nd edn (London, 1611).

[50] Quoted in Chloe Chard, *Pleasure and Guilt on the Grand Tour: Travel Writing and Imaginative Geography, 1600–1830* (Manchester: Manchester University Press, 1999), pp. 52–53.

[51] C. E. Bosworth, "William Lithgow of Lanark's Travels in Greece and Turkey, 1609–1611," *Bulletin of the John Rylands University Library of Manchester*, 65 (1983), 8–36, especially 10–12, 27–28.

[52] Elizabeth S. Leedham-Green, *Books in Cambridge Inventories: Booklists from Vice-Chancellor's Court Probate Inventories in the Tudor and Stuart Periods*, 2 vols. (Cambridge: Cambridge University Press, 1986).

[53] Linda Levy Peck, "Hobbes on the Grand Tour: Paris, Venice, or London?" *Journal of the History of Ideas*, 57 (1996), 177–83 and Linda Levy Peck, "Constructing a New Context for Hobbes Studies," in Howard Nenner (ed.), *Politics and the Political Imagination in Later Stuart Britain, Essays Presented to Lois Green Schwoerer* (Rochester, NY: University of Rochester Press, 1997), 161–79.

In addition to theology and politics, the mainstay of the library, it contained many works on history, language, and travel. The Cavendish library reflected the ideal of the Renaissance courtier now set in a global context. To begin, there was Castiglione's *The Courtier* in several languages, Henry Peacham's *The Compleat Gentleman*, the works of Lipsius, and the essays of Bacon. Language books in the library included Florio's dictionaries, a Spanish dictionary and Spanish grammar, an Italian grammar, the *French Academy*, and *French Schoolmaster*. The books on travel ranged widely including Fynes Morrison's *Itinerary*, an influential work on European travel of the late sixteenth century, and those popular books, George Sandys's *Travels*, Robert Dallington's *A Survey of the Great Duke's State of Tuscany* (London, 1605), and *Coryat's Crudities*.

The library's focus was worldwide, including histories of Great Britain, Ireland, France, Spain, the Low Countries, Venice, Sicily, Hungary, Portugal, Turkey, the Indies, Florida, Mexico, Japan, China, and Leo Africanus's *History of Africa*. It contained works on world exploration by Hakluyt, Magellan, and Raleigh, as well as Mercator's atlas, and maps by Ortelius. The library also included maps in octavo size, presumably suitable for carrying, and Dr. Hood on the use of the globes. Both Cavendish and Hobbes served on the board of the Virginia Company. Cavendish owned Gerard Malynes, *Maintenance of Free Trade*, one of the important contributions to the 1620s debate on East India Company trade, Wheeler's *Treatise of Commerce*, and several volumes on the East and West Indies, Virginia, and Bermuda. The Cavendish library reflected not only a strong interest in countries and cultures around the world but the creation of networks with Europeans whom Cavendish and Hobbes met on their travels to Europe. Among the Cavendish manuscripts was the Italian correspondence with Michael Mersenne whom Cavendish and Hobbes had met in Venice, who wished to be in touch with them once they were back in England.[54]

Thomas Howard and Aletheia Talbot, Earl and Countess of Arundel, who owned Benvenuto's *The Passenger*, also put together an important library that reflected the Howard family's interest in language, law, and travel and their own interests in art and building.[55] The library grew as the Earl and Countess traveled, writing their names in books purchased abroad, carefully noting the place of purchase. The Arundel library

---

[54] Trustees of the Chatsworth Settlement Trust, Chatsworth Library, E.1 a. I am grateful to the trustees for permission to quote from the library catalog.
[55] Peck, "Uncovering the Arundel Library at the Royal Society," 3–24.

included the books of his great-uncle Henry Howard, Earl of Northampton, who, although he did not travel to the continent, collected continental books. These included grammar and language books such as *Principal Rules of the Italian Grammar and a Dictionary for better understanding of Bocaccio, Petrarch and Dante* and *Observations on the Language of Castiglione* as well as works on French, Hebrew, Greek, and Chaldaic. Northampton had owned histories of China and the Indies, Guido Benzoni's *History of the New World* of 1579, and Sebastian Muenster's *Cosmographia Universelle* of 1575 with its elaborate engravings.[56]

Indeed, engravings and plans appeared in many books in the Arundel library. Reflecting Arundel's esteem for Palladio, the Earl owned Pietro Felini's treatise on building in Rome, embellished with engravings of famous sculpture and buildings done by Palladio. He had Giovanni Lomazzo's treatises on art of 1585 and 1590 and two works by Georgio Vasari including his *Lives of the Most Excellent Painters*. The library included works by Alberti and Cellini. Arundel bought Buonanito Lorini's elaborately illustrated work on fortifications, and Faustis Vorantius's *Machie Novae*, published in Venice in 1600, filled with illustrations of buildings and engineering. He had two copies of Vitruvius and two books on architecture by the popular Vredeman de Vries. Arundel bought Petrus Opmeer, *Opus Chronographicum Orbis*, in 1611. Arundel's own purchases of works on Italian language and law included Enrico Bacco, *Il Regno di Napoli* (1611) and Giovanni Griffio *Il Summario di Tutte Le Leggi et Parti Ottenute Nel . . . Senato [of Venice]* of 1558 which he bought in 1620.[57]

Interest in foreign literature and travel was not limited by gender. The Countess of Arundel bought books too on her continental travels and took the Arundel library to the continent during the English Civil War. On 1 April 1618 she wrote her name on the title page of Fabio Colonna's *Fabii Columnae Lyncei Minus Congitarum Plantarum Pars Prima & Secunda Pars* (Rome, 1616), a beautifully illustrated scientific work on plants.[58] Colonna, the path-breaking Neapolitan naturalist, was a leading member of the Academia dei Lincei, the important Italian scientific academy founded in 1603 by Frederico Cesi, which counted Galileo among its members. This Arundel volume suggests connections between the Lynceans and English *virtuosi*.

In addition to the libraries created by Hobbes and Arundel, Lady Anne Clifford's famous portrait of 1646 displays a wealth of books that identified

[56] *Ibid.*   [57] *Ibid.*   [58] *Ibid.*, p. 5.

her as a connoisseur of European literature, geography, and architecture. These included Abraham Ortelius, *Theatrum orbis terrarum*, *The French Academy*, which Cavendish also owned, *The Feigned History of Don Quixote*, Guillaume de Saluste Du Bartas's, *Works*, Montaigne's *Essays*, Charron's *Of Wisdom*, Plutarch's *Lives* in French, Gucciardini's *Works* in French, as well as Sir Henry Wotton's *The Elements of Architecture*.[59]

Thus, whether they were armchair travelers or inveterate tourists, the well-to-do in the first half of the seventeenth century bought books, prints, and maps that put them in touch with the history, politics, and material culture of Europe, the Americas, Asia, and Africa. Didactic literature on travel emphasized the importance of contact and investigation of foreign cultures even as it stressed the virtues of England. Stuart horizons increased further when peace with Spain in 1604 made travel abroad easier for both men and women.

CURIOSITY, TRAVEL, AND LUXURY CONSUMPTION

William Cecil, third Lord Burleigh, wrote to the Earl of Shrewsbury from Italy on 23 July 1609 to laud the lavish new *pietra dura* chapel of the Medici and to advise the purchase of Venetian wall paintings to celebrate Shrewsbury's grandeur. After recommending the artists Gianbologna and Scipione Pulzone (Il Gaetano), Burleigh wrote "if your Lordship desire to increase your magnificence then my Lord let me have the honour to persuade you to employ Mr. Coke to provide you of the works of Benedicto Palma at Venice, who exceeds in doing large pictures as much as the whole side of a great-chamber upon cloth and the subject of history."[60] Shrewsbury, representative of a great noble family, father of Aletheia, Countess of Arundel, herself a great traveler and collector, later had the opportunity to display his status, not with liveried retainers or land but with Venetian art. Magnificence, the virtue celebrated by fifteenth-century Italian humanists, was available for sale through the history paintings of Palma.

Thomas Coke, whom Lord Burleigh recommended as an agent, worked for the Shrewsbury family and for Arundel. Granted passports in 1608 and 1612, Coke traveled to the continent and wrote back commentaries on what

[59] Graham Parry, "The Great Picture of Lady Anne Clifford," in David Howarth (ed.), *Art and Patronage in the Caroline Courts: Essays in Honour of Sir Oliver Millar* (Cambridge: Cambridge University Press, 1993), pp. 202–19.

[60] Quoted in J. Irene Whalley, "Italian Art and English Taste: An Early-Seventeenth-Century Letter," *Apollo*, 94 (1971), 184.

he saw from architecture for the living to commemoration of the dead.[61]
Two months after Burleigh's letter, on 30 October 1609, Coke wrote to the
Countess of Shrewsbury of "the fair buildings of marble in these countries." Coke described the Cappella dei Principi in Florence. "This chapel is
intended to be the receptacle of the dead of this Duke's house of Medici
and in truth I think they will hardly find a more curious one till they come
to paradise, but it will be divers years before it be finished."[62] Travel,
particularly to France and Italy, increasingly became part of a well-to-do
Briton's education in the early modern period and offered opportunities to
patronize new artists and purchase new goods. Travel offered aspirants
to government service familiarity with continental languages and politics.
Travel also provided merchants with trading partners, religious dissidents
with cities of refuge, military men the opportunity to serve in continental
wars and, later, royalists with places of exile.

Travel was encouraged and controlled by the Crown. Travel licenses had
a long history, dating back at least to the reign of Edward I. In the late
sixteenth century, Queen Elizabeth granted licenses for various periods of
time from six months to three years, usually with a stricture against
traveling to Rome. Roger Ascham published a strong attack on travel to
Rome in his popular work *The Scholemaster* in the 1570s,[63] and in the
second half of the sixteenth century, it was thought dangerous, spiritually
if not physically, for English Protestants to visit Rome. Later, Charles I
stopped licenses granted since 14 July 1630, "being informed of notable
abuses at this time in licenses for travel, some under pretense of going to the
Spa, and others upon other occasions."[64] Rome, however, quickly became
one of the objects of the trip. Sir Robert and Lady Shirley had their
portraits painted by Van Dyck in Rome in 1622.[65] English travelers paid
attention not only to Roman architecture and sculpture, ancient and
modern, but also to the museum of Abraham Kircher, a Jesuit scholar,
who put together a scientific collection that was a popular tourist site
in Rome.

[61] BL Add. Mss. 69,873, Coke Papers, series II, f. 135, License to travel to Thomas Coke, 15 July 1608,
"as well to gain the languages, as also for the increase of his knowledge and experiences," f. 137,
License to Thomas Coke, "upon necessary business sent over into the parts beyond the seas unto our
very good Lord the Earl of Arundel," 30 September 1612.
[62] Quoted by Whalley, "Italian Art and English Taste," p. 189.
[63] Sara Warneke, *Images of the Educational Traveler in Early Modern England* (London: E. G. Brill,
1995), p. 7.
[64] *CSPD 1629–31*, p. 312, 27 July 1630, Nonsuch.
[65] Karen Hearn, "Sir Anthony Van Dyck, Portrait of Sir William Kiligrew, 1638," *British Art in Focus*,
Patrons' Papers 6 (London: Tate, 2003).

Parliament enacted a statute in 1604 which limited travel by women and children unless they had a license from the King himself or six members of the Privy Council. In 1606 King James lightened this burden by issuing a proclamation allowing women and children to use travel passes issued by commissioners in the ports of London.[66] Travelers could take both money and servants out of the country. Licenses allowed travelers to take anywhere from L30 to L200 depending on their status. Thus, Thomas Smith, Viscount Strangeford, was allowed four servants "and money allowed unto a person of his quality."[67] In 1629 James, Duke of Lennox, received a license to travel for up to three years with Dr. Topham, Dean of Lincoln, John St. Alman, and eight other servants, with L200 in money.[68] Contemporary travel literature recommended that travelers take bills of exchange rather than cash. Travelers could obtain bills of exchange from London merchants who had networks on the continent. Paying the merchant at the outset of the trip enabled the traveler to pick up local currency throughout his travels from foreign merchants who had ties to London. Letters of credit provided instant access to money from merchants since they were signed by someone of probity and standing.[69] But letters of credit created immediate debt to the traveler and he or she was advised only to turn to letters of credit after bills of exchange had been exhausted.[70] For those who traveled to Italy, Leghorn, as the English called Livorno on the western coast, was a significant stop. Livorno had developed as a center of English trade in the late sixteenth and early seventeenth centuries as the Venetians lost their control of Mediterranean trade and English trade expanded. There, English merchants who imported luxury textiles such as silk and velvet, had their headquarters. They served also as post boxes for the transport of luxury goods back home and as banks, providing local currency for bills of exchange.

Most travel was undertaken to educate, some to serve in the military. In 1635 John Greaves, MA, of Oxford, wished to go abroad "the better to enable him to do service thereafter." He had license to go for two years

---

[66] *Stuart Royal Proclamations*, (ed.) James F. Larkin and Paul L. Hughes, 2 vols. (Oxford: Clarendon Press, 1973), I, p. 147, "A Proclamation touching passengers," 23 August 1606.

[67] *CSPD 1629–31*, p. 52.   [68] *Ibid.*, p. 67, 29 September 1629.

[69] See Maczak, *Travel in Early Modern Europe*, pp. 85–91.

[70] For examples of Bills of Exchange, see BL Add. Mss. 69,873, Coke Papers, series II, ff. 143, 145. William Hand to Thomas Coke. Philip Burlamachie was paid L77 for a Bill of Exchange to the Guadagini in Florence to pay Coke "the full sum," without any loss to you" 9 February 1613/14. Sir Roger Townshend's agent paid "Burlamachi by your appointment 23 October 1628 upon a bill of exchange from Venice for so much money delivered there to Mr. John Spelman, L48–3–10." BL Add. Mss. 41,656, Townshend Accounts and Inventories, f. 119v.

"provided he repair not to Rome without license from his Majesty."
Edward Noy was given permission to travel to France and Spain with
two servants and necessary carriages while James Small and William
Thorpe received licenses to go to France. Thomas Verney, son of
Edmund Verney, Knight Marshall, received permission to travel in foreign
parts for three years, with a proviso that he not go to Rome as did John
Bussy, William Herbert, John Matthers, and John Pritchard, all of
Glamorganshire. Captain Thomas Bardsey and Jeffrey Cuckow were given
permission to go to the Low Countries while George Synnot, colonel of a
regiment of foot under the French king, received a pass to go to France with
his wife and two children. Several were given safe conduct to go to Persia.[71]

The Grand Tour and the Giro d'Italia, undertaken with a tutor, called
for a time in France or Switzerland to study the French language and
French court manners, followed by travel over the Alps to Venice and
Florence to study Italian antiquities and Renaissance art and architecture.
Thus Thomas Hobbes, accompanying the Earl of Devonshire to France in
the 1630s, intended to "live this summer, in some town near the Loire, and
not to come to Paris till toward winter, and then to stay all winter there."[72]
In 1642 James Howell prescribed an enticing and well-established routine
for the Grand Tour which would enable young gentlemen to learn French
and to appropriate French material culture. He urged them to be careful in
religious matters and to attend a university near the Loire in order to learn
French before taking up residence in Paris. Thus prepared, the gentleman
was ready to spread his wings. Then "he may take adventure upon Paris and
the court and visit ambassadors and, going in the equipage of a young
nobleman, he may entertain a cook, a lackey, and some youth for his page."
Each servant would cost him about L50 a year. "And for his own expenses
he cannot allow himself less than L300. I include herein all sorts of exercise,
his riding, dancing, fencing, racket, coach hire, with other casual charges,
together with his apparel which, if it be fashionable, it matter not how plain
it is, being a ridiculous vanity to go gaudy amongst strangers." Howell
pointed out that there were several academies in Paris at which one might
learn "to manage arms, to dance, vault, and ply the mathematics."[73]
Contemporaries often criticized young gentlemen who returned in
Spanish or French dress with foreign manners. Nevertheless, the Grand
Tour created desires for new manners, new clothes, and new artifacts that

---

[71] *CSPD 1635*, pp. 532, 549, 558, 565, 577, 591, 603, 610.
[72] Quoted in Hobbes, *The Correspondence*, I, p. 21. Hobbes to Sir Gervase Clifton, 27 March 1634.
[73] Howell, *Instructions for Forreine Travel*, pp. 20–21, 26–27, 65.

could be met by the importation, copying, and adapting of continental material culture. Imports of these luxury goods carried with them the imprimatur of the Medici, the Doge of Venice, and even the Pope. Inigo Jones made drawings for the first Lord Carnarvon of articles that he had brought back from the Grand Tour.[74]

In 1611–12 Sir Charles Somerset, son of the Earl of Worcester, kept a much more detailed diary than Spencer had of his travels through Italy, France, Germany, and the Low Countries. Michael Brennan, who edited the diary, points out that he discussed "military and naval fortifications, national and civil administration, and urban design," and showed great interest in classical antiquity and continental developments in architecture and garden design.[75] While Somerset emphasized the damage done by the French Wars of Religion,[76] he also had a keen eye for goods and merchandise. He stopped first at Dieppe which he described as "a fair town and a brave harbor, it hath very fair streets, well paved, clean and sweetly kept, a town of much merchandise, it hath many goodly vessels belonging unto it that traffic into the East Indies and into Spain." Of Rouen he wrote "It is a town of very great merchandise, consisteth much of that from all partes, they come into the river that bringeth them to the town wall at Newhaven." Linen was the most important commodity in Normandy and Somerset commented on how the French diverted rivers to run their mills. Venice was much admired by the English in the early seventeenth century for its extraordinary location in the lagoon, its art and architecture, its resistance to the papacy, and its trade. Somerset pronounced "this town is one of the greatest towns of Christendom for merchandise; for they are all even the best themselves are merchants, aye the Duke himself deals in merchandise."[77] Somerset spent L1,315 on his trip, more than half, L782, on "apparel, gifts, and commodities bought in diverse places, and sent into England, and other expenses extraordinary."[78]

As part of their training as importers, merchants were sent abroad as apprentices. Thus Sir Paul Pindar, a leading member of the Levant Company, was apprenticed to an Italian current merchant and at eighteen went to Venice as his factor.[79] He later served as ambassador to Turkey and brought back extraordinary diamonds and Arabic and Persian manuscripts

---

[74] T. B. Trappes-Lomax, "Some Houses of the Dormer Family," *Recusant History*, 8 (1965–66), 175–87.

[75] Brennan (ed.), *The Travel Diary of Sir Charles Somerset*, pp. 3–4.

[76] My thanks to Jonathan O'Gorman for this point.

[77] Brennan (ed.), *The Travel Diary of Sir Charles Somerset*, pp. 51, 64–65, 248.   [78] *Ibid.*, p. 15.

[79] Richard Grassby, *The Business Community of Seventeenth-Century England* (Cambridge: Cambridge University Press, 1995), pp. 195–96.

to England. He gave or loaned diamonds to James I and Charles I and donated rare manuscripts to the new Bodleian Library at Oxford.[80] Pindar later became financier to the early Stuarts, a farmer of the customs and the alum works. He built a great new house in Bishopsgate. Pindar's mansion was much admired for its elaborate carved oak front and leaded glass windows. Dismantled in the 1890s, the front is displayed at the Victoria and Albert Museum.[81]

Richard Grassby points to the number of gentlemen who became apprenticed to the great international trading companies, the Merchant Adventurers, the East India Company, and especially the Levant Company.[82] He stresses the large percentage of gentry in the business community, perhaps 30 percent, which "distinguished England clearly from other pre-industrial societies."[83] Such increasing interpenetration of gentry and merchant communities may have helped to make interest in other cultures and desire for foreign luxury goods much more widely dispersed in English society.

Sir William Brereton visited Holland in 1634 and 1635. He compared the Amsterdam Exchange unfavorably with London's Royal Exchange. "It is not so state and richly adorned in respect of the ornaments and pictures there, whereof this is naked overhead . . . the ware therein . . . are but baubles and trifles in comparison of the Old Exchange, London."[84] Nevertheless, Brereton bought almost 200 tiles for his fireplaces, 80 on martial themes, 50 flowers and 50 birds, along with gilt and painted door knobs. He purchased genre pictures of the Hen and Chickens and the Banquet as well as portraits of the Queen of Bohemia and the Prince of Orange. As gifts for his father-in-law, Sir George Booth, he bought religious paintings, including Lazarus and Christ's Ascension, and two pictures of Jepthah, the greater for himself, the lesser for Booth. Each cost eighteen guilders.[85] Brereton purchased two dozen heads of the Roman emperors done in Plaster of Paris. He also negotiated for "a couple of those perspectives, which show the new found motion of the stars about Jupiter the price sixty guilders for both."[86] Brereton thought the Prince of Orange's garden "the fairest and most

---

[80] "Sir Paul Pindar," *Dictionary of National Biography*, (ed.) Sidney Lee (London: Smith, Elder and Co., 1896), vol. 45, pp. 310–12.
[81] John Summerson, *Architecture in Britain, 1530–1830* (Harmondsworth, Middlesex: Penguin, 1955), p. 53.
[82] Grassby, *The Business Community of Seventeenth-Century England*, pp. 161–62.
[83] *Ibid.*, pp. 169–70.
[84] Sir William Brereton, *Travels in Holland, the United Provinces, England, Scotland, and Ireland, 1634–1635*, (ed.) Edward Hawkins (London: Printed for the Chetham Society, 1844), p. 55.
[85] *Ibid.*, pp. 59–60. [86] *Ibid.*

spacious" he had ever seen and bought tulips from the Prince of Orange's gardener at five guilders the hundred.[87] Having purchased two chests, Brereton arranged with a Hull shipper to transport his goods.[88]

In the 1640s, Robert Bargrave, a member of a gentry family on his way to join the Levant Company, visited Italy for three weeks after the ship he was sailing on pulled into port at Livorno, the English entrepôt. Bargrave spent two weeks in Siena in "the daily divertisements of music, horse riding … courting our palates with their curious fruits and delicate Muscatella wine." He went to the opera and admired Siena's famous cathedral. In Florence he found "rarities … such in number and such for quality, as the whole world can scarce equal, much less exceed." These included the Medici chapel with its precious stones, which had already been noted by Thomas Coke, the Uffizzi "furnished with all kinds of riches and curiosities, for worth not to be prized," palaces, fountains, houses, convents, monasteries, villas, the Boboli Gardens, and "their noble silken traffic." Returning to Livorno he described it as a small city "but a very valuable one, in respect of its traffic … nor does it want the conveniency of a handsome mould for ships, nor the embellishments of a fair piazza (from which ours in Covent Garden took its pattern)." Whether or not Inigo Jones patterned Covent Garden after Livorno's piazza, contemporaries' love of Italian architecture would have made the association seem likely.[89] Bargrave, from a royalist family from Kent, steeped himself in the sights and sounds of Italy even as he went off to make his fortune in Turkey. Bargrave claimed to have learned Italian in three weeks. He brought back a collection of rarities too including antique coins.[90]

English travelers and diarists, openly competitive, often argued, as did Brereton, that English shops and their luxury goods were superior, especially to the French. Always curious, they learned, admired, compared, and sought to appropriate the luxuries and manufactures they encountered on their travels. In the 1590s Robert Dallington deemed Parisian shops "thick, but nothing so full of wares, nor so rich as they of London."[91] In 1610 Coryat thought the built environment of the Palais du Justice wanting in comparison to the Royal Exchange: "As for their Exchange where they sell

---

[87] *Ibid.*, pp. 28, 34.   [88] *Ibid.*, p. 60.

[89] Michael G. Brennan (ed.), *The Travel Diary of Robert Bargrave, Levant Merchant (1647–1656)* (London: Hakluyt Society, 1999); Stephen Bann, *Under the Sign: John Bargrave as Collector, Traveler and Witness* (Ann Arbor: University of Michigan Press, 1994), pp. 9–17, 53.

[90] Brennan (ed.), *The Travel Diary of Robert Bargrave*, introduction, p. 15.

[91] Quoted in John Lough, *France Observed in the Seventeenth Century by British Travellers* (Stocksfield, Northumberland, and Boston: Oriel Press, 1984) p. 54.

many fine and curious things, there are two or three pretty walks in it, but neither for length, nor for the roof, nor the exquisite workmanship is it any way to be compared with ours in London." Howell, who visited Lyons in 1621, found it "a stately rich town, and a renowned mart for the silks of Italy and other Levantine commodities, and a great bank for money, and indeed the greatest of France."[92] While denigrating Parisian artificers and their houses, as well as the cutlery and gloves on offer, Howell grudgingly admired its fashion. "A tailor can tick you up after the best and newest fashion ... they are very perfect at tooth-picks [and] beard brushes." But he went on, "I persuade myself that the two several ranks of shops in Cheapside can show more plate, and more variety of mercery wares, good and rich, than three parts of Paris."[93]

In the 1650s seventeenth-century commentators continued to examine the luxury goods available in Paris and to stress the increasingly rich plate and clothing on display in London. Peter Heylen described the boutiques of Paris.

Presently without the Chapel is the Burse, Le Gallerie des Merchands, a rank of shops, in show, but not in substance, like to those in the Exchange in London ... On the bottom of the stairs and round about the several houses, consecrated to the execution of Justice, are sundry shops of the same nature, meanly furnished if compared with ours; yet I persuade myself the richest of this kind in Paris.[94]

WOMEN AS TRAVELERS

Studies of the Grand Tour have traditionally focused on scions of the nobility completing their education, diplomats angling for jobs back home, and tutors shepherding their flock. More recently, scholars of modern England have begun to examine the travels and travel narratives of women from the eighteenth century on and the way in which gendered language inflected portrayal of other cultures and peoples.[95] Yet the travels of individual women in the seventeenth century have been less well documented. Sara Warneke suggests that "after the demise of pilgrimage, women found it difficult to travel abroad except as the wives, daughters, sisters or servants of male travelers." Although women often accompanied their husbands or their representatives, well-to-do women did travel without their male relatives much as they went shopping and attended the

---

[92] *Ibid.*, p. 64. [93] *Ibid.*, p. 55. [94] *Ibid.*, pp. 54–55. [95] See footnote 34 above.

theater.[96] As we have seen, on 23 August 1606, King James issued a proclamation at Farnham Castle making it easier for women and children under twenty-one to get licenses to cross the sea.[97]

Women traveled most often to Spa in the Low Countries, whose waters had long been publicized. The English came to drink the healthful waters and settled down into a summer season of visits and sightseeing, a vacation they often repeated.[98] On 24 April 1608, Sir Oliver Butler was granted a license to travel for four years to and from Spa in the company of his wife and Goddard Oxenbridge.[99] Jean Beaulieu, one of the ambassadorial staff at Brussels, accompanied the ambassador's wife Lady Edmonds and two other women.[100] But women also appear to have traveled without male relatives or officials. On 5 July 1622, Lady Savage, wife of Sir Thomas Savage, received license to travel to Spa[101] and on 20 May 1623, Lady Wallingford was licensed to go to Spa for six months and to take over eight coach horses.[102] On 21 May a pass to Spa was prepared for Mrs. Ursula Wildgoose. The Countess of Rutland, too, was a traveler. On 25 June 1622, she was given license to go to Spa with as many servants as she wanted and £100 in money.[103] Women often used Spa as a jumping off place to go to France and Italy. For some this included the chance to attend Roman Catholic service openly. On 20 August 1606, Lady Jane Lovell wrote to Salisbury that she was prevented by rains from going to the Spa. Although loyal to her king and country, she attended Catholic service.[104]

Aletheia Talbot, Countess of Arundel, daughter of the Countess of Shrewsbury to whom Thomas Coke wrote of the glories of Italy, was one of the most prominent women at the courts of the early Stuarts and the most notable woman traveler in the period.[105] At times she traveled separately from the Earl. While Arundel conformed to the established church, Aletheia was a Roman Catholic. Both Arundels moved beyond travel and the purchase of foreign luxury goods to identify themselves as European nobles and patrons. As much as her husband, Aletheia Talbot

---

[96] Warneke, *Images of the Educational Traveler in Early Modern England*, p. 5.

[97] *Stuart Royal Proclamations*, I, p. 147.

[98] Stoye, *English Travelers Abroad, 1604–1667*, pp. 207–08.

[99] *CSPD 1603–10*, p. 424, 24 April 1608.   [100] Stoye, *English Travellers Abroad, 1604–1667*, p. 207.

[101] *CSPD 1619–23*, p. 420, 5 July 1622.   [102] *Ibid.*, p. 586, 20 May 1623.

[103] *Ibid.*, p. 412, 25 June 1622.   [104] *CSPD 1603–10*, p. 329, 20 August 1606.

[105] On the Countess of Arundel as architectural patron, see Elizabeth V. Chew, "The Countess of Arundel and Tart Hall," in Edward Chaney (ed.), *The Evolution of English Collecting: The Reception of Italian Art in the Tudor and Stuart Periods* (New Haven and London: Yale University Press, 2003), pp. 285–314; David Howarth, "The Patronage and Collecting of Aletheia, Countess of Arundel, 1606–1654," *Journal of the History of Collections*, 10 (1998), 125–37. On her political role see Helen Payne, "Aristocratic Women and the Jacobean Court, 1603–1625" (Ph.D. Thesis, London, 2001).

saw herself as a European noble and patron. Both were ardent consumers of European goods. They bought books, manuscripts, classical marbles, sixteenth- and seventeenth-century paintings and brought home artists and artifacts from their travels. Imported luxuries of all sorts became crucial to their identity. We look first at the Countess of Arundel and secondly at the Earl.

Arundel first traveled to Spa in 1612. In 1613–14 both the Earl and Countess of Arundel toured Italy with Inigo Jones and others, a trip that helped to shape Jones's architecture and the Arundels' collecting for a lifetime. Called back to London because of the death of his uncle, Henry Howard, Earl of Northampton, the Arundels were feted by the Duke of Turin who gave them two Spanish horses.[106] They stopped in Paris to see King Louis XIII and his queen, Anne of Austria. "The Earl and Countess will have the honour of kissing the hands of the King and Queen here." There had been some difficulty in providing "my Lady a tabouret, which is a low stool that is allowed to Princesses and Duchesses only to sit on before the Queen, but in view of the status of my Lady, any objections will soon be waived." Since Arundel had a claim to be Duke of Norfolk, the premier dukedom in Britain that the fourth Duke had lost when he was attainted of treason in 1572, this problem was quickly solved. To be regarded as of high rank and great refinement abroad as well as at home was important to the Earl and Countess. Both were praised for their "deportment and charm." Aletheia made a particularly good impression on Anne of Austria, who "hath showed much to like and favor her."[107] Although Northampton died in June, the Earl and Countess did not come home until October.

Aletheia eagerly took part in the material culture of the courts of France, Italy, and the Spanish Netherlands. She became Peter Paul Rubens's first English patron in 1620 when she commissioned her own portrait and sat for him in Antwerp. The Countess of Arundel also had close ties to Rubens's star pupil, Anthony Van Dyck. Van Dyck, who made his first trip to London in 1620–21 probably at the request of Arundel, joined the Countess in Italy in 1622. In 1623 Rubens dedicated six plates of his Battle of the Amazons to the Countess.[108] While on a trip to Italy, Inigo Jones made extensive notes on the Palazzo del Te, the extraordinary summer

---

[106] HMC *Downshire*, V, p. 61, Dudley Carleton to William Trumbull, 17 November 1614.
[107] HMC *Downshire*, V, pp. 35, 46. Jean Beaulieu to William Trumbull, 13 October 1614, p. 35; 27 October 1614, p. 46.
[108] Griffiths, *The Print in Stuart Britain*, p. 75.

house that Guido Reni built for the Duke of Mantua. Aletheia, too, asked for a model as she planned her villa for entertainment, Tart Hall.[109]

The Countess of Arundel's closest connections were with Venice and the Venetians. Her two sons were educated in nearby Padua. In 1618, at a dinner given by Queen Anne for the departing Venetian ambassador, the Countess of Arundel sat next to the ambassador. He described her as "the chief lady of the court and kingdom, no other taking precedence of her either for descent or in the queen's favour. The lady is extremely partial to the city and aristocracy of Venice where she received much favour and courtesy a few years ago, of which she retains grateful recollection."[110] In December 1619 she gave a large gift to Alessandro Gatti, the Venetian chaplain who had written a work on the hunt, on the occasion of his returning to Venice. Travel intertwined with politics, and ambassadors kept a close watch on the rise and fall of political favorites. In August 1620 the Venetian ambassador reported that Viscount Purbeck, the brother of the King's favorite, the Duke of Buckingham,

left here to go to the baths of Spa in Flanders, with his wife and some other ladies. The Countess of Arundel has also left for the same place. I hear that the viscount wishes to go on to Italy and to see Venice out of curiosity, and the countess to go to Padua to see her sons. It would be advantageous to show appropriate honour to the former ... for the sake of his brother upon whom fair fortune continues to shine ... The latter is well known to your Excellencies.

In October 1620, the Venetian secretary at Milan reported that the Countess's efforts to pass informally through Milan had caused uproar because the Duke "desired to do her honour."[111]

In 1621 Aletheia took her children to the Veneto. There, on New Year's Day, she wrote to Dudley Carleton, formerly English ambassador to Venice, that she was "among his ancient acquaintances at Venice."[112] She remained in touch with Secretary of State Calvert, commented on events at court, and hoped that the Parliament would

[109] Jeremy Wood, "Taste and Connoisseurship at the Court of Charles I: Inigo Jones and the Work of Giulio Romano," in Eveline Cruickshanks (ed.), *The Stuart Courts* (Stroud: Sutton, 2000), pp. 118–40; Howarth, "The Patronage and Collecting of Aletheia, Countess of Arundel," 125–37; Chew, "The Countess of Arundel and Tart Hall," pp. 285–314.

[110] *CSPV, 1617–19*, p. 315, 14 September 1618, Horatio Busino to the Signori Giorgio, Francesco and Zaccharia Contarini. When Queen Anne died in 1619, Aletheia Talbot took the role of chief mourner.

[111] *CSPV, 1619–21*, p. 85, Girolamo Lando, Venetian ambassador in England to the Doge and Senate, 20 December 1619; p. 350, Lando to the Doge and Senate, 6 August 1620; p. 428, Giacomo Vendramin, Venetian secretary at Milan, to the Doge and Senate, 7 October 1620.

[112] *CSPD, 1619–23*, p. 211, 1? January 1621.

give the King satisfaction.[113] While in Venice, she became involved in the fall of Antonio Foscarini, the former Venetian ambassador to England. The Countess insisted on coming before the Doge and the Council of Ten accompanied by Sir Henry Wotton, the English ambassador, where she protested her love of Venice and claimed that she had not met with Foscarini.[114] Despite this uproar, the Countess remained in Venice until 1623, because of the illness of her son. John Chamberlain thought it strange that she would go before the Doge to justify herself from idle rumors, and sniffed at her staying so long on so little pretense.[115] The Earl of Arundel presented the episode differently to Carleton. The Countess had been accused of allowing Antonio Foscarini to meet secretly the Pope's Nuncio, and other foreign ministers, at her house. On complaining to the State, "she received ample satisfaction, and was even seated by the Doge in the Colleggio," an honor presumably similar to the tabouret. Arranging her return from Venice, she sent "seventy bales of goods all sealed and exempted from customs by order of the Doge."[116] Continuing her travels to heads of state, the Countess of Arundel planned to see Queen Elizabeth of Bohemia, King James and Queen Anne's daughter, on her way home to England.[117]

"THE PRIME THINGS TO BE SEEN": SEEING THE SIGHTS, DEFINING THE SELF

The Earl of Arundel distilled decades of Italian travel when, on 25 April 1646, he wrote *Remembrances of Things Worth Seeing in Italy* for his young friend John Evelyn.[118] Unlike the model outlined in the Spencer manuscript or the pattern prescribed by Bacon, Arundel's advice focused on Italian art and architecture both ancient and modern that he had seen over a lifetime. Arundel was not just a sightseer; he wrote with an eye to possession. He did not draw on the didactic literature of the period and the canonical view of the Grand Tour so much as he described the specific places, collections, pictures, and classical sites that animated his desire to

[113] *Ibid.*, p. 226, 24 February 1621.   [114] *CSPV, 1621–23*, pp. 293, 299–304.

[115] *CSPD 1619–23*, p. 390, Chamberlain to Carleton, 11 May 1622.

[116] Howarth, "The Patronage and Collecting of Aletheia, Countess of Arundel," 125–37. Prudence Leith-Ross, *The John Tradescants, Gardeners to the Rose and Lily Queen* (London: P. Owen, 1984), p. 165.

[117] *CSPD 1619–23*, p. 394, Arundel to Carleton, 16 May 1622.

[118] Thomas Howard, Earl of Arundel, *Remembrances of Things Worth Seeing in Italy: Given to John Evelyn, 25 April 1646*, ed. John Martin Robinson (London: Roxburghe Club, 1987).

purchase, display, and replicate his masterpieces. Arundel's *Remembrances* present him as one of the great English consumers of European art, interested, even in his last months, to buy Leonardos and Titians to accompany those he already owned. Arundel's views received wider circulation through their influence on John Evelyn's writings.

From his bed in Padua, Arundel recalled ancient and modern buildings, interiors, gardens, and collections that Evelyn should see in Vicenza, Verona, and Milan as he made his way back to England. In Vicenza, "the prime things to be seen are the buildings ordered by Andrea Palladio," ranging from the Theatro Olympico to the basilica in the public square, and private palaces, especially the suburban Rotunda. At Verona, he stressed "the antique amphitheatre called the Arena, which is the most entire in Italy, and the garden of Conte Giusti, besides the seat and country about it which is counted the best in Italy." In Milan, Arundel recommended the Duomo, the castle, and two suburban villas and the bishop's palace designed by an architect of Phillip II's Escorial. Arundel called attention to Madonnas by Leonardo and Raphael at the church of Saint Celso and despaired of Leonardo's fresco of the Last Supper at the Monastery of Madonna Della Gratia. So admired by Francis I that he wished to "have carried it into France for love of that picture, being the rarest thing that ever Leonardo did … now it's wholly destroyed."[119]

Arundel remembered those Italians he had met, from counts and civil lawyers to apothecaries, whose collections of pictures and drawings were worth looking at. At Castellacchio, he urged Evelyn to see Cavaliere Arconato who had some of Leonardo's designs. "I was told he was desirous to sell, but did not enquire of the price. I would be glad by some means to have the lowest price known, he hath good paintings of Parmensis (Parmigianino) and Titian in some other rooms, I think he will sell any thing being old and having but one daughter which is married."[120] When Evelyn left Arundel, the Earl was in tears as he lamented woes of family and civil war.[121] Although he wished to return to his home in Albury in Surrey, Arundel died a few months later in Padua. Evelyn recorded visits to many of Arundel's sights in his diary, noting guiltily that he had not been able to see the Rotunda in Vicenza because of an uncooperative companion.[122]

The *Remembrances*, layered with memories of Arundel's travels on the continent and especially to Italy, also reflect the experience of exile. For many royalists, exile, however bitter, was in some ways an extension of the

---

[119] Arundel, *Remembrances*, pp. 23–26.   [120] Arundel, *Remembrances*, pp. 27–28.
[121] *Ibid.*, p. 23.   [122] *Ibid.*, pp. 35–37.

Grand Tour as we shall see in a later chapter. Together the Earl and Countess went into exile in 1641 in the Low Countries. Arundel and Evelyn traveled together to see the sights in Bruges shortly after their arrival from England. While the Countess continued in Antwerp, Arundel moved to Padua. Royalist exiles like Evelyn returned to Britain in between civil wars in the 1640s, during the Protectorate in the 1650s, and at the Restoration in 1660. They brought with them the vision, the goods, the experience, the networks, and the memories of what they had seen and experienced.

Through their relationship to precious objects, books, manuscripts, pictures, sculpture, and claims through court etiquette to sit before the Queen of France and the Doge of Venice, the Arundels defined their own identity and relationship to others, not only as English nobility whose families had won their titles long ago on the battlefield, but as international cognoscenti. Arundel sought to share knowledge and understanding of his collections by publishing books illustrating his ancient marbles and coins, encouraging the reproduction of some of his paintings and drawings, and opening his house to all interested gentlemen.[123] In the next chapter we shall see how Arundel sought to make his collections available to a wider public through print.

To Arundel the collector must also be added Arundel the entrepreneur. He had his Italian secretary, Francesco Vercellini, recruit Clemento Coltreci to establish a restoration studio in London for what David Howarth describes as "the ever-increasing number of antiques coming from Italy and the Levant."[124] Further, in 1634 Arundel sent Coltreci along with Mr. Page to Ireland to develop a trade in marble. Writing to Thomas Wentworth, Earl of Strafford, Arundel asked that Page, who was well known to Wentworth,

inform himself of marbles the best he may, and to that purpose, have sent along with him, one Sigr Clemento an excellent Sculptor who works for me, and knows well marbles, to the end that . . . I may not only make use of them myself for a little room I am about, but set up a trade of them hither; and increase shipping with the good of both kingdoms and benefit to the undertakers.[125]

---

[123] See chapter 4 below.

[124] David Howarth, "Lord Arundel as an Entrepreneur of the Arts," *Burlington Magazine*, 122 (1980), 690–92.

[125] Quoted in Howarth, "Lord Arundel as an Entrepreneur of the Arts," 690. Arundel to Strafford, 14 August 1635, Arundel House.

A servant of the Arundels recalled carrying "several of the said marbles, stones, and pillars and other stones from the city wharf to Arundel wharf where they were worked on by the said Earl's servants ... the said marbles were taken and disposed of by the said Earl and his agents."[126] The quarry continued to be worked in the 1630s and Inigo Jones may have used the marble to repair Old St. Paul's.[127]

The Arundels presented their sense of self in a series of portraits from 1616. These drew attention to their foreign travel, the goods that they had gathered from abroad, and their enthusiasm for exploration. In one important double portrait of 1616, the Earl and Countess point to their sculpture and painting collections in special galleries decorated with Italian chairs.[128] In 1620 Rubens represented the Countess as a great European noble seated in a chair of state, accompanied not by her husband but by Dudley Carleton, Ambassador to Venice, surrounded with her hound, hounds man, and dwarf, with the Howard family arms crossed with Talbot floating over head.[129] In the 1630s, Arundel enthusiastically took up the Madagascar project for the colonization of the island off Africa. To mark the project, Arundel commissioned an imposing double portrait from Van Dyck in which the Earl, in garter robes, points to Africa and specifically Madagascar on the globe while the Countess, in coronation robes, holds the navigation instruments.[130]

"AFRICA YIELDS MOST EXCELLENT THINGS FIT FOR THE USE OF MAN": EMBASSIES AND LUXURY CONSUMPTION

Embassies deliberately used luxury to mark the power and magnificence of the monarch. In addition, ambassadors used their travels to bring back the curious and rare. Gift-giving, a central feature of ambassadorial ritual, highlighted the exchange of contemporary luxury goods. James I sent a gilded coach, originally commissioned by Queen Elizabeth, to Tsar Boris Godunov in 1603 with scenes of Christians fighting Muslims.[131]

---

[126] *Ibid.*, p. 692.   [127] Howarth, "Lord Arundel as an Entrepreneur of the Arts," 690–92.

[128] Daniel Mytens, Thomas Howard, Earl of Arundel, ?1616; Aletheia Talbot, Countess of Arundel, ?1616, Arundel Castle.

[129] Peter Paul Rubens, Aletheia, Countess of Arundel, Alte Pinakothek, München.

[130] See, for instance, Ernest B. Gilman, "Madagascar on My Mind: The Earl of Arundel and the Arts of Colonization," in Peter Erickson and Clark Hulse (eds.), *Early Modern Visual Culture: Representation, Race, Empire in Renaissance England* (Philadelphia: University of Pennsylvania Press, 2000), pp. 284–314.

[131] V. S. Goncharenko and V. I. Narozhnaia, *The Armoury: Moscow Kremlin State Museum: A Guide*, 2nd edn (Moscow: Red Square Publishers, 2000).

The English Muscovy Company brought presents of silver plate to the Tsars between 1553 and 1649 to gain trading rights.[132] In 1605 Charles Howard led an embassy to Spain to reopen diplomatic relations after the Anglo-Spanish Peace Treaty. Sir James Carlisle brought an elaborate cortege in 1615 to visit the French court, slipping silver wheels on the carriages before his entry into Paris. Endymion Porter sent back luxury goods to his wife Olive while on Prince Charles's embassy to Spain in 1623.[133] Embassies became increasingly magnificent under Charles II and James II. In 1663 an embassy led by Charles Howard, Earl of Carlisle, reopened trade with Russia. He brought 100 followers and presented an opulent array of silver plate. These lavish embassies to famous and far-flung destinations were enthusiastically retold in print in text and pictures.

Henry Howard, Arundel's grandson, spent years in exile in Antwerp and Padua both before and after the Restoration. Because he was a Catholic he could not take a full role in the political life of Charles II's Britain. He could, however, bring the grandeur of the old nobility to diplomatic missions. Thus in 1664–65 he accompanied Lord Leslie, chief minister to the Holy Roman Emperor, from Vienna on an embassy to Adrianople and Constantinople to Sultan Mahomet IV.[134] John Burbury's *A Relation of a Journey of the Right Honourable my Lord Henry Howard* (London, 1671), celebrated the embassy.[135]

In 1669, Howard undertook a journey to Tangier for Charles II to negotiate a commercial treaty with Sultan Rashid II, the Emperor of Morocco, known as "the Great Tafiletta."[136] Tangier had come to the Crown through Charles's marriage to the Portuguese princess Catherine of Braganza, and it was hoped that Tangier would become an important outpost in overseas trade. The King had built up its fortifications. Howard brought along Wenceslaus Hollar, who had accompanied Arundel on his embassy to the Emperor in 1636, to make drawings of the settlement at Tangier.[137] Howard's trip aimed to display the power and status of the

---

[132] Elspeth Moncrieff, "Politics and Plate: English Silver from the Kremlin," *Apollo*, 133 (1991), 50–52; John Culme, *English Silver Treasures from the Kremlin*, a loan exhibition (London: Sotheby's, 1990).

[133] *CSPD 1619–23*, p. 590, 28 May 1623.

[134] John Martin Robinson, *The Dukes of Norfolk: A Quincentennial History* (Oxford: Oxford University Press, 1982), p. 125.

[135] Burbury dedicated the tract to the eldest son of Lord Henry Howard much as William Crown's diary of Arundel's embassy of 1636 had been dedicated to his grandson Henry Howard.

[136] Robinson, *The Dukes of Norfolk*, pp. 125–26; Enid M. G. Routh, *Tangier: England's Lost Atlantic Outpost, 1661–1684.* (London: J. Murray, 1912).

[137] See F. C. Springell, "Unpublished Drawings of Tangier by Wenceslaus Hollar," *Burlington Magazine*, 106 (1964), 68–74.

British king, to investigate Africa on behalf of the Royal Society, and to explore the commercial possibilities of opening up the continent.

Howard and his brother Charles were active members of the Royal Society. Sir Robert Moray, president of the Royal Society, saw the mission to Tangier as an opportunity to learn, explore, and bring back ancient manuscripts and new goods. Moray and Henry Oldenburg, Secretary of the Royal Society, crafted a detailed list of thirty-six questions to Howard. Some resembled those questions on situation, quality, inhabitants, and rarities posed earlier by the anonymous writer of the "Things principally to be Observed" in the Spencer manuscript. But the Royal Society was as interested in botany, anthropology, engineering, medicine, and technology, as on the workings of the royal court.

Thus, the Royal Society inquired about climate, meteors, disease, medicines, perfumes, soil, ores, and people. They wanted to know the position of Mount Atlas, the mines and springs nearby, and its plants. They asked Howard to bring back specimens of plants, seeds, ores, earths, and clays as well as "designs of their palaces and temples." The Royal Society asked about "men and women, [their] ... diet, economy ... their strength, agility, stature, shape etc ... Whether it be true, that those in Numidia (in the land of Dates) live long, though they lose the teeth soon; and that the Negroes are short lived though their teeth continue sound to their death?" They inquired about their arts and technology, including issues of current interest, "particularly, what varnishes they have among them? and what ways of tempering their iron and steel." They asked about perfume and aphrodisiacs: "what is the composition called Lhasis which 'tis said, that whosoever takes an ounce of it, shall fall a laughing and sporting, and be like one half drunk, and very amorous?"

The Royal Society tried to recover the early history and culture of North Africa.

Whether there be any inscriptions or coins with characters neither Latin nor Arabic? And what coins and other antiquities are or have been found around Fez and at Densir? And whether at Thelosia there be any marble pillars with sentences and epigrams in Latin characters? To inquire into the ancient manuscripts that may probably have been translated out of the ancient Greek, either in geometry, astronomy, physique, or chemistry?

Drawing on classical accounts, they asked "Whether at Morocco they keep still their public act of scholars? And if so, what is therein performed ... Whether any African writers give any account of the ancient Punic learning." They asked about African libraries: "what books of geography, genealogies, history, alchemy, medicine, magic, etc. are extant amongst them?" In particular, they asked about works cited by Leo Africanus, the sixteenth-century Andalusian humanist who lived in Fez and converted to Islam, including genealogies by Ibn Rachu, cosmography by Bichri, and books on magic by Margian and Ibn Khaldun. "And whether it be true, what the same Leo Africanus relates, that the fortune-tellers at Fez, by pouring some drops of oil into a glass of water, can represent creatures, and show them to bystanders; and speaking to them, receive an answer by words or signs?"

Testing further the reports of Leo Africanus, whose works could be found in English libraries, the Royal Society asked about birds perched on crocodiles, a lizard who drank no water; "whether it be true, that the lions about Pietra Rosta are so tame as to come into the streets and gather bones and at Agla the lions so cowardly that they fly at the voice of a child ... Whether camels will travel many days without provender and drink, and ordinary in traveling have no drink allowed them but once in three or four days?" They wanted to know "what the ostrich feeds upon? To get one dried." The Royal Society asked Howard to carry out barometric experiments at sea level and on Mt. Atlas using Robert Boyle's portable barometer.

While the Royal Society focused on Africa's flora and fauna, the body and health of its inhabitants, technology, longitude and latitude, and cultural artifacts, it also inquired about kingdoms with gold such as "Tacrure, three or four hundred leagues distant from the Guiny Shore, governed by an Emperor and rich in gold etc." and of rivers "whether they carry any Golden Sands in them?"[138]

Howard, arrayed with trumpeters and with Wenceslaus Hollar to record the scene, waited fruitlessly for a year for the appearance of the Emperor of Morocco. While waiting, he offered to bring back African curiosities to his friends. Sir Henry Sheere was the engineer in charge of building a new harbor in Tangier. When Sheere went to Genoa, Howard sent greetings to the Marquess Durazo, with whom he had traveled in Turkey, and asked: "If there be any curiosity here in Africa where I am like to go that his lordship would be served in, for when I had the honour of being his comrade in Turkey I perceived how curious he was in all things."

Howard himself was interested in the curious and rare and donated a mummy, if not a dried ostrich, to the Royal Society museum. At the same

[138] Royal Society, RBO. RBC. 3.130–134. "Inquiries for Barbary Recommended by the Royal Society to the favour and care of his excellency the Lord Henry Howard His Majesty's Ambassador Extraordinary to the Emperor of Morocco."

time, however, he wanted European luxuries that he had seen and used. Howard asked Sheere to purchase speckled marble for his chimney piece and instructed him at great length on the perfumes, perfumed linens, and perfume bottles he wished him to buy in Genoa and have sent in special cases to Arundel House.

(As I am the greatest lover and hunter after sweets [perfumes] in the world) . . . [get] what quantity you can of the spirit . . . of orange flowers, which is the most delicate smell in the world such as the Dominican apothecary once furnished me with at Florence, and I never saw elsewhere . . . also for delicate waters such as the aqua di cordova in Spain and Portugal or in Italy, the aqua d'angely or aqua narisa etc and I desire of all sorts . . . bring samples only for a trial and settle for me a correspondence how I may send for, pay, and receive them in England, to which place it ought be directed for me addressed thus for Mr. Thomas West at Arundel House in London. There is a delicate red usually put up in little glasses to be used with juice of lemon to red ladies faces.[139]

While Howard was familiar with these products from his travels, a literature on perfume offered these goods to the stay-at-home consumer. Sir Hugh Platt's *Delights for Ladies: To Adorn their Persons, Tables, Closets and Distillatories* (London, 1628) and Jean Fargeron's, *Catalogue des Marchandises* (Montpellier, 1665) discussed embellishments, compounds, perfumes, and powder for the teeth for men and women. They described to English and European consumers the wide range of perfumes and cosmetics on offer.

Howard's mission ended unsuccessfully when the Emperor Tafiletta failed to meet him in Tangiers, unimpressed or unaware of the grand

---

[139] BL Add. Mss. 19,872, Papers relating to Tangiers 1669–1700, f. 1r–2v. "My Lord Howard's Instructions in his own hand at my going into Genoa 29 August 1669." Howard inquired after Roman Catholic priests and Jesuits in Rome. Sheere reported that "My Lord sought a speckled kind of marble for his chimney piece and not to bestow above L5 or L6. He takes notice of certain boxes wherein perfumes of all sorts are put . . . the tops . . . show the flowers whereof the perfumes are made," p. 44. On perfume see Gioia di Consiglio, *Collezionare la profumeria italiana d'epoca* (Rome: Fratelli Palombi, 1997); Heiner Meininghaus, Christa Habrich, and Tanja Volz, *Düfte und edle Flakons aus fünf Jahrhunderten – Five Centuries of Scent and Elegant Flacons* (Stuttgart: Arnoldsche, 1998). "By the Baroque period, apothecaries shops carried special narrow necked bottles with tightly fitting ground in glass stoppers and balsam jars with tin or silver lids that screwed on . . . Turners and silversmiths created marvels of technology like miniature apothecaries chests filled with tiny compartments," p. 44. Scent was used in linen cabinets and "throughout the reign of Louis XIV, people even wore miniature scent holders and 'acorns' under their clothes." Francoise de Bonneville, *The Book of Fine Linen* (Paris: Flammarion, 1994), pp. 66–67. See A. Manners "An Account of Perfumery Supplied for the Use of King James I," *Proceedings of the Society of Antiquaries of London*, 2nd series 4 (1867–70), 435–37; L. G. Matthews, *The Royal Apothecaries* (London: Wellcome Historical Medical Library, 1967); Hugh Platt, *Delightes for Ladies: to adorne their persons, tables, closets and distillatories* (London, 1628); Jean Fargeron, *Catalogue des Marchandises* (Montpellier, 1665).

embassy waiting for him. The four trumpeters and kettle drummer who had cost L100 were to no avail.[140] Howard himself spent part of the year in Europe. The British gave up Tangier in 1683 and destroyed its fortifications. Hollar's views, sketched during Howard's embassy, provide their only depiction. Howard reported on his mission to the Royal Society but had to tell them that he never found ancient manuscripts, palaces, and treasure. Despite such disappointment, the mission reinforced increasing interest in African goods and trade.

A member of Howard's entourage published *A Letter from a Gentleman of the Lord Ambassador Howard's Retinue to his Friend in London*, dated at Fez, 1 November 1669, in which he gave "a full relation ... of the present state of the countries under the power of Taffaletta, Emperor of Morocco. With a brief account of the marchandizing commodities of Africa. As also the manners and customs of the people there." The tract, "published for public satisfaction" in 1670, sold for sixpence.

The *Letter* addressed in print many of the inquiries posed by the Royal Society. "God's Providence hath therefore planted that part of the world with such good and healing roots as might oppose the malice and prevent the mischiefs of venomous creatures." Monstrous creatures were to be found: "Beyond the City of Fez there is a great wilderness full of wild beasts and fowls. The Arabs do live in all the fruitful places, but in the land nothing is to be seen but mountains of sand, that are very dreadful in a storm of Wind." Jackals, lions, and leopards, he reported, attacked humans.

But the author focused on Africa's resources not on latitude and longitude or experiments on Mount Atlas. Instead, he provided "A Brief Account of the Native Commodities of Africa." These included hides, honey, "silk stuff that is made by the citizens of the Sea-Shore, of the bark of trees. Here is also raw silk; the country breeds silkworms in great abundance about Fez and Morocco." He not only emphasized the range of Africa's commodities but the importance of establishing control over trade to Africa.

Africa yields most excellent things fit for the use of man ... The commodities of this country [are] very many; it were a happy thing to have a prince there that did command all the land and that were a lover of trade; then caravans might go safe from place to place without fear of robbing: but the nature of the Arabs inclines

---

[140] Arundel Castle, G1/194. "Warrant for four trumpeters and a kettle drummer to attend Henry Lord Howard in his embassy to the Emperor of Morocco 1669, L100."

them to thieving and violence; so that although one should have a passport from the prince, it is a great hazard, if you be not provided with a good guard.

The writer drew particular attention to gold:

If peace were established in the country, and with our nation, then we might fetch from Guiny, and the Negro's country, the rich commodity of gold dust. Now every month some of the blacks do adventure to Fez, with camels loaden with that superfluous earth, of which they have too much, and carry back other trifles that are esteemed amongst them. Some say that the sun hath burnt the sand of the wilderness in some places, and that it is become perfect gold. It is certain that in the sandy deserts the blacks do gather up gold; this gold is the best in the world, it is as pliable almost as paper, and doth not so easily consume and waste. If some would adventure in the land, to search out the country, and bring a just and a true report, he must discover many things which our traders might improve to their advantage.

The tract described Africans who traded gold for trifles in much the same way as Hartlib did Native Americans who, it was hoped, would trade silk for English goods. Both argued that English control of trade would bring improvement although Hartlib was more interested in civilizing and converting the indigenous peoples. The author concluded: "Were that country in the hands of an ingenious and laborious people, it is not to be doubted, but that it would furnish the rest of the world with excellent productions. But since the conquest of the country by the Arabs, war and oppressions have hindered the inhabitants from the improvement of their soil."[141]

Curiosity about Africa and Asia was not new. The transmission of classical texts through Arabic was well known to humanists. Chairs had been established in Arabic at Oxford and Cambridge in the 1630s. But throughout the seventeenth century, interest in gold, slaves, and other products had grown. An English company established a right to trade in Guinea and Benin in 1619 and bought slaves from Arab traders. In search of gold in 1660 an English company went up the Gambia river and the Royal Adventurers were trading to Africa in 1663. Several tracts appeared in the early 1660s about efforts to make a peace treaty with the ruler of Morocco. In 1667 the African traders "invited all His Majesty's native subjects to join their joint stock company" in connection with James, Duke of York. "They announced the company's

---

[141] S. L., *A Letter from a Gentleman of the Lord Ambassador Howard's Retinue* (London, 1670), pp. 34–36.

resolutions to furnish his Majesty's American plantations negroes at certain and moderate rates."[142]

Howard's mission took place in 1669, the tract was published in 1670. Two years later in 1672, The Royal African Company was established with personal connections to James, Duke of York.[143] Hollar's views were published by John Overton in 1673 entitled *Prospects in and about Tangier.*[144] Anthony Disney points out that in the interaction of Europeans with Africa two processes overlapped, the first to understand, the second to exploit.[145] The Royal Society's inquiries and Griffith's tract demonstrate both.

Howard presented a second paper to the Royal Society in 1676/77 entitled "A Description of the Diamond Mines ... [of] the Coast of Coromandel," apparently provided by the East India Company. Jean-Baptiste Tavernier's *Six Voyages to India* had not yet been translated into English in which Tavernier discussed the diamond mines of India. Howard's paper, probably written by Nathaniel Chumley of the East India Company, reported on thirty-eight mines, many more than Tavernier had mentioned, and provided details on living conditions along the Coromandel coast.[146] The author claimed he had "visited several

---

[142] *A Proclamation Declaring His Majesties Pleasure to Settle and Establish a Free Port at his City of Tanger in Africa* (London, 1662); *A Brief Relation of the Present State of Tangier, and of the Advantages Which his Excellence the Earl of Tiveot has Obtained Against Gayland* (London, 1664); *A Description of Tangier, the Country and People Adjoining* (London, 1664); *Articles of Peace Concluded and Agreed Between His Excellency the Lord Bellasyse His Majesty's Governor of his City and Garrison of Tangier in Africa ... and Cidi Hamet Hader Ben Ali Gayland* (London, 1666); Sir Henry Sheeres, *A Discourse Touching Tanger: In A Letter to a Person of Quality* (London, 1680). *The Several Declarations of the Company of Royal Adventurers* (London, 1667).

[143] Anthony Disney, *Historiography of Europeans in Africa and Asia, 1450–1800* (Aldershot, Hampshire: Variorum, 1995), p. 57. For early narratives of Africa see P. E. Russell, "Veni, Vidi, Vici: Some Fifteenth-Century Eyewitness Accounts of Travel in the African Atlantic before 1492," *Historical Research*, 66 (June, 1993), 115–28.

[144] Wenceslaus Hollar, *Divèrs Prospects in and about Tangier ... etched in copper and are to be sold*, (London: Printed by John Ogilby, 1673).

[145] Disney, *Historiography of Europeans in Africa and Asia, 1450–1800*, introduction, xviii.

[146] Royal Society, CP, IX (1) 32. "A description of the diamond mines." Read 22 March 1676/1677. Jean-Baptiste Tavernier, *Travels in India*, trans. and ed. Valentine Ball, 2nd edn, 2 vols. (London: Oxford University Press, 1925), II, pp. 352–54. Ball commented, "There is a very important early description of the diamond mines of these regions, which is of special interest, as it gives a clue to the original sources of many names of diamond sites which are to be found in the modern literature of the subject. It was published in the *Philosophical Transactions*, XII, 1677, p. 907, having been presented to the Royal Society by the Earl Marshal of England, who was then Henry Howard, afterward Duke of Norfolk. His term of office as Earl Marshal lasted from 1672–83. I am inclined to think it may have been written by Mr. Cholmly, who is described by Sir Stryensham Master as having been engaged for several years before 1679 in making the annual purchases of diamonds for the Company, especially at the mines of Gollapalle and Mjalvalle ... this paper, published only a year after Tavernier's first edition appeared, enumerates 23 mines in the Kingdom of Golkonda, and 15 in the Kingdom of Bijapur – in all 38." Ball planned to published this paper with annotations.

22. Wenceslaus Hollar accompanied Lord Henry Howard on his embassy to Tangier where he produced several engravings of the fort and settlement for publication.
The Folger Shakespeare Library, ART 230514, Wenceslaus Hollar, Prospect of the Inner Part of Tangier (London, 1673).

of, these mines, and am able to say something of it."[147] This paper was published in the Society's *Philosophical Transactions*, and translated into French.

The paper also presented the romance of diamond mining. It told the story of a Portuguese gentleman who had begun to work a diamond mine in Currure, spending L45,000 searching for diamonds without success. On the brink of suicide, his workers found a great diamond. He took the stone to Goa where he erected a stone tablet: "Your wife and children sell, sell what you have, / Spare not your clothes, nay, make yourself a slave, / But money get, then to Currure make haste, / There search the mines, a prize you'll find at last."[148]

Luxury goods carried many meanings in seventeenth-century England: comfort, novelty, fashion, gentility, respectability, emulation, and refinement. In addition to the role of retailers, merchants, authors, artists, and publishers in creating new wants through imports and print, consumers took an active role in creating their own desires for new goods based in part on seeing, reading, and travel. Travel created intellectual, social, political, and economic networks and laid the basis for new industry, trade, science, exploration, and exploitation. To the appeal of continental manners, mentality, and refinement embodied in luxury goods, the lure of the exotic must be added. In future chapters we shall look at more of the luxury goods that travelers admired and copied and book publishers purveyed, from rarities, pictures, sculpture, building, furnishings, and gardens, to scientific instruments and inventions. Information, print, and travel created new wants that some English moved energetically to fill.

---

[147] Royal Society, CP, IX (1), 32.   [148] *Ibid.*; Tavernier, *Travels in India*, II, p. 42.

CHAPTER 4

"Anything that is strange": from rarities to luxury goods

In 1625 John Tradescant, gardener to the Earl of Salisbury and to King James I, laid out an ambitious program to collect rarities for George Villiers, Duke of Buckingham, the royal favorite who controlled most of the bounty dispensed by James I and Charles I between 1616 and 1628. Tradescant enlisted merchants, diplomats, and sea captains who traded to the New World, Asia, and Africa to aid in the quest. Writing to Sir Edward Nicholas, then Secretary of the Navy and later Secretary of State, Tradescant claimed that Buckingham wanted the biggest and strangest flora and fauna from "all places."[1] Buckingham had just returned from a diplomatic mission to Paris where he had met Peter Paul Rubens, from whom he commissioned a portrait of himself on horseback costing L500, and the Duke of Chevreuse, whose barber he hired and whose collections of "strange fowls" he admired and wished to imitate. Buckingham also brought back plants from France for Tradescant to plant at New Hall and Burley.[2] Buckingham's imports ranged from art and artificers to botanical and exotic material culture. The key words in Tradescant's program were "rare," "strange," and "biggest."

Deal with all merchants from all places but especially the Virginia and Bermuda and Newfoundland men that ... they will take care to furnish His Grace with all manner of beasts and fowls and birds alive or if not with heads, horns, beaks, claws, skins, feathers, slips or seeds, plants, trees, or shrubs. Also from Guinea or Benin or Senegal.

Tradescant suggested that Nicholas contact Sir Thomas Roe, the English envoy in Turkey and a major agent in the making of Caroline collections, as well as "Captain North to the New Plantation towards the Amasonians," and merchants and sea captains sailing to the East Indies. In particular,

---

[1] On Tradescant see Arthur MacGregor (ed.), *Tradescant's Rarities. Essays on the Foundation of the Ashmolean Museum* (Oxford: Clarendon Press, 1983).
[2] Roger Lockyer, *Buckingham: The Life and Political Career of George Villiers, First Duke of Buckingham 1592–1628* (London: Longman, 1981), p. 239.

Tradescant asked "the merchants of the Guinea Company and those who traded to the west coast of Africa" for "one elephant's head with the teeth in it, very large; one river horse's head of the biggest kind that can be gotten; one seacow's the biggest that can be gotten; one seabull's head with horns."[3]

Tradescant's interests trace themes that begin with sixteenth-century *Wunderkammern* and look forward to the Royal Society's anthropological and natural history investigations. He asked for snake skins and all kinds of fruits and flowers. Tradescant also requested the material culture of the peoples of Africa, "their habits, weapons and instruments . . . [and] their ivory long flutes." He concluded by asking generally for "anything that is strange."[4]

Defined by political, cultural, and economic discourses and practices, rarities, like luxury goods, were situated in networks of exchange forged by courtiers, diplomats, and merchants.[5] Thus, English collecting changed alongside expanding trade with Europe, Asia, Africa, and the New World in the sixteenth and seventeenth centuries. The English proved eager consumers of the novel and the exotic, domesticating, copying, displaying, and selling foreign artifacts whether they were pictures, prints, sculpture, tapestries, glass, scientific instruments, or rare flora and fauna. Political power helped to define access to these goods which were then specifically used to solicit and display political favor.

Many of the merchants and diplomats from whom Tradescant solicited rarities were clients of Buckingham's. Some took part in royally chartered joint-stock companies. The rarities Tradescant requested served as markers of patronage relationships alongside more traditional luxury goods such as gold cups and chains. For instance, Humphrey Slaney, a London merchant, who traded with Guinea, had infringed the patent of the Guinea Company. In June 1624 Secretary Conway ordered that "Upon the arrival of the next ship belonging to them or his partners, the goods are not to be allowed to land til the king's pleasure there is known."[6] Filling the Buckingham and Tradescant

---

[3] Quoted in MacGregor (ed.), *Tradescant's Rarities*, pp. 19–20. On the Guinea company see P. E. H. Hair and Robin Law, "The English in Western Africa to 1700," in Nicholas Canny (ed.), *The Oxford History of the British Empire*, 5 vols. (Oxford: Oxford University Press, 1998), I, pp. 241–63. See also John W. Blake, "The English Guinea Company, 1618–1660: An Early Example of the Charter Company in Colonial Development," *Proceedings and Reports of the Belfast Natural History and Philosophical Society*, 3 (1945/46), 14–27.

[4] MacGregor, *Tradescant's Rarities*, pp. 19–20.

[5] Arjun Appadurai (ed.), *The Social Life of Things, Commodities in Cultural Perspective* (Cambridge: Cambridge University Press, 1986); Chandra Mukerji, *From Graven Images: Patterns of Modern Materialism* (New York: Columbia University Press, 1983).

[6] *CSPD 1623–25*, p. 268, Secretary Conway to the officers of the port of London (6 June 1624).

shopping list in 1625 could only help Slaney's position. In 1626, Slaney requested Buckingham's help in the return of his ship taken by pirates.[7]

This chapter continues to examine how new wants were created, specifically, at the connection of collecting to luxury consumption. It looks at the ways in which collectors and their agents formed two types of new collections, first natural history and second, painting and sculpture, the cultural meanings attached to these goods by their owners, and how observers read them. Publication of natural history and artistic collections through books and prints displayed these collections to the public. Thus, collecting stimulated a larger audience's desire for new luxury goods through report, copying, the secondhand market, prints, and early museums. Indeed, alongside the shop, the theatre, and public gardens, early museums provided well-to-do men and women with a new and important public space in which to meet and to gaze on the foreign, the exotic, the precious, and the curious. Finally, the chapter considers the critique that accompanied new sorts of collecting, a critique with political as well as moral overtones.

WUNDERKAMMERN

English collections in the seventeenth century included *Wunderkammern* and *studiolo* which emulated new forms of collecting that had developed from the fifteenth century in Burgundy, Italy, and at the Habsburg court.[8] Coins, medals, gems, and sculpture, uncovered in Italy, Greece, and Turkey became the object of collectors in Western Europe. In fifteenth-century France, Jean Duc de Berry expanded the traditional medieval treasure of regalia, relics, and illustrated manuscripts by collecting natural curiosities from expeditions such as ostrich eggs and coconuts, alongside antique coins and sculpture.[9]

Sixteenth-century encyclopedic collections of strange animals, plants, and artifacts reflected Renaissance philosophy and its burning desire to understand the natural and physical world. The Italian *studiolo*, put together by leading collectors such as the Medici, brought together rarities in a special room or cabinet for examination and study, a place to display the wonderful to amazed viewers.[10] Continuing this tradition, Jacobean and Caroline collectors, like the Earl of Arundel and William Murray, built special cabinets in the 1620s and 1630s to display their collections of

---

[7] *CSPD 1625–26*, p. 251, 8 February 1626.
[8] Arthur MacGregor, "Collectors and Collections of Rarities in the Sixteenth and Seventeenth Centuries," in MacGregor (ed.), *Tradescant's Rarities*, pp. 70–97.
[9] *Ibid.*   [10] *Ibid.*

paintings, drawings, gems, and medals. The *studiolo* also proved a pre-cursor to early scientific academies. When Georgio Vasari planned a series of wall decorations for the *studiolo* next to the treasure room in the palace of Francesco de Medici, he included an alchemical laboratory, glass works, and dyers with a heated vat lined with copper or lead.[11]

Alongside the curiosities of the animal and plant world, the *Wunderkammer* displayed the material culture of other peoples. In the sixteenth century, Spanish explorers sent back gold, silver, and stone treasures from Mexico, one of the great sources for these wonders.[12] Displaying different cultures together helped to underpin a narrative of classic and barbarian, pagan and Christian contact.[13] It has been argued that there were few *Wunderkammern* in England. Some scholars suggest that collecting and connoisseurship were pastimes for melancholic aristo-crats down on their luck.[14]

Many English collectors, such as William Camden, Sir Robert Cotton, and Lord William Howard of Naworth, were more interested in English antiquities than in natural wonders.[15] They put together important collec-tions of Roman British, Anglo-Saxon, and medieval artifacts and manu-scripts. These collections of British antiquities shaped new types of organizations such as the Elizabethan Society of Antiquaries. At monthly meetings from 1587, antiquaries, heralds, and gentlemen gathered to dis-cuss Britain's ancient institutions, using their own collections of manu-scripts and coins to support their arguments. Their papers circulated in manuscript. Some were published during the English Civil War and collected in print in the eighteenth century.[16] Yet, while English collectors

---

[11] Charles J. Singer, A. Rupert Hall, and Eric J. Holmhyarde (eds.), *From the Renaissance to the Industrial Revolution, c. 1500–c. 1750*, vol. III of *A History of Technology*, 8 vols. (Oxford: Clarendon Press, 1955–1978), plate 2813.

[12] John Elsner and Roger Cardinal (eds.), *Cultures of Collecting* (London: Reaktion Books, 1994).

[13] Anthony Alan Shelton, "Cabinets of Transgression: Renaissance Collections and the Incorporation of the New World," in Elsner and Cardinal (eds.), *Cultures of Collecting*, pp. 177–203; Thomas Da Costa Kaufmann, "From Treasury to Museum: The Collections of the Austrian Hapsburgs," in Elsner and Cardinal (eds.), *Cultures of Collecting*, pp. 137–54.

[14] William Eamon, *Science and the Secrets of Nature: Books of Secrets in Medieval and Early Modern Culture* (Princeton: Princeton University Press, 1994), p. 304.

[15] See Kevin Sharpe, *Sir Robert Cotton, 1586–1631: History and Politics in Early Modern England* (Oxford: Oxford University Press, 1979), pp. 17–48. On Camden and the collections he inspired, see Leslie W. Hepple, "William Camden and Early Collections of Roman Antiquities in Britain," *Journal of the History of Collections*, 15 (2003), 159–73. *Sir Robert Cotton as Collector: Essays on an Early Stuart Courtier and his Legacy*, ed. C. J. Wright (London: British Museum, 1997).

[16] On the Elizabethan Society of Antiquaries see Linda Van Nordern, "The Elizabethan Society of Antiquaries" (Ph.D. dissertation, UCLA, 1946); Thomas Hearne, *A Collection of Curious Discourses Written by Eminent Antiquaries upon Several Heads in our English Antiquities*, 2 vols. (London, 1771).

were not as interested in *Wunderkammern* as continental collectors in Italy, Germany, Scandinavia, France, and the Low Countries, rarities did interest more people of different social status than usually thought. This chapter suggests that, in addition to its philosophical meanings, *Wunderkammern*, and English collecting more generally, reflected European trade, exploration and exploitation, and new historical and scientific investigation.

Wunderkammern demanded an audience. Prestige was conferred not merely by private ownership but by public display. The materials for *Wunderkammern* were almost always imported and included not only foreign flora and fauna but also artifacts created with the new optics including wonders such as a chess set within a hazelnut and a cherrystone with sixty faces carved on it.[17] While the goods were rare and not for sale, their display to well-connected visitors, recorded in continental paintings and prints,[18] resembled the display of luxury goods in the shops in the inner sanctum of the New Exchange. The gaze of admiring visitors conferred honor on both collector and viewer alike.

Sir Walter Cope possessed the best-known *Wunderkammer* in England in the late sixteenth and early seventeenth centuries. Cope, who held office at both the Elizabethan and Jacobean courts, had close ties to the Earl of Salisbury.[19] A member of the Elizabethan Society of Antiquaries, Cope and his collections reflected the geographical range of English trade and the rage for novelty. Thomas Platter, who visited Cope in 1599, described his apartment as "stuffed with queer foreign objects . . . a long narrow Indian canoe, with the oars and sliding planks, hung from the ceiling of this room." Platter noticed all sorts of exotic clothing, instruments, and furnishings from Africa and Asia such as "an African charm made of teeth . . . beautiful Indian plumes . . . shoes from many strange lands." Goods from the New World included "A Madonna made of Indian feathers," the sort of artifact much prized by the Spanish. There were wonders of natural history such as "the horn and tail of a rhinoceros, is a large animal like an elephant," "a unicorn's tail," and "flies which glow at night in Virginia instead of lights, since there is often no day there for over a month." Platter noted that there were others "in London interested in curios, but this gentleman is superior

---

[17] The Tradescant museum included a cherrystone "upon one side St. George and the Dragon, perfectly cut: and on the other side 88 emperors faces," John Tradescant, Jr., *Musaeum Tradescantianum* (London, 1656), a2–a3.

[18] On the emergence of cabinet pictures see Jonathan Brown, *Kings and Connoisseurs: Collecting Art in Seventeenth-Century Europe* (Princeton: Princeton University Press, 1994), pp. 153–58.

[19] Julia F. Merritt, "The Cecils and Westminster, 1558–1612: The Development of an Urban Power Base," in Pauline Croft (ed.), *Patronage, Culture and Power: The Early Cecils, 1558–1612* (New Haven: Yale University Press, 2002), pp. 234, 239–40.

to them all for strange objects, because of the Indian voyage he carried out with such zeal."[20] Cope also owned goods from China including "ornaments and clothes," "an artful little Chinese box," earthen pitchers, and porcelain. As we have seen, such china was increasingly imported, sold, and imitated in seventeenth-century England.[21]

John Tradescant, who energetically sought the most exotic flora and fauna for the Duke of Buckingham, first became a botanical collector through his work as a gardener for the Earl of Salisbury while Hatfield House was under construction in 1609.[22] The Hatfield gardens were stocked with 30,000 vines which the Queen of France and the wife of the French ambassador sent to Salisbury.[23] In 1611 Tradescant went to the Low Countries and to France to bring back fruit trees and flowers. While in Paris, Tradescant saw his friend Jean Robin, gardener to the French king, who sold him pomegranate and fig trees and "other rare shrubs."[24] On this trip, Tradescant brought back almost one thousand plants to adorn Hatfield. While Salisbury's growing interest in fruit trees borrowed French court style, it also reflected King James's campaign, in imitation of Henry IV, to grow mulberry trees in England. Later, under Charles I, Tradescant became Keeper of the Mulberry Gardens in St. James.[25] The Mulberry Gardens, begun as part of the silk project, became a favorite place for Londoners to socialize in public.

At the same time, Tradescant created another new public space. After leaving Buckingham's employ, Tradescant moved to South Lambeth where he publicly displayed his natural history collections in his museum called "The Ark." Tradescant's collecting for Salisbury, Buckingham, and King Charles brought him flora and fauna from all over the world alongside the cultural artifacts of far-flung cultures. Tradescant's rarities drew visitors to admire, to wonder, and to contribute.

The *Musaeum Tradescantianum*, published in 1656, lists over 100 donors to Tradescant's collections.[26] It documents gifts from a wide range of Jacobean and Caroline courtiers, officeholders, merchants, diplomats,

[20] *Thomas Platter's Travels in England, 1599*, ed. Clare Williams (London: Jonathan Cape, 1937), pp. 171–73. Cope also had a collection of coins and pictures. Philip, Duke of Stettin, visited Cope's collection in 1602. MacGregor, "The Tradescants as Collectors of Rarities," in *Tradescant's Rarities*, p. 18. Platter noted that "in one house on the Thames bridge I also beheld a large live camel."

[21] See chapter 1 above.

[22] MacGregor (ed.), *Tradescant's Rarities*, pp. 3–16; Prudence Leith-Ross, *The John Tradescants, Gardeners to the Rose and Lily Queen* (London: P. Owen, 1984).

[23] MacGregor (ed.), *Tradescant's Rarities*, p. 4.

[24] Quoted in *ibid*, p. 5.   [25] Leith-Ross, *The John Tradescants*, pp. 9–34.

[26] John Tradescant, Jr., *Musaeum Tradescantianum* (London, 1656), a2–a3.

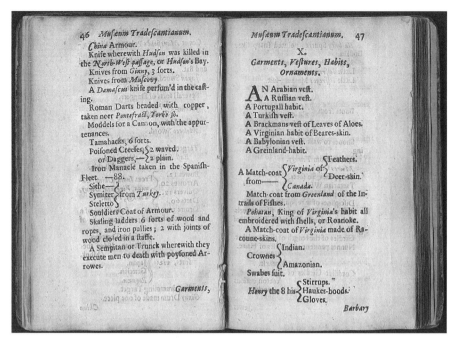

23. John Tradescant created the first natural history museum in London in the early seventeenth century made up of rarities from around the world contributed by courtiers, merchants, and sea captains. His son published this catalog in the 1650s.
 The Folger Shakespeare Library, 154794, John Tradescant, Jr., *Musaeum Tradescantianum* (London, 1656).

and sea captains. Tradescant's letter of 1625 had evidently not been in vain. Tradescant's patrons included a larger group of enthusiasts for the curious and the exotic than scholars have usually pictured and shows how the Tradescant collection was put together. Although published in the 1650s, the donor list reflects collecting from the beginning of the reign of James I through the 1620s and 1630s.[27]

English men and women with interests in art and science contributed to Tradescant's collections. Tradescant's benefactors include the first and second Earls of Salisbury, Salisbury's decorators Rowland Buckett and Richard Butler, and Michael Hicks, a Jacobean officeholder with strong ties to the Cecils. The Duke of Buckingham and several of his relatives,

---

[27] Leith-Ross, *The John Tradescants*, pp. 163–80; April London, "Musaeum Tradescantianum and the Benefactors to the Tradescants' Museum," in MacGregor (ed.), *Tradescant's Rarities*, pp. 24–39. Although the catalog was published in 1656 the evidence suggests that its holdings were in place by the 1630s, p. 25.

both male and female, and Aletheia Talbot, Countess of Arundel, and her daughter-in-law, Lady Maltravers, contributed to Tradescant's Ark. Secretary Nicholas, to whom Tradescant appealed for rarities in 1625, gave as did Archbishop Laud. The Bacon circle, including Sir Nathaniel Bacon, the landscape artist, Mary, Lady Killigrew, Bacon's niece and wife of Sir Robert Killigrew, Van Dyck's patrons,[28] and Thomas Bushell, Bacon's secretary, made gifts to Tradescant. Later, in the 1630s, Bushell created his own grotto and collected mummies.[29]

Leading diplomats such as Sir Henry Wotton, Sir Thomas Roe, and Dudley Carleton, Viscount Dorchester, who were agents in the making of English art collections, also provided Tradescant with rarities, as did collectors such as Sir Clipsby Crew, Sir Kenelm Digby, William Murray, George Goring, and George Gage. Merchants such as Baptist Hicks, John Slaney, and William Courteen, whose son became a notable collector, contributed to Tradescant. Courtiers with connections to the trading companies, such as Dudley Digges with interests in Virginia and the Levant and Henry Cary, Viscount Falkland, with investments in New World fishing, presented gifts to Tradescant. Tradescant had accompanied Digges and Sir William Boswell to Russia and kept a journal of the trip.[30] Navy officials, including Sir John Trevor and Phineas Pett, and eleven ship captains, contributed artifacts to the Tradescant Museum. So did Francis Cleyn, the artist and designer of the Mortlake tapestries, Richard Butler, one of the great London glass designers who worked for the Earl of Salisbury,[31] and Caspar Kalthoff, a Dutch inventor and patentee who worked for the second Earl of Worcester. Beginning in 1628, Kalthoff created engines to raise water from mine shafts and to propel boats and carriages, some of which Worcester later presented to the Royal Society.[32]

The Tradescant list of benefactors suggests that men and women of different social status in early Stuart England became part of the process of acquiring and admiring exotic objects for Tradescant's *Wunderkammer* even if they did not put one together for themselves. The Tradescant treasures included both natural and artificial objects. One contemporary

[28] Karen Hearn, "Sir Anthony Van Dyck, Portrait of Sir William Killigrew, 1638," *British Art in Focus*, Patrons' Papers 6 (London: Tate, 2003).

[29] On Bushell see Leith-Ross, *The John Tradescants*, p. 176.

[30] London, "Musaeum Tradescantianum and the Benefactors to the Tradescants' Museum," in MacGregor (ed.), *Tradescant's Rarities*, pp. 29, 18. On Courten, see Carole Gibson-Wood, "Classification and Value in a Seventeenth-Century Museum: William Courten's collection," *Journal of the History of Collections*, 9 (1997), 61–77.

[31] Leith-Ross, *The John Tradescants*, p. 177.   [32] *Ibid.*, p. 179 and see chapter 8 below.

visitor to the Ark in 1634 described the range of artifacts: "beasts, fowl, fishes, serpents, worms, . . . precious stones and other arms, coins, shells, feathers . . . of sundry nations . . . a little garden with diverse outlandish herbs and flowers, whereof some that I had not seen elsewhere but in India, being supplied by noblemen, gentlemen, sea commanders . . . with such toys as they could bring or procure from other parts."[33]

Tradescant's 1656 catalog included the curious, the foreign, the useful, and the strange. "Outlandish fruits from both the Indies, with seeds, gums, roots, woods, and divers ingredients medicinal and for the art of dying" mingled with "warlike instruments" from around the world. Tradescant displayed curious clothing and ornament including "Pohatan, King of Virginia's habit all embroidered with shells."[34] Significantly, *Musaeum Tradescantianum* gave English names to many items even those "less familiar and as yet unfitted with apt English terms . . . for the ready satisfying whomsoever may desire a view thereof."[35]

The contemporary celebration and appropriation of nature and nature's wonders had its critics. In 1634 John Milton wrote *Comus* as an entertainment for the inauguration of the Earl of Bridgewater as Lord President of Wales at Ludlow Castle. Comus, son of Circe, lives in the woods, the leader of an antic crew. Comus exalts the bounty of nature and links it to worldly wealth, possession, and display in a way that might not sound strange to the silk projectors, the Duke of Buckingham, Tradescant, and Bernard Mandeville at the end of the seventeenth century:

> Wherefore did nature pour her bounties forth
> With such a full and unwithdrawing hand,
> Covering the earth with odors, fruits and flocks,
> Thronging the seas with spawn innumerable,
> But all to please and sate the curious taste?
> And set to work millions of spinning worms
> That in their green shops weave the smooth-hair'd silk
> To deck her sons; and that no corner might
> Be vacant of her plenty, in her loins
> . . . if all the world
> Should in a pet of temperance feed on pulse,
> Drink the clear stream, And nothing wear but friese,
> The all-giver would be unthankt, would be unprais'd,
> Not half his riches known, and yet dispis'd

---

[33] Quoted in Leith-Ross, *The John Tradescants*, p. 154.

[34] Quoted in Bent Juel-Jenson, "Musaeum Clausum, or Bibliotheca Abscondita, Some Thoughts on Curiosity Cabinets and Imaginary Books," *Journal of the History of Collections*, 4 (1992), 132.

[35] Tradescant, Jr., *Musaeum Tradescantianum*, a2v–a3.

And we should serve him as a grudging master,
As a penurious niggard of his wealth.[36]

According to Comus, nature offered her bounty to fulfill the unending wants of those who explored and exploited its riches. But for Milton, to appropriate nature's riches "to please and sate the curious taste," was nothing less than luxury and, therefore, immoral. Milton's heroine, "The Lady," whom Comus waylaid, argues against those who monopolize nature's bounty and are immoderate in their desires.

> If every just man that now pines with want
> Had but a moderate and beseeming share
> Of that which lewedly-pamper'd luxury
> Now heaps upon some few with vast excess,
> Nature's full blessings would be well dispens't.

Milton condemns the misuse of natural abundance and the taste for the "curious," so common among his contemporaries. Though women were traditionally accused of luxurious appetites, Milton uses "The Lady" to censor them in Comus.

In contrast to such criticism, the dedicatory poem to John Tradescant in *Musaeum Tradescantianum*, published in the midst of the Protectorate in 1656, argues that his collecting reflected a prelapsarian view of the world and sought to minimize Tradescant's connections to the Stuart court.

> Nor court, nor shop-crafts were thine arts but those
> Which Adam studied ere he did transgress:
> The wonders of the creatures, and to dress
> The worlds great garden. Sure the sun ne'er rose
> Nor couch'd, but blush'd to see thy roof enclose
> More dainties than his orb. Can death oppress
> Such honest art as this, or make it less?
> No: fame shall still record it, and expose
> Industrious care to all eternity.
> Die the body may, and must: arts cannot die.

In the midst of the Interregnum, John Tradescant, Jr., sought to expand the audience for his father's collection to include scientists, artisans, and the nation as a whole. He explained "To the Ingenious Reader" why he had put together the catalog. "That the enumeration of these rarities (being more for variety than any one place known in Europe could afford) would be an honour to our nation, and a benefit to such ingenious persons as would

---

[36] John Milton, *Comus* (London, 1637), lines 709–26.

become further enquirers into the various modes of nature's admirable works, and the curious imitators thereof."[37] Elias Ashmole gave the Tradescant collection to Oxford University in 1677 where it formed the basis for the Ashmolean Museum.[38] As we shall see, ingenuity, curiosity, and imitation, hallmarks of English collecting in the early seventeenth century, led in two directions, to connoisseurship and to invention, manufacture, and marketing.

PAINTINGS AND SCULPTURE

Painting and sculpture were integral parts of the performance of royal and aristocratic power at Renaissance courts.[39] Pictures, even objects of devotion released from a place on the church wall, became collectors' items in fifteenth-century Italy. Henry VII and Henry VIII brought Italian artists to their courts in the first half of the sixteenth century. By the seventeenth century, separate art galleries and libraries grew up alongside the *Wunderkammern*, both in Italy and northern Europe.[40] Art works became luxury objects as they increasingly became the medium of exchange between ambassadors and favorites, kings and courtiers, and clients and patrons. The fevered search for sixteenth-century Italian pictures became a phenomenon. Although prices never reached dizzying heights, copying increased to meet demand. The display and reproduction of these pictures made them available to a wider audience.

In his article on art and economics, David Ormrod poses a central question: how can we explain "the growing urge to own and display pictures as commodities?"[41] Distinguished analysts including Oliver Millar, Francis Haskell, and David Howarth have focused on the Caroline court as the center of the new taste and connoisseurship for Italian pictures in England.[42] Yet this taste did not begin with Charles I but expanded earlier during the reign of James VI of Scotland and Anne of Denmark, who

---

[37] Tradescant, Jr., *Musaeum Tradescantianum*, "To the Ingenious Reader."

[38] MacGregor (ed.), *Tradescant's Rarities*, pp. 40–45.

[39] See David Howarth, *Images of Rule: Art and Politics in the English Renaissance, 1485–1649* (Berkeley: University of California Press, 1997); R. Malcolm Smuts, *Culture and Power in England, 1585–1685* (New York: St. Martin's Press, 1999).

[40] Kaufmann, "From Treasury to Museum: the Collections of the Austrian Habsburgs," pp. 137–54.

[41] David Ormrod, "Art and its Markets," *Economic History Review*, 52 (1999), 544–51.

[42] Oliver Millar (ed.), "Abraham van der Doort's Catalogue of the Collections of Charles I," *Walpole Society*, 37 (1960); Francis Haskell, "Charles I's Collection of Pictures," in Arthur MacGregor (ed.), *The Late King's Goods: Collections, Possessions and Patronage of Charles I in the Light of the Commonwealth Sale Inventories* (Oxford: Oxford University Press, 1989), pp. 203–31; David Howarth, *Lord Arundel and his Circle* (New Haven: Yale University Press, 1985). See also Jeremy

ascended the English throne in 1603. On his first trip to England in 1629, Peter Paul Rubens wrote that

This island seems to me to be a spectacle worthy of interest of every gentleman ... not only for the splendour of the outward culture, which seems to be extreme ... but also for the incredible quality of excellent pictures, statues, and ancient inscriptions which are to be found in this court ... Certainly in this island I find none of the crudeness which one might expect from a place so remote from Italian elegance.[43]

Splendor and elegance became aspirations to be met, in part, through the purchase of continental art and classical monuments.

Rubens's analysis of English collecting might have been far different in 1599, the year that Thomas Platter lauded Sir Walter Cope's *Wunderkammer*. In the Elizabethan period, serried ranks of ancestors lined the long galleries of Elizabethan country houses. Most picture collections contained portraits of family members and the great, copies given or bought by patrons, kin, and admirers. Thus, portraits of Queen Elizabeth in all sizes proliferated, produced by workshops, and sold in London and the countryside.[44] If the collector was eminent enough, such as the Earl of Leicester, foreign leaders presented their likeness to him as diplomatic gifts.[45]

Inventories taken at death often do not accurately reflect the holdings of those who may have already given away some of their possessions. Nevertheless, they provide some insight into the role of art works in constructing identity. The inventory of 1596 of Lettice Knollys, the widowed Countess of Leicester,[46] certainly reflects only a small part of the Earl of Leicester's picture collection.[47] But it records portraits of the Prince of Orange, his wife and son, and Mary of Hungary, Regent in the Netherlands. Leicester probably acquired such portraits when he led the English forces in the Netherlands in the 1580s. There were also seven small

Wood, "Van Dyck and the Earl of Northumberland: Taste and Collecting in Stuart England," in Susan T. Barnes and Arthur K. Wheelock (eds.), *Studies in the History of Art* (Washington, DC: National Gallery, 1994), pp. 280–324.

[43] Quoted in Christopher White, *Peter Paul Rubens: Man and Artist* (New Haven: Yale University Press, 1987), p. 225.

[44] Sir Roy Strong, *The Cult of Elizabeth: Elizabethan Portraiture and Pageantry* (London: Thames and Hudson, 1977); *The English Icon: Elizabethan and Jacobean Portraiture* (London: Paul Mellon Foundation for British Art, in association with Routledge and Kegan Paul, 1969).

[45] Oxford, Bodleian, Mss. Eng. Hist. c. 120, f. 35ff. An inventory 23 April 1596 of goods of the Countess of Leicester and Sir Christopher Blount. Simon Lester Adams, *Leicester and the Court: Essays on Elizabethan Politics* (Manchester: Manchester, University Press, 2002).

[46] Oxford, Bodleian, Mss. Eng. Hist. c. 120, f. 35ff.

[47] See J. O. Halliwell-Phillips, "An Inventory of the Plate, Household Stuff, Pictures etc in Kenilworth Castle, Taken after the Death of Robert Earl of Leycester, 1588," in *Ancient Inventories ... Illustrative of the Domestic Manners of the English in the 16th and 17th Centuries* (London, 1854). See Adams, *Leicester and the Court*.

Flanders pictures and eight maps. Surprisingly, Lettice Knollys's inventory does not include a portrait of Queen Elizabeth although there are portraits of Robert Cecil, members of the Knollys family, the Countess's relatives, women friends, and an unfinished picture of a woman with roses, perhaps herself.[48]

Portraits, from full length to miniature, continued to be a major part of English art collections in the seventeenth century. The most eminent subjects were on display in public rooms; the most personal saved for the bedroom or the closet, the inner sanctum off the gallery. For example, Henry Howard, Earl of Northampton, placed his large art collection throughout Northampton House on the Strand and his house in Greenwich. It included some religious pictures but most were portraits of the Howard family and its connections, including two of Mary Queen of Scots. In his bedroom, he gazed on the images of King James, Mary, Queen of Scots, and the Virgin Mary.[49] Lionel Cranfield, London merchant and, later, Lord Treasurer, displayed portraits of the Countess of Buckingham, King James, Henry IV of France, King Charles, several court ladies, and the Infanta, ruler of the Spanish Netherlands, in his great gallery at Chelsea. In his closet, he placed folding pictures of Luther and of Jesus.[50]

The royal households of King James, Anne of Denmark, Prince Henry, and Prince Charles, and the urban aristocracy that surrounded them in London, established new patterns of art collecting.[51] James created a new British elite, made up of some members of the Scottish aristocracy, such as the Dukes of Lennox, and the Marquis of Hamilton; great English noble families like the Howards and the Percys whose ambitions were unfulfilled by Queen Elizabeth; and Elizabethan officials, most notably Robert Cecil, Earl of Salisbury.[52] This new elite sought to emulate continental court taste. Their demand for continental pictures and antique sculpture shaped demand for more than a century.[53] Even the Civil War could not rupture it.

---

[48] Oxford, Bodleian, Mss. Eng. Hist. c. 120. The same inventory provides "A note of the late Earl of Essex his goods," which includes armor, jewels, and books but no pictures.

[49] Linda Levy Peck, "The Mentality of the Jacobean Grandee," in Linda Levy Peck (ed.), *The Mental World of the Jacobean Court* (Cambridge: Cambridge University Press, 1991), pp. 148–68.

[50] Centre for Kentish Studies, Sackville papers, U269/1, E 16.

[51] R. Malcolm Smuts, "Cultural Diversity and Cultural Change at the Court of James I," in Peck (ed.), *The Mental World of the Jacobean Court*, pp. 99–112.

[52] See Croft, *Patronage, Culture and Power*; Linda Levy Peck, *Northampton: Patronage and Policy at the Court of James I* (London: Allen and Unwin, 1982).

[53] See Smuts, "Cultural Diversity and Cultural Change at the Court of James I," pp. 99–112; also R. Malcolm Smuts, *Court Culture and the Origins of a Royalist Tradition in Early Stuart England* (Philadelphia: University of Pennsylvania Press, 1987); and J. C. Robertson, "Caroline Culture: Bridging Court and Country," *History*, 75 (1990), 388–416.

24. Miniatures provided a popular sixteenth- and seventeenth-century form in which to present important portraits. Collections of miniatures were displayed in cabinets in the closet or in the bedroom. Images of the monarch and his family were especially popular. The Folger Shakespeare Library, Painting m11, King James I. Miniature, *c.* 1620?

25. The Folger Shakespeare Library, Painting m12, Anne of Denmark. Miniature, *c.* 1620?

26. The Folger Shakespeare Library, Painting m13, Peter Oliver, Henry Frederick, Prince of Wales. Miniature, early 1610s.

Jacobeans imported pictures, sculptures, and the decorative arts as early as the first decade of the new reign. In contrast to the sixteenth-century focus on the Low Countries and English portraiture, James's courtiers and officials collected Italian art. Venetian artists were already fashionable. Sir Philip Sidney had commissioned Veronese to do his portrait while he was in Venice in the 1580s.[54] The Earl of Leicester displayed Venetian paintings both in London and in the country in the 1580s.[55] As we saw in the previous chapter, William Lord Burghley had urged the Earl of Shrewsbury to buy large Venetian canvases in 1609.[56] Prince Henry himself began a collection which included Italian sculpture and pictures. James I bought a cabinet of medals belonging to Abraham Gorlaeus, the Antwerp collector, for

---

[54] See Blair Worden, *The Sound of Virtue: Philip Sidney's Arcadia and Elizabethan Politics* (New Haven: Yale University Press, 1996).

[55] Paul Shakeshaft, "Too Much Bewiched With Thoes Intysing Things": The Letters of James, Third Marquis of Hamilton and Basil, Viscount Feilding, Concerning Collecting in Venice 1635–1639," *Burlington Magazine*, 128 (1986), 116.

[56] J. Irene Whalley, "Italian Art and English Taste: An Early-Seventeenth-Century Letter," *Apollo*, 94 (1971), 184.

Prince Henry in 1610.[57] Perhaps the earliest Venetian pictures to arrive at the English court came in Sir Philip Burlamachi's shipment for Prince Henry also in 1610.[58] Northampton's collections reflected the increasing Jacobean interest in Italian works of art. When he died in 1614, he owned "fourteen Venetian paintings of one bigness" brought back from Italy by his great nephew and namesake, Henry Howard, son of Thomas Howard, Earl of Suffolk.[59]

The Duke of Tuscany gave Prince Henry fifteen statuettes by Giovanni Bologna (Gianbologna) in 1612 as a gift to promote the marriage of the Prince of Wales to his sister, Caterina de Medici. Indeed, the Medici had used Gianbologna's bronzes as diplomatic gifts since the 1560s. By 1612, however, a single bronze would not suffice. After Gianbologna's death, his workshop reproduced considerable numbers of his models. The Prince, thrilled with the sculptures, placed them himself in his cabinet at Richmond.[60]

Women were active patrons, ordering pictures, commissioning build-ings, and purchasing luxury goods.[61] Queen Anne commissioned Inigo Jones to design the Queen's House at Greenwich in 1616 as well as the decorative gate and silk house at Oatlands. She filled her London palace, Denmark House, with exotic furnishings including ebony cabinets, Chinese carpets, porcelain, and looking glasses.[62] The Queen loved jewelry and amassed a major collection of gems.[63] The inventory taken after her death in 1619 showed portraits of European royalty, Jacobean courtiers, Italian, English, and Dutch landscapes, and Dutch interior scenes. The Queen, who had converted to Roman Catholicism, had in her bedroom

---

[57] Ashmolean Museum, *Thomas Howard, Earl of Arundel: Patronage and Collecting in the Seventeenth Century*, ed. David Howarth and Nicholas Penney (Oxford: Ashmolean Museum, 1985), p. 71. Timothy Wilks, "The Court Culture of Prince Henry and his Circle, 1603–1613" (D.Phil. thesis, Oxford, 1987). Roy Strong, *Henry, Prince of Wales, and England's Lost Renaissance* (London: Thames and Hudson, 1986).

[58] Timothy Wilks, "Art Collecting at the English Court from the Death of Henry, Prince of Wales, to the Death of Anne of Denmark," *Journal of the History of Collections*, 9 (1997), 31–48.

[59] E. P. Shirley, "An Inventory of the Effects of Henry Howard, K. G., Earl of Northampton, Taken on his Death in 1614, Together with a Transcript of his Will," . . . *Archaeologia*, 42 (1869), 364; Peck, "The Mentality of the Jacobean Grandee," p. 166.

[60] Katharine Watson and Charles Avery, "Medici and Stuart: A Grand Ducal Gift of 'Giovanni Bologna' Bronzes for Henry Prince of Wales (1612)," *Burlington Magazine*, 115 (1973), 493–507.

[61] See chapter 1 above and chapter 5 below.

[62] M. T. W. Payne, "An Inventory of Queen Anne of Denmark's 'Ornaments, Furniture, Householde Stuff, and Other Parcells' at Denmark House, 1619," *Journal of the History of Collections*, 13 (2001), 23–44.

[63] Diana Scarrisbrick, "Anne of Denmark's Jewelry Inventory," *Archaeologia*, 109 (1991), 193–238.

several pictures of Jesus and one of Mary Magdalen.[64] Her Lady in Waiting, Lucy Harrington, Countess of Bedford, spent much of her time at court where she joined the quest for Italian pictures.[65] The Earl and Countess of Arundel made their crucial visit to Italy with Inigo Jones in 1613–14, setting the pattern of collecting not only for themselves but also for many others at the English court.

Royal favorites also took an important role in seventeenth-century collecting.[66] Robert Carr, Earl of Somerset, and George Villiers, Duke of Buckingham, became proponents of the taste for new continental designs, luxury goods, and art. Until the recent work of A. R. Braunmuller and Timothy Wilks, Carr, the young Scot, had not been known as an art collector.[67] In fact, he began to be interested in European art as early as 1612. Writing on Carr's behalf, Sir Thomas Overbury asked William Trumbull, the English ambassador in the Low Countries, "If upon the death of any great man in that country, you can help my Lord of Rochester to any good bargain of excellent hangings at second-hand, or pictures or any household stuff which they have there better than ours, it would be a very acceptable service to my lord."[68] The inventory of Carr's goods taken immediately after his fall in 1615 shows a full-fledged collection of Italian High Renaissance, and Mannerist pictures. Dudley Carleton, then English ambassador in Venice and later ambassador to the Hague, put it together for him.[69]

The Duke of Buckingham was one of the great collectors of the early seventeenth century. Along with Charles I, Arundel, and the second and third Marquises of Hamilton, he collected Italian pictures, European decorative arts, and antique sculpture. Buckingham bought Rubens's gem collection in 1626 and in 1627 bought the painter's collection of pictures and sculpture.[70] His imported furniture reflected his collecting interests

---

[64] Payne, "An Inventory of Queen Anne's Household," 23–44.

[65] Karen Hearn, "Lucy Harrington, as Art Patron and Collector" (MA thesis, Courtauld Institute, 1990).

[66] Sir John Elliott and Laurence Brockliss, *The World of the Favourite* (New Haven: Yale University Press, 1999).

[67] A. R. Braunmuller, "Robert Carr, Earl of Somerset, as Collector and Patron," in Peck (ed.), *The Mental World of the Jacobean Court*, pp. 230–50; T. Wilks, "The Picture Collection of Robert Carr, Earl of Somerset," *Journal of the History of Collections*, 1 (1989), 167–77; Wilks, "Art Collecting at the English Court," 31–48.

[68] Quoted in Henry Vining Ogden and Margaret Sinclair Ogden, *English Taste in Landscape in the Seventeenth Century* (Ann Arbor: University of Michigan Press, 1955), p. 19 n. 5, citing HMC *Downshire* III, 369.

[69] Folger L. b. 638; Oxford, Bodleian Mss. Eng. Hist. Mss. c. 120.

[70] François Portier, "Prices Paid for Italian Pictures in the Stuart Age," *Journal of the History of Collections*, 8 (1996), 58.

too. In 1628 Buckingham acquired a tortoiseshell cabinet from Antwerp, perhaps through Van Dyck, decorated with copies of pictures by Paolo Veronese and Domenico Feti.[71] Indeed, fame gained from collecting and display became a new aspect of aristocratic identity alongside accomplishments on the battlefield. Power was made manifest not only through hosts of retainers but also by emulation of the greatest collectors at the Spanish, Italian, French, and Low Countries courts.[72]

Arundel spelled out the ideological meaning of his own taste, connecting family, fame, and collecting, in the will he drafted in 1617.[73] Although descended from the Dukes of Norfolk who, from the Wars of the Roses on, had distinguished themselves on the battlefield, Arundel was neither a military leader nor a county magnate. King James had restored him to most if not all of his titles at his accession. His father died in the Tower as a recusant under Elizabeth. Arundel himself was not wealthy. Of the King he wrote, "My house still smarts for the wounds it hath received for his mother and him."[74] To support his collecting, he sold Norfolk lands. During his first trip to Italy, he pawned two gold rings set with diamonds in Genoa in 1614 which he repaid and reclaimed some months later.[75] His marriage to the wealthy heiress Aletheia Talbot rescued his fortunes and enabled them both to become major collectors. Arundel's will praised his wife, to whom he gave most of his goods and chattels, and his mother, urging them both to see that his children were educated in virtue, "that they may never see the horrible and impious breeding ... which this latter age is fallen into." Arundel asked his young son James to

succeed me in my love and reverence to antiquities and all things of art, I give unto him all my statues and pictures whatsoever with all inscriptions or monuments of stone which I desire he may take so much a love unto as that he may increase those I leave. Howsoever, I charge him deeply that he never part with any of those things, which (God knoweth), I have gathered with so much travail and charge. I give him all my books, manuscripts or others that he may delight in learning and languages, fit for a nobleman.

---

[71] Monique Riccardi-Cubitt, "The Duke of Buckingham's Cabinet d'Amateur," *British Art Journal*, 1 (2000), 77–86.

[72] See Sarah Schroth, "The Private Picture Collection of the Duke of Lerma" (Ph.D. thesis, New York University, 1990). Neither Carr's holdings nor Buckingham's could match the largest European collection. Philip III's favorite, the Duke of Lerma, in the first decade of the seventeenth century had 2,000 pictures.

[73] John Newman, "A Draft Will of the Earl of Arundel," *Burlington Magazine*, 122 (1980), 692–96. Howarth, *Lord Arundel and his Circle*, pp. 105, 209–10.

[74] Newman, "A Draft will of the Earl of Arundel," 696.

[75] BL Add. Mss. 15,970, ff. 3–4, 7 September 1614.

Arundel made special mention of the regalia of the Order of the Garter, which had come down to him both from the Howard and Talbot families. He also asked that Inigo Jones make new tombs for his parents and grandmother at Arundel, "plain without painting or gilding but either in good marble or brass." Dedicating his collections to the fame of his family, Arundel hoped "to inflame the heirs of my House with the love of things virtuous & noble."[76]

Arundel's eldest son did share these values with him. Acting for Arundel in 1633, Maltravers wrote to William Petty that his father was glad "to hear of the things which you have bought him at Milan and Venice," adding in another letter that Arundel knew the "pieces of Correggio at Milan which you write of though he thinks the prices somewhat high."[77] For Arundel, English virtue and nobility included the continual search for, possession of, and display of foreign art and antiquities. Even as he lay dying in Padua, he longed for more Leonardo drawings to add to those he already owned.[78]

Charles I shared this vision of culture, becoming an art collector himself in a way that his father never had. The King's collections, developed alongside Buckingham's and Arundel's, were enhanced by his trip to Spain in 1623 and crowned with his purchase of the Duke of Mantua's collection in 1630.[79] Those who sought royal bounty often saw collecting as a political instrument with which to win the King's favor.

The second Marquis of Hamilton, Scottish privy councillor and English courtier, put together an important collection of pictures by his death in 1625. It included paintings by Rubens, "old Tintoret," Bassano, Brueghel, and Caravaggio.[80] His son, a favorite of Charles I, put together an even greater collection of Italian art, with the help of Basil Feilding, Earl of Denbigh, English ambassador to Venice in the 1630s.[81] The younger Hamilton, who declared himself "much in love with pictures," followed the King's taste, admiring sixteenth-century Venetian artists, Leonardo, and Dürer. Displaying his collections at Wallingford House, located even closer to Whitehall Palace than Buckingham's York House on the Strand, Hamilton sought to

---

[76] Howarth, *Lord Arundel, and his Circle*, p. 105; Newman, "A Draft will of the Earl of Arundel," 696.

[77] BL Add. Mss. 15,970, Henry Howard, Lord Maltravers to William Petty, 15 February 1632–33, f. 7; Maltravers to Petty, 28 February 1632–33, f. 8. Arundel to Petty, 8 March 1632–33, f. 10.

[78] Thomas Howard, Earl of Arundel, *Remembrances of Things Worth Seeing in Italy: Given to John Evelyn, 25 April 1646*, ed. John Martin Robinson (London: Roxburghe Club, 1987).

[79] Brown, *Kings and Connoisseurs*, pp. 40–42.

[80] See inventory in Appendix III in Hearn, "Lucy Harrington, as Art Patron and Collector."

[81] Shakeshaft, "To Much Bewiched with Thoes Intysing Things" 114–32.

command the King's affections through the purchase of important Venetian pictures. He explicitly competed with the Earl of Arundel for important Venetian collections and attacked the Earl for "greed" and bidding up prices.[82]

In particular, Hamilton sought to buy the de la Neve collection with which King Charles was "so extremely taken." Urging Feilding to buy the collection no matter what the price, Hamilton claimed that it was a "point of honour": he had promised to buy it for the King who had provided him with some of the monies. "I shall never leave troubling you til you have sent me word that you have bought La Neve's study . . . for I am engaged to the king to bring that collection to England."[83] When Feilding warned him that he was making a bad bargain, Hamilton described the overlapping wants that drove him: "I love cheap bargains and chiefly such thing not for the money but in regard the desires it breeds amongst us that loves such rarities yet I must tell you that I should be very sorry to miss of that collection . . . chiefly because I have undertaken to his Majesty to buy it."[84] He added on another occasion, "the truth is my Lord Arundel's jesting will trouble me more than losing double their value."[85] The purchase of the de la Neve collection and other pictures "will cast a shadow upon my lord of Arundel's collection and some say even upon himself; for I believe except the King's that there are not such pieces in England." Hamilton repeatedly urged that his Venetian pictures be packed very carefully, if possible in their frames, and carefully stowed so as not be damaged, especially by the Venetian currants, another important import, in the hold.[86] Hamilton's favor with King Charles ultimately proved disastrous. After his execution in 1649, Hamilton's collection, seized by the Commonwealth, was sold to the Habsburg Archduke Leopold Wilhelm in 1651. The Archduke celebrated the acquisition of the Hamilton collection publicly by commissioning David Teniers to paint the "Italian Collection of Archduke Leopold-Wilhelm."[87]

THE PROCESS OF COLLECTING AND THE ROLE OF AGENTS

In 1603 there were few if any shops and no auctions in England in which to buy art. The lack of such a local infrastructure did not, however, prevent

---

[82] Quoted in *ibid.*   [83] Quoted in *ibid.*, 126, 130.
[84] Quoted in *ibid.*, 126.   [85] Quoted in *ibid.*, 129.   [86] *Ibid.*, 123–24. 125, 129, 130.
[87] Neil De Marchi and Hans J. Van Miegroet, "Art, Value, and Market Practices in the Netherlands in the Seventeenth Century," *Art Bulletin*, 76 (1994), 457.

collectors from pursuing their new passion.[88] Buyers depended on agents abroad, especially ambassadors and merchants, to supply the luxury goods they desired, in addition to purchases made on their own travels.[89] Dealers and agents, who served as important intermediaries in the consumption of art, helped to transform the unique object into a luxury good for the many. As we shall see later, by the middle of the century the market in original pictures and copies flourished as did an even larger market for prints in London. By the 1670s both shops and auctions sold pictures in England.[90]

In contrast, in the Netherlands by the 1620s galleries sold pictures, sculpture, and decorative arts. Contemporary painters portrayed the archdukes of the Spanish Netherlands and other high-ranking officials surrounded by a profusion of art on display for study and sale.[91] Moreover, by the middle of the seventeenth century, Netherlands art dealers targeted both the rich and less well off. For the rich, dealers brought together Italian works of the sixteenth and seventeenth centuries with the work of contemporary Dutch artists. At the lower end, works by little-known contemporary artists, whose output may have been controlled by their dealers, were for sale. Secondhand dealers of art, many of them women, sold their wares in taverns and inns.[92] Neil de Marchi and Hans J. Miegroet stress that contemporary dealers sought to shape the product to the preferences of the local marketplace.[93]

---

[88] John Michael Montias, "Art Dealers in Seventeenth-Century Netherlands," *Simiolus*, 18 (1988), 244–56, argues that "the demand for cultural artefacts rises faster than per capita income in market economies."

[89] On collectors and agents see David Howarth, "Merchants and Diplomats: New Patrons of the Decorative Arts in Seventeenth-Century England," *Furniture History*, 20 (1984), 10–17; Howarth, *Lord Arundel and his Circle*; Wood, "Van Dyck and the Earl of Northumberland," pp. 280–324; and Jeremy Wood, "The Architectural Patronage of Algernon Percy, 10th Earl of Northumberland," in John Bold and Edward Chaney (eds.), *English Architecture: Public and Private, Essays for Kerry Downes* (London: Hambledon Press, 1993), pp. 55–80.

[90] Brian Cowan, "Arenas of Connoisseurship: Auctioning Art in Later Stuart England," in Michael North and David Ormrod (eds.), *Art Markets in Europe, 1400–1800* (Aldershot, Hampshire: Ashgate Publishing, 1998) pp. 153–66; Carol Gibson-Wood, "Picture Consumption in London at the End of the Seventeenth Century," *Art Bulletin*, 84 (2002), 491–500.

[91] De Marchi and Van Miegroet, "Art, Value, and Market Practices in the Netherlands in the Seventeenth Century," 457.

[92] Montias, "Art Dealers in Seventeenth-Century Netherlands," *Simiolus*, 245.

[93] De Marchi and Van Miegroet, "Art, Value, and Market Practices in the Netherlands in the Seventeenth Century," 451. For instance, in 1623 an Antwerp art dealer sent a consignment of pictures to his cousin in Spain with this advice. "You are dealing in items of pleasure and must extol the product; but if the paintings are not up to the expected quality or are priced too high the thing to do is not push too hard; we will send fewer ... Watch out for what is wanted there and sellable ... this is all just testing the market. And if it proves impossible to turn a profit on paintings, we will simply put the money into another line of business."

27. Collectors' cabinets and art galleries drew together the virtuosi to look at pictures, sculpture, rarities, books, and instruments. Paintings in this genre became popular in the Netherlands in the early and middle seventeenth century.
The Walters Art Gallery, Baltimore, Jan Brueghel I and Hieronimus Frucken II, "Archdukes Albert and Isabella Visiting a Collector's Cabinet," *c.* 1621.

Studies of the Netherlands art market have examined the range of ownership, prices, workshop practice, and social networks amongst artists and dealers but there have been few such studies of the art market in early seventeenth-century England.[94] Lack of dealers' inventories for the first half of the century obscure English art dealing although there is important new work on the economics of the art market after 1660.[95] What seems clear is that Jacobeans initially collected continental art primarily through agents abroad or, later, through foreign dealers who traveled to London.[96]

[94] David Ormrod, "The Origins of the London Art Market, 1660–1730," in North and Ormrod (eds.), *Art Markets in Europe, 1400–1800*, p. 167.

[95] See Cowan, "Arenas of Connoisseurship," pp. 153–66; Gibson-Wood, "Picture Consumption in London at the End of the Seventeenth Century," 491–500; Iain Pears, *The Discovery of Painting, The Growth of Interest in the Arts in England, 1680–1768* (New Haven: Yale University Press, 1988); Antony Griffiths, *The Print in Stuart Britain, 1603–1689* (London: British Museum Press, 1998), pp. 13–23.

[96] Griffiths, *The Print in Stuart Britain*, p. 18.

Italian and Low Countries pictures were comparatively inexpensive in the Jacobean period, certainly less expensive than elaborate court clothing, court masques, and diplomatic missions, although prices climbed in the 1630s.[97] Agents' correspondence makes clear that prices depended on the painter, the genre, whether history, portraits, or landscape, the size and the number of figures pictured.[98] Thus, in 1636, King Charles wanted "to know the story, and what bigness it is, and the price" of a "rare" Venetian picture.[99] In addition, the value of paintings resided not only in their maker but also in the quality of their previous owner.[100]

The English ambassadors in Venice, Sir Henry Wotton and Sir Dudley Carleton, helped to fashion the Stuart taste for High Renaissance and seventeenth-century Italian pictures. The close ties between the English Crown and the Venetians in their battle against the papal interdict in 1605 led to closer connections with Italian culture. Both Wotton and Carleton were in touch with gentlemen on the Grand Tour. Thus Henry Howard, son of the Earl of Suffolk, thanked Carleton for "your noble remembering me so often." He promised on his return to Venice from Florence to meet the ambassador.[101] In a gift-giving society, in which exchange of gloves, deer, and gold cups marked patronage relationships, Wotton, ambassador to Venice during the Venetian Interdict, made art an important new gift at the early Stuart court. He presented Italian and Low Countries pictures to Prince Henry and Robert Carr, the King's favorite.[102] Sir Walter Cope, Salisbury's close associate, advised Carleton in 1611 that "if you meet with any ancient masterpieces of paintings at a reasonable hand, you cannot send anything more gracious to the Prince or my Lord Treasurer" while he was willing to "bestowe a few crowns for myself . . . if such rarities come your way."[103] Carleton and his wife sought to advance his career, especially his efforts to become Secretary of State or Provost of Eton, through gifts to the great of art and magnificent furniture including Italian marble fireplaces.[104] But

[97] Portier, "Prices Paid for Italian Pictures in the Stuart Age," 54–58. Smuts, "Cultural Diversity and Cultural Change at the Court of James I," p. 302n35.

[98] See Shakeshaft, "To Much Bewiched with Thoes Intysing Things," 114–32.

[99] *Ibid.*, p. 123

[100] De Marchi and Miegroet, "Art, Value, and Market Practices in the Netherlands in the Seventeenth Century," 453–55, 463.

[101] PRO SP 99/13, f. 315, Henry Howard to Carleton.

[102] Linda Levy Peck, *Court Patronage and Corruption in Early Stuart England* (London: Unwin Hyman, 1990), pp. 62–67.

[103] Quoted in Shakeshaft, "To Much Bewiched with Thoes Intysing Things," 117, and Robert Hill, "Ambassadors and Art Collecting in Early Stuart Britain: The Parallel Careers of William Trumbull and Sir Dudley Carleton, 1609–1625," *Journal of the History of Collections*, 15 (2003), 212.

[104] Peck, *Court Patronage and Corruption*, pp. 12–15, 18–20, 163–84.

Carleton's collection for Robert Carr, Earl of Somerset, was not a gift. When Carr fell from power in 1615 just as the pictures and sculpture reached the London docks, Carleton quickly claimed that he had acted merely as Carr's broker and required payment.[105] He sold three paintings from the collection to Lord Henry Danvers and twelve to Arundel for L200.[106]

In the Low Countries, ambassadors such as Sir William Trumbull also sought to curry favor through the decorative arts. In 1606 Trumbull supplied tapestries to Thomas Howard, Earl of Suffolk, and in 1612, plants and fruit trees to the Earl of Salisbury.[107] Trumbull's news of the sale of the Duke of Aerschot's estate interested several Jacobeans. In 1613 Carr's secretary asked for details of "the Duke of Aerschot's jewels, plate of agate, crystal, etc." but the favorite decided against the purchase.[108] Robert Sidney, Viscount Lisle, wrote Trumbull "I do not want pictures or medals nor hangings of very great value, but for a handsome suite of fine pieces I would willingly give L100."[109] Lord Darcy wanted to buy tapestries "to hang a room of 34 yards in compass and I would bestow L300,"[110] and Thomas Lake, Secretary of State, was interested in the Duke's books.[111] Trumbull supported early Stuart taste for Netherlandish art of the sixteenth and seventeenth centuries.[112] He tried to sell Buckingham a picture by Frans Snyder in 1620[113] and Arundel asked him to look into bronzes belonging to the estate of a Brussels architect.[114]

Sir Thomas Roe, from whom John Tradescant had sought rarities on behalf of Buckingham, served as ambassador to the courts of Shah Jahangir, the Mughal emperor, and later to the Turkish Sultan. He accepted Arundel's orders for antiquities and sent back luxury goods from India and Turkey.[115] Arundel wrote to Roe to thank him for the medal of Alexander which had arrived and to ask for his favor to John

---

[105] SP14/80/88, "Account of such things as I have bought for the Earl of Somerset."

[106] Albert R. Braunmuller, "Robert Carr, Earl of Somerset, as Collector and Patron," in Peck (ed.), *The Mental World of the Jacobean Court*, p. 234.

[107] Hill, "Ambassadors and Art Collecting in Early Stuart Britain," 211–28, 212.

[108] HMC *Downshire*, IV, 233, John Packer to Trumbull, 23 October 1613.

[109] *Ibid.*, 169, Robert, Viscount Lisle, to Trumbull, 22 July 1613.

[110] *Ibid.*, 160, Lord Darcy to Trumbull, 4 July 1613   [111] *Ibid.*, 212, 215.

[112] David Howarth, "William Trumbull and Art Collecting in Jacobean England," *The British Library Journal*, 20 (1994), 140–62. Hill, "Ambassadors and Art Collecting in Early Stuart Britain:" 211–28.

[113] See David Howarth, "The Arrival of Van Dyck in England," *Burlington Magazine*, 132 (1990), 709; Lockyer, *Buckingham*, p. 214. Howarth, "William Trumbull and Art Collecting in Jacobean England," 140–62.

[114] Hill, "Ambassadors and Art Collecting in Early Stuart Britain," 218.

[115] Howarth, *Lord Arundel and His Circle*, pp. 87–95.

Markham, who went to Turkey to purchase antiquities for him.[116] When Markham wanted to be consul of Cio, a post in the gift of the Turkey Company, he asked the Countess to ask Arundel's uncle, Northampton, for letters on his behalf to the Archbishop of Canterbury, George Abbot, whose brother Maurice was the chief Turkey merchant.[117] The search for antiquities was embedded in elaborate transnational networks.

Even as ambassadors helped to create the taste for High Renaissance and seventeenth-century pictures, their patrons began to shop for themselves through their own agents. The Arundels used a variety of agents to purchase art for them in addition to Roe and Markham, principally, William Petty, Balthazar Gerbier, Nicholas Lanier, and George Gage.[118] Van Dyck celebrated George Gage's role as agent in a famous portrait in which he represents Gage, a close neighbor and friend of the Countess of Arundel, viewing a painting with a sculpture presented by a dealer and his assistant.[119] Even when he was in exile in 1646, Arundel wrote to a Spanish agent about paintings by Velasquez.[120]

Buckingham sent Balthazar Gerbier to Italy in 1621 to search for pictures for him.[121] Basil Feilding, ambassador to Venice in the 1630s, sought out collections of Italian pictures and sculpture for King Charles and the Marquis of Hamilton. As he traveled around Italy, Feilding wrote to Hamilton about the pictures available for sale, warning him, in 1637, that he would be unable to supply further pictures until he paid for those already delivered. "My credit is fallen so low by reason of the slow payment made in England that I must ingeniously confess the merchants would not venture further with me, til they find all debts duly discharged." Nevertheless, Feilding spent 500 duckets on original pictures "by modern painters ... the best of these times."[122] Artists served as dealers too. Van Dyck and Rubens both collected and sold art. Dudley Carleton traded a collection of antiquities for nine Rubens paintings.[123] Lucas Vosterman, the engraver who had worked for Rubens, dealt in art after Arundel persuaded him to come to London after 1623.[124]

[116] *CSPD 1619–23*, p. 467, Thomas Howard, Earl of Arundel to Sir Thomas Roe, 9 December 1622, Arundel House.

[117] BL Add. Mss. 69,873, Coke Papers, Series II, f. 146.

[118] Howarth, *Lord Arundel and his Circle, passim*.

[119] See Wood, "Van Dyck and the Earl of Northumberland," pp. 280–324; Wood, "The Architectural Patronage of Algernon Percy," pp. 55–80.

[120] Howarth, *Lord Arundel and His Circle*, p. 218.   [121] Lockyer, *Buckingham*, pp. 214–15.

[122] Quoted in Shakeshaft, "To Much Bewiched with Thoes Intysing Things," 124.

[123] Brown, *Kings and Connoisseurs*, p. 20   [124] Griffiths, *The Print in Stuart England*, pp. 74–75.

Dealers in Italy through whom the English purchased goods included Daniel Nys, Peter Fitton, and Sir Walter Montagu. Nys was a major dealer in the Venetian art market from the 1610s. He had connections to Aletheia, Countess of Arundel, and arranged the sale of the Mantuan collection to Charles I.[125] Arundel bought Nys's cabinet of gems, described by Vincenzo Scamozzi, in *L'Idea della Archettura Universale* (Venice, 1615), for L10,000.[126] Arundel's son, Lord Maltravers, wrote to William Petty, Arundel's greatest agent, that "I am glad Signor Neece's jewels and the forty drawings prove so well."[127] Nys also arranged the sale of some of Carr's pictures to the Earl of Arundel, including five Tintorettos, three Veroneses, one Bassano, one Titian, one Schiavone for L200.[128]

William Petty met Peter Fitton, an English secular priest, in Rome in 1635. Fitton competed with Sir Walter Montagu, brother of the Earl of Manchester, for the trade of English collectors including King Charles. Fitton wrote in 1632, "here is a Flemish merchant that hath bought a number of statues and curiosities for our King of England. Yesterday he obtained leave of Cardinal Barberini to send them out of Rome. I should be glad if you could learn whether the King hath employed any Englishman here in this affair and who he is."[129]

Sir Walter Montagu supplied pictures to English people of various rank.[130] Amongst his papers is an invoice for six pictures forwarded to Mrs. Mary Cox and Mr. Florenus Kelly with charges for packing and customs.[131] On a grander scale Montagu managed a major commission to copy antique Roman sculpture for the King. Inigo Jones wrote to Sir Henry Garway, head of the Great Farm of the Customs, on the King's behalf and Garway sent on the letter to the merchant Samuel Boothouse in Leghorn.

The king's majesty having ordered certain molds to be made at Rome of such statues and other things as he desireth to have, since the originals are not to be got for money, the which molds being all made and well packed up and sent for Ligorne by Mr. Walter Montague who procured them, from whence they are to be shipped for England, his Majesty commanded me to signify his pleasure unto you ... write unto your factor at Livorne to see the said molds carefully shipped and sent away by the first ship that come for England.[132]

---

[125] Howarth, *Lord Arundel and his Circle*, pp. 159–60.   [126] *Ibid.*, pp. 61, 232n12.

[127] BL Add. Mss. 15,970, f. 65, quoted in Mary Hervey. *The Life, Correspondence, and Collections of Thomas Howard, Earl of Arundel* (Cambridge: Cambridge University Press, 1921), p. 406.

[128] Portier, "Prices Paid for Italian Pictures in the Stuart Age," 53–69, 55.

[129] Quoted in Howarth, *Lord Arundel and his Circle*, p. 136.   [130] *Ibid.*, p. 136.

[131] North Misc. B.17 Montague Papers.   [132] Quoted in Howarth, *Lord Arundel and his Circle*, p. 203.

Charles II rewarded Montagu for his efforts on behalf of his father.[133]

Merchants also participated in the network of art exchange. Philip Burlamarchi loaned money to King Charles to buy the Mantuan collection.[134] Richard Grassby points out that Sir John Shaw was among the English merchants abroad who dealt in pictures and antiquities. He bought fifty pictures for Charles including a Tintoretto, a Van Dyck, and a Brueghel.[135] Sir Henry Garway carried Arundel's collections in his holds as well as those molds of antique sculpture for the King. Garway's factor, Samuel Boothouse, was an important middleman in the importation of Italian art.[136]

In addition, merchants and diplomats promoted new artists and new goods, such as *pietra dura* or leather hangings, that they hoped would please the court in London. Basil Feilding offered to send a Flemish artist trained in Rome who specialized in decorating leather hangings to the Caroline court.

He hath a new way never practis'd but at Rome, of making great designs and representing histories upon leather hangings in chiaroscuro which would be though done upon bare walls, of great ornament to a house ... I have often heard of his Majesty's design of building a royal palace for the adorning whereof this man being very proper I thought fit to divert him from settling upon any dependance, til I know his Majesty's pleasure.[137]

Bills of exchange drawn on merchant accounts provided the means to pay for these luxury goods. For example, the Marquis of Hamilton used his merchant, Moorhead, to transfer monies to Basil Feilding to buy collections of Italian art in the 1630s.[138]

As a result of this lively art market, merchants in Italy and the Low Countries, whose main trade was in textiles, dabbled in art to meet the demands of the English market. Daniel Skynner, a cloth merchant in Antwerp, was in continual correspondence between 1611 and 1625 with

---

[133] Algernon, 10th Earl of Northumberland, wrote to the Earl of Leicester that "My Lord of St. Albans and Lord Almoner or Lord Abbot (for so Mr Walter Montague is now called) would be very glad of your Lordship's company." KAO U1475 C85/32 8 December 1662.

[134] Portier, "Prices Paid for Italian Pictures in the Stuart Age," 58–59.

[135] Richard Grassby, *The Business Community in Seventeenth-Century England* (Cambridge: Cambridge University Press, 1995), pp. 356–58.

[136] Howarth, "Merchants and Diplomats," 10–17; David Howarth, "Samuel Boothouse and the English Artistic Enterprise in Seventeenth Century Italy," *Italian Studies Birmingham*, 32 (1977), 86–96.

[137] Quoted in Shakeshaft, "To Much Bewiched with Thoes Intysing Things," 131. Howarth, "Merchants and Diplomats," 10–17.

[138] Shakeshaft, "To Much Bewiched with Thoes Intysing Things," 131.

William Trumbull, the King's agent at the Hague. Skynner offered information, wrote newsletters, and complained about his problems with customs officials. In addition, he imported goods that Trumbull wanted, asked for protection from Dutch officials, and bought Italian and sixteenth-century Flemish pictures which he sought to sell in London.[139] Thus he wrote to Trumbull in 1625, "I have sent herewith a note of such Italian pieces as I have at London. And so far as I can learn, the like will not be found here ... I pray if you can help me, I may vent some of my pieces at London."[140] Skynner offered pictures attributed to major sixteenth- and seventeenth-century artists. The pieces in London included a large painting of Adam and Eve that Skynner bought because it was attributed to Titian; Bassano's *The Angel Appearing to the Shepherds*; Palma's *St. Jerome*; "one great piece of Cavalier Balione of Lot and his two daughters for which the Marquis of Hamilton offered Mr. Fletcher forty pieces which I wish he had taken"; as well as Bassano's *Lucretia*, a damaged piece by Raphael, and several other "good pieces."[141]

EXPANDING THE MARKET FOR ART

The demand and market for art expanded in the early seventeenth century through imports, exchange, gifts, copying, the secondhand market, and prints. King Charles's cabinet at Whitehall displayed gifts of continental art from the King's courtiers. Sir Francis Cottington, the English ambassador to Spain, presented Charles with *The Negro Venus*, thought to be an antiquity but now believed to be a sixteenth-century Italian sculpture.[142] Sir Henry Mildmay, Master of the Jewel House, bought a bronze of a sleeping cupid by Francesco Duquesnoy in Rome which he presented to the King.[143] The Marquis of Hamilton presented a Laocoon; the Earl of Denbigh gave an East Indian idol "brought back from his embassy to the Great Mughal."[144] Sir Henry Wotton and Sir Henry Vane presented gifts as did the widow of George Herriot, the King's jeweler, who presented two bronzes after Gianbologna.[145] The Lord Chamberlain presented the

[139] On Skinner, see HMC *Downshire*, 3, 4, 5, and 6 *passim*. BL Add. Mss. 72,310. Howarth, "William Trumbull and Art Collecting in Jacobean England," 140–62, prints two of Skynner's letters on art.
[140] Quoted in Howarth, "William Trumbull and Art Collecting in Jacobean England," 140–41.
[141] *Ibid.*
[142] David Howarth, "Charles I, Sculpture and Sculptors," in MacGregor (ed.), *The Late King's Goods*, pp. 73–113.
[143] *Ibid.*   [144] *Ibid.*   [145] *Ibid.*

King with a picture of the Virgin by the Renaissance master Andrea del
Sarto in exchange for a watercolor of Queen Henrietta Maria.[146] Such an
unequal exchange made it clear that the del Sarto was a gift and the
watercolor its graceful royal acknowledgment.

Charles himself tried to disseminate his collections. He allowed favored
courtiers to copy portraits or pictures in his collection. Copies from famous
collections carried their own cachet. William Murray, son of a Jacobean
Scot who served King James, had Francis Cleyn, designer of the Mortlake
tapestries, develop the Green Closet off the gallery in his residence, Ham
House, between 1637 and 1639.[147] Murray filled the cabinet with miniatures, pictures, and bronzes which echoed the layout, holdings, and display
of King Charles's cabinet at Whitehall. Cleyn decorated the room in white
and gold after Whitehall palace, and the pictures in the Green Closet, like
the pictures at Whitehall, were most often framed with ebony. Murray
owned copies of pictures by Titian, Correggio, Bloemart, Breenburgh,
Bassano and Van Dyck, presumably copied from the King's collection as
a mark of royal favor. In addition, Murray's Green Closet was hung with
pictures "by or after Rottenhammer, Breenbergh, Brouwer, and Stella."[148]
Murray, who had attended Charles on his trip to Spain in 1623, gave the
King a bronze of Moses and a Dutch picture by Rottenheimer for his
Whitehall cabinet.[149]

Arundel House on the Strand became famous, as its owner hoped, for
the antique marbles, sculpture, European pictures, books and manuscripts,
pietra dura, and porcelain that the Arundels collected on their travels,
especially in Italy. They also brought home the artists themselves, such as
the Netherlands silversmith Christian, son of Adam, Wenceslaus Hollar, the
Czech artist, Lucas Vosterman, the engraver, and Francois Dieussart, the
French sculptor.[150] The Arundels ensured that their collections would
be available to a wider audience. First, in his draft will of 1617 Arundel
had urged that the collections be kept together at Arundel House and "that

---

[146] Portier, "Prices Paid for Italian Pictures in the Stuart Age," 62.
[147] Christopher Rowell, "A Seventeenth-Century 'Cabinet' Restored, The Green Closet at Ham
      House," *Apollo*, 143 (1996), 18–23.
[148] *Ibid.*; Peter M. Thornton and Maurice Tomlin, *The Furnishing and Decoration of Ham House*,
      Furniture History Series, 16 (London: Furniture History Society, 1980).
[149] Howarth, "Charles I, Sculpture and Sculptor," pp. 103–104. Christopher Rowell, "A Seventeenth-
      Century 'Cabinet' Restored: The Green Closet at Ham House," *Apollo*, 143 (1996), 18–23.
[150] Howarth, *Lord Arundel and his Circle*, pp. 162, 172. Griffiths, *The Print in Stuart Britain*, p. 71.
      Philippa Granville, *Silver in Tudor and Early Stuart England.* (London: Victoria and Albert Museum,
      1990), p. 472.

all gentlemen … or artists which are honest men may always be used, with courtesy & humanity when they shall come to see them."[151] Second, they commissioned Inigo Jones to design an extension in which some of the collection was on display.[152] Third, Arundel commissioned John Selden to publish a scholarly edition of Arundel's ancient inscriptions and marbles which had been collected in Italy and Turkey.[153] Fourth, Wenceslaus Hollar, the Czech artist whom Arundel had met on his diplomatic mission to Prague, painted watercolors of that important but unsuccessful trip.[154] Hollar engraved some of Arundel's pictures and drawings as well as his collection of natural history prints.[155] Arundel publicized his collections by having Hollar and Lucas Van Vosterman reproduce not only pictures but also drawings, a new departure, David Howarth suggests, for seventeenth-century collectors. In particular, Hollar reproduced some of Arundel's Leonardo drawings.[156] Other collectors put together albums of prints of the Arundel collection.[157] After the Arundels went into exile in 1641–42, Hollar went into exile too and prepared prints of some pieces of the Arundel collection for the commercial market on the continent in the 1640s.[158] Visitors still came to visit the collections of Arundel House during the 1650s, now in the hands of Arundel's heir. The residue of Arundel's collection remained on display. It ranged from a large Madonna by Raphael to works by Dürer, Holbein, Michelangelo, Gulio Romano, and Isaac Oliver. "In the long gallery are divers ritrattos and the old Earl and his gallery of statutes … . and he pointing you to it."[159]

---

[151] Arundel Castle Manuscripts T9. Newman, "A Draft Will of the Earl of Arundel," 692–96.

[152] David Howarth, "Lord Arundel as an Entrepreneur of the Arts," *Burlington Magazine*, 122 (1980), 690. Howarth discusses the creation by Arundel of a cabinet room in which to display Arundel's extraordinary collection of books of drawings of Michelangelo, Raphael, and Leonardo. Howarth suggests that it was designed by Inigo Jones. Jane Roberts, Curator of Drawings, the Royal Collection, suggests that some of the Leonardo drawings in the Royal Collection, some of which were reproduced by Wenceslaus Hollar, came from the Arundel Collection.

[153] John Selden, *Marmora Arundelliana* (London, 1628).

[154] Griffiths, *The Print in Stuart Britain*, pp. 87–89.   [155] *Muscrum Scarabeorum* (Antwerp, 1646).

[156] Howarth, *Lord Arundel and his Circle*, pp. 182–83.

[157] Griffiths, *The Print in Stuart Britain*, p. 97. David Howarth and Nicholas Penney (eds.), *Thomas Howard, Earl of Arundel: Patronage and Collecting in the Seventeenth-Century* (Oxford: Ashmolean Museum, 1985), p. 43. Griffiths questions whether Arundel intended such a project. Michael Vickers, "Hollar and the Arundel Marbles," *Country Life* (1979), 916–17.

[158] Griffiths, *The Print in Stuart Britain*, pp. 89–90.

[159] Mary Beal, *A Study of Richard Symonds: His Italian Notebooks and their Relevance to Seventeenth Century Painting Techniques* (New York: Garland, 1984), pp. 298–99.

28. Wenceslaus Hollar reproduced some of the rarities, paintings, and drawings from the collection of Thomas Howard, Earl of Arundel, one of the greatest seventeenth-century collectors.
The Folger Shakespeare Library, ART 25435, Wenceslaus Hollar, From his set of etchings *Muscrum scarabeorum . . . varie figure*, 1646. Butterflies in the collection of Thomas Howard, Earl of Arundel.

Most art historians agree that "until the 1650s purchasers of Italian art had been forced to buy abroad."[160] Yet the importation of continental collections to England in the early seventeenth century did create a second-hand English art market for European pictures and luxury goods that has been little studied. For instance, Lionel Cranfield bought pictures that had belonged to Sir Adam Newton, Prince Henry's tutor, from Richard Colbeck, a dealer or possibly Newton's heir, in the 1630s.[161] "The chiefest and best of them are these that follow: A great piece of the deluge worth L15; A small piece of Pilate's washing his hands worth L7; A large night piece on cloth L10; A long piece on board of the prodigal L4; a piece on board of St. Anthony's temptation worth L6. The total spent was L95–10.[162] In the 1630s, the servants of Basil Feilding, English ambassador in Venice, Francis Cottington, one-time English ambassador to Spain, and the Earl of Northumberland, an important collector, combined to import a

[160] Portier, "Prices Paid for Italian Pictures in the Stuart Age," 67.
[161] KAO, Sackville Papers, U269/1, F8.   [162] *Ibid.*

large group of Venetian pictures to sell in London. "There is a collection of pictures come home brought, as I hear, by your servant Bassford. He has two partners, servants to Northumberland and Cottington, it is reported that they stand them in 700 pounds. They are most of them copies, and hardly there will be got half that money for them."[163] The relatively low cost of paintings allowed the little-known Mary Cox to buy, Bassford to speculate, and the Whitehall group at court to collect.

"WITH PICTURES GAY": THE CRITIQUE OF COLLECTING

Art collecting worried even its keenest promoters such as the diplomats Sir Henry Wotton and Sir Thomas Roe. Wotton concluded his work, *The Elements of Architecture* of 1624, by defending what he called "ornament." "Against which me thinks I hear an objection, even from some well-meaning man; that these delightful crafts may be divers ways ill applied in a land. I must confess indeed, there may be a lascivious and there may be likewise a superstitious use, both of picture and of sculpture."[164] Wotton worried that interest in art and architecture would be identified with Counter-Reformation Italy. In fact, the fashion for Italian pictures bridged disagreements about religion and politics, bringing together Roman Catholics and the godly, and, later, royalists, parliamentarians, and members of the New Model Army.[165]

Sir Thomas Roe feared that collecting might be thought effeminate. He wrote to Arundel from Constantinople in 1621 that he was sending him ancient coins, "rare pieces of white coral" for his fountains; and a piece of Priam's palace in Troy for its antiquity. Roe had discovered how to get ancient marbles from Delphi, which in due course Arundel received, but manuscripts were more difficult. Marveling at what was available in the Ottoman Empire, Roe wrote:

I find the gentlest arts and sciences rather despised and neglected, than worn out; as if they were means to soften and civilize those natures, whose end and proposition is war, blood, and conquest ... I think they would here follow the precept of a barbarous Goth, not to destroy, but leave and deliver them to us for our corruption, to divert us from the thought or use of arms. But they are absurdly

---

[163] Shakeshaft, "Too Much Bewiched with Thoes Intysing Things," 123.

[164] Henry Wotton, *The Elements of Architecture* (London, 1624), p. 121.

[165] Oliver Millar, "Philip, Lord Wharton, and his Collection of Portraits," *Burlington Magazine*, 136 (1994), 517–30. Francis Haskell's lectures on the dispersal of Charles I's collection show that members of the New Model Army bought "The Late King's Goods."

mistaken; for civility and knowledge do confirm and not effeminate good and true spirits.[166]

Rejecting the traditional critique that luxury softened the spirit of the nation, Roe argued in the 1620s that collecting reflected civility and refinement not luxury.

King James, who prided himself on bringing peace and plenty to his kingdoms, presided over a court in which these issues had important resonance. The Venetian ambassador to England in the 1620s commented critically on the King's failure to support the Elector Palatine and Princess Elizabeth, James I's daughter, during the Thirty Years' War.

The power and spirit of nations do not always maintain the standard of ancient example and disclose at bottom the weakness generated by long and ill regulated ease, amid pleasure, wealth and display, results sometimes produced by an excessive desire for peace.[167] ... His [King James's] liberality and munificence flow like rivers and seas and continually fatten his favorites. His excessive donations, his expenditure in receiving and sending ambassadors consume mountains of gold, a single one costing 40,00 to 50,000 sterling and even more, such as that of Viscount Doncaster to Germany for a few months ... The magnates are mostly hated for their vain ostentation, better suited to their ancient power than their present condition."[168]

But the expenditure and ostentation which the Venetian condemned did not include collecting Venetian pictures. At the same time, he praised Prince Charles for his "modesty and prudence: he loves old paintings, especially those of our province and city."[169]

The Venetian ambassador's critique of peace and luxury at the English court appeared in the 1630s in Amsterdam. In 1636 a Dutch broadside used the powerful image of the sleeping prince and his corrupt favorite to rouse the English to war against Spain. The broadside depicts the English fleet anchored at Dover while Charles I dozes. Louis XIII tries to awaken Charles to defend the Palatinate but "De Engelsch gespaniolezeenede Favorit" fends him off, supported by the Spanish ambassador offering a trunk filled with gold plate. At the rear, the Earl of Arundel enters from his fruitless diplomatic mission to Prague (during which he hired Hollar and bought the Pirckheimer Library). Within months, the broadside was

---

[166] Sir Thomas Roe, *The Negotiations of Sir Thomas Roe in his Embassy to the Ottoman Porte From the Year 1621 to 1628 Inclusive* (London, 1740), p. 16. Howarth, *Lord Arundel and his Circle*, p. 88.

[167] *CSPV, 1621–23*, p. 423. "Relation of England of Girolamo Lando, Venetian Ambassador 21 September 1622."

[168] *Ibid.*, p. 437.   [169] *Ibid.*, p. 452.

translated into English and published in London. In the translation, "The English Favourite" gives a more elaborate speech than in the Dutch version, stressing his concentration on court revels, art, hunting, corruption by Spanish gold, and disdain for war. Thus, the favorite exclaims to Louis XIII:[170]

> Holla, French King, who taught you to be so rude,
> So near our King who sleeps thus to intrude?
>
> . . .
>
> Tis better dance, be merrie, jovial still,
> With Spanish pistollets our purses fill,
> Better with pictures gaie to feed our sight
> Than naked corpses gor'd with blood in fight
> In hunting spend our time than all in vain
> With loss of men and money war with Spaine[171]

Buckingham, the Stuart's greatest favorite, had been assassinated eight years before the print appeared, but the cluster of attributes ascribed to him by the broadside (and by other contemporary literature) continued to appear in contemporary propaganda. James and Buckingham, the King devoted to peace and the favorite devoted to collecting and display, resonated as emotive icons in the 1630s.

In the early eighteenth century the issue of effeminacy continued to be deployed, but now in the context of a burgeoning auction market in which women bought many of the pictures. Lord Shaftesbury argued, rather like Sir Thomas Roe, that real connoisseurship and knowledge were masculine but that the growing market for pictures to decorate the home was effeminate. Shaftesbury criticized a public that identified the art market with luxury goods: "whilst we look on painting with the same eye, as we view commonly the rich stuffs and coloured silks worn by our ladies, and admired in dress, equipage, or furniture, we must of necessity be effeminate in our taste, and utterly set wrong as to all judgement and knowledge in the kind."[172]

---

[170] BM *Catalogue of Political and Personal Satires*, ed. Frederic George Stephens and M. Dorothy George, II vols. (London: British Museum Publications, 1978), I, #133 "The Kingly Cocke," 1636.

[171] *Ibid.* Dorothy George argues that the Dutch print alludes to Sir Francis Cottington, formerly English ambassador to Spain. The English version, however, labels the favorite as the Duke of Buckingham. Moreover, George notes that the English version of the Spanish Ambassador's speech refers not to Charles but to James.

[172] Quoted in Gibson-Wood, "Picture Consumption in London at the End of the Seventeenth-century," 491–500; Cowan, "Arenas of Connoisseurship," pp. 153–66.

This chapter has argued that collecting based on the importation of art and artifacts from Europe and from trade routes around the world was one type of luxury consumption. Great nobles, aspiring gentry, well-to-do citizens, men and women used luxury goods, whether pictures, rarities, curiosities, or decorative arts, to identify themselves as cultivated, refined, learned, and European. The process of collecting brought together merchants, scholars, nobles, gentlemen, officeholders, and sea captains. Such collecting was deeply imbedded in an expanding commercial society that linked travel, trade, and colonization. From Sir Walter Cope's house in the City to Tradescant's Ark in Lambeth and Arundel House on the Strand, these collections were on display in London. Copies of pictures circulated among king and courtiers, while prints of portraits and paintings, books on antique sculpture and natural history could be found for sale at the New Exchange. Collecting was not only a private passion but also a public performance, which created new wants and new wares. These wares were increasingly available for view and for sale in seventeenth-century London even before the Civil War.

Charles I engaged Rubens to paint the ceiling of Inigo Jones's Banqueting House which the King hoped would be part of the new Whitehall Palace. Rubens had completed a cycle on behalf of Marie de Medici that honored her dead husband Henry IV, father of Henrietta Maria, and agreed to do a comparable cycle lauding King James. The original program, perhaps devised during James's own reign, had highlighted King James as writer, with pen and book in hand. The long panels alongside each major panel contained quotations from the psalms.[173] Later, Rubens, King Charles, and Inigo Jones revised the program: the psalms became putti and the "Apotheosis of King James" became the central panel. Everyone who entered the Banqueting House, whether courtiers, ambassadors, officeholders, or visitors, saw a baroque ceiling worthy of the praise that Rubens himself had lavished on English collectors in 1629.

The English appropriation of European luxury artifacts described in this chapter changed the pattern of consumption among the nobility, gentry, and well-to-do during the seventeenth century. It paralleled that documented by Richard Goldthwaite for Italy between 1300 and 1600.[174] It provided the basis for the culture of gentility documented by Lois Carr,

---

[173] Gregory Martin, "The Banqueting House Ceiling: Two Newly Discovered Projects," *Apollo*, 139 (1994), 29–34.

[174] Richard Goldthwaite, *Wealth and the Demand for Art in Italy, 1300–1600* (Baltimore and London: Johns Hopkins University Press, 1993).

Lorena Walsh, Richard Bushman, and Woodruff Smith.[175] In the next chapter we will consider another dimension of this phenomenon: how builders and their patrons cultivated domestic comfort from a variety of designs and luxurious furnishings brought from abroad.

---

[175] Lois Green Carr and Lorena Walsh, *Inventories and the Analysis of Wealth and Consumption Patterns in St. Mary's County, Maryland, 1658–1777* (Chicago: Newberry Library, 1977); Richard Bushman, *The Refinement of America: Persons, Houses, Cities* (New York: Knopf, 1992); Woodruff D. Smith, *Consumption and the Making of Repectability, 1600–1800* (London and New York: Routledge, 2002).

CHAPTER 5

"Examine but my humours in buildings, gardening, and private expenses": cultural exchange and the new built environment

Building had long signified political power and social consequence in city and country. Raising a pile or adding "a handsome apartment" offered the individual and family the opportunity to project power, wealth, identity, and taste to neighbors, superiors, and subordinates. Fixed in materials meant to last generations, building was the greatest family and, indeed, generational economic investment and cultural statement. Building thus appears a less likely site of short-term changes in luxury consumption than "French wares" on sale in the New Exchange in the 1630s. Yet building bore striking similarities to other forms of luxury consumption. As we shall see, the transmission of information about novelty, style, and the exotic took place through on-site inspections at home and abroad, skilled craftsmen, print, and trade. At a time when there were few if any architects, masons worked not from architectural designs but from patterns and verbal instruction.[1] Print culture, especially continental pattern books, provided the external aspects of houses such as fenestration and their internal details such as fireplaces and wrought-iron gates. Furnishing those houses in city and country brought new fashions from all over the world into the market, distributed and redistributed again through purchase, gift, loan, and bequest.

Building responded quickly to changing political relationships as well as to new fashions and display. With the accession of James I in 1603, royal policy intertwined with a burst of individual and communal desires to build houses and churches and improve the urban infrastructure. King James spent much more on royal building than Elizabeth had from the beginning of his reign.[2] For his larger family, new apartments were added

---

[1] Christy Anderson, "Learning to Read Architecture in the English Renaissance," in Lucy Gent (ed.), *Albion's Classicism: The Visual Arts in Britain, 1550–1660* (New Haven: Yale University Press, 1995), pp. 239–86. Elizabeth McKellar, *The Birth of Modern London: The Development and Design of the City, 1660–1720* (Manchester: Manchester University Press, 1999).

[2] Howard M. Colvin, *The History of the King's Works*, 6 vols. (London: HMSO, 1975–82), III, 1485–1660 (Part 1); IV, 1485–1660 (part 2).

29. James I commissioned Inigo Jones to design a new banqueting house for Whitehall Palace after the earlier one burnt down. After the King's death in 1625, Jones and Rubens planned a series of ceiling paintings to commemorate James's reign, which were installed in the 1630s.
The Royal Commission on Historical Monuments (England), London, Inigo Jones, The Banqueting House.

to the eight standing palaces. He developed plans for the rebuilding of Whitehall Palace, added rooms for Queen Anne, and commissioned Inigo Jones's Banqueting House when his first burnt down. In addition, King James built hunting lodges, Queen Anne added to Somerset House and commissioned Inigo Jones to build the Queen's House at Greenwich, Prince Henry built at Richmond, and Inigo Jones designed new lodgings and outbuildings at Newmarket for Prince Charles.[3] Church building from the richest parishes to the poorest increased during the first decade of James's reign.[4]

Because the Stuart monarchs made fewer public progresses after 1604, the need to house and entertain the court on progress decreased. Desire to

---

[3] *Ibid.*, III, p. 119, IV, pp. 32–33.
[4] Julia F. Merritt, "Puritans, Laudians, and the Phenomenon of Church-Building in Jacobean London," *The Historical Journal,* 41 (1998), 935–60.

live closer to the court and City stimulated building or renting in London and its suburbs. As a result, expanding population presented real estate speculators with opportunities to develop new types of housing for the well-to-do as well as to subdivide tenements for the less well off. London maps, documenting the increasingly built-up areas of the metropolis, demonstrate how important building was for the patron, the developer, the mason, and itinerant worker.[5] The early Stuarts regulated building in London, promoted the creation of shops, gardens, waterworks, churches, and hospitals, and allowed the creation of townhouses for the well-to-do in St. Martin in-the-Fields, Covent Garden, and Lincoln's Inn. These efforts were so successful that they felt impelled to issue proclamations ordering the gentry and nobility to return to their homes to carry out their duties as sheriffs, justices of the peace, and lord and deputy lieutenants. Nevertheless, the gentry spent more and more time in London.

The most important industry in England alongside the cloth trades, building boomed in city and country. In the early seventeenth century, patrons translated their reading and travel into new architectural forms reflecting the changing functions of houses. Country houses became more compact and lost their courtyards because, increasingly, the traditional duty of providing expansive hospitality to the neighborhood ceased to be uppermost in builders' minds. Instead, new outbuildings such as banqueting houses, riding houses, arcades, and elaborate gardens celebrated the refinement of the builder.[6] Architectural style in the early seventeenth century was a good deal more eclectic than the later penchant for classicism would suggest. Italy, France, and the Low Countries offered styles that the well-to-do eagerly adapted to the English city and countryside. Jacobean and Caroline builders added Italian gates and balconies, Low Countries' hipped roofs, French interiors, and Italian and French gardens. London style was quickly diffused to the countryside through emulation, patterns, and the skills of master

[5] See Christopher G. A. Clay, *Economic Expansion and Social Change: England, 1500–1700*, 2 vols. (Cambridge: Cambridge University Press, 1984), I, pp. 208–209. Jeremy Boulton, *Neighbourhood and Society: A London Suburb in the Seventeenth Century* (Cambridge: Cambridge University Press, 1987).

[6] Anderson, "Learning to Read Architecture in the English Renaissance," pp. 239–86; Malcolm Airs, *The Tudor and Jacobean Country House: A Building History* (Stroud: Alan Sutton, 1995); Malcom Airs, *The Making of the English Country House, 1500–1640* (London: Architectural Press, 1975); Mark Girouard, *Robert Smythson and the Elizabethan Country House* (New Haven: Yale University Press, 1983); Mark Girouard, *Robert Smythson and the Architecture of the Elizabethan Era* (London: Country Life, 1966); Anthony Wells-Cole, *Art and Decoration in Elizabethan and Jacobean England: The Influence of Continental Prints, 1558–1625* (New Haven: Yale University Press, 1997); Lucy Worsley and Tom Addyman, "Riding Houses and Horses: William Cavendish's Architecture for the Art of Horsemanship," *Architectural History*, 45 (2002), 194–229.

masons.[7] Architects and master craftsmen copied newly imported architectural details, such as windows, gates, balconies, and fountains, from new London buildings onto country mansions and then replicated them again on other country houses.[8] At the same time, well-to-do men and women filled their houses with luxury goods from Europe and Asia.[9]

This chapter examines the aspirations and architectural education of English men and women and suggests some of the ways in which building and furnishing became an increasingly important site for the expansion of luxury consumption and the dissemination of continental style. It looks specifically at the importance of new London building and the meanings contemporaries attached to their houses, interiors, and gardens. Indeed, building for the ages reflected not only changing contemporary politics and social relationships, but also identity and self creation. Sir Henry Wotton, who helped shape the Jacobean taste for Italian and Italianate art as English ambassador to Venice, described "every man's proper mansion house and home," as "the theatre of his hospitality, the seat of self-fruition, the comfortablest part of his own life, the noblest of his son's inheritance, a kind of private princedom."[10]

LIONEL CRANFIELD BUILDS

Lionel Cranfield's building projects define significant changes in aspirations and display between 1603 and 1640. As Cranfield moved from London merchant to peer, from importer to Lord Treasurer, he projected his increasing importance through what the Jacobeans took to be "modern" European architecture. Cranfield's building commanded attention, influenced other builders, and forged connections with members of the Stuart elite.

A major London merchant engaged in the expanding importation of luxury textiles including Italian silks, velvet, and taffeta in the 1590s, Cranfield tripled his wealth between 1598 and 1601.[11] In 1603, as a sign of his prosperity, Cranfield decided to build in Wood Street, just off Cheapside in the City where he had his business. But Cranfield had problems with his

---

[7] Nicholas Cooper, *The Houses of the Gentry 1480–1680* (New Haven and London: Yale University Press, 1999).

[8] *Ibid.*, pp. 155–94.

[9] See, for instance, the furnishings of Aletheia Talbot, Countess of Arundel, discussed below and David M. Mitchell, "A Passion for the Exotic," in Mireille Galinou, *City Merchants and the Arts, 1670–1720* (London: Published by Oblong for the Corporation of London, 2004), pp. 68–82.

[10] Sir Henry Wotton, *The Elements of Architecture* (London: Longmans Green and Co., 1903), p. 65.

[11] Menna Prestwich, *Cranfield: Politics and Profits Under the Early Stuarts: The Career of Lionel Cranfield, Earl of Middlesex* (Oxford: Clarendon Press, 1966), pp. 30, 55.

builders. On 19 November 1603, Thomas Gardiner wrote urgently of the need to finish "a botcher's beginning." The builder had already ruined the foundation and the windows. First, "the columns that bear your new building must be removed one foot further outward and a new foundation made, for he hath left the jetty so great the joints sink already ... If Mr. Thornton, whom Mr. Stow commended to you, had not taken the work in hand ... your charge and work before had been spoiled." Second, he had cut a window "so far under size ... that it would not serve for neither of hall nor parlour window."[12] Thornton, recommended to Cranfield by John Stow, perhaps the author of the *Survey of London*, rescued a bad job, ennobled the increasingly important parlor, and provided the taste (or sense) that the builder lacked. In November 1604, Cranfield paid L20 to Thornton for the great parlor window.[13] Such a homely letter suggests that in building his house at Wood Street Cranfield did not engage an architect, did not use a drawing or a model but, like most contemporaries, relied on his own ideas and those of his builders.[14]

Cranfield's difficulties should be contrasted with his next major building projects. In 1611 Cranfield bought his first country estate, Pishobury in Hertfordshire, built by Sir Walter Mildmay, the Elizabethan Chancellor of the Exchequer, in 1585. Even as he calculated his income from the manor's rents, Cranfield began to refurnish the house and remake the gardens on a grander scale. In 1612 he sent one hundred fine trees, "the best I think you have seen," to create handsome walks and groves. He ordered the trees "set as their beauty may appear" and placed "together in walks some pretty distance asunder." He also planned to build a new orchard.[15] Three years later, Cranfield commissioned Inigo Jones to design a door or porch for Pishobury.[16] His innovations attracted attention. Sir Roger Townshend,

---

[12] The "botcher" had complained to his livery company but they acknowledged his error. HMC *Calendar of the Manuscripts of Major-General Lord Sackville*, edited by Charles John Sackville-West and Arthur Percival Newton, 2 vols. (London: HMSO, 1940–). HMC *Sackville*, I, 59–61, 270–71. For a discussion of the increasing importance of the parlor in the seventeenth century see Frank E. Brown, "Continuity and Change in the Urban House: Developments in Domestic Space Organisation in Seventeenth-Century London," *Comparative Studies in Society and History*, 28 (1986), 583.

[13] KAO U 269/1, E2, 17 November 1604.

[14] See Girouard, *Robert Smythson and the Elizabethan Country House*; John Schofield, *The Building of London: From the Conquest to the Great Fire* (London: British Museum Press in association with the Museum of London, 1993).

[15] Prestwich, *Cranfield: Politics and Profits Under the Early Stuarts*, pp. 89–90. HMC *Sackville*, I, 236–45, 247–51, 310–11 (October 1612), Cranfield to Richard Shepherd.

[16] John Harris and Gordon Higgott, *Inigo Jones: Complete Architectural Drawings* (London: Zwemmer, 1989), p. 84. These accounts no longer exist but BL Eg. 1933 contains the bailiff's account for an estate of Sir Lionel Cranfield's in 1615 which includes a carpenter working on a malt house and kitchen garden.

a Norfolk country gentleman who was building Raynham Hall, came to see Cranfield's house in October 1619 as part of his mission to view new domestic architecture.[17]

By 1621 Cranfield, now Master of the Court of Wards, and soon to be named Lord High Treasurer of England, had bought Beaufort House, the Chelsea mansion which had once belonged to Sir Thomas More.[18] He enlarged the park and hired Inigo Jones to design an elaborate gate and entrance.[19] When Sir Henry Wotton published *The Elements of Architecture* in 1624, he sent specially bound copies to leading officials including Cranfield. As he extolled the virtues of Vitruvius, Alberti, and Palladio,[20] Wotton cited in particular Palladio's views that the "principal Entrance was never to be regulated by any certain dimensions but by the dignity of the master; yet to exceed rather in the more, than in the less, is a mark of a generosity and may always be excused with some noble emblem ... or inscription as that of the Conte di Berilacqua, under his large gate at Verona."[21] The inept artisan in Wood Street was forgotten. For Cranfield, as for other Jacobeans, continental magnificence had replaced the "botcher's beginning."

Unfortunately, Lionel Cranfield's political star was on the wane. He was impeached by Parliament for extorting bribes from the suppliers of luxury goods and defrauding the Crown shortly after Wotton sent him *Elements of Architecture* in 1624. In his vigorous but vain defense, Cranfield denied the charges and argued that he had always paid full price to all the royal suppliers. "I bought my cloth of gold, silver and tissues, my velvets, satins, damasks, and taffetas, and my hangings, carpets and all other things of value of the merchants at the first and best hand with ready money and charged His Majesty with no other prices than I paid them."[22] After his fall, Cranfield sold his Chelsea mansion and lived in the City during term

---

[17] Linda Campbell, "Documentary Evidence for the Building of Raynham Hall," *Architectural History*, 32 (1989), 52–67. "Item given at Sir Lionel Cranfield his house viz to a man 5s, to a maid there 5s, to a boy there 12d (21 October 1619)."

[18] Beaufort House had belonged to Robert Cecil and he had planned to rebuild it. See Walter Hindes Godfrey (ed.), *The Parish of Chelsea*, 4 vols. Survey of London, vols. 2, 4, 7, 11 (London: London County Council, 1913–27), IV, Part II, pp. 18–27. While Cranfield was wealthier in 1621 than in 1603 he was able to buy Beaufort House for L3,000, about the value of the Wood Street properties. See Prestwich, *Cranfield: Profits and Politics under the Early Stuarts*, pp. 27, 384.

[19] KAO, U 269/1, E 15/1, Inigo Jones to Cranfield, 4 April 1620. Jones's designs for Cranfield are in Harris and Higgott, *Inigo Jones: Complete Architectural Drawings*, pp. 128–31.

[20] Wotton, *The Elements of Architecture*, pp. 65–66.

[21] Wotton, *The Elements of Architecture*, p. 120. The proportions of the gate were not strictly classical. See Gordon Higgott, "'Varying with Reason': Inigo Jones's Theory of Design," *Architectural History*, 35 (1992), 51–77.

[22] Quoted in Geoffrey Beard, *Upholsterers and Interior Furnishing in England, 1530–1840* (New Haven: Yale University Press, 1997), p. 56.

30. Lionel Cranfield commissioned Inigo Jones to design a gate for Beaufort House in Chelsea, one of several commissions he gave to Jones. The gate was incorporated into Chiswick House by Lord Burlington.
Inigo Jones Gate, commissioned by Lionel Cranfield, now part of Chiswick House.

time where his long-standing interest in building and furnishing continued. His accounts show that he hired carpenters, plasterers, bricklayers, and joiners to work on his house in St. Bartholomew's, rented part of the Earl of Holland's House, and had other houses for his family in the new squares of Covent Garden and Lincoln's Inn Fields.[23] Cranfield and his circle built

---

[23] Oxford, Bodleian, Bankes Mss. 62/31. KAO U 269, A389, Accounts. 1630, A462/4, receipts signed by Nicholas Stone.

and furnished with enthusiasm. Lord Newburgh wrote of letting his house and furnishing another,[24] and Bishop Godfrey Goodman wrote to Cranfield that he was employing a Scotsman in painting and engraving.[25] Cranfield also commissioned Van Dyck to do a portrait of his daughter Lady Frances before her marriage to Richard Sackville, heir to the Earl of Dorset. The proud father hung the picture with a rich gold frame supplied by George Geldorp, the art dealer.[26]

All that survives today of Cranfield's building *is* Inigo Jones's elaborate gate. A century later the Earl of Burlington incorporated it into Chiswick House, the epitome of the eighteenth-century Palladian revival. Cranfield may not have gone on the Grand Tour, but he had international connections and he knew what was in fashion. Indeed, it is incorrect to suggest that "no-one from the trading or banking classes" sought Inigo Jones's service.[27] Cranfield used him repeatedly. Merchants as well as courtiers adapted what they understood to be the magnificence and splendor of continental style in building, interiors, and gardens.[28]

EDUCATING THE EYE

Sixteenth-century England had seen a burst of construction in the countryside in what W. G. Hoskins called "The Great Rebuilding." In the 1570s the Earl of Shrewsbury wrote crossly to his wife that he did not like the way she kept so many of his men when he needed them for building.[29] In 1587 William Harrison emphasized the growing comfort of English houses in recent decades. "So magnificent and stately as the basest house of a baron doth often match in our days with some honours of princes in old time. So that if ever curious building did flourish in England, it is in these our years, wherein our workmen excel and are in manner comparable in skill with old Vitruvius, Leon Battista, and Serlio."[30] Lawrence Stone argues that in the

---

[24] KAO, U 269/1, CP 92. [25] KAO, U 269/1, CP 51.

[26] Alastair Laing, *In Trust for the Nation: Paintings from National Trust Houses* (London: National Gallery Publications, 1995), p. 22.

[27] Gent (ed.), *Albion's Classicism*; Harris and Higgott, *Inigo Jones: Complete Architectural Drawings*, pp. 298–99.

[28] On Pindar's house in Bishopsgate, see John Summerson, *Architecture in Britain, 1530–1830* (Harmondsworth, Middlset: Penguin, 1955), p. 53.

[29] Folger, X. d. 428 (97), George Talbot Earl of Shrewsbury to Elizabeth Countess of Shrewsbury, *c.* 1575. W. G. Hoskins, "The Rebuilding of Rural England, 1570–1640," *Past and Present*, 4 (1953), 44–59.

[30] William Harrison, *The Description of England*, ed. Georges Edelen (Washington, DC: Folger Shakespeare Library; New York: Dover Publications, 1994), p. 199. This reproduces the 1587 edition.

period 1580–1620, "England was largely rebuilt in the new materials with new standards of comfort and privacy." Large "Prodigy Houses," such as Theobalds, Holdenby, and Hardwick, displayed the honor of their owners who were able to house the Elizabethan court while on progress. With the inflation of honors under James, Stone argues, building increased.[31] Nicholas Cooper documents the expansion of gentry housing between 1480 and 1680.[32] Colin Platt emphasizes the importance of the appropriation of Italian and French design in the early seventeenth century and describes the second great rebuilding in the later seventeenth century.[33]

In particular, Inigo Jones influenced English building in the first half of the seventeenth century as Surveyor of the King's Works, member of the London Buildings Commission, architect to the affluent, and rebuilder of St. Paul's.[34] Jones was strongly influenced by continental design drawn from his own reading and from his earliest trips to the continent.[35] Jones bought a 1601 edition of Palladio's *Quattro Librii* in Venice which he immediately began to annotate.[36] His building drew on examples from Roman antiquity, Florentine and Bolognese Mannerism, and especially sixteenth-century architects such as Sebastiano Serlio, Palladio, and Palladio's pupil, Scamozzi, whom Jones met in Venice.[37] Jones also created designs for retail shopping at the New Exchange and for manufacturing and warehouses in Lothbury. As early as 1606, the antiquary Edmund Bolton hoped that through Inigo Jones "all that is praiseworthy in the elegant arts of the ancients may one day find their way across the Alps into England."[38]

Continental books shaped English design more generally. There were only two original works on architecture published in England in the sixteenth century, Leonard Digges's, *A Book Named Tectonicon* in 1556 and John Shute's, *First and Chief Grounds of Architecture* in 1563.[39] From

---

[31] Lawrence Stone, *The Crisis of the Aristocracy, 1558–1641* (Oxford: Clarendon Press, 1965), p. 552. W. G. Hoskins, "The Rebuilding of Rural England, 1570–1640," 44–59.

[32] Cooper, *The Houses of the Gentry 1480–1680*.

[33] Colin Platt, *The Great Rebuildings of Tudor and Stuart England: Revolutions in Architectural Taste* (London: University College of London Press, 1994).

[34] Colvin, *The History of the King's Works*, III, pp. 129–59.

[35] Anderson, "Learning to Read Architecture in the English Renaissance," pp. 239–86.

[36] John Newman, "Inigo Jones's Architectural Education before 1614," *Architectural History*, 35 (1992), 18–50.

[37] Harris and Higgott, *Inigo Jones: Complete Architectural Drawings*, p. 16. Giles Worsley, "Inigo Jones: Lonely Genius or Practical Exemplar?" *Journal of the British Archaeological Association*, 146 (1993), 102–12.

[38] Quoted in Harris and Higgott, *Inigo Jones: Complete Architectural Drawings*, p. 63.

[39] John Bold, *John Webb: Architectural Theory and Practice in the Seventeenth Century* (Oxford: Oxford University Press, 1989), p. 18. Jones and Webb owned and annotated the 1601 edition of Palladio and owned the 1619 edition of Serlio, p. 19. Eileen Harris, *British Architectural Books and Writers*,

the Elizabethan period on, English builders such as Sir Thomas Tresham collected continental works on architecture.[40] Robert Peake translated Serlio into English in 1611 and dedicated the volume to Prince Henry in order "to benefit the public." Serlio's books, which included illustrations of antique building, modern churches, secular architecture, and street scenes, provided a "source book for details."[41] The works of Vredeman de Vries, Wendel Dietterlin, and Palladio also proved influential.[42]

Arundel owned works by Vitruvius, Palladio, Leon Baptista Alberti, and Benvenuto Cellini. The Arundels' trip to Italy with Inigo Jones in 1613–14 influenced all three with a love of classical antiquity and Renaissance architecture. Arundel bought a fifteenth-century manuscript copy of Vitruvius's *De Architectura libri decem* on 14 June 1614 in Siena.[43] Arundel also borrowed books from Henry Percy, Earl of Northumberland, who compiled the most important architectural library in the early seventeenth century. One of Arundel's two copies of the work of Vredeman de Vries bears the inscription, "This book I had from my Lord of Northumberland."[44]

At the beginning of King James's reign, Henry Percy, ninth Earl of Northumberland, built Syon House on the outskirts of London. Northumberland, who had chaffed under Elizabeth's rule in the 1590s and corresponded with James VI of Scotland, had been named to James's Privy Council when he became king in 1603. In joyful spirits, Northumberland wrote to Robert Cecil in 1603 "now that I am a builder, I must borrow of my knowledge of Theobalds, somewhat out of every place of mark where curiosities are used."[45] His political success was short lived. In 1605 his brother took part in the Gunpowder Plot and was executed.

1556–1785 (Cambridge: Cambridge University Press, 1990), pp. 182–83, 418–22. Rudolf Wittkower argues that there were no English theoretical works on architecture in the seventeenth century while Elizabeth McKellar points to translations of works by Italians: e.g. Joseph Moxon published his translation of Vignola in 1655; William Leybourn published *The Compleat Surveyor* in 1653, McKellar, *The Birth of Modern London*, p. 139.

[40] Grouard, *Robert Smythson and the Elizabeth Country House*, p. 15.

[41] Bold, *John Webb*, p. 18. Harris, *British Architectural Books and Writers*; J. V. Field, "Why Translate Serlio?" in Francis Ames-Lewis (ed.), *Sir Thomas Gresham and Gresham College: Studies in the intellectual history of London in the sixteenth and seventeenth centuries*, (Aldershot, Hampshire: Ashgate Publishing, 1999), pp. 198–221.

[42] Bold, *John Webb*, pp. 18–19.

[43] BL Arundel Mss. 122, "M. Vitruvii Pollionis de Architectura libri decem," with Arundel's signature and date.

[44] Linda Levy Peck, "Uncovering the Arundel Library at the Royal Society: Changing Meanings of Science and the Fate of the Norfolk Donation," *Notes and Records of the Royal Society*, London, 52 (1998), p. 11, fig. 4.

[45] Quoted in Paul Hunneyball, "Status, Display, and Dissemination: Social Expression and Stylistic Change in the Architecture of Seventeenth-Century Hertfordshire" (D. Phil. thesis, Oxford University, 1994), p. 43. See G. R. Batho (ed.), *Household Papers, Henry Percy, Ninth Earl of Northumberland, 1564–1632* (London: Royal Historical Society, 1962).

31. Sebastiano Serlio, one of the most popular continental writers on architecture, provided illustrations of buildings and interiors used by English builders. To demonstrate perspective, this engraving shows an idealized Renaissance street scene for a play.
The Folger Shakespeare Library, STC 22235, f. 25v, Sebastian Serlio, *Architecture* (London, 1611).

Northumberland defended himself by claiming that he was too busy to plot treason: "examine but my humours in buildings, gardening, and private expenses these two years past."[46] Nevertheless, he was sentenced to the Tower.

As part of his devotion to building, Northumberland circulated his significant library of Latin, Italian, and French architecture books among his friends and acquaintances. In 1610 Northumberland loaned his books to Sir John Holles. He included works by "Vitruvius, the father of all the rest; Vignola, Jacques Androuett, Lorenzo Sirigatt, Jacques Perret; Philibert de L'Orme ... Sebastiano Serlio, Wendelino Dietterlin, Leon Baptista Alberti ... Palladius you have already." He encouraged Holles to "use them as long as you will, but lose none of them for some cannot be gotten again." When Northumberland later requested the return of the books, Holles replied from London that he had left both Vignola and Guigati in the country and asked to keep the Vitruvius a little longer, adding sententiously that "the pleasure of building, being a more permanent work, [was] many times better than getting of children or other posterity."[47]

Sir John Coke, who made a fortune from office as Secretary of State, spent L6,600 remodeling Melbourne Hall and sent thirty-two pages of instructions to his builders in 1629.[48] While Coke focused on economy and recycling materials, he also emphasized regularity in building. Amongst the books in Coke's library was Wotton's *The Elements of Architecture*.[49] Even at the end of the century, Sir John Van Brugh drew few designs for his extraordinary Castle Howard.[50] Instead, the account book of the mason and carpenters at Castle Howard includes a transcription of chapters 1 and 2 of Palladio's Second Book of Architecture.[51]

Writers and publishers took advantage of the growing market for books on continental architecture in the early seventeenth century. In addition to Robert Peake's translation of Serlio in 1611, Henry Peacham included

[46] Quoted in Mark Nicholls, *Investigating Gunpowder Plot* (Manchester, Manchester University Press, 1991), p. 144.

[47] HMC *Portland*, IX, 152, 115. Neither letter is dated. Girouard suggests that Northumberland's letter dates from 1610. Girouard, *Robert Smythson and the Architecture of the Elizabethan Era*, pp. 28–31. Holles's letter may have been written after 1612 when he had lost favor at court after the death of his patron, Prince Henry. Peter Seddon (ed.), *Letters of John Holles*, 3 vols. (Nottingham: Thoroton Society Record Series, 1975–86).

[48] Michael Young, *Servility and Service: The Life and Work of Sir John Coke* (Woodbridge, Suffolk: Boydell Press 1986), p. 225. Cooper, *The Houses of the Gentry, 1480–1680*, pp. 45, 217.

[49] BL Add. Mss. 69,883B, Coke Papers, Series II, ff. 58–59, "List of books at Greys Inn"; Cooper, *The Houses of the Gentry, 1480–1680*, pp. 45, 216–18, 254–55.

[50] McKellar, *The Birth of Modern London*, p. 119.

[51] Charles Saumarez-Smith, *The Building of Castle Howard* (London: Faber, 1990), p. 26.

a chapter on architecture in his *The Compleat Gentleman* (London, 1622).
Bacon wrote about building in his essays and, as we have seen, Wotton
published *The Elements of Architecture* in 1624.[52] Later in the century, Pierre
Le Muet, architect to Louis XIV, published the *Art of Fair Building
represented in the figures of several uprights of houses with their ground plots
fitting for persons of all qualities* in 1675. Like Hannah Woolley, whose
A Supplement to the Queen-Like Closet was published in 1674, the author
sought to make comfort and refinement more widely available. "To lodge
most pleasantly and stately ... is one of the most delightful contents of
this life." Muet aimed, as had Peake in 1611, at the "benefit of the public."
His publisher, Robert Pricke of Cripple Gate, advertised that his shop had
"other books of architecture and also ... maps, copy-books, books of
beasts, birds, flowers and fruits and likewise Italian, Dutch and French
prints."[53] In 1683 Joseph Moxon continued to recommend Serlio, Vignola,
Scamozzi, Palladio, and Sir Henry Wotton, all published in England by the
early seventeenth century.[54] Clearly there was a boom in architectural
literature in Jacobean England that continued through the century.

Well-to-do patrons did more than read and collect architecture books.
Some went on the Grand Tour in France, Italy, and the Low Countries and
studied at Geneva and Padua. At home they went to see the buildings going
up around them. Thus, Sir Roger Townshend, who visited Cranfield's
house in 1619, also visited Inigo Jones's work on the Prince's lodgings at
Newmarket;[55] Hatfield House, still unfinished when Lord Treasurer
Salisbury died in 1612; Audley End, which Suffolk built in 1614; and the
Earl of Arundel's house at Highgate. In London he viewed Inigo Jones's
improvements to Somerset House;[56] saw Fulke Greville's new residence
called Bath House (also drawn by John Smythson when he came to
London in 1619); and had William Edge, his bricklayer and plot drawer,
go to Wimbledon House "to take a view" both of the house and the
gardens. Then, in 1619 Townshend went abroad and took William Edge
with him.[57] When, in 1622, Townshend continued his building at
Raynham Hall, he adopted a style that architectural historians consider
precociously classical.[58] Whether or not such a label is appropriate,

[52] Girouard, *Robert Smythson and the Architecture of the Elizabethan Era*, p 31.
[53] Pierre Le Muet, *The Art of Fair Building represented in the figures of several uprights of houses with their ground plots fitting for persons of all qualities* (London, 1675), "To the reader" and title page.
[54] See McKellar, *The Birth of Modern London*, p. 139.
[55] Colvin, *The History of the King's Works*, III, p. 138; IV, pp. 176–79.   [56] *Ibid.*, IV, pp. 254–60.
[57] Campbell, "Documentary Evidence for the Building of Raynham Hall," 57 and 65–66, notes 65, 68, 69, 73, 74, 75, 80.
[58] *Ibid.*, pp. 57 and 65–66.

Townshend consciously aimed to infuse his building with contemporary and continental style.

LONDON: ROYAL POLICY

London was always a magnet to those in power. It had been an important metropolis and entrepôt since Roman times and the site of government and of the ecclesiastical elite since the Middle Ages. Caroline Barron points out that in the twelfth and thirteenth centuries bishops and abbots had inns in the City of London as did some secular lords. This wealthy aristocracy used their London houses for offices, warehouses, and entertainment.[59] London's overall population quadrupled from 50,000 in 1550 to 200,000 in 1630.[60] Like continental monarchs, the Tudors and early Stuarts drew their elite to London. Frequented by the gentry when the law courts were in session and when Parliament met, London became the site of conspicuous consumption as F. J. Fisher pointed out.[61]

Jacobean aristocratic culture was increasingly urban. Elizabethan nobility and officeholders had been more likely to rent housing during term time than to build. That changed with the accession of King James because, in contrast to Queen Elizabeth, James I stopped traveling on progress around the countryside. He made London even more of a magnet for those who came to seek preferment, follow cases at law, petition the courts, hear sermons, participate in trading companies, pay visits, and take part in the marriage market. Although Lawrence Stone contrasted the French aristocracy who built city palaces with the English who built country houses,[62] in fact, many of the early Stuart nobility built city palaces and suburban villas. Furthermore, by the end of the seventeenth century, some country gentry

[59] Caroline Barron, "Centres of Conspicuous Consumption: The Aristocratic Townhouse in London, 1200–1550, *London Journal*, 20 (1995), 1–16. Christopher Dyer, *Standards of Living in the Later Middle Ages: Social Change in England* (Cambridge: Cambridge University Press, 1989).

[60] Schofield, *The Building of London*, p. 157; Vanessa Harding, "Early Modern London 1550–1700," *London Journal*, 20 (1995), 34–45.

[61] F. J. Fisher, "The Development of London as a Centre of Conspicuous Consumption in the Sixteenth and Seventeenth Centuries," *TRHS*, 4th series 30 (1948), 37–50; Richard Goldthwaite, "The Empire of Things: Consumer Demand in Renaissance Italy," in Francis W. Kent, Patricia Simons, and J. D. Eade (eds.) *Patronage, Art and Society in Renaissance Italy* (Canberra Humanities Research Centre and Oxford: Clarendon Press, 1987), pp. 153–76. See also Peter Burke, "Investment and Culture in Three Seventeenth-Century Cities: Rome, Amsterdam, Paris," *Journal of European Economic History*, 7 (1978), 311–36.

[62] See Lawrence Stone, "The Residential Development of the West End of London in the Seventeenth Century," in Barbara C. Malament (ed.), *After the Reformation: Essays in Honor of J. H. Hexter* (Philadelphia: University of Pennsylvania Press, 1980), pp. 167–212.

were spending as much as nine months a year in London.[63] Richard Goldthwaite argues that the city – Florence, Rome, Venice – was the engine of consumption in Renaissance Italy.[64] London was the chief engine of the English economy and building was one of London's most important trades.

James I celebrated himself as a Roman Emperor from his accession to the English throne and sought to make London a new Rome.[65] He appointed Simon Basil, who had close ties to Salisbury, Surveyor of the King's Works. According to Howard Colvin, Basil's tenure witnessed "vastly increased expenditure representing a royal building program more ambitious than England had seen for over half a century."[66] From the appointment of Inigo Jones as Surveyor in 1615, the plans for the King's works became self-consciously Italianate.[67] King James followed his pattern of promoting luxury production by repeatedly issuing proclamations from 1603 regulating London building.[68] James called for brick instead of timber and "uniform order and form."[69] In a proclamation of 1615 he praised several new building projects undertaken in London since his accession that had enhanced "public use."

Now that our city of London is become the greatest or next the greatest city of the Christian world, it is more than time that there be an utter cessation of further new-buildings ... [We] do exceedingly approve and commend all edifices, structures, and works, which tend to public use and ornament, in and about our said city, as the paving of Smithfield, the planting of Moorfields, the bringing of the new stream unto the western parts of the cities and suburbs, the pesthouse, Sutton's hospital, Britain's Burse, the re-edifying of Aldgate, Hicks Hall, and the like work, which have been erected and performed in greater number in these twelve years of our reign than in whole ages heretofore as it was said by the first Emperor of Rome, that he had found the city of Rome of bricks, and left it of marble, so that we whom God hath honored to be the first King of Great Britain mought be able to say in some proportion, that we found our city and suburbs of London of sticks, and left them of bricks, being a material far more durable, safe from fire, beautiful and magnificent.[70]

[63] Susan E. Whyman, *Sociability and Power in Late-Stuart England: The Cultural Worlds of the Verneys, 1660–1720* (Oxford: Oxford University Press, 1999).

[64] Goldthwaite, "The Empire of Things," pp. 153–76.

[65] Linda Levy Peck (ed.), *The Mental World of the Jacobean Court* (Cambridge: Cambridge University Press, 1991), pp. 5, 7–8, 9.

[66] Colvin, *The History of the King's Works*, III, p. 107.   [67] *Ibid.*, IV, pp. 3–34.

[68] *Stuart Royal Proclamations*, ed. James F. Larkin and Paul L. Hughes (Oxford: Clarendon Press, 1973); vol. I: *Royal Proclamations of James I, 1603–1625*; Vol. II: *Royal Proclamations of Charles I, 1625–1646*.

[69] *Stuart Royal Proclamations*, I, no. 51, 1 March 1604–1605.

[70] *Ibid.*, no. 152, 16 July 1615. Norman Brett-James, *The Growth of Stuart London* (London: George Allen and Unwin, 1935), p. 9.

Not only did the Crown play an important role in refining and regulating London building, it supported, albeit with some misgivings, new aristocratic housing.

London's intense population growth brought pressure on the housing stock. London landlords subdivided houses to increase their income from letting. Jeremy Boulton suggests that "all ranks of society took in lodgers."[71] James aimed, as had Elizabeth, to prevent disease caused by overcrowding through the division of tenements. Both monarchs insisted that new buildings must be established on old foundations. Thus, within a month of James's accession, the Privy Council prohibited Arnold James from building in Cheapside, "higher than the shed which stood there before, lest it injure the lights of the Golden Key," belonging to the Mercers' Company whose rents supported a grammar school.[72] James used the Privy Council and the Star Chamber to proceed against violators.

Most significantly, the King moved to fulfill his vision of London as a new Rome by creating a Commission on New Buildings. He named the Earl of Arundel to head it with Inigo Jones as its principal advisor. Sir Henry Wotton and Lionel Cranfield also were members.[73] As we have seen, all these men shared and shaped the love of continental design. The Commission had powers to enforce the King's proclamations, to hear complaints, and to fine.[74]

Whatever James's good intentions, contemporaries such as John Chamberlain immediately labeled the Commission a financial scheme of the Crown.[75] Royal efforts to regulate London building raised political questions about the King's power to control private property and levy taxes without Parliament. In 1615 James denied that its purpose was to raise money. Nevertheless, in 1624 Parliament listed the Commission as a grievance. In reply, King James told members of parliament that "I have a grievance as well as you. First that you make a matter of building about London a grievance ... I have no end in it but the honour of the kingdom, I have maintained it; and I marvel much that you have condemned the

---

[71] Boulton, *Neighbourhood and Society*, pp. 85–86.   [72] *CSPD 1603–10*, p. 4, 20 April 1603.

[73] *Acts of the Privy Council, 1615–16*, pp. 97–98, 121–22, 303–304, 413, 428, 483–86. See Thomas G. Barnes, "The Prerogative and Environmental Control of London Building in the Early Seventeenth Century: The Lost Opportunity," *California Law Review*, 58 (1970), 1332–63. David Howarth, "The Politics of Inigo Jones," in Howarth (ed.), *Art and Patronage in the Caroline Courts: Essays in Honour of Sir Oliver Millar* (Cambridge: Cambridge University Press, 1993), pp. 68–89. Brett-James, *The Growth of Stuart London*, pp. 140–47; Colvin, *The History of the King's Works*, III, pp. 142–47.

[74] Barnes, "The Prerogative and Environmental Control of London Building," 1332–63.

[75] N. E. McClure (ed.), *The Letters of John Chamberlain*, 2 vols. (Philadelphia: American Philosophical Society, 1939), I, p. 601.

commissioners."[76] When it became clear that they could not practically demolish large numbers of buildings, the Commission on New Building settled for fining owners and getting them to rebuild.

The Commission on New Building continued into Charles I's reign. Shortly after his accession, King Charles issued an extensive proclamation specifiying dimensions and demanding regularity in London building. Thomas Barnes suggests that Inigo Jones was responsible for the requirements that both Stuarts set out for windows, numbers of stories, and thickness of walls as well as the prohibition of protrusions over the street.[77] But contemporary critics saw the proclamation as yet another aspect of the Personal Rule between 1629 and 1640, claiming that its purpose was to extract fines to benefit projectors and the Crown. Such criticism stimulated strong counterclaims. Thus John Cusacke argued that it was "high treason in a subject to say that the streets of the city of London or of any other city within His Majesty's dominions of England or Ireland are not His Majesty's proper possessions and that the building on or over any of them raised are not held in capite," that is by feudal tenure.[78] Yet, even if the Commission aroused political debate about Crown finance, its intent was to make London a modern European capital. Indeed, that very intent generated some of the criticism. Thus, James Howell explained that Arundel, "observing the uniform and regular way of stone structure up and down Italy, hath introduced that form of building to London and Westminster, and elsewhere, which though distasteful at first, as all inno-vations are, for they seem like bug-bears, or gorgons' heads, to the vulgar; yet they find now the commodity, permanence, and beauty thereof, the three main principles of architecture."[79]

The explosive growth of London worried the Crown. Despite repeated proclamations aimed at sending the gentry back to the country, inquests revealed gentry living in many of London's wards[80] or claiming that they

---

[76] *Stuart Royal Proclamations*, I, p. 597n2.

[77] Barnes, "The Prerogative and Environmental Control of London Building," 1349; Cooper, *The Houses of the Gentry, 1480–1680*, p. 172.

[78] John Cusacke, "Via Regia," Oxford, Bodleian Library, Rawlinson D 693. Cusacke argued that the King had the right to regulate London housing because he had a title "in capite to all jettings of houses into the streets of cities or boroughs or into public highways of England and Ireland." He inquired whether houses which were "demolished and changed into brick buildings . . . extinguish the king's former lawful claim by a tenure in capite." Linda Levy Peck, "Beyond the Pale: John Cusacke and the Language of Absolutism in Early Stuart Britain," *The Historical Journal*, 41 (1998), 121–49.

[79] Quoted in Oliver Hill and John Cornforth, "English Country Houses: Caroline, 1625–1685," *Connoisseur*, 164 (1967), 266.

[80] Felicity Heal and Clive Holmes, *The Gentry in England and Wales, 1500–1700* (Basingstoke, Hampshire: Macmillan; Stanford: Stanford University Press, 1994). Oxford, Bodleian Library,

had no country home at all.[81] The poet, "Sir John Suckling ... and his family ... lodged in the house of William Sharowe, tailor, in Fleet Street"[82] and "Sir Fulke Greville ... for his abode in the country he has none we can learn."[83] Yet, whether they built great palaces on the Strand, villas in the suburbs, rented new houses in Covent Garden, or took rooms with the tailor in Fleet Street, the nobility and gentry were increasingly urban and, in the early seventeenth century, intermingled with the London populace.[84] That urban aristocracy fueled consumption of imported luxury goods and style in the early seventeenth century.

CITY PALACE, URBAN SQUARE, AND SUBURBAN VILLA

The early seventeenth century saw the increasing importance of the city palace and new types of building in the form of squares, such as Covent Garden and Lincoln's Inn Fields, and the villa, such as Syon, Ham House, Tart Hall, and Albury.[85] John Adamson has analyzed the building of aristocratic palaces between 1600 and 1660. In 1600 there were twelve major houses; by 1642 there were twenty-six, twelve of them along the river. These were owned by the highest-ranking nobles, two dukes and twenty-one earls, who, he argues, lived in greater state than the King himself. He points out that household ordinances became more elaborate in the 1620s and 1630s, and that ambassadors stayed in great peers' houses. Questioning the notion of aristocratic financial distress during the Civil War, he demonstrates that the great nobility continued to build in the 1640s.[86]

Bankes Mss. 62/32. Gentry often claimed that they were in London to pursue lawsuits or were the King's servants. Church wardens tried to protect some of their gentry as an "ancient parishioner" and "good benefactor to our poor, and other needful occasions."

[81] Oxford, Bodleian Library, Bankes Mss. 62/18. Sir Christopher Darcy even claimed downward mobility: he was a younger son, the little land that he owned was let to farmers, and he had married into the family of a London doctor.

[82] Oxford, Bodleian Library, Bankes Mss. 14/2. In January 1634–35, in Farringdon Ward Without, St. Brides, the common council certified that: "The Earl of Northumberland has taken Dorset House in Salisbury Court for five years and has been resident there one year and came thither about 3 November 1633 and stayed there until 3 March following, and came thither again about ... November last, and he and his family were the last in the country at his mansion house at Petworth and at Syon in Middlesex."

[83] Oxford, Bodleian Library, Bankes Mss. 14/4.

[84] Sir Henry Gater and Edwin Paul Wheeler, *The Parish of St. Martin-in-the-Fields*, Part II, *The Strand*, Survey of London, vol. 18 (London: London County Council, 1937). Northampton House was surrounded by the victualer, the sadler, and the vintner.

[85] Cooper, *The Houses of the Gentry, 1480–1680*, pp. 128–54.

[86] John Adamson, "Princely Palaces: Aristocratic Town Houses, 1600–1660," presented at conference, Centre for Metropolitan History, Institute of Historical Research, University of London, 15–17 July 1993.

Among the new elite that James's accession swept into power were Henry Howard, Earl of Northampton, his nephew Thomas Howard, Earl of Suffolk, and his great-nephew Thomas Howard, Earl of Arundel. The houses of these three Jacobeans, Northampton House, Audley End, and Arundel House, not only reflect Howard ambitions but also the relationship of building to changing court culture. Henry Howard, Earl of Northampton, descended from the Dukes of Norfolk, was the younger son and brother of two Tudor traitors, the Earl of Surrey and Thomas Howard, fourth Duke of Norfolk. Within the first two years of the new reign, he built the largest London house of the Jacobean period on the Strand diagonally across from the Whitehall Tilt yard. By its 162 feet of frontage on the Strand and proximity to the court, Northampton House proclaimed the power of the Lord who resided within. Size and location were its most important features: Northampton House was closer to the King than Salisbury, Bedford, York, Dorset, and Essex Houses. Its architecture appeared to refer to Elizabethan prodigy houses, a square with commanding towers on each corner and an entry gate smothered in Flemish strap work.[87] The Earl of Northampton also established a country residence in Greenwich Park on the model of a hunting lodge, a new building type of the Jacobean period. When Northampton died in 1614, his nephew, Thomas Howard, Earl of Suffolk, inherited his house on the Strand and immediately renamed it Suffolk House. Suffolk took down Tudor outbuildings and put in a garden.[88]

One striking aspect of the building boom of the first decade of the seventeenth century was that some of these new aristocratic palaces were *remodeled* beginning in the 1630s and continuing throughout the Civil War, Commonwealth, and Restoration. The English nobility rebuilt not because the city palaces were in poor repair but because they were old-fashioned. Thus, in the 1640s, when Northampton House came into the hands of the Percys, Earls of Northumberland, they rebuilt it, first, in 1642,

---

[87] Linda Levy Peck, *Northampton: Patronage and Policy at the Court of James I* (London: Allen and Unwin, 1982), p. 73; E. Beresford Chancellor, *The Private Palaces of London Past and Present* (London: Kegan Paul, Trench, Trubner & Co., 1908), pp. 10–20; Gater and Wheeler, *The Parish of St. Martin-in-the-Fields*, Part III, *Trafalgar Square and Neighbourhood*, Survey of London, Vol. 20. (London: London County Council, 1940). On the rebuilding of Northumberland House see Jeremy Wood, "The Architectural Patronage of Algernon Percy, 10th Earl of Northumberland," in John Bold and Edward Chaney (eds.), *English Architecture, Public and Private: Essays for Kerry Downes*, (London: Hambledon Press, 1993), pp. 55–80; Adamson, "Princely Palaces: Aristocratic Town Houses, 1600–1660."

[88] David Howarth, "The Houses of the Howards," Paper Presented at The Aristocratic Town House in London Conference, Centre for Metropolitan History, Institute of Historical Research, University of London, 15–17 July 1993.

according to the designs of Inigo Jones, and, second, in the 1650s, according to those of John Webb, Jones's associate.[89] The Howards and Percys, descendants of great medieval magnates, now built on the Strand and collected pictures from the Rialto.

Suffolk built Audley End, the largest private house in Jacobean England, after he became Lord Treasurer in 1614. Its purpose, like that of Northampton House, was to display the restored power of the Howards. Suffolk designed Audley End to house the court when the monarch, on progress, came to visit. Its size caused wonder. But royal tastes had changed. Because King James no longer traveled around the countryside to meet his local governors and citizens after the difficulties of his first progress in 1604, Audley End quickly became a white elephant and came into the hands of the Crown.[90] In contrast, Arundel added an art gallery designed by Inigo Jones to his house on the Strand in order to display his collections.[91] Franciscus Junius, the family tutor, lauded the Arundels who "expose these jewels of art to the public view in the academy at Arundel House." Amongst the visitors, Abraham Booth of the Dutch East India Company, described "this court as worth seeing before all others."[92]

King James's favorites, Robert Carr, Earl of Somerset, and George Villiers, Duke of Buckingham, also became proponents of the new taste in building and interior furnishings. While Carr did not have time to build, we have already seen his desire to buy continental furnishings from at least 1612. As we shall see, his 1615 inventory shows how successful he was in buying pictures, furniture, and hangings. The Duke of Buckingham commissioned Inigo Jones to draw up plans for his lodging at Whitehall, to remodel a townhouse about 1619–21, and work on a gallery, chapel, armory, and stable at New Hall in Essex.[93] For New Hall, Jones designed "an elaborate Italianate ceiling . . . blue white and gold." Buckingham filled York House and his Chelsea villa with sculpture and pictures.[94]

Alongside city palaces, London's strong population growth provoked more general real estate speculation. The increasing density of the City and the West End is visible in contemporary maps such as William Fairthorne's

---

[89] See Wood, "The Architectural Patronage of Algernon Percy," pp. 55–80.
[90] Colvin, *The History of the King's Works*, IV, p. 28.
[91] David Howarth, *Lord Arundel and his Circle* (New Haven: Yale University Press, 1985), p. 57.
[92] Quoted in Elizabeth V. Chew, "The Countess of Arundel and Tart Hall," in Edward Chaney (ed.), *The Evolution of English Collecting: The Reception of Italian Art in the Tudor and Stuart Periods* (New Haven: Yale University Press, 2003), pp. 285–314.
[93] John Harris and A. A. Tait, *Catalogue of the Drawings By Inigo Jones, John Webb and Isaac de Caus at Worcester College Oxford* (Oxford: Oxford University Press, 1979), pp. 10–11.
[94] Simon Jervis, "Furniture for the First Duke of Buckingham," *Furniture History*, 33 (1997), 48–74.

of 1658.[95] Small tradesmen, carpenters, bricklayers, and merchants were prosecuted for putting up illegal tenements in the City and its eastern suburbs between 1590 and 1602. Thomas Barnes points out that, "By the 1630s, the majority of West End developers were very substantial persons."[96]

Robert Cecil, Earl of Salisbury, who had catered to the luxurious tastes of the well-to-do by building the New Exchange in 1609, developed the adjacent real estate in the parish of St. Martin in-the-Fields to provide them with suitable West End residences. On his nine acres, he leased plots for thirty-one years and allowed lessees to design their houses, provided they maintain the residential nature of the neighborhood.[97] When, in the 1620s, high-ranking members of the elite moved in, the second Earl of Salisbury insisted that they build in brick. His tenants included courtiers and officeholders who continued to renew their leases up to 1640.[98]

The fourth Duke of Bedford developed Covent Garden north of the Strand by 1629 with the support of the Crown. The family had owned the land since the dissolution of the monasteries. Bedford engaged Inigo Jones to produce a new aristocratic townhouse for an urban gentry based on continental models. This early example of speculative building was influenced by the piazza at Leghorn [Livorno], the center of English merchant activity in Italy, and the Place des Vosges in Paris.[99] Dianne Duggan argues that King Charles himself insisted on the model of regularity for the townhouses and that Inigo Jones serve as designer. The King and the Commission on New Building oversaw the initial plans.[100]

Despite anxiety about gentry living in town rather than the country, the Crown also applauded the development of aristocratic housing in Lincoln's Inn Fields near the Inns of Court.[101] It granted William Newton licenses to build in Great Queen Street and Lincoln's Inn Fields.[102] John Holles, Earl

[95] William Fairthorne, "An Exact Delineation of the Cities of London and Westminster and the Suburbs" [1658] (London: The London Topographical Society, 1905).

[96] Barnes, "The Prerogative and Environmental Control of London Building" 1338–39.

[97] Lawrence Stone, *Family and Fortune: Studies in Aristocratic Finance in the Sixteenth and Seventeenth Centuries* (Oxford: Clarendon Press, 1973), pp. 109–12.

[98] Stone, *Family and Fortune: Studies in Aristocratic Finance in the Sixteenth and Seventeenth Centuries*, pp. 109–111. Westminster Archives, 10/356.

[99] Dianne Duggan, "'London the Ring, Covent Garden the Jewel of that Ring': New Light on Covent Garden," *Architectural History*, 43 (2000), 140–61. Schofield, *The Building of London*, p. 168.

[100] Duggan, "London the Ring, Covent Garden the Jewel of that Ring," 140–61. Dianne Duggan, "The Fourth Side of Covent Garden Piazza, New Light on the History and Significance of Bedford House," *The British Art Journal*, 3 (2003), 53–65.

[101] Schofield, *The Building of London*, p. 170.

[102] Colvin, *The History of the King's Works*, III, p. 145.

of Clare, who had borrowed architecture books from the Earl of Northumberland in 1610, was one of the major developers in this project. In the 1630s, real estate speculators in the West End included other courtiers such as John Moore, Clerk of the Signet, and William Price, Groom of the King's Privy Chamber. In fact, the Earl of Clare, Moore, and Price were called up before Star Chamber in the 1630s for violating the King's proclamations on building.[103] The Arundels too participated in the speculative building in the 1630s. The Countess purchased a piece of land near Covent Garden and then built, decorated, and rented out a house to the Marquis of Vieuville by 1643.[104] While he was serving in the second Bishops' War in the summer of 1640, the second Earl of Bridgewater worried about new building near his house in the Barbican: "I hope … my neighbors … [do not] take advantage of my absence to erect their buildings to my annoyance." His steward reassured him that "There have not as yet any body offered to erect any building near your Lordship's walls."[105]

Along with city palaces and new urban squares, the Stuart elite shaped the capital with villas, important houses on the edges of the green spaces surrounding the city. Syon House, Northumberland's suburban house, stood near Richmond. Cranfield and other courtiers had houses in Chelsea. In 1610 Thomas Vavasour, a Jacobean courtier, built a suburban mansion, called Ham House. After Vavasour's death, William Murray, the son of one of the Jacobean Scots who had accompanied James south, bought Ham House and enlarged it in the 1630s.[106] Ham House was remodeled again in the 1650s by his daughter Elizabeth, Lady Dysart, later Countess of Lauderdale.[107] Sir Adam Newton, tutor to Prince Henry, built Charlton House which was, according to Pevsner "apart from Holland House, the only Jacobean mansion of the first order in the precincts of London." Wendel Dietterlin's *Architectura* (1593), one of the most influential books on architecture, served as a major source for Charlton House, as well as for Bramshill, in Hampshire, built by Lord Zouch between 1606 and 1612.[108]

---

[103] Barnes, "The Prerogative and Environmental Control of London Building," 1339.

[104] David Howarth, "The Patronage and Collecting of Aletheia, Countess of Arundel 1606–54," *Journal of the History of Collections*, 10 (1998), 135.

[105] HEH, Bridgewater Mss. 6560, Earl of Bridgewater to Richard Harrison, 17 August 1640, 6561, Harrison to Bridgewater, 22 August 1640. I am grateful to Barbara Donagan for these references.

[106] Cathal Moore, Christopher Rowell, and Nino Strachey, *Ham House* (London: National Trust, 1995). Peter M. Thornton and Maurice Tomlin, *The Furnishing and Decoration of Ham House*, Furniture History Series 16 (London: Furniture History Society, 1980), pp. 1–33.

[107] Thornton and Tomlin, *The Furnishing and Decoration of Ham House*, pp. 33–35.

[108] Nikolaus Pevsner and David Lloyd, *Hampshire and the Isle of Wight* (Harmondsworth: Penguin, 1967), p. 38.

32. Inigo Jones modeled the Queen's House on a Medici villa and ideas drawn from Scamozzi and Palladio.
Worcester College, Oxford, Inigo Jones, The Queen's House, Greenwich. Reproduced by permission of the Provost and Fellows of Worcester College, Oxford.

In 1616 Queen Anne commissioned Inigo Jones to create one of the most important buildings of the early Stuart period, the Queen's House in Greenwich. According to Howard Colvin, Jones modeled the Queen's House directly on Poggio a Caiano, the Medici villa built by Sangallo in the 1480s as well as Scamozzi's Villa Molini to which he added ideas drawn from Palladio's *Quattro Librii*.[109] Salomon de Caus laid out new gardens in front.[110] Left unfinished at the Queen's death, the project was taken up again by Henrietta Maria, again with Inigo Jones's help, and in the 1630s preparations were made for the insertion of the ceiling paintings by Orazio Gentileschi. By 1637–40, Nicholas Stone had prepared pedestals for the installation of marble sculpture.[111]

Like Inigo Jones, her traveling companion, the Countess of Arundel's love of Italy inspired her when, in the 1630s, she built Tart Hall.[112] Located on the edge of St. James's Park, next to the present site of Buckingham

[109] Colvin, *The History of the King's Works*, IV, pp. 114–15.

[110] *Ibid.*, pp. 112–23.   [111] *Ibid.*, pp. 119, 120.

[112] Howarth, "The Patronage and Collecting of Aletheia, Countess of Arundel," 125–37. Dianne Duggan, "'A Rather Fascinating Hybrid,' Tart Hall: Lady Arundel's Casino at Whitehall," *The British Art Journal*, 4 (2003), 54–64; Nikolaus Pevsner, *The Buildings of England* (Harmondsworth: Penguin, 1951–74). Pevsner suggests that the trio of houses on the site of Buckingham Palace, belonging to George Gage, George Goring, and the Countess of Arundel, drew on the designs of Wendel Dietterlin. BL Maps, Crace Collection, Portfolio XI, 61, "A Platt and Description of Tart Hall House with the Gardens showing how far the Parish of St. Martin-in-the-Fields and St. Margaret's in Westminster extended into the said house and gardens." I am grateful to Elizabeth Chew for this citation.

Palace, beside roads to Westminster and Chelsea, Tart Hall's expansive gardens stretched beside those of her neighbors, George Gage, the cosmopolitan art dealer, and George Goring, Lord Arlington, the Caroline collector.[113] Dianne Duggan suggests that, with the advice of George Gage, she based the house, at least in part, on the Venetian palazzi and Brenta villas she had visited in the early 1620s.[114] The Palazzo del Te, the suburban villa of the Gonzagas in Mantua, may have been another influence. We know that Inigo Jones had made notes on Palazzo del Te which he and the Arundels visited.[115] In 1623 the Countess asked Count Alessandro Striggio for a scale model of the Palazzo del Te on behalf of Prince Charles, "to show every detail together with a clear description of the principal things to be seen inside by way of sculpture and painting ... And, if it were possible to have the original model that was used for the same building, he would be even more grateful."[116] Duggan also suggests similarities between Tart Hall and Sir John Danvers's house in Chelsea, which he built in 1622–23 after returning from Italy.[117]

Alongside the heady boom in new domestic architecture, new buildings for manufacture went up in London. The patent to make farthing tokens was awarded to Henry Frederick, Lord Maltravers, the Arundels' son, and Sir Francis Crane, director of the Mortlake tapestry works, in 1636. Two years later Inigo Jones drafted plans that draw strongly on Serlio for Maltravers's house, office, and warehouse in Lothbury, a center for metal workers in the City of London.[118] Although art historians have doubted whether Jones's designs were ever built, property transactions suggest that they were.[119] In 1639 Crane's executor, his brother Richard, sold his interest in lands and tenements in Lothbury to Maltravers for L1,750. Located on Lothbury and Coleman Street, the property bordered on the gardens of two Caroline courtiers, Sir Robert Killigrew, for whom Inigo Jones built a house, and Richard, Earl of Warwick.[120] The charter is marked "Lothbury

---

[113] BL Maps, Crace Collection, #61.

[114] Duggan, "Tart Hall: Lady Arundel's Casino at Whitehall," 54–64.

[115] Jeremy Wood, "Taste and Connoisseurship at the Court of Charles I: Inigo Jones and the Work of Giulio Romano," in Eveline Cruickshanks (ed.), *The Stuart Courts* (Stroud: Sutton, 2000), pp. 118–40.

[116] *Ibid.*, pp. 120–21, translation from the Italian, p. 127. David Howarth suggests that she asked on behalf of Prince Charles, "The Patronage and Collecting of Aletheia, Countess of Arundel," 125–37, 130.

[117] Duggan, "Tart Hall: Lady Arundel's Casino at Whitehall," 54–64.

[118] See Harris and Higgott, *Inigo Jones: Complete Architectural Drawings*, pp. 16, 17, 18, 84–85, 256, 257; Worsley, "Inigo Jones: Lonely Genius or Practical Exemplar?" 109–10.

[119] Harris and Higgott, *Inigo Jones: Complete Architectural Drawings*, pp. 84–85, suggest that it was not built.

[120] Worsley, "Inigo Jones: Lonely Genius or Practical Exemplar?" 105.

House" and the purchase price suggests substantial building.[121] Giles Worsley notes the similarities between the Lothbury design and Sir Benjamin Rudyard's West Woodhay Park, Berkshire.[122] In addition, comparing maps of 1633 and 1658, Lothbury shows considerable development and the filling in of houses, even perhaps Jones's Lothbury House.[123] In 1659–60, Sir William Petty bought the Lothbury property from those who had purchased it two years earlier from the heirs of Maltravers and his mother, the Countess of Arundel. The deed refers to five houses already built and others whose foundations had been dug. After the Great Fire, one of Petty's first worries was how it had affected his Lothbury property. Perhaps Inigo Jones's Lothbury House had burnt down.[124]

DIFFUSION

The diffusion of style from London to the countryside occurred quickly.[125] Paul Hunneyball has recently analyzed in detail the appearance of new architectural styles in Hertfordshire, pointing out how quickly London fashions reached the county elite.[126] Examining local architecture as a commodity, he suggests that "most elite fashions had some link to the capital, either through the copying of built examples or the use of London based craftsmen." For example, the remodeling of Blickling Hall drew on Salisbury's great Hatfield House.[127] Most often new fashions were expressed in improvements and additions to existing houses. Attuned to visual innovation, the Hertfordshire elite, including newcomers from the City of London, adopted new styles as a important way of displaying their status.

Among the most important architects of the era were the Smythsons. In 1609 and 1619, Robert Smythson and his son John came to London to sketch the new buildings going up there. In 1609 Robert Smythson drew

---

[121] BL Additional Charter 76,982 A and B, 8 March 1659, BL Additional Charter 76,971, Indenture 1 January 1638–39, "Lothbury House," 1 January 14 Charles I, "Assignment of the House."

[122] Worsley, "Inigo Jones: Lonely Genius or Practical Exemplar?" 105, 109–10.

[123] See BL Maps, Crace Collection, Portfolio 1, no. 31, London General Plan, 1633; Fairthorne, "An Exact Delineation of the Cities of London and Westminster and the Suburbs," 1658.

[124] BL Additional Charter 76,971, Indenture 1 January 1638–39, "Lothbury House," 1 January 14 Charles I, "Assignment of the House;" BL Add. Mss. 72,907, 8 March 1659–60, ff. 13–20, transcript of the purchase deed of land in Lothbury by Petty and Gaunt; BL Add. 76,966, A, B, Counterpoint of lease by Edmund Wurcupp and his trustees of property in the parish of St. Margaret, Lothbury. BL Maps 18.d.5.

[125] See Paul Hunneyball, *Architecture and Image-Building in Seventeenth-Century Hertfordshire*, Oxford Historical Monographs (Oxford: Oxford University Press, 2004).

[126] *Ibid.*, pp. 5, 12–13, 17.

[127] Hunneyball, "Status, Display, and Dissemination," pp. 7, 15–18, 103.

The Front of Bathe House: S^{ir} foulke gryvelles: in houlborne
1619

33. The Smythsons sketched new building in London in 1609 and 1619. The front of Fulke
Greville's house includes a new fashion, an Italian pergola.
The Royal Institute of British Architects, "The Front of Bathe House: Sir Foulke Gryvelles:
in Houlborne 1619, " sketched by John Smythson. Reproduced by permission of RIBA
Library Drawings Collection.

Northampton's new house and garden, the New Exchange, Ham House,
and a summer house in Chelsea. In 1619 John Smythson sketched Lady
Coke's house, Sir Fulke Greville's new Italian pergola, and Edward Cecil's
house on the Strand designed by Inigo Jones. Smythson also drew Jones's
new building at Arundel House, including "the Italian gate over the water,"
"A new Italian window/the gallery at Arundel House," and "the new Italian
gate at Arundel House in the garden." The Smythsons incorporated
London fashions into several of the country houses they built for the
Cavendishes.[128] In particular, Smythson incorporated Jones's design at

---

[128] See Girouard (ed.), "The Smythson Collection of the Royal Institute of British Architects,"
pp. 23–184; Girouard, *Robert Smythson and the Architecture of the Elizabethan Era*; Cooper, *Houses
of the Gentry, 1480–1680*, p. 190.

Bolsover, the romantic castle built for William Cavendish, Earl of Newcastle, with the addition of a riding house to match the Earl's interests.[129] In addition to the direct copying by builders like the Smythsons, Nicholas Cooper suggests that London craftsmen introduced "metropolitan practices to the countryside."[130] Thomas Crewe, lawyer and Speaker of the House of Commons under James and Charles, used local craftsmen to add a Renaissance arcade to his house at Steane Park, Northamptonshire, and a classical entrance to the church. Gerard Christmas, a popular Jacobean Low Countries sculptor, designed Crewe's funeral moment, which resembled Archbishop Abbot's who died in 1633.[131]

Women were active patrons both in town and country despite the common-law doctrine of coverture which denied them control over property unless they were widows. Lady Jane Berkeley, Sir Roger Townshend's mother, separated from her husband, built her own unconventional villa, Ashley Park, at Walton on Thames in Surrey, and had a house in London at the Barbican.[132] The dowager Countess of Pembroke, mother of the third and fourth Earls of Pembroke, built Houghton Conquest, Bedfordshire, with classical loggias probably by Inigo Jones which were then imitated at Hambledon Hall.[133] Dorothy Catesby, widow of Sir William Dormer, a member of a leading recusant Buckinghamshire family, added to the family home at Eythorpe before 1613. Her grandson, first Earl of Carnarvon, had Inigo Jones add "a handsome apartment" to Wing, which, by the 1630s, had become the family's principal residence.[134]

An important strand of Jacobean culture was imperial: a modest sort of classical architecture had perhaps reached Bermuda as early as 1619.[135] In the 1630s Thomas Wentworth, Earl of Strafford, built a new mansion in Jigginstown, Ireland, that had a frontage with marble columns and pavements of 360 feet, larger than Salisbury's Hatfield House, at a cost of

---

[129] Girouard (ed.), "The Smythson Collection of the Royal Institute of British Architects," 21–184. Worsley and Addyman, "Riding Houses and Horses," 194–229.

[130] Cooper, *The Houses of the Gentry, 1480–1680*, p. 190.

[131] Katherine Esdaile and Arthur Oswald, "The Chapel at Steane Park, Northamptonshire," *Country Life*, 84 (2 July 1938), 12–17. Christmas's sons carried out the construction of the Crewe monument and that of his daughter.

[132] Campbell, "Documentary Evidence for the Building of Raynham Hall," 64, notes 25 and 28. Cooper, *Houses of the Gentry 1480–1680*, p. 137.

[133] Harris and Higgott, *Inigo Jones: Complete Architectural Drawings*, pp. 84–85. Cooper, *The Houses of the Gentry, 1480–1680*, pp. 190, 205, 333n72. Paula Henderson, "The Loggia in Tudor and Early Stuart England: The Adaptation and Function of Classical Form," in Gent (ed.), *Albion's Classicism*, pp. 109–46.

[134] T. B. Trappes-Lomax, "Some Homes of the Dormer Family," *Recusant History*, 8 (1965–66), 175–87.

[135] I am grateful to Karen Kupperman for this point.

L22,000.[136] Built of brick, decorated with marble, crafted by imported craftsmen, Strafford claimed to imitate royal splendor: "I have in a manner finished it and so contrived it for the rooms of state and other accommodations which I have observed in His Majesty's houses."[137]

INTERIORS

William Harrison had stressed the increasing richness of interiors in the late Elizabethan period for all social groups from the nobility and merchants to farmers and artisans.

The furniture of our houses also exceedeth and is grown in manner even to passing delicacy; and herein I do not speak of the nobility and gentry only but likewise of the lowest sort in most places of our south country ... in noblemen's houses it is not rare to see abundance of arras, rich hangings of tapestry, silver vessel, and so much other plate as may furnish sundry cupboards, to the sum oftentimes of L1,000 or L2,000 at the least ... Likewise in the houses of knights, gentlemen, merchantmen, and some other wealthy citizens, it is not ... [uncommon] to behold generally their great provision of tapestry, Turkey work, pewter, brass, fine linen, and thereto costly cupboards of plate ... these sorts do far exceed their elders and predecessors and, in neatness and curiosity, the merchant all other ... now it is descended yet lower, even unto the inferior artificers and many farmers.[138]

Harrison attributed the costly moveables of farmers to their long leases, presumably at low rents, which allowed them "to garnish their cupboards with plate, their joint beds with tapestry and silk hangings, and their tables with carpets and fine napery, whereby the wealth of our country (God be praised ...) doth infinitely appear."[139] Supporting Harrison's description, Joan Thirsk and Craig Muldrew have described the spread of goods and credit in the sixteenth century.[140] Geoffrey Beard emphasizes "the increase in refinement and luxury ... during the latter part of the sixteenth and early years of the seventeenth century." He draws attention to the striking

[136] Hugh Kearney, *Strafford in Ireland, 1633–41: A Study in Absolutism* (Cambridge: Cambridge University Press, 1959, 1989), pp. 172–73, 178. Con Costello, "Jigginstown House," *Journal of County Kildare Archaeological Society*, 14 (1969), 375–76; Maurice Craig, "New Light on Jigginstown," *Journal of County Kildare Archaeological Society*, 15 (1971), 50–58. I am grateful to Jane Ohlmeyer and Anne Laurence for these citations.
[137] Quoted in Craig, "New Light on Jigginstown," 50–58.
[138] Harrison, *Description of England*, pp. 200–201.   [139] *Ibid.*
[140] Joan Thirsk, *Economic Policy and Projects: The Development of a Consumer Society in Early Modern England* (Oxford: Clarendon Press, 1978). Craig Muldrew, *The Economy of Obligation: The Culture of Credit and Social Relations in Early Modern England* (Houndmills, Basingstoke: Macmillan; New York: St. Martin's Press, 1998).

difference between the goods left by Sir George Shirley in 1622 and those
left by his ancestor Sir Ralph Shirley in 1517. Sir George had elaborate bed
furnishings of red taffeta all "suitable to the bed," and a pair of tables in the
great parlor in the French style of du Cerceau with supports of carved
"men."[141]

Indeed, Jacobean aspirations to splendor and magnificence extended to
interior furnishings as well as architecture. These goods articulated political, social, and economic relationships through their circulation and display. In London, most of the evidence of early seventeenth-century
furnishing has disappeared. What remain are extensive inventories and
correspondence for interiors and houses that no longer exist. This documentary evidence, however, suggests the influence of French taste and
importation of Asian luxury goods in the Jacobean period, eagerly adopted
by the court and disseminated widely throughout the century.

French and Italian women introduced new fashions in seventeenth-century
interior design. Mme. de Ramboullet, an Italian aristocrat whose husband
was Master of Ceremonies to Louis XIII, redesigned Hotel de Ramboullet in
Paris in 1619.[142] At much the same time, Marie de Medici was furnishing her
newly built Palais du Luxembourg. Characterized by comfort and regularity,
these interiors also reflected, among other things, what Peter Thornton has
described as "the art of the upholsterer."[143] The new French style was often
expressed in complete suites of bed-hangings, curtains, and wall hangings,
symbolized in Mme. de Ramboullet's "Chambre Bleu."[144]

The transmission of this style to England took place in several ways.
Abraham Bosse's engravings of well-to-do French life and interiors circulated in England in the 1630s and 1640s, while decorative French prints
presented particular elements of interior designs such as chimney pieces.
Charles I's consort, Henrietta Maria, daughter of Marie de Medici, became
an important influence in her own right when she engaged in her own
building and gardening programs at Greenwich and Oatlands. She repeatedly requested "French fashion" from her upholsterer, such as "the
conversion of an English bed into 'the French fashion,'" and ordered
fruit trees and "rare outlandish flowers."[145] Van Dyck painted the Queen

---

[141] Beard, *Upholsterers and Interior Furnishings in England*, p. 58.

[142] Peter M. Thornton, *Seventeenth-Century Interior Decoration in England, France and Holland*,
(New Haven: Yale University Press, 1979), pp. 7–10.

[143] *Ibid.*   [144] *Ibid.*

[145] *Ibid.*; Susan Sykes, "Henrietta Maria's 'House of Delight,' French Influence and Iconography in the
Queen's House, Greenwich," *Apollo* (1991), 332–36. Beard, *Upholsterers and Interior Furnishings in
England*, pp. 60–62.

with her dwarf, Jeffrey Hudson, with rich fabric and an orange tree in the background. Well-to-do Londoners such as Humphrey Weld purchased upholstery from French tapissiers in Paris in the 1630s.

Northampton had neither family home nor fine furniture when he became privy councillor to King James in 1603. As we have seen, he built quickly, establishing the largest city palace on the Strand and an innovative lodge in Greenwich Park. Northampton's inventory of 1614 reveals the richness of aristocratic interiors in the early years of the seventeenth century. His furnishings were both splendid and exotic, including lacquer chests from Asia that became ever more popular over the century.[146] He had a suite of bedroom furniture of purple velvet trimmed with silver lace "all suitable to the bed" in the French style,[147] a crimson leather couch in a Spanish style in which the leather was deeply embossed like a book cover, and a China gilt cabinet upon a frame. After his death, the Countess of Suffolk bought the Earl's household stuffs from his trustees "the like whereof then could not elsewhere be gotten."[148] The Earl of Arundel bought his library and some other household goods for L529.[149]

The Earl of Somerset's inventory, taken at the moment of his arrest in 1615, displayed the international character of Jacobean interiors, particularly the impact of Asian luxury goods.[150] It listed many carpets from Persia, Turkey, and Egypt, and imported lacquered chests, including a "cabinet of ebony with a frame." While the fashion for chinoiserie is ascribed to the eighteenth century,[151] Somerset had furniture and hangings of china work, including "six pieces of hangings of crimson China velvet embroidered China fashion," a China chest, one "oval china table," a little china table, and a china chest gilt and painted.[152] Not only was chinaware listed in the inventories of the great, but, as we have seen,

---

[146] E. P. Shirley (ed.), "An Inventory of the Effects of Henry Howard, K. G., Earl of Northampton, Taken on his Death in 1614, Together with a Transcript of his Will," *Archaeologia*, 42 (1869), 347–78. Linda Levy Peck, "The Mentality of a Jacobean Grandee," in Linda Levy Peck (ed.), *The Mental World of the Jacobean Court* (Cambridge: Cambridge University Press, 1991), pp. 148–68.

[147] Thornton, *Seventeenth-Century Interior Decoration in England, France and Holland*, p. 104.

[148] Quoted in Anthony Upton, *Sir Arthur Ingram, c.1565–1642* (Oxford: Oxford University Press, 1961), p. 80.

[149] Library of Congress, British Manuscripts Project, National Library of Wales, Carreglwyd Mss. 372, BMab 651/1, 27 September 1616.

[150] Folger L. b. 638, Somerset Inventory, 1615.

[151] David L. Porter, "Monstrous Beauty: Eighteenth-Century Fashion and the Aesthetics of the Chinese Taste," *Eighteenth-Century Studies*, 35 (2002), 411.

[152] Folger L. b. 638, Somerset Inventory 1615.

"china houses" appear in the Jacobean city comedies of Jonson, Brome, and Massinger.[153]

Somerset's furnishings also displayed the early seventeenth-century movement toward unified sets of upholstered pieces with "two great chairs of white silver velvet with gold and silk fringe ... two long cushions, two seat cushions, two ... stools and twelve high stools of the same stuff." The great parlor contained six pieces of hangings of crimson Chinese velvet embroidered China fashion" and, "in a china chest, one pavilion bed of the same with a counterpoint and all furniture suitable."[154] Furthermore, Somerset's plate reflected the lavish gifts showered on the royal favorite. It included "A basin and ewer Nuremberg work gilt, the ewer like an elephant, in black leather cases" and "another basin and ewer Nuremberg work with a great rugged pearl in the midst of the basin, the ewer round with a sprig like a branch on the top, in black leather cases."

Somerset's efforts to buy the moveables of leading continental collectors may well have succeeded.[155] Tapestries of the Trojan War lined the walls of the great parlor. Somerset also owned "six pieces of hangings of new tapestry thirteen foot deep, with a border of beasts, birds, and fishes; eight pieces of hangings of new tapestry, nine foot deep, with a border of beasts, birds and fishes; two pieces of hangings of a Roman story, thirteen foot deep," and "one old piece of coarse hanging, the rest whereof is at the Tower," where the Earl and Countess of Somerset themselves had been sent after their conviction for murdering Sir Thomas Overbury.[156]

Queen Anne's inventory, taken after her death in 1619, shows that she too filled Denmark House with elaborate upholstery for her beds with matching chairs and stools, such as "a field bed of carnation satin wrought with gold and silver with a broad lace of gold with spangles, a counterpoint of carnation satin embroidered with gold, five curtains of carnation satin wrought in flowers suitable to the bed." The Queen displayed Persian and Turkey carpets, tapestries, ebony cabinets, and porcelain with silver gilt mounts. Three elaborate clocks wrought with gold and jewels were, no doubt, presentation pieces to the Queen. These included "a rich cabinet of ebony inlaid with silver white and gilt with flowers and beasts, a clock in the top thereof, with an image holding a globe of silver with a pair of

---

[153] I am grateful to A. R. Braunmuller for this point. James Knowles, "Jonson in China: Maritime Trade with China," unpublished paper presented to the National Maritime Museum and Institute of Historical Research seminar series, 25 January 2000.

[154] Folger L. b. 638, Somerset Inventory 1615.   [155] See chapter 4 above.

[156] Folger L. b. 638, 29 November 1615, f. 3v. A. J. Kempe, *The Loseley Manuscripts* (London: J. Murray, 1836), 408–409.

balances"; an ebony coach with a clock, with silver wheels, silver passengers, and two silver lions drawing it; and a silver tortoise garnished with pearls, emeralds and a ruby, "and a clock in the body of the tortoise."[157] After the Queen's death, King James looked over all her goods, kept the most valuable, designated some for ambassadorial gifts, some of her gowns for her ladies-in-waiting, and consigned the rest to resale.[158]

The Duke of Buckingham furnished York House to reflect the new French fashion for uniform furnishings and the Italian taste for new decorative arts.[159] The King's Bedchamber, hung with green velvet, had a French bed with green embroidered velvet with its curtains, "double valence, head cloth, four cups and four feathers to the same."[160] At Chelsea, in his picture and sculpture galleries, the Duke also had large sets of "gilt stools" which Simon Jervis identifies as similar to the Italian *sgabelli* chairs in Daniel Myten's 1618 portrait of Aletheia, Countess of Arundel. Mentioned in the inventory of Tart Hall, these chairs were also owned by other early Stuart nobility. Jervis suggests that "marble and *pietra dure* tables, antique sculpture, Italian or Italianate paintings, painted cassoni, carved, painted, and gilt sgabelli constitute a consciously Italian language of interior decoration."[161] As we have seen, Buckingham also commissioned three tapestries from the Mortlake tapestry works in 1623 on the subjects of the Months, on Vulcan, and on the Queen of Sheba. Sir Francis Crane, the director, decided that the favorite's favor was more important than payment and presented them to him as a gift.[162] The inventory for Chelsea House lists "two rich suites of hangings, the one of the history of Vulcan and Venus in nine pieces, the other, the history of the twelve seasons being six pieces."[163]

Ham House, owned by the Caroline courtier, Sir William Murray, had unified bedroom upholstery by the 1630s. Murray created the Green Closet at Ham House to present his collections of paintings and miniatures, commissioning ceiling paintings from Francis Cleyn the designer of the Mortlake tapestry works.[164] Two decades later, Elizabeth Murray, Countess of Dysart, later Duchess of Lauderdale, who inherited Ham House from

---

[157] M. T. W. Payne, "An Inventory of Queen Anne of Denmark's 'Ornaments, Furniture, Householde Stuffe, and Other Parcells' at Denmark House, 1619," *Journal of the History of Collections*, 13 (2001), 23–44.

[158] *Ibid.*, p. 25.   [159] Simon Jervis, "Furniture for the First Duke of Buckingham," pp. 48–74.

[160] *Ibid.*   [161] *Ibid.*

[162] Wendy Hefford, "The Duke of Buckingham's Mortlake Tapestries of 1623," *Bulletin du CIETA*, 76 (1999), 90–103.

[163] Jervis, "Furniture for the First Duke of Buckingham," p. 74.

[164] Christopher Rowell, "A Seventeenth-Century 'Cabinet' Restored: The Green Closet at Ham House," *Apollo* 143 (1996), 18–23.

her father, furnished her bedchamber magnificently with "curtains of crimson damask bordered with heavy fringe and gold drops," with matching bed coverings and quilt.[165] The inventory of 1654 includes those signifiers of advanced taste, lacquer furniture cabinets, and leather hangings.[166]

The Countess of Arundel celebrated her autonomy and innovation in Tart Hall, which she furnished in eye-catching fashion. While the inventories are not complete, they make for startling reading. Filled with "Indian" textiles and furniture alongside Italian chairs, French and Spanish tables, Persian and Turkish rugs, Tart Hall had red and yellow leather floor covers that matched coordinated hangings. Her collections of porcelain outshine all others and her interest in Indian furniture, supplied perhaps by Sir Thomas Roe, the East India Company, or the Arundels' agents, is pathbreaking.[167]

The Countess built a special Dutch "Pranketing" Room to entertain and to display her large collection of porcelain vessels on columns of shelves around the room, over the mantle, and atop the dresser. The taste for such ensembles of porcelain increased after the Restoration and hit its peak with the collections of Queen Mary II in the 1690s, but the fashion began in the early seventeenth century.[168] The Countess had vases and basins and ewers of all sorts, "a long drinking pot" and, "for ornament," figures of men, women, and animals, including a dolphin, lion, hind, frog, and a fish head. The Countess set off her porcelain with crystal, brass candlesticks and basins, Indian dishes, tortoiseshell salters, and Dutch baskets. The Countess had an unusual pot whose purpose the inventory maker did not understand: "a very large deep vessel of porcelain and therein a turned stick with a bar at the end: gagged of wood to make some sort of liquor with." Pictures of fowl and fish, alive and "dressed in a dish," ornamented the room. Lit by a large brass candelabra, the pictures in the gallery celebrated

---

[165] E. D. H. Tollemache, *The Tollemaches of Helmingham and Ham* (Ipswich: W. S. Cowell, 1949), p. 59.

[166] Thornton, *Seventeenth-Century Interior Decoration in England, France and Holland*, p. 104. Thornton and Tomlin, *The Furnishing and Decoration of Ham House*, pp. 6–32.

[167] Lionel Cust, "Notes on the Collections Formed by Thomas Howard, Earl of Arundel and Surrey, K. G.," *Burlington Magazine*, 20 (1911), 97–100, 233–36, 341–43. Arundel Castle Mss. Inventory 1, "An Inventory of all the parcells of purselin, glasses & other goods." See Chew, "The Countess of Arundel and Tart Hall," pp. 285–314. Howarth, "The Patronage and Collecting of Aletheia, Countess of Arundel," 125–37. Duggan, "Tart Hall: Lady Arundel's Casino at Whitehall," 54–64.

[168] Thornton, *Seventeenth-Century Interior Decoration in England, France and Holland*, pp. 249, 383 and note 22, cited in John Ayers, Oliver Impey, and J. V. G. Mallet, *Porcelain for Palaces: The Fashion for Japan in Europe 1650–1750* (London: Oriental Ceramics Society, 1990), p. 57n6. Howarth, "The Patronage and Collecting of Aletheia, Countess of Arundel," 125–37. Charles Kingsford, "Bath Inn or Arundel House," *Archaeologia*, 72 (1922), 243–77. Duggan, "Tart Hall: Lady Arundel's Casino at Whitehall," 54–64.

dining and plenty with pictures of a cook, a fisherman, a fowler, and a fruiterer with their produce, such as "hares, hartichokes, and pigeons" and "hartichokes, plums and cherries."[169] The Great Room, next to the Pranketing House, was filled with pictures and "nine great Italian chairs of walnut trees with arms covered with red leather set with brass nails."[170]

Most unusually, Tart Hall was filled with Indian or, more generally, Asian goods. The parlor held "a large cupboard fashioned Indian cabinet, a large trunk of mother of pearl, an Indian chest, a low Indian table with a little Indian chest thereupon, a little black Indian table, thereon a pair of tables of Indian, with men therein of Indian stuff . . . two Indian looking glasses hanging by the walls." Mr Howard's bedchamber had an Indian armchair and three other Indian chairs, amidst yellow and red damask hangings and a yellow bedstead standing on yellow leather.[171]

The expansion of building and decorating among the well-to-do provided work for a variety of luxury artificers and retailers. Somerset's inventory captures his grandeur, his debt, and the re-circulation of luxury goods. At the time of his fall, some of Somerset's furnishings were still "at M. Goddard's house, the upholster's house at the Crown in the Poultry," including hangings for a bed of tawny satin. Others were "at pawn for the Earl's debts" including "six pieces of hanging of green velvet embroidered with China gold and silk after the manner of China work." The Earl and Countess's silver, which included the Earl of Cumberland's wedding gift, organized, as we have seen, at some cost by John Tailor and John Daccombe, was "all at pawn with W. Havers excepting one basin and two ewers." An elaborate chain with diamonds, not yet been paid for, was returned to George Herriot, the renowned goldsmith.[172]

On a less exalted scale, throughout the 1620s, Sir John Coke and his family lived at the Gatehouse in St. John's, London, even as he built and furnished Melbourne House. Coke used two upholsters, William Angel and Mr. Webb, to supply the upholstery he needed. Angel produced two suites of new hangings composed of five pieces, ten foot deep, based on biblical stories, one, the story of Abraham, the other of Joseph. Webb

[169] Arundel Castle Mss. Inventory 1, "An Inventory of all the parcells of purselin, glasses & other goods." Ayers, Impey, and Mallet, *Porcelain for Palaces*, pp. 56–59, 74–75, 84, 105, 138, 229.

[170] Cust, "Notes on the collections formed by the Earl of Arundel," *Burlington Magazine*, 20 (1911), 97–100, 233–36, 341–43.

[171] *Ibid.*

[172] Folger L. b. 638, Somerset Inventory, 1615, ff. 3, 5, 7v, 12v. "In a tailor's house, one M Curteys in Trinity Lane," Somerset's new clothes remained including "the outside of a cloak embroidered with perfumed leather" and a "Spanish cloth jerkin."

supplied a bedstead, painted it, and provided four cups on top, canvas to line the valence of "three Indian beds" with featherbeds, bolsters, cushions and hangings, and a "couch chair of Turkey work" to be sent to Melbourne.[173] In 1628 Sir Roger Townshend designed a new bed requiring goods from the upholsterer, Mr. Bromell, figured satin from the draper Mr. Constable, and fringe and lace from the silkman, Mr. Benion.[174]

The rental furniture business has not been studied but must have become important as increasing numbers of the new elite lived in many wards of the City of London and its suburbs, whether in their own houses, in inns, or in furnished lodgings with the barber, the scrivener, the apothecary, and the grocer. While in London, they hired furniture from merchants such as William Ockould, an upholsterer. Thus in October and November 1620, the Earl and Countess of Cumberland rented household furniture from Ockould for L14 during their stay near Blackfriars. The Countess "at her going from London to Lansborough did bring with her in her coach a green rug of William Ockould's which is unpaid."[175] Ralph Grynder, the Queen's upholsterer, hired out tapestries, beds, blankets, rugs, and leather chairs to the Duc and Duchesse de Chevreux and their retinue when they escorted Henrietta Maria to England in 1625.[176]

THE CIRCULATION OF GOODS

Furnishings circulated throughout the countryside by purchase, gift, loan, rental, the secondhand market, and bequests.[177] Spencers, Cokes, Talbots, and Townshends sent silver, linen, furniture, bed hangings, carpets, and pictures ahead for use and display on their arrival whenever they changed their residence.[178]

The importance of linen is indicated by its placement just after silver plate in contemporary inventories. Linen counted when books often did not and pictures were often delineated only by size. Lady Jane Cheyne, daughter of the Duke of Newcastle, had the linen sheets she used at

---

[173] BL Add. Mss. 69,877, Coke Papers, series II, ff. 10–11; 69,880, f. 49. Receipted bill, William Angel, Upholsterer, 10 June 1630. Young, *Servility and Service: The Life and Work of Sir John Coke*, p. 225.

[174] BL Add. Mss. 41,656, Townshend Accounts and Inventories, ff. 120–120v.

[175] Chatsworth Mss. Household, Miscellaneous Cliffords, M28, M 32.

[176] Beard, *Upholsterers and Interior Furnishings in England*, p. 60.

[177] BL Add. Mss. 75,326: Inventories at Althorp, 1610–36; Chatsworth Mss., Lonsborough Papers, G. Inventories, 9/10.

[178] BL Add, Mss. 41,656, f. 125, Townshend Accounts and Inventories, 26 January 1636–37, plate delivered "for present use in house at Stiffkey." Folger Cavendish Talbot Mss. X. d. 428 (97), George Talbot, Earl of Shrewsbury, to Elizabeth, Countess of Shrewsbury, *c.* 1575.

Welbeck Abbey brought to Ashridge, the residence of her sister Elizabeth, Viscountess Brackley, when she visited, and then to Chelsea where she lived with her husband, Charles Cheyne. She broke up some of the linen for towels and gave some away. Lady Jane Cheyne also bought linen second-hand, specifically pieces that had belonged to Mr. Baggs and Mr. Gage. It was obviously acceptable to buy at secondhand the linen that George Gage, the art connoisseur and the Countess of Arundel's neighbor at Tart Hall, had imported.[179] In addition to extensive holdings of tablecloths, napkins, and bedding, inventories of linen reflected contemporary style. For instance, black embroidery on pillows was fashionable. The Countess De Lisle had two pairs of pillow cases "wrought with black silk and gold."[180] Similarly, in 1620, Dorothy Shirley, widow of Sir Henry Unton, left her niece Gertrude Gibbes £100 and "the bedding and furniture of the chamber I use to lie in at Farrington" including "my sheet wrought with black, and two pillow beers wrought with black."[181]

The well-to-do also borrowed goods from one another. For christenings, high-ranking family or friends sent ermine.[182] Cranfield sought to ingratiate himself with Buckingham by loaning him hangings and other household furnishings.[183] The fourth Earl of Dorset requested from Cranfield not only a buck but also the loan of silver dishes.[184] Philippa Glanville has demonstrated the great expenditure on plate exhibited on the buffet in the sixteenth and seventeenth centuries and its important place in social display. She points to the importance of women buying, sharing, and bequeathing silver plate in their wills.[185]

Indeed, bequests served as one means to re-circulate goods.[186] Testators who left household goods in their wills sometimes defined their personal meaning through their location in their homes. Anne, Viscountess Dorchester, widow of the diplomat Dudley Carleton, Lord Dorchester, who had influenced the taste for Venetian art at the Jacobean court, left her hangings, furnishings, and Persian rugs in her will. Now living in retirement in Gosford Hall, Essex, she identified her bequests by the rooms in which

---

[179] HEH Ellesmere Mss. EL 11,143, Lady Jane Cavendish account book, 1635–63.
[180] KAO U 1475, E48, Inventory of plate and linen, June–July 1621.
[181] John Gough Nichols, *The Unton Inventories* (London: Printed for the Berkshire Ashmolean Society, by John Bowyer Nichols and son, 1841), pp. 15–36.
[182] Folger X. d. 428 (2), Talbot manuscripts, Thomas Howard, Earl of Arundel, to Elizabeth, Countess of Shrewsbury, 27 June 1607.
[183] KAO U 269/1, CP 1–23, Mary, Countess of Buckingham, to Cranfield.
[184] KAO U 269/1, CP 39, Fourth Earl of Dorset to Cranfield.
[185] Philippa Glanville, *Silver in Tudor and Early Stuart England*, pp. 36–45, 57–58.
[186] Nichols, *The Unton Inventories*, pp. 15–36.

they were placed in the house at Westminster where she and Carleton lived in state appropriate to Carleton's high office and dearly won peerage. She bequeathed eight or ten pieces of hangings from her dining room in Westminster along with the Turkey carpet used there. In addition, she left

my canopy, couch stools, and chairs which did stand in my gallery at Westminster, my great tawny velvet cabinet which was in my chamber at Westminster ... my tawny embroidered cloth bed which was wrought in my house with the carpets, sideboard, clothes, stools and all things belonging to it ... my purple plush couch canopy which did stand at my house at Westminster with the carpets, stools and chairs thereunto belonging.

Her bequests reflect the French "art of the upholsterer" including her "carnation flowered satin for a bed ... in measure ninety yards" and all its furniture; a white suite of hangings coordinated with white Turkey carpets, "and the long one that John Frithe wrought to it," and twelve chairs. She also bequeathed her "best suite of hangings with the beasts being eleven pieces," and her best Persian carpet that had belonged to Lord Dorchester. Her bequests also cast light on the secondhard market and its role in recycling goods. The Countess left "my new suite of hangings which I bought at second hand and cost me two hundred pounds."[187]

Dorothy Shirley's bequests of silver, linen, hangings, and pictures to several of her nieces, friends, and household servants show the diversity of contemporary luxury goods and the significance of new fashions in silver for the buffet and new lacquered tables.[188] Lady Anne Gibbs, her "well beloved niece," received back "two flat sallett [salad] dishes, and six silver plates, which sallett dishes and plates she gave me." To Lady Unton Dering, Dorothy Shirley left "five pieces of Arras hangings, which are wrought with the story of Sampson and three of my best silver candlesticks." To Jane Hawley, she gave £100, "my coach and coach horses and coach horse beasts and my silver livery basin and ewer which are usually set upon my cupboard, my black cabinet, or one of my other cabinets at her choice and election." She bequeathed Sir Thomas Edmondes, Treasurer of the King's Household and director of her charities, an agate cup and her stepson's wife a little agate watch. To her friend Sir Robert Pye, Dorothy Shirley left furniture, pictures, as well as the furnace in her brewhouse "and all my story pieces in my gallery there, unless [except] the picture of Sir Henry Unton which I do give and bequeath to my loving niece the

---

[187] Quoted in Beard, *Upholsterers and Interior Furnishings in England*, pp. 290–91.
[188] Nichols, *The Unton Inventories*, pp. 15–36.

Lady Dering." The portrait of Sir Henry Unton, recapitulating his life from birth to death, is one of the most famous of Elizabethan pictures.

GARDENS AND PLANTS

Gardens and gardening, extensions of the house and its furnishings, provided an additional site of cultural borrowing and luxury display. In the late sixteenth and early seventeenth centuries, large numbers of new plants introduced from North America, India, and China, and especially Turkey, marked England's international trade. At the same time, books of herbals and directions for gardening, both Platonic and practical, described plants newly imported from around the world. Designs borrowed from the Italians, the Dutch, and the French appeared in English gardens while nurserymen made links with far-flung traders to Turkey, North and South America, and Africa.[189]

Gentlemen on the Grand Tour paid careful attention to continental gardens. The papers of Sir John Coke include notes about plants and herbs in Italian, and French along with "plants of the north."[190] John Coke junior, in Geneva in 1642 to learn French, kept a commonplace book in which he described the gardens at Blois at length.[191] As the Arundels imported artists, and artisans, so too they imported gardeners. William Trumbull provided "Benedetto the gardener" to the Earl and Countess of Arundel in 1618–19.[192]

John Tradescant, gardener to Robert Cecil, Earl of Salisbury, brought plants from the Low Countries, France, and Russia. His purchases included anemones, currants, and cherry trees from C. Helin of Harlem, cyprus trees from John Robin, the French botanist who was director of the Jardin des Plantes, orange trees from Paris, quince from Brussels, and tulips from Harlem. He also got apricots from the gardener to the Archduke of the Netherlands.[193] On his Russian trip Tradescant brought back Muscovy roses and in his notebook made the "earliest list of Russian flora."

[189] Richard Gorer, *The Flower Garden in England* (London: Batsford, 1975). On seventeenth-century gardens, see Sir Roy Strong, *The Renaissance Garden in England* (London: Thames and Hudson, 1979); John Dixon Hunt, *Garden and Grove: The Italian Renaissance Garden in the English Imagination, 1600–1750* (London: Dent, 1986).

[190] BL Add. Mss. 69,883B, Coke Papers, series II, ff, 24, 30, 31.

[191] BL Add. Mss. 69,888, Coke Papers, series II, f. 30, 4 April 1642 to December 1642.

[192] Robert Hill, "Ambassadors and Art Collecting in Early Stuart Britain: The Parallel Careers of William Trumbull and Sir Dudley Carleton, 1609–1625," *Journal of the History of Collections*, 15 (2003), 211–28.

[193] R. T. Gunther and John Goodyer, *Early British Botanists and their Gardens* (Oxford: Oxford University Press, 1922), pp. 328–29.

Tradescant told John Parkinson about the plants he had seen in North Africa and that he had brought back the "Argier Apricocke."[194]

Parkinson's *Paradisi in Sole, A garden of all sorts of pleasant flowers* (1629), a large book with extensive illustrations, incorporated Tradescant's findings and displayed Turkish imports.[195] One of the most popular books on plants, Tradescant listed "his own acquisitions" of the 1630s in his copy of Parkinson.[196] The Reverend Walter Stonehouse made a list of his own garden plants in 1640–44 which included specimens from Virginia, New England, and Guinea, some of which he probably got from the Tradescants.[197]

The popularity of these works brought rare plants to the general public. Gardens and rare plants became a luxury good. In England, rare plants were displayed in the greatest gardens such as Wilton, coveted by gardeners such as Major General John Lambert who borrowed French plants from a leading royalist in Paris in the late 1650s, and celebrated by John Evelyn in *Elysium Britannicum*.[198]

Exotic plants and flowers also became the subjects of designs for embroidery, clothing, and wallpaper. Parkinson's *Paradisi* was not just for gardening afficionados. In 1643, for example, Lady Franklin, wife of Sir John Franklin, a member of the Long Parliament, gave a copy of *Paridisi* to her "dear sister, Anne Purefoy," who colored in some of the illustrations.[199] Peter Stent advertised prints of flowers to embroider.[200]

The styles of popular gardens ranged from the Elizabethan gardens that Francis Bacon celebrated in his essays to the French and Italian styles adapted in the Jacobean period and promoted especially by Salomon and Isaac de Caus.[201] On his trip to London in 1609, Robert Smythson sketched the garden at Sir Thomas Vavasour's Ham House which may have been based on Henry IV's gardens at St Germain-en-Laye planned by Claude Mollet.[202] When Sir John Danvers returned from France and Italy in the early 1620s, he built an innovative house in Chelsea with widely admired

[194] *Ibid.*, p. 344 and note 2.
[195] Dorothy Gardiner, *The Tradescants and their Times, c. 1600–1662*, reprinted from *Journal of the Royal Horticultural Society*, 53, part 2 (1928); Gorer, *The Flower Garden in England*, p. 26.
[196] Gorer, *The Flower Garden in England*, p. 29.
[197] Gunther and Goodyer, *Early British Botanists and their Gardens*, pp. 350–51.
[198] Arthur MacGregor (ed.), *Tradescant's Rarities: Essays on the Foundation of the Ashmolean Museum* (Oxford: Clarendon Press, 1983), p. 4; see chapter 6 and John Evelyn's *Elysium Britannicum and European Gardening*, ed. Therese O'Malley and Joachim Wolschke-Bulmahn (Washington. DC: Dumbarton Oaks Research Library and Collection, 1998).
[199] The Folger Shakespeare Library copy has this inscription and partially colored plates.
[200] I am grateful to Rachel Doggett for these references.
[201] Strong, *The Renaissance Garden in England*, pp. 73–165.
[202] Moore, Rowell and Strachey, *Ham House*, p. 3n1.

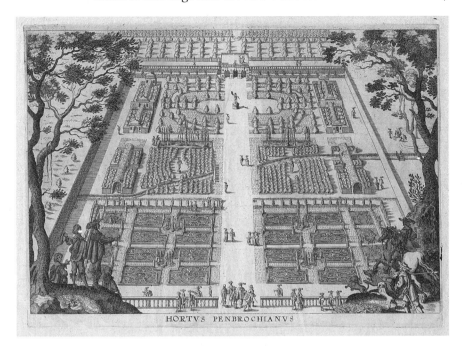

HORTVS PENBROCHIANVS

34. The Earls of Pembroke, great builders and collectors in the early seventeenth century, continued to build in the 1640s and 1650s. Isaac de Caus engraved the gardens and grotto of Wilton House, which he published, in the 1640s.
The Folger Shakespeare Library, ART 249058, Isaac de Caus, *Hortus Penborchianus* (Garden at Wilton), (Cologne, 1655).

gardens.[203] Many Jacobean and Caroline gardens displayed new garden structures, such as grottos. Thomas Bushell built a grotto in the 1620s, the Earl of Arundel entertained visitors in his grotto at Albury, and Isaac de Caus created grottos for the Earl and Countess of Bedford at Woburn Abbey, and for the Earl of Pembroke at Wilton House.[204] De Caus published these designs in the 1640s and Wenceslaus Hollar engraved Arundel's grotto, as he had Arundel's art collections, to bring the new, the rare, and curious to the public and, perhaps, to serve as a model for others.

The continuing effort to develop new gardens, adopt new plants, and create new styles from the Elizabethan period to the late seventeenth century can be traced in the gardens of Kirby Hall, which were among

---

[203] Cooper, *The Houses of the Gentry 1480–1680*, p. 141, 184.
[204] Isaac de Caus, *Wilton Garden: New and Rare Inventions of Waterworks* (London, 1645). Strong, *The Renaissance Garden in England*, pp. 130–33, 174–75, 139–44.

the finest in England.[205] Sir Christopher Hatton, Queen Elizabeth's Lord Chancellor, completed Kirby Hall between 1570 and 1575. In the 1580s Thomas Tresswell surveyed the gardens. As a result, Hatton moved the nearby village and enclosed its common land between 1586 and 1591. Between 1605 and 1619, his cousin and heir, Sir Christopher Hatton, created the Great Garden. King James visited the house in 1612 and 1619. Nicholas Stone, Jr., modernized Kirby Hall and its gardens during the 1640s for Christopher Hatton, later first Baron Hatton, drawing on elements in Serlio.[206] Hatton stocked the garden with rare plants between 1658 and 1662. A royalist returning from exile, he ordered trees from Paris and considered plants for sale from John Rose, Charles II's gardener. In the 1660s, Hatton, a member of the Royal Society, composed a list of "certain seeds and plants growing in the Barbados," a topic of interest to the Society's Georgic Committee.[207] The Hattons restocked the garden again between 1676 and 1702. In the 1690s another major remodeling of the terraces of the Great Garden transformed the Renaissance garden, where each "room" of the garden was a surprise, into a "garden which opened up the enclosed aspect . . . with formal vistas and avenues linked to the surrounding country-side."[208] The long-term development of the Kirby Hall gardens demonstrates that the desire for rare plants and new garden designs did not belong to a single historical moment but was a long-term theme in the expansion of luxury consumption from the sixteenth century onwards.

CONCLUSION

Cultural borrowing from the continent and Asia shaped architecture, interior furnishings, and garden design throughout the seventeenth century. Such borrowings were not new. But the process gained momentum through print, travel, and personal visits by enthusiastic Jacobean builders. Patrons, both men and women, ranged from royal favorites, great nobles, Jacobean Scots, and privy councilors, to well-to-do gentry and merchants. Early Stuart builders in the countryside eagerly took up style and ornament newly displayed in London. Court, city, and country were linked in

---

[205] Brian Dix, Iain Sader, and Tara Hilton, "Kirby Hall and its Gardens: Excavations in 1987–1994," *Archaeological Journal,* 152 (1995), 291–380. Teresa Sladen, "The Garden at Kirby Hall, 1570–1700," *Journal of Garden History,* 4 (1984), 139–56.
[206] *Ibid.*
[207] Sladen, "The Garden at Kirby Hall, 1570–1700," 139–56. See chapter 8 below on the Georgic Committee of the Royal Society.
[208] Dix, Sader, and Hilton, "Kirby Hall and its Gardens," 291–380.

extravagant expenditure on building up to 1640. As Bishop Godfrey Goodman later wrote, "No kingdom in the world spent so much in building as we did."[209]

What happened, then, during the Civil War and Interregnum? The celebration of house turned to longing for home. Personal identity, crystallized around home and hearth, found expression in print in the 1640s and 1650s. William Cavendish, Duke of Newcastle, had engravings of his several houses made in the 1630s. Plates of Welbeck Abbey, Bolsover Castle, and Ogle as well as their new riding houses feature prominently in Newcastle's *Methode et Invention Nouvelle de Dresser les Chevaux*, which was printed in Antwerp in 1657.[210] Wenceslaus Hollar, who had worked for the Arundels since 1636, produced engravings of the Four Seasons in the 1640s for distribution on the continent. They featured Arundel houses in the background of three of them.[211] Did luxury consumption cease during the decades of political instability? When Charles I withdrew to York and then to Oxford, did the nobility, gentry, and merchants connected to the court stop building and buying? Did the well-to do, whatever their political stance, change their patterns of consuming? These crucial issues will be addressed in the next chapter.

[209] Quoted in Lawrence Stone and Jeanne Fawtier Stone, *An Open Elite? England 1540–1880*, abridged edn (Oxford: Oxford University Press, 1986), p. 205.

[210] Mark Girouard, "Early Drawings of Bolsover Castle," *Architectural History*, 27 (1984), 510–18.

[211] Duggan, "Tart Hall: Lady Arundel's Casino at Whitehall," 54–64.

CHAPTER 6

"The pictures I desire to have ... must be exquisitely done and by the best masters": luxury and war, 1640–1660

In spring 1647 the English reached a crossroads: the Long Parliament, victorious in war against Charles I, negotiated with the defeated king and ordered the New Model Army to disband. But the New Model refused to disperse, seized King Charles in June, and debated the future shape of government at Putney on the outskirts of London in October 1647. As the army fought Presbyterian leaders for supremacy, each claiming to represent the people, another Londoner took a different type of action.

Between March and September 1647, Humphrey Weld of Covent Garden, grandson of a Lord Mayor of London and son of an alderman, cupbearer to Queen Henrietta Maria, and Roman Catholic, ordered paintings by contemporary Roman artists for his London townhouse. Weld secretly commissioned Peter Fitton, the Jesuit art dealer now in Paris, to buy history pictures, religious paintings, and still lifes. "The pictures I desire to have, some must be bespoke ... the sizes I would have them at ... are not usual in Rome, others may be of any size ... both must be exquisitely done and by the best masters."[1] Throughout the summer of 1647 Fitton tried to procure these works. "Send me a measure in thread of the breadth and length of each picture and the masters' names by whom you would have them made. I will send them to one at Rome, who will advertise me whether the masters you desire will undertake to make the pictures and at what rate and, withal, I would wish you to send me the stories you desire the pictures to be made of."[2] He urged Weld to procure a bill of exchange to pay for the pictures directed first to Venice, "to be made over from thence to Rome."

In the end, Fitton could not fulfill Weld's "shopping list," not because of upheaval or iconoclasm in England but because some of the painters, the

[1] J. P. Ferris, "A Connoisseur's Shopping-List, 1647," *Journal of the Warburg and Courtauld Institutes*, 38 (1975), 339–41.
[2] Quoted in *ibid.*

230

best known of them Salvatore Rosa (1615–73), were working for Cardinal Mazarin. The New Model Army's control of London and the rhetoric of the Putney Debates did not dampen Weld's pursuit of the exquisite though it contrasts vividly with Colonel Rainsborough's evocative claims at Putney for "the poorest he" in England. Weld's desires for new pictures, new houses, and new furnishings, satisfied through the importation of continental material culture, highlight the themes of luxury consumption and cultural borrowing that we have been examining. But more unexpectedly, they raise important questions about the ways in which the Civil War, Commonwealth, and Protectorate affected luxury consumption.

Weld's order marked his family's very successful transition, beginning in the middle of the sixteenth century, from the Grocers' Company to landed gentry, an ascent reflected in the purchase of increasingly valuable moveables for Weld House in London's West End and Lulworth Castle in Dorset. King James had knighted Weld's father, a London alderman, in 1603.[3] Weld himself attended Trinity College, Cambridge, and the Middle Temple. Obtaining a license to travel in the 1630s, he went to Paris and probably Rome where he may have seen the work of the artists whose pictures he ordered. After his return, between 1638 and 1642, he wooed Claire Arundel, daughter of an ancient Catholic family,[4] and secured an appointment in Queen Henrietta Maria's household. In these same years, Weld began to furnish his houses in contemporary French style, purchasing furnishings, upholstery, and curtains from a *tappisier* in Paris in 1638.[5]

Throughout the 1640s and 1650s, Weld developed his property holdings in city and country. In 1640, as war broke out with Scotland, he sold the family property in the City and moved to the fashionable West End. He bought property from the Caroline collector and art broker, George Gage, in Aldwych Close for L2,600 and added adjacent land in 1649. Weld developed the parcel in the 1650s, building several new houses at a cost of L15,600. The lane on which it stood became known as Weld or Wild Street.[6] He himself amalgamated two mansions on the site to create Weld House, an important new London mansion. In 1657 he added a chapel. Accusing Weld of being a papist and surrounding himself with Catholic servants, the government ordered him to build a wall to prevent access to the chapel from the rear of

---

[3] Joan Berkeley, *Lulworth and the Welds* (Gillingham, Dorset: Blackmore Press, 1971), pp. 35–81.

[4] Lord Arundel was not directly related to Thomas Howard, Earl of Arundel.

[5] Berkeley, *Lulworth and the Welds*, pp. 57–58. Weld's mother, Dame Mary Weld, left a charitable bequest to be administered by the Haberdashers' Company, Guildhall, Ms. 15,903, Parts 1 and 2.

[6] W. E. Riley and Sir L. Gomme, *The Parish of St. Giles-in-the-Fields*, 2 vols., Survey of London (London: London County Council, 1912–1914), II, pp. 93–97, 100.

the house.[7] One wing of his mansion, let to the Spanish or French ambassadors, became a center for Catholic gatherings and worship.[8]

In 1641 Weld bought Lulworth Castle, built by Thomas Howard, Viscount Bindon, in 1609, from Theophilus Howard, second Earl of Suffolk. Like Bolsover Castle, built by the Cavendishes for entertaining and retreat, Lulworth Castle evoked the chivalric past, but was, in fact, a new Jacobean lodge.[9] Lulworth Castle became a center of Roman Catholicism and subsequently fell to a parliamentary garrison which carried away its paneling. In 1643 the Committee for Compounding, which imposed taxes to support the parliamentary army, fined Weld the hefty sum of L4,000 for recusancy and refusing to take the Oath of Abjuration. The same year, goods seized from Weld House and distrained at the Guildhall in London were ordered sold. Summoning him to take the Oath of Abjuration on penalty of seizure of his estate in 1650 and 1651, the Dorset County Committee complained that because he was living in London, they could not tender him the oath.[10]

Such scrutiny did not deter Weld. Despite fines, the sequestering of his goods in the 1640s, and complaints against him in the 1650s, Weld played an important role in protecting royalist land holdings. When the Commonwealth regime sold royalist lands in 1651 and 1652, Weld bought them, acting as a trustee not only for his father-in-law, Lord Arundel, but for many others as well. He held the lands until the families could recover them.[11] At the Restoration, Weld received his reward from the Crown. He served as a member of parliament, as a deputy lieutenant in Dorset, and as a heartily disliked justice of the peace in London in the 1670s.[12] A mob attacked Weld House in 1671.[13] Weld himself lost his office in 1679 for allowing access to

[7] PRO *Calendar of Proceedings of the Committee for Compounding, 1643–1660, preserved in the State Paper Department of Her Majesty's Public Record Office,* ed. Mary Anne Everett Green, 5 vols. (London: HMSO, Eyre and Spottiswoode, 1889–1892), II, p. 1447. I am grateful to Barbara Donagan for this reference. On 6 August 1646 Weld claimed to have contributed four pieces of cannon for parliament. Because his estate had been made into a garrison and the rest of his estate seized, he was obliged to flee to Oxford where his mother had a small estate. See also 6 March 1647, 15 July, 28 October, 22 December, 5 January 1648, 28 February 1648, 1 March 1648, 1 July 1648.

[8] Riley and Gomme, *The Parish of St. Giles in the Fields,* II, p. 95n.

[9] Colin Platt, *The Great Rebuildings of Tudor and Stuart England: Revolutions in Architectural Taste* (London: University College London Press, 1994), pp. 96–98.

[10] PRO *Calendar of the Committee for Compounding,* II, 1447. PRO *Calendar of the Proceedings of the Committee for Advance of Money, 1642–1656, preserved in the Public Record Office,* ed. Many Anne Everett Green, 3 vols. (London: HMSO, Eyre and Spottiswoode, 1888), part 1, p. 242; part 2, pp. 983–85. Berkeley, *Lulworth and the Welds,* p. 6.

[11] PRO Calendar of the Committee for Compounding, II, 1447; Berkeley, *Lulworth and the Welds,* p. 67

[12] *CSPD 1671,* pp. 241–42. Basil Duke Henning (ed.), *The House of Commons, 1660–1690,* 3 vols. (London: Secker and Warburg, 1983), III, pp. 682–83.

[13] *CSPD 1671,* pp. 241–42.

Roman Catholic services in his private chapel.[14] The Portuguese and Spanish ambassadors bought his London residence after Weld's death. A mob sacked it after James II fled London.[15]

Weld's conspicuous consumption draws attention to the active markets for luxury goods, art, building, and furnishing alongside investment in land and development of London real estate throughout the Civil War and Interregnum. Just as important, it suggests the reluctance of successive regimes between 1640 and 1660 to crack down on luxury consumption. This chapter addresses both issues.

Taxation, impressment, and plunder affected royalists, parliamentarians, and the uncommitted throughout England.[16] Christopher Clay suggests that "at least 150 to 200 houses of major local importance were more or less reduced to ruins, and the true total may have been very much higher ... During the decade or so after the cessation of hostilities in England, making good the damage their homes had suffered must have been a major financial preoccupation of the gentry."[17] Beginning in the early 1640s all the English were taxed much more heavily and thoroughly than before. Committees for Advancing Money and Committees for Compounding moved systematically against royalists. Some had to sell their lands to meet these new obligations. The end of war did not end this financial pressure. In 1651 and 1652 Parliament passed Acts of Confiscation which confiscated the land of over 700 royalists who had supported both the first and second civil wars. John Habakkuk, Joan Thirsk, and John Broad have analyzed royalist sales, arguing that they varied in different parts of the country and were often conveyed to trustees.[18] Most estates were reassembled before the Restoration.

---

[14] He was accused of allowing "as free access to the chapel as before." HMC, House of Lords Mss., App. to 11th Rep., Part II, p. 127, Quoted in Riley and Gomme *The Parish of St. Giles-in-the-Fields*, II, 95n.

[15] Riley and Gomme, *The Parish of St. Giles in the Fields*, II, pp. 93–97.

[16] Martyn Bennett, *The Civil Wars Experienced: Britain and Ireland, 1638–1661* (London and New York: Routledge, 2000); John S. Morrill (ed.), *Revolution and Restoration: England in the 1650s* (London: Collins and Brown, 1992); John S. Morrill (ed.), *The Impact of the English Civil War* (London: Collins and Brown, 1991); Charles Carlton, *Going to the Wars: The Experience of the British Civil Wars, 1638–1651* (London: Routledge, 1992).

[17] Christopher G. A. Clay, "Landlords and Estate Management in England," in Joan Thirsk (ed.), *The Agrarian History of England, 1640–1750*, V, Part II of *The Agrarian History of England and Wales*, general ed. H. P. R. Finberg, 8 vols. (Cambridge: Cambridge University Press, 1967–), p. 134. See also Nicholas Cooper, *The Houses of the Gentry, 1480–1680*, (New Haven: Yale University Press, 1999), pp. 225–32, 351n52.

[18] Joan Thirsk, "The Sales of Royalist Land during the Interregnum," *Economic History Review*, new series 5 (1952), 193–94. John Broad, "Gentry Finances and the Civil War: The Case of the Buckinghamshire Verneys," *Economic History Review*, new series 32 (1979), 183–200. H. J. Habakkuk, "Landowners and the Civil War," *Economic History Review*, 18 (1965), 130–51; Habakkuk, "The Land Settlement and the Restoration of Charles II," *TRHS*, 5th series, 28 (1978) 201–22.

The Royalist Composition papers document the sequestration and fining of the estates of nobility, gentry, and merchants who had supported King Charles. Although land sales may have had fewer deleterious effects than once thought on royalists, the grimness of composition, advancing money for the army, the fall in rents surely, it is suggested, inhibited spending. Yet, Christopher Clay suggests that the long-term consequences of the Civil War on landowners were limited because the new regime did not attempt to destroy the position of their foes – and kin – as landowners. It did not question who bought royalist land and sought to "punish delinquency" but "prevent ruin."[19] For instance, Lord Charles Howard of Naworth began as a royalist, went into exile, and returned as a parliamentarian. Upon his return, he found his rents of L1,200 from his Cumberland estates in 1651 higher than they had been in 1633. By 1659 they had doubled to L2,300.[20] The impetus to acquire and to build that had been expanding throughout the early seventeenth century, a reflection, in part, of the expansion in the size of the nobility and the gentry and increased prosperity, continued despite heavier taxation and fines, from 1642 to 1660.

LONDON RETAILING AND THE CIVIL WAR

Parliament held London, center of demand and sale of luxury goods, throughout the wars although royalist support remained.[21] Stephen Porter suggests that the war had different effects on the London economy. On the positive side, contracts for clothing and arms spurred the London economy and enriched some. The city attracted those fleeing the fighting. One contemporary argued that building fortifications would "encourage our friends to frequent her [London] and to come with their estates to inhabit in her by multitudes, whereby she will grow mighty, famous and rich even in times of war."[22] On the negative side, London did suffer from

---

[19] Quoted in Clay, "Landlords and Estate Management," p. 148. J. Shedd, "Legalism Over Revolution: The Parliamentary Committee for Indemnity and Property Confiscation Disputes, 1647–1655," *The Historical Journal*, 43 (2000), 1093–1107, points out that the indemnity committee often upheld royalist property rights.

[20] C. Roy Hudleston (ed.), *Naworth Estate and Household Accounts, 1648–1660* (Durham: Surtees Society, 1958).

[21] For recent historiography of the impact of Civil War, see Morrill (ed.), *The Impact of the English Civil War*; Morrill (ed.), *Revolution and Restoration*; Robert Ashton, *Counter-Revolution: The Second Civil War and its Origins, 1646–8* (New Haven: Yale University Press, 1994); Bennett, *The Civil Wars Experienced*; Carlton, *Going to the Wars*.

[22] Quoted in Stephen Porter (ed.), *London and the Civil War* (Basingstoke, Hampshire: Macmillan, 1996), p. 176. See also Ben Coates, "Poor Relief in London during the English Revolution Revisited," *London Journal*, 25 (2000), 40–58. Jeremy Boulton, "London 1540–1700," in Peter Clark (ed.), *The Cambridge Urban History of Britain, Vol. II, 1540–1820* (Cambridge: Cambridge University Press, 2000), p. 342.

the conflict. Royalist armies diverted some cloth supplies. As a result, hallage receipts fell between 1643 and 1645 to two-thirds of the receipts in 1638–42, although by 1646 they had returned to prewar levels.[23] Attendance at the Inns of Court was down by 30 percent.[24] Fashionable districts such as St. Martin in-the-Fields and Covent Garden lost population and their rents declined.[25]

In 1642 R. Poole described "all trade being at a stand."[26] The Venetian ambassador wrote in 1643 that "all the shops are kept shut by order of Parliament with loss to the merchants and inconvenience to the inhabitants."[27] Tradesmen and artisans worried about few customers and hard times. Nehemiah Wallington complained "workmen are gone and trading is dead."[28] The committee for the militia petitioned the House of Commons: "Our rich men are gone because the City is the place of taxes and burdens; trade is decayed, and shops shut up in a great measure; our poor do much increase."[29] The royalist newspaper, *Mercurious Aulicus*, asserted in 15 July 1644 that "12,000 houses and shops were empty."[30] Jeremy Boulton suggests that the late 1640s "represented the worst slump in Londoners' living standards since the 1590s."[31] Ben Coates argues that poverty increased during the first civil war. Many parishes could not maintain poor relief especially in newly urbanized areas. Nevertheless, he suggests that "the impact of the Civil War on the London economy was at its worst in late 1643 and early 1644."[32]

The New Exchange offers an important case study in the fortunes of luxury retailers in the West End during the 1640s and 1650s and, as we saw earlier, presents a somewhat less bleak picture than scholars have drawn.[33] Although it had been easy enough to rent these shops at the end of the 1630s, during the Civil War trade did fall off. The second Earl of Salisbury leased some of the shops for a half year, rather than the customary three or five. On 19 December 1639, for example, Thomas Johnson of the Strand took a lease for five years of shops in the lower part of the New Exchange at

---

[23] Porter, *London and the Civil War*, p. 185.   [24] *Ibid.*, pp. 187–88.   [25] *Ibid.*, pp. 190–91.

[26] BL Add. Mss. 78,315, Evelyn Papers, f. 8. R. Poole to John Evelyn, 13 January 1641–42.

[27] *CSPV, 1643–44*, p. 14, 4 September 1643, Geralamo Agostini to the Doge. Bennett, *The Civil Wars Experienced*, p. 128.

[28] Quoted in Porter, *London and the Civil War*, p. 191.   [29] *Ibid.*

[30] *Ibid.* Ian Gentles, "London Levellers in the English Revolution: The Chidleys and Their Circle," *Journal of Ecclesiastical History*, 29 (1978), 297–303.

[31] Jeremy Boulton, "Food Prices and the Standard of Living in London in the 'Century of Revolution,' 1580–1700," *Economic History Review*, 2nd series 53 (2000), 475.

[32] Coates, "Poor Relief in London during the English Revolution Revisited," 51.

[33] See chapter 1 above.

the yearly rent of L12. Five years later, on 2 October 1644, Mary Turpin, spinster, took a shop in the lower part for half a year for L3.[34] Some shopkeepers petitioned Salisbury for release from their leases because trade was poor in "these unhappy times."[35] On the other hand, several important shopowners from the 1630s continued to rent their shops in 1647 and their wills suggest that Hugh Pope and Josias Fendall left considerable estates.[36] Other evidence exists about continued trade. A libel published in 1650 attacked aristocratic women for frequenting the New Exchange, claiming that it was a place of assignation.[37]

London retailing revived after the end of the first civil war in 1646. In Cheapside land values and rents saw a small slip in the 1640s. By 1650 these values had returned to the level of the 1630s.[38] Alan Simpson's study of Thomas Cullum, a leading London merchant, provides striking evidence of the liveliness of the London economy in the later 1640s and 1650s.[39] Granted the Excise Office in 1645, which brought him L1,300 a year, Cullom became a member of the East India Company in 1647. Cullom began to invest in London property in 1644 and, like Humphrey Weld, bought property there in 1649. He spent more than L10,000 on which he received an annual income of almost 9 percent. Between 1645 and 1650 Cullom estimated that he had made between L3,800 and 4,700 each year from "trade, office, and rents."[40]

London livery companies reflected continuing demand for specialized luxury goods. The clockmakers actively monitored quality and imports. In the 1630s, the company kept a close watch on imports "which had been brought in from beyond the seas, and not brought to the common hall to

---

[34] Hatfield, Cecil Mss., Estate Papers Box R5.

[35] HMC *Salisbury*, XXIV, 281 and note. Anne Segar to William, Earl of Salisbury, before 10 May 1647, 289. Benjamin Copley to William, Earl of Salisbury, before 4 December 1668. John Rowe and George Franklin also wished to give up their shops sometime before 1668, 288–89.

[36] Hugh Pope, PRO PROB 11/253, 29 March 1656; *Index of Wills Proved in the Prerogative Court of Canterbury*, vol. 7, 1653–56, ed. Thomas M. Bragg and Josephine Skeate Moir (London: The British Record Society, 1925), Hugh Pope, gentleman, Covent Garden, St. Martin-in-the-Fields, Middlesex, 1656, f. 93; Josias Fendall, PRO PROB 11/229, joiner, Covent Garden, Middlesex, 1653, f. 221.

[37] Henry Neville, *Newes from the New Exchange, or the Commonwealth of Ladies* (London, 1650). James Grantham Turner, "'News from the New Exchange': Commodity, Erotic Fantasy, and the Female Entrepreneur," in Ann Bermingham and John Brewer (eds.), *The Consumption of Culture, 1600–1800: Image, Object, Text* (New York: Routledge, 1995), pp. 419–39.

[38] Derek Keene, *Cheapside Before the Great Fire* (London: Economic and Social Research Council, 1985), pp. 19–32.

[39] Alan Simpson, "Thomas Cullum, Draper, 1587–1664," *Economic History Review*, 2nd series 11 (1958), 19–34.

[40] *Ibid.*

meeting."[41] Despite the fall off in trade in the 1640s, clockmaking remained an attractive business. Artisans without training set themselves up as clockmakers against the rules. In 1642 Francis Starley, who had not been apprenticed, and Victor Ball, a tailor, were forbidden the trade of clockmaker. In 1646 Thomas Farmer was forbidden to make cases for clocks. In the 1650s there were more than forty members of the company along with numerous watchmakers. They continued to ferret out "bad work" and praise the good, such as the master work of James Letts who, they thought, produced the first watch to show the day of the month in 1656.[42]

Demand for London luxury goods continued in the 1650s. The Townshends of Raynham Hall bought glass, five large pieces of china, salts, a sugar box, and "12 spoons of the Italian fashion" engraved with the family coat of arms. On one object, Lady Townshend paid to have a coat of arms taken off and another engraved on it. In 1652 Lady Townshend received a mercer's bill from Richard Blake for L51–02–06 (which she satisfied by paying L50) for making clothes, including one of lemon color silver stuff, with stays, buckram and bone, calico, and ribbon.[43] In 1655, while redecorating her dining room and parlor, Mary Coke asked her husband Thomas, son of Charles I's secretary of state, who was in London, "pray send down the cloth and forget not the glasses, and if you think it convenient, I would have one dozen of cane chairs, half great chairs and half a dozen of Turkey work chairs to suit with ours; and half dozen cushions to suit with those we have."[44]

New public spaces, alongside the pulpit, the theatre, the shop, and the public garden, emerged in the 1650s. The first coffeehouse in London opened in 1650, celebrating coffee and tobacco, luxury commodities newly available in the seventeenth century. It created a primarily masculine venue in which Londoners could discuss politics and read newspapers and tracts.[45] Its natural ally, of course, was the bookstore.

Booksellers continued to thrive during the Civil War and Interregnum. For instance, John Holden leased the Blue Anchor in the Lower Walk of the New Exchange from 1648/1649 to 1652. Holden compiled a distinguished book list that reflected the demand for philosophy, plays,

[41] Guildhall Ms. 2710, Clockmakers Company, Minute Books, vol. 1, ff. 45–60.
[42] *Ibid.* [43] BL Add. Mss. 41,656, Townshend Papers, ff. 126–37. [44] HMC *Cowper* II, 343.
[45] Steven C. A. Pincus, "Coffee Politicians Does Create: Coffeehouses and Restoration Political Culture," *Journal of Modern History*, 67 (1995), 807–834. Brian Cowan, "Arenas of Connoisseurship: Auctioning Art in Later Stuart England," in Michael North and David Ormrod (eds.), *Art Markets in Europe 1400–1800* (Aldershot, Hampshire: Ashgate Publishing, 1998).

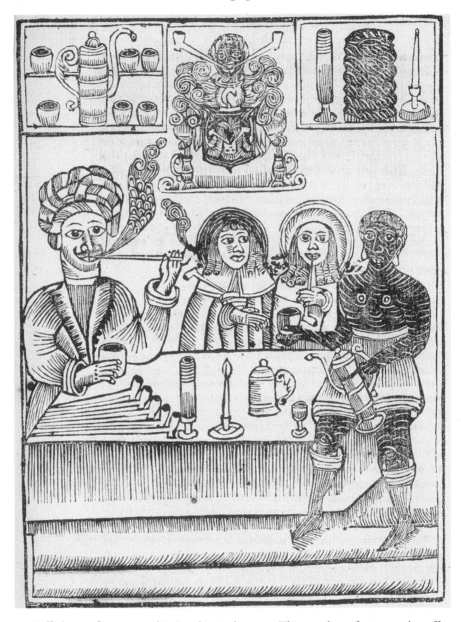

35. Coffeehouses first appeared in London in the 1650s. This woodcut of 1672 attacks coffee drinking and tobacco smoking as immoral and foreign. Exotic figures mingle with other coffeehouse customers.
The Folger Shakespeare Library, J147, woodcut of a coffeehouse from *A Broadside against Coffee* (London, 1672).

romances, and French translations during the Commonwealth.[46] Indeed, Holden's stock suggests that one could walk down the Strand and buy works by some of the leading authors of the day, many of them royalists. In 1651, for example, he offered René Descartes on Method and Thomas Hobbes on Human Nature, an English translation of the first part of *On the Elements of Law*.[47] In addition, he had on hand Joseph Hall's religious writings, plays by Massinger and Cowley, and William Davenant's *Gondibert*, the writer's most important work, with prefaces by Hobbes and Davenant himself dated from Paris, 1650.[48] Derek Hirst asks, "who could have failed to notice that Hobbes's and D'Avenant's . . . *Gondibert* (1651) carried the Parisian address of the political exile?"[49]

Holden also sold several translations from the French that swelled the market in the 1650s such as La Calprenede's *Cassandra*, which Sir Charles Cotterell translated. After serving in the royalist army, Cotterell had become Master of Ceremonies at the court in exile of Elizabeth of Bohemia and, later, the court of Henrietta Maria. His fluent translation made *Cassandra* popular into the eighteenth century.[50] Holden also promoted a translation of a work on the passions by La Chambre, physician to the Lord Chancellor of France. The continuation of royalist influence in London and Westminster and the Commonwealth's reluctance to censor books meant that royalist literature continued to be published and sold in the heart of London.

According to Annabel Patterson and Lois Potter, romance appeared especially as a royalist genre in the 1650s.[51] Thus, Holden advertised a folio edition of "An excellent New Romance, entitled, The Wall-Flower, written by Doctor Bayly very pleasant and delightful." Both Bayly, a royalist controversialist, and Davenant were imprisoned by the Republic when Holden sold their books on the Strand. Indeed, Holden's

---

[46] Donald G. Wing, *Short Title Catalog of Printed Books . . . 1641–1700*, 4 vols. (New York: Index Committee of the Modern Language Association of America, 1982–1998) IV, Publisher and Printer Index, p. 462. George Edward Briscoe Eyre (ed.), *A Transcript of the Registers of the Worshipful Company of Stationers from 1640–1708* (London, 1913–14), pp. 362. 366, 388, 402.

[47] For the Engagement Controversy in 1650 and 1651 during which this work appeared see Quentin Skinner, *Hobbes and Civil Science*, vol. III of *Visions of Politics* (Cambridge: Cambridge University Press, 2002), p. 303.

[48] Derek Hirst, "The Politics of Literature in the English Republic," *Seventeenth Century*, 5 (1990), 133–55.

[49] *Ibid.*, p. 144.

[50] HMC Appendix to the Second Report, "The Manuscripts of C. Cottrell Dormer, Esq., Rousham, near Oxford," pp. 82–84; Edwin Kuehn, "France into England, 1652: The Cotterell Translation of La Calprenede's Cassandra," *Romance Notes*, 18 (1977), 107–17.

[51] Annabel M. Patterson, *Censorship and Interpretation: The Conditions of Writing and Reading in Early Modern England* (Madison: University of Wisconsin, 1984). Lois Potter, *Secret Rites and Secret Writing: Royalist Literature, 1641–1660* (Cambridge: Cambridge University Press, 1989).

frontispiece advertised Bayly's imprisonment with a large engraving of Newgate Prison.[52] Holden also published *Ibraham or the Illustrious Bassa*. His customers, however, were not always impressed. The royalist, Dorothy Osborne, who had read the French original, wrote dismissively of this translation: "I have no patience for these translators of romances; I met with *Plexandre* and *L'Illustre Bassa*, both so disguised that I, who am their old acquaintance, hardly knew them, besides that they were still so much French in words and phrase that 'twas impossible for one that understood not French to make any thing of them."[53]

Holden also co-published books with Humphrey Mosely, the leading royalist bookseller.[54] In 1652 they jointly published translations of La Calprenede's *Cleopatra* and Sandoval's *History of the Civil Wars in Spain*.[55] At the same time, Holden hedged his bets, investing in two Latin panegyrics dedicated to Oliver Cromwell. Entitled *Irenodia Gratulatoria*, the volume had two portraits of Cromwell, a dedication to Lord President Bradshaw, and a publication date of 1652 or, as the title page added, "Libertatis Angliae, IIII."[56] Holden's bookshop demonstrates the diversity of opinion available in print in Commonwealth London.

When Holden died in 1652 his wife Susanna took over the business but soon transferred her interest in the books to Mosely. Henry Herringham began his forty years' occupancy of the Blue Anchor in 1653. One of the most important booksellers of the period, Herringham published Dryden and other playwrights of the Commonwealth and Restoration. Samuel Pepys often dropped by the Anchor when it was owned by Herringham.

ROYALISTS AND EXILE

"From Anno Domini 1641 till Anno Domini 1646, in our unnatural wars, no man understanding the true grounds of it, most of the ancient gentry

---

[52] Thomas Bayly, D. D., *Herba Parietis, or the Wall-Flower. As it grew out of the stone-chamber belonging to the metropolitan prison of London, called Newgate* (London, 1650).

[53] Quoted in Kuehn, "France into England, 1652: The Cotterell Translation of La Calprenede's *Cassandre*," 113–14.

[54] Potter, *Secret Rites and Secret Writing*, pp. 20–22, 36–37, 89, 161.

[55] Seigneur de Gaultier de Coste La Calprenede, *Cleopatra: A New Romance* (London, 1652). Prudencio de Sandoval, *The Civil Wars of Spain in the Beginning of the Reign of Charls the 5t, Emperor of Germanie and King of that nation* (London, 1652).

[56] BL Thomason Tracts, E 796 (30). See entry in *Stationers Register*, 9 January, 1651–52. Holden had become a freeman of the Stationers through William Sheares, a prolific London bookseller who owned two fashionable shops, one at the New Exchange and one in Covent Garden.

were either extinct or undone … Dearth, plunder, sales and sequestrations sent them to another world or beggar bush, and so all – or most – shires."[57] Popularly, royalists have been pictured as selling the family pictures and plate, suffering poverty and imprisonment at home or sickness and death in a foreign land, plotting and bickering with Charles II's advisors. Out of sight has been out of mind! Historians, other than Paul Hardacre and, more recently, Neil Reynolds, have made little systematic study of royalists in exile.[58]

Royalist letters capture the pain of exile. The Earl of Arundel wrote repeatedly from Antwerp to Sir Richard Browne, Charles I's representative in Paris, requesting travel passes for himself and his family, asking for advice on cheap accommodations in Paris, lamenting "having no money nor rental paid me in England," sending and asking for political news, and praying for peace.[59] The Arundels took some of their collections into exile. Their secretary made "A note of the things put up in the chests which are with his Lordship beyond seas."[60] Complaining of ill health, Arundel repeatedly asked in 1643 and 1644 for a pass to France "as ample as may be, for myself, my wife, children, with our servants, horses, goods, and baggage that we may not be troubled with officious searches we, resolving to carry nothing but our own proper goods and with as many clauses of favour and protection as may be, which are needful in these dangerous times especially in France."[61] Arundel assured Browne that the Duke of Vendome and the Duchess of Chrevreuse, friends from before the war, would support his request. By 1644 Arundel had reached Rheims. "I intend … to seek some quiet and cheap place where I may have some horsemanship for my children."[62] The Countess of Arundel, who remained in Antwerp, used Browne to send on her packet of letters to the Earl.[63] By 1646 the Earl had moved to Padua with their children while the Countess remained in the Netherlands.

---

[57] Francis Bamwell (ed.), *A Royalist's Notebook: The Commonplace Book of Sir John Oglander, Kt. Of Nunwell* (London: Constable and Company, 1936), p. 109.

[58] Paul H. Hardacre, *The Royalists during the Puritan Revolution* (The Hague: Nijhoff, 1956); Paul H. Hardacre, "The Royalists in Exile during the Puritan Revolution, 1642–60," *Huntington Library Quarterly*, 16 (1953), 353–70. Neil Reynolds, "The Stuart Court and Courtiers in Exile, 1644–1654" (Ph.D. thesis, Cambridge University, 1996).

[59] BL Add. Mss. 78,193, Browne Papers, Earl of Arundel to Browne, f. 3, 26 February 1642–43; f. 9, 2 July 1643.

[60] Arundel Castle, IN 39.

[61] BL Add. Mss. 78,193, Browne Papers, Earl of Arundel to Browne, f. 3, Antwerp, 26 February 1642–43.

[62] *Ibid.*, f. 61.

[63] BL Add. Mss. 78,193, Countess of Arundel to Browne, ff. 66–67, 14 October, 28 October 1644.

Upon ye second Arch towards ye Louure, there
is ye representation of ye Samaritan woman
powring water for our Sauiour.

The Jesuites Church called la petit St Louis
is very magnificent both for structure and pro-
portion, ye pillars about ye Altar are of black
and white marble, ye ends whereof are
kept with siluer and richly gilded, ye pulpit
is of steel gilt, given by ye Duke of Orleans
and cost 1000. liuers.

The Louure ye ordinary lodging of ye King
there is a famous galery all a long ye river
side 666. paces long.

The Gardens of ye Tuyleryy are curious, in one
whereof is a very high labirinth of Ceder
trees. In ye Citty wee saw ye palace of Justice, a
very large place and stately, there are some
walkes not unlike to ye exchange In
London where they sell all manner of mercers
stuffe.

Nostre dame ye Cathedrall Church, hath a
faire Frontispeice withall ye Kings of France
at ye entrance is to be seene against one of the
pillars a mighty statue of St. Christopher
in ye shape of a Gyant all of one stone.

In ye Vniversity (which covereth ye Citty
in forme of a hat) wee saw ye Royall garden
furnished with all manner of simples in y^e
faulbourg de St Victor.

the

36. During the Civil War, royalists traveled on the continent. This traveler discusses the sights in Paris and, in particular, the Palais du Justice, which contained shops he compares to London's Exchange.
The Folger Shakespeare Library Ms. V. a. 428, Travels Through France, Italy, Naples, Sicily, Malta. Manuscript, 1647–49.

Yet, for some royalists, periods of exile in the 1640s and 1650s proved to be an extension of the Grand Tour.[64] They self-consciously used their time abroad as a means to learn about the buildings, the collections, and the technology in the Netherlands, France, and Italy. Despite the pass system, the Commonwealth and Protectorate governments made little effort to control the comings and goings of ordinary English royalists into and out of England. Royalists flocked to Henrietta Maria's court in exile in Paris and Elizabeth of Bohemia's court in the Hague, joined foreign armies from Germany to Turkey,[65] resided in Amsterdam, traveled to Italy, and admired the French court and Parisian fashion and Italian science and art. Royalists in the East and West Indies, the American colonies, and the Ottoman Empire fought for control of commercial networks that continued to function.[66] Royalists also used their time on the continent to look, to learn, to buy, and to bring back new goods and new processes. At home they went to war or laid low and, by the 1650s, emerged to find a republic which provided them with the space to publish, to build, and to acquire as they had before.

Surprisingly, luxury consumption arose as a byproduct of war. For example, during the first civil war, between 1642 and 1646, royalists at Oxford with Charles I engaged William Dobson to paint their portraits. Dobson had replaced Van Dyck as the English court painter after the latter returned to the Netherlands in 1641. Royalist portraits showed them in armor, the royal children in military attire, and officials, such as the Master of Requests, holding documents that defined their office. Dobson painted Sir Charles Cotterell, Henrietta Maria's chief of staff, and his wife in 1645. These pictures recorded their identity as supporters of the King under extraordinary circumstances.[67]

The Queen had traveled to France in 1641 to pawn the Crown jewels and to bring back men and money to support the war effort.[68] When that failed, she had returned to Paris where she created a court

---

[64] See chapter 3 above and Edward Chaney, *The Evolution of the Grand Tour: Anglo-Italian Cultural Relations since the Renaissance* (London: Frank Cass, 1998), and Edward Chaney, *The Grand Tour and the Great Rebellion: Robert Lassels and "The Voyage of Italy" in the Seventeenth Century*, (Geneva: Slatkine, 1985).

[65] I am grateful to Geoffrey Parker for this point.

[66] Carla Gardina Pestana, *The English Atlantic in the Age of Revolution, 1640–41* (Cambridge, MA: Harvard University Press, 2004).

[67] Malcolm Rogers, *William Dobson, 1611–46* (London: National Portrait Gallery, 1983); Linda Levy Peck, *Court Patronage and Corruption in Early Stuart England* (London: Unwin Hyman, 1990), p. 12.

[68] Jens Engberg, "Royalist Finances during the English Civil War, 1642–1646," *Scandinavian Economic History Review*, 14 (1966), 73–96.

in exile for herself and her children. There, where she ranked as a French princess, Caroline ceremonial life continued. The Queen created a large household establishment of both English and French courtiers in the south wing of the Louvre. When, after the death of Charles I, her son Charles II became king, Henrietta Maria's position at the French court was further reinforced.[69] While the exile court of her sister-in-law Elizabeth of Bohemia, at the Hague, was a more modest affair, both courts served as magnets for royalists in exile.[70] Thus, continental travel, now enhanced by exile, continued to be a staple of a gentleman's education.

Earlier prescriptions for travel, to learn languages, civil law, history, and politics, continued, now enhanced by interest in mathematics, current court fashion, art, ancient monuments, rarities, and science. In 1643–44 Sir Edward Nicholas, Charles I's secretary of state, instructed his son to go to Orléans or Blois to learn French. He urged him to "keep a book" in which he entered all his observations and to learn the names and alliances of the great nobility, noting those "of the reformed religion." Nicholas also reinforced his son's Protestantism, by reminding him to read the Bible daily in "French or in some other tongue," to attend the Protestant Church in France, and to avoid Jesuits.

Translating French will render you soonest able to write it; but frequent discourse with French people will make you readiest in speaking and most exact in pronouncing it. If you can meet with a good tutor (as there are many in France), you shall do well to learn the mathematics, the knowledge of the grounds whereof is very useful in most employments. Let your principal study be history and the civil law; and while you are in France you will with most profit read the history of that kingdom. And you may there, in their court parliaments, learn the practice of the civil law ... For exercise use fencing and dancing and, if your allowance will reach to it, you may for a month or two learn to ride the Great Horse ... You must once a week visit the king's ambassador or agent while you remain at Paris and go to the court, that you may know the persons of great officers and observe the fashion there.[71]

Nicholas soon joined his son in exile. Although he was impoverished, he continued to work for the royal family and to correspond with other royalists such as Sir Christopher Hatton and Endymion Porter.[72]

[69] Reynolds, "The Stuart Court and Courtiers in Exile, 1644–1654," pp. 48–50.
[70] *Ibid.*   [71] BL Egerton Mss., 2558, ff. 1–2v, 15 February 1643–44.
[72] *The Nicholas Papers: Correspondence of Sir Edward Nicholas, Secretary of State*, ed. George F. Warner, 4 vols. (London: Camden Society, 1886–1920).

37. William Cavendish, Duke of Newcastle, was in exile in Paris where he established a riding school. In 1657 he published a large volume filled with illustrations on dressage. He used his English houses as the background for these illustrations. In this case, an African servant holds a horse in front of Welbeck Abbey.
The Folger Shakespeare Library, 291113, William Cavendish, 1st Duke of Newcastle, *Methode et Invention Nouvelle de Dresser les Chevaux* (Antwerp, 1657).

The Duke of Newcastle went into exile after leading royalist forces to defeat, leaving his daughters Jane and Elizabeth at home to defend Welbeck Abbey against the parliamentary army. While Newcastle joined the court in exile in Paris, Lady Jane successfully fought with the local sequestration committee in 1650 for the fifth of the family's landed income to which she and her siblings were entitled.[73] Meanwhile, Newcastle established a riding school in Paris and then in Antwerp and published his famous illustrated volume on the art of the horse, *Methode et Invention Nouvelle de Dresser les Chevaux* in 1657, with prints by Lucas Vosterman. In the volume, Newcastle presents himself on horseback in front of Welbeck Abbey, Bolsover Castle, and Ogle attended by servants, both African and

[73] *The Royalist Composition Papers: being the proceedings of the Committee for Compounding, AD 1643–1660*, 1 April 1650 and 26 November 1650, p. 1732.

English. The volume used designs of the houses made as early as the 1630s and brought from England.[74] Newcastle transmitted the courtly attitudes and consumption of the French court both to his pupils and, through his publications, to an English audience in the 1650s.[75]

Science, scientific instruments, and technology attracted the attention of the English abroad as we shall see at greater length in a later chapter. Another royalist, Charles Cheyne, traveled in Europe in the late 1640s and early 1650s. Visiting Rome, he, like other European travelers, was especially impressed with Athanasius Kircher's famous scientific museum, one of the principal sites on the seventeenth-century tourist map. Back in England, Cheyne requested a model of the apparatus for distillation from the famous Jesuit scientist and polymath.[76] Cheyne later married Lady Jane Cavendish, thereby becoming the Duke of Newcastle's son-in-law. His interest in Italian art, architecture, and science influenced his building in the Restoration.[77]

John Evelyn provides the best documented example of the relationship of exile and innovation. Evelyn immersed himself in continental material culture and disseminated it in England through personal contact and publication from the 1640s on.[78] His papers document the experience of exile of a large circle of royalists. Evelyn, then in his twenties, first went abroad in June 1641.[79] Before embarking, he sat for his portrait by Hendrick van der Brocht, an artist and dealer, in London on 28 June at his sister's request, "upon my resolutions to absent myself from this ill face of things at home."[80] Van der Brocht, who looked after the Arundels' collections, proved to be one of Evelyn's important correspondents. Evelyn began his tour as a sightseer not an exile. Crossing to the Low Countries, he went to the court of Elizabeth of Bohemia at the Hague where "I had the honor to kiss her hand." He also visited her "palace or country house, built after the Italian manner." In addition, he took part in army maneuvers and had a suit of armor made.[81] Recording the artistic and architectural sights

---

74 Mark Girouard argues that pictures of the houses were done in the 1630s; others suggest that they were done in the 1650s. See chapter 5, note 210.

75 Lucy Worsley and Tom Addyman, "Riding Houses and Horses: William Cavendish's Architecture for the Art of Horsemanship," *Architectural History*, 45 (2003), 194–229.

76 HEH EL 11,123, Chaloner to Cheyne, 17 January 1671.   77 See chapter 7 below.

78 Michael Hunter, "John Evelyn in the 1650s," in his *Science and the Shape of Orthodoxy: Intellectual Change in Late Seventeenth Century Britain* (Woodbridge Suffolk: Boydell Press, 1995), pp. 67–98.

79 BL Add. Mss. 78,315, Evelyn Papers, f. 2, Jane Newton to Evelyn, May 1637; f. 3, William Newton to Evelyn, 5 February 1637–38; f. 26, William Newton to John Evelyn, May 1644.

80 John Evelyn, *The Diary of John Evelyn*, ed. E. S. de Beer, 6 vols. (Oxford: Clarendon Press, 1955), II, p. 29, 29 June 1641.

81 *Ibid.*, pp. 33–37, 55; Evelyn was present at Dort in September "at the reception of Queen Mother Maria de Medices, Dowager of France, widow of Henry the Great, and mother to the king Lewes

of major Dutch cities and small towns, Evelyn noted their wealth and commerce, neatness and order. Evelyn thought Gresham's Royal Exchange superior to Amsterdam's but admired the ships and waterways that underpinned Dutch trade and shipping.[82] "The most busy concourse of mortal men, now upon the face of the whole earth and the most addicted to commerce: Nor must I forget the ports and issues of the town, which are very noble pieces of architecture, some of them modern; and so are their churches."[83]

Always curious, Evelyn sought to learn not only about art and architecture but also about diversity of religious beliefs and invention. In Amsterdam he visited synagogues and Jewish cemeteries, admired stately funeral monuments, and plucked pages of Hebrew text from books entombed with rabbis. He sought novelty and innovations in technology.[84] Pictures, houses, gardens, fountains, porcelain, ingenious machinery, and other aspects of luxury consumption in the early seventeenth century continued to attract visitors' interest in the 1640s. Evelyn also went shopping. From Rotterdam Evelyn sent home pictures. "Their annual mart or fair, so furnish'd with pictures (especially landskips, and drolleries as they call those clownish representations), as I was amaz'd: some of these I bought and sent into England."[85] In Leyden he visited printing houses and looked at exotic plants and other natural curiosities.[86]

Evelyn returned to England and spent the early war years in London, where he continued to receive rents from his tenants in Surrey. Evelyn's diary records his own enthusiasm for entertainment and viewing art and architecture. These served as the means to continue his previous way of life in the midst of upheaval, and to fill the vacancy of an absent court. In 1642 Evelyn spent time "studying a little; but dancing and fooling more."[87] In March 1643, in the midst of the first civil war, Evelyn visited "my L[ord] of Salisbury's palace at Hatfield; where the most considerable rarity besides the house, (inferior to few for its architecture then in England) was the garden and vineyard rarely well water'd and planted." He admired the picture of Secretary Cecil in "mosaic-work very well done by some Italian hand."[88] On 15 April 1643, he toured Balls Park, Hertford, "Sir J. Harris[on]'s his house new built," and returned by way of the

---

XIII of France, and Queen of England, whence she newly arriv'd toss'd to and fro by the various fortune of [her] life. From this city she designed for Cologne conducted by the Earl of Arundel and the Herr van Brederode" (II, 57).
[82] Evelyn, *Diary*, pp. 33–35, 46, July 1641.   [83] *Ibid.*, p. 48, August 1641.
[84] *Ibid.*, pp. 42–43, 20–21 August 1641.   [85] *Ibid.*, p. 39, 13 August 1641.
[86] *Ibid.*, pp. 39, 52–54, August 1641.   [87] *Ibid.*, p. 78, 29 January–5 March 1642.
[88] *Ibid.*, p. 80, 11 March 1643.

house and gardens of Theobalds.[89] Harrison, a London merchant and one of the farmers of the customs under Charles I, bought the property in 1637 which he rebuilt in a style akin to that of Inigo Jones in the 1630s. Knighted in 1640, Harrison later claimed that "during the time of the war, he lost by the rebels above one hundred and thirty thousand pounds, and yet he left his son sixteen hundred pounds a year in land, and ... his daughter above twenty thousand pounds."[90]

In 1642 and 1643 Evelyn bought art from Hendrick van der Brocht. Before van der Brocht left for the continent, he wrote to Evelyn that he had "come to London with the picture cases safely here" although he had run into some soldiers. Van der Brocht had sold pictures both to Evelyn and to his brother before and now asked for payment. "I left the nearest price of the Adoration for seven pounds, if times were otherwise I could not leave it for L10. The two other sea pieces for 30 shillings a piece ... Your things which you had of me were a little landskip in watercolour at 15 shillings, a little tempest, 10 shillings, a boy of bronze, 30, which maketh L2/15/3 ... If times were otherwise or that I did not go away I should not trouble you."[91] Once ensconced in Alkmaar, in the Netherlands, with the Countess of Arundel, van der Brocht sent several letters to Evelyn enclosing "some prints ... of Sir Anthony Van Dyck's etched by Mr. Hollar who is very much esteemed in these parts and especially in Antwerp where he is now dwelling. Many lovers of art make collections of his works."[92] Both Hollar and Pierre Lombart engraved portraits for the English market in the 1640s and 1650s.

In 1643 Evelyn also left for the continent. Claiming to have supplied horses and arms to the King, he obtained a license to travel from Sir Edward Nicholas, the Secretary of State, who was a family friend. Upon arrival in Paris, Evelyn visited Sir Richard Browne, "his Majesty's Resident with the French King." Evelyn later married Browne's daughter. When he returned to England, he became an important source of news to his father-in-law.

Evelyn maintained correspondence with a large royalist network in exile interested in art, learning, and material culture. The language of compliment, crafted within social networks at home, continued, now adapted to the experience of exile. One of his correspondents, Christopher Caley [Kaley], called Evelyn's "letters the veins that bring the blood ... to us. ... Rome cannot be but a place fit for such a noble spirit as

---

[89] *Ibid.*, p. 81.
[90] *Ibid.*; Anne Harrison, Lady Fanshawe, *The Memoirs of Lady Fanshawe* (London: Henry Colburn, 1829), p. 32. BL Stowe 184, f. 161, "Losses by sequestration, 1643–49."
[91] BL Add. Mss. 78,315, Evelyn Papers, f. 13, 15 December 1642.   [92] *Ibid.*, f. 17, 1 April 1643.

38. Pierre Lombart reproduced a portrait made by Van Dyck of Lady Anne Carr, daughter of the Earl of Somerset and Frances Howard, as part of a series entitled "The Countesses" for the commercial market.
The Folger Shakespeare Library, ART 232571, Pierre Lombart engraving after Van Dyck, portrait of Lady Anne Carr, c. 1650.

yours ... I must ... want the sight of those antiquities you are busy in and, for those present magnificences, they tempt me not did you please to write them ... I shall come to admire all those rarities and among the chiefest you."[93] Another exile, Clipsby Crew, wrote from Tours recommending the Duke of Vendome's house: "you shall not see the like in all your travels."[94] From Rome in 1644, Evelyn wrote to John Collier, a Leghorn merchant who organized Evelyn's finances and arranged transport of his trunks, that "being now at Rome ... I find a place so furnished with divertissements to my genius that I am half afraid it will be very difficult for me to think of a removal this winter."[95]

In contrast, William Ducie sent Evelyn a very gloomy forecast from home in 1644, writing about failed negotiations and troop movements. "I hope you find in France all that contentment and pleasure you expected there ... Believe it sir you may think yourself happy to be out of the calamities that are like to befall us in this kingdom the next summer."[96]

Evelyn continued his travels in Italy in 1645. Friendships flourished in exile. Thomas Henshaw, who joined him in Rome, served in the French army and traveled to Italy and Spain during his exile. He translated a history of the Chinese monarchy from the Italian and, at the Restoration, became French tutor to Charles II and member of the Royal Society.[97] Another acquaintance, Robert Abdy, wrote to Evelyn in the spring of 1645 from Padua requesting that he "look again upon the square ruby which I had a mind to buy." Asking Evelyn to "give what your judgement thinks fitting," he asked him to "look out another diamond." Abdy sent his services to Mr. Hobson, the leading English merchant in Venice, and Mr. Campion, "my school fellow ... if we have your company any time for you go to France I'll beg your leave to transcribe some of your Italian songs and the catalogue of your things."[98] Anna Baretieri sent Evelyn figures from Florence presumably bronzes.[99]

---

[93] *Ibid.*, ff. 33, 38, 40, 42, 11 September 1644–1 December 1644.
[94] *Ibid.*, Clipsby Crewe to Evelyn, July 1643.
[95] *Ibid.*, f. 36, Rome 25 November 1644; f. 52, notes to Collier about trunks, chests and boxes sent to Livorno for Evelyn and Henshaw.
[96] *Ibid.*, f. 25, 22 February 1643–44.
[97] Royal Society, Sackler Archive; Stephen Pasmore, "Thomas Henshaw FRS (1618–1700)," *Notes and Records of the Royal Society*, 36 (1982), 177–88.
[98] BL Add. Mss. 78,315, Evelyn Papers, f. 46. Mr. Abdy, Padua, 26 March 1645. Robert Abdy was a London merchant who was one of the trustees of the will of Robert Abbot, from whom Evelyn borrowed money. Guildhall Mss. L78, Clayton Papers, Ms. 2931, Robert Abbott account book A, 1645/6–52, f. 113, 9 May 1649.
[99] BL Add. Mss. 78,315, Evelyn Papers, ff. 48, 50, Anna Baritieri, Florence, April 1645.

Hendrick van der Brocht longed to join him and assumed that Evelyn
was making copies of what he saw to bring home. Van der Brocht wished
that they could

together enjoy the sights of those rare pictures in those parts. I do not doubt of the
increase of the love and skill you have in pictures and that you do exercise your self
in it having had so good a beginning. I was last year in England and did see at
Wotton your fine trout pond; no doubt you will see some fine grottos for
fountains which may serve you for a pattern ... I do not doubt but you go
often (at your being at Venice) unto the island of St. George to see the rare
great picture of Veronese and the goodly pictures of Titian at Frari and other
places.[100]

Evelyn returned to England after the first civil war ended in 1646. Like
Humphrey Weld and many others, Evelyn felt secure enough to return to
prewar types of consumption. In late November 1647, as Humphrey Weld
ordered his Roman pictures, Evelyn sought to buy Venetian mirrors through
John Hobson, consul of the Levant Company in Venice, with whom Evelyn
had dined and who had previously shipped goods from Venice for him.
Hobson, who provided prices and sizes, pointed out that Venetian technology had improved, and that prices had fallen by more than half. "They were
never cheaper since I knew Venice, for whereas formerly 'twas a difficult
matter to find a glass of five quarters which is an English yard ... I now can
meet with many of that size for half the money and under."[101] Venetians now
framed looking glasses with exotic woods such as ebony but Hobson thought
that Evelyn could have the frames done in London.[102]

At home, Evelyn recorded visits to several royalist collectors who themselves had been in exile on the continent, including Sir Clipsby Crew,
Thomas Henshaw, and Endymion Porter.[103] At Crew's, Evelyn admired
"fine Indian hangings and a very good chimney-piece of water colours done
by Breugel which I bought for him."[104] During the trial of Charles I in
January 1649, Evelyn looked at perspectives by Steenwyck at Thomas
Henshaw's.[105] In May 1649 he met Endymion Porter at the house of the
artist and dealer George Geldorp and noticed a "rare cabinet of one

[100] *Ibid.*, f. 56. Antony Griffiths, *The Print in Stuart Britain, 1603–1689* (London: British Museum
Press, 1998), pp. 96–98, 115. Cf. transcription of Letters in Robert Harding, "John Evelyn, Hendrick
van der Brocht the Younger and Wenceslaus Hollar," *Apollo*, 144 (1996), 39–44.
[101] Evelyn, *Diary*, II, p. 476, 22 March 1646–47.
[102] BL Add Mss. 78,315, Evelyn Papers, f. 106, 29 November 1647.
[103] Evelyn, *Diary*, II, p. 540; 28 February 1648. Crew traveled to France in February 1644 with Peter
Rycaut and his wife and J. Denne, BL Add. Mss. 28,010.
[104] Evelyn, *Diary*, II, pp. 540, 546, 554–55.   [105] *Ibid.*, p. 546, 2 January 1649.

Delabarrs."[106] But on 20 June 1649, several months after the execution of the King, Evelyn decided to go into exile again. "I went to Putney and other places on the Thames to take prospects in crayon, to carry into France, where I thought to have them engrav'd."[107] In Paris, Evelyn himself made the first English landscape engravings, presenting the views he had sketched before leaving London.[108] For Evelyn, Putney, the site of the army leveller debates over a future constitution, meant the picturesque not the political.

When Evelyn returned to England once more in 1652 after two years in France, he forswore politics. He toured Whitehall "whereof many years, I had not been, and found it very glorious and well furnished."[109] He found many fellow exiles back home again. For example, Evelyn dined with Lord Bruce, "my fellow traveller in Italy" with whom he had gone to the opera in Venice in 1645.[110] He visited Hobbes, "the famous philosopher of Malmesbury with whom I had been long acquainted in France."[111] Hobbes had gone into exile a royalist and returned to England in 1651, ready, as were many, to accommodate the new regime. Hobbes described his tranquil life at home to correspondents.[112]

Evelyn's building and gardening during the Interregnum reflected the interest in grottos and water works that had emerged before the Civil War among well-to-do builders. To these he added what he had seen on the continent,[113] books like Walter Blith's, *The Improver Improved* of 1652, and conversations with contemporaries such as John Beale, an associate of Samuel Hartlib's, about the ideal garden.[114] In 1655 he admired the garden

---

[106] *Ibid.*, pp. 554–56, 12 May 1649; p. 555, 19 May 1649.   [107] *Ibid.*, p. 57.

[108] Antony Griffiths, "The Etchings of John Evelyn," in David Howarth, (ed.), *Art and Patronage in the Caroline Courts: Essays in Honor of Sir Oliver Millar* (Cambridge: Cambridge University Press, 1993), p. 63.

[109] Evelyn, *Diary*, III, p. 166, 11 February 1656.

[110] *Ibid.*, p. 166, 14 February 1656.

[111] *Ibid.*, p. 163, 14 December 1655.

[112] Thomas Hobbes, *The Correspondence*, ed. Noel Malcolm, 2 vols. (Oxford: Clarendon Press, 1994), I, p. 201. Thomas de Mantel to Hobbes, 26 August/5 September 1654 from Paris, "It gave me great happiness to know that you were content and enjoying the benefit of a tranquil life while this kingdom (especially Paris) was undergoing these disturbances."

[113] BL Add. Mss. 78,334, Padua, Garden of Simples.

[114] Timothy Mowl, "New Science, Old Order: The Gardens of the Great Rebellion," *Journal of Garden History*, 13 (1993), 16–34; *John Evelyn's "Elysium Britannicum" and European Gardening*, ed. Therese O'Malley and Joachim Wolschke-Bulmahn (Washington, DC: Dumbarton Oaks Research Library and Collection, 1998); Douglas Chambers, "Wild Pastoral Encounter: John Evelyn and the Regeneration of the Pastoral in the Mid-Seventeenth Century," in Michael Leslie and Timothy Raylor (eds.), *Culture and Cultivation in Early Modern England: Writing and the Land* (Leicester: Leicester University Press, 1992); Douglas Chambers, *The Planters of the English Landscape Garden: Botany, Trees and the Georgics* (New Haven: Yale University Press, 1993).

at Deepdene which Charles Howard, Arundel's grandson, created, describing it as "an amphitheatre garden, or solitary recess, being 15 acres, environ'd by a hill."[115] Oxford friends urged Evelyn to complete his "Elysium Britannicum" so that "other Italian glories and pompous beauties may one day be brought (so far as the temper of the climate will give leave) into English gardens."[116]

If Evelyn did not complete this great work on gardens, he did design gardens for himself and others.

Resolving to possess myself in some quiet if it might be, in a time of so great jealousy, I built (by my brother's permission) . . . a little study over a cascade, to pass my melancholy hours shaded there with trees, and silent enough. This trifle, however despicable, was the occasion of my brother's vast expense, when some years after, he enlarged the gardens, built the portico, and cut the mount into the present shape it now is of, with the fountains in the parterre, which were amenities not frequent in the best noblemen's gardens in England. This being finished whilst I was abroad, was conducted by a relation of ours, George Evelyn, who had been in Italy, but was mistaken in the architecture of the portico, which tho' making a magnificent show, has great faults.[117]

Timothy Mowl suggests that Evelyn underestimated the importance of his cousin George's innovation.[118] He borrowed architecture books from Evelyn including "the French book he was pleased to lend me that describeth several doors and gates adorned with pillars of the three Grecian orders . . . and the famous book of architecture, the name he hath forgotten."[119] Evelyn's interest in building extended beyond his own houses and gardens. In 1655 he contributed to Sir Nicholas Crisp's dockside development in Deptford[120] and designed gardens for Henry Howard, sixth Duke of Norfolk.

Evelyn had become a connoisseur in the company of the Earl of Arundel. In the 1640s and 1650s, he documented continental and domestic art collections, buildings, and technology. He engraved landscapes and built houses and gardens in the Italian and French style. He bought luxury goods for himself and for friends and family on the continent and, once back in England, continued to order art and artifacts. But Evelyn did not seek merely to distinguish himself from others within a courtly society,

[115] Quoted in Mowl, "New Science, Old Order: The Gardens of the Great Rebellion," 26.
[116] Quoted in John Dixon Hunt, *Garden and Grove: The Italian Renaissance Garden in the English Imagination, 1600–1750* (London: Dent, 1986). Mowl considers this tepid praise.
[117] Evelyn, *Diary*, II, p. 81, 17 May 1643; III, pp. 60–61, 22 March 1652.
[118] Mowl, "New Science, Old Order: The Gardens of the Great Rebellion," 16–34.
[119] BL Add. Mss. 78,316, Evelyn Papers, f. 75. [120] *Ibid.*, ff. 90, 93, 94, 95, 96, 97, 98, 1655–1656.

to become a rarity himself as his correspondent Christopher Caley suggested. Rather, Evelyn worked diligently to import, to copy, to improve goods, processes, and the built environment. Throughout the 1650s he wrote to French writers such as Abraham Bosse, the engraver and author of books on the art; scientists such as Dr. N. Lefebvre who informed him about the process for making varnish; and Claude Russelde, an alchemist.[121] In England he was in close contact with the Wilkins circle at Oxford and the Hartlib circle in London. The flattering letters he received both from English and foreign friends throughout the 1640s and 1650s mirrored his construction of himself as a transmitter of European culture and innovation.

The young Peter Pett, later a founding member of the Royal Society, summed up these themes nicely in a sycophantic letter to Evelyn from All Souls, Oxford, in 1654. Pett linked aristocratic honor, curiosity, and refinement to continental culture while he demeaned English backwardness. Referring to Evelyn's interest in the project for a history of languages, Pett wished that he could present his service in all the languages of the world "which do surmount the scantness of our English dialect (the knowledge of which tongues your spacious understanding doth so perfectly comprehend . . . for you can, sir, no more expect curiosity or refinedness of fancy from one whose education hath been empounded within the island where he was born."[122] Pett sent thanks from Dr. Wilkins for the rarities that Evelyn had sent him and thanks from Mr. Barlow for the offer of Bembus's tables for the All Souls Library.

As a result of these gifts, Evelyn's name was listed in the library's book of enrollment, already a site for college fundraising. "Our library doth indeed for the gift of forty shillings or the value thereof, allow the donors a perpetual receptacle for their names: and we observe that our monumental books of enrollment do sometimes prove successful engines to us, whereby to serve up the purses of some London citizens as they visit our coasts . . . wherein these piteous cockneys are not a little proud of their purchasing forty shillings worth of immortality." But Evelyn's name, unlike the "piteous cockneys," "which is so much known and loved in the European world, hath grandeur enough in it eternally to gild and adorn our register."[123]

---

[121] *Ibid.*, f. 42. N. Lefebvre, 3 June 1652, Paris.   [122] *Ibid.*, f. 72, December 1654.
[123] *Ibid.*, f. 72, December 1654.

PARLIAMENTARIANS AND ENTREPRENEURS

If some royalists used the period of exile to appropriate continental material culture, what impact did the Commonwealth and the Protectorate have on the luxury trade at home? The answer seems obvious. The values of those who challenged Charles I, drawn together most of all by religious belief more than any other single issue, seemed to oppose the sumptuous, and sometimes Catholic, material culture of the court, its courtiers, great merchants, and artisans. Iconoclasm challenged the visual; the word undermined other routes to knowledge and belief. The new regime shut down the theatres, threatened the shops, and sold off the King's goods. As we have seen, Anne Lady Halkett worried that she had erred as a young woman when, like many others, she had gone with friends to the Spring Garden and to the theatre.[124] In his magisterial study, *The State's Servants*, Gerald Aylmer argues that conspicuous consumption lessened during the English Republic from 1649 to 1660, pointing out that, for some, excess investment went into joint-stock ventures. Fewer built houses than those who served Charles I and several of the Protectorate's most important officials did not build new houses or expand old ones at all.[125]

Nevertheless, this chapter argues that the Civil War underwrote the expansion of luxury consumption for some, especially for those in London. The sitting of the Long Parliament increased the numbers of those who lived in London while the war in other parts of the country brought refugees to the city. While increased taxation was a new burden, the revenue from compositions went to members of the army, who then had more to spend. New coats of arms were granted throughout the period 1640–60 and heraldic visitations were bruited in 1658–59 during Richard Cromwell's rule.[126] Most importantly, the Commonwealth chose not to ruin its opponents like Weld, not to prevent exiles like Evelyn from returning, not to censor publication, and not to prevent luxury consumption.

We have already seen that, in London, retail shopping recovered quickly from the first civil war and that Thomas Cullum and Humphrey Weld

---

[124] John Gough Nichols (ed.), *The Autobiography of Anne Lady Halkett*, Camden Society, new series 13 (1875), p. 3. Linda Levy Peck, "Women in the Caroline Audience: The Evidence from Hatfield," *Shakespeare Quarterly*, 51 (Winter, 2000), 474–77.

[125] Gerald E. Aylmer, *The State's Servants: The Civil Service of the English Republic, 1649–1660* (London: Routledge, 1973), p. 280.

[126] *Ibid.*

began to buy London property in the 1640s. Some members of the elite continued their earlier patterns of luxury consumption throughout the 1640s and 1650s; others fashioned a new identity through the purchase of luxury goods. For example, parliamentary leaders such as Sir Thomas Barrington and his wife, Lady Judith, became residents in London where the visit and the coach became important aspects of aristocratic social life.[127] Barrington took a long lease on a new house in Queen's Street in 1641, moving from lodgings in Fleet Street when it became apparent that Parliament would sit indefinitely. Part of a terrace of houses built as a speculative development near Covent Garden, the house with its Corinthian columns reflected the classical style of the 1630s. The Barringtons continued to work on the new house, re-glazing windows and improving the water supply. They brought their own furniture from the country and purchased more from a Mrs. Darby in London. The puritan Barringtons also bought a new coach in 1640, trading in the scarlet coach they had just bought from the diplomat Sir William Becher for L50. Both Sir Thomas and Lady Judith used the coach, the latter to pay visits to Lady Carlisle and Lady Devonshire and to sightsee, to view the tombs in Westminster Abbey, and the great room at the Charterhouse. Their neighbors included prominent parliamentary peers and ambassadors. Sir Thomas also worked on his pew at St. Giles church, providing thirty-two yards of mat, raising the height of the pew, and adding his coat of arms just before he died in 1645.[128]

Some entrepreneurs, optimistic about profits from luxury trades, sought to make their fortunes at the end of the first civil war. By 1646 Robert Abbott, William Petty, and Peter Lely, a banker, a scientist, and an artist, set up new businesses in London. Two, Petty and Lely, came from travel abroad in France and the Netherlands; the third, Abbott, had just come out of prison. Like Weld and Evelyn, they saw the end of the first civil war as offering a return to order, promotion, and profit. They remained enthusiastic despite the second civil war, the execution of the King, and the Interregnum.

Robert Abbott, a London scrivener, went to prison in 1643 for participating in Edmund Waller's plot to secure London for the King. The ringleaders were executed although Waller himself went into exile in

---

[127] Susan E. Whyman, *Sociability and Power in Late-Stuart England: The Cultural Worlds of the Verneys, 1660–1720* (Oxford: Oxford University Press, 1999).

[128] Arthur Searle, "Sir Thomas Barrington in London, 1640–1644," *Essex Journal*, 2 (1967), no. 1, 35–41 and no. 2, 63–70.

Italy where he traveled with John Evelyn. Although sentenced to death, Abbott languished in prison, his goods appropriated by Parliament. Released in 1645, he successfully requested the return of his goods so that he could earn a living for his family. In the late 1640s, he set up his business taking deposits and loaning money, especially to royalists who rewarded his loyalty. Abbott's business was an early form of deposit banking.[129] Thus, in 1648, on behalf of Robert Smith, Abbott paid Mr. Portman for a jewel, Mr. Carter and Mr. Shute for horses, Mr. Seele for a bed and bolster, made payments to the East India Company, and lent money to John Prettyman.[130]

Abbott's clients also included several women who took an active role in managing their money and estates, a role that the wars made more important. His clients included Jane Lady Hart, Jane Waring, Anne Huxley, Lady Anne St. John (later Countess of Rochester), Anne Kingston, Elizabeth, Countess of Dirletoun, Lady Hatton, Mary Taylor, and Lady Whorwood.[131] Some had large amounts of money on deposit with him. For instance, between 1646 and 1649, Anne Huxley had a credit of L1,359; Jane Waring had L481 on deposit in 1646; Lady Hart, a relative of Evelyn's, had L2,500 which Abbott then paid to the East India Company for her in 1651.[132] Colonel Owen deposited L500 for the Countess of Dirletoun which Abbott then paid to her.[133] Abbott apparently laundered money for King Charles and remitted money to Paris to royalists in exile without a problem. Jane Whorwood conveyed money to the King while he was in captivity at Hampton Court in 1647–48. In 1649 she had an additional L319 on deposit.[134] During the Interregnum, Abbott commissioned his own portrait as a young aristocrat in the style of Van Dyck.[135] Robert Clayton, Abbott's relation and apprentice, took over the business at

---

[129] Frank T. Melton, *Sir Robert Clayton and the Origins of English Deposit Banking, 1658–85* (Cambridge: Cambridge University Press, 1986). Melton does not discuss women who were Abbott's clients.

[130] Guildhall Mss., L78, Clayton Papers, Ms. 2931, Robert Abbott account book, 1645-46–1652, ff. 77, 101, 156. Abbott handled some of Thomas Lord Windsor's finances in the 1650s. Guildhall Mss., L78 Clayton Papers, Ms. 2931.

[131] Guildhall Mss., L78, Clayton Papers, Ms. 2931, Robert Abbott, account book, ff. 101, 20, 161, 125, 17, 123. 181, 140, 190. On loyalist women see Melissa Franklin, "The Language of Loyalism Among Royalist Women" (MA thesis, University of Rochester, 1996); N. H. Keeble, "Obedient Subjects? The Loyal Self in Some Later Seventeenth-Century Royalist Women's Memoirs" in Gerald M. McLean (ed.), *Culture and Society in the Stuart Restoration: Literature, Drama, History* (Cambridge: Cambridge University Press, 1995).

[132] *Ibid.*, ff. 16v–17; 13v–14; 181.   [133] *Ibid.*, f. 140.

[134] Guildhall Mss., L78, Clayton Papers, Ms. 2931, Robert Abbott account book, f. 125.

[135] National Portrait Gallery, London. There are two portraits of Abbott although the older may be Maurice Abbott.

Abbott's death in 1658, becoming the most important banker during the Restoration. Elected Lord Mayor in 1679, Clayton's mayoralty was characterized by splendor and hospitality. He built an impressive mansion in the city.[136]

William Petty, the son of a draper, took ship as a young man and, after many adventures, wound up in Paris where he joined the circle around Mersenne, the French mathematician, which included Thomas Hobbes.[137] Petty returned to England after the first civil war. One of the most important economic thinkers and planners of the seventeenth century, Petty composed a list of ways to make his fortune through patents, education, medicine, print, and patronage in 1648–49.[138] Petty's ways to win wealth reflected the importance of improvement and innovation that characterized the circle of Samuel Hartlib, of which he was a member, and the mentality of patentees, artists, and courtiers who understood the importance of patronage and advertisement.

1. By procuring privileges for public designs of universal use 2. By making models and directing private works and engines 3. By selling some works made by myself and friends 4. By giving, selling transcripts of secrets [and] artifices ... 5. By printing the same afterwards 6. By drawing in adventurers upon the credit of former performance ... 8. By honorary pension from great persons 9. By the practice of physic, setting up and maintaining a *Noscomium Academicum.*

Petty intended to "maintain servants" by "transcribing, translating, and drawing my own communications" and by "showing rarities to the curious."[139] He began by inventing a mechanical copying machine and, in 1648, went into business with John Holland, who put up the capital to invest in "such adventures as Petty had perfected and knew the correctness of, for public good and private advantage."[140]

At the same time that Petty planned how to make money, he also planned ways to spend it. In 1648–49, he recorded shops in which to purchase luxury goods including "The Frying Pan in Leadenhall Street,

---

[136] Guildhall Ms. Jaspar A. R. Abbott, "Robert Abbott, 'City Money Scrivener and his Account Book, 1646–52," *Guildhall Miscellany*, 1 (1956), 31–39; Evelyn, *Diary*, IV, pp. 185–86; Melton, *Sir Robert Clayton and the Origins of English Deposit Banking.*

[137] Lord Edmund Fitzmaurice, *The Life of Sir William Petty, 1623–1687* (London: John Murray, 1895), pp. 5–13.

[138] BL Add. Mss. 72,891, Petty Papers, f. 8v, 1647–48.   [139] *Ibid.*, f. 8v, 1647–48.

[140] Quoted in Fitzmaurice, *The Life of Sir William Petty*, p. 13.

to buy ebony, aligzant wood, speckled wood, stript wood, redwood, box etc."[141] He also listed twenty-three London tradesmen including a gunsmith, spectacle maker, ivory turner, perfumer, molder in wax, a clockmaker, and a glass seller, a brewer, dyer, and druggist, along with those in the building trades.[142]

The Dutch artist and art dealer, Peter Lely, the most prominent portrait painter of the Restoration, arrived in London in 1646 and became a member of the Painter-Stainers Company the next year. His early career in England demonstrated the continuation of a lively art market in the late 1640s and 1650s. Living in and operating a studio in Covent Garden, Lely received commissions from the parliamentary peers, Algernon Percy, Earl of Northumberland, Viscount Lisle, Philip, Lord Wharton, the Earl of Pembroke, as well as the Countess Dysart of Ham House.[143] Lely himself put together a major collection of pictures, drawings, and sculpture, some drawn from the King's collections, which included large numbers of pictures and sketches by Van Dyck, Veronese, and Titian, and drawings that had belonged to the Earl of Arundel. He also owned Bernini's bust of Thomas Baker. Commissioned to do a bust of Charles I based on studies by Van Dyck, Bernini had produced one of the King's agent Baker as well. Lely claimed to have the best collection of drawings and prints in Europe. It included several formerly owned by Rembrandt. At Lely's death, ninety-nine eager buyers among the English elite purchased his pictures, drawings, and bronzes.[144] They included Thomas Povey, a City merchant and member of the Royal Society, who had interests in the West Indies and great love of pictures and Henry Mordaunt, Earl of Peterborough, who added Lely's pictures to his collections alongside his Mortlake tapestries and the cabinet of gems that had once belonged to the Earl of Arundel.[145]

Politics did not dictate art patronage. Sometime before 1653, Lely, Sir Balthazar Gerbier, Buckingham's old client, and George Geldorp proposed to the Long Parliament the making of grand portraits to celebrate its achievements. At each end of the Whitehall Banqueting House, below Rubens's ceiling paintings celebrating the reign of James I, they "proposed two large group-portraits in the Dutch tradition: the

---

[141] BL Add. Mss. 72,891, Petty Papers, f. 8.   [142] *Ibid.*, f. 8.

[143] Oliver Millar, *Sir Peter Lely 1618–80, Exhibition Catalog* (London: National Portrait Gallery, 1978).

[144] Diana Dethloff, "The Executors' Account Book and the Dispersal of Sir Peter Lely's Collection," *Journal of the History of Collections*, 8 (1996), 15–51.

[145] *Ibid.*; Diana Scarrisbrick, "The Arundel Gem Cabinet," *Apollo*, 144 (1996), 45–48.

whole Assembly of Parliament at one end, the Council of State at the other."[146] While that idea failed, in 1654 Lely was commissioned to paint the Lord Protector, Oliver Cromwell. Shortly afterwards he did a group portrait of the royalist Sir Edward Hales and his family surrounded with classical columns, lavish drapery, and contemporary garden sculpture. Hale's grandfather, the first baronet, had supported Parliament but Hales himself led a royalist uprising in 1648 that aimed to free King Charles. Sometime after he inherited the baronetcy in 1654, he commissioned the Lely portrait.[147]

The cluster of parliamentary peers, Northumberland, Lisle, Lord Wharton, and Pembroke, who commissioned Lely, continued to build, buy, furnish, collect, and commission during the 1640s and 1650s, much as early Stuart patrons had done. For instance, in the early 1640s Algernon Percy, tenth Earl of Northumberland, hired Inigo Jones to rebuild both Northumberland House on the Strand and Syon House in the London suburbs. After Charles I's execution, Northumberland moved to Syon where he continued to rebuild and to work in his gardens for which he imported exotic plants.[148] Evelyn visited Northumberland House in 1658 and admired the pictures by Andrea del Sarto, Georgione, and Leonardo, as well as portraits by Van Dyck and Titian, which Northumberland bought from Van Dyck, who was not only a painter but a collector and dealer.[149]

Viscount Lisle, son of the second Earl of Leicester and Northumberland's nephew, sat in the House of Commons from 1640, became a commissioner for the trial of Charles I and, from 1649, served as a member of the Council of State. Even as Lisle took a leading ceremonial role in the Protectorate, he served as one of the commissioners to dispose of King Charles's collections. Hilary Madicott has shown that "by 1660, Lisle had ... created what was almost certainly the largest collection in this country of works of art from the former royal palaces."[150] Purchasing through members of the New Model Army and syndicates of royal creditors, Lisle took advantage of his position to acquire more than sixty paintings and sixty works of sculpture. His selections resembled

---

[146] Millar, *Sir Peter Lely, 1618–1680*, pp. 9–14, 24–25. [147] The portrait is at the Guildhall.

[148] Jeremy Wood, "The Architectural Patronage of Algernon Percy, 10th Earl of Northumberland," in John Bold and Edward Chaney (eds.), *English Architecture, Public and Private: Essays for Kerry Downes* (London: Hambledon Press, 1993), pp. 55–80.

[149] Evelyn, *Diary*, V, p. 247.

[150] Hilary Maddicott, "A Collection of the Interregnum Period: Philip, Lord Viscount Lisle, and his Purchases from the 'late King's Goods,' 1649–1660," *Journal of the History of Collections*, 11 (1999), 1.

Arundel's taste for drawings and works by Holbein and Weld's interest in paintings by Roman artists. In the 1650s, at the same time that he bought art, Lisle built a mansion in West Sheen, Richmond, close to Northumberland's Syon House.[151] There, he displayed some of King Charles's sculpture in his new gardens.

Protectorate supporters as well as royalists continued to value the Grand Tour. James Chaloner, whose father Thomas had been Lord Chamberlain to Henry, Prince of Wales, was a parliamentarian, a regicide, and governor of the Isle of Man. He sought to place his seventeen-year-old son Edward with a tutor in France in 1652. To do so, he wrote to a royalist in exile for help.[152] "Sir, it is now diverse years since that you went out of this nation where I had the honour and happiness to be known to you." Although they had written at first, their correspondence had been "now for a long time discontinued ... only a pair of my worthy kinsmen, Mr. Fleetwood and Mr. Cheyne, had in their travels the good fortune to meet with you ... By which favour I saw I was not forgotten by you." Chaloner hoped Edward might live with a French family for three years "where he may improve his Latin and Greek and be instructed in the arts; using at convenient times dancing and fencing; and that where fewest English resort, who are like to draw on expenses ... if not greater inconveniences. I shall not allow him above one hundred marks by the year which is L66–13–4 sterling" in order to keep him "closer to his learning."[153]

BUILDING

Even the most expensive form of consumption, building, continued between 1640 and 1660. Gerald Aylmer identifies at least sixteen important builders among the parliamentarians. Lord Fairfax, the great military leader of the New Model Army, Edmund Ludlow, the republican who challenged Cromwell, and Colonel Edward Harley were among them.[154] Fairfax wrote from Yorkshire to his cousin James Chaloner in London in 1650 about the

---

[151] Maddicott, "A Collection of the Interregnum Period," 1–24. J. Cloake, *Richmond's Great Monastery: The Charterhouse of Jesus of Bethlehem of Shene* (Richmond: Richmond Local History Society, 1990).

[152] BL Add. Mss. 71,448, f. 52, James Chaloner to (?), c. 1652; BL Add, Mss. 78,193. Henry Frederick, Earl of Arundel, who had succeeded his father in 1646, asked Sir Richard Browne in 1648 for a pass for his son Charles and two servants to pass through Flanders on their way to Holland and France.

[153] BL Add. Mss. 71,448, f. 52.

[154] Aylmer, *The State's Servants*, p. 280; Timothy Mowl and Brian Earnshaw, *Architecture Without Kings: The Rise of Puritan Classicism under Cromwell* (Manchester: Manchester University Press, 1995).

designs Edward Carter had prepared for him. Carter, son of Francis Carter, the surveyor of the New Exchange, was himself Surveyor of the King's Works from 1643.[155] Fairfax wanted a handsome and convenient design not a stately home. "I perceive his model is for a larger and costlier house than I intended though I shall be willing to do something to make it fair as well as convenient."[156] Fairfax sent a plan of the site, adding "I like a gallery in a house . . . though it take up lodging room, yet in a city they may best be spared. I would not bestow above L2000; more may make a stately house but this as convenient and handsome."[157] He asked that Carter send a precise model, the sort presumably Sir Henry Wotton had prescribed in his *The Elements of Architecture*. Fairfax rejected, however, Chaloner's suggestion that he buy some of the Duke of Buckingham's collections. "I received lately a letter from you concerning the Duke of Buckingham's estate. I am unfit every way to undertake such a business neither have I any desire to purchase great things."[158] He did give orders for appropriate repairs to York House to attract a tenant.[159] Other Protectorate officials who built included Edmund Prideaux, Attorney General, who rebuilt Forde Abbey, Dorset, and Oliver St. John who built Thorpe Hall, which Evelyn admired as a "stately palace."[160] Contemporary satirists with an axe to grind in 1659 and 1660 attacked "their great parks and new houses."[161]

Parliamentarians, royalists, and neutralists continued to feel that building was key to their status and estate. *Wilton Garden* was published in the 1640s with views of the new garden at Wilton House created in the 1630s.[162] The Earls of Pembroke undertook the most important building of the Interregnum, reconstructing Wilton House after a fire in the late 1640s with the help of Inigo Jones and John Webb. "Commonwealth in date as the rooms and the pediments of the towers above them undoubtedly are, they represent a continuity of the monarchy's Franco-Palladian Mannerism well into the Interregnum. And it was the chief architect of the monarchy who still provided the invention to shape that continuity."[163]

---

[155] Howard M. Colvin, *The History of the King's Works*, 6 vols. (London: HMSO, 1975–82), Vol. III: 1485–1660, (Part I), pp. 161–65.

[156] BL Add. Mss. 71,448, f. 3, Lord Fairfax to James Chaloner, 14 February, 1650/1651.

[157] *Ibid.*, f. 5, Fairfax to Chaloner, 25 February 1650/1651.

[158] *Ibid.*, f. 7, Fairfax to Chaloner, 13 June 1651.

[159] *Ibid.*, ff. 21, 36, Fairfax to Chaloner, 12 October 1655.

[160] Quoted in Maddicott, "A Collection of the Interregnum Period," 16.

[161] Quoted in David Farr, "Kin, Cash, Catholics, and Cavaliers: The Role of Kinship in the Financial Management of Major-General John Lambert," *Historical Research*, 74 (2001), 46.

[162] Isaac de Caus, *Wilton Garden: New and Rare Inventions of Waterworks* (London, 1645).

[163] Mowl and Earnshaw, *Architecture without Kings*, pp. 47, 53. Jones had been fined in 1646 but was pardoned and living in Somerset House.

The extraordinary Double Cube Room, redesigned about 1650 to display Pembroke's Van Dycks, had a ceiling by Emanuel de Critz.[164]

Other country houses were built or added onto even in the 1640s.[165] The Earl of Salisbury had "the ruins and decay" of Cranborne House, Dorset, surveyed in 1646. The next year he had the older parts renovated while erecting new sections.[166] Haunt Hill House, Great Weldon, Northamptonshire, was built in about 1643, in the midst of war; Red House, Herefordshire, influenced by London architecture, was built in 1647. Wood Lane Hall, North Yorkshire, and Norgrove Court, Worcestershire, with a mantle copied from Vredeman de Vries, were both built in 1649.[167]

With peace, wealthy royalists and republicans built new houses, enlarged and redecorated their old ones, often in what they thought to be modern Italian or French style, and cultivated their gardens in the 1650s.[168] Raynham Hall, Norfolk, which Sir Roger Townshend built in a new style in the 1620s, had additions in the late 1650s. Print, catalogs, and personal contact continued to serve as the source of information as they had earlier in the century. In the 1650s new translations of Italian designers appeared with William Leybourn, *The Compleat Surveyor* (1653) and Joseph Moxon's *Vignola* (1655). A reprint of the 1611 translation of Sebastiano Serlio appeared in 1658 entitled *A new-naturalized work of a learned stranger. Or, An exquisite tutor powerful to benefit the publick, and convey unto Englishmen, especially architects and artificers of all sorts.*

Roger Pratt was one of the most important architects of the Interregnum period. A friend of John Evelyn's, he returned to England after the execution of the King and rebuilt a house for his cousin Sir George Pratt of Coleshill, Oxfordshire, in 1650. John Summerson has suggested that the new style of Coleshill reflects the "seventeenth-century Italian baroque."[169] Pratt became an architect in London after he returned from

---

[164] *Ibid.*   [165] Cooper, *The Houses of the Gentry, 1480–1680*, pp. 209, 215.

[166] HMC *Salisbury*, XXIII, 281.

[167] Cooper, *The Houses of the Gentry, 1480–1680*, pp. 285, 228–29; Mowl and Earnshaw, *Architecture without Kings*, pp. 123, 124, 175, 184–86.

[168] Lord Henry Herbert built Badminton House, in Gloucestershire, after 1655. Edmund Waller, who had attempted a royalist uprising, built Hall Barn, Buckinghamshire, in 1656. Cooper, *The Houses of the Gentry 1480–1680*, p. 249. On Interregnum gardens see Mowl, "New Science, Old Order: The Gardens of the Great Rebellion," 16–35.

[169] John Summerson, *Architecture in Britain, 1530–1830* (Harmondsworth, Middlesex: Penguin, 1958; Yale University Press, 1993), p. 138. R. T. Gunther (ed.), *The Architecture of Sir Roger Pratt* (Oxford: Oxford University Press, 1928); Timothy Mowl and Brian Earnshaw argue that Inigo Jones built Coleshill to which Pratt later made additions. Mowl and Earnshaw, *Architecture without Kings*, pp. 31, 33, 48–59.

exile and published a book on architecture in the 1660s in which he urged "the study of continental models, in Italy and France, or, failing that, on the plans published in Italian and French books, citing in particular Palladio, Freart, and Scamozzi," the guiding lights of builders in the early seventeenth century.[170]

William Murray, as we saw earlier, had redecorated Ham House in the latest French styles in 1637–39, about the time that Humphrey Weld went shopping in Paris. When war broke out, Murray joined the King and, after Charles's execution, lived in Holland and Scotland, dying in Edinburgh in 1655. According to an inventory compiled at his death, Murray owned Italian and Flemish pictures as well as copies of Titians and Correggios from the collections of Charles I and Philip IV of Spain. His daughter Elizabeth, who had married Sir Lionel Tollemache, lived primarily at Hemingham Hall and in a house in Covent Garden. But, she redecorated Ham House herself from the 1650s to the 1670s buying new and exotic furniture including Japanese lacquer and ivory cabinets made in Antwerp in a fashion begun by the Jacobeans.[171]

The most vivid description of building during the 1650s is that of John Egerton, second Earl of Bridgewater. The first and second Earls of Bridgewater, both royalists, never went into exile. The second Earl of Bridgewater, arrested and imprisoned in 1651, was accused of plotting against the Commonwealth. After posting bail and sureties of L15,000, he retired to Ashridge, his country house, where he spent his money and time building. In 1668, almost twenty years later, he wrote an extensive apology to his heirs entitled "some reasons why I am in debt."[172] Bridgewater argued that he had rebuilt his house, riding house, bowling alley, mills, barns, and gardens in the country because, unlike other royalists, he could not leave the country, "the troubles I was in debarred me from going abroad with any safety." In his apologia, Bridgewater pondered the issue of necessity to make the case that his elaborate building supported both his position and his profit.

Bridgewater strove to sustain his family's status, honor, "decency," and convenience at Ashridge in the midst of social upheaval.[173] He enlarged his

---

[170] Gunther, *The Architecture of Sir Roger Pratt*, p. 4.

[171] Peter M. Thornton and Maurice Tomlin, *The Furnishing and Decoration of Ham House*, Furniture History Series 16 (London: Furniture History Society, 1980), pp. 4–35; Cathal Moore, Christopher Rowell, and Nino Strachey, *Ham House Guidebook* (London: National Trust, 1995), pp. 60–61. See chapter 5 above.

[172] HEH Ellesmere Mss. EL 8117, "Some reasons given by me why I am in debt," 6 June 1668, with later additions, 20 December 1673 and 25 March 1674.

[173] See Paul Hunneyball's discussion of Bridgewater and Ashridge. Paul Hunneyball, *Architecture and Image-Building in Seventeenth Century Hertfordshire*, Oxford Historical Monographs (Oxford: Clarendon Press, 2004).

park, created a second one, and then enlarged that one too. "Those who after me shall enjoy the satisfaction and [ex]tent of them, will be ready and willing to forgive me the charge of them, although I must account it as none of the smallest of my expenses." Bridgewater enclosed his warren: "a thing of no small charge but yet I think cannot be condemned when the time in which it was done and the roughness of it to persons of quality are considered … surely whether I should have suffered myself to have been utterly deprived of a warren or no will admit of no question." He also defended his spending on his gardens: "I have not done amiss in this part of my charge, nor in the new gates, which I made to the garden for the better embellishing of it."

Bridgewater admitted that the riding house and the bowling alley were not necessary to maintain his estate. Further, "The new [m]ill house may not be looked upon as quite so necessary, yet that may deserve favourable sentence when the necessity of having distilled waters in a large family (and that in the country too)." But his new mills and bridge at Watford would provide "considerable rent, current profit and future maintenance." Bridgewater redid the kitchen and the great chamber, rebuilt the old lodge, and created new coach houses. "The like necessity (I must confess) I cannot plead for what I have done to my parlour at Ashridge and the rooms by it next the garden but decency and convenience have ever weighed much with me and I hope they are not so quite excluded out of other men's thoughts … My libraries both at Ashridge and at Bridgewater House [in London] I only reckon as part and that considerable of my expenses. I say nothing for the justification of it. I know learning both hath and deserves a greater respect then that there should be any quarrel pick't at them."

Finally, Bridgewater dwelt emotionally on the funeral monument he built to honor his wife, Elizabeth, younger daughter of the Duke of Newcastle, who died in 1663. She had died in childbirth while accompanying him to London where he had been remanded into custody over a duel.[174] He embodied his sorrow in "the monument, which I have erected in little Gaddesden Church to the memory of my father and my mother and that most invaluable and unprizeable jewel with which God once blessed me, my entirely beloved and truly loving wife."[175] Bridgewater also enriched the church of Little Gaddesden. He built new pews and provided new furnishings for the pulpit and a new communion table

---

[174] Douglas Coult, *A Prospect of Ashridge* (London: Phillimore, 1980), pp. 122–24; HEH Ellesmere Mss. El 8348, certificate and account of burial, 17 July 1663.
[175] HEH Ellesmere Mss. EL 8360, "Bridgewater family monuments."

"for the use of the House of Almighty God which (before I did what I did to it) was irreverently and even scandalously neglected by the whole Parish who (both by law and religion) ought to have take better care of it." Church, funeral monument, house, interiors, garden, park, bowling alley, riding house, mills, stables, barns, Bridgewater built and rebuilt all of them throughout the Interregnum and into the 1660s. Visitors in 1681 praised Bridgewater's gardens and park as well as "this ancient house, grown more famous in the country by the present Lord's great house-keeping."[176] Bridgewater's father had died L27,000 in debt; he died L50,000 in debt.[177]

ART

As we have seen, luxury retail shops continued to function even in the middle and late 1640s, and building expanded in the 1650s. Nonetheless, Iain Pears argues that there was no art market until the 1680s and no direct connection between the great collectors of the early seventeenth century and the Restoration period. The Earl of Arundel and the Duke of Buckingham, he claims, "acted in a vacuum ... The catastrophe of the Civil War made the situation even worse as many of the Englishmen apprenticed to foreign painters lost their masters and the best of the great collections were broken up."[178] In contrast, I have already presented evidence of the continuing consumption of continental art. I will argue here that the republic's own policies helped to expand the market in England for fine art, reproductions, and prints.

Shortly after Charles I's execution, the new commonwealth ordered inventories of "the king's goods" in all royal palaces and put most of them up for sale.[179] While this action suggests an ideological attack on the material presentation of monarchy, its purpose was more likely financial. First, the regime held on to some of Charles's most important acquisitions, including Raphael's cartoons of the Acts of the Apostles used for the Mortlake tapestry works, Andrea Mantegna's "Triumph of the Caesars," and antique sculpture. The Protectorate hung tapestries in the Banqueting House on great occasions, kept some furniture as well as

---

[176] Quoted in Coult, *A Prospect of Ashridge*, p. 125.

[177] HEH Ellesmere Mss. EL 8117, "Some reasons given by me why I am in debt."

[178] Iain Pears, *The Discovery of Painting: The Growth of Interest in the Arts in England, 1680–1768* (New Haven: Yale University Press, 1988), pp. 1, 106.

[179] Arthur MacGregor (ed.), *The Late King's Goods: Collections, Possessions and Patronage of Charles I in the Light of the Commonwealth Sale Inventories* (Oxford: Oxford University Press, 1989).

some portraits and Dutch pictures. As we saw, the critical Evelyn pronounced Whitehall, "very glorious and well furnished." Second, the goods were used to pay off the Crown's creditors and supporters of the regime, some of whom kept the items for themselves. In May 1650, the Commonwealth put the King's paintings and furniture on display at Somerset House. Oliver Millar, Jonathan Brown, and Francis Haskell have analyzed the dispersal of the art collections of Charles I, Buckingham, Arundel, and Hamilton and the lively art market it created.[180] The Crown's creditors formed syndicates who took art as payment. According to Francis Haskell, leaders of the syndicates of creditors included a court jeweler, tailor, draper, upholsterer, and lawyer, all people familiar with the luxury market. Thus Edmund Harrison, embroiderer to James I and Charles I, received Titian's *Pope* and Rubens's *War and Peace* as payment while David Murray, the King's Tailor, took a Dürer self-portrait and Correggio's *Satyr Unveiling Venus.*[181] Haskell notes that "For the very first (and for the very last) time a huge range of great artistic masterpieces was widely distributed among the ordinary citizens of England."[182] The primary purchasers included members of the New Model Army and officeholders. In some cases, they immediately sold these items to the French and Spanish ambassadors.[183]

But just as interesting as the dispersal of the great collectors' Rubens, Titians, and Van Dycks is the resale market that developed in London, both of originals and of copies. Evelyn had wondered at the extraordinary number of landscapes and other Dutch pictures owned by Netherlands burghers; within a decade it was possible for the English, too, to buy copies of famous works, often with a courtly provenance. Richard Symonds went into exile on the continent after serving in the royalist army. In Italy, he visited artists, museums, and collectors and learned art techniques that he brought back to England.[184] Once back in London, Symonds wrote about artistic practice and documented the burgeoning English art market then

---

[180] *Ibid.*; Brown, *Kings and Connoisseurs*, pp. 59–93; Oliver Millar, *The Inventories and Valuations of the King's Goods, 1649–1651* (Glasgow: Walpole Society, 1972). Francis Haskell, Paul Mellon Lectures, Oxford, 1995, lecture on the dispersal of Charles I's collection.

[181] Francis Haskell, Mellon Lectures, Oxford, 1995.

[182] Haskell, "Charles I's Collection of Pictures," in MacGregor (ed.), *The Late King's Goods*, p. 227.

[183] *Ibid.*, pp. 227–28; Jonathan Brown, *Kings and Conoisseurs in Seventeenth-Century Europe* (Princeton: Princeton University Press, 1994), pp. 59–63. The Buckingham and Hamilton collections were sold to Archduke Leopold Wilhelm, Brown, *Kings and Connoisseurs*, pp. 59–60.

[184] Mary Beal, *A Study of Richard Symonds: His Italian Notebooks and their Relevance to Seventeenth-Century Painting Techniques* (New York: Garland, 1984); Anne Brookes, "Richard Symonds and the Palazzo Farnese, 1649–50," *Journal of the History of Collections*, 10 (1998), 139–57.

in its infancy. He recorded the names and addresses of collectors, shops, and shopkeepers who supplied not only the secondary market for the late King's goods, but also copies of famous paintings from the great collections.[185]

Symonds paid particular attention to copyists, including John Bradshaw, a heraldic painter, Mrs. Boardman, a copyist, and Jan van Belcamp, a minor Dutch painter and a Keeper of the King's pictures. "At a merchant's in St. Swithin's Lane, pictures which were of Belcamp lately dead . . . . This Belcamp was an under copier to another Dutchman that did fondly keep the king's pictures and when any nobleman desired a copy, he directed them to Belcamp." Different dealers championed different artists. "Mr. Pierce in Bishopsgate street says Bradshaw is the only man that doth understand perspective of all the painters in London." "Walker cries up Decreet [Emanuel De Critz] for the best painter in London. He demands L50 for the copy of Titian's woman naked and a man playing on the organs. Hutchinson has the original." "For his Venus putting on her smock which was the king's, so Mrs Boardman told me that copied it, he prizes it at L63."[186]

Colonel John Hutchinson, a well-known puritan, and leader of the New Model Army, became a major figure in the Rump parliament and signed the King's death warrant.[187] He bought several important pictures from King Charles's and the Earl of Arundel's collections, including Titian's *Pardo Venus* and *Venus with Organ Player*. The latter was described as "a very pretty piece that is esteemed as one of the best by Titian, which is a nude woman and a man playing the organ, life-size."[188] In 1653 Hutchinson sold the *Pardo Venus* to Antoine de Bordeaux, Cardinal Mazarin's representative, at a sizeable profit.[189] But Hutchinson was not just a broker. With these pictures and other luxury goods, he created a new persona for himself, at some distance from one he had presented only a few years before. Deprived of power when Cromwell dissolved the Rump, Hutchinson retired to the country, supervised his sons' and daughters' educations, gave up hawking, took up the viol, and bought art. His wife, the puritan writer Lucy Hutchinson, described his life in the 1650s.

---

[185] Beal, *A Study of Richard Symonds*, pp. 298–311.
[186] *Ibid.*, 307–11. Symonds listed the residue of Arundel's collection, "in the closet of the Lady Ann Mary Howard now in Arundel House 1653."
[187] Lucy Hutchinson, *Memoirs of the Life of Colonel Hutchinson*, ed. James Sutherland (London: Oxford University Press, 1973).
[188] Quoted in Brown, *Kings and Connoisseurs*, p. 86.   [189] *Ibid.*, p. 90.

The only recreation he had during his residence at London was in seeking out all the rare artists he could hear of, and in considering their works in paintings, sculptures, gravings, and all other such curiosities, insomuch that he became a great virtuoso and patron of ingenuity. And loath that the land should be disfurnisht of all the rarities that were in it, which being set to sale in the King's and divers noblemen's collections, he lay'd out about L2000 in the choicest pieces of painting then set to sale, most of which were bought out of the King's goods which were given to his servants to pay their wages; and . . . the Colonel gave ready money for them, of whom he bought so good pennieworths that they were valued much more worth than they cost. These he brought down into the country, intending a very neat cabinet for them; and these, with the surveying of his buildings and improving by enclosure the place he liv'd in, employ'd him at home . . . thus please'd himself in these innocent recreations during Oliver's mutable reign.[190]

Hutchinson worked side by side with Viscount Lisle on purchases of Charles I's goods.[191] Clearly, for Hutchinson, the collecting of Venetian paintings, beloved by Charles I and the Earl of Arundel, not to mention Phillip II of Spain, posed no issue of luxury that he needed to reject. Hutchinson's attention to building, enclosure, and improving while in retirement during the Interregnum parallels Bridgewater's.

In the same period, another leading army officer, Major-General John Lambert, moved to Kensington at the close of the civil wars although he originally came from Yorkshire.[192] In 1652 he bought Wimbledon and, later, part of Nonsuch, Henry VIII's pleasure palace, for which he purchased pictures from Charles I's collection.[193] Lambert devoted himself to painting, botany, and gardening, especially after he fell out with Oliver Cromwell. He hired Jean Baptist Gaspars as his art tutor and specialized in painting flowers. Satirized on contemporary playing cards as "The Knight of the Golden Tulip," Lambert filled Wimbledon's extensive gardens with rare plants brought from abroad. In 1656, while still in office, Lambert corresponded with the royalist Christopher Hatton in exile in Paris. Hatton, who had reported on Henrietta Maria's court to Sir Edward Nicholas, now wanted to return to London.[194] Addressing him with the

---

[190] Hutchinson, *Memoirs of the Life of Colonel Hutchinson,* p. 207.
[191] Maddicott, "A Collection of the Interregnum Period," 1–24.
[192] William Harbutt Dawson, *Cromwell's Understudy: The Life and Times of General John Lambert and the Rise and Fall of the Protectorate* (London: William Hodge, 1938). Farr, "Kin, Cash, Catholics, and Cavaliers," 44–62.
[193] MacGregor (ed.), *The Late King's Goods,* pp. 32, 34.
[194] *The Nicholas Papers,* ed. Warner.

pen name, Simond Smyth, Lambert asked him to purchase rare flowers for Lambert's gardens.

For the anemones they are by the description of their colours so rare and unknown here as I shall desire your Lordship to add what more to them you judge fit and also the same for the irises; and for the tulips I chiefly desire the praecox, and that I may know the prices of [the] dearest before your Lordship come to [make a con]tract.[195]

In exchange Lambert offered Hatton half a dozen plants which were neither in the Duke of Orléans's nor M. Morin's catalogs. "If they be strangers your Lordship may command them." Hatton returned in 1656 and received permission to reside in London in 1657 from Oliver Cromwell.[196] John Evelyn described Hatton's Kirby Hall, built in the 1570s and remodeled between 1638 and 1640, as "built à la moderne" a term of approval he applied to several houses as he toured.[197] Lord Hatton created an important garden of rare plants at Kirby Hall after returning from exile.[198]

PRINTS AND LUXURY BOOK PRODUCTION

Alongside the thriving art market, a lively commercial market for prints developed in the 1640s and 1650s. In the first half of the seventeenth century, most prints were imported from Amsterdam. Antony Griffiths suggests that printmaking might be thought to have been devastated by the Civil War since its leading practitioners, such as Hollar, went abroad, but in the long term it was not.[199] First, Hollar continued to produce prints during the first civil war. Between 1641 and 1644, before he left England, Hollar designed three series of the Four Seasons in different lengths. One set presented women in fashionable dress in front of landscapes that included Tart Hall, Arundel House, and Albury in Surrey, homes to his patrons, the Earl and Countess of Arundel, who were already in exile.[200] Second, when Hollar went into exile in the Netherlands, he continued to produce commercial engravings. Exile provided new material and new subjects. Hendrick van der Brocht asked John Evelyn to sketch various women's dress as he toured the

---

[195] Quoted in Dawson, *Cromwell's Understudy: The Life and Times of Colonel John Lambert*, pp. 280–81; 177–79; 277–81; 451, 453–54. Farr, "Kin, Cash, Catholics, and Cavaliers," 44–62. I am grateful to Barbara Donagan for the example of Lambert.
[196] BL Add. Mss. 29,548, f. 14.   [197] Evelyn, *Diary*, p. 134.
[198] Brian Dix, Iain Sader, and Tara Hilton, "Kirby Hall and its Gardens: Excavations in 1987–1994," *Archaeological Journal*, 152 (1995), 291–380.
[199] Griffiths, *The Print in Stuart England*, p. 166.   [200] *Ibid.*, pp. 110–15.

39. In the 1640s Hollar produced prints showing current fashions in clothing and accessories. This engraving includes furs, muffs, gloves, hats, lace and fans.
The Folger Shakespeare Library, ART 250011, Wenceslaus Hollar, Antwerp, 1647.

continent so that Hollar could engrave them.[201] Third, while in exile, English printmakers learned continental technique.

By 1650 Hollar and others had returned to England. Some English printmakers had learned French techniques while they were abroad. For example, William Fairthorne worked with French masters. George Vertue claimed that "he graved the best of his works between 1650 and 1660."[202] French printmakers came to England in the 1650s. Pierre Lombart, a French engraver, visited Evelyn in order to see his collections in 1653 and collaborated with John Ogilby on his luxury edition of Vergil. Lombart later did two portraits of Cromwell, one after Edward Walker's portrait, the other an adaptation of Van Dyck's portrait of Charles I on horseback with a page.[203] In the 1650s John Evelyn engraved landscapes, bought prints in Rome, and translated the work of the outstanding French engraver Abraham Bosse which he published as *Sculptura* in 1662.[204] Francis Barlow, who specialized in painting birds, dedicated to Evelyn an engraving of Titian's Venus and the organ player owned by

[201] BL Add Mss. 78,315, Evelyn Papers, f. 56.
[202] Quoted in Griffiths, *The Print in Stuart England*, p. 176.   [203] *Ibid.*, pp. 178–83.
[204] *Ibid.*, pp. 129–31. Griffiths, "The Etchings of John Evelyn," pp. 51–67.

Colonel Hutchinson.[205] Later in the century, English printers were able to export their prints to the Dutch market.[206]

During the 1650s new luxury goods included elaborate books produced by subscription which claimed the virtues of magnificence and splendor usually associated with the accoutrements of great offices of state. John Ogilby published expensive editions of Vergil and Homer and travel books on Africa, Asia, and America with each page decorated with the coats of arms of his subscribers.[207] Ogilby's first Vergil was published as a quarto in 1649; five years later he transformed it, declaring,

from a mean octavo, a royal folio flourished, adorned with sculpture and illustrated with annotations, triumphing with the affixed emblazons, names and titles of a hundred patrons, all bold assertors in vindication of the work, which (what e're my deserts) being publish'd with that magnificence and splendour, appear'd anew, and taking beauty, the fairest that till then the English press ever boasted.[208]

These luxury editions publicly displayed the erudition and taste of their subscribers. The book had plates by Wenceslaus Hollar, Francis Cleyn, the Mortlake designer, and William Fairthorne. Lely's portrait of Ogilby faced Cleyn's portrait of Virgil with a map of Aeneas' journeys by Hollar. Most of Ogilby's subscribers were royalists who had fought for King Charles, gone into exile, and returned in the 1650s.[209] The appeal of the edition to them lay not only in display but also in the story of Aeneas, a prewar Eden, and a wandering hero, perhaps a reference to Charles II in exile. According to Nigel Smith, Ogilby's translation analyzes the ills of the royalists, while asserting their "superiority to the Commonwealth."[210]

Ogilby dedicated the volume to William Seymour, Marquis of Hertford. As a youth, Hertford had secretly married Arabella Stuart, King James I's cousin, and spent four years in France from 1611 to 1615 in disfavor. With the death of Arabella he returned to England. Although he was one of the peers who petitioned King Charles to call Parliament in 1640, he joined the King and became Groom of the Stool in 1643–44. In 1654, at the time of Ogilby's publication, he lived in Essex House in London, which he shared

---

[205] *Ibid.*, p. 171. Evelyn, *Diary*, p. 573, 22 December 1656.

[206] Griffiths, *The Print in Stuart Britain*, p. 27. Jan van der Waals, "The Print Collection of Samuel Pepys," *Print Quarterly*, I/4 (1984), 236–42, 247–57.

[207] Katherine Van Eerde, *John Ogilby and the Taste of his Times* (Folkestone, Kent: Dawson, 1976). Sarah L. C. Clapp, "The Subscription Enterprises of John Ogilby and Richard Blome," *Modern Philology*, 30 (1933), 365–79.

[208] *Ibid.*   [209] *Ibid.*

[210] Nigel Smith, *Literature and Revolution in England, 1640–1660* (New Haven and London: Yale University Press, 1994), p. 8.

with his brother-in-law, Arthur Capell, the Earl of Essex, whose father had been beheaded in 1649. Hertford's wife, Frances, his sons, daughters, and in-laws, all had pages in their honor in Ogilby's Vergil. At the Restoration Charles II restored him to the Dukedom of Somerset.

Ogilby's subscribers included other intellectual circles of the Protectorate. They included Elias Ashmole, the poet Edward Sherburne, Edward Bysshe, Garter King of Arms under Cromwell, Anthony Ashley Cooper, later Earl of Shaftesbury, Dorothy Osborne, the royalist writer, and Charles Dormer, son of the Earl of Caernarvon. Katherine Van Eerde points out that Ogilby felt safe enough to dedicate the second edition (1658) to William, son of the Earl of Strafford, who was executed in 1641 and for whom Ogilby had worked. For that edition 75 percent of the initial subscribers signed up again.[211]

Thus, in the 1650s, the elaborately illustrated book sponsored by subscription became an additional form of luxury consumption. Ogilby's subscription enterprise of the Protectorate continued into the Restoration, broadening its subjects and its audience. Ogilby proceeded to publish Homer, works of travel, and maps of the world. In 1669 he published *An Embassy from the East-India Company of the United Provinces to the Grand Tartar Cham, Emperor of China* and a series of lavish works on Africa, Asia, America, and Europe. For *Britannia*, Ogilby sought subscribers further afield. "For the better ease and conveniency of the gentry that live far remote," he appointed booksellers in other towns where they could examine volumes already published as well as the county information that would appear. *Britannia* was thought to cost L14,000 and members of the royal family and nobility contributed L1,900.[212]

CONCLUSION

Luxury consumption always takes place in the context of institutions, policies, and cultures that support or suppress it. Despite their religious and moral views, the policies of the Civil War and Interregnum governments did not curtail luxury consumption. Between 1628 and 1640 imports had increased by almost 50 percent.[213] Although we lack statistics on imports and exports during the Civil War and Interregnum, port statistics for 1640 and 1663 show that

---

[211] Van Eerde, *John Ogilby and the Taste of his Times*; Clapp, "The Subscription Enterprises of John Ogilby and Richard Blome," 365–79.

[212] Quoted in Clapp, "The Subscription Enterprises of John Ogilby and Richard Blome," 370.

[213] A. M. Millard, "The Import Trade of London, 1600–1640" (Ph.D. thesis, University of London, 1956), p. 218.

imports doubled between those years despite the political upheaval.[214] Ralph Davis points out that coastal trade grew and "the colonial trades, of only moderate significance before 1642, had already emerged in 1660 as among the greatest of English trades."[215] In fact, the Commonwealth's Council on Trade eagerly sought to aid the English economy. The Navigation Act of 1651, reenacted at the Restoration,[216] required that all goods traded between England and any of its possessions be carried in English boats.

The Navigation Act's provisions were not new. James I's Privy Council had tried to promote English trade by ordering that goods imported from the Mediterranean be carried only in English ships, a requirement which it extended to the Baltic trade in 1622. In 1624, the Privy Council sought to forbid Dutch trade with the American colonies.[217] Whatever the complex motives in the shaping of the Navigation Act, its long-term effect was to promote British trade around the world.[218] With a substantial navy able now to enforce the Navigation Act and a series of successful wars against the Dutch, English shipping, trade, and maritime power increased throughout the rest of the century.

Commonwealth policies also displayed an impressive and continuing interest in putting people to work. For instance, James I's favorite project, silk production and the growing of mulberry trees in Virginia, was revived in the 1650s. At the very time that the Massachusetts Bay Colony banned the wearing of "gold and silver lace, great boots . . . silks and tiffany hoods by any whose estate was worth less than L200,"[219] a flurry of pamphlets appeared beginning in 1650 promoting silk production in Virginia. Samuel Hartlib, the unflagging advocate for universal reformation, was only one of those who repeatedly urged the revival of Jacobean policy to cultivate the

---

[214] Christopher G. A. Clay, *Economic Expansion and Social Change: England 1500–1700*, 2 vols. (Cambridge: Cambridge University Press, 1984), II, 155, 157. Neville Williams, "The London Port Books," *Transactions of the London and Middlesex Archaeological Society*, 18 (1956), 13–26.

[215] Ralph Davis, *The Rise of the English Shipping Industry in the Seventeenth and Eighteenth Centuries* (London: Macmillan, 1962), p. 15.

[216] *The Statutes of the Realm*, 11 vols. (London: G. Eyre and A. Strahan, 1810–22), 12 Charles II, c. 4, V, pp. 181–205. The statute authorizing tonnage and poundage listed a wide variety of goods with their rates inward and outward, 12 Charles II, c. 4.

[217] Ralph Davis, *English Overseas Trade, 1500–1700*, Prepared for the Economic History Society (London: Macmillan, 1973), pp. 29, 35.

[218] Steven C. A. Pincus, "From Holy Cause to Economic Interest," in Steven C. A. Pincus and Alan Houston (eds.), *A Nation Transformed: England after the Restoration* (Cambridge: Cambridge University Press, 2001), pp. 272–98; Steven C. A. Pincus, "England and the World in the 1650s," in Morrill (ed.), *Revolution and Restoration*, pp. 129–47.

[219] Stephen Innes, "Puritanism and Capitalism in Early Massachusetts," in J. A. James and Mark Thomas (eds.), *Capitalism in Context: Essays on Economic Development and Cultural Change in Honor of R. M. Hartwell* (Chicago: University of Chicago Press, 1994), p. 111.

silkworm. "It is not only my opinion that silkworms will thrive here; but the . . . judgement of King James and his council confirmeth the same; as you may see by his letter to the deputy lieutenants of every country wherein also many weighty reasons are contained to convince men of the same." Hartlib emphasized that silk was more profitable than tobacco. "The silk-trade (unless we will be deaf to reason and experience) cannot be denied the precedency of all trades that are at this day a foot, in either world: and that in regard of its great and certain gain in so small a time."[220]

Such pleas did not fall on deaf ears. The Virginia legislature adopted policies to encourage the crop, revived the Virginia Company law "requiring the planting of a specified number of mulberries . . . [and] offered bounties for the production of silk and other crops beside tobacco."[221] Treating silk as an important export, not an unnecessary show of vanity or indulgence, the Commonwealth pamphlet literature promoting silk production expressed no misgivings as to how it would be used or by whom. Of course, the critique of luxury continued throughout the Civil War, finding reflection, for instance, in the Commonwealth attack on the early Stuart court.[222]

Less noticed than the Navigation Acts and the initiatives of the Council on Trade, certain Commonwealth and Protectorate policies helped indirectly to promote luxury consumption. These included a relatively free press and relatively free travel. Furthermore, royalist fines, sale of Crown land, profits from trade, such as that of the East India Company, created a heady land market that ultimately reinforced the gentry's hold on the land. Finally, the reluctance of the Commonwealth and Protectorate governments to ruin their opponents made moveables and property more secure and helped to reunite the ruling elite.

Thus, as this chapter argued, luxury consumption and government support for it continued and expanded in the midst of political change. Royalists who came back from exile returned to their patterns of consumption alongside parliamentarians and the non-aligned who shared their interest in building, buying luxury goods, and collecting. London retailing

---

[220] BL E628 (13) Hartlib 1651, p. 69 (D3). Edward Williams wrote *Virgo Triumphans or Virginia Richly and Truly Valued* (London, 1650) and *Virginia's Discovery of Silke-Wormes with their benefit and the Implanting of Mulberry Trees* (London, 1650). See chapter 2 above. On Hartlib see Mark Greengrass, Michael Leslie, and Timothy Raylor, *Samuel Hartlib and Universal Reformation: Studies in Intellectual Communication* (Cambridge: Cambridge University Press, 1994).

[221] Wesley Frank Craven, *The Southern Colonies in the Seventeenth Century, 1607–1689* (Baton Rouge: Louisiana State University Press, 1949), pp. 252–53.

[222] See Anthony Weldon, *The Court and Character of King James* (London, 1650); Arthur Wilson, *The History of Great Britain Being the Life and Reign of King James I* (London, 1653); Francis Osborne, *Traditional Memoirs of King James I* (London, 1658).

generally continued to operate in the 1640s and 1650s despite criticism. The Commonwealth created an art market by disposing of the late King's goods; building boomed in the 1650s, whether to recover from war damage or to display traditional or newly assumed status and power. In addition, as John Morrill points out, "most of the new farming technologies, new crops, and new rotations were imported into England from the Netherlands. The experience of royalist exiles in the 1650s in learning about these developments and pioneering them upon their return is a very obvious, if very oblique consequence of the revolution."[223]

The next two chapters look at these consequences for luxury consumption in the Restoration. The first studies the adoption of continental luxury in a suburban Anglican church and the second maps the connections forged between science, technology, and luxury consumption through international networks of exchange.

---

[223] Morrill (ed.), *Revolution and Restoration*, p. 99.

CHAPTER 7

"Rome's artists in this nature can do no more": a Bernini in Chelsea

From the general impact of the Civil War and Interregnum on luxury consumption, we turn to a case study that situates luxury consumption in church and illuminates several themes that we have been tracing: the importance of continental imports, the influence of travel and print, London fashion, and the construction of identity through new luxury goods. Royalists' desires for continental art and technology, reinforced in exile, shaped Charles Cheyne's two important commissions in 1670: the first, a funeral monument designed and crafted in Rome by close associates of Gian Lorenzo Bernini, and the second, a telescope made by Rome's preeminent instrument maker, Eustachio Divini. Shipped together in thirty cases from Livorno to Chelsea, "the monument and the tube," as the agent called them, provide extensive evidence of the negotiations that marked the appropriation of continental material culture by English patrons. The importance of the funeral monument lies not in its mistaken ascription to the great Bernini but in the aspirations and cosmopolitan taste that shaped Cheyne's decision to commission and import a Roman baroque monument and make it fit an Anglican parish church. One of the few English funeral monuments to be imported, the Cheyne monument presents the cosmopolitanism of death and presages the series of grand eighteenth-century funeral monuments of the great and the good by the French sculptor François Roubiliac at Westminster Abbey.[1]

THE MONUMENT

Eastern and Western Christian churches had a longstanding commitment to the role of luxury goods to enhance devotion in the form of frescoes, icons, pictures, mosaics, stained glass, church silver, elaborate costume, and

[1] See David Bindman and Malcolm Baker, *Roubiliac and the Eighteenth-Century Monument: Sculpture as Theater* (New Haven: Yale University Press, 1995).

special architecture. Great churchmen and cardinals, patrons of artists, sculptors, and architects had their equal in Cardinal Wolsey.[2] Despite the English Reformation's rejection of many aspects of visual worship, in the early seventeenth century, Arminians and Laudians emphasized the "beauty of holiness" centered on the sacrament of the Eucharist and encouraged the laity's donation of silver for its celebration.[3] The gentry edified their pews and continued the tradition of building family funeral monuments within the church or laying brasses to commemorate the dead.[4]

In 1670 Charles Cheyne commissioned a funeral monument to commemorate his wife, Lady Jane Cavendish, a royalist heroine and writer, whose substantial fortune had enabled him to buy the manor of Chelsea. Cheyne chose not to go to the Southwark monument makers so popular in sixteenth- and seventeenth-century England.[5] Instead, he ordered the tomb from Rome, from the son of Gian Lorenzo Bernini, the architect of baroque Rome, and Antonio Raggi, one of Bernini's closest associates.[6]

Cheyne's choice was unique. It was extremely rare to commission and import funeral monuments from abroad at any time, although high-ranking Caroline patrons had busts done in Rome.[7] Cheyne's agent in Rome wrote flatteringly that "renown speaks to me and others [of] your deserving self. Therefore much more to be courted and admired for the rareness of such examples at present in the British Islands."[8] Moreover, most seventeenth-century funeral monuments, even of those with court connections, were built in the country.[9] Although Lady Jane's family seat was in Devonshire and Charles Cheyne's in Buckinghamshire, Cheyne chose to put up this impressive monument in Chelsea. His unusual commission shows the

---

[2] Thomas P. Campbell, "Cardinal Wolsey's Tapestry Collection," *Antiquaries Journal*, 76 (1996), 73–137.

[3] Peter Lake, "The Laudian Style: Order, Uniformity, and the Pursuit of the Beauty of Holiness in the 1630s," in Kenneth Fincham (ed.), *The Early Stuart Church, 1603–1642* (Basingstoke: Macmillan, 1993), pp. 161–85. Charles Oman, *English Church Plate, 1597–1830* (London: Oxford University Press, 1959); Oman, *Caroline Silver, 1625–1688* (London: Faber, 1970).

[4] Nigel Llewellyn, *Funeral Monuments in Post-Reformation England* (Cambridge: Cambridge University Press, 2000).

[5] See, for instance, Alice T. Friedman, "Patronage and the Production of Tombs in London and the Provinces: The Willoughby Monument of 1591," *Antiquaries Journal*, 65 (1985), 390–401.

[6] Rudolf Wittkower, *Art and Architecture in Italy, 1600–1750* (Baltimore: Penguin Books, 1958), p. 204, describes Raggi as "Bernini's most intimate and most prolific pupil."

[7] See Katherine Ada Esdaile, "The Monuments in Chelsea Old Church," in Weston Henry Stewart (ed.), *Chelsea Old Church . . .*, revised and reissued with an intro. by Reginald Blunt (London: Oxford University Press, 1932). Llewellyn, *Funeral Monuments in Post-Reformation England*, p. 275, "Canova did this once or twice, Pierre Monnot once, Thorwaldsen once; but such works are rare exceptions at every period."

[8] HEH, Ellesmere Mss. EL 11, 125, Edward Altham to Charles Cheyne, 1/11 April 1671.

[9] Nigel Llewellyn, *Funeral Monuments in Post-Reformation England*, p. 147.

transformation of cultural meaning as objects moved across cultures and into new contexts.

Why, to begin with, did Cheyne choose to import this lavish funeral monument from Rome? Letters amongst family members in 1656, two account books, eulogies in 1670, and the agents' letters about the commission suggest that four reasons converged to produce his decision. First, with this monument Cheyne commemorated his devotion to Lady Jane and celebrated the godly pattern of his wife's life even as he inscribed himself in the memorial as the grieving husband. Second, he expressed his deep sense of obligation and gratitude for her dowry and social connections to the peerage, particularly to her father, William Cavendish, Duke of Newcastle, royalist commander and tutor to Charles II. Newcastle and his second wife Margaret Cavendish, Duchess of Newcastle, were still alive when Cheyne commissioned Lady Jane's monument. While Cheyne's own family were ancient Buckinghamshire gentry, he had no title. The 1657 Antwerp edition of the Duke of Newcastle's *Methode et Invention Nouvelle de Dresser les Chevaux* presents the family watching his two sons on horseback. "Monsieur Chenie et Madame Jane sa femme" are seated to the far right not according to her status but his, while her younger sister, who had married the Earl of Bridgewater, sits at her father's right hand. As we have seen, Bridgewater erected an important memorial to Elizabeth in the 1660s.

Third, Cheyne had traveled in Italy, visiting Rome in the 1640s as a young royalist exile. His Italian agent assumed that he was sympathetic to Roman Catholicism and an admirer of Italian art and culture. Cheyne, an Anglican, demonstrated great interest in churches and church building not only in Chelsea but also in the country and in Ireland.[10] With this monument Cheyne not only repaid his debt to his wife and her family but also demonstrated his own piety and taste.[11] Fourth, as Lord of the Manor, Cheyne aimed to develop the fashionable London suburb of Chelsea. A Bernini in Chelsea strengthened the attraction of the historic village and its church as destinations of importance. Earlier agents such as Sir Thomas Roe and Sir Henry Wotton had worried that Roman art would be thought papist. By the 1670s, however, this luxury consumer and London real estate developer no longer worried about this issue.

While Bernini had few English patrons, he had many admirers at the Caroline court. Most notably, with the permission of the pope, Bernini had crafted a bust of Charles I in 1635 from the triple portrait by Van Dyck.

---

[10]   HEH Ellesmere Mss. EL 11,145, Cheyne account book, 1669–73, August, 1670.
[11]   Bindman and Baker, *Roubiliac and the Eighteenth-Century Monument.*

A companion bust of Henrietta Maria was put aside with the outbreak of
the war with the Scots.[12] In 1636 Thomas Howard, Earl of Arundel,
commissioned a sculptor in Florence to recreate in marble the Van Dyck
portrait of himself and his grandson. At the same time he wrote, "I could
wish Cavalier Bernino, or Francesco Fiamengo might do another."[13]
Nicholas Stone, Jr., son of the leading sculptor in England, had visited
Bernini in 1638 and been welcomed "to spend my time with the other of his
disciples."[14] Thomas Baker sat for the sculptor himself on the eve of the
Civil War.[15] English artists continued to be fascinated with Bernini,
although Richard Symonds, who visited Rome in 1650–52, preferred the
work of Alessandro Algardi.[16]

Cheyne's commission also reflected cosmopolitan fashion after the
Restoration. The court of Charles II and its elite, to which Cheyne had
ties, emulated the taste of Louis XIV and the French court. The French
king had invited Bernini to Paris in 1665 to do his own bust from life and to
remodel the Louvre.[17] Christopher Wren and John Evelyn both admired
Bernini. Evelyn wrote, "Bernini was the most famous: skilled in statue,
painting, architecture and music … This was another Michelangelo. It
was he who cut that incomparable bust in white marble from three
paintings of King Charles the first … painted by Van Dyck."[18]

By 1670, when Cheyne ordered the funeral monument, Bernini not only
enjoyed the patronage of Louis XIV and a succession of popes but also
controlled much of the sculpture business in Rome.[19] In England, sculptors
such as John Bushnell and artists such as Cibber and Grinling Gibbons
borrowed from Bernini from the 1670s on. Sir Peter Lely, whose own
paintings drew on the baroque aesthetic, bought Bernini's bust of Thomas
Baker. By 1705 the Cheyne memorial was popularly said to be by Bernini

[12] See Ronald Lightbown, "Bernini's Busts of English Patrons," in Moshe Barasch, Lucy Freeman
Sandler, and Patricia Egan (eds.), *Art, the Ape of Nature: Studies in Honor of H. W. Janson* (New York:
Abrams, 1981), pp. 439–76.

[13] Quoted in David Howarth, *Lord Arundel and his Circle* (New Haven: Yale University Press, 1985),
p. 162. As he went into exile, Arundel left instructions for his tomb including a sculpture of himself
by Francesco Fancelli.

[14] *The Notebook and Account Book of Nicholas Stone*, (ed.) Walter L. Spiers, Walpole Society, 7 (Oxford,
1919), 170–71.

[15] R. J. Ninnnis, "The Hewer Memorial at Clapham," *Antiquaries Journal*, 54 (1974), 262.

[16] Mary Beal, *A Study of Richard Symonds: His Italian Notebooks and their Relevance to Seventeenth
Century Painting Techniques* (New York: Garland, 1984). Anne Brookes, "Richard Symonds and the
Palazzo Farnese, 1649–50," *Journal of the History of Collections*, 10 (1998), 139–57.

[17] Rudolf Wittkower, *Gian Lorenzo Bernini: The Sculptor of the Roman Baroque* (London: Phaidon,
1955).

[18] BL Add. Mss. 78,340, Evelyn Papers, p. 325.   [19] Wittkower, *Gian Lorenzo Bernini*, pp. 39–40.

40. Gian Lorenzo Bernini began work on the funeral monument for Beata Ludovica Albertoni about the time that Paolo Bernini designed the monument for Lady Jane Cheyne. The differences suggest the adaptation of Italian baroque style to the desires of an English patron.
Gian Lorenzo Bernini, Blessed Ludovica Albertoni, San Francesco a Ripa, Rome. Scala/Art Resource, NY. ART 70182.

himself. Other tombs of the British aristocracy were attributed erroneously to Bernini, and Bernini memorials were being copied in Clapham.[20]

Gian Lorenzo Bernini began work on his monument for the Blessed Ludovica Albertoni in the Altieri Chapel, San Francesco a Ripa, Rome, some time in 1671. Bernini's theatrical and ecstatic monument to Ludovica, who was beatified in 1671, forces us to inquire how Paolo Bernini approached the Cheyne commission.[21] The monument itself provides important evidence.

[20] Eric MacLagen, "Sculpture by Bernini in England," *Burlington Magazine*, 40 (1922), 56–63, 112–20. Margaret Whinney, *Sculpture in Britain 1530–1830* (London: Penguin, 1988), 93–102. See Jennifer Montagu, "Bernini Sculptures not by Bernini," in Irving Lavin (ed.), *Gianlorenzo Bernini: New Aspects of his Art and Thought* (University Park: Pennsylvania State University Press, 1985), pp. 25–61.

[21] Shelley Perlove, *Bernini and the Idealization of Death: The Blessed Ludovica Albertoni and the Altieri Chapel* (University Park: Pennsylvania State University Press, 1990).

A twenty-foot tall "semi-circular temple" surrounds the life-size and life-like effigy of Lady Jane on a black marble tomb chest. Dressed in an off-the-shoulder gown with necklace and earrings, she rises from a pillow which rests on the Bible, while her fingers hold open a smaller book, as if in the midst of reading. A coronet lies at her feet. Multicolored marble columns surround her. Light entering through the cupola of the monument illuminates the figure. At the top, an elaborate metal cross, unusual in Protestant churches, and flaming hearts on urns, borrow from the baroque visual vocabulary. The flaming heart had begun to appear in English parish churches in the 1630s as part of a Laudian revival of religious art.[22] It had appeared as the frontispiece in Francis Quarles's *Emblems* of 1635 which "brought to Protestant England – in a suitable guise – the emotional ardors and religious ecstasies of the Catholic Counter-Reformation, aptly illustrated on the title page by the heart, burning with divine love, and rising above the world."[23]

Yet the monumental body of Lady Jane Cheyne does not reflect the emotional ecstasy of Bernini's St. Theresa of the 1640s and the Blessed Ludovica Albertoni of the 1670s. The effigy also differs from Antonio Raggi's work in the 1660s and 1670s, including the death of St. Cecilia (1660–67) and his work for the Jesuit Church Il Gesu (1669–83).[24] Thus, the Cheyne monument makes explicit the problems posed for a provincial patron and the solutions chosen to accommodate baroque conventions to an Anglican parish church. It also provides a striking example of the way in which agents and artists did – and did not – adapt their goods to fit the local market.[25]

Nigel Llewellyn argues that funeral monuments aimed at public consumption not private contemplation. They were "expensive objects of display and consumption intended to confront the viewer with important social and ethical truths."[26] Often planned during the lifetime of those memorialized, funeral monuments were the most important commissions

[22] Kenneth Fincham, "The Restoration of Altars in the 1630s," *Historical Journal,* 44 (2001), 919–40; Karl Josef Holtgen, "Francis Quarles's Emblems and Hieroglyphikes," in Ayers L. Bagley (ed.), *Telling Image: Explorations in the Emblem* (New York: AMS Press, 1996), pp. 1–28.

[23] Karl Josef Holtgen, "Catholic Pictures Versus Protestant Words?: The Adaptation of the Jesuit Sources in Quarles's Emblemes," *Emblematica* 9 (1995), 221–38.

[24] Wittkower, *Art and Architecture in Italy*, pp. 202–204, plate 116; see also Patrizia Cavazzini, "The Ginetti Chapel at S. Andrea delle Valle," *Burlington Magazine*, 141 (1991), 401–13.

[25] See Michael North and David Ormrod (eds.), *Art Markets in Europe, 1400–1800,* (Aldershot, Hampshire: Ashgate Publishing, 1998).

[26] Nigel Llewellyn, *The Art of Death: Visual Culture in the English Death Ritual, c. 1500–c. 1800* (London: Published in association with the Victoria and Albert Museum by Reaktion Books, 1991), p. 115.

41. Paolo Bernini designed the funeral monument for Lady Jane Cheyne, including multicolored marble columns, a black marble urn on yellow marble supporters with a sculpture by Antonio Raggi, a large cross on top, and flaming hearts beside it.
The Courtauld Institute, Conway Library, London, All Saints, Chelsea, Tomb of Lady Jane Cheyne.

for sculpture in the early modern period. In 1653 a member of the Verney
family was advised "to see Dr. Donne's and other tombs at Paul's at
Westminister or elsewhere before you speak with the workmen."[27] Funeral
monuments expressed both dynastic concerns and personal grief[28] and shed
light on contemporary constructions of social identity, self, status, and
gender.

LADY JANE CHEYNE

Lady Jane was the eldest daughter and co-heir of William Cavendish, Duke
of Newcastle, and his first wife Frances Blore, widow of Henry Howard, son
of Thomas Howard, Earl of Suffolk. Lady Jane managed the Cavendish
family estate, defended their property from the parliamentary army, saved
the family's collection of Van Dycks from Welbeck Abbey and Bolsover
Castle, and applied for compensation while her father was in exile in
France in the 1640s and 1650s.[29] In April 1647 she petitioned for one-
fifth of her father's estate on behalf of her brothers and sisters. In
November she complained that, although the Council had allowed her
the fifth, the county council of Northumberland refused it. She was
granted the fifth once more. She sent money to Newcastle and his young
second wife, Margaret Cavendish, in Paris.[30]

Jane and her sisters, Elizabeth and Frances, remained at home at
Welbeck during the Civil War. Jane and Elizabeth wrote poetry and
religious meditations as well as a satirical play in the manner of Caroline
court masques that lamented the absence of friends and family. They
bound their writings, which emphasized women's "self-possession" and
companionate marriage, for their father, Newcastle, who had encouraged
their education and their writing since childhood. Both sisters continued to
write after their marriages.[31] The Countess of Bridgewater primarily wrote
religious verse, although she occasionally used material culture in her

---

[27] Quoted in Llewellyn, *Funeral Monuments in Post-Reformation England*, pp. 166–67.
[28] Bindman and Baker, *Roubiliac and the Eighteenth-Century Monument*, p. 187.
[29] PRO *Calendar of the Proceedings of the Committee for Compounding . . . 1643–1650: preserved in the State Paper Department of Her Majesty's Public Record Office*, (ed.) Mary Anne Everett Green, 5 vols. (London: HMSO, Eyre and Spottiswoode, 1889–92), III, p. 1732.
[30] *Ibid.*
[31] See Margaret J. M. Ezell, "'To be your Daughter in your Pen': The Social Functions of Literature in the Writings of Lady Elizabeth Brackley and Lady Jane Cavendish," *Huntington Library Quarterly*, 51 (1988), 281–96; "Lady Jane Cavendish and Elizabeth Brackley," in Germaine Greer et al. (eds.), *Kissing the Rod: Anthology of Seventeenth Century Women's Verse* (London: Virago, 1988), pp. 106–18; Jane Cavendish and Elizabeth Cavendish, "The Concealed Fancies: Poems," in Marion Wynn-Davies (ed.), *Women Poets of the Renaissance* (New York: Routledge, 1999), pp. xxvi–viii, 255–59;

poems to draw moral conclusions as in "A Contemplation upon the Sign of a Cushion," "Made on a Sight of the Countess of Bridgewater's Picture," and "Spoken upon Receiving a Cake of Perfume Made up in the Shape of a Heart."[32] The few letters of Lady Jane's that have survived reflect the sociability of the town, the pull of kinship, and the centrality of marriage and pregnancy in women's lives. Together, they suggest the epistolary novel *avant la lettre*.

Bright, well-educated, and closely connected to her family, Lady Jane was said to have proclaimed that she would only marry a royalist. In 1654, during the Protectorate, she married Cheyne, who was some six years younger than she. William Davenant, the royalist poet and dramatist, celebrated the union, while emphasizing Lady Jane's reluctance to be drawn from her poetically constructed retirement.[33]

> Why from my thoughts sweet rest, sweeter to me
> Then young ambition's pros'prous travails be,
> Or love's delicious progresses,
> And is next death the greatest ease;
> Why from so calm a heav'n
> Dost call me to this world, all windy grown;
> Where the light crowd, like lightest sand is driven,
> And weighty greatness, even by them, to air is blown?

Lady Jane's sisters made more socially distinguished matches. Her husband's sense of obligation to the family into which he married was expressed strongly in letters to his brother-in-law in which he wrote of "the vassalage I owe"[34] and her own frequent efforts to send her husband's compliments to her brother.

Charles Cheyne was the eldest surviving son of a well-known gentry family of Drayton Bassett and Chesham Bois, Buckinghamshire, who had served as sheriffs and justices of the peace in the county for two centuries. The Cheynes had been numbered among the godly in the late sixteenth

---

Betty S. Travitsky, " 'His Wife's Prayers and Meditations': MS Egerton 607," in Anne M. Haselkorn and Betty S. Travitsky (eds.), *The Renaissance Englishwoman in Print: Counterbalancing the Canon* (Amherst: University of Massachusetts Press, 1990), pp. 241–60.

[32] Travitsky, "His Wife's Prayers and Meditations," p. 245; Wynn-Davies, *Women Poets of the Renaissance*, p. 5.

[33] Davenant, "Upon the Marriage of the Lady Jane Cavendish with Mr. Cheney," in A. M. Gibb (ed.), *The Shorter Poems and Songs from the Plays and Masques* (Oxford: Clarendon Press, 1972), pp. 131–132. Davenant had close connections to members of the Caroline Court and served under her father in the Civil War.

[34] NUL, Portland Papers, Pw1/83, 9 April 1656, Charles Cheyne to Charles Cavendish, Viscount Mansfield, Welbeck Abbey.

century, but ties of kinship cut across religion in Buckinghamshire and most of the family remained neutral in the Civil War.[35] Son of Francis Cheyne of Cogenho, Northamptonshire, and Anne, daughter of Sir William Fleetwood, the Jacobean lawyer and antiquary knighted by James I on his first progress, Cheyne attended Brasenose College, Oxford, in 1640 and Lincoln's Inn in 1642. He inherited the manor of Chesham Bois in 1644 at the age of eighteen.[36] He served in the royalist army, went into exile during the Civil War, and traveled in Spain and Italy between 1643 and 1650.[37] His Italian agent assumed he was fluent in Italian. "I should have translated the whole account into English had you not been in Italy and therefore do not doubt but the language will be understood easily by you."[38] Cheyne was accused of popery in 1650. Although he became a justice of the peace upon his return to Buckinghamshire in 1652, he was later expelled from the bench until the Restoration in 1660.[39]

In the 1650s, the Cheynes rented a house in Chelsea as they looked for a permanent seat in the southern suburbs. As part of his marriage settlement, Cheyne had sold the manor and advowson of his family home in Cogenho, Northamptonshire, in 1655 and created a settlement for his properties in Buckinghamshire.[40] Despite Lady Jane's position as an heiress, the payment of her portion appears to have been delayed. In 1656 she thanked her brother for his "real intentions concerning my having my portion and I am extremely well satisfied you have done what you can in it."[41]

When her brother, Charles Cavendish, Viscount Mansfield, urged the Cheynes to purchase a house, Lady Jane set out her requirements. The house and seat, the aristocratic country ideal transposed to town, would not only have to please themselves but also impress others. Her brother suggested the house of Alderman Allen (Thomas Alleyn). Her reply provides important information about metropolitan rents and the cost of living on the south bank during the Protectorate.

---

[35] See Linda Levy Peck, *Court Patronage and Corruption in Early Stuart England* (London: Unwin Hyman, 1990), pp. 76, 79, 105, 245n16.

[36] VCH, *Buckinghamshire*, III, 219.

[37] Basil Duke Henning (ed.), *The House of Commons, 1660–1690*, 3 vols. (London: Secker and Warburg, History of Parliament Trust, 1983), II, pp. 51–52.

[38] HEH Ellesmere Mss. EL 11,134, 9/19 March 1672, Rome, Edward Altham to Charles Cheyne.

[39] Henning (ed.), *The House of Commons, 1660–1690*, II, pp. 51–52.

[40] VCH, *Northamptonshire*, III, 237.

[41] NUL, Portland Papers, Pw1/89, Lady Jane Cheyne to Charles Cavendish, Viscount Mansfield, 7 May 1656. She thought that Margaret Cavendish's agent was interfering with her income, NUL, Portland Papers, Pw1/90, Lady Jane Cheyne to [Frances, Countess of Ogle], 2 July 1668.

it is, as you say, a very noble house and I hear was never built for less than the sum you mention, but the seat is not good, which is a great impediment to the sale of it. We have for one year more taken this house. Which is so cheap a rent that I knew not where we can be beaten, til we can seat ourselves to our liking both for house and seat, that being our desires, and paying no more than L50 a year for this, I would not wish Mr Cheyne to buy unless it were such a place wherein both the house and seat might please, as well the opinions of others as our own. I know very good houses at present offered for sale whereof ... Mr Morreyes [Morris] at Twitnam [Twickenham], Sir Nicholas Crisp's at Hammersmith, but neither of these shall we think of, the latter being no seat and the other being on the contrary [south] side of the water. I do believe those that live on that side of the water it stands them in no less than L100 a year ... though our occasions would not be so much of sending to and fro yet I believe it would come at least to L50 which is as much as the rent of this house, wherein we have no less than 11/12 rooms of a floor, besides offices and servants' lodgings and as long as we can have so much room and convenience at the cheap rate of L50 a year, we shall not think of purchasing.[42]

Chelsea had been a fashionable refuge since the time of Henry VIII. Its thirty or forty houses including several aristocratic mansions bordered Little Chelsea, in the later seventeenth century, an area of mixed income housing along the Fulham Road. Its rents were similar to those in the West End.[43] In 1657 Lady Jane's substantial fortune allowed Cheyne to buy the estate of Chelsea and, in 1660, the manor from the Duke and Duchess of Hamilton. The Cheynes lived in the manor house originally owned by Henry VIII and Sir Thomas More.[44]

While she hunted for houses, Lady Jane bought luxury goods in London in the 1650s. With her allowance of L50 each quarter, Lady Jane immediately paid her outstanding bills for cloth, rugs, linen, and jewelry. For instance, she noted in her account book that she owned L1,600 worth of jewelry in September 1656. Early the next year, she delivered 161 diamonds to make a pair of bracelets.[45] She gave six silver fruit dishes to her sister Elizabeth's son, Lord Brackley, which the Earl of Bridgewater recorded

---

[42] *Ibid.* Lady Jane refers probably to Thomas Alleyn who became an alderman in 1653–54. Henry Murray, Esq. had a house in Twickenham as did one Morris who was a justice of the peace in 1649. Alan Charles Bell Urwin, *Twicknam Parke: An Outline of the History of Twickenham Park ... to the Present Day* (Twickenham, Middlesex: Alan C. B. Urwin, 1965), pp. 76–77. See Alfred Beaven, *The Aldermen of the City of London Temp Henry III–1908*, 2 vols. (London: E. Fisher & Co., 1908–13), II, p. 81. Sir Nicholas Crisp was a royalist and inventor.

[43] Peter Clark (ed.), *Cambridge Urban History of Britain, vol. II: 1540–1820* (Cambridge: Cambridge University Press, 2000), p. 665. Susan E. Whyman, *Sociability and Power in Late-Stuart England: The Cultural Worlds of the Verneys, 1660–1720* (Oxford: Oxford University Press, 1998), pp. 69–70.

[44] Randall Davies, *Chelsea Old Church* (London: Duckworth, 1904), p. 57.

[45] HEH Ellesmere Mss. EL 11,143, Lady Jane Cavendish account book, 1635, 1650s.

decades later in his will.[46] She borrowed money too, including L45 from Jane Freeman in 1663.[47] Lady Jane bought expensive imported linen secondhand, specifically pieces that had belonged to Mr. Baggs, a Caroline official, and George Gage, the art connoisseur.[48]

Lady Jane cemented family ties through letters and visits. She had strong links to her brothers and sisters with whom she corresponded frequently. In 1656 Lady Jane wrote faithfully to her brother at Welbeck, saying "every week I read my own happiness in your most loving letters." Her brother's letters, were "the best and only company that I have in Mr. Cheyne's absence for though I affect to keep the house being with child yet I am willing he should sometimes visit his friends and acquaintances in which time your letters are my best companion." She praised her brother's wit and fancy and she hoped that her sister-in-law would soon be pregnant too.[49] When her brother showed concern about Cheyne's absence, Jane sought to reassure him. "I have his letters, and did I not know myself married, I should think by what he writes, that he was still a wooer, which puts me in mind of your words, for you told me it would be always so, being the nature of the person."[50]

In 1656, when both Lady Jane and her sister Elizabeth were pregnant, the importance of childbirth to family strategy and its dangers were uppermost in all their minds. Yet both sisters made public visits in London late in their pregnancy. Her brother reminded Jane that she "was not Samson." In the later stages of her pregnancy she reported that, although she was sick at night, she was well during the day. Her husband advised her not to go to Lady Clifton's funeral while she was pregnant and her brother urged her not to go out in a coach.[51] Nevertheless, she dined out with the Duke of Devonshire, a cousin, and planned to "wait on my sister Bridgewater as often as I can who is expected this day in town and if the greatness of her big belly will give her leave to come . . . I intend to wait of her tomorrow, and by the next give you an account how she doth."[52] The Countess of Bridgewater had already written to her brother that she planned to go to town for Easter. "My sister Jane is not yet they say near as big as I am. She breeds the best that ever I knew: for she makes nothing of a great belly."

---

[46] *Ibid.*, 8104, Earl of Bridgewater's will, 2 April 1685.

[47] *Ibid.*, 11,143, Lady Jane Cavendish account book.   [48] *Ibid.*

[49] NUL, Portland Papers, Pw1/86, Lady Jane Cheyne to Charles Cavendish, Viscount Mansfield, 27 March 1656.

[50] *Ibid.*, Pw1/88, Lady Jane Cheyne to Charles Cavendish, Viscount Mansfield, 29 April 1656.

[51] *Ibid.*, Pw1/86, Lady Jane Cheyne to Charles Cavendish, Viscount Mansfield, 27 March 1656.

[52] *Ibid.*, Pw1/87, Lady Jane Cheyne to Viscount Mansfield, 9 April 1656.

Jane reported that her sister's health was "perfect and looks very well, although she is very big."[53] Although Bridgewater House was in the Barbican in the City, on 17 May Jane's sister, Elizabeth, wrote to their brother, "I ventured to go to Chelsea on Thursday last by reason it was my sister Cheyne's wedding day. My Lord's business is now done and he went to give the Protector thanks. I went to Chelsea and after we supped with my sister Bolingbroke."[54] Her son, Henry, was born two weeks later after a very difficult labor.[55] Elizabeth had nine or ten pregnancies and during one wrote a "A Prayer in Time of Labour."[56]

On 18 May 1656, two weeks before her sister, Lady Jane gave birth to her first child, a daughter. The baby was not expected for another ten days and Charles Cheyne reported to his brother-in-law, "its weakness made us give it presently a sprinkling of Christianity." Lady Jane wanted the child named Elizabeth after her sister, although "tis traditional not to request for godmother any one with child." The godparents were Lady Bolingbroke and one of Cheyne's aunts and Lord Bolingbroke who stood in for the Duke of Newcastle. But Puritan sensibilities intruded on the christening. "Such was my dear lady's desire and his kindness but some unchristian Justice, it being Sunday, made him pay L10 for breaking the Sabbath and gave him then a license to do it. Such use we make of the law of God and man."[57]

Did Lady Jane like living in Chelsea? Remaining somewhat aloof from the public spaces of the town, she acknowledged that sociability was the reigning value. "As to Hyde Park, you judge very rightly of my inclination, for I like much better the solitary walks of Welbeck than the crowd and dust of that park. I have not as yet been there, for which I am much wondered at, by those that affect such pleasures. I see little in them nor should I at any time go but to shun singularity which most condemn though without cause."[58] Nevertheless, a few weeks later, she reassured her brother that she did not lack company: "I have company with me not only every day but all day, Chelsea being as pleasant a place for inviting of

[53] *Ibid.*

[54] *Ibid.*, Pw1/118–20, Elizabeth, Countess of Bridgewater to her brother Viscount Mansfield, from Ashridge.

[55] *Ibid.*, Pw1/121, John Egerton, second Earl of Bridgewater, to his brother-in-law Charles Cavendish, Viscount Mansfield, 3 June 1656 from Bridgewater House.

[56] BL Egerton Ms. 607, ff. 49–53, quoted in Patricia Crawford and Laura Gowing, *Women's Worlds in Seventeenth-Century England* (London: Routledge, 2000), p. 20.

[57] NUL, Portland Papers, Pw1/84, Charles Cheyne to Lord Viscount Mansfield at Welbeck from Chelsea, 20 May 1656.

[58] *Ibid.*, Pw1/86, Lady Jane Cheyne to Charles Cavendish, Viscount Mansfield, 27 March 1656.

company as any I know, and being not far from Hyde Park, we can not miss of seeing often our friends and acquaintance."[59]

In 1660 Charles Cheyne assumed the local offices of a country gentleman, even as Chelsea remained the center of his activities where he entertained Buckinghamshire connections like the Verneys.[60] He served as justice of the peace for Buckinghamshire and became a deputy lieutenant of the county in 1665. That year, he also became a justice of the peace for Middlesex. In addition to these local offices, Cheyne served in Parliament from 1660 as a moderate Tory.[61] He spoke for bills to naturalize foreign Protestants and to ensure that all members had taken the Oath of Allegiance and the Anglican Sacrament according to the Test Act but spoke against the marriage of James, Duke of York, to Mary of Modena and supported a petition for the withdrawal of the Declaration of Indulgence. Even as he negotiated for the funeral monument from Rome, he managed a parliamentary conference on the growth of popery, although he noted privately that the bill was likely to be "null."[62] Cheyne opposed a provision on behalf of Roman Catholics who had borne arms or lost their estates to support the King.

Cheyne became Commissioner of Customs with a salary of L1,020 in 1675 and was rewarded by Charles II with the Scottish title, Viscount Newhaven, in 1681. But if he supported Charles II, he also upheld the powers of Parliament. In 1685 he questioned the continuation of the customs before Parliament had met to regrant it to James II. His pension of £1,200 was cancelled at the Glorious Revolution.[63]

REPRESENTING THE SELF

Charles Cheyne commemorated Lady Jane's life not in words of grief alone but with the most luxurious and imposing monument that he could commission for their Chelsea parish church. The monument that commemorates the life of Lady Jane also illuminates larger issues: first, the construction of the social identity of early modern women and second, the

---

[59] *Ibid.*, Pw1/89, Lady Jane Cheyne to Charles Cavendish, Viscount Mansfield, 7 May 1656. Lady Jane had a satirical eye for the foibles of urban society commenting on the "bravery of Sir George Sandys . . . the gallant of the town."

[60] Whyman, *Sociability and Power in Late-Stuart England*, pp. 69–70.

[61] "Charles Cheyne," in Henning (ed.), *The House of Commons, 1660–1690*, II, pp. 51–52.

[62] HEH Ellesmere Mss. EL 11,145, Charles Cavendish Account Book, Sunday 19 February 1670–71.

[63] "Charles Cheyne," in Henning (ed.), *The House of Commons, 1660–1690*, II, pp. 51–52.

difference between Protestant and Roman Catholic baroque conventions in the presentation of the monumental body.[64]

Adam Littleton, the scholar whom Cheyne had named to the post of rector at Chelsea Old Church in 1669–70, based his funeral sermon for Lady Jane on Proverb I. 30, "Favour is deceitful, and beauty is vain: but a woman that feareth the lord, she shall be praised." After praising Lady Jane as the pious and private wife characteristic of Renaissance prescriptive literature, Littleton went on to laud her education, her management of the estate, and her writing. Indeed, Littleton argued for Lady Jane's equality with men through her own reason, education, and the workings of the holy spirit.

> The equality of the woman's merits and rights with man … alike capable of those improvements, which by the efforts of reason and the methods of education and the instincts of the Blessed Spirit are to be made upon it, and no less fitted in her natural ingenuity for all kind of studies and employments: though custom, like a salique law, hath excluded them from public offices and professions; and confin'd them, mostly to the narrow territories of home …. A learned woman of Utrecht, has in a printed discourse fairly in this behalf vindicated the reputation of her sex.[65]

Littleton's reference to *Whether a Christian Woman Should Be Educated* by Anna Maria Van Schurman, the foremost feminist of the period, is striking. He must have known that it would please Cheyne, Newcastle, and Lady Jane's stepmother Margaret Cavendish, who corresponded with Van Schurman.[66]

At the same time, an elegy on Lady Jane's death characterized her as a saint.[67] Indeed, that elegy specifically addresses the problem of how to worship at the shrine of a Protestant woman.

---

[64] On "early modern subjectivities," see Lyndal Roper, *Oedipus and the Devil: Witchcraft, Sexuality, and Religion in Early Modern Europe* (London: Routledge, 1994), pp. 4–34; Jonathan Sawday, "Self and Selfhood in the Seventeenth Century," in Roy Porter (ed.), *Rewriting the Self: Histories from the Renaissance to the Present* (London: Routledge, 1997), pp. 29–48.

[65] Adam Littleton, *A Sermon at the Funeral of the Right Honourable the Lady Jane, Eldest Daughter to his Grace William, Duke of Newcastle, and Wife to the Honourable Charles Cheyne, esq; at Chelsea. Novemb. 1 being All-Saints day by Adam Littleton, priest* (London: 1669), pp. 19–20.

[66] On Van Schurman see Joyce L. Irwin (ed.), *Whether a Christian Woman Should Be Educated and Other Writings from her Intellectual Circle* (Chicago: University of Chicago Press, 1998); Irwin, "Anna Maria Van Schurman: The Star of Utrecht (Dutch, 1607–1678)," in Jeanne R. Brink (ed.), *Female Scholars: A Tradition of Learned Women Before 1800* (Montreal: Eden Press Women's Publications, 1980), pp. 68–85. I am grateful to Hilda Smith for discussion of Van Schurman.

[67] "An elegy on the death of the thrice noble and virtuous Lady, the Lady Jane Cheyne, eldest daughter to William, Duke of Newcastle, by a person of quality and neighbour in Chelsey," in Littleton, *A Sermon*, H2–3v. See Margaret Aston, "Gods, Saints, and Reformers: Portraiture and Protestant

> Farewell (dear lady) now a blessed saint:
> Did not religion on us lay restraint,
> Our vows and prayers soon would turned be
> From praying for, to praying unto three;
> But these as fruitless are, as those are vain;
> Thou feelest none, nor pitied our pain,
> Our eyes will better shew the love we bore,
> Where to lament's more fit, then to implore.[68]

The Cheyne monument clearly posed the problem of how to present a pious noble woman in a Protestant culture with a baroque vocabulary.[69] Sixteenth-century Protestant reformers had denied that saints had a place in a reformed church.[70] Later, Caroline clerics, including Calvinists such as John Prideaux, played with the language of sainthood within the culture of the court.[71] Richard Crashaw, a Caroline poet and royalist exile, wrote poems to Mary Magdalene and St. Theresa. Lady Jane Cheyne herself composed a fierce poem on her sister Elizabeth's death in childbirth in 1663 in which she called her a saint: "For none can give example like her life, / To friendship, kindred, family or wife / A greater saint the earth did never bear / She lived to love, and her last thought was care."[72]

Presentation of the self as saint was a frequent motif in Restoration portraiture of aristocratic women. Peter Lely painted portraits of the Countess of Castlemaine as the Madonna, St. Catherine, and the Repentant Magdalen, while Mrs. Pepys was painted as St. Catherine "following the fashion set by the Catholic Queen Catherine of Braganza."[73] Godfrey Kneller made portraits of court women as St. Cecilia.[74]

England," in Lucy Gent (ed.), *Albion's Classicism: The Visual Arts in Britain, 1550–1660* (New Haven: Yale University Press, 1995), pp. 181–220; Marcia Pointon, *Strategies for Showing: Women, Possession, and Representation in English Visual Culture, 1665–1800* (Oxford: Oxford University Press, 1997).

[68] "An elegy ... on Lady Jane Cheyne," H2. Another elegy on Lady Jane was written by Richard Flecknoe, a writer who converted to Catholicism while in Italy in the 1640s. Davies, *Chelsea Old Church*, p. 73.

[69] Ninnnis, "The Hewer Memorial at Clapham," 261, addresses the adaptation of Bernini's monument to Maria Raggi to Hewer. He argues that "In Protestant England, at the time, the primary symbol of the Christian faith, the cross ... was generally avoided in the interior arrangements of churches."

[70] See Aston, "Gods, Saints, and Reformers," pp. 181–220.

[71] See Peck, *Court Patronage and Corruption*, pp. 29, 209.

[72] HEH Ellesmere Mss. EL 8353, "On the death of my dear sister the Countess of Bridgewater dying in childbed, Delivered of a dead infant, a son, the 14th day of June 1666," quoted in Greer et al. (eds.), *Kissing the Rod*, p. 118.

[73] Ninnnis, "The Hewer Memorial at Clapham", 261.

[74] Pointon, *Strategies for Showing*, pp. 268–69.

Bernini's St. Theresa, Blessed Ludovica, and Maria Raggi offered models for the presentation of saintly women: all three were portrayed in a moment of ecstasy (or death) with both hands pressed to their breasts. One of Antonio Raggi's most important commissions was a scene with St. Cecilia. But the effigy of Lady Jane Cheyne is not a copy of these. Rather, the Anglican Lady Jane, the writer of poetry, plays, and religious meditations, is presented as a cultivated, aristocratic woman in the fashionable attire of Restoration England. Yet she too has one hand clasped to her bosom.

This representation of elegance, education, and virtue emerged from the negotiation of conflicting views of religion and gender in Rome and London. Cheyne was an active patron in the making of his wife's funeral monument.[75] He took a keen interest in the design, the multicolored marble, the height of the memorial, and the effigy. Cheyne wished to present Lady Jane as wife, mother, and heiress. He wanted a coronet on her head to express her rank as the daughter of a duke and a small figure to represent his daughter Katherine, who died months after her mother. Yet the heraldic vocabulary typical of seventeenth-century English monuments[76] is missing from the Cheyne monument because of the negotiations with Rome. Indeed, Cheyne's desire to present Lady Jane's high status through a coronet was rejected by the architect as appropriate only to the presentation of the Virgin Mary. The crown would have to be added in London.

For the crown pendent which you mention, you if you think fit may have it done there when the monument arrives, for the sense here of the artists (that undertake things of this quality) is that the custom of this Church is not to crown any of the saints though canonized and have lamps at their shrines. It being an honour only above the rest due to the Regina Sanctorum Omnium as Mother of God, and Queen of Heaven.

But there was another option:

Yet because the lady was the eldest daughter of a duke it is very requisite that there should be some sign or token of that honour and worth to accompany the monument and therefore the artists have thought fit to place a crown at her feet as neglected and not esteemed in her lifetime; which if I mistake not is part of your

---

[75] HEH Ellesmere Mss. EL 11,121, Rome, 25 October 1670, Edward Chaloner to Charles Cheyne, esq. See Graham Parry. "Cavendish Memorials," in *The Seventeenth Century,* special issue: *The Cavendish Circle,* 9 (1994), 275–87.

[76] See Llewelyn, *Funeral Monuments in Post-Reformation England,* pp. 309–11, 373.

design mentioned in your letter and may prove conformable to your conception if not altogether yet in some nature.[77]

The figure of Katherine, his daughter, which would have marked the effigy as that of a mother and wife, was ultimately lost in confusion over the scale of the monument. Cheyne did, however, get a large cross that he didn't order!

Cheyne's plans to memorialize Lady Jane went beyond creating the monument itself to reconstructing its setting in Chelsea Old Church. The need to enlarge Chelsea Old Church had been stated as long ago as 1631. "Forasmuch as the small parish of Chelsea hath of late years been greatly increased by the buildings, resort, and residence of divers great and noble personages whereby the church is become too little for the parishioners by which means also many of the ancient inhabitants and their families are too commonly put from their seats."[78] But such efforts were delayed. Lady Jane Cheyne had agreed to pay for the roof before her death. Adam Littleton pointed out that "of her charity to this place I question not but we shall see in a short time some fair testimonies erected."[79]

Indeed, the church was redone to coincide with the arrival of the extraordinary funeral monument. After the death of Lady Jane and, five months later, his daughter Katherine, Cheyne toured several parish churches in the course of a trip to and from Dublin.[80] Upon his return he tore down the old nave and the west tower of Chelsea Old Church, replaced the roof, created a family vault beneath the chancel, and planned the monument for the north wall.[81] Burial in the chancel was considered most prestigious because it was so near the altar.[82] Cheyne certainly intended to impress the court, upwardly mobile gentry and citizens, and his in-laws with this monument. But also he conveyed the centrality of the making of this monument to his own sense of self, defined through his marriage, in the inscription for the funeral vault which he built in the Chelsea Old Church.[83]

[77] HEH Ellesmere Mss. EL 11, 126, Altham to Cheyne, 3/13 June 1671.
[78] Davies, *Chelsea Old Church*, p. 9.
[79] Walter Hindes Godfrey (ed.), *The Parish of Chelsea*, 4 vols., Survey of London, vols. 2, 4, 7, 11 (London: London County Council, 1913–27), IV, Part II, p. 3, "subscription towards the rebuilding were asked for in 1669–1670 and Mr. Randall Davies has shown that the work was probably not begun until after Lady Cheyne's funeral, 1st November 1669. It was completed in January 1671–2 with the exception of the tower which was finished in 1674."
[80] HEH Ellesmere Mss. EL 11,145, Cheyne account book, August 1670.
[81] Godfrey (ed.), *The Parish of Chelsea*, Part 3: *The Old Church*, p. 19.
[82] Llewellyn, *Funeral Monuments in Post-Reformation England*, p. 148.
[83] See the inscription on the Cheyne monument in Thomas Faulkner, *An Historical and Topographical Description of Chelsea and its Environs*, 2 vols. (London, 1829), I, pp. 224–25.

This burial place was purchased and made by Charles Cheyne Esq for his most dearly beloved wife, the most incomparable and pious lady the Lady Jane eldest daughter to his Grace William Duke of Newcastle who lately deceased lyeth here interred, by the help of whose portion he became Lord of this Manor of Chelsea and desires that by her he and his may at their appointed times be here likewise interred and rest inviolate till all shall arise and come to judgment. Here under an angel with a trumpet to be carved.[84]

With this inscription, Cheyne made plain his love, his wife's high social status, his financial obligation, and his family's "purchase" on Chelsea Old Church. While his funeral monument, like others, celebrated family and religion, Cheyne's commission was a remarkable import, grand, stately, lifelike, Roman, and rich.

NEGOTIATING THE BAROQUE BODY: ARTISTS, PRICING, AND PRODUCTION

The logistics of Cheyne's commission were as extraordinary as the monument itself and illuminate the role of agents and artists in shaping the patron's desires.[85] Cheyne's agents in Rome served as brokers between patron and artists, addressing the problems of price, models, size, and transport. The "architect," described variously as Bernini's heir, son, and nephew, made substantial changes to the design as it progressed. The sculptor of the effigy, Antonio Raggi, played a subsidiary role to the architect, but one superior to the stonemasons. The agents arranged the network of merchants who transferred monies and delivered the monument. It proved an expensive and difficult task to coordinate the work of different artists and artisans located all over Rome, and delays in correspondence raised repeated problems.

Ideology and religious difference proved even more difficult to negotiate. Cheyne and his agents had to navigate the shoals of differing religious and ideographic values characteristic of Catholic Rome and Protestant Britain. Roman artists instructed Cheyne not only that the heraldic claims of English funeral monuments had to give way to baroque Catholic conventions but also that the effigy had to look lifelike, adorned with the jewelry, costume,

---

[84] HEH Ellesmere Mss. EL 11141: "These for Dr. Littleton."

[85] Jennifer Montagu, *Roman Baroque Sculpture: The Industry of Art* (New Haven: Yale University Press, 1989), pp. 37–47, discusses the commission at length drawing on the Bridgewater Mss. at the Huntington.

and portrait of the deceased. Contemporary English values about the commemoration of the dead gave way to the style of baroque Rome.[86]

To order the monument, Cheyne had to find an agent in Rome. He began with his cousin Edward Chaloner and his account book shows meetings with Chaloner before he left for Rome in 1670 to join the entourage of the English ambassador there.[87] Chaloner was obviously grooming himself for preferment at court and with good reason. While his grandfather, Sir Thomas, had been a high-ranking official at the court of James I and much favored, his father and uncle were both regicides. Chaloner sought to prove that he was loyal to Charles II.[88] Cheyne's agents' correspondence (his side of the correspondence has not survived) illuminate every stage of the process of negotiations with the architect, the sculptor, and the marble cutters. While the mail could take a month, the correspondents often wrote back on the same day.

By October 1670 Chaloner had sent Cheyne three models, probably on paper, with prices provided by the architect, which were, in the end, to prove much too optimistic.[89] The next step was a three-dimensional model. In January 1671 Chaloner wrote, "the model of your monument in wood is now made which in my apprehension shows very noble but the account of the several prices and quantity of stones which I promised you in my last is not yet made."[90] The uncertainty in pricing stemmed from the number of artisans involved and the evolving design for the monument. The architect's original figures which suggested a price of L250–300 for the monument proved too low. In the end the monument cost about L500.[91]

---

[86] "Monumental body" is Nigel Llewellyn's term, in *Funeral Monuments in Post-Reformation England*, pp. 363–75.

[87] HEH Ellesmere Mss. EL 11,145, Cheyne account book, December, 8 January, 1669–70, "given to the scrivener that made the bond at Sir Thomas Bludworth's for security for my cousin Chaloner's Exch 2–6."

[88] "Sir Thomas Chaloner," Oxford DNB, X, 897–98.

[89] HEH Ellesmere Mss. EL 11,121 Chaloner to Cheyne, 25 October 1670.

[90] HEH Ellesmere Mss. EL 11,123 Chaloner to Cheyne, 17 January 1671.

[91] HEH Ellesmere Mss. EL 11,124, Altham to Cheyne, 11/21 March 1671. "I have received three hundred and fifty-five crowns of Roman money ten Gaels to the crown which according as the exchange goes is the value of one hundred pounds sterling.... There was more than one mistake made in the account sent you about the monument which partly proceeded from the architect whose computation made of the expense was writ you but he (afterwards we found) was no competent judge, it belonging to the Capo-Maestro of the stone cutters to understand the exact sum and the true expenses of the design who would have eight hundred crowns for the making of it as the architect had designed it, but we brought him to seven hundred crowns and lower he would not fall ... In conclusion I hope to made a good election of not only two able men but honest (likewise) as I perceive from the marble they have made choice of. I perceive ... you wrote Mr. Chaloner that you thought the statue entered into the same account but it is not so for that belongs to a sculptor which is here another profession ... He will not undertake to do it for less then fifty pistols, or there about. I will strive to have it done by the best master and at the best price as can be possible."

In the midst of the commission, Chaloner decided that French culture and language, rather than Italian, was the wave of the future. He asked Cheyne's advice as one who was well traveled. Complaining of how costly Rome was, although it helped that he was one of the ambassador's company, Chaloner complained about his allowance. "I find it but sufficient . . . to keep me in meat, drink, and clothes, without any accidental expenses in a sedentary life and you very well know that the expense of journeying must of necessity be above double."[92] Chaloner decided to leave for France to learn the language in much the same way as early seventeenth-century travelers had done: "intending to reside at Orleans or some other town upon the Loire all the next summer for the attaining some knowledge in the French tongue which will be much more advantageous upon all accounts than the Italian. Notwithstanding these my resolves your more sage and experienced judgement and advice is desired which shall be my compass."[93]

Upon his departure from Rome Chaloner left Edward Altham, an English merchant, in charge of the commission for the monument. Altham, the son of a gentleman, had hoped to be ordained. A royalist exile, he had left England in the early 1640s but returned in 1647. In 1648 he departed for Rome, where he studied Hebrew. In 1652 he became a Roman Catholic with connections to the English College in Rome. His brother Leventhorp was a wine merchant in London and Edward himself became a merchant dealing with exports.[94]

The monument was already underway when Altham became involved in the project. As he presented the bills to Cheyne, he wrote flatteringly: "I hope I am not mistaken in making election of the best workmen this city affords supposing you to be a person of that quality as has been represented to me and will not think much to pay well to be better served. I can assure you were it not that the present Pope is no ways inclined to building nor sculpture both statue and monument would have cost a great deal more then now it will."[95]

Because Antonio Raggi, the sculptor, insisted that the effigy look as lifelike as possible, Altham asked Cheyne "the lineaments of the face, whether, long or round, and the proportion of nose, lips, forehead, fat or lean, of which in part I am somewhat already informed by Mr Sanderson

[92] HEH Ellesmere Mss. EL 11,121.   [93] *Ibid.*

[94] Jennifer Montagu, "Edward Altham as a Hermit," in Edward Chaney and Peter Mack (eds.), *England and the Continental Renaissance: Essays in Honour of J. B. Trapp* (Woodbridge, Suffolk: Boydell Press, 1990), pp. 271–82.

[95] HEH Ellesmere Mss. EL 11,127, Altham to Cheyne, 17/27 June 1671.

who was both the Lady's kinsman and acquaintance; but I shall expect
more to that purpose from your self."[96] Cheyne complied, sending a
portrait for the sculptor. A portrait and miniature of Lady Jane are at
Welbeck Abbey and a sketch of one of these may have been used.[97] Altham
replied,

The . . . draught of the face came very well conditioned to hand and well liked by
such as have skill to understand things of that nature. The sculptor . . . does not
doubt but to imitate its likeness. He is one of the best in Rome at his art and
consequently the dearest, a quondam scholar of that famous Algardi who has
immortalized himself in describing the history of Attila when he came to destroy
Rome which is expressed in noble sculptures in white marble set up in the Church
of St. Peter's in the days of Pope Innocent the Tenth. This artificer is called
Antonio Raggi with whom as yet I am not agreed, he demanding fifty pistols for to
make the single statue and, if a small figure of the daughter to the Lady be annexed
to accompany the statue as we were once thinking of, he will have no less then one
hundred and eighty crowns but that small figure shall not be made till such time as
I shall have your approbation for it.

Not only did the sculptor insist on the face being as lifelike as possible, he
wanted Lady Jane's clothing and jewelry to be lifelike too. Indeed Raggi
believed, according to Altham, that these luxury ornaments were crucial to
her likeness. "The sculptor is of the opinion to follow the style of this
country in the habiliments of the figure and as they are represented in the
draught so to form them with necklace pendents etc. as if alive without
which ornaments very difficultly can be represented the likeness to
acquaintances." Altham disagreed: "the reposing posture of the figure on
the urn did not require such a lively representation of the person as being
dead or supposed to be upon the bed of languishing. To which he [Raggi]
made no reply but the custom of this place was to make the figure as like as
may be."[98] Altham consulted other masters to make sure that Raggi was
correct. "The dress or drapery of the statue will be such as the best
judgements of artists shall think fit for I am not content to have the opinion
of one sculptor but do take advice of painters concerning this particular
who will have the *panegiatura* as it is called here done as much as may be to
the life that it may the better represent the likeness of the person."[99]

[96] HEH Ellesmere Mss. EL 11,124, 11/21 March 1671, Edward Altham to Charles Cheyne.
[97] Richard W. Goulding, *The Welbeck Abbey Miniatures Belonging to His Grace the Duke of Portland, A
    Catalogue Raisonné* (Oxford: Printed by Frederick Hall at the University Press, 1916), p. 164, #247;
    Richard W. Goulding, *Catalogue of the Pictures Belonging to his Grace the Duke of Portland, K. G.*
    (Cambridge: Cambridge University Press, 1936), p. 3 #2, Lady Jane Cheyne, School of Van Dyck.
[98] HEH Ellesmere Mss. EL 11,125 1/11 April 1671, Altham to Cheyne.
[99] HEH Ellesmere Mss. EL 11,126 3/13 June 1671.

42. Antonio Raggi, one of Gian Lorenzo Bernini's most important collaborators, designed the elegant figure of Lady Jane Cheyne with a coronet at her feet.
The Courtauld Institute, Conway Library, London, All Saints, Chelsea, figure of Lady Jane Cheyne by Antonio Raggi.

The architect designed the Cheyne monument with the finest marbles and engaged seven marble cutters for more than two months.[100] Bernini's interests in the use of multicolor marbles, black and yellow, green, red and white, are reflected too in the Cheyne memorial.[101] Altham delighted in enumerating their luxury, their color, and provenance.

Two excellent white marble stones of a likeness and of the best sort that comes from Massa di Carara of this material is the base made and the capitelli over the two pillars. The two pillars, are to be made of an excellent speckled stone tending to red and white which is called breccia di Francia. It is costly but much better than an inferior sort of the like stone that is used in Rome. ... The urn is to be all black; the feet of it yellow. You need not fear but there will be an excellent concordance of colours for, in this kind, Rome has

[100] HEH Ellesmere Mss. EL 11,125, 1/11 April 1671.
[101] Montagu, *Roman Boroque Sculpture*, p. 46.

such a variety of different objects as that no nation is more exact in the inflexions then this."[102]

HEIGHT: ENGLISH FEET OR ITALIAN PALMS?

The major crisis of the commission, which occurred in the midst of cutting the marbles, concerned the height of the monument. The architect had planned a monument twenty feet tall with a cross at the top but there were only fourteen feet to the window in Chelsea Old Church. Altham asked in one letter: "when you next write to express me the grandeur of the chancel where this monument is to stand and whether there are more windows than one … and how placed … I suppose the chancel stands east."[103] Chaloner, now in Venice, advised Altham of a great mistake, "that there is but fourteen foot height of place in the chancel where the monument is to be erected; we received from your note of twenty foot place and accordingly the architect's design was conformable to that space, but how now to accommodate this difference will be somewhat difficult; unless the cross … be omitted, which happily you never intended should be put there as was designed."[104] Altham reminded Cheyne of the difference between the smaller Italian palm and the English foot.

I send you inclosed the precise measure of an Italian palm and so you may be pleased to do in your letter to me to send a thread … of the exact height of the place that the monument is to stand in. Mr Chaloner told me that there is a window which is over this monument, and if so I do not apprehend but that the cross may, if you please, stand some two or three foot in the space of the window which cannot hinder much the light … The stones being brought most of them and the workmen engaged I do not see how to remedy the inconvenience without your loss if you will not have the design go on.[105]

Altham considered ways to cut down the monument: "some part of the frontispiece being most for ornament of architecture may be omitted and without any prejudice to the monument be rendered capable to stand in the compass of fourteen foot."[106] Indeed, as he considered the problem, Altham drew on baroque conventions to demonstrate that the monument's extension above the window would enhance the view of those who came to gaze at it.

---

[102] HEH Ellesmere Mss. EL 11,124, 11/21 March 1671.
[103] HEH Ellesmere Mss. EL 11,125, 1/11 April 1671.
[104] HEH Ellesmere Mss. EL 11,124, 11/21 March 1671.   [105] *Ibid.*   [106] *Ibid.*

Supposing some small part of the monument should extend itself some few palms in the light of the window, I cannot conceive it of much prejudice to the chancel: and to the monument it must be beneficial whose cupola has an open oval figure in the top of it, on purpose to receive the light which is to render the statue (in a reposing posture upon the urn) better visible to spectators.[107]

Cheyne reassured Altham that the project could proceed.[108] However, in Altham's concern over the height of the monument, the crucial issue of the monument's site in Chelsea Old Church was lost sight of, as we shall see.

The time taken on the height of the monument meant that the figure of young Katherine Cheyne had to be dropped. But, as the monument came to completion, Altham became rhapsodic, pointing out how grand the statue was on its own.

Upon mature consideration the artist reputed it better to be single, which lies after this fashion, at length the upper part of the body somewhat upright leaning upon a cushion, the left hand and arm visible reposing upon a book open. The right hand and arm bent towards the breasts in a pious posture, the visage looking upwards from whence the devout soul may be considered (by the spectators) as full of expectation and highly concerned in the thoughts of another life. The habiliments are conformable to the dress of the upper part which is done as much to the likeness of the portrait that was sent, as the artist could arrive for. The coronet is carved in a convenient place not far from the feet. The marble proves excellent and very white which will appear better to the eye being to be laid upon an urn of black marble polished which is to be supported by two yellow marble bases. The frontispiece of the monument will be all white polished marble, the two pillars of speckled marbled white and red ... the supporters of the pillars inlaid with a greenish kind of marble which in diverse parts of the frontispiece is inlaid and very delicate.[109]

When Cheyne inquired at the beginning of August 1671 about the progress of the monument, Altham responded vividly by describing the difficulties of organizing artists and craftsman in Rome for the project because of the different quarters of the city in which each practiced as well as the summer heat.[110]

Finally, monument, sculpture, and marble were ready to be shipped to London in "thirty great cases." It was magnificent, so said Altham and the Roman artists who had worked on it.

[107] HEH Ellesmere Mss. EL 11,125, 1/11 April 1671.
[108] *Ibid.*, HEH EL 11,126, Altham to Cheyne, Rome 3/13 June 1671.
[109] HEH EL 11,127, 17/27 June 1671.   [110] *Ibid.*, 11,129, 8/18 September 1671.

But now at last (I bless God) this enterprise is finished and the greatest part of the monument incased, the statue is put up likewise and with what care and diligence you will be able to write me when you see it … I could now please myself with a high degree of flattery in telling you the opinion of the Romans concerning the statue and monument but I will mortify myself in this particular and take off the edge of your expectation. Let it be sufficient only to say this: Rome's artists in this nature can do no more.[III]

"CHARGES DO AUGMENT BEYOND IMAGINATION"

In the same letter in which he lauded the monument, Altham discussed the bills and the complexities of production in baroque Rome.[112]

When Mr Chaloner writ you concerning the three designs sent you we took the word for the expenses specified only from the architect but when we came to discourse with the head masters stone cutters they made it appear vastly different nor did these speak plainly but rather diminished than augmented the expenses to engage us in the design … The head masters complain that the architect has added many things which was not in the design … To the architect I cannot give less than ten pistols having been very sedulous and has followed in this design his uncle's way of architecture which is to have the stones cut sloping not in a right line which is very difficult … . Then does there enter in another expense of the custom house which will have three or four per cent for such commodities as leave Rome. In conclusion I cannot tell what will be the sum.[113]

In October the monument was dispatched complete with "do it yourself" directions showing how to put it together with each piece marked from AA to GGG. Altham ordered "that the line or mortar must not touch the marble because they stain it."[114] Altham's correspondents, George Northcliffe and William Hodges, forwarded the monument to his brother Leventhorp Altham in London. Altham wrote again in November while the monument was in transit sending along several more observations from the architect. Later, he invoked the great name of Bernini in his efforts to gain payment. "The architect is not as yet paid to whom I cannot think it convenient to give less then ten if not fifteen pistols. He is kinsman to the famous Cavalier Bernino, and his heir besides and, what most imports, an honest man."[115]

The monument finally arrived in January 1672 almost a year and a half after it had been ordered. Leventhorp Altham served as the middleman for

---

[III] *Ibid.* II,129; HEH Ellesmere Mss. EL II,131, 14/24 October 1671.   [112] *Ibid.*   [113] *Ibid.*
[114] HEH Ellesmere Mss. EL II,133, 25 November/15 December 1671; HEH Ellesmere Mss. EL II,139.
[115] HEH Ellesmere Mss. EL II,134, 9/19 March 1672.

payments and post. Cheyne paid for the monument by sending money to Italy via Leventhorp and recorded payments to Leventhorp's porter for letters from Rome.[116] Leventhorp also dealt with the custom house about the arrival of the marbles; the customs officers rated the monument cheaply at L20 which meant that the customs duties would be twenty shillings.[117] A small boat brought the cases down river to Chelsea. Cheyne's own accounts document the unloading and setting up of the monument in Chelsea Old Church. Between 15 and 20 January, he paid 2–6 to "the laborers about the stone cases for drink"; 13–6 to "Carpenter Hodges and three more for their pains at the stone cases"; another 2–6 to Tom Burt for the same; 2–6 to Mr Altham's porter and he tipped three boys for sweeping the church.[118]

Cheyne soon wrote to Altham that the monument had arrived. The agent wanted to know whether it met expectations and continued to press to get the bills paid. "Your obliging lines from Chelsea January 11 were extremely welcome . . . your swift quill has proved a dove to bring me early good tidings from the abyss of many waters for . . . which good success I can sacrifice no less than a Te Deum Laudamus."[119] The account included additions the architect had made to the original design, "beneficial to the work in hand which liberty he pretended to have as architect and not to be contradicted by the stone cutters."[120] The problem of the height of the monument had caused delay and in the end the workmen had to work harder to produce the monument according to schedule.[121]

Despite the successful arrival of the monument, there was one glaring error. Altham had mistaken its location. Instead of standing in the chancel, the monument was placed on the north wall. As a result, the effigy of Lady Jane did not look toward the altar as was customary but out the door of Chelsea Old Church! To Cheyne's question about "the posture of the figure lying with the feet to the west," the Roman Catholic Altham responded that custom meant little in a Reformed church.

The truth is if in England that custom is not observed it may seem somewhat indecent to bring in a contrary custom. But seeing the situation would not permit it, it may be excused and such a small error in a Reformed church will be the easier pardoned, being a step out of the way from antiquity . . . will appear nothing in respect of those large strides which the reformists have taken in things of great

---

[116] HEH Ellesmere Mss. 11,145, Cheyne's account book, p. 53.
[117] HEH Ellesmere Mss. EL 11,122, Leventhorp Altham to Cheyne 12, January 1672.
[118] HEH Ellesmere Mss. EL 11,145, Cheyne's account book, p. 53, January 1671–72 2–6, "given to Mr Altham's porter for a letter from Rome; several more payments to Mr Altham's porter on the 5th, the 8th.
[119] HEH Ellesmere Mss. EL 11,134, 9/19 March 1672. [120] *Ibid.* [121] *Ibid.*

importance from ancient church ceremonies. Mr. Chaloner, who has been at Geneva, will be of my opinion.[122]

Whatever he thought of Altham's explanation, Cheyne saw the monument as central to his own self-definition. He wrote the inscription for the monument that stressed Lady Jane's role as wife and mother and benefactor to the church. He asked Littleton to translate them into Latin "whereto I covet not embroidery, but rather a few words of such value as you think suitable."[123] Littleton sought guidance from Mr. Carew: "Good sir Your opinion whether plain inscription in prose or a verse, if verse whether those may be made? if prose whether parted by unequal lines or sit all together. Pray, dash out what you dislike in either."[124]

The monument to Lady Jane and the funeral vault under the altar in Chelsea Old Church were amongst the most important projects of Cheyne's life, joining family piety and a virtuoso's taste with the promotion of Chelsea. Given the important role of Lady Jane Cavendish in household decisions, and the rapidity with which Cheyne ordered the monument, it is not impossible that she had shared in planning it before she died.

Cheyne's monument to Lady Jane is in striking contrast to her sister's, her brother-in-law's, and her father's, "one of the most notable existing examples of a tomb created by a foreign sculptor resident abroad to be set up in England."[125] The two Cavendish sisters' funeral monuments show striking differences even as both husbands firmly recorded their grief both in words and marble. Elizabeth died during pregnancy in 1663 while visiting her husband, the Earl of Bridgewater, in jail in London on a charge of dueling. He wrote movingly about her and the loss he felt. His heartfelt inscription accompanies a striking but simple tomb erected to her and other relatives in Little Gaddesden, Hertfordshire, some six years later.[126] When the Duke of Newcastle died in the 1670s, he was buried in Westminster Abbey in a tomb designed for his wife Margaret Cavendish and himself. His heir insisted that his father be buried privately, at night, and accompanied only by relations in no more than four coaches, "my brother Cheyne," Lord Bridgewater, and his son Lord Brackley, if they were in town.[127] The Duke and Duchess of Newcastle were commemorated by an anonymous English tombmaker.[128] Margaret Cavendish wears a coronet, the usual heraldic sign of her status as a duchess.

[122] HEH Ellesmere Mss. EL 11,135.   [123] HEH Ellesmere Mss. EL 11,141, "These for Dr. Littleton."
[124] *Ibid.*   [125] Esdaile, "The Monuments," p. 74.   [126] See chapter 6 above.
[127] BL Add. Mss. 37,998, f. 241, 11 January 1676–77.   [128] See Parry, "Cavendish Memorials," 275–87.

43. The Earl of Bridgewater, married to Lady Jane Cheyne's sister Elizabeth, commissioned a simple tomb for her and other relatives with heraldic decoration and lengthy inscriptions. The Courtauld Institute, Conway Library, Little Gaddesden (Herts.), Bridgewater Monument.

Cheyne continued to develop the borough of Chelsea throughout his life. As London expanded westward, Cheyne tried to attract new residents to Chelsea not only through new housing but also through the creation of new public spaces. He leased land for the creation of the Chelsea Physic Garden. He helped arrange land purchases for Chelsea College, a royal institution.[129] Just before his own death in 1698 he wrote from the country to the rector of Chelsea Old Church hoping to hear that Chelsea was

full as ever. I wish your best houses were so too, and I hope I shall live to see it so ... The Church doth indeed want a gallery, even for the inhabitants you have, and I shall ever be ready to help you to more, if I could myself, or get others to build more houses. I would be glad to let land for that purpose, and particularly put down a tavern and bowling-green, for your designs of better and more sober purposes, as my man Williams may inform you.[130]

Cheyne died in 1698 and was buried in Chelsea Old Church. There is no monument to him. Instead, an inscription on Lady Jane's, presumably placed by his second wife at Cheyne's request, reads: "sacred to the memory of Charles Cheyne, Viscount Newhaven, of the kingdom of Scotland, Lord of this Manor of Chelsea, who erected this monument to the memory of the Lady Jane Cheyne, his first wife, who died twenty-nine years since; and now he himself (alas too soon) lies buried in the same vault (as he ordered by his last will) and with her expects a blessed resurrection."[131]

THE TUBE

Even as he ordered Lady Jane's funeral monument, Cheyne used the same agents to order a telescope from Eustachio Divini, the great Roman instrument maker. Scientific instruments had become new luxury goods in the early seventeenth century. Cheyne's father-in-law, the Duke of Newcastle, already interested in optics, had Dr. Joseph Webbe working on telescopes in 1631.[132] Newcastle ultimately put together a collection of seven telescopes made by Italian makers including Eustachio Divini. In 1648 he sold them to his cousin, the Earl of Devonshire, for L80 through the agency

---

[129] Thomas Birch, *The History of the Royal Society of London for Improving of Natural Knowledge, From its First Rise*, 4 vols. (London: A. Millar, 1756–57), II, pp. 371, 378, 434.
[130] Faulkner, *An Historical and Topographical Description of Chelsea*, I, pp. 334–35.   [131] *Ibid.*, I, p. 225.
[132] Thomas Hobbes, *The Correspondence*, (ed.) Noel Malcolm, 2 vols. (Oxford: Clarendon Press, 1994), I, pp. 19–20, and note 10.

of Thomas Hobbes.[133] When Cheyne himself visited Rome in the 1640s, he visited Kircher's famous museum, and twenty years later remained interested in Kircher's work. Although not a member of the Royal Society, Cheyne had connections with those who were.[134] Even as Cheyne imported his own telescope from Rome, John Doddington, an English diplomat in Venice and the Royal Society's correspondent, sent Henry Oldenburg, Secretary of the Royal Society, "two telescopes and two microscopes of the Signior Eustachio Divini, and Giuseppe Campani, with such other curiosities as Padre Kircherus will impart to me."[135]

Divini had begun making clocks and lenses in Rome in the mid-1640s.[136] In 1648 he created a compound microscope with cardboard sliding tubes and convex lenses and worked on the construction of long telescopes. He used these for astronomical observation, publishing a map of the moon and later the rings of Saturn in 1649. Divini and Campani warred over whose telescope had discovered the moons of Jupiter and the comparative claims of their telescopes were put to the test in 1664 before the Academia del Cimento in Florence.[137] When Louis XIV invited the astronomer Cassini to France, he used Campani's telescope to make further discoveries. Divini also engaged in a prolonged fight with Christopher Huygens over precedence.[138]

Enthusiasm for scientific instruments was reinforced in the 1660s and 1670s from several directions. In the 1660s the Royal Society displayed both continental telescopes and microscopes. At meetings in 1666, the members heard a report about the ongoing "contest" between Divini and Campani about who made better lenses and whose telescope was used to discover the spots on Jupiter.[139] The Royal Society's *Philosophical Transactions* published an article on the Divini microscope in 1668.[140] King Charles II, John Evelyn, Sir Paul Neile, and William Brouncker looked at Saturn through a

[133] On Divini and the Royal Society, see Birch, *History of the Royal Society of London*, pp. 481, 482, 562, 564. On Newcastle's telescopes, see Hobbes, *The Correspondence*, (ed.) Malcolm, I, pp. 19–20 and note 10.

[134] HEH Ellesmere Mss. EL 11,123, Chaloner to Cheyne, 17 January 1671.

[135] Royal Society, LBC 4. 254, John Doddington to Henry Oldenburg, 23 January 1670–71. He suggests that "he send anything of bulk to M. Humph Sidney at Livorno for me, or leave it with Mr. George Ravenscraft a merchant well known in St. Helen's and he will convey it to me."

[136] Silvio A. Bedini, "Seventeenth Century Italian Compound Microscopes," *Physis*, 5 (1963), 383–97; Silvio A. Bedini, "Divini," in Charles Coulston Gillispie, *Dictionary of Scientific Biography*, 16 vols. (New York: Scribner, 1970–80), IV, p. 128.

[137] Henry King, *The History of the Telescope* (London: Charles Griffen and Co., 1955), pp. 58–65.

[138] *Ibid.*   [139] See, for instance, Birch. *History of the Royal Society of London*, II, pp. 97–98, 102–103.

[140] "A Description of a Microscope of a New Fashion," *Philosophical Transactions*, II.

44. The Greenwich Observatory, founded in 1672, demonstrates the contemporary interest in telescopes and astronomy. This engraving shows the long telescopes that Eustachio Divini and others began to make in the 1660s and 1670s.

A study in the house of John Flamsteed, Astronomer Royal, next to the Greenwich Observatory, from an engraving in *Historia Coelestis* (1712). Science Museum, London, Snark/Art Resource, NY ART 180595.

telescope in the Whitehall Privy Gardens.[141] The Royal Observatory in Paris was founded in 1670, followed in 1672 by the Royal Observatory at Greenwich.

Cheyne's order for a Divini telescope sheds new light on the international market in scientific instruments, technological improvement, and pricing. To begin with, Cheyne requested a remake of his old telescope, perhaps one that belonged to Newcastle. Cheyne had a telescope of perhaps 7 palms (five to seven feet) with three lenses which he now sought to have refashioned. Divini urged a different approach. Claiming that his technique for grinding the lenses had improved, he urged Cheyne to purchase a new telescope of 11 or 12 palms (seven to nine feet). The new telescope would cost at least 30 crowns but for that Chaloner promised to "procure you a little hand flask into the bargain."[142]

The fashion for extraordinarily long telescopes was in full swing and Divini was its greatest exponent.[143]

For your further information concerning the length and prices of the tubes which Sigr Eustachio makes I here insert the particulars; one palm and half, 2 palms, 3 & 4 palms with 4 glasses in each, 25 crowns; 5 and 6 palms, 30 crowns; 7 palms, 35 crowns; 8 palms, 40 crowns; 10 and 11 Palms, 45 crowns; 15 palms, 60 crowns; 18 palms, 70 crowns; 24 palms, 90 crowns; 35 palms, 150 crowns; 50 palms, 400 crowns; 65 palms, 500 crowns; 93 palms, 1000 crowns.[144]

At ninety-three palms, the longest telescope was almost seventy feet.

Science and humanities combined in Divini's practice. He tested his telescopes by looking at a quotation from the Italian poet Tasso.

One passage I must relate to you concerning the tube which upon the trial of it seemed extravagant. Eustachio put it out of his window towards an object which at a convenient distance he had placed on purpose to prove his tubes. The first verse of Tasso written upon a place which could neither be read nor the letters visible but with the tube were most clearly legible on which he and I more then once or twice fixed our eyes and by degrees lost the object so that through the tube we could see nothing but a mist or cloud: which I wondering at, he went to check nigh the window and perceived that the sun had heated the upper part of the tube which caused the humidity of the paper to retreat inward and so obfuscated the glass which being taken out we observed it all covered with such a humidity as if it

---

[141] Evelyn, *Diary*, pp. 285–86.

[142] HEH Ellesmere Mss. EL 11,123, Chaloner to Cheyne, 17 January 1671.

[143] "Divini," *Dictionary of Scientific Biography*, IV, p. 128. HEH Ellesmere Mss. EL 11,124, 11/22 March 1671.

[144] HEH Ellesmere Mss. EL 11,123, Chaloner to Cheyne, 17 January 1671.

had been breathed upon. Such accidents as these may be easily prevented if perceived and for want of experience may prove troublesome.[145]

Finally the telescope that Cheyne had ordered was finished. "Now sir concerning the tube of eleven palms with four glasses which Eustachius has had in hand a long time it is at last accomplished and very politely done and I hope much to your satisfaction."[146]

Charles Cheyne's personal aspirations for the new and the ingenious bore fruit in the monument and the tube. After a period of exile, Cheyne returned to London in the 1650s to construct a refined urban life despite his politics. While Lady Jane had doubts about the sociability of public spaces like Hyde Park, the increasing attraction of London for the gentry brought them visits from country friends and family. They shopped for an estate and settled in Chelsea.

Furthermore, Cheyne made the rebuilding of Chelsea Old Church and the creation of Lady Jane's funeral monument central to his own identity and a centerpiece of his expenditure. The Bernini funeral monument, inspired by cosmopolitan taste and shaped by conflicting demands of artists and patrons, served as a beacon to attract spectators to Chelsea. George Virtue proclaimed its importance in 1705 when he noted that "in Chelsea Church dedicated to St. Luke . . . is a fine monument, in a niche is represented the Lady Jane Cheyne, in white marble as big as the life lying on her right side, leaning on a Bible, this monument was done by the famous Signor Bernini an Italian and cost 500 pounds."[147]

At the same time, Divini's long telescope, "polite" and fashioned with Italian marbled paper, represented another sort of luxury good, one that signified Cheyne's expansive interests in science as a virtuoso. On one occasion John Evelyn noted, "I made my Lord Cheyne a visit at Chelsea and saw those ingenious waterworks invented by Mr. Winstanley wherein were some things very surprising and extraordinary."[148] The contemporary interest in the curious, the ingenious, and the foreign as part of a refined lifestyle led not only to imports such as the monument and the tube but also an increasing interest in understanding the processes by which such goods were made. The early work of the Royal Society centered in part in learning how to make luxury goods that ranged from marble and telescopes to porcelain, as we shall see in the next chapter.

---

[145] HEH Ellesmere Mss. EL 11,126, 3/13 June 1671.   [146] *Ibid.*
[147] George Vertue, *Note Books*, 6 vols. (Oxford: Walpole Society, Oxford University Press, 1930–55), I, p. 88.
[148] "Sir Charles Cheyne," in Henning (ed.), *The House of Commons, 1660–1690*, II, pp. 51–52.

CHAPTER 8

"The largest, best-built, and richest city in the world": The Royal Society, luxury manufactures, and aristocratic identity

While in France in the 1650s, John Evelyn began a commonplace book on the mechanical arts in which he described how to dye, enamel, and gild, make Venetian soap, create "a cement for cracked porcelain and other fragile ware," refresh marble and silver plate, and remove grease spots from hats. Before describing new tools for engraving, an art that he himself practiced and publicized, Evelyn, the virtuoso, turned to varnish.[1] Of Japanese varnish in particular, Evelyn wrote: "this I first communicated to the workmen, coach makers, cabinet makers, and others [in] 1653, since which it has been generally, and successfully used . . . but omitting to get a patent in due time, when his Majesty was restored, as indeed not thinking it worthwhile, others prevented me, to their greater enriching: Much good may it do them."[2]

Evelyn's was no casual boast. In 1657 his friend and traveling companion in exile, Thomas Henshaw, urged him on behalf of one Mr. Paston, "not to make the receipt of the gold varnish common, for he having received it of me and made experiment of it, did very much esteem and affect it; and was passionately troubled when the Plaster of Paris man at Charing Cross told him you had promised to teach it to him."[3] Demand for lacquer was widespread: when Asian supplies proved insufficient, new kinds were developed in

---

[1] BL Add. Mss. 78,340, Evelyn Papers, pt. 2, pp. 301ff, "Artes Illiberales et Mechanick." See Michael Hunter, "John Evelyn in the 1650s," in his *Science and the Shape of Orthodoxy: Intellectual Change in Late Seventeenth Century Britain* (Woodbridge, Suffolk: Boydell Press, 1995), pp. 67–98. Frances Harris suggests that Evelyn began the collection in France in the 1650s.

[2] BL Add. Mss. 78,340, Evelyn Papers, pt. 2, p. 306. To these comments Evelyn added, "see receipt 39, p. 310 and the best improved receipt 116, p. 322." See Charles J. Singer, A. Rupert Hall, and Eric J. Holmhyarde (eds.), *From the Renaissance to the Industrial Revolution, c.1500–c.1750*, vol. III of *A History of Technology*, 8 vols. (Oxford: Clarendon Press, 1955–78), p. 696. Evelyn provided several recipes for cement for broken glass and porcelain, one of which he claimed came from the Indies.

[3] Quoted in Hunter, "John Evelyn in the 1650s," p. 81.

Paris, London, Holland, and Germany.[4] In 1688 John Stalker and George Parker published *A Treatise of Japaning and Varnishing* which included pictures of "above an hundred distinct patterns for Japan-work, in imitation of the Indians, for tables, stands, frames, cabinets, boxes, etc."

Evelyn's commonplace book, based in part on his discussions with French chemists,[5] reflects the seventeenth-century focus on invention, improvement, and refinement through cultural borrowing that stretches from Francis Bacon and his contemporaries to Samuel Hartlib. His interests continue those put forward earlier in the century by the Crown and its projectors. Now, after years of exile in France, Italy, and the Low Countries, Evelyn brought home foreign materials and processes, many of them for producing luxury goods. These he contributed to the Royal Society's "History of Trades," an enterprise which the new scientific organization eagerly took up at its founding by drawing on the agenda put forward decades earlier by Sir Francis Bacon.[6]

In *The New Atlantis* of 1605, Francis Bacon had divided his utopian scientific enterprise called Salomon's House into those who did experiments, those who studied mechanics, and those who "sail into foreign countries ... who bring us the books and abstracts and patterns of experiments of all other parts."[7] The early Royal Society based its enterprise not only on its own experiments and reports but also on international networks of exchange created by its members and fostered by Henry Oldenburg, its indefatigable secretary.[8] The Royal Society constructed extensive sets of inquiries deliberately aimed at searching out new discoveries, new processes, and new wares, learning how to imitate or improve them, and publishing them so that they could be produced at home. Building on decades of interest in experiment and invention, the Royal Society offered a public forum in which its members – aristocrats, citizens, and artisans alike – demonstrated a new sensibility that combined the curious and the

---

[4] See *Titles of Patents of Invention Chronologically Arranged from March 2 1617 (14 James I) to October 1, 1852 (16 Victoriae)*, (ed.) Bennet Woodcroft (London: Eyre and Spottiswoode, Queen's Printing Office, 1854), p. 57, patent #293. Edward Hurd offered lacquering after the manner of Japan "to such a degree of curiosity and durableness as to any brought from India," 24 March 1692–93.

[5] See, for instance, BL Add. Mss. 78,316, Evelyn Papers, no. 42, N. Lefebvre to Evelyn, 3 June 1652, Paris.

[6] Kathleen Ochs, "The Failed Revolution in Applied Science: Studies of Industry by Members of the Royal Society of London, 1660–1688," (Ph.D. thesis, University of Toronto, 1981).

[7] Quoted in Ernan McMullin, "Openness and Secrecy in Science: Some Notes on Early History," *Science, Technology and Human Values*, 10 (1985), 20.

[8] Paula Findlen, "The Economy of Scientific Exchange in Early Modern Italy," in Bruce Moran (ed.), *Patronage and Institutions: Science, Technology, and Medicine at the European Courts, 1500–1750* (Woodbridge, Suffolk: Boydell Press, 1991), pp. 5–24.

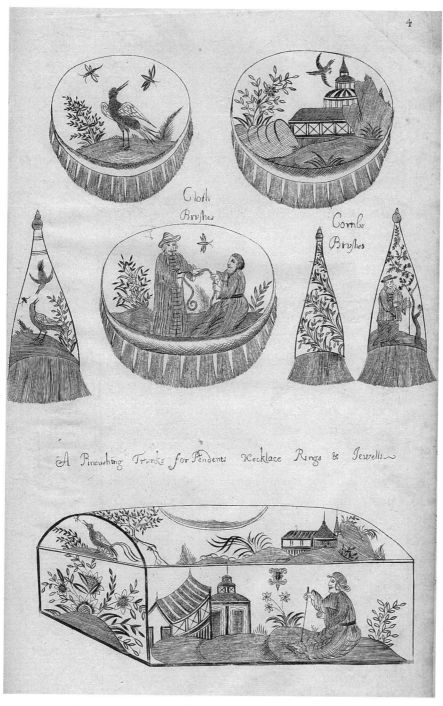

45. Interest in lacquer furniture, that began in the Jacobean period, reached print in the Restoration.
The Folger Shakespeare Library, 207232, pl. 4, John Stalker and George Parker, *A Treatise of Japaning and Varnishing*, (Oxford, 1688).

useful. The society supported the creation and refinement of new artifacts to support this mentality. Finally, faced with the effects of the Great Fire, the Royal Society enthusiastically drew on continental city planning to urge the rebuilding of London as the engine of the economy with retail commerce at its hub as well as the seat of a powerful monarch. The Royal Society did not, as some contemporaries and later historians point out, encompass all British scientific investigation and invention.[9] Nevertheless, its capacious interests in its early years supported innovation and cultural borrowing of all types. This chapter examines several strands connecting seventeenth-century science to the manufacture and consumption of luxury goods. Increased luxury consumption proved to be one unexpected outcome of the Bacon/Hartlib program. Science, its proponents and practice, sought technical improvement in manufactures, agriculture, and the arts; science created new desires and new identities for the well-to-do; science created new artifacts that underpinned this identity, and science supported new town planning and building.

SCIENCE AND LUXURY MANUFACTURES: THE HISTORY OF TRADES

Under Elizabeth I, efforts to diversify the economy and provide work led to the granting of many patents for import substitution.[10] As we have seen, James I took up the issues of manufacture and trade from the beginning of his reign. He stressed the importance of replacing imports and creating new exports to enhance trade and customs as well as providing work for the poor.[11] In 1605 Bacon described the work of Salomon's House on such ventures as "flying in the air" and "boats for going under water" as well as manufacturing "papers, linen, silks, tissues . . . [and] excellent dyes,"[12] all of which were proposed in early seventeenth-century patents.[13]

---

[9] Christine MacLeod, *Inventing the Industrial Revolution: The English Patent System, 1660–1800* (Cambridge: Cambridge University Press, 1982), pp. 201–206.

[10] Joan Thirsk, *Economic Policy and Projects: The Development of a Consumer Society in Early Modern England* (Oxford: Clarendon Press, 1978). The earliest patent, issued by Henry VI in 1449, provided the privilege of making colored glass for college chapels. Stephen Van Dulken, *British Patents of Invention, 1617–1977: A Guide for Researchers* (London: British Library, 1999), p. 2.

[11] See chapter 2 above.

[12] Quoted in Rose-Mary Sargent, "Bacon as an Advocate for Cooperative Scientific Research," in Markku Peltonen (ed.), *The Cambridge Companion to Bacon* (Cambridge: Cambridge University Press, 1996), p. 161.

[13] Oxford, Bodleian Library, Bankes Mss., cited in Linda Levy Peck, *Court Patronage and Corruption in Early Stuart England* (London: Unwin Hyman, 1990), pp. 140, 266–67. *Specifications of Patents, Old Series, 1617–1852* (London: Eyre and Spottiswoode, Queen's Printing Office, 1859).

Bacon spelt out an extensive project for a History of Trades in *Parasceve*, part of his *New Organum* in 1620.[14] Understanding the principles of a plethora of trades, he argued, would provide insight into the fundamental workings of nature. With intellectual roots that went back to sixteenth-century humanism and the vision of Juan Luis Vives, Bacon's History of Trades agenda combined natural philosophy and utility to advance science and to improve manufactures.[15] Amongst the trades to be investigated, he included the production of luxury goods such as gold, silk textiles, leather, pottery, glass, coaches, paper, clocks, watches, and mathematical instruments. In addition, Bacon called for histories of the building trades and architecture.[16]

As Attorney General, Bacon had to approve patents and he began a process of vetting that continued off and on throughout the century. Bacon himself fostered a circle of projectors including Nicholas Geffe who, as we have seen, argued for silk production in England in 1607. These initiatives did not go unchallenged. In 1621, when Parliament sought to impeach Bacon, the charges grew in part out of his approval of monopolies and projects. Nevertheless, when Parliament outlawed monopolies in 1624, it left room for projects that promoted new techniques and industries to produce goods usually imported from abroad.[17]

The growth in luxury consumption in the early seventeenth century fostered increasing demand for government protection of the property rights of inventors and suppliers. Throughout the 1630s, Attorney General John Bankes received projects for improvements in agriculture and manufacturing including several to produce luxury goods. The themes of Bacon's *Parasceve* continued in these Caroline proposals for new ways to make glass, gold and silver thread, madder for dying, Flanders tile, sword blades, paper, cases for looking glasses, and beaver hats. In 1637, for example, Edmund Gregory got a patent for "ornamenting fabrics with shells . . . sometimes mixed with silver and gilt" which on linen or taffeta "will be fit for hangings for beds and many other uses."[18] Bombarded with patent applications, Bankes referred them to committee. Based on their reports, he turned some down, a procedure usually credited to Attorney General Somers in the 1690s.[19]

[14] Walter E. Houghton, Jr. "The History of Trades: Its Relation to Seventeenth-Century Thought as Seen in Bacon, Petty, Evelyn, and Boyle," *Journal of the History of Ideas*, 2 (1941), 33–60; Ochs, "The Failed Revolution in Applied Science."

[15] Houghton, "History of Trades," 33–60.

[16] Ochs, "The Failed Revolution in Applied Science," pp. 249–50.

[17] *The Statutes of the Realm*, 11 vols. (London: G. Eyre and A. Strahan, 1810–22), IV, pt. 2, 1212–1214, 21 Jac., c. 3.

[18] *Specifications of Patents, Old Series, 1636–1676*, #101.

[19] See Oxford, Bodleian Library, Bankes Mss. Cf. Christine MacLeod, "The 1690s Patents Boom: Invention or Stock Jobbing?" *Economic History Review*, new series 39, (1986), 552.

In the late 1640s and 1650s, Samuel Hartlib and his circle sought universal improvement and included a History of Trades amongst their aims.[20] Thus, as we have seen, when William Petty returned from the continent in the late 1640s, he planned to make his fortune by "procuring privileges for public designs of universal use," and selling "secrets and artifices not sufficiently understood."[21] Petty placed these personal ambitions for profiting from inventions in the larger context of improvement. In 1648 he published a proposal to Hartlib for an institution modeled on Bacon's Salomon's House. Petty urged that all children, whatever their status, learn "some gentle manufacture in their minority."[22] Their education should include making watches and jewelry, printing on glass and etching, grinding glasses, crafting musical instruments, distilling perfume, refining metals, and making mariners' compasses, globes, and other magnetic devices, as well as studying architecture and gardening. Through such studies, Petty argued, the rich would become more industrious. Indeed, gentlemen would want to excel ordinary workmen. With an eye to the challenges of the Civil War, Petty argued that such knowledge would be a "great ornament in prosperity, so it will be a great refuge and stay in adversity."[23] Petty concluded that "we see that all countries where manufactures and trades flourish, as Holland, etc. become potent and rich. For how can it otherwise be?"[24] The state would benefit from increased customs, beggars would have work, and barren land would be made fruitful, all arguments set out in early Stuart patents.

The virtuosi, of whom Evelyn was the greatest, are often said to have been interested in the strange and the wonderful for their own sake.[25] For many, however, including Evelyn, the curious *included* the useful. In the 1650s and 1660s virtuosi and experimenters saw themselves as joined together in an enterprise for improvement. Thus, upon his return to England in the 1650s, Evelyn developed strong ties to the Hartlib circle.[26] His interests included art, architecture, books, botany, and anatomy. He

---

[20] Ochs, "The Failed Revolution in Applied Science"; Ochs, "The Royal Society of London's History of Trades Programme: An Early Episode in Applied Science," *Notes and Records of the Royal Society of London*, 39 (1985), 129–58. Houghton, "History of Trades," 33–60; Charles Webster, *The Great Instauration: Science, Medicine and Reform, 1626–1660* (London: Duckworth, 1975). Mark Greenglass, Michael Leslie, Timothy Raylor, *Samuel Hartlib and Universal Reformation: Studies in Intellectual Communication* (Cambridge: Cambridge University Press, 1994).

[21] BL Add. Mss. 72,891, Petty Papers, f. 8v.

[22] William Petty, *The Advice of W.P. to Mr. Samuel Hartlib for the Advancement of Some Particular Parts of Learning* (London, 1648), pp. 5–6.

[23] *Ibid.*, p. 6.   [24] *Ibid.*, pp. 22–23.

[25] Walter E. Houghton, Jr., "The English Virtuoso in the Seventeenth Century: Part I," *Journal of the History of Ideas* 3 (1942), 51–73; Part II, 190–219.

[26] Hunter, "John Evelyn in the 1650s," pp. 78, 83–84.

had seeds and plants from the Tradescant garden and tables of "veins, arteries, and nerves," taken from cadavers, which he had purchased in Padua in 1646.[27] In 1661 Evelyn drew up an extensive list of trades entitled "The History of Arts Illiberal and Mechanick." His categories, based on status and gender, drew attention to luxury goods and their place in polite society. He listed "1. Useful and purely mechanic; 2. Mean and less honourable; 3. Servile; 4. Rustical; 5. Female; 6. Polite and More Liberal; 7. Curious; 8. Exotic and very rare secrets."[28] Evelyn's emphasis on status difference was more vivid than Petty's, but both drew on Bacon's program. Both urged that children be educated in manufactures.[29]

While Evelyn's categories were encyclopaedic, he himself was most interested in the curious and exotic, which focused especially on refinement in contemporary decorative arts. Reflecting the expanding demand for a wide variety of luxury goods in the decorative arts, Evelyn included enameling, oil painting, miniatures, mosaics, fresco and grostesco, a type of Italian fresco; gilding and bronzing of frames, casting brass sculpture, "plastica," that is, molding or modeling; engraving, etching, and printing.[30] Drawing on seventeenth-century fashion, Evelyn wanted to learn how to make porcelain and inlay furniture in imitation of Venetian *pietra comessa*. Evelyn claimed that his "exotic and very rare secrets" drew on Chinese, Persian, and Indian sources as well as European practice. Like Bacon, he was interested in cloth, leather, glass, optics, and mathematical instruments such as "clocks, watches, dials, and all automata." He drew attention to all sorts of improvements in textiles including camlets, expensive Eastern fabrics that combined angora and silk or other fibers, stained Indian calico, cotton, leather, and plastron, that is, the breastplate used in fencing. He discussed improvements to moisture proof cloth as well as inventions to take spots out of cloth and silk.[31] Several of these, such as weatherproofing and the Turkish way of making camlets, had been Jacobean and Caroline projects.[32]

The Royal Society explicitly took up Bacon's program for a History of Trades as laid out in *Parasceve*.[33] Evelyn, Petty, and Christopher Merrett presented their own programs for the history of trades.[34] In 1664

---

[27] John Evelyn, *The Diary of John Evelyn*, (ed.) E. S. de Beer, 6 vols. (Oxford: Clarendon Press, 1955), III, p. 501.

[28] Royal Society, CP, iii (1), #1. BL Add. Mss. 78,339, "Exotic Arts and Trades," f. 2v. See A. Forbes Sieveking, "Evelyn's 'Circle of Mechanical Trades,'" *The Newcomen Society Transactions*, 4 (1923), 40–47.

[29] Petty, *The Advice of W. P. to Mr. Samuel Hartlib.*   [30] Royal Society CP, iii (1).

[31] *Ibid.*   [32] *Titles of Patents of Invention, Part I*, #17 (1620) and #40 (1637).

[33] Thomas Sprat, *History of the Royal Society* (London, 1667), pp. 257–59, lists the "histories of nature, arts, or works" that the society considered.

[34] See Petty's list of over 200 trades in BL Add. Mss. 72,891, 229r–230.

"Dr. Merrett brought in his catalogue of trades ... for the several fellows to look over it and to choose what trade they would give or procure the history of."[35] The Bishop of Exeter also claimed that he too had a printed catalog of the history of trades. The society asked him to compare it with Merrett's and make any necessary additions.[36]

In 1663 the Royal Society named eight committees in its major areas of interest.[37] Three committees, mechanics, the History of Trades, and agriculture, drew the greatest interest of members. The committee on mechanics, the largest of the eight, had sixty-eight members, including seventeen noblemen and twenty-two knights. The president of the society, Sir Robert Moray, as well as such active members as Robert Boyle, John Evelyn, Robert Hooke, Christopher Wren, and William Petty, were among them. Thirty-five members sat on the committee for the History of Trades. In contrast, the committee on astronomy and optics had only fifteen members.[38] While the committee structure was in place for only a few years the strength of interest in manufactures including luxury goods is clear.

Both the committees on mechanics and the History of Trades produced reports on production linked to the luxury trade. They explicitly aimed to improve these manufactures by consulting foreign and domestic producers. Thus the mechanics and trade committees issued papers on the cloth industry that included several on dyeing by William Petty;[39] felt-making by Robert Hooke;[40] watches, a new kind of candlestick, and jewelry based on the practices of Nuremberg.[41] John Beale reported in "The art of making parchment, vellum, glue, etc." that "Matthew Wills, alias Coxe of Yeavill, makes the best parchment in England. Challengeth the best in the world ... From himself I received these following instructions."[42] Beale also investigated silk.[43] Sir Edmund Bacon of Norfolk recounted how to

---

[35] Royal Society, Ms. Journal Book, 1664–67, p. 51, 19 October 1664.

[36] *Ibid.*, p. 80, 7 December 1664.

[37] Charles Wilson, *England's Apprenticeship, 1603–1763*, 2nd edn (London: Longman, 1984) takes note of these committees, p. 100.

[38] Royal Society, Ms. Journal Book, 1660–64, pp. 301–305, "A List of the several committees of the society." See Michael Hunter, "An Experiment in Corporate Enterprise: The Royal Society's Committees of 1663–1665 with a Transcript of the Surviving Minutes of their Meetings," in his *Establishing the New Science: The Experience of the Early Royal Society* (Woodbridge, Suffolk: Boydell Press, 1989), pp. 73–122.

[39] BL Add. Mss. 72,897, Petty Papers, includes Petty's papers on dyeing textiles, wool, pumping water, and tannery. Royal Society, CP, III, 5, 6.

[40] Royal Society, CP, XX, 96.   [41] Royal Society, CP, II (1) Mechanicks.

[42] Royal Society, CP, III, 18.

[43] Royal Society, *Philosophical Transactions*, II (1666), 424; Ochs, "The Failed Revolution in Applied Science," p. 89.

paint on agate.[44] President Moray proposed a history of masonry while Robert Boyle planned a history of tin.[45] Improvements in the making of glass, of central concern to the Jacobean regime and one of its most successful forms of import substitution, continued to interest both the Royal Society and contemporary English patentees. Christopher Merrett's translation of Antonio Neri's *Art of Glass* in 1662 referred to improvements in glassmaking over the previous two decades.[46] Robert Hooke received a parcel of silk from the East India Company. Examining the textiles under the microscope he proposed the production of artificial silk.[47]

The *Philosophical Transactions*, edited by Oldenburg, published papers that also addressed the History of Trades and luxury production.[48] Between 1660 and 1670, papers appeared on such topics as varnishes, masonry, hats, paper, leather, tapestry, parchment, enamelling, engraving, and making red glass among others.[49] The *Philosophical Transactions* displayed a continuing interest in the manufacture of porcelain which, as we have seen, had been imported as early as the 1600s. Oldenburg presented "An intimation of a way found in Europe to make China dishes." He reported that a Parisian had discovered an Italian in Milan with "the secret of making as good porcelain as is made in China itself and transparent . . . addith that he had seen him make some. This as it deserves, so it will be further inquired after, if God permit."[50] Oldenburg also published reports on leather working from around the world including New France, Russia, India, and Turkey.[51] The purpose of these papers and reports was not only to understand the principles underlying nature but also to enhance English manufactures.

Evelyn's commonplace book and other collections served as the basis for his later reports to the Royal Society on practical ways to engrave and make marbled paper accompanied by the tools and processes necessary to

[44] Royal Society, CP, III, 41.

[45] Ochs, "The Failed Revolution in Applied Science," pp. 21, 46; Robert Boyle, "Memoirs for the Natural History of Tin," in Michael Hunter and Edward B. Davies (eds.), *The Works of Robert Boyle*, 14 vols. (London: Pickering and Chatto, 2000), XIV, pp. 135–37.

[46] Antonio Neri, *The Art of Glass . . . translated into English, with some observations on the author; whereunto is added an account of the glass drops made by the Royal Society, Meeting at Gresham College*, trans. by Christopher Merrett (London, 1662).

[47] Maria Zytaruk, "Robert Hooke's 'Pretty Objects': Consumerism, Empire and the Micrographia," in Michael Cooper and Michael Hunter (eds.), *Hooke 2003* (London: Royal Society, 2003), p. 196.

[48] Ochs, "The Failed Revolution in Applied Science," pp. 38–39.

[49] *Ibid.*, pp. 46–47. Evelyn annotated several papers in his own copy of the Royal Society's *Philosophical Transactions* now at the British Library.

[50] Royal Society, *Philosophical Transactions*, I, p. 127.

[51] Ochs, "The Failed Revolution in Applied Science," p. 209.

produce them. He had published *Sculptura* in 1661, a translation of the work of Abraham Bosse, the great French engraver with whom he had been in correspondence in the 1650s.[52] Evelyn then presented a detailed report to the Royal Society on "the great convenience . . . of having a rolling press to be able to accomplish that new way of engraving so lately described and celebrated and to pursue (as far as my talent reaches) that part of the History of Trades promoted by our illustrious assembly."[53] He suggested to the Royal Society "A book of the tools, models, and all the utensils pertaining to the several trades etc. designed in perspective and exactly proportioned."[54] Robert Hooke, the director of the Society's experiments and a strong proponent of the History of Trades, also presented the Society with illustrations of tools and manufacturing processes.[55]

Contemporary patents mirrored the increasing range of luxury goods in Restoration England. Although eighteen patents were granted during the Interregnum, they were not recognized at the Restoration because they had not received the Great Seal.[56] When the patent system officially resumed in 1660, luxury goods continued to be an important focus as they had been since the Jacobean period. In 1660 Charles Howard, grandson of the Earl of Arundel and, later, a leading member of the Royal Society, patented a new way to tan leather.[57] Martin Clifford and Thomas Poulden claimed a new way of making crystal glasses "as good if not better than any [that] comes from Venice." Thomas Tilson, a merchant, promised to make both crystal and looking glasses. Francis Smethick presented a new invention to grind optic glasses.[58] Sir Philip Howard and Francis Wallson received patents for graving, garnishing, and coloring of ships and other vessels, and for the coloring of wood, iron, stone, and plaster from certain grain growing in England.[59]

Restoration patents may not be an index of all contemporary inventions but they demonstrate the continuation of themes articulated in earlier

---

[52] BL Add. Mss. 78,316, Evelyn Papers, no. 57, Abraham Bosse to John Evelyn, Paris.

[53] Royal Society, CP, III (1), 2, 14 May 1662.

[54] Royal Society, CP, III (1), 1, Evelyn, 16 January 1660–1661.

[55] Royal Society, CP, XX, 96; Ochs, "The Failed Revolution in Applied Science," pp. 12, 13, 209, 252.

[56] Stephen Van Dulken, *British Patents of Invention, 1617–1977* (London: British Library, 1999), p. 2.

[57] *Titles of Patents of Invention, Part I*, #130, 27 October 1661.

[58] *Ibid.*, pp. 29–33, #134, Martin Clifford and Thomas Poulden for making crystal glasses; #140, Thomas Tilson, merchant, making of crystal glasses and looking glasses, 19 October 1663; #141, 4 February 1664, Francis Lord Willoughby and Lawrence Hyde, one Davie de Meurato has found a new way of making and framing sugar mills; #147, 16 February 1666, Charles Hildeyerde, making blue paper used by sugar bakers; #149, 14 May 1667, Francis Smethick, new invention to grind optic glasses in figures that are not spherical.

[59] *Ibid.*, #158, 2 March 1669.

projects and paralleled the Royal Society's efforts to promote new manufacturing processes including luxury industries.[60] Indeed, both Charles II
and, later, Queen Anne issued orders that the Royal Society vet *all* patents,
a function the French Academy of Science undertook beginning in the
1690s. Although the Royal Society apparently did not undertake this task,[61]
it took a strong interest in technical progress. Catherine MacLeod has
argued of the 1690s that "technical progress seems to have been as far from
official minds as it was from the consciousness of all but a handful of
economic writers at this time," but the language of early Stuart projects and
the intense interest of the Royal Society in the 1660s suggests otherwise.[62]

Robert Merton, A. R. Hall, and Michael Hunter have debated the
relative importance of technology and utility in the proceedings of the
early Royal Society. Arguing for the essential connections between
puritanism, technology, and science, Merton linked early Royal Society
papers and experiments to contemporary patents. Drawing on the work of
J. U. Nef, who sought to demonstrate a sixteenth-century industrial revolution, Merton argued that the Royal Society showed a particular interest in
mining and manufacturing, reflecting the interests of its middle-class
members.[63] In contrast, Hall argued that scientific innovation went back
to the fifteenth century and could not therefore be connected with
Protestantism.[64] Hunter countered the Merton thesis first, by demonstrating the variety of interests from agriculture to zoology displayed by the
early Royal Society and, secondly, by pointing out, as had Lotte and Glenn
Mulligan, that large numbers of its members were Anglican aristocrats and
officeholders, not members of a puritan bourgeoisie.[65] In contrast to the
earlier views of Christopher Hill, Robert Merton, and Charles Webster,
Hunter argues that most of the members of the Royal Society from 1660 to
1700, professional and landed, were associated with government and the
court.[66] Approaching the issue from another direction, Catherine
MacLeod argues that the Royal Society, while in favor of invention, was

---

[60] Royal Society, *Philosophical Transactions*, I, *passim* and chapter 2 above.
[61] See Hunter, *Establishing the New Science.*   [62] MacLeod, "The 1690s Patent Boom," 554.
[63] Robert K. Merton, *Science, Technology and Society in Seventeenth-Century England* (New York:
H. Fertig, 1970), p. 142.
[64] A. Rupert Hall, "Merton Revisited," *History of Science*, 2 (1963), 1–16.
[65] Lotte Mulligan points out the connections to Anglicanism and the court: "Civil War Politics,
Religion and the Royal Society," *Past and Present*, 59 (1973), 92–116.
[66] See Hunter, "Reconstructing Restoration Science," in *Establishing the New Science*, pp. 339–55; Lotte
Mulligan and Glenn Mulligan, "Reconstructing Restoration Science: Styles of Leadership and
Social Composition of the Early Royal Society," *Social Studies of Science* 11 (1981), 327–64.

of two minds about the patent system.[67] As we have seen, Evelyn did not get a patent for his varnish, preferring to argue, at times, as did many others, that science and improvement should be open for the benefit of the public. MacLeod suggests that invention developed in seventeenth- and eighteenth-century England outside of the patent system and minimizes the importance of the Royal Society to contemporary patents.[68] As a result, historians appear to have abandoned the connection between the History of Trades and patents.

Nevertheless, continuing interest in new manufactures throughout the seventeenth century and demand for luxury goods did find reflection in contemporary patents and in the Royal Society's activities. In fact, Royal Society reports on mining sat next to new ways of making luxury goods. Patentees, twenty of them members of the Royal Society, did not just claim privileges for engines and cauldrons but luxury goods such as coaches and clocks. The Royal Society itself put together a joint patent in the name of Abraham Hill, one of its members, in 1665. The Letters Patent, which describe Hill as "Fellow of the Royal Society of London for the improving of natural knowledge," granted patents for multiple inventions that included new carriages and coaches, new guns, a powder horn, an engine to break and dress hemp, and a watch to find the longitude.[69]

Eighteenth-century manufactures grew out of these seventeenth-century projects and investigations. Maxine Berg has listed patents for new products, ornamenting, and finishing in the United Kingdom from 1627 to 1825 that show growth across two centuries.[70] Many deal with luxury goods that were, as we have seen, of great interest to early Stuart patentees and the Royal Society. These include glass and porcelain, printing and ornamenting cloth, embossing and gilding, engraving and etching, papier-mâché and japanned ware, ornaments for buildings, coaches, painting, and varnishes, printing, and stamping paper. While most inventors did not take out patents, those who did often specified that they were imitating foreign processes.[71] Berg stresses the important role of the Society for the Encouragement of Arts, Manufactures, and Commerce, founded in 1754, in underwriting and promoting new forms of eighteenth-century manufacturing.[72] But, because Berg's statistics are not broken down for the seventeenth century, they don't indicate how many luxury products were

---

[67] MacLeod, *Inventing the Industrial Revolution*, pp. 185–90.   [68] *Ibid.*

[69] *Titles of Patents of Invention, Part I*, #143, March 1665.

[70] Maxine Berg, "The Idea of Modern Luxury and the Invention of British Consumer Goods," paper presented at the North American Conference on British Studies, Toronto, 3 November 2001.

[71] *Ibid.*   [72] *Ibid.*

already patented before the eighteenth century.[73] Because patent specifications are not available before the early eighteenth century, the nature of seventeenth-century innovation remains hidden. It is clear, however, that many eighteenth-century patents promoted those luxury goods and processes that were already desired in the early seventeenth century, appropriated from abroad over the course of the century, patented under the early Stuarts, and investigated by the Royal Society in the 1660s and 1670s. Indeed, if we look at the manufactures that the Society of Arts, Manufactures, and Commerce promoted between 1754 and 1756, they include cobalt to color glass; madder for dyeing; leather; tinning; American silk cultivation; papermaking, and crucibeles.[74] As we have seen, all found important places on the agenda of seventeenth-century patentees and the Royal Society's History of Trades.

Moreover, those luxury goods discussed in Jacobean patents and Royal Society reports appeared in the domestic environment before the turn of the eighteenth century. Most consumption studies begin with the Restoration at the earliest. Lorna Weatherill demonstrates that ownership of luxury goods such as china, clocks, and looking glasses grew from 1675 to 1725 among men and women of differing status groups. By 1675 these goods had already appeared in probate inventories of the lower gentry, professionals, and tradesmen and showed significant growth by 1725. While pewter and silver objects were widespread, china was owned by fewer but ownership was growing fast.[75] Weatherill suggests "the late seventeenth and early eighteenth centuries were marked by brisk changes, some based on industrial expansion, others on increasing imports of consumer items."[76] Wedgwood may have finally learned the secrets of porcelain manufacture, but the early Stuarts and Oldenburg and his Royal Society colleagues took leading roles in the search.

---

[73] *Ibid.*

[74] D. G. C. Allan and John L. Abbott (eds.), *The Virtuoso Tribe of Arts and Sciences: Studies in the Eighteenth-Century Work and Membership of the London Society of Arts* (Athens and London: University of Georgia Press, 1992), xv–xvi.

[75] Lorna Weatherill, *Consumer Behaviour and Material Culture in Britain 1660–1760*, 2nd edn (London: Routledge, 1996), pp. 168, 44. She points out that, by 1725, 51% of the lesser gentry had clocks, 62% looking glasses, and 33% pictures. Amongst those in trades of high status, clergy and professions, 34% had clocks, 62% looking glasses, and 35% pictures while amongst tradesmen whose trades were unknown, 29% had clocks, 57% looking glasses, and 32% pictures. In London inventories generally 29% had clocks, 74% looking glasses, and 37% pictures.

[76] *Ibid.*, pp. 25–28.

FROM THE COLLECTOR TO THE SCIENTIST

In its early years the Royal Society included virtuosi and collectors of the previous generation and the experimenters from Oxford and Gresham College. Counter-Reformation Catholics joined latitudinarians in the Royal Society. The new science supported new forms of luxury consumption by expanding gentlemen's interests to include scientific investigation, improvement in manufactures and agriculture, and application of technology, much as William Petty had hoped. New luxury goods, such as telescopes and microscopes, historical artifacts, such as mummies, and exotic imports from the East and West Indies, such as tea, cacao, and exotic plants, became topics for investigation. Innovations in collecting ascribed to Sir Hans Sloane in the late seventeenth and early eighteenth centuries were already underway.[77] Thomas Sprat's *The History of the Royal Society*, an institution whose charter was then only a few years old, claimed scientific innovation for Charles II and a constellation of aristocrats. One of Oldenburg's correspondents wrote,

Like a second Apollo the king himself presides as supreme moderator and governor of this band of stars, among whom are to be found the sons of kings, princes, dukes, magnates, landowners, counts, barons, great patrons of learned men, and a host of men of all orders distinguished for their learning and wisdom.[78]

Members of the nobility and gentry were positively encouraged to join the Royal Society, which admitted privy councillors and those above the rank of baron without review.[79] Their names – and Sprat's *History of the Royal Society*[80] – were used to propagandize for the new institution. Together with Oxford dons, London doctors, City merchants and artisans, English aristocrats took up the interest in the new science.

Some noblemen were already interested in science. Elizabethan circles around John Dee and, later, the Earl of Northumberland, had become

---

[77] British Museum, *Enlightenment Discovering the World in the Eighteenth Century*, ed. Kim Sloan, with Andrew Burnett (London: British Museum Press, 2003).

[78] Stiernhielm to Henry Oldenburg, 17 May 1670. Quoted in Michael Hunter, *The Royal Society and its Fellows, 1660–1700: The Morphology of an Early Scientific Institution*, (Chalfont St. Giles, Bucks: British Society for the History of Science, 1982), p. 10.

[79] Hunter, *The Royal Society and its Fellows*, pp. 9–10. Hunter emphasizes that the Royal Society was based in London, p. 6. Citing Alban Thomas, *A List of the Royal Society of London . . . with the places of abode of most of its members* (1718), Hunter points out that of 133 addresses listed only 19 had "addresses further outside London than Kensington, Clapham or Hackney," p. 8.

[80] *Ibid.*

interested in experimental science as well as alchemy.[81] Northumberland's circle, including Thomas Harriott who viewed the moon through a telescope in 1609, continued its scientific studies even while the earl spent years in prison as a conspirator in the Gunpowder Plot of 1605.[82] The Cavendishes, William and Charles, engaged in scientific activity from the 1630s.[83] Later, as part of the Grand Tour, English travelers visited Athanasius Kircher's Museum in Rome, acquired books by members of the famous Florentine scientific academy, the Academia dei Lincei, and bought telescopes, as we have seen, from the great Roman telescope makers, Eustachio Divini and Giuseppe Campani.[84] When Evelyn was given a stone from Cairo filled with hieroglyphics in 1645, he copied them and sent them to Thomas Henshaw to give to Kircher.[85] Evelyn bought the "principal veins and arteries, and nerves" of a man excised during autopsy in Padua which he displayed on four large tables and later presented to the Royal Society.[86] Others, like Martin Lister and Sir Philip Skippon, members of the Royal Society, went to France and Germany in the second half of the century, where they studied medicine and copied new kinds of machinery.[87]

Steven Shapin calls Robert Boyle "at once the most noble and the most intellectually central of the early Royal Society's active fellowship."[88] But he questions the scientific interest of other noblemen and gentlemen arguing that "the new science secured little legitimacy within seventeenth- or eighteenth-century gentlemanly society," a point Houghton made too in his pioneering work on the virtuosi.[89] Drawing on seventeenth- and eighteenth-century prescriptive literature, Shapin suggests that its efforts to create a new role of scholar and gentleman failed. He does note that the Arundel circle sponsored the "virtuosity" of seventeenth-century gentlemen, and that the Royal Society called itself "a great assembly of gentlemen," but

[81] William Sherman, *John Dee: The Politics of Reading and Writing in the English Renaissance* (Amherst: University of Massachusetts Press, 1995).

[82] Gordon Batho, "The Wizard Earl of Northumberland: An Elizabethan Scholar-Nobleman," *Historian*, 75 (2002), 19–23.

[83] Stephen Clucas, "The Atomism of the Cavendish Circle: A Reappraisal," *Seventeenth Century*, 9 (1994), 247–73.

[84] Evelyn visited Kircher while in Rome, 8 November 1644, *Diary and Correspondence of John Evelyn*, ed. William Bray (London: H. G. Bohn, 1859–62).

[85] Houghton, "The English Virtuoso in the Seventeenth Century," Part II, 207n.

[86] Evelyn's copy of Nehemiah Grew's *Musaeum Regalis Societatis* (London, 1681).

[87] On Sir Philip Skippon and Martin Lister, see *DNB* and also John Stoye, *English Travellers Abroad, 1604–1667: Their Influence in English Society and Politics* (New Haven: Yale University Press, 1989).

[88] Steven Shapin, "'A Scholar and A Gentleman': The Problematic Identity of the Scientific Practitioner in Early Modern England," *History of Science*, 29 (1991), 279–327.

[89] *Ibid.*, 291–92. See Houghton, "The English Virtuoso in the Seventeenth Century," Part I, 51–73; Part II, 190–219.

argues that the scientist later became identified with the pedant in satirical literature.[90] In contrast, I want to emphasize that in practice, aristocratic members sought to incorporate their interest in art, books, and curiosities into the agenda of the new Royal Society and many, like Sir Hans Sloane in later decades, took up science with enthusiasm.[91]

For example, Henry and Charles Howard, whose activities have been little noticed, provided crucial support to the fledgling organization. Henry Howard, the grandson of the Earl of Arundel, spent years in exile in Italy and the Low Countries. His family returned to England in the 1650s and at the Restoration began to enjoy some of the prominence it had lost in the preceding twenty years. From its outset Henry and his brother Charles were enthusiastic members of the Royal Society. Henry Howard, not Boyle, was the highest ranking nobleman in the society in 1677, when he became Duke of Norfolk, although by that time he was inactive. His brother Charles, a founding member, chaired its most active committee, the Agriculture Committee, from the beginning of the Society.[92] Together, the Howards' relationship with the Royal Society helped to connect the new institution with future agricultural improvement, and networks of exchange in Europe, the New World, Africa, and India as well as with early seventeenth-century patterns of collecting.

Networks of exchange and transmission of information and artifacts were key to the development of the new science. Henry Howard arranged important continental contacts for the new society and sent back rarities for the Society's new repository from his diplomatic travels. In 1666 Henry Oldenburg, who had long-standing relations with the Howard family,[93] flattered Howard's "own happy genius" to ask "if by your interest we might obtain some philosophical correspondents in the chief cities of Italy, and particularly at Florence, Pisa, Bologna, Milan, Venice, Naples, Rome, Riccio, Cassini, Gottignies, Fabri, Redi, Borelli, Settala, Campani are no inconsiderable persons for such a commerce; and they may be assured, that I shall make it a part of my study to make some return."[94] Oldenburg's list

[90] Shapin, "A Scholar and A Gentleman," 296.

[91] Arthur MacGregor, *Sir Hans Sloane: Collector, Scientist, Antiquary, Founding Father of the British Museum* (London: British Museum Press, 1994).

[92] Hunter, "An Experiment in Corporate Enterprise," pp. 73–122.

[93] Oldenburg had written earlier, in 1655, to a third Arundel grandson, Philip Thomas, who had taken orders as a Dominican Friar. Oldenburg tried to convince him to leave the Roman Catholic Church. Philip was then in England raising money for a Dominican College on the continent. He returned after the Restoration, joined the household of Catherine of Braganza, wife of Charles II, and was made a Cardinal in 1675.

[94] Henry Oldenburg, *The Correspondence of Henry Oldenburg*, ed., A. Rupert Hall and Marie Boas Hall, 10 vols. (Madison: University of Wisconsin Press, 1965–75), III, pp. 200–201.

included Italian writers on geometry (Ricci), astronomers (Cassini), instrument makers and engineers (Campani and Settala), Jesuit writers on math, medicine, and astronomy (Fabri and Gottignies), and members of the Florentine academy (Borelli and Redi).[95]

In June 1667 Oldenburg wrote to Manfred Settala, the well-known engineer who had developed "burning mirrors," whom he asked Howard to contact, "that if anything out of the way, philosophically speaking, becomes known to you or to other learned men in your noble city and its neighbourhood, you will be so kind as to impart it to us." He added in a postscript "As your merits, distinguished Sir, reported to me by others, were strongly confirmed by the kindness of the Hon. Henry Howard of Norfolk, a high-ranking member of the Royal Society, if the answers with which you gratify me in the future are now addressed to Arundel House in London (where the Hon. Mr. Howard lives) they will certainly be well looked after."[96]

Oldenburg made other requests of Howard that reflect contemporary interests in luxury materials and processes. In July 1667 Oldenburg wrote to Howard, "Methinks, it were worth knowing whether there are not now some persons in Italy, that know the old Roman way of plastering and the art of tempering tools to cut porphyry (the hardest of marbles). There is a certain artificial marble, adorning the Elector of Bavaria's whole palace at Munchen, which we should be glad to learn the preparation of."[97] The Royal Society carried out an experiment to color marble based on a recipe by Athanasius Kircher, on 4 December 1665.[98] In response, Evelyn noted that "Mr. Bird of Oxford had long since discovered how to do this," and mentioned a piece he had seen or heard of "a lively red" done by Bird.[99] In 1668 Richard Calthorp, a gentleman, received a patent for a new way of sawing and polishing of marble "being his own invention and never before

---

[95] *Ibid.*

[96] *Ibid.*, pp. 440–41. "It is intended that its members be learned men from all quarters who strive to promote the useful sciences and arts, not by speculation alone, but on the sure foundation of observation and experiment … I understand that you are engaged upon successful study of the secrets of nature and art … cooperation and friendliness between learned men greatly foster and illuminate the liberal arts and our knowledge of things … through the experimental investigation of things in nature the foundations of philosophy may be rendered more solid – the old ones being subjected to criticism and equally fruitful new ones made publicly known," pp. 441n4, 201n8.

[97] *Ibid.*, p. 200.

[98] "An Experiment of a Way of Preparing a Liquor, That Shall Sink Into, and Colour the Whole Body of Marble, Causing a Picture, Drawn on a Surface to Appear Also in the Inmost Parts of the Stone," *Philosophical Transactions*, I, 125–27, 4 December 1665.

[99] Royal Society, *Philosophical Transactions*, I, pp. 125–27. Evelyn's copy now at the British Library. Evelyn also included a receipt for cutting porphyry in his commonplace book, BL Add. Mss. 78,340, p. 314, #63.

used in England" that would enable the use of domestic quarries such as those in Devon.[100]

When the Royal Society met on 9 May 1666, it displayed its wide-ranging interests. Members saw experiments by Robert Hooke, heard reports on the competing Italian telescope makers, Eustachio Divini and Giuseppe Campani, as to whose telescope was used to discover the spots on Jupiter; and discussed magnetism. In addition, Charles Howard "gave in a relation from his brother at Vienna, wherein the emperor's historio-grapher, Petrus Lambecius, J. U. D. desires to correspond with the society." Howard presented a book by Lambecius with an "account of the emperor's library . . . consisting of about eighty thousand books, manuscripts, and printed; whereof a part are several libraries, as that of Tycho Brahe, Kepler, Maestlinus, and the relics of the Royal Hungarian library of Buda, etc., consisting besides of near sixteen thousand medals; a collection of curiosities both of nature and art."[101]

Lambeck published eight volumes on the Imperial Library.[102] He probably sent the Royal Society the first or second volume in which he described the library, how he had reorganized it, and the court's art and coin collections.[103] Lambeck also described his other work, *Historia Litteraria*, of 1659, which gave "an account of the rise, progress, fall, and restoration of languages, sciences, and arts, from the beginning of the world to this age; as also of the men famous for the increasing and promoting of knowledge."[104] In reply, Oldenburg laid out the aims of "the Royal Scientific Society founded by his Britannic Majesty in this city" as "the development of both the sciences and the useful arts."[105]

At the same meeting, the members asked Charles Howard to remind his brother Henry that he had promised to present a mummy to the society's repository.[106] The mummy, when it was duly received, enjoyed pride of place in the catalog of the Royal Society's collections published in 1681. The description of this exotic object showed deference to the donor and described the winding sheets with values drawn from the contemporary

---

[100] *Specifications of Patents, Old Series, 1636–1676*, #152, 29 February 1668.
[101] Royal Society, Ms. Journal Book, 1664–67, p. 197, 9 May 1666.
[102] *Commentarium de Augustissima Bibliotheca Caesarea Vindobonensi*, 8 vols. (Vienna, 1665–79); *La Grande Encyclopédie*, 60 vols. (Paris: Larousse, 1971–76) 21, 818.
[103] Ernst Trenkler, "Peter Lambeck und seine 'Commentarii'," *Biblos*, 26 (1977), 164–84.
[104] Royal Society, Ms. Journal Book, 1664–67, pp. 197–98, 9 May 1666. *Philosophical Transactions*, II, 575–76, 9 December 1667.
[105] Oldenburg, *Correspondence*, III, p. 120.
[106] Thomas Birch, *The History of the Royal Society of London for Improving of Natural Knowledge, From its First Rise*, 4 vols. (London, A. Millar, 1760), II, pp. 88–89.

cloth trade: "an Aegyptian mummy given by the illustrious Prince Henry, Duke of Norfolk. It is an entire one taken out of the royal pyramids. In length five feet and ½ defended with several linen covers, all woven like ordinary flaxen cloth. But by the spinning, distinguished into three kinds. The utmost is like flaxen cloth of two shillings an ell; the inmost, of half a crown; the middlemost, of three shillings."[107]

After the Great Fire in 1666, Henry Howard provided the Royal Society with a home in Arundel House on the Strand for seven years from January 1666/1667 to 1673.[108] On 1 October 1667, Oldenburg wrote to Boyle that

> summons are this very day sent about for the re-assembling of our Society on Thursday next [3 October] in Arundel House. And though the Council expressed to Mr. Howard their tenderness and scruple of continuing their meetings there, seeing his sons are come home, who need many rooms with their attendants; yet is the Society urged by that noble person to go on there as they have begun, alleging it to be an honour and reputation to him, to do so. Some of us are so sanguine, as to believe, we shall have a College of our own created before the end of next summer.[109]

In November 1667, Oldenburg wrote to Boyle that they had held their largest meeting ever at Arundel House. "On Saturday last we had a very numerous meeting at Arundel House, never so great an one before; we being about threescore, and of them about 50 at dinner, for which his Majesty sent in a doe, as Mr. Howard another."[110]

The Royal Society met amidst reminders of Arundel's collections. Sprat celebrated this evocative setting and the Society's mission. "In Arundel House there is a perfect representation, what the real philosophy ought to be: as there we behold the new inventions to flourish among the marbles, and images of the dead: so the present arts that are now rising, should not aim at the destruction of those that are past, but be content to thrive in their company."[111]

Indeed, the Royal Society planned to build its new home on the grounds of Arundel House.[112] Christopher Wren designed a lavish version of Salomon's House. When that proved too expensive, the Royal Society turned to Robert Hooke. Henry Howard himself presented his own design. None was ever built. But Michael Hunter suggests that had the

---

[107] Nehemiah Grew, *Musaeum Regalis Societatis* (London, 1681), B.

[108] On Arundel House see Birch, *History of the Royal Society of London*, II, pp. 73, 113–14, 345, 346, 351, 371, 377–78, 480.

[109] Oldenburg, *Correspondence*, III, p. 505.   [110] *Ibid.*, IV, p. 5, 3 December 1667.

[111] Sprat, *History of the Royal Society*, p. 253.

[112] Michael Hunter, "A College for the Royal Society," in *Establishing the New Science*, pp. 156–84.

proposed college at Arundel House been realized, London would have had "a purpose-built baroque scientific research institute south of the Strand."[113]

Because Howard was a Roman Catholic he could not take part fully in the political life of Charles II's Britain. He could, however, bring the grandeur of the old nobility to diplomatic missions. In this capacity, Howard established connections for the Royal Society in central Europe, Turkey, and Morocco as well as Italy and cemented ties with the Levant and East India Companies. As we have seen, in 1664–65 he accompanied Lord Leslie, Chief Minister to the Holy Roman Emperor, to Adrianople and Constantinople to wait on Sultan Mahomet IV.[114] John Burbury, Howard's secretary, later described the embassy in *A Relation of a Journey of the Right Honourable my Lord Henry Howard* (London, 1671).[115]

On this embassy Howard met Paul Rycaut, soon to be consul to the Levant Company and ambassador to Turkey with whom he established a warm relationship and who provided him with rarities from Asia. In 1666 Howard nominated Rycaut to membership in the Royal Society.[116] When, in February 1666–67, Howard brought a Society meeting "a stone taken out of the dead-sea, burning and stinking," members desired him to procure more.[117] Rycaut responded from Deal where he was about to take ship. Expressing his pleasure at receiving "more fresh commands from the Royal Society" he promised to send more of the stones.[118]

Howard's grandfather Arundel had sought antiquities through Sir Thomas Roe, ambassador to Constantinople. Much as Roe had written to Arundel, Rycaut reported to Howard that "antiquities and paintings are very rarely to be found in the Eastern parts of the world where the barbarism of

---

[113] *Ibid.*, pp. 171–72, 179. The first mention of Howard's offer of Arundel House to the Society came in a letter of 25 September 1666 from Oldenburg to Boyle. Referring to a meeting at Gresham College, he wrote: "which perhaps will be the last meeting in that place, the City striving hard to get that College totally into their hands for this time of distress: which if they obtain, the Society are provided with another place to meet in, to wit, in Arundel-house by the generosity of Mr. Howard." In February, 1666/67 Colepresse wrote to Oldenburg, "I can not but congratulate the beneficence of Mr. Howard towards the Royal Society." When the Council met on 12 September it ordered the officers to find another meeting place. On 19 September "the Council agreed to meet in Arundel House on the invitation of Charles Howard." Oldenburg, *Correspondence* III, pp. 233, 333, 227n3.

[114] John Martin Robinson, *The Dukes of Norfolk: A Quincentennial History* (Oxford: Oxford University Press, 1982), p. 125.

[115] John Burbury, gent., *A Relation of a Journey of The Right Honourable My Lord Henry Howard* (London, 1671).

[116] Royal Society, Sackler Archive, Rycaut; Sonia Anderson, *An English Consul in Turkey: Paul Rycaut at Smyrna, 1667–1668* (Oxford: Clarendon Press, 1989).

[117] Birch, *History of the Royal Society of London*, II, p. 149. Quoted in Oldenburg *Correspondence*, III, pp. 343–44 and note.

[118] Oldenburg, *Correspondence*, III, p. 343, Rycaut to Oldenburg.

the Turks could destroy them, yet where I make my journeys, if any of that nature occurred, I shall not only give you a description of them, but also a rude copy to communicate to the Royal Society."[119] Rycaut described the Turks' favorable treatment of merchants with an image later made famous by Bernard Mandeville. In his very influential work of 1666, *The Present State of the Ottoman Empire*, Rycaut wrote "they commonly abstain from the spoil and plunder of merchants' estates ... and as their own comparison is like to the labourious bee which brings honey to the hive, and is innocent, industrious, and profitable; and therefore an object of their compassion and defence."[120] Rycaut sent Howard his own manuscript on the pseudo messiah Sabbatai Zevi. Howard arranged to have Evelyn publish it as part of the very popular *History of the Three Late Famous Imposters* in 1669.[121]

As we have seen, in 1669 Howard undertook a year-long mission to Tangier for Charles II to negotiate a commercial treaty with the Emperor of Morocco.[122] The next year, he presented a paper to the Royal Society responding to its long list of questions about Africa, including its natural history, inhabitants, and gold.[123] In 1676–77 Howard presented a paper on newly discovered diamond mines in India. John-Baptiste Tavernier's *Six Voyages to India* had just been published in France.[124] European travel accounts of India tended to "ignore the staple products of the country because their interest was confined mainly to the limited class of goods which could bear the heavy cost of transport to Europe."[125] Howard's paper, probably written by Nathaniel Chumley who worked for the East India Company, provided details of thirty-eight mines, many more than Tavernier had described, and discussed living conditions along the Coromandel coast.[126] The Royal Society ordered the paper, "A Description of the Diamond Mines ... [of] the Coast of Coromandel," published in its *Philosophical Transactions*; it was later translated into French.[127]

As a sign of his commitment to the Royal Society, Henry Howard made an unparalleled gift to the fledgling organization. He donated the "Library

[119] *Ibid.*, pp. 343–44. On Rycaut and his connections to Howard, see Anderson, *An English Consul in Turkey, 1667–1678*, pp. 39–48, 210–15, 229–43, 260–61, 270.

[120] Paul Rycaut, *The Present State of the Ottoman Empire* (London, 1668), chapter 9, p. 89.

[121] Anderson, *An English Consul in Turkey, 1667–1668*, pp. 213–14.

[122] Robinson, *The Dukes of Norfolk*, pp. 125–26.   [123] See chapter 3 above.

[124] John-Baptiste Tavernier, *The Six Voyages of John Baptista Tavernier, a noble man of France now living, through Turkey into Persia and the East-Indies, finished in the year 1670* (London, 1678).

[125] Meera Nanda, *European Travel Accounts During the Reigns of Shahjahan and Aurangzeb* (Kurukshetra: Nirmal Book Agency 1994), p. 60.

[126] Royal Society, CP, IX (1) 32, "A description of the diamond mines."

[127] Robinson, *The Dukes of Norfolk*, p. 124; John-Baptiste Tavernier, *Travels in India*, trans. and ed. Valentine Ball, 2nd edn, 2 vols. (London: Oxford University Press, 1925), II, p. 42.

of Arundel House" to the Royal Society after it took up residence there following the Great Fire.[128] John Evelyn took credit for initiating the donation. Looking back two decades later he wrote to Samuel Pepys: "The Royal Society's [library] is a mixture (though little proper to the institution and design of that worthy assembly, yet) of many excellent books, given (at my instance) by the late Duke of Norfolk."[129] Evelyn wanted to ensure the survival of the library. Made up of several different libraries, that had belonged to Wilibaldus Pirckheimer, the German humanist, Henry Howard, Earl of Northampton, and Thomas Howard and Aletheia Talbot, Earl and Countess of Arundel, this famous Renaissance library was the most important donation the Royal Society received in its first century. Although it did not fit the aims of some members, the Society officially welcomed the library which marked its legitimacy and authority as a learned academy.[130] Howard desired "only that in case the Society should come to fail, it might return to Arundel House; and that this inscription 'Ex dono Henrici Howard Norfolciensis' might be put upon every book given them . . . . The Society received this noble donation with all thankfulness, and ordered that Mr. Howard should be registered as a benefactor."[131]

Amongst the Norfolk volumes that remain at the Royal Society today is Fabio Colonna's *Fabii Columnae Lyncei Minus Congitarum Plantarum Pars Prima & Secunda Pars* (Rome, 1616). Colonna, famous for his botanical studies and drawings of plants, was a leading member of the Academia dei Lincei, the scientific academy founded in 1603 by Frederico Cesi. As we have seen, Colonna's book, probably presented as a gift, belonged to the Countess of Arundel, who signed her name on the title page and dated it 1 April 1618.[132] The volume provides a unique link between the Lynceans

---

[128] See Linda Levy Peck, "Uncovering the Arundel Library at the Royal Society: Changing Meanings of Science and the Fate of the Norfolk Donation," *Notes and Records of the Royal Society*, 52 (1998), 3–24. On Northampton's library see Linda Levy Peck, "The Mentality of a Jacobean Grandee," in Peck (ed.), *The Mental World of the Jacobean Court* (Cambridge: Cambridge University Press, 1991), pp. 148–68 and Nicholas Barker, "The Books of Henry Howard, Earl of Northampton," *Bodleian Library Record*, 13 (1990), 375–81.

[129] University of Texas, Austin, Carl H. Pforzheimer Library, English Manuscripts, MS35I, John Evelyn to Samuel Pepys, 26 August 1689, Deptford. He lamented that part of "that rare collection of good authors and valuable manuscripts, which by the industrie of Fr: Junius, Mr Selden and the purchase of Pinellis library etc and was nobly furnish'd, but out of which, the best were . . . conveyed away, through the negligence of those his grand-father had committed the care of them to, whilst that magnificent Earl and Maecenas, was in Italy, where he died."

[130] Lisa Jardine points out that the reaction to the Norfolk donation was mixed among fellows of the Royal Society.

[131] Birch, *History of the Royal Society of London*, II, p. 136.

[132] Peck, "Uncovering the Arundel Library at the Royal Society," 3–24.

and the Royal Society founded almost sixty years later and signifies the importance of gift exchange in seventeenth-century society in general and science in particular.[133]

In 1678, after the Royal Society moved back to Gresham College, the Arundel books and manuscripts were transferred to the new site. In 1677 at William Dugdale's suggestion, fifty-four heraldic manuscripts were given to the College of Arms.[134] The Society published a catalog of the more than 4,000 Norfolk books and manuscripts in 1681 and placed them separately, as the donor wished, with an inscription in gold commemorating the donation.[135] Later, changing meanings of science made the Norfolk donation an anomaly. The Royal Society got rid of most of the books and manuscripts in the nineteenth and twentieth centuries by trading them with the British Museum for scientific books or selling them through Quartich and Sotheby's.[136]

In the same years, Charles Howard, Henry's younger brother, was one of the founder members of the Royal Society, a botanist with interests both in manufacturing and gardening. He patented a new method of tanning, which he advertised in a broadsheet.[137] Howard was an enthusiastic chairman of the Agricultural Committee,[138] which met at Howard's lodgings in Arundel House. The committee systematically collected seeds and plants from around the globe. For its contribution to the History of Trades, the committee planned "a history of agriculture and gardening, in order to improve the practice thereof."[139] Lord Christopher Hatton who had returned from exile in 1656 and collected and planted rare species at his home at Kirby Hall, became a member of the committee.[140]

Charles Howard took a particular interest in plants from the New World. He suggested at the meeting on 6 February 1668 "that some particulars relating to the plants of the Bermudas might be [enclosed] in the ... letter for Mr. Norwood."[141] Howard explained how to care for the fruits, seeds, berries, roots, plants, grasses, grains, herbs, and trees sent back from Bermuda, by drying them out and wrapping them in paper. He advised that "young trees may be set in half-tubs of earth arched over with hoops and covered with mats to preserve them from the dashing of the

---

[133] *Ibid.*; Findlen, "The Economy of Scientific Exchange in Early Modern Italy."
[134] Peck, "Uncovering the Arundel Library at the Royal Society," 3–24.
[135] *Ibid.*   [136] *Ibid.*
[137] Michael Hunter, *Science and Society in Restoration England* (Cambridge: Cambridge University Press, 1981), p. 192. *Titles of Patents of Invention, Part I,* #130, 27 October 1661.
[138] See Hunter, "An Experiment in Corporate Enterprise," pp. 73–122.
[139] Royal Society, Domestic Mss., V, #65.   [140] See chapter 6 above.
[141] Quoted in Oldenburg *Correspondence*, IV, p. 169n.

sea-water in their coming home, and remember to give them air every day in fair weather and let them be watered with fresh water once a day ... Send ... all the sorts of potatoes in earth."[142] Howard himself contributed to the Royal Society's repository. "Dr. Wilkins moved that Mr. Howard, being furnished with various flowers of a strawy consistence, might be desired to increase the Society's repository with them."[143] Charles Howard became known as a scholar-hermit, famous for his own garden and for his experimental work on plants. Later in life he continued his alchemical researches.[144]

The Royal Society offered Henry and Charles Howard the opportunity to take part publically in the new scientific culture, to display their new interests, and to receive public honor and acclaim. The Howards linked the consumption, collections, and networks of their grandfather and his circle with the new scientific body. Indeed the Roman Catholicism of the man who gave the Royal Society a home in Arundel House between 1667 and 1673 may have led to the pamphlet literature that accused the Royal Society of being Roman Catholic. In much the same way that Henry Wotton had worried in the early seventeenth century that European art was popish, Henry Stubbe claimed that the science of the Royal Society was popish. In 1670 Stubbe, a persistent critic, published *Campanella Revived, or An Enquiry into the History of the Royal Society, whether the virtuosi there do not pursue the projects of Campanella for the reducing England unto popery* (London). Nevertheless, the Howards, scions of the premier ducal family in England and the important collectors of the early seventeenth century, remained enthusiasts for the new Royal Society. Indeed, Howard wrote flattering to Oldenburg that providing a home for the Royal Society enhanced his honor and reputation.[145] Despite diatribes and satire, the expansion of aristocratic identity through science found expression not only in scientific investigation but also in recasting the arts as objects of the History of Trades.

CURIOSITY, USE, AND IMPROVEMENT

As we have seen, the History of Trades agenda at the Royal Society ranged widely from basic industries such as dyeing, felt-making, tin, and masonry to luxury trades such as optics and painting. Thomas Povey, one of the

---

[142] *Ibid.*, pp. 168–69.
[143] Birch, *History of the Royal Society of London*, II, p. 73, 21 March 1665/1666.
[144] Charles Howard, *Oxford DNB*, vol. 28, p. 324.
[145] Oldenburg, *Correspondence*, III, p. 505, Oldenburg to Boyle, 1 October 1667.

founder members of the Royal Society, son of Anne of Denmark's auditor and grandson of a City embroiderer, was described by Evelyn as "a nice contriver of all elegancies, and exceedingly formal."[146] Educated at Gray's Inn, Povey sat as an MP, first for Liskeard, Cornwall in 1646 and second for Bossiney in 1659, and served as a member of the Council for the Colonies in 1657. At the Restoration he took up several official positions, serving as the Duke of York's Treasurer, Receiver General for the rents and revenues of the plantations in Africa and America, and Master of Requests. Povey had a house in Lincoln's Inn Fields and a country house, The Priory, in Hounslow, Middlesex. Along with interests in the West Indies and Africa, he was treasurer for Tangier and surveyor-general of victualling, yielding both offices to Samuel Pepys whom he sponsored for membership in the Royal Society.[147]

Povey became active in the new Royal Society as early as 1661.[148] When Robert Boyle brought him books in 1661, Povey responded with a fulsome letter of thanks in which he declared Boyle himself "a full and noble library." Povey enclosed "a small quantity of pepper of Jamaica" for analysis by Boyle and Sir Robert Moray.[149] Povey's interests ranged from the "qualities of the herb called tea or Chee"[150] to an invention for raising water.[151] He presented rarities from the West Indies to the Society,[152] and "curiosities of silk works" for the repository.[153] In August 1664, as a member of the Committee on Correspondence which included President Moray, John Hoskins, Henry Slingsby, Dr. Wilkins, Mr. Hooke, and Mr. Oldenburg, he looked at "books of voyages to be perused for inquiries ... to be sent into all parts of the world with particular ones for the East India Company."[154] Povey's activities suggest that the virtuosi were eager to combine the curious with the useful.

In April 1666 Povey presented a paper to the society on new methods of painting by Robert Streater who had painted the hall of his Lincoln's Inn

[146] Evelyn, *Diary*, IV, p. 84.
[147] "Thomas Povey," *Oxford Dictionary of National Biography*, ed. H. C. G. Mathews and Brian Harrison (Oxford: Oxford University Press, 2004), XLV, 67–68.
[148] Royal Society, Sackler Archive.
[149] Royal Society, Boyle Papers, BL. 4.146, Povey to Boyle, 8 May 1661, f. 146. Povey wrote "The Method, Manner and Order of the Transmutation of Copper into Brass," *Philosophical Transactions*, 17, 735–36.
[150] BL Sloane, 1039, f. 139 (1686).   [151] "Thomas Povey," *Oxford DNB*, XLV, 68.
[152] Birch, *History of the Royal Society of London*, II, p. 128, Povey presents curiosities from West Indies, 27 November 1666.
[153] Birch, *History of the Royal Society of London*, II, p. 76.
[154] Royal Society, Domestic Mss., V, #68, Minutes of the Committee of Correspondence 19 August 1664. The Committee met at Povey's house.

mansion so that it produced no glare. Streater, whom Povey described as "a general and excellent master of the pencil," enjoyed the patronage of the great and good in the early Restoration.[155] Born in Covent Garden, the son of a painter, Streater was instructed by Du Moulin and influenced by sixteenth- and seventeenth-century Italian painting. He specialized in large architectural scenes and landscapes.[156] After Evelyn visited Povey's house in Lincoln's Inn Fields, he noted that "the perspective in his court painted by Streater is indeed excellent, with the vasas in imitation of porphyry and fountain."[157] In 1669 Pepys visited Streater, the "famous history painter ... where I found Dr. Wren and other virtuosos looking upon the paintings he is making of the new theatre at Oxford."[158] His ceiling for the Sheldonian is one of the few of his works to survive. In 1672 Evelyn visited Sir Robert Clayton, who had succeeded his uncle Robert Abbott as one of London's most important scriveners and bankers, where he admired "the cedar dining-room ... painted with the history of the Giants' War incomparably by Mr. Streater but the figures are too near the eye."[159]

As Richard Symonds had returned with recipes from Italian artists in the 1650s so Povey reported on contemporary artists' practice in the 1660s.[160] Povey presented the Royal Society with Streater's recipe, combining three or four beaten eggs with one or two small pieces of green figs or their branches. The resulting watery fluid, he claimed, could be used by the painter without further addition.[161] The issue interested both the society's virtuosi and experimenters because it provided the means of copying Italian practice. In August 1666 President Moray reported that he and a group of members of the Royal Society, including Mr. Henry Slingsby, Mr. Povey, Dr. Walter Charlton, Mr. Hooke and Mr. Oldenburg, had met with Streater to repeat the experiment and reported that it worked.[162] Povey himself reported that they "went afterwards to my house where they saw a chimney piece wrought thus by Dankhurst in landscape, who having studied long in Italy, had seen many things which had been done this way especially a large cabinet in the Pope's Palace."[163] Although the process had been understood by the ancients, Povey claimed that it had been forgotten.

[155] Royal Society, CP, II, 24.   [156] "Robert Streater," *Oxford DNB*, LIII, 50–51.

[157] Evelyn, *Diary*, III, p. 375.

[158] "Robert Streater," *Oxford DNB*, LIII, 50, Pepys, *Diary*, IX, 434; see Horace Walpole's *Anecdotes of Painting in England* (Strawberry Hill, London, 1762).

[159] Evelyn, *Diary*, III, pp. 625–26.   [160] See chapter 6 above.   [161] Royal Society, CP, II, 24.

[162] Birch, *History of the Royal Society of London*, II, pp. 107–108, 6 August 1666.

[163] Royal Society, CP, II, 24.

There are extant some pieces finished this way by Correggio which I have heard persons of the highest judgement in painting say, are most valuable for their delicacy in work and beauty in colouring ... And they were held not able to be over-prized at one thousand pounds each, they being indeed worthy of the utmost price that can be set upon painting or the highest efforts of art and were considered as jewels in the rich collection his late Majesty had of the best paintings."[164]

Yet even as he wrote lyrically of the lost collections of Charles I, in his report of 19 December 1667, Povey sought to bring art within the compass of the Royal Society's History of Trades through a study whose aim would be improvement and use as well as curiosity. He urged that Peter Lely, Samuel Cooper, and Streater, "the chief masters of these times," meet with a committee of the Royal Society to help write this history in much the same way that Robert Hooke had advocated meeting with artisans to understand the mysteries of their trade.

Something yet new and undiscovered may spring up to further improvement which ought to be and is the most honourable part of that you aim at: that you may not seem to entertain yourselves with curiosity and speculation only: but may by that various and universal learning which meets here, as it were in council, leave something new or improved to the succeeding world and still go on to inflame this age by a generous emulation abroad, to envy and imitate what you have more happily, first opened and essayed: that it may not be said by the malicious that you discourse and make flourishes and subsist chiefly upon what is delivered to by you by them that lived before you.[165]

Painting "hath been the study, delight, and ornament of all ages and nations where peace or civility have not been abandoned." Povey suggested a volume that combined history with practice, to look at artists' "several ways of working, the degrees of improvement of this art, the varity of their colours." He suggested that lesser arts such as bronzing, staining, engraving, and etching be considered in an appendix.[166]

Povey's interests were not, of course, unique. In its first decade the Royal Society looked into many technical aspects of art from colors and how they were made, marble and how it was colored, polished, and cut, varnish, and engraving.[167] Povey suggested that some members of the society meet to develop questions for Lely, Cooper, and Streater. A new committee,

---

[164] *Ibid.* The paper is left unascribed and is misdated to 18 April 1665. The text indicates that it was prepared after Povey's first introduction of the subject.

[165] Royal Society, Ms. Journal Book, 1667–71, pp. 70–71, 19 December 1667. Royal Society CP, II, 24, pp. 11–12, 18. For the date see Birch, *History of the Royal Society of London*, II, p. 227.

[166] Royal Society, CP, II, 24.

[167] See, for instance, *Philosophical Transactions*, I (1665), pp. 125–27; VIII (1673), pp. 6010–15.

consisting of Povey, Sir Philip Carteret, Sir Theodore de Vaux, John Evelyn, Thomas Henshaw, Dr. William Croone, John Hoskins, Mr. Edmund Wylde, and Robert Hooke was appointed to meet.[168] Povey's proposal accorded with the early Royal Society's interests even if it was not taken further. In the 1660s, the capacious agenda of the Royal Society included the luxury products of the leading court portraitist, miniaturist, and landscape painter.

CREATING A MARKET FOR SCIENTIFIC INSTRUMENTS

Alongside its investigations into luxury manufactures, scientific inquiry also created new luxury goods. As Thomas Hankins and Robert Silverman point out, "instruments moved easily from natural philosophy to art and to popular culture,"often predating the scientific experiments they made possible.[169] Telescopes had been known since the sixteenth century, with authorship ascribed to Dutch spectacle makers among others.[170] Using a borrowed telescope, Galileo had made his discoveries of the moons around Jupiter in 1609. Galileo's discoveries and their report in print thereby created a luxury market for books on astronomy and telescopes. Indeed, in 1634, Thomas Hobbes wrote to his employer, the Duke of Newcastle, that

My first business in London was to seek for Galileo's dialogues; I thought it a very good bargain, when at taking my leave of your Lordship I undertook to buy it for you, but ... it is not possible to get it for money. There were but few brought over at first, and they that buy such books, are not men as to part with them again. I hear say it is called in, in Italy, as a book that will do more hurt to their religion then all the books have done of Luther and Calvin, such opposition they think is between their religion, and natural reason. I doubt but that translation of it will here be publicly embraced, and wish extremely that Dr. Webbe would hasten it.[171]

As we have seen, Newcastle was already interested in optics and had bought several telescopes including some from Divini by the late 1640s.[172] The telescopes of Divini and Campani had filled the meetings of the Royal Society as well as the pages of the *Philosophical Transactions*.[173]

[168] Birch, *History of the Royal Society of London*, II, p. 231.
[169] Thomas Hankins and Robert Silverman, *Instruments and the Imagination* (Princeton: Princeton University Press, 1995), p. 5.
[170] Henry C. King *The History of Telescopes* (London: Charles Griffin, 1955), p. 30.
[171] Thomas Hobbes, *The Correspondence*, ed., Noel Malcolm, 2 vols. (Oxford: Clarendon Press, 1994), I, pp. 19–20, and note 10.
[172] *Ibid.*, I, xlviii, II, 621 and note 3.
[173] See, for instance, Birch, *History of the Royal Society of London*, II, pp. 88, 97, 99, 102, 152, 313.

Isaac Barrow delivered his optical lectures in Oxford in 1667 and 1668.[174] His protégé, Isaac Newton, followed suit in 1670–72, shortly after Charles Cheyne ordered his telescope from Divini. Describing his reasons for presenting these lectures Newton wrote:

The recent invention of telescopes has so occupied most geometers that they seem to have left to others nothing in optics untouched nor any room for further discovery. Moreover, since the lectures that you heard here not so long ago brought together such a great variety of optical topics and a vast quantity of discoveries with their very accurate demonstrations, it might perhaps seem a vain endeavor and futile effort for me to undertake to treat this science again But since I observe that geometers have hitherto erred with respect to a certain property of light pertaining to its refractions, ... I judge it will not be unappreciated if I subject the principles of this science to a rather strict examination, adding what I have conceived concerning them and confirmed by numerous experiments to what my reverend predecessor last delivered in this place.[175]

With this, Newton announced his findings which led to the development of the reflecting telescope. By the early eighteenth century, it displaced the refracting telescopes of Divini and Campani. The Royal Society, taken with Newton's findings, made him an honorary member.[176]

Domestic shops selling technically advanced telescopes developed from the 1670s. The trade centered in London around St. Paul's and Covent Garden. Christopher Cock, son of John, a grinder of lenses, had a royal appointment from Charles II. His shop in Long Acre, Covent Garden, supplied telescopes to the St. Andrews Observatory. Robert Hooke was instrumental in the commercial production of microscopes. Cock worked with him and sold simple microscopes from 1678.[177] By 1696 his shop, the Blue Spectacles, had moved near St. Anne's Church, London. In the same years, John Yarwell sold microscopes and telescopes at The Archimedes and Spectacles in St. Paul's Church Yard and later in Ludgate. Yarwell had

---

[174] Mordechai Feingold, *Before Newton: The Life and Times of Isaac Barrow* (Cambridge: Cambridge University Press, 1990).

[175] Alan E. Shapiro (ed.), *The Optical Papers of Isaac Newton*, vol. I: *The Optical Lectures, 1670–1672* (Cambridge: Cambridge University Press, 1984), p. 47.

[176] King, *The History of the Telescope*, p. 174.

[177] Catherine Wilson, *The Invisible World: Early Modern Philosophy and the Invention of the Microscope* (Princeton: Princeton University Press, 1995), p. 91; Brian Bracegirdle, "Seventeenth-Century Simple Microscopes," in R. G. W. Anderson, J. A. Bennett, W. F. Ryan (eds.), *Making Instruments Count: Essays on Historical Scientific Instruments Presented to Gerard L'Estrange Turner* (Aldershot: Variorum, 1993), pp. 295–305.

a royal appointment from William III.[178] Newton, by then president of the Royal Society, praised domestic instrument makers.

Over the course of the seventeenth century, telescopes and microscopes moved from novelties in Italian courts to luxury goods available to well-to-do consumers in London shops. The Royal Society participated in the creation of this market for scientific instruments. Henry Oldenburg said as much when he wrote to Thomas Hobbes that "For, the benefit of a science known not only in gross, but also by retail and in parcels, move the mind to a more eager and vigorous pursuit of acquiring the same."[179] Indeed, through its meetings and publications, the Royal Society transmitted the technology, such as the grinding of optical glasses and the invention of the microscope, to supply the demand it had helped to nourish.

RECONSTRUCTING THE CITY

Members of the Royal Society whose mission emphasized improvement and the useful arts had the opportunity to apply their expertise, gathered at home and abroad, after the Great Fire of London in 1666. Many of its members were part of the urban elite.[180] Oldenberg and the Fellows saw the Great Fire as an opportunity.

'Tis incredible, how little the sufferers, though great ones, do complain of their losses. I was yesterday in many meetings of the principal citizens, whose houses are laid in ashes, who instead of complaining, discoursed almost of nothing, but of a survey of London, and a design for rebuilding, and that in such a manner (with bricks, and large streets . . .) that for the future they may not be so easily subject to the like destruction. I hope, that some of our Society will signalize themselves in this survey . . . which when done to the satisfaction of the King may by His Majesty be offered and recommended to the Parliament. I was this very morning with our President, and suggested this business to his Lordship who liked it so well that he intends to move it tomorrow at the council of the Society.[181]

When the time came to provide models for the rebuilding of London in 1666, Christopher Wren, John Evelyn, William Petty, and Robert Hooke drew on their travels and reading to produce plans for a modern city. Petty argued that the new London would offer "foreign travel to the youth of

---

[178] Gloria Clifton, *Directory of British Scientific Instrument Makers 1550–1851* (London: Zwemmer, National Maritime Museum, 1995), pp. 59, 60, 307.

[179] Hobbes, *The Correspondence*, I, p. 211, Henry Oldenburg to Hobbes, 6/16 June 1655.

[180] Hunter, *The Royal Society and its Fellows*, pp. 8–10.

[181] Oldenburg, *Correspondence*, III, p. 226, Oldenburg to Boyle, 10 September 1666.

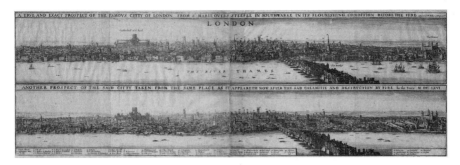

46. Hollar had produced an engraving of the City of London just before the Great Fire. He added a view of the desolation and published both together.
The Folger Shakespeare Library, Map L85c no. 1, Wenceslaus Hollar, *A true and exact prospect of the ... citty of London ... before the fire [and] Another prospect of the sayd citty ... as it appeareath now, after the sad calamitie* (1666).

England."[182] They envisioned a city whose structure resembled Paris, Rome, and Venice and celebrated both royalty and retail.

The year before, while visiting France, Wren promised a correspondent "I shall bring you almost all France in paper."[183] During his trip Wren spent time with French scientists, admired collections of rarities, studied French architecture, and met Bernini, who was then working on the bust of Louis XIV and a new wing for the Louvre. In a long letter he described what impressed him most and what he meant to import.

I have busied myself in surveying the most esteem'd fabrics of Paris, and the country round; the Louvre for a while was my daily object, where no less than a thousand hands are constantly employ'd in the works some in laying mighty foundations, some in raising the stories, columns, entablements, etc. with vast stones, by great and useful engines; others in carving, inlaying of marbles, plastering, painting, gilding, etc. Which altogether make a school of architecture, the best probably, at this day in Europe.[184]

Wren made or bought drawings. He had wanted a copy of Bernini's design for the Louvre, but the Italian architect and sculptor allowed him to see it only for a few minutes. "It was five little designs in paper, for which he

---

[182] Quoted in Norman Brett-James, *The Growth of Stuart London* (London: George Allen and Unwin, 1935), p. 322. While Wren and Evelyn were devoted to antique sculpture and architecture, they were just as clearly concerned with the modern. On their participation in the battle of the books see Joseph Levine, *Between Ancients and Moderns: Baroque Culture in Restoration England* (New Haven: Yale University Press, 1999).

[183] Quoted in Lydia M. Soo, *Wren's "Tracts" on Architecture and Other Writings* (Cambridge: Cambridge University Press, 1998), p. 105.

[184] Quoted in *ibid.*, p. 103.

[Bernini] hath receiv'd many thousand pistoles."[185] Later, Wren was forced to draw it from memory. When he returned to London Wren addressed the rebuilding of London fresh from his study in France.

Wren preferred the older Palais Mazarine to Versailles. Versailles, he thought, was a product of feminine taste and ephemeral fashion.

Not an inch within but is crowded with little curiosities of ornaments: the women, as they make here the language and fashions, and meddle with politics and philosophy, so they sway also in architecture; . . . and little knacks are in great vogue; but building certainly ought to have the attribute of eternal, and therefore the only thing uncapable of new fashions. The masculine furniture of Palais Mazarine pleased me much better where is a great and noble collection of antique statues and bustos, (many of porphyry) good basso-relieves, excellent pictures of the great masters, fine arras, true mosaics . . . Vasas of porcelain painted by Raphael, and infinite other rarities, the best of which now furnish the glorious apartment of the Queen Mother at the Louvre which I saw many times.[186]

Wren, like his contemporaries, sought out collections of great art and sculpture, the curious and the rare. Like Evelyn, who had visited in 1644, Wren admired "the curious rarities of the Duke of Orleans library, well fill'd with excellent intaglios, medals, books of plants, and fowls in miniature."[187] He visited academies "of painters, sculptors, architects, and the chief artificers of the Louvre." Beginning with Bernini, Wren named the leading architects, sculptors, plasterers, and engravers whom he admired. Turning to painters he named those who did history, portraits, flower painting, enamel and gardening. Wren hoped to return at Christmas and "by that time to perfect what I have on the anvil: 'Observations on the present State of Architecture, Arts, and Manufactures in France.'"[188]

Evelyn brought the experience of the Grand Tour and exile to his plans for London. Specifically, he drew on the layout of the streets of Rome which he visited in 1644–45, the Rialto bridge in Venice, and sites in Florence, Amsterdam, and Paris. In 1666, immediately after the Great Fire, Evelyn wrote *Londinum Redivivum, or London Restored not to its pristine, but to far greater beauty commodiousness and magnificence*. In it he described how London could become superior to all other cities in the World: "fitter for commerce, apter for government, sweeter for health, more glorious for beauty." He called on the "ablest men, merchants, architects, and workmen," to work together to rebuild London.[189] He

[185] *Ibid.*, p. 105   [186] Quoted in *ibid.*, pp. 104–105.   [187] *Ibid.*, pp. 103–106.   [188] *Ibid.*, p. 106.
[189] John Evelyn, *Londinum Redivivum, or London Restored not to its pristine, but to far greater beauty commodiousness and magnificence* (London, 1666), pp. 54–55, 31.

suggested that Sir Jonas Moore, who mapped Tangier, draw the plan.[190] After his return from exile, Evelyn had contrasted London with Paris, the former "so mad and lowd a Town, is no where to be found in the whole world."[191] In 1659 he described London as "nobly situated" on the Thames but "wooden, northern, and an artificial congestion of houses" and warned of the danger of fire.[192] In 1662 Charles II appointed him one of the Commissioners of Sewers.

The cultural geography of London should be shaped for "competent breadths for commerce and intercourse, cheerfulness and state." Levelling potholes and uneven roads, Evelyn thought, would provide "more ease of commerce, carriages, coaches, and people in the streets, and not a little for the more handsome ranging of the buildings," better declivities to the Thames than in Genoa. Churches should be "so built after the modern architecture without and contrivance within, as may best answer their pious designation ... in the piazzas should be keep the several markets, in others the coaches may wait, and in some should be public fountains placed ... [to] show their crystal waters, as in most of the best cities of Europe they do, save this of ours." Triumphal gates with statues would ring the city. "The gates and entrees of the city, which are to be rebuilt, might be the subjects of handsome architecture, in form of triumphal arches, adorned with statues, relieves, and apposite inscriptions, as prefaces to the rest within."[193]

London Bridge should have "a substantial baluster of iron, decorated with statues upon their pedestals," a reference to European models, including Bernini. Evelyn would do away with the London Bridge shops, "Or if they will needs have shops, let them be built of solid stone, made narrow and very low, like to those upon the Rialto at Venice." The Guild Hall should be rebuilt like the State Hall in Amsterdam. The Royal Exchange in the City should be rebuilt too. "It will be necessary to amplify the old design, which was much too narrow for the assemblies. If it should be erected near the Thames, let there be spacious piazzas about it, either for dwellings, or public ware-houses." Evelyn placed the College of Physicians

in one of the best parts of the town, encircled with an handsome piazza for the dwelling of those learned persons, with the chirurgeons [surgeons], apothecaries, and druggists in the streets about them; for I am greatly inclined to wish, that all of a mystery should be destined to their several quarters. Those of the better sort of shopkeepers, who sell by retail, might be allotted to the sweetest and most eminent streets and piazzas.

---

[190] *Ibid.*, pp. 30–31.   [191] *Ibid.*, p. 7n.   [192] *Ibid.*, p. 5.   [193] *Ibid.*, pp. 34–36, 37, 38, 40–41, 50–51.

Evelyn suggested that paving stones emulate those of the Dutch and Romans, and indeed Evelyn became a projector for these in 1666.[194]

Thomas Sprat, too, celebrated the opportunity for improvement and invention created by the Great Fire. "A new city is to be built, on the most advantageous seat of all Europe for trade and commerce. This therefore is the fittest season for men to apply their thoughts, to the improving of the materials of building and to the inventing of better models for houses, roofs, chimneys, conduits, and streets all of which have been already under the consideration of the Royal Society."[195] Charles II appointed commissioners, including the architect Sir Roger Pratt, to meet with the City's representatives, whose delegation included Robert Hooke. While the King admired the plans of the Royal Society Fellows, they were not adopted. Furthermore, Parliament agreed with the City magistrates that the City should be built on the old plan. But some reforms were adopted: houses had to be built of brick, streets widened to accommodate coaches, the Royal Exchange, St. Paul's, and the Guildhall reconstructed, and city houses built to just a few patterns with no overhangs.[196] Wren rebuilt St. Paul's and most of the City's churches.

James I's design to create a modern capital based on borrowing from the ancients and contemporary Europe came to fruition after the Great Fire. But it was speculators and builders like Nicholas Barbon, not Wren, Evelyn, Petty, and Hooke, who remade the City and the West End.[197] In 1673 the Royal Society returned to Gresham College. As builders developed the Strand, Henry Howard tore down Arundel House and redeveloped the property into streets, and commercial and residential buildings.[198] The home of the great collector and of the Royal Society between 1667 and 1673 was turned into luxury housing for the gentry, who came to London to live and to shop for longer and longer periods of time in the late seventeenth century.[199]

Barbon saw London and building as the engine of the economy, just as Evelyn did. In *An Apology for the Builder*, Barbon wrote that "those houses in the Strand and Charing Cross are worth now fifty and threescore pounds

[194] *Ibid.*, pp. 51, 41, 42, 49, 52.   [195] Sprat, *History of the Royal Society*, pp. 122–23.

[196] Elizabeth McKellar, *The Birth of Modern London: The Development and Design of the City, 1660–1720* (Manchester, England: Manchester University Press, 1999).

[197] *Ibid.*

[198] Arundel Castle Mss. MD 1514; John Stow, *A Survey of the Cities of London and Westminster, and the Borough of Southwark*, 2 vols. (1720), II, pp. 117–18; Brett-James, *The Growth of Stuart London*, pp. 327–28.

[199] Susan E. Whyman, *Sociability and Power in Late-Stuart England: The Cultural Worlds of the Verneys, 1660–1720* (Oxford: Oxford University Press, 1999), pp. 87–110.

per annum, which within this thirty years were not let for above twenty pounds."[200] New houses provided increased work for the building trades and their new inhabitants spent more on food, clothing, and furnishing. Barbon is often associated with the new mentality that asserted the importance of consumption to the economy while Evelyn is associated with early Stuart court culture and the virtuosi.[201] But, though Evelyn did not like the aesthetic results of the speculative building that followed the Great Fire, his goals and Barbon's were similar. Twenty years after the Great Fire, Barbon echoed Evelyn's vision: "the artists of this age have already made the city of London the metropolis of Europe, and if it be compared for the number of good houses, for its many and large piazzas, for its richness of inhabitants, it must be allowed, the largest, best built, and richest city in the world."[202]

---

[200] Nicholas Barbon, *An Apology for the Builder, or, a Discourse Shewing the Cause and Effects of the Increase of Building* (London, 1685), p. 2.
[201] McKellar, *The Birth of Modern London*, pp. 30–31.   [202] Quoted in *ibid.*, pp. 32–33.

CHAPTER 9

New wants, new wares: luxury consumption, cultural change, and economic transformation

John Evelyn wrote a paean of praise to Sir William Petty in 1675. Evelyn called him a genius who was unequaled as

a superintendent of manufacture and improvement of trades ... When I, who knew him in mean circumstances, have been in his splendid palace he would himself be in admiration how he arrived at it; nor was it his value or inclination for splendid furniture and the curiosities of the age, but his elegant Lady could endure nothing mean, or that was not magnificent. He was very negligent himself, and rather so of his person, and of a philosophic temper. "What a to-do is here!" would he say, "I can lie in straw with as much satisfaction."[1]

William Petty, the father of "political arithmetic," had dreamed in 1648 of using his knowledge of invention gained abroad to improve manufactures and education at home in order to support himself in sufficient style to afford servants.[2] He had succeeded beyond his wildest dreams. Petty now lived on the north side of Piccadilly, on the same street as Clarendon House and Burlington House.[3] Nicholas Barbon offers a contemporary's analysis of how this had happened. "The wants of the mind are infinite," he wrote, "Man naturally aspires and as his mind is elevated, his senses grow more refined, and more capable of delight; his desires are enlarged, and his wants increase with his wishes, which is for every thing that is rare, can gratify his senses, adorn his body and promote the ease, pleasure and pomp of life."[4]

In this conclusion, Petty's example frames our arguments about the increasing importance of individual and family aspirations to acquire

[1] John Evelyn *Diary and Correspondence of John Evelyn*, ed. William Bray (London: G. Bohn, 1859–62), pp. 345–46.
[2] BL Add. Mss. 72,891, Petty Papers, f. 8v (1647–48). See chapter 6 above.
[3] *The Correspondence of Thomas Hobbes*, ed. Noel Malcolm, 2 vols. (Oxford: Clarendon Press, 1994), II, pp. 753 and 755n3.
[4] Quoted in Christopher Berry, *The Idea of Luxury: A Conceptual and Historical Investigation* (Cambridge: Cambridge University Press, 1994), p. 112.

luxury goods in seventeenth-century English society and culture, the expanded institutional support for luxury manufactures, the impact of luxury on gender roles and law, and the contribution of the eighteenth-century luxury debate to our understanding of seventeenth-century consumption.

ASPIRATIONS AND LUXURY CONSUMPTION

The analysis of seventeenth-century English luxury consumption and cultural borrowing offers an additional framework for seventeenth-century studies. As we have seen, luxury affected identity and ideology, behavior and social relations, as well as the economy and politics. Luxury challenged gender roles and transformed objects from rarities to manufactured goods. Luxury goods served not only as marks of distinction but as ties to bind different segments of society. Fueled by the increasing numbers of those who claimed the life of the gentry, luxury goods circulated throughout society through gift, bequest, sale and resale. English society as a whole used new as well as traditional luxury goods to mark relationships of patron and client, master and servant, and good neighbors through gift exchange.[5] Men and women knowingly used luxury goods to display status, to create social ties, to gain favor, to reinforce memory, and to worship. The "demoralization" of luxury was well under way in the early seventeenth century.

Luxury consumption grew through expanding demand for existing goods, the creation of new wants and new ways to sell wares, the Crown's promotion of luxury industries, and the import of luxury goods from Europe, the New World, Asia, and Africa. Over the course of the first three-quarters of the seventeenth century, the English elite bought an increasingly diverse range of luxury goods from abroad.

As we have seen, they appropriated not only the material goods themselves but also their rich and exotic meanings. From Italian building design, textiles, glass, and scientific instruments, and Parisian interiors, garden designs and "French wares" to Chinese porcelain, Indian textiles, antiquities from Greece and Turkey, and rarities and exotic groceries from the East and West Indies, Asia and Africa, these goods identified their consumers as fashionable, cosmopolitan, and, as King Charles and John Evelyn called it, "modern." The knowledgeable and self-conscious shopper

---

[5] Linda Levy Peck, *Court Patronage and Corruption in Early Stuart England* (London: Unwin Hyman, 1990).

who struck bargains in person and through agents ranged from those who bought ribbon from the local mercer and nobles who ordered goods from London for themselves and their neighbors in the north, to courtiers who built great collections of art and sculpture, and the country gentleman who imported a Roman funeral monument.

Luxury did not lessen sociability. The well-to-do did not simply withdraw from public performance of duties surrounded by retainers to the private enjoyment of pictures and rarities. Instead, increasing luxury brought increasing public display, not in the form of a profusion of followers, but in processions of coaches. The gridlock of early seventeenth-century London traffic, was spelt out in Henry Peacham's *Coach and Sedan, Pleasantly Disputing for Place and Precedence*.[6] Luxury created new sites for public display which grew alongside new ways to entertain in private. Some new luxury goods popular in the late seventeenth century such as toilet sets and tea services enhanced women's abilities to entertain friends and admirers privately. But women's luxury consumption in the seventeenth century took place publicly too, in the New Exchange, in the theatre, in the coach, in the coffeehouse, at public sermons, and in the new public gardens. Although they risked criticism there, these new public spaces provided both women and men venues in which to spend leisure time and money.

The late sixteenth and seventeenth centuries saw the creation of a greater infrastructure for luxury consumption, a national market, and new retail shops in which to buy luxury goods. While the marketplace had served as a center for buying and gossip since the Middle Ages, now shopping increasingly became an entertainment and pastime for men and women. The court's outer presence chambers were open to respectable Londoners[7] but even those who could not attend the Stuart court could buy perfume from the Queen's perfumer at the New Exchange.

While much of the luxury trade was concentrated in London, it quickly reached the countryside. Luxury consumption worked through networks of credit and exchange that increasingly linked the capital with national markets and England with the continent. Knowledge of the new developed through display, print, and travel, whether to London, to Europe, and other continents, through the activity of intermediaries such as

---

[6] [Henry Peacham], *Coach and Sedan, Pleasantly Disputing for Place and Precedence* (London, 1636).
[7] See Robert O. Bucholz, "Going to Court in 1700: A Visitor's Guide," *The Court Historian*, 5 (2000), 181–215.

47. The fashion for chinoiserie continued into the Restoration. This elaborate toilet set in silver has Chinese designs.
The Metropolitan Museum of Art, Metalwork-Silver, English (London), 17th century (1683–84), William Fowl (act. 1681–84), toilet set, 1 mirror, 2 casket, 7, 8 candlesticks; toilet service with scenes of chinoiserie, presented by Charles II to Duchess of Richmond, 1680s, Fletcher Fund, 1963, (63.70.1,2,7,8). Photograph, all rights reserved, The Metropolitan Museum of Art.

ambassadors, tutors, architects, agents, builders, skilled craftsmen, and scientists.

From William Harrison's contemporary observations in the 1570s and 1580s,[8] to the important work of Joan Thirsk,[9] Christopher

[8] William Harrison, *The Description of England*, 2nd edn (London, 1587).
[9] Joan Thirsk, *Economic Policy and Projects: The Development of a Consumer Society in Early Modern England* (Oxford: Clarendon Press, 1978).

48. The Metropolitan Museum of Art, Metalwork-Silver, English (London), 17th century (1687–88), Maker: D., London (*c.* 1682–97), toilet set, 15 pin cushion, 13 scent bottle, 16 snuffers, 17 tray for snuffers, Fletcher Fund, 1963 (63.70, 15, 13, 16, 17). Photograph, all rights reserved, The Metropolitan Museum of Art.

Clay,[10] and Craig Muldrew,[11] we know that the incomes of the well-to-do increased in the sixteenth century and their outlay on more comfortable houses and personal possessions increased even faster. They spent more on manufactured goods. Craig Muldrew paints a picture of widespread consumption in the sixteenth century that included luxury goods and accompanying modes of credit in rural areas.

Jan de Vries analyzes the change in aspirations to acquire by demonstrating that in the late sixteenth century, even as wages declined, families

---

[10] Christopher G. A. Clay, *Economic Expansion and Social Change, England 1500–1700*, 2 vols. (Cambridge: Cambridge University Press, 1984), II, p. 26.

[11] Craig Muldrew, *The Economy of Obligation: The Culture of Credit and Social Relations in Early Modern England* (Houndmills, Basingstoke: Palgrave, 1998).

increased their productivity in order to consume.[12] During the sixteenth century, the number of those doing wage labor increased. While wages showed an uneven history, Christopher Clay suggests that "by 1700 labouring people were coming to possess accoutrements of dress such as coloured stockings, gloves, buckled shoes ... and ribbon-trimmed hats, and their households to contain brass pots, iron frying pans, cutlery and glazed earthenware, none of which had been owned by their predecessors of the mid sixteenth century. A mass market was thus developing for a considerable range of manufactures."[13]

R. M. Hartwell points out that culture and institutions were as important to development as was the role of the state in supporting private property and profit-seeking.[14] While luxury exists in most societies, the cultural and institutional support for luxury consumption and luxury manufactures present in 1600 was not present in earlier centuries. The opportunities offered by print, renewed contact with and travel to the continent, the opening up of the East and West Indies, and the migration of skilled labor, offered an extraordinary opportunity to English rulers which they took up with alacrity.

The court and the aristocratic households around it formed an economic institution whose policies and practices promoted luxury to the whole society. The Jacobean court not only patronized luxury craftsmen, who were an important part of the London economy,[15] but also sponsored luxury manufactures, the development of London, international trade, and the creation of new colonies which offered the raw materials for luxury goods. Patents of monopoly substituted domestic production for imports such as silk, glass, and tapestries. Policies to diversify the economy begun by Lord Burghley in the 1570s continued under James I, to provide work for an increasing population, and to improve skilled labor either through migration or by copying continental practice. Peace with Spain opened a period of increasing trade to and from the East and West Indies. English common law and equity protected the rights of retailers and traders as well as landed property. Litigation for debt grew much faster than litigation over land over the course of the sixteenth century so that by 1640 it comprised 88 percent of the business of the Court of Common Pleas.

---

[12] Jan de Vries, "Between Purchasing Power and the World of Goods: Understanding the Household Economy in Early Modern Europe," in John Brewer and Roy Porter (eds.), *Consumption and the World of Goods* (London: Routledge, 1992), pp. 85–132.

[13] Clay, *Economic Expansion and Social Change*, II, 31.

[14] See John A. James and Mark Thomas (eds.), *Capitalism in Context: Essays on Economic Development and Cultural Change in Honor of R. M. Hartwell* (Chicago: University of Chicago Press, 1994).

[15] Ian Archer, "City and Court in the Reign of Elizabeth I" (unpublished paper).

Those litigating were those who benefited from the burgeoning economy, merchants and artisans as well as gentry.[16]

Civil wars and religious ideology made little dent in these forms of luxury consumption and, I argue, promoted cultural borrowing. By 1670 luxury consumption was deeply imbedded in English culture, society, and economy, despite political and religious conflict. Abroad, the capture of trade networks, such as the Italian silk trade, allowed the English to export the silk goods they had once imported and then sought to replace. Now, too, they were able to develop a trade based on re-export of goods bought in the Indies as predicted by Thomas Mun in the 1620s debates over balance of trade.[17]

These findings challenge the hypothesis that middle-class consumers in the eighteenth century created a new kind of luxury consumption through new goods, new wants, and new ways to sell them. John Brewer, Peter Earle, and Maxine Berg suggest that sixteenth- and seventeenth-century luxury consumption was narrowly focused on the court, giving way in the early eighteenth century to urban consumption and demand for goods by a middle-class public, supporting the theory of the development of the bourgeois public sphere laid out by Jürgen Habermas.[18] I argue that, in many respects, that public was already in place. The steady growth of luxury consumption from the first half of the sixteenth century had reached more and more people by the eighteenth century, but its practices, sites, and mentalities developed in the sixteenth and early seventeenth centuries. Indeed, the innovations of the Jacobean period are inextricably linked to economic growth in the middle of the seventeenth century and beyond. The role of Crown, aristocracy, and merchants who facilitated the increasing luxury consumption of the seventeenth century needs to be placed alongside the current focus on middling groups as creators of luxury consumption. New luxury consumption: urban, social, and expansive, was in place in the early seventeenth century augmented in variety and scale throughout the century.

---

[16] C. R. Brooks, *Pettifoggers and Vipers of the Commonwealth* (Cambridge: Cambridge University Press, 1986), pp. 68–70, 94–95. Muldrew, *The Economy of Obligation*.

[17] Thomas Mun, *England's Treasure by Forraign Trade* (London, 1664).

[18] John Brewer and Roy Porter (eds.), *Consumption and the World of Goods* (London: Routledge, 1993). Peter Earle, *The Making of the English Middle Class: Business, Society and Family Life in London, 1660–1730* (Berkeley and Los Angeles: University of California Press, 1989); Maxine Berg and Helen Clifford (eds.), *Consumers and Luxury: Consumer Culture in Europe, 1650–1850* (Manchester: Manchester University Press, 1999). Jürgen Habermas, *The Structural Transformation of the Public Sphere*, trans. Thomas Burger (Cambridge, MA: MIT Press, 1991).

Moreover, many of the themes of luxury consumption in the late seventeenth century were also in place: retail shopping as entertainment, the growth of the London season,[19] the development of public leisure centers like arcades and public parks, later copied in regional towns,[20] and the continuing expansion of the art market with the arrival of auctions.[21] Late seventeenth-century English art, the offspring of the cultural borrowings from Rubens and Van Dyck in the early seventeenth century, nestled within the Protestant, parliamentary, and commercial regime of which it was symbolic capital. The spoils of the Grand Tour were displayed in great country houses and suburban villas that marked the connoisseurship of their aristocratic owners, such as Chatsworth, Castle Howard, and Chiswick House where in the early eighteenth century, Lord Burlington appropriated the classical gate that Inigo Jones designed for Lionel Cranfield.[22]

LAW AND GENDER

Women, who always exercised an important role in the consumption decisions of the family, created autonomous selves through the purchase, bequest, and display of luxury goods. The critique of luxury purveyed in sermons, plays, and pamphlets, reiterated the traditional accusation that women caused luxury which weakened and effeminated men. The anxieties exposed in this prescriptive literature, which reflected the growing importance and spread of the consumption of luxury goods beyond the court aristocracy, were expressed in a legal decision that affected consumption throughout English society.

In 1663 the Court of Exchequer heard the case of *Manby v. Scott*. Scott, estranged from his wife, refused to pay the bill of Manby, a well-known mercer, who, despite Mr. Scott's prohibition, had extended credit to Mrs. Scott for her purchases. Although Mrs. Scott wished to return to her husband, he would not cohabit with her. The court held that the "silk and velvet to the value of L40 . . . is found suitable to the degree of her husband." Although the doctrine of coverture prevented married women from making contracts under common law, case law on "necessaries" since the fifteenth

[19] Susan E. Whyman, *Sociability and Power in Late-Stuart England: The Cultural Worlds of the Verneys, 1660–1720* (Oxford: Oxford University Press, 1999).

[20] Peter Borsay, *The English Urban Renaissance: Culture and Society in the Provincial Town, 1660–1770* (Oxford: Oxford University Press, 1989).

[21] Brian Cowan, "Arenas of Connoisseurship: Auctioning Art in Later Stuart England," in Michael North and David Ormrod (eds.), *Art Markets in Europe, 1400–1800* (Aldershot, Hampshire: Ashgate Publishing, 1998), pp. 153–66.

[22] See chapter 5 above.

century had declared that "if a woman buy things suitable to the degree of her husband, he shall be bound by it."[23] Of course, poor women received little protection from the doctrine of necessaries.[24]

The judges did not make the decision lightly. They worried that it would enable women to spend and despise their husbands. Furthermore, Chief Justice Robert Hyde reserved decisions on necessaries to judges rather than jurors, the usual triers of fact, because of jury bias.

It is objected, that the jury is to judge what is fit for the wives' degree, that they are trusted with the reasonableness of the price, and are to examine the value, and also the necessity of the things or apparel. Alas poor man! What a judicature is set up here to decide the private differences between husband and wife; the wife will have a velvet gown and a satin petticoat, the husband thinks a mohair or farendon for a gown, and watered tabby for a petticoat, is as fashionable, and fitter for his quality; the husband says that a plain lawn georget of 10s pleaseth him, and suits best with his condition, the wife will have a Flanders lace or pointed handkerchief of 40 l. and takes it up at the Exchange. A jury of mercers, silk-men, sempsters and exchange-men are very excellent and very indifferent judges to decide this controversy ... are not a jury of drapers and milliners bound to favor the mercer or exchange men today that they may do the like for them tomorrow?[25]

Over the century, the necessaries that the wife could claim grew to include houses and furnishings. During the reign of William and Mary, "a tradesman, who sold lace and silver fringes for a petticoat and side-saddle, which amounted to L94, and all within four months, to the wife of a sergeant at law, formerly a judge, recovered against him."[26] By the early

---

[23] Anon, *Baron and Feme, A Treatise of Law and Equity Concerning Husbands and Wives*, 3rd edn (London, 1738), p. 274. Margot Finn, "Women, Consumption, and Coverture in England, c. 1760–1860," *Historical Journal*, 39 (1996), 703–22. I am grateful to Margot Finn for discussion of women and credit. Manby was a well-known mercer from whom Charles Cheyne bought clothes.

[24] Women traders were responsible for their own maintenance. See Finn, "Women, Consumption, and Coverture in England," 703–22.

[25] *Modern Reports*, vol. 8, 124–43, Term. Trin. 15 Car. II. 1663. Judge Hyde's Argument in the Exchequer-Chamber. Judge Hyde sought to send a message to well-to-do female consumers. If the decision to favor the wife "departing from her husband against his will, and taking of clothes upon trust, contrary to his prohibition, shall come abroad to all women; and it shall be repeated that her husband by the opinion of the judges must pay for the wares which she so took up, whilst she lived from him, then shall their husbands be despised in their eyes. But when it shall be known throughout the realm, that the law doth not charge the husband in this case, all the wives shall give to their husbands honour, both great and small." For case law on necessaries see in addition to *Baron and Feme, Stroud's Judicial Dictionary of Words and Phrases*, 4th edn, ed. John S. James, 5 vols., (London: Sweet and Maxwell, 1973), III, pp. 1734–35. William Holdsworth, *A History of English Law* (London, 1923), vol. III, pp. 528–30.

[26] Anon, *Baron and Feme*, p. 285. Finn, "Women, Consumption, and Coverture," 710.

eighteenth century, Lady Calvert had her mercer, linen draper, and others sue her estranged husband for L3,000 in "necessaries."[27]

From Jacobean city comedy to Restoration drama and the decision in *Manby v. Scott*, men pictured women as shoppers who plotted to make their husbands pay for luxuries.[28] Yet legal decisions continued to expand the scope of "necessaries" not because of the rapacity of women but, at least in part, because the range of luxury goods considered necessary to the status and degree of men increased along with the growth of luxury trade and manufacture.

DEBATING LUXURY

This book has argued that luxury consumption, its goods, practices, and newly built environment of the sixteenth and seventeenth centuries, promoted the "endless wants" discerned by Nicholas Barbon at the end of the seventeenth century, celebrated by Bernard Mandeville, and defined by David Hume in the early eighteenth century.[29] Of course, efforts to emulate the Dutch, to copy French skills and Italian glass began under the Tudors, and James I harnessed the printing press to support the Crown's efforts to improve manufactures. The luxury consumption of the early seventeenth century and the royal policies and tracts that supported it are directly connected to the writings on political economy of the late seventeenth century and eighteenth century. For luxury was situated not only in traditional discourses of virtue and vice and war and peace, but also in the discourse of trade and manufacture. While the fruitful pamphlet literature of the 1650s, especially from the Hartlib circle, is very important to the development of political economy, I have tried to show that their interests and writings are linked to the writings of early Stuart pamphleteers and the policies of the early Stuarts.

The eighteenth century "Luxury Debate" has been much studied.[30] Enlightenment writers such as Montesquieu, for instance, differentiated

---

[27] *Ibid.*, 703–22, and Lawrence Stone, *Broken Lives: Separation and Divorce in England 1660–1857* (Oxford: Oxford University Press, 1993).

[28] See chapter 1 above.

[29] Berry, *The Idea of Luxury*, pp. 112, 126–34, 142–52. John Sekora, *Luxury: The Concept in Western Thought, Eden to Smollett* (Baltimore: Johns Hopkins University Press, 1977). Maxine Berg and Elizabeth Eger (eds.), *Luxury in the Eighteenth Century: Debates, Desires and Delectable Goods* (Basingstoke, Hampshire: Palgrave, 2003).

[30] See Berry, *The Idea of Luxury*; Sekora, *Luxury: The Concept in Western Thought, Eden to Smollett*; Neil de Marchi, "Adam Smith's Accommodation of 'Altogether Endless' Desires," in Berg and Clifford (eds.), *Consumers and Luxury*, pp. 18–36.

the ancient luxury of the Persian court, extractive and unproductive, from the modern luxury of contemporary Paris, created through invention and manufacture and widely circulated throughout society.[31] David Hume, Sir James Steuart, and Adam Smith, icons of the Scottish Enlightenment, sought to understand the demand for luxury goods. Adam Smith's suggestion that "the desire of the conveniencies and ornaments of building, dress, equipage, and household furniture seems to have no limit or certain boundary"[32] applied as much to Elizabeth Lady Compton's demands of 1610 and William Petty's new London house, as it did to his own contemporaries.

In particular, Sir James Steuart, a Jacobite exile who wrote his *Inquiry into the Principles of the Political Economy* in the 1760s, offers an analysis of luxury that reminds us of the purpose, practice, and outcome of early seventeenth-century policy. Steuart argued that luxury was central to both the economy and society because the multiplication of wants and the luxury consumption of the rich drove the circulation of goods throughout the economy to the benefit of the poor up to the limits of the margins of cultivation. "The rich will call for superfluities; the free hands will supply them, and demand food in their turn ... when once this imaginary wealth (money) become well introduced into a country, luxury will very naturally follow; and when money becomes the object of our wants, mankind become industrious, in turning their labour towards every object which may engage the rich to part with it; and thus the inhabitants of any country may increase in numbers until the ground refuses further nourishment."[33]

Aspirations to magnificence and splendor were good for the economy, Steuart argued. Looking at contemporary France, Steuart countered Mirabeau's claim that luxury consumption hurt the populace. Like William Petty, Steuart linked luxury and skilled labor. Steuart wrote "elegance of taste and in living, which has for its object the labour and ingenuity of man; and as the ingenuity of workmen begets a taste in the rich, so the allurement of riches kindles an ambition, and encourages an application to works of ingenuity, in the poor." Indeed, French workmen, fertile inventors with "their reputation for the elegance of their taste in

[31] Charles De Secondat, Baron de Montesquieu, *The Persian Letters*, trans. and intro. George Healey (Indianapolis and Cambridge: Haslett Publishing, 1999).

[32] Quoted in Berry, *The Idea of Luxury*, p. 183.

[33] Sir James Steuart, *An Inquiry into the Principles of Political Economy*, ed. and intro. Andrew S. Skinner, 2 vols. (Chicago: University of Chicago Press, 1966), vol. I, p. 45.

matters of dress, have got into possession of the right of prescribing to all Europe the standards of taste in articles of mere superfluity."[34]

Steuart argued that the statesman should take an active role in managing the economy. His prescription reminds us of the policies of James I to promote luxury industries. When foreign trade declined, Steuart suggested "the introduction of luxury may be a rational and prudent step of administration; . . . an able statesman will soon throw industry into a new channel, better calculated for reviving foreign trade, and for promoting the public good, by substituting the call of foreigners instead of that of domestic luxury."

But like James I, Steuart thought the statesman should aim to support the export of luxuries. "Joining all the advantages of ancient simplicity to the wealth and power which attends upon the luxury of modern states . . . we must encourage economy, frugality, and a simplicity of manners, discourage the consumption of every thing that can be exported, and excite a taste for superfluity in neighboring nations." He concluded,

by such means, elegance of taste, and the polite arts may be carried to the highest pitch. The whole of the inhabitants may be employed in working and consuming; all may be made to live in plenty and in ease, by the means of a swift circulation which will produce a reasonable equality of wealth among all the inhabitants. Luxury can never be the cause of inequality, though it may be the effect of it. Hoarding and parsimony form great fortunes, luxury dissipates them and restores equality.[35]

In the late nineteenth and early twentieth centuries, Werner Sombart and Max Weber undertook their own analyses of luxury consumption. Sombart, like Sir James Steuart, argued that luxury was key to the development of capitalism. For Sombart, capitalism arose not through Max Weber's "Protestant Ethic," in which industry and thrift, flowing from the Protestant emphasis of working in the world, produced accumulation, but through the interplay of courts, cities, women, and sexuality. All led to the growth in the production and circulation of luxury goods which ignited capitalist exchange.[36] Weber, however, believed that court luxury was not sufficient and focused instead on the fusion of court, war, and a larger consumer market as essential to the origins of industrialization.[37]

---

[34] *Ibid.*, I, pp. 135–39, 46, 250. "Vice is not more essentially connected with superfluity, than virtue with industry and frugality."

[35] *Ibid.*, pp. 228–29, 281–82.

[36] Werner Sombart, *Luxury and Capitalism*, trans. W. R. Dittmar, intro. Philip Siegelman (Ann Arbor: University of Michigan Press, 1967).

[37] Max Weber, *General Economic History*, trans. Frank M. Knight (New York: Collier Books, 1961), pp. 229–30.

Each theory finds some support in this book's argument. During the early seventeenth century, when England was at peace, the royal court and London were central to the growth of luxury consumption. Sombart suggested that the division of retail shopping from wholesale took place in the later seventeenth century and the move, for instance, of the mercers away from Paternoster Row and the later development of commodity stores.[38] In fact, as we have seen, retail shopping was reinforced in the Royal Exchange in the City in the 1570s and was established in the West End by the Earl of Salisbury in his New Exchange of 1609. Moreover, throughout the seventeenth century, luxury consumption built upon regional consumer industries and credit already in place in the sixteenth century. In the middle and late seventeenth century, war played a greater role in shaping and expanding luxury consumption. Evelyn's representation of Petty's amazement at his palatial London home and accumulation of luxury goods due to hard work in manufactures and Mrs. Petty's taste for magnificence, splendor, and refinement happily combine the protean theories of Max Weber's *Protestant Ethic* and Werner Sombart's *Luxury and Capitalism*. Both describe the transformation of the economy in the early modern period.

CULTURAL BORROWING AND ECONOMIC CHANGE

Yet, neither Sombart nor Weber emphasize the importance of cultural borrowing, whether invention or skilled labor, to economic change. From James I to the Royal Society, contemporaries sought a knowledge-based economy.[39] At the beginning of the seventeenth century, the English were imitators and importers of goods; gradually over the century they began to learn how to make and export copies of continental and Asian goods and, just as importantly, to capture trade networks from European competitors. The English Crown's continuing concern with cultural borrowing, manufacture, and trade was clearly stated from the beginning of James I's reign by the King himself and his officials. Francis Bacon urged that those who "sail into foreign countries ... bring us the books and abstracts and patterns of experiments of all other parts."[40] The early Stuarts adopted

---

[38] Sombart, *Luxury and Capitalism*, pp. 131–33.
[39] I am grateful to Margaret Jacob for discussion of this point.
[40] Quoted in Ernan McMullin, "Openness and Secrecy in Science: Some Notes on Early History," *Science, Technology and Human Values*, 10 (1985), 20.

the policy with enthusiasm. At the Restoration, the Royal Society took up Bacon's plan, supplemented by that of Samuel Hartlib.

At the beginning of the eighteenth century, Daniel Defoe, that acute and oft-quoted observer, wrote,

It is a kind of proverb attending to the character of Englishmen, that they are better to improve than to invent, better to advance upon the designs and plans which other people have laid down, than to form schemes and designs of their own and which is still more, the thing seems to be really true in fact, and the observation very just.[41]

While Defoe coupled English identity with quickened manufactures and commercial activity at the opening of the eighteenth century, his protean comment helps frame the issues of luxury consumption, cultural borrowing, and manufactures a century earlier.

When, in 1754, the Society of Arts, Manufactures, and Commerce offered premiums for technological improvements, its agenda, as we saw earlier, mirrored that of Jacobean patentees and the Royal Society. It followed in the footsteps of Queen Elizabeth and King James, Lord Burghley, Bacon, Hartlib, and the Royal Society.[42] Cultural borrowing and luxury consumption had already taken strong root in seventeenth-century England.

In conclusion, while this book has sought to cast light on the role of luxury and cultural borrowing in early modern England, it does not insist on the uniqueness of the English experience. Instead, it underlines the importance of analyzing the social and cultural values and practices that surround luxury in other societies in other times and places. England's openness to other cultures through print, travel, and migration, its eagerness for information, and its willingness to copy and invent, may even suggest parallels with other once marginal economies such as nineteenth-century America, twentieth-century Japan and Asia, and twenty-first century China.

---

[41] Quoted in Catherine MacLeod, *Inventing the Industrial Revolution: The English Patent System, 1660–1800* (Cambridge: Cambridge University Press, 1982), p. 208.

[42] D. G. C. Allen and John L. Abbot (eds.), *The Virtuoso Tribe of Arts and Sciences: Studies in the Eighteenth Century and Membership of the London Society of Arts*, (Athens and London: University of Georgia Press, 1992), pp. xv–xvi. See chapter 8 above.

Bibliography

MANUSCRIPT SOURCES

ARUNDEL CASTLE

Arundel Castle Mss. G1/194, Embassy to the Emperor of Morocco 1669
Arundel Castle Mss. IN 1, Inventory of Tart Hall 1641
Arundel Castle Mss. N 39, Items Arundel took into exile
Arundel Castle Mss. T9, Arundel's draft will

BRITISH LIBRARY

Add. Charter 76,982, A and B, Lease to William Petty in St. Margaret, Lothbury
Add. Charter 76,971, Indenture 1 January 1638–39, Henry, Lord Maltravers, messuage and garden in St. Margaret, Lothbury
Add. Mss. 15,561, Long Family of Wiltshire
Add. Mss. 15,970, Arundel and Maltravers correspondence
Add. Mss. 19,872, Papers relating to Tangiers 1669–1700
Add. Mss. 28,010, J. Denne, notes on trips to France with Sir Clipsby Crew and Peter Rychaut 1644
Add. Mss. 28,714, Inventory, Thomas Bulmer, citizen and draper, 1594
Add. Mss. 37,998, Papers of Sir Edward Walker relating to the Order of the Garter
Add. Mss. 41,656, Townshend Accounts and Inventories
Add. Mss. 62,092, Margaret Spencer Account Book, 1610–13.
Add. Mss. 69,873, Coke Papers series II, Correspondence
Add. Mss. 69,877, Coke Papers, series II, Sir John Coke, Household Accounts, 1623–38
Add. Mss. 69,880, Coke Papers, Personal and Household Accounts, 1587–1655
Add. Mss. 69,883B, Coke Papers, series II, Miscellaneous papers
Add. Mss. 69,888, Coke Papers, series II, Commonplace book, 4 April 1642 to December 1642.
Add. Mss. 71,448, James Chaloner correspondence
Add. Mss. 72,310, Trumbull Papers, Daniel Skynner correspondence
Add. Mss. 72,709, Elizabeth Lady Raleigh to her brother Sir Nicholas Carew
Add. Mss. 72,891, Petty Papers
Add. Mss. 72,897, Petty Papers on dying textiles, woollen manufacture, tannery, 1662–1687

Add. Mss. 72,907, Petty Papers, lease of St. Margaret, Lothbury

Add. Mss. 75,303, Althorp Papers, account book for journey to Duke of Wurtemberg 1603

Add. Mss. 75,304, Althorp Papers, mission to invest Duke of Wurtemberg with Order of the Garter including Spencer's travel diary

Add. Mss. 75,326, Spencer inventories for Althorp 1610–36

Add. Mss. 75,350, Althorp Papers, "Account of France, history, geography, administration"

Add. Mss. 75,352, Earl and Countess of Cumberland, correspondence with men of business, 1600–36

Add. Mss. 76,966, A, B, St. Margaret, Lothbury, 1567

Add. Mss. 78,193, Arundel correspondence with Richard Browne, 1640s

Add. Mss. 78,315, Evelyn Papers

Add. Mss. 78,316, Evelyn Papers

Add. Mss. 78,334, Evelyn Papers

Add. Mss. 78,339, Evelyn Papers

Add. Mss. 78,340, Evelyn Papers, "Artes Illiberales et Mechanick"

Arundel 122, Vitruvious, "Architectura libri decem"

Egerton 1933, Household accounts for an estate of Sir Lionel Cranfield, 1615

Egerton 2558, Papers of Sir Edward Nicholas

Harl. 4258, Steward's Account for the Earl of Bath, 1602–1604

Royal Ms. 16 E xxvi, François de Verton, "Traicté des proprietez des meuriers & instruction par le gouvernement des vers a soye," *c.* 1605–10

Sloane Pr. xxxv

Sloane Mss. 857, Michael Mersey, John Greene to Alessio Morelli in Venice, 1667–71

Sloane, 1039, f. 139, Thomas Povey, Qualities of the herb called Tea or Chee, transcribed from a paper of 1686

Stowe 184, Sir John Harrison, Losses by sequestration, 1643–49, f. 161

Stowe 184, Sir Peter Lely, Proposal to paint the memorable achievements of Parliament, *c.* 1651, f. 283

BRITISH LIBRARY, MAP COLLECTIONS

Crace Collection, Portfolio I, 15, "A Plan of London, Westminster, and Southwark ... as they were survey'd ... toward the latter end of the reign of Queen Elizabeth"

Crace Collection, Portfolio I, no. 31, London General Plan, 1633

Crace Collection, Portfolio I, 35 and 36, Fairthorne, William, "An Exact Delineation of the Cities of London and Westminster and the Suburbs" (London, 1658)

Crace Collection, Portfolio xi, 61, Tart Hall and gardens, copy of plan drawn by Richard Baynes 1633

BRITISH MUSEUM, PRINTS AND DRAWINGS

"The Kingly Cocke," 1636

Mercer's Chapel with adjoining shops and houses as rebuilt after the Fire. Engraving from William Morgan, *London Survey'd*, 1681–82

CENTRE FOR KENTISH STUDIES

U 269 A389, Cranfield Papers, Accounts 1630, A462/4, receipts signed by Nicholas Stone
U 269/1, Cranfield Papers, CP 1–23, Mary, Countess of Buckingham, to Cranfield
U 269/1, Cranfield Papers, CP 39, Fourth Earl of Dorset to Cranfield
U 269/1, Cranfield Papers, CP 51
U 269/1, Cranfield Papers, CP 92
U 1475, E48, Inventory of plate and linen, June–July 1621.
U 1475 C85/32 8 December, 1662. Algernon, 10th Earl of Northumberland to the Earl of Leicester

CHATSWORTH

Chatsworth Mss., Library, E.1 a
Chatsworth Mss., Household, Miscellaneous Cliffords, M28, M 32
Chatsworth Mss., Lonsborough Papers, G. Inventories, 9/10

FOLGER SHAKESPEARE LIBRARY

Folger, 600, Humphrey Mildmay's Diary
Folger, V. a. 179 G., H. "The Goldsmith's Storehouse, in Two Books" (1604)
Folger, V. b. 232, Thomas Trevilian, Commonplace book, 1608
Folger, X. d. 428 Cavendish Talbot Mss., 97, 99, *c.* 1575, George Talbot, Earl of Shrewsbury to Elizabeth Countess of Shrewsbury; 2, 118, Arundel christening, 1607
Folger, Ms. Add. 727, Ms. list of Elizabeth of Bohemia's expenses, 1622
Folger, Ms. V. a. 318, f. 15, Hugh Alley, *A caveatt for the citty of London.* "Cheapside," Ms. 1598
Folger, L. b. 638, Somerset Inventory
Folger, Letter X. c. 49 Smith Correspondence, 1620

GUILDHALL LIBRARY

Guildhall, Mss., L78, Clayton Papers, Ms. 2931, Robert Abbott, account book
Guildhall, Ms. 15903, parts 1 and 2
Guildhall, Ms. 2710, Clockmakers Company, Minute Books, vol. 1, ff. 45–60

HATFIELD HOUSE

Hatfield, Cecil Mss., Accounts 35/2 1638, St. Martin's Lane, List of tenants and rents

Hatfield, Cecil Mss., Accounts 123/7, 1620

Hatfield, Cecil Mss., Accounts 127/8, Account of the Privy Purse for one year ending at Michaelmas 1638.

Hatfield, Cecil Mss., Accounts 160/1, 1610: accounts; building Britain's Burse

Hatfield, Cecil Mss., Bills 34 A and B, M485/104. George Skargill, 24 December 1608. Microfilms deposited at the British Library and Folger Shakespeare Library

Hatfield House Manuscripts, Bills 40–44, M485/105. 9 June 1609

Hatfield, Cecil Mss., Bills 189, 1637–38

Hatfield, Cecil Mss., Deeds, 41/2, Articles Concerning the Upper Part of the Burse, 24 December, 14 Charles I

Hatfield, Cecil Mss., Deeds 106/21, Indenture 20 April 22 James I between Hugh Pope and William Earl of Salisbury

Hatfield, Cecil Mss., Deeds, 146/2

Hatfield, Cecil Mss., Estate Papers, Box F3

Hatfield, Cecil Mss., Estate Papers, Box G3, accounts, 1611–12, with names of shopkeepers for 1611

Hatfield, Cecil Mss., Estate Papers Box H4

Hatfield, Cecil Mss., Estate Papers, Box R5 1633–34, Britain's Burse, leases of 1633–47

Hatfield, Cecil Mss., General 3/9

Hatfield, Cecil Mss., General 50/4

Hatfield, Cecil Mss., General 72/35

Hatfield, Cecil Mss., General 101/17

Hatfield, Cecil Mss., Legal 64/5, 1627

Hatfield, Cecil Mss., Legal 38/11, Letters Patent granting Salisbury, in consideration of his having built Britain's Burse, license to sell merchandise there, especially new draperies

Hatfield, House Manuscripts, Legal 231/23

Hatfield, "Family Papers," 1629–41, ed. R. T. Gunton, vol. 6

Hatfield, "Family Papers," 1642–59, ed. R. T. Gunton, vol. 7

Hatfield, "Family Papers, Supplement," 1637–92, ed. R. T. Gunton

Hatfield, "Family Papers, Second Supplement," 1617–64, ed. R. T. Gunton

HUNTINGTON LIBRARY, SAN MARINO, CALIFORNIA

HEH Ellesmere Mss. EL 6521 January 1634/35

HEH Ellesmere Mss. EL 6560, Earl of Bridgewater to Richard Harrison, 17 August 1640

HEH Ellesmere Mss. EL 6561 Harrison to Bridgewater, 22 August 1640

HEH Ellesmere Mss. EL 8104 Earl of Bridgewater's will, 2 April 1685

HEH Ellesmere Mss. EL 8117, Earl of Bridgewater: "Some Reasons Given by Me Why I Am in Debt," 6 June 1668, with later additions, 20 December 1673 and 25 March 1674

HEH Ellesmere Mss. El 8348, certificate and account of burial, 17 July 1663

HEH Ellesmere Mss. EL 8353

HEH Ellesmere Mss. EL 8360, Bridgewater family monuments

HEH Ellesmere Mss. EL 11,121–11,141, Correspondence of Edward Chaloner, Edward Altham, and Leventhorp Altham and Charles Cheyne, Esq. about orders for funeral monument and telescope, 1670–72

HEH Ellesmere Mss. EL 11,141, Cheyne's instructions to Dr. Littleton about inscription

HEH Ellesmere Mss. EL 11,143, Lady Jane Cavendish account book, 1635–63

HEH Ellesmere Mss. EL 11,145, Cheyne account book, 1669–73

HEH Hastings Mss., HAF, Box 8, nos. 20, 34, 37, 38. No. 32 lists the expenses of the journey to Bath

NATIONAL LIBRARY OF WALES

Carreglwyd Mss. 372, Henry Howard, Earl of Northampton, household goods, 27 September 1616, BMab 651/1

NOTTINGHAM UNIVERSITY LIBRARY

NUL, Portland Papers, Pw1/83–85, Letters of Charles Cheyne to Charles Cavendish, Viscount Mansfield, 1656

NUL, Portland Papers, Pw1/86–89, Lady Jane Cheyne to Charles Cavendish, Viscount Mansfield, 1656

NUL, Portland Papers, Pw1/90, Lady Jane Cheyne to Frances, Countess of Ogle, 1668

NUL, Portland Papers, Pw1/118–20, Elizabeth Countess of Bridgewater to her brother Viscount Mansfield, from Ashridge

NUL, Portland Papers, Pw1/121–22, John Egerton, second Earl of Bridgewater, to his brother in law Charles Cavendish, Viscount Mansfield, 3 June 1656 from Bridgewater House

NUL, Portland Papers, Pw1/668, "Directions for the Prospective Glasses," n.d.

OXFORD UNIVERSITY

Bodleian Library, Bankes Mss., petitions and grants of patents and licenses, 1630s

Bodleian Library, Ms. North c 47, "Inventory of William Earl of Down, late of Wroughton in the county of Oxon, 8 June 1631"

Bodleian, Eng. Hist. Mss.c. 120, f. 35ff. An inventory 23 April 1596 of goods of the Countess of Leicester and Sir Christopher Blount

Bodleian Library, Rawlinson D 693, John Cusacke, "Via Regia"

PUBLIC RECORD OFFICE

PROB11/229 will of Josias Fendall, joiner, Convent Garden, Middlesex, 1653

PROB 11/253 will of Hugh Pope gentleman, Covent Garden, St. Martin in the Fields, Middlesex, 1656

SP 14 State Papers of James I
SP 99/13 Carleton Correspondence

ROYAL SOCIETY, LONDON

Royal Society, Boyle Papers, BL. 4.146, Povey to Boyle, 8 May 1661, f. 146.
Royal Society, Classified Papers, II, 1660–1740, Surveying, Optics, Perspective, Painting, Music, Mechanicks
Royal Society, Classified Papers, II, 24 [Thomas Povey] "An Account of a Secret in the Use of Painting in Answer to the Commands of the Royal Society"
Royal Society, Classified Papers, III (1), 1660–1740, Mechanicks, #1
Royal Society, Classified Papers, III (2), 30, Sir Thomas Lombe's new machine for silk weaving, 1729–30
Royal Society, Classified Papers, IX (1) 32. "A Description of the Diamond Mines"
Royal Society, Classified Papers, X, 1660–1740, Botany, Agriculture
Royal Society, Committee Papers, III, 1, #2. 14, May 1662
Royal Society, Domestic Mss. vol. 5, #37, petition for alum mines; #68, Committee for Correspondence, 19 August 1664
Royal Society, Ms. Journal Book, 1660–64, pp. 301–305, committees of society
Royal Society, LBC 4. 254, John Doddington to Henry Oldenburg, 23 January 1670–71
Royal Society, RBO. RBC. 3.130–134. "Inquiries for Barbary Recommended by the Royal Society to the Favour and Care of His Excellency the Lord Henry Howard His Majesty's Ambassador Extraordinary to the Emperor of Morocco"
Royal Society, Sackler Archive

UNIVERSITY OF TEXAS, AUSTIN

University of Texas, Austin, Carl H. Pforzheimer Library, English Mss. MS35I, John Evelyn to Samuel Pepys, 26 August 1689

WESTMINSTER ARCHIVES

10/356, St. Martin in-the-Field parish rates 1632

PRINTED PRIMARY SOURCES

"The Account Book of Nicholas Stone," Walpole Society, 7 (London, 1918–19).
Acts of the Privy Council of England [Public Record Office]. New Series, ed. J. R. Dasent. (London: Stationery Office, Published under the direction of the Master of the Rolls, 1890–).
Alley, Hugh, *Hugh Alley's Caveat: The Markets of London in 1598, Folger. Ms. V. a. 318*, ed. Ian Archer, Caroline Barron, and Vanessa Harding, London Topographical Society, 137 (1988).

Articles of Peace Concluded and Agreed Between his Excellency the Lord Bellasyse His Majesty's Governor of His City and Garrison of Tangier in Africa . . . and Cidi Hamet Hader Ben Ali Gayland (London, 1666).

Astell, Mary, *A Serious Proposal to the Ladies . . .* (London: 1695).

  Astell Political Writings, ed. Patricia Springborg (Cambridge: Cambridge University Press, 1996).

The Autobiography of Anne Lady Halkett, ed. John Gough Nichols, Camden Society, new series 13 (London, 1875).

Bacon, Francis, *The Letters and Life of Francis Bacon*, 7 vols., ed. James Spedding (London: Longman, Green, Longman and Roberts, 1861–74).

  The Essayes or Counsels, Civill and Morall, ed. Michael Kiernan (Oxford: Clarendon Press, 2000).

  The New Organon, ed. Lisa Jardine and Michael Silverthorne (Cambridge: Cambridge University Press, 2000).

Barbon, Nicholas, *An Apology for the Builder, or, a Discourse Shewing the Cause and Effects of the Increase of Building* (London, 1685).

  A Discourse of Trade (London, 1690).

Baron and Feme: A Treatise of Law and Equity Concerning Husbands and Wives, 3rd edn (London, 1738).

Batho, G. R., ed., *Household Papers, Henry Percy, Ninth Earl of Northumberland, 1564–1632* (London: Royal Historical Society, 1962).

Bayly, Thomas, D. D., *Herba parietis, or the Wall-Flower. As it grew out of the stone-chamber belonging to the metropolitan prison of London, called Newgate* (London, 1650).

Benvenuto, *The Passenger of Benvenuto Italian Professor of his Native Tongue, for These Nine Years in London* (London, 1612).

Bettey, J. H., ed., *Calendar of the Correspondence of the Smyth Family of Ashton Court, 1548–1642* (Gloucester: Printed for the Bristol Record Society by Alan Sutton, 1982).

Billingsley, Martin, *A Copie Book Containing a Variety of Examples of All the Most Curious Hands Written*, 2nd edn (London, 1637).

Birch, Thomas, *The History of the Royal Society of London for Improving of Natural Knowledge, From its First Rise*, 4 vols. (London: A. Millar, 1756–57, 1760).

Blith, Walter, *The English Improver Improved*, 2nd edn (London, 1652).

Blount, Henry, *A Voyage into the Levant* (London, 1636).

Bonoeil, John, *His Majesty's Gracious Letter to the Earl of Southampton, Treasurer, and to the council and company of Virginia here, commanding the present setting up of silk works, and planting of vines in Virginia* (London, 1622).

Botero, Giovanni, *The Magnificence of Cities* (London, 1606).

Brennan, Michael G., ed., *The Travel Diary (1611–1612) of an English Catholic . . . Sir Charles Somerset* (Leeds: Leeds Philosophical and Literary Society, 1993).

  (ed.), *The Travel Diary of Robert Bargrave, Levant Merchant 1647–1656*, (London: Hakluyt Society, 1999).

Brereton, Sir William Bart., *Travels in Holland, the United Provinces, England, Scotland, and Ireland, 1634–1635*, ed. Edward Hawkins (London: Printed for the Chetham Society, 1844).

A Brief Relation of the Present State of Tangier, and of the Advantages Which his Excellence the Earl of Tiveot has Obtained Against Gayland (London, 1664).

By the King. A Proclamation Declaring His Majesties Pleasure to Settle and Establish a Free Port at his City of Tanger in Africa (London, 1662).

British Museum, *Catalogue of Prints and Drawings in the British Museum*, ed. Frederic Stephens and M. Dorothy George, 11 vols. (London, 1870–1954).

    Catalogue of Political and Personal Satires, ed. Frederic Stephens and M. Dorothy George, vol. I (London: British Museum Publications, 1978).

Bullock, William, *Virginia Impartially Examined and Left to Publick View . . .* (London, 1649).

Burbury, John, *A Relation of a Journey of the Right Honourable my Lord Henry Howard* (London, 1671).

Calendar of the Proceedings of the Committee for Advance of Money, 1642–1656: preserved in the Public Record Office, ed. Mary Anne Everett Green, 3 vols. (London: HMSO, Eyre and Spottiswoode, 1888).

Calendar of the Proceedings of the Committee for Compounding . . . 1643–1660: preserved in the State Paper Department of Her Majesty's Public Record Office, ed. Mary Anne Everett Green, 5 vols. (London: HMSO, Eyre and Spottiswoode, 1889–92).

Calendar of State Papers, Domestic Series 1547–1625 (London: Longman, 1856–72).

Calendar of State Papers, Domestic Series 1625–1649 (London: Longman, 1858–97).

Calendar of State Papers, Domestic Series 1671 (London: Longman, 1860).

Calendar of State Papers and Manuscripts Relating to English Affairs . . . in the Archives and Collections of Venice, 1619–23, 1643–44 [Public Record Office] (London: Stationery Office, 1864–1947).

Cavendish, Jane, and Elizabeth Cavendish, "The Concealed Fancies: Poems," in Marion Wynn Davies, ed., *Women Poets of the Renaissance* (New York: Routledge, 1999), 255–59.

Cavendish, William, Duke of Newcastle, *Methode et Invention Nouvelle de Dresser les Chevaux* (Antwerp, 1657).

Chamberlain, John, *Letters of John Chamberlain*, ed. N. E. McClure (Philadelphia: American Philosophical Society Proceedings, 1939).

Chamberlayne, John, *The Natural History of Coffee, Thee, Chocolate, Tobacco . . . collected from the writings of the best physicians and modern travellers* (London, 1682).

[Child, Sir Josiah], *A Treatise Wherein is Demonstrated, 1. that the East India Trade is the Most National of all Foreign Trade . . .* (London, 1681).

Commissioners of Patents for Inventions

    Titles of Patents of Invention Chronologically Arranged from March 2 1617 (14 James I) to October 1, 1852 (16 Victoriae), ed. Bennet Woodcroft (London: Eyre and Spottiswoode, Queen's Printing Office, 1854).

Specifications of Patents, Old Series, 1617–1852 (London: Eyre and Spottiswoode, Queen's Printing Office, 1859).

Subject Matter Index ... of Patents of Invention from March 2, 1627 (14 James I) to October 1, 1852 (16 Victoriae), ed. Bennet Woodcroft, 2 pt (London: Eyre and Spottiswoode, Queen's Printing Office, 1854).

Coryat, Thomas, *Coryat's Crudities* (London, 1610).

Dallington, Robert, *The View of France* (London, 1604).

   A Method for Travel Shewed by Taking the View of France as it Stood in the Year ... 1598 (London, 1605).

Davenant, William, *Gondibert: An Heroic Poem* (London. 1651).

   "Upon the Marriage of the Lady Jane Cavendish with Mr. Cheney," in A. M. Gibb, ed., *The Shorter Poems, and Songs from the Plays and Masques* (Oxford: Clarendon Press, 1972), pp. 131–32.

De Caus, Isaac, *Wilton Garden: New and Rare Inventions of Waterworks* (London, 1645).

A Description of Tangier, the Country and People Adjoining. (London, 1664).

D'Ewes, Simonds, *The Journal of Simonds D'Ewes from the Beginning of the Long Parliament to the Opening of the Trial of the Earl of Strafford* (New Haven: Yale University Press, 1923).

A Direction for Travailers taken out Justus Lipsius and enlarged for the behoof of the yong Earle of Bedford, being now ready to travel (1592).

Erondelle, Pierre, *The French Garden: For English Ladies and Gentlewomen to Walk in ... thirteen dialogues in French and English* (London, 1605).

Esdaile, Katherine Ada, "The Monuments in Chelsea Old Church," in Weston Henry Stewart (ed.), *Chelsea Old Church ...* , revised and reissued with an introduction by Reginald Blunt (London: Oxford University Press, 1932).

Evelyn, John, *Londinum Redivivum, or London Restored not to its pristine, but to far greater beauty, commodiousness and magnificence* (London, 1666).

   Diary and Correspondence of John Evelyn, ed. William Bray (London: H. G. Bohn, 1859–62).

   London Revived: Considerations for its Rebuilding in 1666, ed. E. S. de Beer (Oxford: Clarendon Press, 1938).

   The Diary of John Evelyn, ed. E. S. de Beer, 6 vols. (Oxford: Clarendon Press, 1955).

   Tyrannus or the Mode with a Discourse of Sumptuary Laws (London, 1661); reprinted in *The Writings of John Evelyn*, ed. Guy de la Bedoyere (Woodbridge, Suffolk: Boydell Press, 1995), pp. 163–72.

"An Experiment of a Way of Preparing a Liquor, that Shall Sink into, and Colour the Whole Body of Marble, Causing a Picture, Drawn on a Surface to Appear also in the Inmost Parts of the Stone," *Philosophical Transactions*, I (1665–66), 125–27.

Fairholt, F. W., "On an Inventory of the Household Goods of Sir Thomas Ramsay, Lord Mayor of London, 1577," *Archaeologia*, 40 (1866), 311–42.

Fairthorne, William, "An Exact Delineation of the Cities of London and Westminster and the Suburbs" [1658] (London: London Topographical Society, 1905).

Fanshawe, Anne Lady, *The Memoirs of Lady Fanshawe* (London: Henry Colburn, 1829).

Fargeron, Jean, *Catalogue des Marchandises* (Montpellier, 1665).

Fleming, Giles, *Magnificence Exemplified: and the repair of St Paul's exhorted unto* (London, 1634).

Fowler, Rev. J. J., "The Account Book of William Wray," *The Antiquary*, 32 (1896).

Gater, Sir Henry and Edwin Paul Wheeler, *The Parish of St. Martin-in-the-Fields*, Part II, *The Strand*, Survey of London, vol. 18 (London: London County Council, 1937); Part III, *Trafalgar Square and Neighbourhood*, Survey of London, vol. 20 (London: London County Council, 1940).

Geffe, Nicholas, *Discourse . . . of the Meanes and Sufficiencie of England, for to Have Abundance of Fine Silke, by Feeding of Silke-Wormes within the Same . . . For the general use and universal benefit of all those his country-men which embrace it* (London, 1607).

Gerbier, Balthazar, *On Magnificence in Buildings* (London, 1662).

Godfrey, Walter Hindes, *The Parish of Chelsea*, 4 vols., Survey of London, vols. 2, 4, 7, 11 (London: London County Council, 1913–27).

Goodman, Godfrey, Bishop of Gloucester, *The Court of King James the First*, ed. John S. Brewer, 2 vols. (London: Richard Bentley, 1839).

Great Britain. Royal Commission on Historical Manuscripts. Historical Manuscript Commission Reports.

First and Second Reports with Appendices (1874), Appendix to the Second Report, "The Manuscripts of C. Cottrell Dormer, Esq., Rousham."

The Manuscripts of the House of Lords, 1678–1688 (1887).

The Manuscripts of the Earl Cowper . . . preserved at Melbourne Hall, Derbyshire, 2 vols. (1888).

The Manuscripts of His Grace the Duke of Portland preserved at Welbeck Abbey, 9 vols. (1891–1923).

The Manuscripts Of The Most Honourable The Marquess Of Downshire Formerly Preserved At Easthampstead Park, Berkshire. 6 vols. (1924–c. 95).

The Manuscripts of the Most Hon. the Marquis of Salisbury . . . preserved at Hatfield House, Hertfordshire, 24 vols. (1883–1976).

The Manuscripts of Major-General Lord Sackville . . . preserved at Knole, Sevenoaks, Kent, 2 vols. (1940–66).

Grew, Nehemiah, *Musaeum Regalis Societatis* (London, 1681).

Hall, Joseph, *Quo Vadis? A Just Censure of Travel as It Is Commonly Undertaken by the Gentlemen of Our Nation* (London, 1617).

Halliwell-Phillips, J. O., "An Inventory of the Plate, Household Stuff, Pictures etc. in Kenilworth Castle, Taken after the Death of Robert Earl of Leycester, 1588," in *Ancient Inventories . . . Illustrative of the Domestic Manners of the English in the 16th and 17th Centuries* (London, 1854).

Harrison, William, *The Description of England*, ed. Georges Edelen (Washington, DC: Folger Shakespeare Library; New York: Dover Publications, 1994). This edition is based on the 1587 folio.

Hartlib, Samuel, *A rare and new discovery of a speedy way, and easy means, found out by a young Lady in England . . . for the feeding of silk-worms in the woods, on the mulberry tree leaves in Virginia* (London, 1652).

    His Legacie or an Enlargement of the Discourse of Husbandry in Brabant and Flanders wherein are bequeathed to the Commonwealth of England more outlandish and domestic experiments and secrets in reference to husbandry (London, 1652).

    The Reformed Common-wealth of Bees. Presented in severall letters and observations to Samuel Hartlib, esq. with the reformed Virginian silk-worm. . . . (London, 1655).

Hearne, Thomas, *A Collection of Curious Discourses Written by Eminent Antiquaries upon Several Heads in our English Antiquities*, 2 vols. (London, 1771).

Heywood, Thomas, *If You Know Not Me, You Know No Body, the Second Part with the Building of the Royal Exchange* (London, 1633).

An Historical and True Discourse of a Voyage Made by the Admiral Cornelis Matelife, the Younger into the East Indies (London, 1608).

H. N., *The Compleat Merchant* (London, 1684, 1690).

Hobbes, Thomas, *The Correspondence*, ed. Noel Malcolm, 2 vols. (Oxford: Clarendon Press, 1994).

Hollar, Wenceslaus, *Divers Prospects in and about Tangier . . . etched in copper and are to be sold*, (London: printed by John Ogilby, 1673).

Howard, Henry, Duke of Norfolk, "A Description of the Diamond-Mines as it was Presented by the Right Honourable, the Earl Marshal of England, to the Royal Society," *Philosophical Transactions*, 12 (1677–78), 907–17.

Howard, Thomas, Earl of Arundel, *Remembrances of Things Worth Seeing in Italy: Given to John Evelyn, 25 April 1646*, ed. John Martin Robinson (London: Roxburghe Club, 1987).

Howell, James, *Instruction for Forreine Travel* (London, 1642).

Hudleston, C. Roy, ed., *Naworth Estate and Household Accounts, 1648–1660* (Durham: Surtees Society, 1958).

Hutchinson, Lucy, *Memoirs of the Life of Colonel Hutchinson*, ed. James Sutherland (London: Oxford University Press, 1973).

Index of Wills Proved in the Prerogative Court of Canterbury, vol. VII, 1653–1656, ed. Thomas M. Bragg and Josephine Skeate Moir (London: The British Record Society, 1925).

Irenodia Gratulatoria, British Library, Thomason Tracts, E 796 30.

Jonson, Ben, *Ben Jonson*, eds. Charles Harold Herford and Percy Simpson, 11 vols. (Oxford: Clarendon Press, 1925–52).

    Epicoene, or the Silent Woman, in Jonson, *Works*, ed. Herford and Simpson, (Oxford: Clarendon Press, 1937–), V, pp. 139–271.

Kempe, Alfred John, *The Loseley Manuscripts* (London: J. Murray, 1836).

Kingsbury, S. M. ed., *The Records of the Virginia Company of London*, 4 vols. (Washington, DC: GPO, 1906–35).

La Grande Encyclopédie, 60 vols. (Paris: Larousse, 1971–76).

Lambeck, Peter, *Commentarium de Augustissima Bibliotheca Caesarea Vindobonensi liber*, 8 vols. (Vienna, 1665–79).

Le Muet, Pierre, *The Art of Fair Building represented in the figures of several uprights of houses with their ground plots fitting for persons of all qualities* (London, 1675).

Letellier, Jean-Baptiste, *Memoirs et instructions pour l'establissement des meuriers, et art de faire la soye en France* (Paris, 1603).

Leybourn, William, *The Compleat Surveyor* (London, 1653, 1674).

Littleton, Adam, *A Sermon at the Funeral of the Right Honourable the Lady Jane, Eldest Daughter to his Grace William, Duke of Newcastle, and Wife to the Honourable Charles Cheyne, esq; at Chelsea. Novemb. 1 being All-Saints day by Adam Littleton, priest* (London: 1669).

Lough, John, *France Observed in the Seventeenth Century by British Travellers* (Stocksfield, Northumberland, and Boston: Oriel Press, 1984).

Malynes, Gerard, *The Center of the Circle of Commerce* (London, 1623).

Mandeville, Bernard, *The Grumbling Hive, or, Knaves Turn'd Honest* (London, 1705). *The Fable of the Bees, or, Private vices, publick benefits* (London, 1714).

Mansell, Robert, *The True State of the Businesse of Glasse of All Kinds, as it now standeth both in the price of glasse and materialls, how sold these fifteen years last past* (London, 1641).

Mare, Eric de, *Wren's London* (London: The Folio Society, 1975).

Middleton, Thomas and Thomas Dekker, *The Roaring Girl or Moll Cutpurse* (London, 1605); reprinted in James Knowles, ed., *The Roaring Girl and Other City Comedies* (Oxford: Oxford University Press, 2001).

Milton, John, *Comus* (London, 1637).

Misselden, Edward, *The Circle of Commerce* (London, 1623).

Modern Reports, vol. 8, 124–43, Term. Trin. 15 Car. II. 1663.

Moffett, Thomas, *The Silkewormes and their Flies* (London, 1599); facsimile edn, ed. Victor Houliston (Binghamton, NY: Medieval and Renaissance Texts & Studies Society, 1989).

Montaigne, Michel de, *The Essays or morall, politike and millitarie discourses of Lo: Michaell de Montaigne*, trans. John Florio (London: 1603).

Montesquieu, Charles de Secondat, *The Persian Letters*, ed. R. Healy (Indianapolis and Cambridge: Mackett Publishing, 1999).

Moxon, Joseph, *Vignola: Or the Compleat Architect* (London, 1655).

Mun, Thomas, *England's Treasure by Forraign Trade* (London, 1664).

Neri, Antonio, *The Art of Glass . . . translated into English, with some observations on the author; whereunto is added an account of the glass drops made by the Royal Society, meeting at Gresham College*, trans. Christopher Merrett (London, 1662).

Neville, Henry, *News from the New Exchange Or the Commonwealth of Ladies* (London, 1650).

New news from the Old Exchange (London, 1650).

The Nicholas Papers: Correspondence of Sir Edward Nicholas, Secretary of State, ed. George F. Warner, 4 vols., (London, Camden Society 1886–1920).

Nichols, John Gough, *The Unton Inventories* (London: Printed for the Berkshire Ashmolean Society by John Bowyer Nichols and Son, 1841).

Oldenburg, Henry, *Correspondence*, ed. A. Rupert Hall and Marie Boas Hall, 13 vols. (Madison: University of Wisconsin Press, 1965–).

Peacham, Henry, *The Compleat Gentleman* (London, 1634).

Coach and Sedan, Pleasantly Disputing for Place and Precedence (London, 1636).

Pepys, Samuel, *Diary of Samuel Pepys: A New and Complete Transcription*, ed. Robert Latham and William Matthews, 11 vols. (Los Angeles and Berkeley: University of California Press, 1970–83).

A Perfect Description of Virginia (London, 1649).

Petty, William, *The Advice of W.P. to Mr. Samuel Hartlib for the Advancement of Some Particular Parts of Learning* (London, 1648).

Platt, Hugh, *Delights for Ladies: To Adorne their Persons, Tables, Closets and Distillatories* (London, 1628).

Platter, Thomas, *Thomas Platter's Travels in England, 1599*, ed. Clare Williams (London: Jonathan Cape, 1937).

Povey, Thomas, "Chai," *Philosophical Transactions*, III (1668).

"The Method, Manner and Order of the Transmutation of Copper into Brass," *Philosophical Transactions*, 17 (1693), 735–36.

Puget de la Serre, Jean, *Histoire de l'Entree de la Reine Mere du Roy ... dans la grande Bretagne* (London, 1639).

The Rates of Merchandizes as They Are Set Down in the Book of Rates (London, 1613).

Riley, W. E., and Sir L. Gomme, *The Parish of St. Giles-in-the-Fields*, Part II, Survey of London, 5 vols. (London: London County Council, 1914).

Roe, Sir Thomas, *The Negotiations of Sir Thomas Roe in his Embassy to the Ottoman Porte, From the year 1621 to 1628 Inclusive* (London, 1740).

A Royalist's Notebook: The Commonplace Book of Sir John Oglander, Kt. Of Nunwell, ed. Francis Bamwell (London: Constable and Company, 1936).

Rycaut, Paul, *The Present State of the Ottoman Empire* (London, 1668).

Sandys, George, *A Relation of a Journey Begun Anno Domini 1610 ... containing a description of the Turkish Empire, of Egypt, of the Holy Land, of the remote parts of Italy and islands adjoining* (London, 1615).

Scamozzi, Vincenzo, *L'idea della Architettura Universale*, 2 vols. (Venice, 1615).

Seddon, Peter, ed., *Letters of John Holles*, 3 vols. (Nottingham: Thoroton Society Record Series, 1975–86).

Serres, Olivier de, *Le Theatre d'Agriculture et Mesnage des Champs* (Paris, 1598).

The Perfect Use of Silk-Wormes and their Benefit ... Done out of the French original of D'Olivier de Serres Lord of Pradel into English by Nicholas Geffe Esquire (London, 1607).

The Several Declarations of the Company of Royal Adventurers (London, 1667).

Sheeres, Sir Henry, *A Discourse Touching Tanger: In a Letter to a Person of Quality* (London, 1680).

Sherley, Sir Anthony, *Sir Anthony Sherley, His Relation of His Travels into Persia* (London, 1613).

Shirley, E. P., "An Inventory of the Effects of Henry Howard, K. G. Earl of Northampton, Taken on his Death in 1614, Together with a Transcript of his Will," *Archaeologia*, 42 (1869), 347–78.

Shirley, James, *The Lady of Pleasure* (London, 1637).

Sholl, Samuel, *A Short Historical Account of the Silk Manufacture in England* (London, 1811).

Smith, Sir Thomas, *A Discourse of the Commonweal of this Realm of England, 1581*, ed. Mary Dewar (Charlottesville: Published for the Folger Shakespeare Library, University Press of Virginia, 1969).

Sprat, Thomas, *History of the Royal Society* (London, 1667).

Stallenge, William, *Instructions for the Increasing of Mulberie Trees* (London, 1609). Originally published in French by Jean-Baptiste Letellier.

The Statutes of the Realm, 11 vols. (London: G. Eyre and S. Atrahan, 1810–22).

Stent, Peter, *A Catalogue of Plates and Pictures that Are Printed and Sould by Peter Stent, dwelling at the sign of the White Horse in Guilt-spur Street* (London, 1654).

Steuart, Sir James, *An Inquiry into the Principles of Political Economy*, ed. and intro. Andrew S. Skinner, 2 vols. (Chicago: University of Chicago Press, 1966).

Stow, John, *A Survey of the Cities of London and Westminister, and the Borough of Southwark*, 2 vols. (London, 1720).

  Annales or a General Chronicle of England, 2nd edn (London, 1632).

Stroud's Judicial Dictionary of Words and Phrases, ed. John S. James, 4th edn, 5 vols. (London: Sweet and Maxwell, 1973).

Stuart Royal Proclamations, ed. James F. Larkin and Paul L. Hughes, 2 vols. (Oxford: Clarendon Press, 1973).

Stubbe, Henry, *The Indian Nectar or a Discourse Concerning Chocolate* (London, 1662).

  "The Remainder of the Observations Made in the Formerly Mention'd Voyage to Jamaica," *Philosophical Transactions*, III (1668), 721–22.

  Campanella Revived, or An Enquiry into the History of the Royal Society, whether the virtuosi there do not pursue the projects of Campanella for the reducing England unto popery (London, 1670).

Tavernier, John-Baptiste, *The Six Voyages of John Baptista Tavernier, a noble man of France now living, through Turkey into Persia and the East-Indies, finished in the year 1670* (London, 1678).

  Travels in India, trans. and ed. Valentine Ball 2nd edn, 2 vols. (London: Oxford University Press, 1925).

Tradescant, Jr., John, *Musaeum Tradescantianum* (London, 1656).

A Transcript of the Registers of the Worshipful Company of Stationers from 1640–1708, ed. George Edward Briscoe Eyre (London, 1913–14).

A True Declaration of the Estate of the Colony in Virginia (London, 1610).

The True English Interest: Or An Account of the Chief National Improvements (London, 1674).

A True Relation and Journall of the Manner of the Arivall and Magnificent Entertainment given to . . . Prince Charles . . . at Madrid (London, 1623).

Van der Passe, Crispijn, *Jardin de fleurs* (Utrecht, 1615).

Vertue, George, *Note Books*, 6 vols. (Oxford: Walpole Society, Oxford University Press, 1930–68).

Villa, Nicole, *Le XVII Siècle vu par Abraham Bosse, Graveur du Roy* (Paris: Les Editions Roger Dacosta, 1967).

Walpole, Horace, *Anecdotes of Painting in England* (Strawberry Hill, London, 1762).

Williams, Edward, *Virginia: More Especially the South Part Therof* (London, 1650).
   Virginia's Discovery of Silk-Worms with their Benefit and the Implanting of Mulberry Trees (London, 1650).
   Virgo Triumphans or Virginia Richly and Truly Valued (London, 1650).

Wing, Donald Goddard, John J. Morrison, Carolyn Nelson, Alfred W. Pollard, *Short Title Catalog of Books Printed in England, Scotland, Ireland, Wales, and British America, and of English Books Printed in Other Countries, 1641–1700*, 4 vols., 2nd edn, revised and enlarged (New York: Modern Language Association, 1972–98).

Woolley, Hannah, *A Supplement to the Queen-Like Closet; or a Little of Everything Presented to All Ingenious Ladies and Gentlewomen* (London, 1674).

Wotton, Sir Henry, *The Elements of Architecture* (London, 1624).

Wycherley, William, *Love in a Wood* (London, 1672).
   The Country Wife (London, 1675).

SECONDARY WORKS

Abbott, Jaspar A. R., "Robert Abbott: City Money Scrivener, and His Account Book, 1646–52," *Guildhall Miscellany* 1 (1956), 31–39.

Adams, Simon, *Household Accounts and Disbursement Books of Robert Dudley, Earl of Leicester, 1558–1561, 1584–1586* (London and New York: Cambridge University Press, 1995).
   The Earl of Leicester and Elizabethan Court Politics (Manchester: Manchester University Press, 2001).

Adburgham, Alison, *Shopping in Style: London from the Restoration to Edwardian Elegance* (London: Thames and Hudson, 1979).

Airs, Malcolm, *The Making of the English Country House, 1500–1640* (London: Architectural Press, 1975).
   The Tudor and Jacobean Country House: A Building History (Stroud: Alan Sutton, 1995).

Allan, D. G. C., and John L. Abbott (eds.), *The Virtuoso Tribe of Arts and Sciences: Studies in the Eighteenth-Century Work and Membership of the London Society of Arts* (Athens and London: University of Georgia Press, 1992).

Anderson, Christy, "Learning to Read Architecture in the English Renaissance," in Lucy Gent, ed., *Albion's Classicism: The Visual Arts in Britain, 1550–1660* (New Haven and London: Yale University Press, 1995), pp. 239–86.

Anderson, Sonia, *An English Consul in Turkey: Paul Rycaut at Smyrna, 1667–1668* (Oxford: Clarendon Press, 1989).

Appadurai, Arjun, ed., *The Social Life of Things: Commodities in Cultural Perspective* (Cambridge: Cambridge University Press, 1986).

Appleby, Joyce Oldham, *Economic Thought and Ideology in Seventeenth-Century England* (Princeton: Princeton University Press, 1978).

Archer, Ian, *The History of the Haberdashers' Company* (Shopwyke Hall, Chichester, Sussex: Phillimore & Co., 1991).

  The Pursuit of Stability: Social Relations in Elizabethan London (Cambridge: Cambridge University Press, 1991).

  "Material Londoners," in Lena Cowen Orlin, ed., *Material London, ca. 1600* (Philadelphia: University of Pennsylvania Press, 2000), pp. 174–92.

Ashley, Maurice, *Financial and Commercial Policy under the Cromwellian Protectorate* (London: Frank Cass, 1962).

Ashton, Robert, *Counter-Revolution: The Second Civil War and its Origins, 1646–8* (New Haven: Yale University Press, 1994).

Aston, Margaret, "Gods, Saints, and Reformers: Portraiture and Protestant England," in Lucy Gent, ed., *Albion's Classicism: The Visual Arts in Britain, 1550–1660* (New Haven: Yale University Press, 1995), pp. 181–220.

Auslander, Leora, *Taste and Power: Furnishing Modern France* (Berkeley: University of California Press, 1996).

Ayers, John, Oliver Impey, and J. V. G. Mallet, *Porcelain for Palaces: The Fashion for Japan in Europe, 1650–1750* (London: Oriental Ceramic Society, 1990).

Aylmer, Gerald, E., *The State's Servants: The Civil Service of the English Republic, 1649–1660* (London: Routledge, 1973).

Bann, Stephen, *Under the Sign: John Bargrave as Collector, Traveler and Witness* (Ann Arbor: University of Michigan Press, 1994).

Barker, Nicholas, "The Books of Henry Howard, Earl of Northampton," *Bodleian Library Record*, 13 (1990), 375–81.

Barnes, Thomas G., "The Prerogative and Environmental Control of London Building in the Early Seventeenth Century: The Lost Opportunity," *California Law Review*, 58 (1970), 1332–63.

Barroll, Leeds, *Anna of Denmark, Queen of England: A Cultural Biography* (Philadelphia: University of Pennsylvania Press, 2001).

Barron, Caroline, "Centres of Conspicuous Consumption: The Aristocratic Townhouse in London, 1200–1550, *London Journal*, 20 (1995), 1–16.

Barrow, Isaac, *The Geometrical Lectures of Isaac Barrow*, trans. James Mark Child (Chicago and London: Open Court Publishing Company, 1916).

Beal, Mary, *A Study of Richard Symonds: His Italian Notebooks and their Relevance to Seventeenth Century Painting Techniques* (New York: Garland, 1984).

Beard, Geoffrey, *Upholsterers and Interior Furnishing in England, 1530–1840* (New Haven and London: Yale University Press, 1997).

Beaven, Alfred, *The Aldermen of the City of London Temp Henry III–1908*, 2 vols. (London: E. Fisher & Co. Ltd., 1908–13).

Bedini, Silvio A., "Seventeenth Century Italian Compound Microscopes," *Physis*, 5 (1963), 383–97.

  "Divini," in Charles Coulston Gillispie, *Dictionary of Scientific Biography*, 16 vols. (New York: Scribner, 1970–80), IV, 128.

Beier, A. L., "Engine of Manufactures: The Trades of London," in A. L. Beier and Roger Finlay, *London 1500–1700: The Making of A Metropolis* (London and New York: Longman, 1986), pp. 141–67.

Beier, A. L., and Roger Finlay, *London 1500–1700: The Making of A Metropolis* (London and New York: Longman, 1986).

Bennett, Martyn, *The Civil Wars Experienced: Britain and Ireland, 1638–1661* (London and New York: Routledge, 2000).

Berg, Maxine, ed., *Markets and Manufacture in Early Industrial Europe* (London and New York: Routledge, 1991).

Berg, Maxine, and Helen Clifford, eds., *Consumers and Luxury: Consumer Culture in Europe, 1650–1850* (Manchester: Manchester University Press, 1999).

Berg, Maxine, and Elizabeth Eger, *Luxury in the Eighteenth Century: Debates, Desires and Delectable Goods* (Basingstoke: Palgrave Macmillan, 2003).

Berg, Maxine, Pat Hudson, and Michael Sonenscher, eds., *Manufacture in Town and Country before the Factory* (Cambridge: Cambridge University Press, 1983).

Berger, Ronald M., *The Most Necessary Luxuries: The Mercers' Company of Coventry, 1550–1680* (University Park: Penn State University Press, 1993).

Berkeley, Joan, *Lulworth and the Welds* (Gillingham, Dorset: Blackmore Press, 1971).

Bermingham, Ann, and John Brewer, eds., *The Consumption of Culture, 1600–1800: Image, Object, Text* (London: Routledge, 1995).

Berry, Christopher J., *The Idea of Luxury: A Conceptual and Historical Investigation* (Cambridge: Cambridge University Press, 1994).

Bettey, J. H., *The Rise of A Gentry Family: The Smyths of Ashton Court, c. 1500–1642* (Bristol Branch of the Historical Association, Bristol University, 1978).

Bindman, David, and Malcolm Baker, *Roubiliac and the Eighteenth Century Monument: Sculpture as Theater* (New Haven: Yale University Press, 1995).

Blake, John W., "The English Guinea Company, 1618–1660: An Early Example of the Charter Company in Colonial Development," *Proceedings and Reports of the Belfast Natural History and Philosophical Society*, 3 (1945/46), 14–27.

Blayney, Peter W. M., *The Bookshops in Paul's Cross Churchyard*, Occasional Papers of the Bibliographical Society, 5 (London: Bibliographical Society, 1990).

Bohls, Elizabeth, *Women Travel Writers and the Language of Aesthetics, 1716–1818* (Cambridge: Cambridge University Press, 1995).

Bold, John, *John Webb: Architectural Theory and Practice in the Seventeenth Century* (Oxford: Oxford University Press, 1989).

Bonneville, Françoise de, *The Book of Fine Linen* (Paris: Flammarion, 1994).

Bosworth, C. E., "William Lithgow of Lanark's Travels in Greece and Turkey, 1609–1611," *Bulletin of the John Rylands University Library of Manchester*, 65, (1983), 8–36.

Boulton, Jeremy, *Neighbourhood and Society: A London Suburb in the Seventeenth Century* (Cambridge: Cambridge University Press, 1987).

"Food Prices and the Standard of Living in London in the 'Century of Revolution,' 1580–1700," *Economic History Review*, 2nd series 53 (2000), 455–92.

"London 1540–1700," in Peter Clark ed., *The Cambridge Urban History of Britain, Vol. II: 1540–1820* (Cambridge: Cambridge University Press, 2000), 315–46.

Bracegirdle, Brian, "Seventeenth-Century Simple Microscopes," in R. G. W. Anderson, J. A. Bennett, and W. F. Ryan, eds., *Making Instruments Count: Essays on Historical Scientific Instruments Presented to Gerard L'Estrange Turner* (Aldershot: Variorum, 1993), pp. 295–305.

Braddick, Michael, *State Formation in Early Modern England* (Cambridge: Cambridge University Press, 2000).

Braunmuller, A. R., "Robert Carr, Earl of Somerset, as Collector and Patron," in Linda Levy Peck, ed., *The Mental World of the Jacobean Court* (Cambridge: Cambridge University Press, 1991), pp. 230–50.

"Shakespeare's fellow dramatists," in Stanley Wells and Lena Cowen Orlin, eds., *Shakespeare: An Oxford Guide* (Oxford: Oxford University Press, 2003), pp. 55–67.

Brett-James, Norman, *The Growth of Stuart London* (London: George Allen and Unwin, 1935).

Brewer, John, and Roy Porter, eds., *Consumption and the World of Goods* (London: Routledge, 1993).

Brewer, John, and Susan Staves, eds., *Early Modern Conceptions of Property* (London and New York: Routledge, 1995).

Broad, John, "Gentry Finances and the Civil War: The Case of the Buckinghamshire Verneys," *Economic History Review*, new series, 32 (1979), 183–200.

Brookes, Anne, "Richard Symonds and the Palazzo Farnese, 1649–50," *Journal of the History of Collections*, 10 (1998), 139–57.

Brooks, Christopher R., *Pettifoggers and Vipers of the Commonwealth* (Cambridge: Cambridge University Press, 1986).

Brown, Frank E. "Continuity and Change in the Urban House: Developments in Domestic Space Organisation in Seventeenth-Century London," *Comparative Studies in Society and History*, 28 (1986), 558–90.

Brown, Jonathan, *Kings and Connoisseurs: Collecting Art in Seventeenth-Century Europe* (Princeton: Princeton University Press, 1994).

Bucholz, Robert O., "Going to Court in 1700: A Visitor's Guide," *The Court Historian*, 5 (2000), 181–215.

Burke, Peter, "Investment and Culture in Three Seventeenth-Century Cities: Rome, Amsterdam, Paris," *Journal of European Economic History*, 7 (1978), 311–36.

Bushman, Richard, *The Refinement of America: Persons, Houses, Cities* (New York: Knopf, 1992).

Campbell, Linda, "Documentary Evidence for the Building of Raynham Hall," *Architectural History*, 32 (1989), 52–67.

Campbell, Thomas P., "Cardinal Wolsey's Tapestry Collection," *Antiquaries Journal*, 76 (1996), 73–137.

Tapestry in the Renaissance: Art and Magnificence, Metropolitan Museum of Art (New Haven: Yale University Press, 2002).

Canny, Nicholas, ed., *The Origins of Empire*, vol. I of *The Oxford History of the British Empire*, 5 vols. (Oxford: Oxford University Press, 1998).

Carey, Sorcha, "The Problem of Totality, Collecting Greek Art, Wonders and Luxury in Pliny the Elder's *Natural History*," *Journal of the History of Collections*, 12 (2000), 1–13.

Carlton, Charles, *Going to the Wars: The Experience of the British Civil Wars, 1638–1651* (London: Routledge, 1992).

Carr, Lois Green, and Lorena Walsh, *Inventories and the Analysis of Wealth and Consumption Patterns in St. Mary's County, Maryland, 1658–1777* (Chicago: Newberry Library, 1977).

Cavazzini, Patrizia, "The Ginetti Chapel at S. Andrea della Valle," *Burlington Magazine*, 141 (1999), 401–13.

Chaloner, William Henry, *People and Industries* (London: Frank Cass, 1963).

Chambers, Douglas, "Wild Pastoral Encounter: John Evelyn, John Beale and the Regeneration of Pastoral in the Mid-Seventeenth Century," in Michael Leslie and Timothy Raylor, eds., *Culture and Cultivation in Early Modern England: Writing and the Land* (Leicester: Leicester University Press, 1992), pp. 173–94.

The Planters of the English Landscape Garden: Botany, Trees and the Georgics (New Haven: Yale University Press, 1993).

Chancellor, E. Beresford, *The Private Palaces of London Past and Present* (London: Kegan, Paul, Trench, Trubner & Co., 1908).

Annals of the Strand, Topographical and Historical (London, Chapman & Hall, 1912).

Chaney, Edward, *The Grand Tour and the Great Rebellion: Richard Lassels and the "The Voyage of Italy" in the Seventeenth Century* (Geneva: Slatkine, 1985).

Chaney, Edward, "Two Unpublished Letters by Sir Henry Wotton to … Duke of Mantua," *Journal of Anglo-Italian Studies* (1991), 156–59.

Chaney, Edward, "Inigo Jones in Naples," in John Bold and Edward Chaney, eds., *English Architecture, Public and Private: Essays for Kerry Downes* (London: Hambledon Press, 1993), pp. 31–53.

Chaney, Edward, *The Evolution of the Grand Tour: Anglo-Italian Cultural Relations since the Renaissance* (London: Frank Cass, 1998).

Chaney, Edward, ed., *The Evolution of English Collecting: The Reception of Italian Art in the Tudor and Stuart Periods* (New Haven and London: Yale University Press, 2003).

Chard, Chloe, *Pleasure and Guilt on the Grand Tour: Travel Writing and Imaginative Geography, 1600–1830* (Manchester: Manchester University Press, 1999).

Chard, Chloe, and Helen Langdon, eds., *Transports: Travel, Pleasure and Imaginative Geography, 1600–1830* (New Haven: Yale University Press, 1996).

Chaudhuri, K. N., *The East India Company: The Study of an Early Joint-Stock Company, 1600–1640* (London: Frank Cass, 1965).

The Trading World of Asia and the English East India Company, 1660–1760 (Cambridge: Cambridge University Press, 1978).

Chew, Elizabeth V., "The Countess of Arundel and Tart Hall," in Edward Chaney, ed., *The Evolution of English Collecting: The Reception of Italian Art in the Tudor and Stuart Periods* (New Haven and London: Yale University Press, 2003), pp. 285–314.

Ciriacono, Salvatore, "Silk Manufacturing in France and Italy in the XVIIth Century: Two Models Compared," *Journal of European Economic History*, 10 (1981), 167–99.

Clapp, Sarah L. C., "The Subscription Enterprise of John Ogilby and Richard Blome," *Modern Philology*, 30 (1933), 365–79.

Clark, Peter, ed., *The Cambridge Urban History of Britain* vol. II, *1540–1840* (Cambridge: Cambridge University Press, 2000).

Clay, Christopher, G. A., "Landlords and Estate Management in England," in Joan Thirsk, ed., *The Agrarian History of England, 1640–1750*, V, part II of *The Agrarian History of England and Wales*, H. P. R. Finberg, general editor, 8 vols. (Cambridge: Cambridge University Press, 1967–).

Economic Expansion and Social Change: England 1500–1700, 2 vols. (Cambridge: Cambridge University Press, 1984).

Clifton, Gloria, *Directory of British Scientific Instrument Makers 1550–1851* (London: Zwemmer, National Maritime Museum, 1995).

Cloake, J., *Richmond's Great Monastery: The Charterhouse of Jesus of Bethlehem of Shene* (Richmond: Richmond Local History Society, 1990).

Clunas, Craig, "Modernity Global and Local: Consumption and the Rise of the West," *American Historical Review*, 104 (1999), 1497–511.

Coates, Ben, "Poor Relief in London during the English Revolution Revisited," *London Journal*, 25 (2000), 40–58.

Cole, Charles Woolsey, *French Mercantilist Doctrines Before Colbert* (New York: Richard R. Smith, 1931).

Coleman, D. C., *Industry in Tudor and Stuart England* (London: MacMillan, 1975).

Colvin, Howard, *The History of the King's Works*, 6 vols. (London: HMSO, 1975–82); vol. III: *1485–1660* (part 1); vol. IV: *1485–1660* (Part 2).

Consiglio, Gioia di, *Collezionare la profumeria italiana d'epoca* (Rome: Fratelli Palombi, 1997).

Cooper, Nicholas, *The Houses of the Gentry 1480–1680* (New Haven and London: Yale University Press, 1999).

Costello, Con, "Jigginstown House," *Journal of County Kildare Archaeological Society*, 14 (1969), 375–76.

Coult, Douglas, *A Prospect of Ashridge* (London: Phillimore, 1980).

Cowan, Brian, "Arenas of Connoisseurship: Auctioning Art in Later Stuart England," in Michael North and David Ormrod, eds., *Art Markets in Europe 1400–1800* (Aldershot, Hampshire: Ashgate Publishing, 1998), pp. 153–66.

Cox, Nancy C., "Objects of Worth, Objects of Desire: Towards a Dictionary of Traded Goods and Commodities 1550–1800," *Material History Review*, 39 (1994), 24–41.

The Complete Tradesman: A Study of Retailing, 1550–1820 (Aldershot, Hampshire: Ashgate Publishing, 2000).

Craig, Maurice, "New Light on Jigginstown," *Journal of County Kildare Archaeological Society*, 15 (1971), 50–58.

Cramsie, John, "Commercial Projects and the Fiscal Policy of James VI and I, *Historical Journal*, 43 (2000), 345–64.

Craven, Wesley Frank, *The Southern Colonies in the Seventeenth Century 1607–1689* (Baton Rouge: Louisiana State University Press, 1949).

Crawford, Patricia, and Laura Gowing, *Women's Worlds in Seventeenth-Century England* (London: Routledge, 2000).

Croft, Pauline, *Patronage, Culture and Power: The Early Cecils* (New Haven and London: Yale University Press, 2002).

Culme, John, *English Silver Treasures from the Kremlin*, a loan exhibition (London: Sotheby's 1990).

Cust, Lionel, "Notes on the Collections Formed by Thomas Howard, Earl of Arundel and Surrey, K. G.," *Burlington Magazine*, 20 (1911), 97–100, 233–36, 341–43.

Cust, Richard, "News and Politics in Early Seventeenth-Century England, *Past & Present* 112 (1986), 60–90.

Davis, Dorothy, *Fairs, Shops and Supermarkets: A History of English Shopping* (Toronto: Toronto University Press, 1966).

Davis, Natalie Zemon, *The Gift in Sixteenth Century France* (Madison: University of Wisconsin Press, 2000).

Davis, Ralph, *The Rise of the English Shipping Industry in the Seventeenth and Eighteenth Centuries* (London: MacMillan, 1962).

English Overseas Trade, 1500–1700, prepared for the Economic History Society (London: MacMillan, 1973).

The Rise of the Atlantic Economies (Ithaca, NY: Cornell University Press, 1973).

Dawson, William Harbutt, *Cromwell's Understudy: The Life and Times of General John Lambert and the Rise and Fall of the Protectorate* (London: William Hodge, 1938).

De Divitiis, Gigliola Pagano, *English Merchants in Seventeenth-Century Italy* (Cambridge: Cambridge University Press, 1997).

De Marchi, Neil, "Novelty and Fashion Circuits in Mid-Seventeenth-Century Antwerp-Paris Art Trade," *Journal of Medieval and Early Modern Studies*, 28 (1998), 201–46.

"Adam Smith's Accommodation of 'Altogether endless' desires," in Maxine Berg and Helen Clifford, eds., *Consumers and Luxury: Consumer Culture in Europe, 1650–1850* (Manchester: Manchester University Press, 1999), pp. 18–36.

De Marchi, Neil, and Hans J. Van Miegroet, "Art, Value, and Market Practices in the Netherlands in the Seventeenth Century," *Art Bulletin*, 76 (1994), 451–64.

Dethloff, Diana, "The Executors' Account Book and the Dispersal of Sir Peter Lely's Collection," *Journal of the History of Collections*, 8 (1996), 15–51.

Dictionary of National Biography (New York and London: MacMillan, 1901–).

Disney, Anthony, *Historiography of Europeans in Africa and Asia, 1450–1800* (Aldershot, Hampshire, 1995).

Dix, Brian, Iain Sader, and Tara Hilton, "Kirby Hall and its Gardens: Excavations in 1987–1994," *Archaeological Journal*, 152 (1995), 291–380.

Douglas, Mary, and Baron C. Isherwood, *The World of Goods: Towards an Anthropology of Consumption* (New York: Basic Books, 1979).

Duggan, Dianne, "'London the Ring, Covent Garden the Jewell of that Ring': New Light on Covent Garden," *Architectural History*, 43 (2000), 140–61.

"The Fourth Side of Covent Garden Piazza: New Light on the History and Significance of Bedford House," *British Art Journal*, 3 (2003), 53–65.

"'A Rather Fascinating Hybrid,' Tart Hall: Lady Arundel's Casino at Whitehall," *British Art Journal*, 4 (2003), 54–64.

Dulken, Stephen Van, *British Patents of Invention, 1617–1977: A Guide for Researchers* (London: British Library, 1999).

Dyer, Christopher, *Standards of Living in the Later Middle Ages: Social Change in England, c. 1200–1520* (Cambridge: Cambridge University Press, 1989).

Eamon, William, *Science and the Secrets of Nature: Books of Secrets in Medieval and Early Modern Culture* (Princeton: Princeton University Press, 1994).

Earle, Peter, *The Making of the English Middle Class: Business, Society and Family Life in London, 1660–1730* (Berkeley and Los Angeles: University of California Press, 1989).

Eighteenth Century Studies, 31 (1997), 87–114, forum on the Grand Tour.

Ekelund, Robert, and Robert Tollison, *Mercantilism as a Rent-Seeking Society: Economic Regulation in Historical Perspective* (College Station, Texas: Texas A & M University Press, 1981).

Elias, Norbert, *The Court Society* (Oxford: Blackwell, 1983).

Elliott, Sir John, and Laurence Brockliss, *The World of the Favourite* (New Haven: Yale University Press, 1999).

Elsner, John, and Roger Cardinal, eds., *Cultures of Collecting* (London: Reaktion Books, 1994).

Engberg, Jens, "Royalist Finances during the English Civil War, 1642–1646," *Scandinavian Economic History Review*, 14 (1966), 73–96.

English, W., "A Survey of the Principal References to Fashion Fabrics in the Diary of Samuel Pepys," *Journal of the Textile Institute*, 40 (1949), pp 23–37.

Erickson, Peter, and Clark Hulse, eds., *Early Modern Visual Culture: Representation, Race, and Empire in Renaissance England* (Philadelphia: University of Pennsylvania Press, 2000).

Esdaile, Katherine Ada, and Arthur Oswald, "The Chapel at Steane Park, Northamptonshire," *Country Life* (2 July 1938), 12–17.

Ezell, Margaret J. M., "Lady Jane Cavendish and Elizabeth Brackley," in Germaine Greer et al., eds., *Kissing the Rod: Anthology of Seventeenth Century Women's Verse* (London: Virago, 1988), pp. 106–18.

"To Be Your Daughter in Your Pen: The Social Functions of Literature in the Writings of Lady Elizabeth Brackley and Lady Jane Cavendish," *Huntington Library Quarterly*, 51 (1988), 281–96.

Fairchilds, Cissie, "Consumption in Early Modern Europe: A Review Article," *Comparative Studies in Society and History*, 35 (1993), 850–58.

Farr, David, "Kin, Cash, Catholics and Cavaliers: The Role of Kinship in the Financial Management of Major-General John Lambert," *Historical Research*, 74 (2001), 44–62.

Faulkner, Thomas, *An Historical and Topographical Description of Chelsea and its Environs*, 2 vols. (London, 1829).

Feingold, Mordechai, *Before Newton: The Life and Times of Isaac Barrow* (Cambridge: Cambridge University Press, 1990).

Feltwell, John, *The Story of Silk* (New York: St. Martin's Press, 1990).

Fermor, Sharon, *The Raphael Tapestry Cartoons: Narrative, Decoration, Design* (London: Scala Books in Association with the Victoria and Albert Museum, 1996).

Ferris, J. P., "A Connoisseur's Shopping-List, 1647," *Journal of the Warburg and Courtauld Institutes* 38 (1975), 339–41.

Field, J. V., "Why Translate Serlio?" in Francis Ames-Lewis, ed., *Sir Thomas Gresham and Gresham College: Studies in the Intellectual History of London in the Sixteenth and Seventeenth Centuries* (Aldershot, Hampshire: Ashgate Publishing, 1999), pp. 198–221.

Fincham, Kenneth, "The Restoration of Altars in the 1630s," *Historical Journal*, 44 (2001), 919–40.

Findlay, Ronald, "Globalization and the European Economy: Medieval Origins to the Industrial Revolution," in Ronald Findlay and Kevin O'Rourke, eds., *Commodity Market Integration, 1500–2000* (Cambridge, MA: National Bureau of Economic Research, 2001), pp. 1–46.

Findlen, Paula, "The Economy of Scientific Exchange in Early Modern Italy," in Bruce T. Moran, ed., *Patronage and Institutions: Science, Technology, and Medicine at the European Court, 1500–1750* (Woodbridge, Suffolk: Boydell Press, 1991), pp. 5–24.

Finlay, Roger, *Population and the Metropolis: The Demography of London, 1580–1650* (Cambridge: Cambridge University Press, 1981).

Finn, Margot, "Women, Consumption, and Coverture in England, c. 1760–1860," *Historical Journal*, 39 (1996), 703–22.

Fisher, F. J., "The Development of London as a Centre of Conspicuous Consumption in the Sixteenth and Seventeenth Centuries," *TRHS*, 4th series, 30 (1948), 37–50.

London and the English Economy, 1500–1700, ed. P. J. Corfield and N. B. Harte (London: Hambledon Press, 1990).

Fitzmaurice, Lord Edmund, *The Life of Sir William Petty, 1623–1687* (London: John Murray, 1895).

Fleming, Juliet, "The French Garden: An Introduction to Women's French," *ELH* 56 (1989), 19–51.

Friedman, Alice T., "Patronage and the Production of Tombs in London and the Provinces: The Willoughby Monument of 1590s," *Antiquaries Journal*, 65 (1985), 390–401.

Galinou, Mireille, ed., *City Merchants and the Arts 1670–1720*, (Oblong: Corporation of London, 2004).

Gardiner, Dorothy, *The Tradescants and their Times, c. 1600–1662*, reprinted from *Journal of the Royal Horticultural Society*, 53, pt. 2 (1928).

Gent, Lucy (ed.), *Albion's Classicism: The Visual Arts in Britain, 1550–1660* (New Haven: Yale University Press, 1995).

Gentles, Ian, "London Levellers in the English Revolution: the Chidleys and their Circle," *Journal of Ecclesiastical History*, 29 (1978), 297–303.

Gibson-Wood, Carol, "Classification and Value in a Seventeenth-Century Museum: William Courten's Collection," *Journal of the History of Collections*, 9 (1997), 61–77.

"Picture Consumption in London at the End of the Seventeenth Century," *Art Bulletin*, 84 (2002), 491–500.

Gilman, Ernest B., "Madagascar on My Mind: The Earl of Arundel and the Arts of Colonization," in Peter Erickson and Clark Hulse, eds., *Early Modern Visual Culture: Representation, Race, and Empire in Renaissance England* (Philadelphia: University of Pennsylvania Press, 2000), pp. 284–314.

Girouard, Mark, *Robert Smythson and the Architecture of the Elizabethan Era* (London: Country Life, 1966).

Robert Smythson and the Elizabethan Country House (New Haven: Yale University Press, 1983).

"Early Drawings of Bolsover Castle: Design and Practice in British Architecture: Studies in architectural history presented to Howard Colvin, 27 *Architectural History* (1984), 510–18.

ed., "The Smythson Collection of the Royal Institute of British Architects," *Architectural History*, 5 (1962), pp. 21–184.

Glanville, Philippa, *Silver in Tudor and Early Stuart England: A Social History and Catalogue of the National Collection, 1480–1660* (London: Victoria and Albert Museum, 1990).

Introduction to David Mitchell, ed., *Goldsmiths, Silversmiths and Bankers: Innovation and the Transfer of Skill, 1550–1750*, Centre for Metropolitan History, Working Papers Series, no. 2 (London: Centre for Metropolitan History, 1995).

Godfrey, Eleanor S., *The Development of English Glassmaking, 1560–1640* (Chapel Hill, NC: University of North Carolina Press, 1975).

Goldthwaite, Richard, "The Empire of Things: Consumer demand in Renaissance Italy," in F. W. Kent, Patricia Simons, and J. D. Eade, eds., *Patronage, Art and Society in Renaissance Italy* (Canberra Humanities Research Centre/Oxford: Clarendon Press, 1987), pp. 153–76.

Wealth and the Demand for Art in Italy, 1300–1600 (Baltimore and London: Johns Hopkins University Press, 1993).

Goncharenko, V. S., and V. I. Narozhnaia, *The Armoury: Moscow Kremlin State Museum – Preserve of History and Culture: A guide*, 2nd edn, (Moscow: Red Square Publishers, 2000).

Gorer, Richard, *The Flower Garden in England* (London: Batsford, 1975).

Gould, J. D., "The Trade Crisis of the Early 1620s and English Economic Thought," *Journal of Economic History* 15 (1955), 121–33.

Goulding, Richard W., *The Welbeck Abbey Miniatures Belonging to His Grace the Duke of Portland: A Catalogue Raisonné* (Oxford: Printed by Frederick Hall at the University Press, 1916).

Catalogue of the Pictures Belonging to his Grace the Duke of Portland, K.G. (Cambridge: Cambridge University Press, 1936).

Gowing, Laura, *Domestic Dangers: Women, Words and Sex in Early Modern London* (Oxford, Clarendon Press, 1996).

"The Freedom of the Streets: Women and Social Space, 1560–1640," in Paul Griffiths and Mark S. R. Jenner, eds., *Londinopolis: Essays in the Cultural and Social History of Early Modern London* (Manchester and New York: Manchester University Press, 2000), 130–51.

Grassby, Richard, *The Business Community of Seventeenth-Century England* (Cambridge: Cambridge University Press, 1995).

Greenblatt, Stephen, *Marvelous Possessions: The Wonder of the New World* (Oxford, Clarendon Press, 1991).

Greenglass, Mark, Michael Leslie, Timothy Raylor, *Samuel Hartlib and Universal Reformation: Studies in Intellectual Communication* (Cambridge: Cambridge University Press, 1994).

Griffiths, Antony, "The Etchings of John Evelyn," in David Howarth, ed., *Art and Patronage in the Caroline Courts: Essays in Honour of Sir Oliver Millar* (Cambridge: Cambridge University Press, 1993), pp. 51–67.

The Print in Stuart Britain, 1603–1689 (London: British Museum Press, 1998).

Gunther, R. T., ed., *The Architecture of Sir Roger Pratt* (Oxford: Oxford University Press, 1928).

Gunther, R. T., and John Goodyer, *Early British Botanists and their Gardens* (Oxford: Oxford University Press, 1922).

Habakkuk, H. J., "Landowners and the Civil War," *Economic History Review*, new series, 18 (1965), 130–51.

"The Land Settlement and the Restoration of Charles II," *TRHS*, 5th series, 28 (1978), 201–22.

Habermas, Jürgen, *The Structural Transformation of the Public Sphere*, trans. Thomas Burger (Cambridge, MA: MIT Press, 1991).

Haley, K. H. D., *The First Earl of Shaftesbury* (Oxford: Clarendon Press, 1968).

Hall, A. Rupert, "Merton Revisited," *History of Science* 2 (1963), 1–16.

Hall, Kim F. *Things of Darkness: Economies of Race and Gender in Early Modern England* (Ithaca, NY: Cornell University Press, 1995).

Hampton, Timothy, "Introduction: Baroques," in "Baroque Topographies: Literature/History/Philosophy," *Yale French Studies*, 80 (1991).

Hankins, Thomas, and Robert Silverman, *Instruments and the Imagination* (Princeton: Princeton University Press, 1995).

Hardacre, Paul H., "The Royalists in Exile during the Puritan Revolution, 1642–60," *Huntington Library Quarterly*, 16 (1953), 353–70.

The Royalists during the Puritan Revolution (The Hague: Nijhoff, 1956).

Harding, Vanessa, "The Population of London 1550–1700: A Review of the Published Evidence," *London Journal*, 15 (1990), 111–28.

"Early Modern London 1550–1700," *London Journal*, 20 (1995), 34–45.

Harding, Vanessa, and Laura Wright, eds., *London Bridge: Selected Accounts and Rentals, 1381–1538* (London: London Record Society, 1995).

Harris, Eileen, *British Architectural Books and Writers, 1556–1785* (Cambridge: Cambridge University Press, 1990).

Harris, Ian, *The Mind of John Locke: A Study of Political Theory in its Intellectual Setting* (Cambridge: Cambridge University Press, 1994).

Harris, John, and Gordon Higgott, *Inigo Jones: Complete Architectural Drawings* (London: Higgott, Zwemmer, 1989).

Harris, John, and A. A. Tait, *Catalogue of the Drawings By Inigo Jones, John Webb and Isaac de Caus at Worcester College Oxford* (Oxford: Oxford University Press, 1979).

Harris, Tim (ed.), *Popular Culture in England, c. 1500–1850* (New York: St. Martin's Press, 1995).

Harte, Negley Boyd, "State Control of Dress and Social Change in Pre-Industrial England," in D. C. Coleman and A. H. John, eds., *Trade, Government and Economy in Pre-Industrial England: Essays Presented to F. J. Fisher* (London: Weidenfeld and Nicolson, 1976), 132–65.

Haskell, Francis, "Charles I's Collection of Pictures," in Arthur MacGregor, ed., *The Late King's Goods: Collections, Possessions and Patronage of Charles I in the Light of the Commonwealth Sale Inventories* (Oxford: Oxford University Press, 1989), pp. 203–31.

Hatch, Jr., Charles E., "Mulberry Trees and Silkworms: Sericulture in Early Virginia," *The Virginia Magazine of History and Biography*, 65 (1957), 3–61.

Hazard, Mary E., "A Magnificent Lord: Leicester, Kenilworth, and Transformation in the Idea of Magnificence," *Cahiers Elizabethains*, 31 (1987), 11–35.

Heal, Felicity, and Clive Holmes, *The Gentry in England and Wales, 1500–1700* (Basingstoke, Hampshire: Macmillan; Stanford: Stanford University Press, 1994).

Hearn, Karen, "Sir Anthony Van Dyck, Portrait of Sir William Killigrew, 1638," *British Art Focus*, Patrons' Papers 6 (London: Tate, 2003).

Hefford, Wendy, "Cardinal Mazarin and the Earl of Pembroke's Tapestries," *Connoisseur*, 195 (1977), 286–90.

"Cleyn's Noble Horses," *National Art-Collections Fund Review*, 87 (1990), 97–102.

"Prince Behind the Scenes," *Country Life*, 184 (4 October 1990), 132–35.

"The Duke of Buckingham's Mortlake tapestries of 1623," *Bulletin du CIETA*, 76 (1999), 90–103.

"Flemish Tapestry Weavers in England, 1550–1775," in Guy Delmarcel, ed., *Flemish Tapestry Weavers Abroad: Emigration and the Founding of Manufactures in Europe* (Louvain, Belgium: Louvain University Press, 2002), pp. 43–61.

Heller, Henry, *Labour, Science and Technology in France, 1500–1620* (Cambridge: Cambridge University Press, 1996).

Henderson, Paula, "The Loggia in Tudor and Early Stuart England: The Adaptation and Function of Classical Form," in Lucy Gent, ed., *Albion's*

Classicism: The Visual Arts in Britain, 1550–1660 (New Haven: Yale University Press, 1995), pp. 109–46.

Henning, Basil Duke, ed., *The House of Commons, 1660–1690*, 3 vols. (London: Secker and Warburg, History of Parliament Trust, 1983).

Hepple, Leslie W., "William Camden and Early Collections of Roman Antiquities in Britain," *Journal of the History of Collections*, 15 (2003), 159–73.

Hill, Oliver, and John Cornforth, "English Country Houses: Caroline, 1625–1685," *Connoisseur*, 164 (1967), 266.

Hill, Robert, "Ambassadors and Art Collecting in Early Stuart Britain: The Parallel Careers of William Trumbull and Sir Dudley Carleton, 1609–1625," *Journal of the History of Collections*, 15 (2003), 211–28.

Higgott, Gordon "'Varying with Reason': Inigo Jones's Theory of Design," *Architectural History*, 35 (1992), 51–77.

Hirst, Derek, "The Politics of Literature in the English Republic," *Seventeenth Century*, 5 (1990), 133–55.

Holdsworth, William, *A History of English Law* (London, 1923).

Holtgen, Karl Josef, "Catholic Pictures Versus Protestant Words?: The Adaptation of the Jesuit Sources in Quarles's *Emblemes*," *Emblematica*, 9 (1995), 221–38.

"Frances Quarle's Emblems and Hieroglyphikes," in Ayers L. Bagley (ed.), *Telling Images Exploration in the Emblem* (New York: AMS Press, 1996), pp. 1–28.

Holderness, B. A., "The Reception and Distribution of the New Draperies in England," in Negley Boyd Harte, ed., *The New Draperies in the Low Countries and England* (Oxford: Oxford University Press, 1997), pp. 217–43.

Hoskins, W. G., "The Rebuilding of Rural England, 1570–1640," *Past and Present*, 4 (1953), 44–59.

Houghton, Walter E., Jr., "The History of Trades: Its Relation to Seventeenth-Century Thought: As Seen in Bacon, Petty, Evelyn, and Boyle," *Journal of the History of Ideas*, 2 (1941), 33–60.

"The English Virtuoso in the Seventeenth-Century," Parts I and II, *Journal of the History of Ideas*, 3 (1942), 51–73, 190–219.

Howarth, David, "Samuel Boothouse and the English Artistic Enterprise in Seventeenth-Century Italy," *Italian Studies Birmingham*, 32 (1977), 86–96.

"Lord Arundel as an Entrepreneur of the Arts," *Burlington Magazine*, 122 (1980), 690–92.

"Merchants and Diplomats: New Patrons of the Decorative Arts in Seventeenth-Century England," *Furniture History*, 20 (1984), 10–17.

Lord Arundel and his Circle (New Haven: Yale University Press, 1985).

"Charles I, Sculpture and Sculptors," in Arthur MacGregor ed., *The Late King's Goods: Collections, Possessions and Patronage of Charles I in the Light of the Commonwealth Sale Inventories* (Oxford and London: Alistair McAlpine in association with Oxford University Press), pp. 103–104.

"The Arrival of Van Dyck in England," *Burlington Magazine*, 132 (1990), 709–12.

"The Politics of Inigo Jones," in David Howarth, ed., *Art and Patronage in the Caroline Courts: Essays in Honour of Sir Oliver Millar* (Cambridge: Cambridge University Press, 1993), pp. 68–89

"William Trumbull and Art Collecting in Jacobean England," *British Library Journal*, 20 (1994), 140–62.

Images of Rule: Art and Politics in the English Renaissance, 1485–1649 (University of California Press, 1997).

"The Patronage and Collecting of Aletheia, Countess of Arundel, 1606–54," *Journal of the History of Collections*, 10 (1998), 125–37.

Howarth, David, and Nicholas Penney, eds., *Thomas Howard, Earl of Arundel: Patronage and Collecting in the Seventeenth Century* (Oxford: Ashmolean Museum, 1985).

Hulme, E. W., "The History of the Patent System Under the Prerogative and at Common Law," *Law Quarterly Review*, 12 (1896), 141–54; 16 (1900), 44–56.

Hunneyball, Paul, *Architecture and Image-Building in Seventeenth Century Hertfordshire*, Oxford Historical Monographs (Oxford: Oxford University Press, 2004).

Hunt, John Dixon, *Garden and Grove: The Italian Renaissance Garden in the English Imagination, 1600–1750* (London: Dent, 1986).

Hunter, Michael, *Science and Society in Restoration England* (Cambridge: Cambridge University Press, 1981).

The Royal Society and its Fellows, 1660–1700: The Morphology of an Early Scientific Institution (Chalfont St. Giles, Bucks: British Society for the History of Science, 1982).

"An Experiment in Corporate Enterprise: The Royal Society's Committees of 1663–1665 with a Transcript of the Surviving Minutes of their Meetings," in Michael Hunter, *Establishing the New Science: The Experience of the Early Royal Society* (Woodbridge, Suffolk: Boydell Press, 1989), pp. 73–122.

"Reconstructing Restoration Science," in Hunter, *Establishing the New Science*, pp. 339–55.

"A College for the Royal Society," in Hunter, *Establishing the New Science*, pp. 156–84.

"John Evelyn in the 1650s," in Michael Hunter, *Science and the Shape of Orthodoxy: Intellectual Change in Late Seventeenth Century Britain* (Woodbridge Suffolk: Boydell Press, 1995), pp. 67–98.

Impey, Oliver R., and Arthur MacGregor, eds., *The Origins of Museums: The Cabinet of Curiosities in Sixteenth- and Seventeenth-Century Europe* (Oxford: Oxford University Press, 1985).

Innes, Stephen, "Puritanism and Capitalism in early Massachusetts," in J. A. James and Mark Thomas, eds., *Capitalism in Context: Essays on Economic Development and Cultural Change in Honour of R. M. Hartwell* (Chicago: Chicago University Press, 1994).

Irwin, Joyce L., "Anna Maria Van Schurman: The Star of Utrecht (Dutch, 1607–1678)," in Jeanne R. Brink, ed., *Female Scholars: A Tradition of*

Learned Women Before 1800 (Montreal: Eden Press Women's Publications, 1980), pp. 68–85.

ed., *Whether a Christian Woman Should Be Educated and Other Writings from her Intellectual Circle* (Chicago: University of Chicago Press, 1998).

Jack, Sybil, *Trade and Industry in Tudor and Stuart England* (London: Allen and Unwin, 1977).

Jardine, Lisa, *Worldly Goods: A New History of the Renaissance* (New York: W. W. Norton, 1996).

The Curious Life of Robert Hooke (New York: HarperCollins, 2004).

Jenner, Mark, and Paul Griffiths, eds., *Londinopolis: Essays in the Cultural and Social History of Early Modern London* (Manchester: Manchester University Press, 2000).

Jervis, Simon, "Furniture for the First Duke of Buckingham," *Furniture History*, 33 (1997), 48–74.

Jones, Ann Rosalind, and Peter Stallybrass, *Renaissance Clothing and the Materials of Memory* (Cambridge: Cambridge University Press, 2000).

Jones, S. R. H., "Technology, Transaction Costs, and the Transition to Factory Production in the British Silk Industry, 1700–1870," *Journal of Economic History*, 47 (1987), 71–96.

Juel-Jenson, Bent, "Musaeum Clausum, or Bibliotheca Abscondita, Some Thoughts on Curiosity Cabinets and Imaginary Books," *Journal of the History of Collections*, 4 (1992), 127–40.

Kaufmann, Thomas Da Costa, "From Treasury to Museum: The Collections of the Austrian Habsburgs," in John Elsner and Roger Cardinal, eds., *Cultures of Collecting* (London: Reaktion Books, 1994), pp. 137–54.

Kearney, Hugh, *Strafford in Ireland, 1633–41: A Study in Absolutism* (Cambridge: Cambridge University Press, 1959, 1989).

Keeble, N. H., "Obedient Subjects? The Loyal Self in Some Later Seventeenth-Century Women's Memoirs," in Gerald McLean, ed., *Culture and Society in the Stuart Restoration: Literature, Drama, History* (Cambridge: Cambridge University Press, 1995), pp. 201–28.

Keene, Derek, "A New Study of London before the Great Fire," *Urban History Yearbook*, 11 (1984), 11–21.

Cheapside Before the Great Fire (London: Economic and Social Research Council, 1985).

"Shops and Shopping in Medieval London," in Lindy Grant, ed., *Medieval Art, Architecture, and Archaeology in London* (Oxford: British Archaeological Association, 1990), pp. 29–40.

"Material London in Time and Space," in Lena Cowen Orlin, ed., *Material London, ca. 1600* (Philadelphia: University of Pennsylvania Press, 2000), pp. 55–74.

Kerridge, Eric, *Textile Manufactures in Early Modern England* (Manchester: Manchester University Press, 1985).

Kettering, Sharon, *Patrons, Brokers, and Clients in Seventeenth-Century France* (New York: Oxford University Press, 1986).

King, Henry C., *The History of the Telescope* (High Wycombe, Bucks: Charles Griffin & Co., 1955; Mineola, NY: Dover Publications, 2003).

Kingsford, Charles, "Bath Inn or Arundel House," *Archaeologia*, 72 (1922), 243–77.

Knowles, James, "Jonson's *Entertainment at Britain's Burse*," in Martin Butler, ed., *Re-presenting Ben Jonson: Text, History, Performance* (Houndmills, Basingstoke: Macmillan, 1999), pp. 114–51.

Knowles, James, ed., *The Roaring Girl and Other City Comedies* (Oxford: Oxford University Press, 2001).

Kowaleski-Wallace, Elizabeth, *Consuming Subjects: Women, Shopping and Business in the Eighteenth Century* (New York: Columbia University Press, 1997).

Kuehn, Edwin, "France into England, 1652: The Cotterell Translation of La Calprenede's Cassandra," *Romance Notes*, 18 (1977), 107–17.

Kuhta, David, *The Three-Piece Suit and Modern Masculinity* (Berkeley: University of California Press, 2002).

Kusamitsu, Toshio, "'Novelty, Give us Novelty': London Agents and Northern Manufacturers," in Maxine Berg, ed., *Markets and Manufacture in Early Industrial Europe* (London and New York: Routledge, 1991), 114–38.

Laing, Alastair, *In Trust for the Nation: Paintings from National Trust Houses* (London: National Gallery Publications, 1995).

Lake, Peter, "The Laudian Style: Order, Uniformity, and the Pursuit of the Beauty of Holiness in the 1630s," in Kenneth Fincham, ed., *The Early Stuart Church, 1603–1642* (Basingstoke: Macmillan, 1993), pp. 161–85.

Lake, Peter, and Michael Questier, *The anti-Christ's Lewd Hat: Protestants, Papists and Players in Post-Reformation England* (New Haven: Yale University Press, 2002).

Landau, David, and Peter Parshall, *The Renaissance Print, ca. 1470–1550* (New Haven: Yale University Press, 1994).

Le Corbellier, Claire, and Alice Cooney Frelinghuysen, *Chinese Export Porcelain* (New York: Metropolitan Museum of Art, 2003).

Leedham-Green, Elizabeth S., *Books in Cambridge Inventories: Book-Lists from Vice-Chancellor's Court Probate Inventories in the Tudor and Stuart Periods*, 2 vols. (Cambridge: Cambridge University Press, 1986).

Leith-Ross, Prudence, *The John Tradescants, Gardeners to the Rose and Lily Queen* (London: P. Owen, 1984).

Lemire, Beverly, "Consumerism in Preindustrial and Early Industrial England: The Trade in Secondhand Clothes," *Journal of British Studies*, 27 (1988), 1–24.

Levin, Richard, "Women in the Renaissance Theatre Audience," *Shakespeare Quarterly*, 40 (1989), 165–74.

Levine, Joseph, *Between the Ancients and the Moderns: Baroque Culture in Restoration England* (New Haven: Yale University Press, 1999).

Levy, Fred J., *Tudor Historical Thought* (San Marino: Huntington Library, 1967).
"How Information Spread Among the Gentry, 1550–1640," *Journal of British Studies*, 21 (1982), 11–34.

Lightbown, Ronald, "Bernini's Busts of English Patrons," in Moshe Barasch, Lucy Freeman Sandler, and Patricia Egan, eds., *Art, the Ape of Nature: Studies in Honor of H. W. Janson* (New York: Abrams, 1981), pp. 439–76.

Llewellyn, Nigel, *The Art of Death: Visual Culture in the English Death Ritual c1500–c1800* (London: Published in association with the Victoria and Albert Museum by Reaktion Books, 1991).

Funeral Monuments in Post-Reformation England (Cambridge: Cambridge University Press, 2000).

Lockyer, Roger, *Buckingham, The Life and Political Career of George Villiers, First Duke of Buckingham 1592–1628* (London: Longman's, 1981).

London, April, "Musaeum Tradescantianum and the Benefactors to the Tradescants' Museum," in Arthur MacGregor, ed., *Tradescant's Rarities: Essays on the Foundation of the Ashmolean Museum* (Oxford: Clarendon Press, 1983), pp. 24–39.

Lough, John, *France Observed in the Seventeenth Century by British Travellers* (Stocksfield, Northumberland, and Boston: Oriel Press, 1984).

Lubbock, Jules, *The Tyranny of Taste: The Politics of Architecture and Design in Britain, 1550–1960* (New Haven: Yale University Press, 1995).

Luu, Lien Bich, "French-Speaking Refugees and the Foundation of the London Silk Industry in the Sixteenth Century," *Proceedings of the Huguenot Society*, 26 (1997), 564–76.

McCray, W. Patrick, "Creating Networks of Skill: Technology Transfer and the Glass Industry in Venice," *Journal of European Economic History*, 28 (1999), 301–33.

MacGregor, Arthur, ed., *Tradescant's Rarities: Essays on the Foundation of the Ashmolean Museum* (Oxford: Clarendon Press, 1983).

"Collectors and Collections of Rarities in the Sixteenth and Seventeenth Centuries," in MacGregor, ed., *Tradescant's Rarities*, pp. 70–97.

MacGregor, Arthur, *Sir Hans Sloane: Collector, Scientist, Antiquary, Founding Father of the British Museum* (London: British Museum Press, 1994).

MacGregor, Arthur, ed., *The Late King's Goods: Collections, Possessions and Patronage of Charles I in the Light of the Commonwealth Sale Inventories* (Oxford and London: Alistair McAlpine in association with Oxford University Press, 1989).

McKellar, Elizabeth, *The Birth of Modern London: The Development and Design of the City, 1660–1720* (Manchester: Manchester University Press, 1999).

McKerrow, Ronald Brunlees, *A Dictionary of Printers and Booksellers in England, Scotland, and Ireland . . . 1557–1640* (London: Printed for the Bibliographical Society, 1910).

MacLagen, Eric, "Sculpture by Bernini in England," *Burlington Magazine*, 40 (1922), 56–63, 112–20.

MacLeod, Christine, *Inventing the Industrial Revolution: The English Patent System, 1660–1800* (Cambridge: Cambridge University Press, 1982).

"The 1690s Patents Boom: Invention or Stock Jobbing?" *Economic History Review*, new series 39 (1986), 549–571.

McMullin, Ernan, "Openness and Secrecy in Science: Some Notes on Early History," *Science, Technology and Human Values*, 10 (1985), 14–23.

Maczak, Antoni, *Travel in Early Modern Europe* (Cambridge: Polity Press, 1995).

Maddicott, Hilary, "A Collection of the Interregnum Period: Philip, Lord Viscount Lisle, and His Purchases from the 'Late King's Goods,' 1649–1660," *Journal of the History of Collections*, 11 (1999), 1–24.

Magnusson, Lars, *Mercantilism: The Shaping of an Economic Language* (London: Routledge, 1994).

Manners, A., "An Account of Perfumery Supplied for the Use of King James I," *Proceedings of the Society of Antiquaries of London*, 2nd series, 4 (1867–70), 435–37.

Marciari, John, *Grand Tour Diaries and Other Travel Manuscripts in the James Marshall and Marie-Louise Osborn Collection*, Yale University Library Gazette, occasional supplement, 2 (New Haven: Beinecke Rare Book and Manuscript Library, 1999).

Martin, Gregory, "The Banqueting House Ceiling: Two Newly-Discovered Projects," *Apollo*, 139 (1994), 29–34.

Martin, Laurence, "Sir Francis Crane," *Apollo*, 113 (1981), 90–96.

Matthews, L. G., *The Royal Apothecaries* (London: Wellcome Historical Medical Library, 1967).

Mauss, Marcel, *The Gift: Form and Functions of Exchange in Archaic Societies*, trans. Ian Cunnison (Glencoe, IL: Free Press, 1954).

Maycock, A. L., *Nicholas Ferrar of Little Gidding*, (London: SPCK, 1963).

Meininghaus, Heiner, Christa Habrich, Tanja Volz, *Dufte und edle Flakons aus fünf Jahrhunderten – Five Centuries of Scent and Elegant Flacons* (Stuttgart: Arnoldsche, 1998).

Melton, Frank T., *Sir Robert Clayton and the Origins of English Deposit Banking, 1658–1685* (Cambridge: Cambridge University Press, 1986).

Merritt, Julia F., "Puritans, Laudians, and the Phenomenon of Church-Building in Jacobean London," *The Historical Journal*, 41 (1998), 935–60.

Imagining Early Modern London: Perceptions and Portrayals of the City from Stow to Strype 1598–1720 (Cambridge: Cambridge University Press, 2001).

"The Cecils and Westminster, 1558–1612: The Development of an Urban Power Base," in Pauline Croft (ed.), *Patronage, Culture and Power: The Early Cecils, 1558–1612* (New Haven: Yale University Press, 2002), pp. 234–40.

Merton, Robert K., *Science, Technology and Society in Seventeenth-Century England* (New York: H. Fertig, 1970).

Millar, Oliver, *The Inventories and Valuations of the King's Goods, 1649–1651* (Glasgow: Walpole Society, 1972).

Sir Peter Lely, 1618–1680, Exhibition at 15 Carlton House Terrace, London SW1 (London: National Portrait Gallery, 1978).

"Viewing a Stuart Legacy," *Country Life* 184 (4 October 1990), 126–31.

"Philip, Lord Wharton, and his Collection of Portraits," *Burlington Magazine*, 136 (1994), 517–30.

Millar, Oliver, ed., "Abraham van der Doort's Catalogue of the Collections of Charles I," *Walpole Society*, 37 (1960).

Mintz, Sidney, *Sweetness and Power: The Place of Sugar in Modern History* (New York: Viking, 1985).

Mitchell, David, ed., *Goldsmiths, Silversmiths and Bankers: Innovation and the Transfer of Skill, 1550–1750*, Centre for Metropolitan History, Working Papers Series, no. 2 (London: Centre for Metropolitan History, 1995).

Moncrieff, Elspeth, "Politics and Plate: English Silver from the Kremlin," *Apollo*, 133 (1991), 50–52.

Montagu, Jennifer, "Bernini Sculptures not by Bernini" in Irving Lavin, ed., *Gianlorenzo Bernini: New Aspects of his Art and Thought* (University Park: Pennsylvania State University Press, 1985), pp. 25–61.

    Roman Baroque Sculpture: The Industry of Art (New Haven: Yale University Press, 1989).

    "Edward Altham as a Hermit," in Edward Chaney and Peter Mack, eds., *England and the Continental Renaissance: Essays in Honour of J. B. Trapp* (Woodbridge, Suffolk: Boydell, 1990), pp. 271–82.

Montias, John Michael, "Art Dealers in Seventeenth-Century Netherlands," *Simiolus*, 18 (1988), 244–56.

Montrose, Louis, "Gifts and Reasons: The Contexts of Peele's *Arraygnement of Paris*," *English Literary History*, 47 (1980), 433–61.

Moore, Cathal, Christopher Rowell, and Nino Strachey, *Ham House Guidebook* (London: National Trust, 1995).

Moreau, Cesar, *Rise and Progress of the Silk Trade in England, from the Earliest Period to the Present Time* (London, 1826).

Morrill, John S., ed., *The Impact of the English Civil War* (London: Collins and Brown, 1991).

    ed., *Revolution and Restoration: England in the 1650s* (London: Collins and Brown, 1992).

Morrison, Kathryn, *English Shops and Shopping: An Architectural History* (New Haven: Published for the Paul Mellon Centre of Studies in British Art by Yale University Press, 2003).

Mowl, Timothy, "New Science, Old Order: The Gardens of the Great Rebellion," *Journal of Garden History*, 13 (1993), 16–34.

Mowl, Timothy, and Brian Earnshaw, *Architecture Without Kings: The Rise of Puritan Classicism under Cromwell* (Manchester: Manchester University Press, 1995).

Muchmore, Lynn, "Gerald de Malynes and Mercantile Economics," *History of Political Economy*, 14 (1969), 336–58.

    "A Note of Thomas Mun's 'England's Treasure by Forraign Trade,'" *Economic History Review*, new series, 23 (1970), 498–503.

Mui, Hoh-Cheung, and Lorna H. Mui, *Shops and Shopkeeping in Eighteenth Century England* (London: Routledge, 1989).

Mukerji, Chandra, *From Graven Images: Patterns of Modern Materialism* (New York: Columbia University Press, 1983).

Muldrew, Craig, *The Economy of Obligation: The Culture of Credit and Social Relations in Early Modern England* (Houndmills, Basingstoke: Macmillan; New York: St. Martin's Press, 1998).

Mulligan, Lotte, "Civil War Politics, Religion and the Royal Society," *Past and Present*, 59 (1973), 92–116.

Mulligan, Lotte, and Glenn Mulligan, "Reconstructing Restoration Science: Styles of Leadership and Social Composition of the Early Royal Society," *Social Studies of Science* II (1981), 327–64.

Nanda, Meera, *European Travel Accounts During the Reigns of Shahjahan and Aurangzeb* (Kurukshetra: Nirmal Book Agency, 1994).

Neely, George, *A Short History of the Clare College Mission, Rotherhithe* (Ramsgate: Church Publishers, 1964).

Neill, Michael, "'Wits Most Accomplished Senate': The Audience of the Caroline Private Theaters," *Studies in English Literature* 18 (1978), 341–60.

Newman, John, "A Draft Will of the Earl of Arundel," *Burlington Magazine* 122 (1980), 692–96.

"The Elizabethan and Jacobean Great House: A Review of Recent Research," *Archaeological Journal*, 145 (1988), 365–73.

"Inigo Jones's Architectural Education before 1614," *Architectural History*, 35 (1992), 18–50.

"Inigo Jones and the Politics of Architecture," in Kevin Sharpe and Peter Lake, eds., *Culture and Politics in Early Stuart England* (Standford: Standford University Press, 1993), pp. 229–55.

Newman, Karen, *Fashioning Femininity and English Renaissance Drama* (Chicago and London: University of Chicago Press, 1991).

"City talk: Femininity and commodification in Jonson's *Epicoene*," in Newan, *Fashioning Femininity and English Renaissance Drama*, pp. 129–43.

Nef, J. U., *Industry and Government in France and England, 1540–1640* (Philadelphia: American Philosophical Society, 1940).

Nicholls, Mark, *Investigating Gunpowder Plot* (Manchester: Manchester University Press, 1991).

Ninnis, R. J., "The Hewer Memorial at Clapham," *Antiquaries Journal*, 54 (1974), 257–67.

North, Michael, and David Ormrod, eds., *Art Markets in 1400–1800* (Aldershot, Hampshire, and Brookfield: Ashgate Publishing, 1998).

Ochs, "The Royal Society of London's History of Trades Programme: An Early Episode in Applied Science," *Notes and Records of the Royal Society of London*, 39 (1985), 129–58.

Ogden, Henry Vining, and Margaret Sinclair Ogden, *English Taste in Landscape in the Seventeenth Century* (Ann Arbor: University of Michigan Press, 1955).

O'Malley, Therese, and Joachim Wolschke-Bulmahn, *John Evelyn's "Elysium Britannicum" and European Gardening* (Washington, DC: Dumbarton Oaks Research Library and Collection, 1998).

Oman, Charles, *English Church Plate, 1597–1831* (London: Oxford University Press, 1959).

Caroline Silver, 1625–1688 (London: Faber, 1970).

Orlin, Lena Cowen, "Boundary Disputes in Early Modern London," in Lena Cowen Orlin, ed., *Material London, ca. 1600* (Philadelphia: University of Pennsylvania Press, 2000), pp. 344–76.

ed., *Material London, ca. 1600* (Philadelphia: University of Pennsylvania Press, 2000).

Ormrod, David, "The Origins of the London Art Market, 1660–1730," in Michael North and David Ormrod, eds., *Art Markets in Europe, 1400–1800* (Aldershot, Hampshire, and Brookfield: Ashgate Publishing, 1998), pp. 167–86.

"Art and its Markets," *Economic History Review*, 52 (1999), 544–51.

Parry, Graham, "The Great Picture of Lady Anne Clifford," in David Howarth, ed., *Art and Patronage in the Caroline Courts: Essays in Honour of Oliver Millar* (Cambridge: Cambridge University Press, 1993), pp. 202–19.

"Cavendish Memorials," *The Seventeenth Century*, special issue: *The Cavendish Circle*, 9 (1994), 275–87.

Pasmore, Stephen, "Thomas Henshaw FRS 1618–1700," *Notes and Records of the Royal Society*, 36 (1982), 177–88.

Patterson, Annabel M., *Censorship and Interpretation: The Conditions of Writing and Reading in Early Modern England* (Madison: University of Wisconsin, 1984).

Payne, M. T. W., "An Inventory of Queen Anne of Denmark's 'Ornaments, Furniture, Householde Stuffe, and Other Parcels' at Denmark House, 1619," *Journal of the History of Collections*, 13 (2001), 23–44.

Pears, Iain, *The Discovery of Painting: The Growth of Interest in the Arts in England, 1680–1768* (New Haven: Yale University Press, 1988).

Peck, Linda Levy, *Northampton: Patronage and Policy at the Court of James I* (London: Allen and Unwin, 1982).

Court Patronage and Corruption in Early Stuart England (London: Unwin Hyman 1990).

"The Mentality of the Jacobean Grandee," in Linda Levy Peck ed., *The Mental World of the Jacobean Court* (Cambridge University Press: Cambridge, 1991), pp. 148–68.

"Hobbes on the Grand Tour: Paris, Venice, or London?" *Journal of the History of Ideas*, 57 (1996), 177–83.

"Constructing a New Context for Hobbes Studies," in Howard Nenner, ed., *Politics and the Political Imagination in Later Stuart Britain: Essays Presented to Lois Green Schwoerer* (Rochester, NY: University of Rochester Press, 1997), 161–79.

"Beyond the Pale: John Cusacke and the Language of Absolutism in Early Stuart Britain," *The Historical Journal*, 41 (1998) 121–49.

"Uncovering the Arundel Library at the Royal Society: Changing Meanings of Science and the Fate of the Norfolk Donation," *Notes and Records of the Royal Society*, London, 52 (1998), 3–24.

"Women in the Caroline Audience: The Evidence from Hatfield House," *Shakespeare Quarterly*, 51 (2000), 474–77.

ed., *The Mental World of the Jacobean Court* (Cambridge University Press: Cambridge, 1991).

Pennell, Sara, "Consumption and Consumerism in Early Modern England," *Historical Journal*, 42 (1999), 549–64.

Perlove, Shelley, *Bernini and the Idealization of Death: The Blessed Ludovica Albertoni and the Altieri Chapel* (University Park: Pennsylvania State University Press, 1990).

Perry, Curtis, ed., *Material Culture and Cultural Materialisms in the Middle Ages and the Renaissance* (Turnhout: Brepols, 2001).

Pestana, Carla Gardina, *The English Atlantic in an Age of Revolution, 1640–1661* (Cambridge, MA: Harvard University Press, 2004).

Pevsner, Nikolaus, *The Buildings of England* (London: Penguin, 1951–74).

Pevsner, Nikolaus, and David Lloyd, *Hampshire and the Isle of Wight* (Harmondsworth: Penguin, 1967).

Pincus, Steven, C. A., "England and the World in the 1650s," in John S. Morrill, ed., *Revolution and Restoration, England in the 1650s* (London: Collins and Brown, 1992), 129–47.

"Coffee Politicians Does Create: Coffeehouses and Restoration Political Culture," *Journal of Modern History*, 67 (1995), 807–34.

"Neither Machiavellian Moment Nor Possessive Individualism: Commercial Society and the Defenders of the English Commonwealth," *AHR* 103 (1998), 705–36.

"From Holy Cause to Economic Interest," in Steven C. A. Pincus and Alan Houston, eds., *A Nation Transformed: England after the Restoration* (Cambridge: Cambridge University Press, 2001), pp. 272–98.

Platt, Colin, *The Great Rebuildings of Tudor and Stuart England: Revolutions in Architectural Taste* (London: University College London Press, 1994).

Platt, Peter G., ed., *Wonders, Marvels and Monsters in Early Modern Culture* (Newark: University of Delaware Press, 1999).

Pointon, Marcia R., *Strategies for Showing: Women, Possession, and Representation in English Visual Culture, 1665–1800* (Oxford: Oxford University Press, 1997).

Porter, David L., "Monstrous Beauty: Eighteenth-Century Fashion and the Aesthetics of the Chinese Taste," *Eighteenth-Century Studies*, 35 (2002), 395–411.

Porter, Stephen, ed., *London and the Civil War* (Basingstoke, Hampshire: Macmillan, 1996).

Portier, François, "Prices Paid for Italian Pictures in the Stuart Age," *Journal of the History of Collections*, 8 (1996), 53–69.

Potter, Lois, *Secret Rites and Secret Writing: Royalist Literature, 1641–1660* (Cambridge: Cambridge University Press, 1989).

Prestwich, Menna, *Cranfield: Politics and Profits Under the Early Stuarts: The Career of Lionel Cranfield, Earl of Middlesex* (Oxford: Clarendon Press, 1966).

Price, W. H., *The English Patents of Monopoly* (Cambridge, MA: Harvard University Press, 1913).

Pugh, T. B., "A Portrait of Queen Anne of Denmark at Parham Park, Sussex," *The Seventeenth Century*, 8 (1993), 171.

Rappaport, Erika, *Shopping for Pleasure: Women in by the Making of London's West End* (Princeton, NJ: Princeton University Press, 2000).

Riccardi-Cubitt, Monique, "The Duke of Buckingham's Cabinet d'Amateur: An Aesthetic, Religious and Political Statement," *British Art Journal*, 1 (2000), 77–86.

Robinson, John Martin, *The Dukes of Norfolk: A Quincentennial History* (Oxford: Oxford University Press, 1982).

Roberts, Mary Louise, "Gender, Consumption, and Commodity Culture," *American Historical Review*, 103 (1998), 817–44.

Robertson, J. C., "Caroline Culture: Bridging Court and Country," *History*, 75 (1990), 388–416.

Roche, Daniel, *The Culture of Clothing: Dress and Fashion in the "Ancien Régime,"* trans. Jean Birrell (Cambridge: Cambridge University Press, 1994).

   "Between a 'Moral Economy' and a 'Consumer Economy': Clothes and their function in the 17th and 18th centuries," in Robert Fox and Anthony Turner, eds., *Luxury Trades and Consumerism in Ancien Régime Paris: Studies in the History of the Skilled Workforce* (Aldershot, Hampshire: Ashgate Publishing, 1998), pp. 219–29.

Rogers, Malcolm, *William Dobson, 1611–46* (London: National Portrait Gallery, 1983).

Roper, Lyndal, *Oedipus and the Devil: Witchcraft, Sexuality, and Religion in Early Modern Europe* (London: Routledge, 1994).

Rowell, Christopher, "A Seventeenth-Century 'Cabinet' Restored: The Green Closet at Ham House," *Apollo*, 143 (1996), 18–23.

Russell, Conrad, *Parliaments and English Politics, 1621–29* (Oxford: Oxford University Press, 1979).

Russell, P. E., "Veni, Vidi, Vici: Some Fifteenth Century Eye-Witness Accounts of Travel in the Africa Atlantic before 1492," *Historical Research*, 66 (1993), 115–28.

Sacks, David Harris, *The Widening Gate: Bristol and the Atlantic Economy, 1450–1700* (Berkeley: University of California Press, 1991).

   "London's Dominion: The Metropolis, the Market Economy, and the State," in Lena Cowen Orlin, ed., *Material London, ca. 1600* (Philadelphia: University of Pennsylvania Press, 2000), pp. 20–54.

Sargent, Rose-Mary, "Bacon as an Advocate for Cooperative Scientific Research," in Markku Peltonen, ed., *The Cambridge Companion to Bacon* (Cambridge: Cambridge University Press, 1996), pp. 146–71.

Sargentson, Carolyn, "The Manufacture and Marketing of Luxury Goods: the *Marchands-Merciers* of Late Seventeenth and Eighteenth Century Paris," in Robert Fox and Anthony Turner, eds., *Luxury Trades and Consumerism in Ancien Régime Paris* (Aldershot, Hampshire: Ashgate Publishing, 1998), pp. 99–137.

Saumarez-Smith, Charles, *The Building of Castle Howard* (London: Faber, 1990).

Saunders, Ann, ed., *The Royal Exchange* (London: London Topographical Society, 1997).

Sawday, Jonathan, "Self and Selfhood in the Seventeenth Century," in Roy Porter, ed., *Rewriting the Self: Histories from the Renaissance to the Present* (London: Routledge, 1997), pp. 29–48.

Scarrisbrick, Diana, "Anne of Denmark's Jewelry Inventory," *Archaeologia*, 109 (1991), 193–238.

"The Arundel Gem Cabinet," *Apollo*, 144 (1996), 45–48.

Schama, Simon, *The Embarrassment of Riches: An Interpretation of Dutch Culture in the Golden Age* (New York: Knopf, 1987).

Schofield, John, *The Building of London: From the Conquest to the Great Fire* (London: British Museum Press in association with the Museum of London, 1993).

Schwoerer, Lois, *The Ingenious Mr. Henry Care, Restoration Publicist* (Baltimore: Johns Hopkins University Press, 1998).

Searle, Arthur, "Sir Thomas Barrington in London, 1640–1644," *Essex Journal*, 2 (1967), no. 1, 35–41 and no. 2, 63–70.

Seaver, Paul, *Wallington's World: a Puritan Artisan in Seventeenth Century London* (Stanford, CA: Stanford University Press, 1985).

Sekora, John, *Luxury: The Concept in Western Thought, Eden to Smollett* (Baltimore: Johns Hopkins University Press, 1977).

Shakeshaft, Paul, "Too much Bewiched with Thoes Intysing Things": The Letters of James, Third Marquis of Hamilton and Basil, Viscount Feilding, Concerning Collecting in Venice 1635–1639," *Burlington Magazine*, 128 (1986), 114–32.

Shammas, Carole, *The Pre-Industrial Consumer in England and America* (Oxford: Clarendon Press, 1990).

Shapin, Steven, "'A Scholar and A Gentleman': The Problematic Identity of the Scientific Practitioner in Early Modern England," *History of Science*, 29 (1991), 279–327.

Shapiro, Alan E., ed., *The Optical Papers of Isaac Newton*, vol. I: *The Optical Lectures, 1670–1672* (Cambridge: Cambridge University Press, 1984).

Shapiro, Barbara, *A Culture of Fact: England, 1550–1720* (Ithaca: Cornell University Press, 2000).

Sharpe, Kevin, *Sir Robert Cotton, 1586–1631: History and Politics in Early Modern England* (Oxford: Oxford University Press, 1979).

Remapping Early Modern England: The Culture of Seventeenth Century Politics (Cambridge: Cambridge University Press: 2000).

Sharpe, Kevin, and Peter Lake, eds., *Culture and Politics in Early Stuart England* (Stanford: Stanford University Press, 1993).

Shearman, John K. G., *Raphael's Cartoons in the Collection of Her Majesty the Queen, and the Tapestries from the Sistine Chapel* (London: Phaidon, 1972).

Shedd, John A., "Legalism over Revolution: The Parliamentary Committee for Indemnity and Property Confiscation Disputes, 1647–1655," *The Historical Journal*, 43 (2000), 1093–107.

Shelton, Anthony Alan, "Cabinets of Transgression: Renaissance Collections and the Incorporation of the New World," in John Elsner and Roger Cardinal, eds., *Cultures of Collecting* (London: Reaktion Books, 1994), pp. 177–203.

Sherman, William, *John Dee: The Politics of Reading and Writing in the English Renaissance* (Amherst: University of Massachusetts Press, 1995).

Sholl, Samuel, *A Short Historical Account of the Silk Manufacture in England* (London: 1811).

Sieveking, A. Forbes, "Evelyn's 'Circle of Mechanical Trades,'" *The Newcomen Society Transactions*, 4 (1923), 40–47.

Simpson, Alan, "Thomas Cullum, Draper, 1587–1664," *Economic History Review*, 2nd series, 11 (1958), 19–34.

Singer, Charles J., A. Rupert Hall, Eric J. Holmhyarde, eds., *From the Renaissance to the Industrial Revolution, c. 1500–c.1750*, vol. III of *A History of Technology*, 8 vols. (Oxford: Clarendon Press, 1955–78).

Skinner, Quentin, *Hobbes and Civil Science*, vol. III of *Visions of Politics* (Cambridge: Cambridge University Press, 2002).

Sladen, Teresa, "The Garden at Kirby Hall, 1570–1700," *Journal of Garden History*, 4 (1984), 139–56.

Sloan, Kim, with Andrew Burnett, eds., *Enlightenment: Discovering the World in the Eighteenth Century* (London: British Museum Press, 2003).

Smith, Nigel, *Literature and Revolution in England, 1640–1660* (New Haven: Yale University Press, 1994).

Smith, Woodruff D., *Consumption and the Making of Respectability, 1600–1800* (London and New York: Routledge, 2002).

Smuts, R. Malcolm, *Court Culture and the Origins of a Royalist Tradition in Early Stuart England* (Philadelphia: University of Pennsylvania Press, 1987).

"The Court and its Neighbourhood: Royal Policy and Urban Growth in the Early Stuart West End," *Journal of British Studies*, 30 (1991), 117–49.

"Cultural Diversity and Cultural Change at the Court of James I," in Linda Levy Peck, ed., *The Mental World of the Jacobean Court* (Cambridge: Cambridge University Press, 1991), pp. 99–112.

Culture and Power in England, 1585–1685 (New York: St. Martin's Press, 1999).

"Material Culture, Metropolitan Influences and Moral Authority in Early Modern England," in Curtis Perry, ed., *Material Culture and Cultural Materialisms in the Middle Ages and the Renaissance* (Turnhout, Belgium: Brepols, 2001), pp. 203–24.

Sombart, Werner, *Luxus und Kapitalismus* (München: Leipzig, 1913).

Luxury and Capitalism, introduction by Philip Siegelman, trans. W. R. Dittmar (Ann Arbor: University of Michigan Press, 1967).

Soo, Lydia M., "Letters from Paris," *Wren's "Tracts" on Architecture and Other Writings* (Cambridge, Cambridge University Press, 1998).

Springell, F. C., "Unpublished Drawings of Tangier by Wenceslaus Hollar," *Burlington Magazine*, 106 (1964), 68–74.

Spufford, Margaret, *The Great Reclothing of Rural England: Petty Chapmen and their Wares in the Seventeenth Century* (London: Hambledon Press, 1985).

Staniland, Kay, "Thomas Deane's Shop in the Royal Exchange," in Ann Saunders, ed., *The Royal Exchange* (London: London Topographical Society, 1997), pp. 59–67.

Stone, Lawrence, "Inigo Jones and the New Exchange," *Archaeological Journal*, 114 (1957), 106–21.

The Crisis of the Aristocracy, 1558–1641 (Oxford: Clarendon Press, 1965).

Family and Fortune: Studies in Aristocratic Finance in the Sixteenth and Seventeenth Centuries (Oxford: Clarendon Press, 1973).

"The Residential Development of the West End of London in the Seventeenth Century," in Barbara C. Malament, ed., *After the Reformation: Essays in Honor of J. H. Hexter* (Philadelphia: University of Pennsylvania Press, 1980), pp. 167–212.

Broken Lives: Separation and Divorce in England 1660–1857 (Oxford: Oxford University Press, 1993).

Stone, Lawrence, and Jeanne Fawtier Stone, *An Open Elite? England 1540–1880*, abridged edn (Oxford: Oxford University Press, 1986).

Stoye, John, *English Travelers Abroad, 1604–1667: Their Influence in English Society and Politics* (New Haven: Yale University Press, 1989).

Strong, Sir Roy, *The English Icon: Elizabethan and Jacobean Portraiture* (London: Paul Mellon Foundation for British Art, in association with Routledge and Kegan Paul, 1969).

The Cult of Elizabeth: Elizabethan Portraiture and Pageantry (London: Thames and Hudson, 1977).

The Renaissance Garden in England (London: Thames and Hudson, 1979).

Henry, Prince of Wales and England's Lost Renaissance (London and New York: Thames and Hudson, 1986).

Styles, John, "The goldsmiths and the London luxury trades, 1550 to 1750," in David Mitchell, ed., *Goldsmiths, Silversmiths and Bankers: Innovation and the Transfer of Skill, 1550–1750*, Centre for Metropolitan History, Working Papers Series, no. 2 (London: Alan Sutton Publishing and Centre for Metropolitan History, 1995), pp. 112–20.

Summerson, John, *Architecture in Britain, 1530–1830* (Harmondsworth, Middlesex: Penguin Books, 1958; Yale University Press, 1993).

Supple, B. E., *Commercial Crisis and Change in England, 1600–1642: A Study in the Instability of a Mercantile Economy* (Cambridge: Cambridge University Press, 1959).

Sykes, Susan, "Henrietta Maria's 'House of Delight,' French Influence and Iconography in the Queen's House, Greenwich," *Apollo* (1991), 332–36.

Thirsk, Joan, "The Sales of Royalist Land during the Interregnum," *Economic History Review*, new series 5 (1952), 193–94.

Economic Policy and Projects: The Development of a Consumer Society in Early Modern England (Oxford: Clarendon Press, 1978).

Thomson, William George, *History of Tapestry from the Earliest Times until the Present Day* (London: Hodder and Stoughton, 1906, 1930).

Thornton, Peter M., "Bizarre Silks," *Burlington Magazine*, 100 (1958), 265–70.

Baroque and Rococo Silks (London: Faber and Faber, 1965).

Seventeenth-Century Interior Decoration in England, France and Holland (New Haven: Yale University Press, 1978).

Thornton, Peter M., and Maurice Tomlin, *The Furnishing and Decoration of Ham House*, Furniture History Series 16 (London: Furniture History Society, 1980).

Thurley, Simon, *The Royal Palaces of Tudor England: Architecture and Court Life, 1460–1547*, (New Haven and London: Yale University Press, 1993).

Tittler, Robert, *Architecture and Power: The Town Hall and the English Urban Community, c. 1500–1640* (Oxford: Clarendon Press, 1991).

Tollemache, E. D. H., *The Tollemaches of Helmingham and Ham* (Ipswich: W. S. Cowell, 1949).

Topik, Steven, and W. G. Clarence-Smith, *The Global Coffee Economy in Africa, Asia and Latin America, 1500–1989* (Cambridge: Cambridge University Press, 2003).

Trappes-Lomax, T. B, "Some Houses of the Dormer Family," *Recusant History*, 8 (1965–66), 175–87.

Travitsky, Betty S., "'His Wife's Prayers and Meditations': MS Egerton 607," in Anne M. Haselkorn and Betty S. Travitsky, eds., *The Renaissance Englishwoman in Print: Counterbalancing the Canon* (Amherst: University of Massachusetts Press, 1990), pp. 241–60.

Trenkler, Ernst, "Peter Lambeck und seine 'Commentari'," *Biblos* 26 (1977), 164–84.

Turner, James Grantham, "'News from the New Exchange': Commodity, Erotic Fantasy, and the Female Entrepreneur," in Ann Bermingham and John Brewer, eds., *The Consumption of Culture, 1600–1800: Image, Object, Text* (New York: Routledge, 1995), pp. 419–39.

Upton, Anthony, *Sir Arthur Ingram, c. 1565–1642* (Oxford: Oxford University Press, 1961).

Urwin, Alan Charles Bell, *Twicknam Parke: An Outline of the History of Twickenham Park . . . To the Present Day* (Twickenham, Middlesex: Alan C. B. Urwin, 1965).

Van der Waals, Jan. "The Print Collection of Samuel Pepys," *Print Quarterly*, I/4 (1984), 236–42, 247–57.

Van Eerde, Katherine S., *John Ogilby and the Taste of his Times* (Folkestone, Kent: Dawson, 1976).

Vickers, Michael, "Hollar and the Arundel Marbles," *Country Life* (1979), 916–17.

The Victoria History of the County of Buckingham, ed. William Page, 4 vols. (London: A. Constable and Co., 1905–27).

The Victoria History of the County of Northampton, ed. William Ryland Dent Adkins, Sir Robert Meyricke Serjeantson, and L. F. Salzman, 4 vols. (Westminster: A. Constable and Co., 1902, 1970).

Villa, Nicole, *Le XVII Siècle vu par Abraham Bosse, Graveur du Roy* (Paris: Les Editions Roger Dacosta, 1967).

Viner, Jacob, "Power Versus Plenty as Objectives of Foreign Policy in the Seventeenth and Eighteenth Centuries," in David Armitage, ed., *Theories of Empire, 1450–1800* (Aldershot: Ashgate Variorum, 1998), 277–305.

Vries, Jan de, "Between Purchasing Power and the World of Goods: Understanding the Household Economy in Early Modern Europe," in John Brewer and Roy Porter, eds., *Consumption and the World of Goods* (London: Routledge, 1992), pp. 85–132.

"Luxury in the Dutch Golden Age in Theory and Practice," in Maxine Berg and Elizabeth Eger, eds., *Luxury in the Eighteenth Century: Debates, Desires and Delectable Goods* (Houndsmill, Basingstoke: Palgrave Macmillan, 2003), pp. 41–56.

Wadsworth, Alfred P., and Julia de Lacy Mann, *The Cotton Trade and Industrial Lancashire, 1600–1780*, Economic History Series, 7 (Manchester: Manchester University Press, 1931).

Walkowitz, Judith R., "Going Public: Shopping, Street Harassment, and Streetwalking in Late Victorian London," *Representations*, 62 (1998), 1–30.

Walsh, Claire, "The Design of London Goldsmiths' Shops in the Early Eighteenth Century," in David Mitchell, ed., *Goldsmiths, Silversmiths and Bankers: Innovation and the Transfer of Skill, 1550–1750*, Centre for Metropolitan History, Working Papers Series, no. 2 (London: Centre for Metropoliton History, 1995), pp. 96–111.

Warneke, Sara, *Images of the Educational Traveler in Early Modern England* (Leiden: E. G. Brill, 1995).

Warner, Alex, and Michael Berlin, "Developing an Interdisciplinary Approach? The Skilled Workforce Project," *Bulletin of the John Rylands Library of Manchester*, 77 (1995), 49–56.

Warner, Frank, *The Silk Industry of the United Kingdom: Its Origin and Development* (London: Drane's, 1921).

Waterfield, Giles, "The Town House as Gallery of Art," *The London Journal*, 20 (1995), 47–66.

Watson, Katharine, and Charles Avery, "Medici and Stuart: A Grand Ducal Gift of 'Giovanni Bologna' Bronzes for Henry Prince of Wales 1612," *Burlington Magazine* 115 (1973), 493–507.

Weatherill, Lorna, "A Possession of One's Own: Women and Consumer Behavior in England, 1660–1740," *Journal of British Studies*, 25 (1986), 131–56.
  Consumer Behavior and Material Culture in Britain, 1660–1720 (London: Routledge, 1988; 2nd edn, 1996).

Weber, Max, *General Economic History*, trans. Frank H. Knight (New York: Collier Books, 1961).
  The Protestant Ethic and the "Spirit" of Capitalism and other writings, ed. and trans., Peter Baehr and Gordon C. Wells (New York: Penguin, 2002).

Webster, Charles, *The Great Instauration: Science, Medicine and Reform, 1626–1660* (London: Duckworth, 1975).

Wells-Cole, Anthony, "Some Design Sources for the Earl of Leicester's Tapestries and Other Contemporary Pieces," *Burlington Magazine*, 125 (1983), 284–85.
  "The Elizabethan Sheldon Tapestry Maps," *Burlington Magazine*, 132 (1990), 392–401.
  Art and Decoration in Elizabethan and Jacobean England: The Influence of Continental Prints, 1558–1625 (New Haven: Yale University Press, 1997).

Weston-Lewis, Aidan, ed., *Effigies and Ecstasies: Roman Baroque Sculpture and Design in the Age of Bernini* (Edinburgh: Scottish National Gallery, 1998).

Whalley, J. Irene, "Italian Art and English Taste: An Early-Seventeenth-Century Letter," *Apollo*, 94 (1971), 184–91.

Wheeler, Sir Robert Eric Mortimer, *The Cheapside Hoard of Elizabethan and Jacobean Jewellery* (London: Museum of London, 1928).

Whinney, Margaret, *Sculpture in Britain 1530–1830* (London: Penguin, 1988).

White, Christopher, *Peter Paul Rubens: Man and Artist* (New Haven: Yale University Press, 1987).

Whyman, Susan E., *Sociability and Power in Late-Stuart England: The Cultural Worlds of the Verneys, 1660–1720* (Oxford: Oxford University Press, 1999).

Wilks, Timothy, "The Picture Collection of Robert Carr, Earl of Somerset," *Journal of the History of Collections*, 1 (1989), 167–77.

"Art Collecting at the English Court from the Death of Henry, Prince of Wales, to the Death of Anne of Denmark," *Journal of the History of Collections*, 9 (1997), 31–48.

Willan, T. S., *The Inland Trade: Studies in English Internal Trade in the Sixteenth and Seventeenth Centuries* (Manchester: Manchester University Press, 1976).

William and Mary Quarterly, 3rd series, 56 (April, 1999), special issue on African and American Atlantic Worlds.

Williams, Neville, "The London Port Books," *Transactions of the London and Middlesex Archaeological Society*, 18 (1956), 13–26.

Williams, Penry, *The Tudor Regime* (Oxford: Clarendon Press, 1979).

Wilson, Catherine, *The Invisible World: Early Modern Philosophy and the Invention of the Microscope* (Princeton: Princeton University Press, 1995).

Wilson, Charles, *England's Apprenticeship, 1603–1763*, 2nd edn (London: Longman, 1984).

Wilson, Kathleen, "The Good, the Bad and the Impotent: Imperialism and the Politics of Identity in Georgian England," in Ann Bermingham and John Brewer, eds., *The Consumption of Culture, 1600–1800: Image, Object, Texts* (London: Routledge, 1995), pp. 237–62.

Wittkower, Rudolf, *Gian Lorenzo Bernini: The Sculptor of the Roman Baroque* (London: Phaidon Press, 1955).

Art and Architecture in Italy, 1600–1750 (Baltimore: Penguin Books, 1958).

Women's Studies, 26 (1997), special issue of women and travel.

Wood, Jeremy, "The Architectural Patronage of Algernon Percy, 10th Earl of Northumberland," in John Bold and Edward Chaney, eds., *English Architecture, Public and Private: Essays for Kerry Downes* (London: Hambledon Press, 1993), pp. 55–80.

"Van Dyck and the Earl of Northumberland: Taste and Collecting in Stuart England," in Susan T. Barnes and Arthur K. Wheelock, eds., *Studies in the History of Art* (Washington, DC: National Gallery, 1994), pp. 280–324.

"Taste and Connoisseurship in the Court of Charles I: Inigo Jones and the Work of Gulio Romano," in Eveline Cruickshanks, ed., *The Stuart Courts* (Stroud: Sutton, 2000), pp. 118–40.

Worden, Blair, *The Sound of Virtue: Philip Sidney's Arcadia and Elizabethan Politics* (New Haven: Yale University Press, 1996).

Worsley, Giles, "Inigo Jones: Lonely Genius or Practical Exemplar?" *Journal of the British Archaeological Association*, 146 (1993), 102–12.

Worsley, Lucy, and Tom Addyman, "Riding Houses and Horses: William Cavendish's Architecture for the Art of Horsemanship," *Architectural History*, 45 (2002), 194–229.

Wright, Louis B., *The Dream of Prosperity in Colonial America* (New York: New York University Press, 1965).

Wrightson, Keith, *Earthly Necessities: Economic Lives in Early Modern Britain* (New Haven: Yale University Press, 2000).

Young, Michael, *Servility and Service: The Life and Work of Sir John Coke* (Woodbridge, Suffolk: Boydell Press, 1986).

Zook, Melinda, *Radical Whigs and Conspiratorial Politics in Late Stuart England* (University Park: Pennsylvania State University Press, 1999).

Zytaruk, Maria, "Robert Hooke's 'Pretty Objects,' Consumerism, Empire and the *Micrographia*," in Michael Cooper and Michael Hunter, eds., *Hooke 2003* (London: Royal Society, 2003).

UNPUBLISHED DISSERTATIONS AND PAPERS

Adamson, John, "Princely Palaces: Aristocratic Town Houses, 1600–1660," paper presented at The Aristocratic Townhouse in London Conference, Centre for Metropolitan History, Institute of Historical Research, University of London, 15–17 July 1993.

Archer, Ian, "City and Court in the Reign of Elizabeth I," unpublished paper.

Berg, Maxine, "Modern Luxury," paper presented at the North American Conference on British Studies, Toronto (3 November 2001).

Franklin, Melissa, "Royalist Women and the Literature of Loyalty," (MA thesis, University of Rochester 1996).

Haskell, Francis, lectures on the dispersal of Charles I's collection.

Hearn, Karen, "Lucy Harrington, as Art Patron and Collector" (MA thesis, Courtauld Institute, 1990).

Howarth, David, "The Houses of the Howards," paper presented at The Aristocratic Town House in London Conference, Centre for Metropolitan History, Institute of Historical Research, University of London, 15–17 July 1993.

Hunneyball, Paul, "Status, Display and Dissemination: Social Expression and Stylistic Change in the Architecture of Seventeenth-Century Hertfordshire" (D. Phil., Oxford University, 1994).

Knowles, James, "Jonson in China: Maritime Trade with China," paper presented to the National Maritime Museum and Institute of Historical Research seminar series, 25 January 2000.

Long, Thomas C., "Samuel Pepys, Devoted Theatergoer: Faithful Client, Luxury Consumer or Ambitious Businessman?" paper presented at Western Conference on British Studies, Denver, Colorado, 11 September 2000.

Millard, A. M., "The Import Trade of London 1600–1640" (Ph.D. thesis, University of London, 1956).

Norton, Marcy, "New World of Goods: A History of Tobacco and Chocolate in the Spanish Empire, 1492–1700," (Ph.D. thesis, University of California, 2000).

Ochs, Kathleen, "The Failed Revolution in Applied Science: Studies of Industry by Members of the Royal Society of London, 1660–1688" (Ph.D. thesis, University of Toronto, 1981).

Payne, Helen, "Aristocratic Women and the Jacobean Court, 1603–1625" (Ph.D. thesis, University of London, 2001).

Reynolds, Neil, "The Stuart Court and Courtiers in Exile, 1644–1654" (Ph.D. thesis, Cambridge University, 1996).

Schroth, Sarah, "The Private Picture Collection of the Duke of Lerma" (Ph.D. thesis, New York University, 1990).

Van Nordern, Linda, "The Elizabethan Society of Antiquaries" (Ph.D. Dissertation, UCLA, 1946).

Wilks, Timothy, "The Court Culture of Prince Henry and his Circle, 1603–1613," (D.Phil. thesis, Oxford University, 1987).

Index